THE LAND
OF THE
BRIGHTON LINE

A field guide to the Middle Sussex and
South East Surrey Weald

DAVID BANGS

© 2018 David Bangs. All rights reserved.

dave@landofthebrightonline.co.uk

www.landofthebrightonline.co.uk

First printed 2018

Design, typesetting and map realisation, Andrew Jamison
andrewjamisondesign@gmail.com

Printed by Bishops Printers, Farlington, Portsmouth

ISBN 978-0-9548638-2-1

Front cover photo: Foyle Tolt on the River Eden

DEDICATION

To you, love, and to my oldest grandson. Big thanks, both of you, for all the fun we've had on so many Wealden walkings.

I want a memory machine

I hope I'll have a memory machine when I get old and wobbly.
I'll sit there and I'll sit there in my easy chair
… and I'll switch it on.

It'll take me back …
… to today,
as I walk,
hand in hand,
with you,
and the twigs of horse chestnut stand out
all winter black against the orange of afternoon sky.

We'll squelch and slip and pick our way along the muddy path
and the poor lame horse will stand so bloomin' miserable
in the wet hassock pasture.

Northwards the Weald lies warm and clear
in weak and limpid watercolour light.

I point (it's always us blokes who do the pushy pointing) and say:
"Look, there's Shipley Mill and Shipley church tower there amongst the trees;
real tiny – miles and miles away".

The woods are clean of leaves and flowers – just trunks and tracery of branches.
The cattle have their woolly coats
and mess the ground around the gates till it's all porridge quagmire.

There's lots of blue up high and stacked up clouds all dulux white,
and there up top of the hanging wood
two gnarled and twisted boles of ancient beech,
so close and tangled that we look and puzzle …
Are those two Siamese twins?
They look so separate, but their roots are fused as one.
Did they always grow together, or have they grown to blend?

* * *

Those and many more are things I want to conjure,
in years ahead when I can walk no longer.

Friday 11th December 2009 … after walking in the Low Weald with you, on the ridge near Beedings, West Chiltington.

CONTENTS

List of maps	7
Acknowledgements	9
Picture and map credits	9
What maps to buy info	10
Preface	11
Introduction	15

SECTION 1
BACKSTORY — 19

Chapter 1
The Wealden landscape's history — 21

Chapter 2
Wealden earth history:
Dinosaurs, tropical swamps and seas, rift valleys, horsetails, tree ferns and quarries — 41

Chapter 3
Landownership and farming — 55

Chapter 4
The big threats — 69

Chapter 5
Woods — 83

Chapter 6
The forests of St Leonard's and Worth — 97

Chapter 7
Rivers, streams, ponds and waterlands — 111

Chapter 8
Archaic pasture, meadow, moor and heath — 125

Chapter 9
Ancient Sussex giants:
The oldest and biggest trees — 139

Chapter 10
More about wildlife — 149

SECTION 2
AREA GUIDE — 161

Chapter 11
Henfield to Albourne and the Downs foot villages:
River, pasture, ploughland and woods — 163

Chapter 12
Ditchling, Clayton and Hurstpierpoint:
A common, mills, fords and small woods — 175

Chapter 13
Westmeston to Wivelsfield Green and Plumpton to South Chailey — 185

Chapter 14
Along the River Ouse:
Hamsey, Barcombe and Newick — 197

Chapter 15
Haywards Heath to Chailey Common and the Bluebell Line — 209

Chapter 16
Between Haywards Heath and Burgess Hill:
Ansty, Heaselands, Ashenground and Bedelands — 221

Chapter 17
Nightingales, waterlands and droves – the heart of the Low Weald:
West Grinstead to Twineham; Cowfold to Shermanbury — 231

Chapter 18
Horsham, Warnham, Shipley Woods, Southwater and Knepp — 241

continued over →

Chapter 19
Sedgwick, Nuthurst, Leonardslee and
Bolney 251

Chapter 20
Rift valley and forest:
The headwaters of the Ouse 261

Chapter 21
The Ardingly Ridgelands:
Balcombe, West Hoathly, Ardingly,
Horsted Keynes 269

Chapter 22
East Grinstead, Crawley Down, Gravetye,
Standen and Weir Wood Reservoir 281

Chapter 23
Worth Forest 291

Chapter 24
St Leonard's Forest's northern plateau 303

Chapter 25
The Rusper Ridgelands – North Horsham
to Ifield:
An old and threatened country 311

Chapter 26
The Reigate and Dorking Low Weald:
The vale of the Mole
The shadow of Gatwick 323

Chapter 27
The Nutfield and Godstone Low Weald:
Horley and Salfords to Lingfield and Oxted 339

Glossary 357

LIST OF MAPS

SECTION 1
BACKSTORY — 14

Area of book	14
Timeline	20
Ancient roads and watersheds	22
'Feld' names	24
Medieval assarts	25
Early medieval planners	26
Medieval drove roads	28
Sausage-shaped farms and manors	30
Medieval parish outliers	31
Lost medieval deer parks	32
Commons, parks and chases (largely heath, moor, grass heath, pasture woodland) between Haywards Heath and Lewes c. 1530	33
Ancient commons to modern towns	36
The geology of the middle Weald	40
Sandrock outcrops	44
Horsham stone pits	48
The middle Sussex 'rift valley'	50
Sticky clays and fertile sands	51
Patterns of landownership in West Sussex and the Brighton Line Weald	56
Moving the goalposts	58
Big flows of development	68
Explosive modern town growth	71
Wealden planning protections	72
How to destroy a statutorily conserved landscape	74
The destruction of the Vale of Holmesdale	79
Ancient woodland	82
Gill woodland	88
The Forest district in late Saxon times, c. 1050 AD	96
St. Leonard's Forest in the late Middle Ages c. 1300–1500	100
The Forests' coup de grace	104
The River Adur catchment / The Sussex Ouse catchment	110
Chalk streams between the River Adur and the River Ouse	112
The River Ouse Navigation	117
The Herrings / Heron Stream	120
Old meadow, heath and pasture	124
The veteran and ancient trees of Balcombe Down and Paddockhurst Park, in Worth Forest	140

SECTION 2
AREA GUIDE — 160

Additionally, all Area Guide chapters have an area map at the beginning.

Key to the Area Guide sub-landscapes	160
Geology and settlement	164

continued over →

Archaic heath, moor, meadow and marsh around Henfield	168
Carr wood, marsh and archaic meadow around Fulking	170
Ditchling Common: How to degrade a nationally important wildlife site	180
East Chiltington wildflower verges	187
What's left of Home Wood	189
Streat and Plumpton Greens	190
Waterlands	191
Marsh and airfield	192
Geology and settlement	198
Ancient woodland loss in modern times	202
The Longford Stream	204
Surviving heath and archaic grassland around Chailey North Commons	210
Cockhaise Brook archaic meadows, Horsted Keynes	216
Danehill Meadows	218
Bedelands: ancient woods and meadows	222
'Northern Arc' woods and ancient meadows	226
Shermanbury: an ancient redoubt in the Adur marshes	234
The waterlands	236
Denne Park, Horsham: some veteran and notable trees	246
The vale of the River Arun and the Horsham Stone scarp	248
Old Leonardslee: heath and meadow	251
Wild Service trees near Cowfold	254
Sedgwick Park Meadows	255
Daffodil country around Haven Farm	257
Old Ansty Wood	265
What's lost: Ardingly Reservoir	273
Ardingly Reservoir	274
East Grinstead's early farms	282
Weir Wood Reservoir	285
Worth Forest daffodils	293
'Pillow mounds' for 'coneys'	294
Worth: a giant forest parish	297
Small Leaved Lime in Worth Forest	299
The Daffodil Forest	304
North Horsham: how to wreck an ancient landscape	313
Woodland change at Ifield	317
Gatwick airport second runway? Trashing our countryside	320
Geology and settlement of the Surrey Brighton Line Weald	324
Wild and wooded	325
The Betchworth tree Ents	330
Reigate commons	334
Sand quarries and lost wetlands	335
Late surviving commons of the Sussex-Surrey county border	341
Some surviving archaic grasslands around Copthorne	343
Some surviving archaic grassland around South Godstone	350

ACKNOWLEDGEMENTS

To Andrew Jamison, book designer. This book bears a huge imprint of your design skills. I can't imagine it having being done without you. You always add value above and beyond what I have asked you to do, and I have asked a lot over a very long time. Thank you.

To Phil Belden, Heather Warne, Chris Smith, Bob Gilbert, Jana Berry and others who critically read part or all of the book's draft and diligently gave me their thoughts on it.

To the many people who have engaged with us and shown interest and friendliness on our meanderings. The dairyman at Plawhatch Farm springs immediately to mind. He moved me to the edge of tears with a few words of welcome when we least expected them. (He had no idea, I'm sure, of the disproportionate effect of his words!)

To those mates and family members who have politely and repeatedly asked about the progress of this book over many years and met the same boring responses … "It'll be out in a year or so / next year / next spring / next Christmas / a few months / a few weeks / a month or so" … and on and on …

PICTURE AND MAP CREDITS

My thanks particularly to Heather Warne for her maps of Medieval Assarts used on page 25, and for her map of Balcombe Down incorporated in the map on page 140; to the late Peter Brandon for the basis of the map of 'Commons, Parks and Chases between Haywards Heath and Lewes c. 1530' on page 33; to John Walters for his photograph of the Tanner Longhorn beetle, *Prionus coriarius,* which appears on the back cover and on page 107; to the Ouse and Adur Rivers Trust for the map of part of those river catchments on page 110; to the Sussex Ouse Restoration Trust, for their map of the River Ouse Navigation on page 117; to the Sussex Biodiversity Records Centre for their Chalk Streams map on page 112, and their maps of Ancient Woodland on page 82 and Gill Woodland on page 88; and to the Sussex Archaeological Society for the photograph of Whalesbeach Farmhouse on page 289.

If I have missed you, then please accept my apologies. I will include you in any future edition.

MAPS

> To get the most out of this book, you may need a copy of the following maps: Ordnance Survey Explorer Maps 122, 134, 135 and 146. These mark all the public rights of way and most statutory Access Land, although much other land open to public access is not marked at present.

PREFACE

The huge wooded vale of the Weald stretches 90 miles west-east between Petersfield, Hampshire and Folkestone, Kent. This book covers the Weald's middle section, some 15 to 17 miles west-east, centred on the London to Brighton railway. I call this area **'The Land of the Brighton Line'**. Its southerly part is bounded by the Rivers Adur and Ouse, and its northerly part by the Horsham to Dorking and East Grinstead to Oxted railways. The area embraces the whole c. 23 mile breadth of the Wealden vale, between the North and South Downs.

I describe all the main geologies and landscape types and as many individual sites as I can within one accessible volume. My focus is on nature. I am motivated by the urgency of the task of informing people of the threats it faces and the need to act to prevent its loss.

Many of the sites I describe have no legal right of public access. This book's description of such sites does not imply any right of public access to them. I leave it up to readers to make their own arrangements for access.

As I wrote in my last book, **'A Freedom to Roam Guide to the Brighton Downs'**, "I have been influenced by the famous series of guides by Nairn and Pevsner called 'The Buildings of England', published on a county by county basis in the 1960s and still available. That series attempted to describe all significant local buildings (exteriors and interiors) quite irrespective of whether they were accessible to the public. In doing so the authors performed a great public service and helped inform the cultural conservation movement". I am influenced, too, by the excellent Climbers' Club Guide, 'Southern Sandstones and the Sea Cliffs of South-East England', which provides information on all of these climbing resources, whilst reminding its readers that they have no right of access to most of them.

The writing of this book took place between 2009 and 2018, and many sites which were visited in the early years of its preparation may not have been re-visited since then. Things are changing rapidly in the Wealden countryside – mostly for the worse – and I warn readers that some of those sites I describe will have deteriorated , been destroyed, or sealed off from public gaze since myself and my informants last visited them. This is particularly true of archaic pasture and meadow sites.

The book is divided into two parts. **Part One: 'The Back Story'** covers the area's geology, landscape history, and land usage, as well as describing its main ecosystems: the forests of the High Weald; the rivers and waterlands; open habitats such as heath and meadow; woodland and ancient trees. My focus is always upon wildlife and the part-cultural, part-natural habitats in which all wild plants and animals live. **Part Two is 'The Area Guide'**. I hope that my delineation of these areas makes geographical sense. Please note, though, that my description in Chapter 20 of the 'rift valley' is partly poetic, and will likely be disowned by proper geologists!

Most sites described are given six figure map references. If you do not know how to read a map reference, you can find out from your Ordnance Survey Explorer maps, which have a simple guide as part of their key.

My treatment of the Surrey Weald is in less depth than that of Sussex. This is because I have known the Sussex Weald for far longer and spent much more time there. I live in Brighton and thus find it more difficult to reach the gorgeous Surrey Low Weald. Some of the material in the Back Story chapters pertains only to Sussex, and the equivalent material pertaining to Surrey is in the two extra-large Area Guide chapters on Surrey, chapters 16 and 17.

Readers will find much about meadows and archaic grasslands, though these are scarce and in declining, often wretched condition, for the most part, in the Weald. I write about them with such emphasis partly because they are the most endangered of the Weald's major ecosystems, and partly because my heritage from the South Downs' chalk grasslands gives me an insight into the delight such places can offer. Readers will find many descriptions of such sites appended with bracketted statements such as **"site now badly damaged, 2016"**. I could have deleted reference to such sites. I think it is more important to record their decline and remember what we are losing. I do not want to be complicit in what is nowadays aptly described as "shifting baseline syndrome" … or in common speech as "moving the goalposts".

Some will ask why this book stops right at the edge of Ashdown Forest and does not include it, despite its national importance. This is because Ashdown Forest is already much written about by many good authors. St Leonards and Worth Forests, however, have no such public profile, and they deserve the serious treatment I seek to give them here.

Some will ask why this book does not cover in detail the ancient buildings and heritage of our hamlets, villages and small country towns. Again, others have done this already in spades.

My concerns are for the green places that no one has written about and few know. It is those places that need friends most urgently.

Respect nature and sustainable crop and livestock farming. Leave only your footprints. Take only your memories. Above all, enjoy and delight in the countryside which is our matrix and our true home. If you do not know it, you cannot fight on its behalf.

What the eye doesn't see, the heart will not grieve over.

AREA OF BOOK

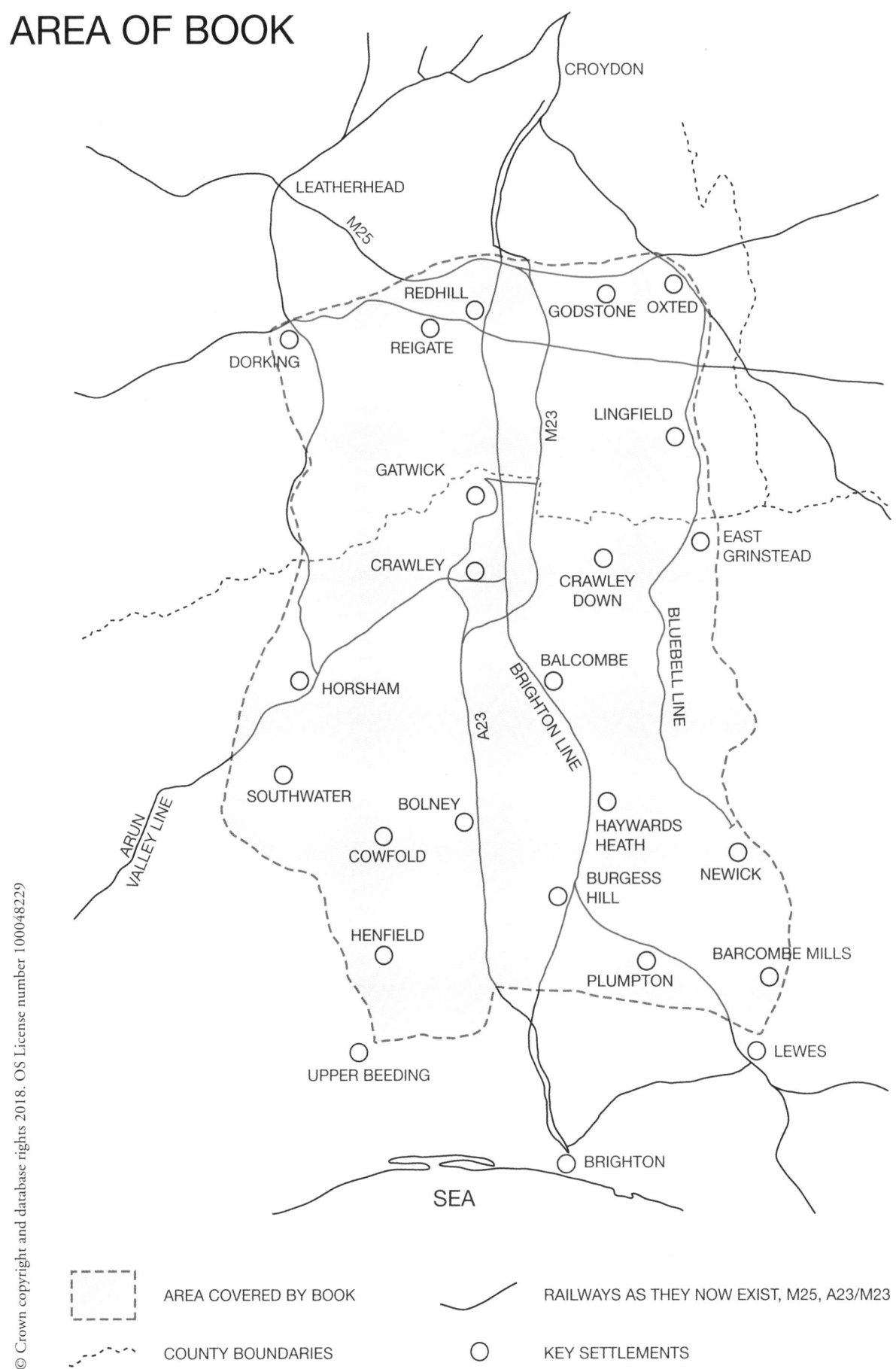

INTRODUCTION

When I was a boy I immersed myself in the Sussex Downs and the Weald. They were my delight, my retreat, and my best mate. That was in the 1960s, which was the most dreadful decade we'd seen so far for the fabric of the countryside. Farmers and developers wrought havoc on our woods, hedgerows and ancient pastures, and drained and poisoned our brooks and floodplains.

Yet the Weald has survived better than most other natural regions of Lowland England. It was, and still is greatly more wooded, and, with its heaths, waterlands, and archaic grasslands, it has more semi-natural habitat.[1] It is *'Ancient Countryside'*[2] with a pattern of fields and woods, lanes, green droves and footpaths, unmodified streams, veteran pollard trees, tiny hamlets and isolated farmsteads, going back largely to Saxon, but also Roman and prehistoric times.

There is much about the Weald that is intimate, mixed, and homely, with time havens that take you back to the wildwood, or to the earliest Saxon 'assarters' – settlers of wild land. The wildlife and microclimate of its deep wooded gills and sandrock outcrops are relics of the Atlantic climatic period, warm and wet, which ended and left them isolated some 5,000 years since.

All this is true, too, of the part of the Weald that I know best, which is The Land of the Brighton Line. I have known it since 1958, when our family returned to the town where my mum was born – Hove – taking the train back down the Brighton Line across the Balcombe Viaduct, with its vista of woods and streams, little fields and blue distant hills, and straining to see the Jack and Jill windmills before we whooshed into the Clayton Tunnel.

It may not be true much longer. In the next generation the process of attrition may destroy what is left of the key qualities of this landscape. Its best places may become mere 'precious fragments' in a subtopian mess of highways, noise, and urban sprawl. That is the trajectory that capitalist development is set upon. It has gone a long way down that path already.

It has already thoroughly done its work in the Thames basin, where the London megacity sprawls from the slopes of the Chilterns to the heights of the North Downs. Who now remembers the landscape of the Great North Wood that stretched from Deptford on the Thames to Selhurst, near Croydon, with its dense coppices, wood pastures and commons? Who now remembers the drowsy Middlesex hay meadows, stretching from Camden Town to Harrow Weald, and around the Nightingale haunted slopes of Hampstead Heath and Horsenden Hill? Who can remember the quiet marshy lushness of the vales of the Rivers Colne, the Lea, and the Wandle … or the meadows, orchards, nursery gardens, and gravelly heaths of the Thames vale way along from Chelsea to Brentford, Walton, Windsor? Those landscapes are thoroughly lost and forgotten when we try to weigh the pluses and minuses of the megalopolis.[3]

A new tranche of London's neighbour landscapes are now being stuffed in its maw. Though naturalists of the Thames Estuary (called by developers the 'Thames Gateway', as though it is only good for passing through) discovered a richness of invertebrate wildlife on its brown field wastes, derelict quarries and sunny rough grasslands that was way over twenty times greater in one square kilometre than the whole of Salisbury Plain,[4] it is now the centre of a giant expansion of the capitalist economy. Tough luck on the Nightingales – some 1.3% of the national population – that find refuge on the Hoo Peninsular.

The Low Weald and our Land of the Brighton Line, together with what's left of the Sussex coastal plain, are amongst the next in capitalism's sights.

THE LOW WEALD

The Low Weald is a land of horizontals and the gentlest contours. It is a soft place. Feelings of quietening, slowing, calm and peace spread through you as you walk its comfortable places. Despite all the past 70 and more years of ruination this is still a landscape of abundant trees, on lane sides and field edges, by ponds, around barns, homes, old pits and streams. So tree'd is it in many parts that thin lines of woodland – shaws – mark the boundaries of its fields, not hedges. Its flatness is thus broken by screen after screen of trees. It is as though each of its fields is a separate room, a self-contained place. If you hear a tractor or a chainsaw, there is no telling if it is in the next field or half a mile away. You may not see it until you come upon it.

Cow Lane, looking towards Wivelsfield's 'Long Ridge'

Close woven with these screens of trees are small and large woods. You may not even realise they are there except by the greater solidity and darker tones of the walls of green that mark their presence – the absence of the spots of sun and light that shine through shaws and field trees. In springtime, those ancient Low Wealden woods bring an intensity of delight that is scarce to be exceeded even in the best of woods elsewhere. Their Bluebells grow so densely that their blooms shine like sheets of lapis lazuli, solid floors of mauve tinted blue. The sun shines through the wood edges and fresh new leaves like beams of gold.

Green flats of river and small stream stretch away, and away again, touched rarely by glimpses of water, sometimes dark, sometimes lit by sky, sometimes marked with thorns and stands of reed. The lines the water takes seem always random, always lazy, always irrational. They turn back on themselves. They split and part their ways, then turn and re-connect. You know them only by the clumps and stands of Alder, Sallow, Willow, Ash, and Oak that guard the hidden waters' banks. These waterlands do not want you to walk in straight lines. They force you to stop, then take another course.

This is a homely countryside; a place of hay, shading trees, streams, cows, woods, corn, meadows, with houses, often ancient, sunk amongst them.

It suffers, in a low key but crucial way, from the preference which generations of rambling activists and government advisers have had for rumpled, heavily contoured landscapes. Only a tiny few of our statutorily protected landscapes are marked by gentle horizontality.[5] Nearly all our National Parks are mountainous or upland. Nearly all our Areas of Outstanding Natural Beauty are hilly. There have been many prepared to advocate for romantic landscapes of hiccupping hills and mountains, tortured valleys, broken rocks, and tumbling screes. Far fewer have been prepared to fight hard for the biological richness and many-layered loveliness of our Low Wealden countryside, leaving it without the statutory protection it so richly deserves.

The Low Weald is under doubled pressure because it is squeezed between the statutorily protected higher ground of the South and North Downs[6] and the High Weald. There is huge pressure from business interests to make available substantial land areas of the Wealden basin for them to damage by their activities. The Thames basin did not satisfy their hunger. In a region of such overall high landscape quality as the Wealden basin, the gentle Low Weald has found fewer allies prepared to defend its qualities, compared to those who settle for aerobic hill climbing and high view points. Only landscapes with relatively small land values and relatively large obstacles to economic exploitation (like steep hills and mountains) tend to be protected.

DIFFERENT LANDSCAPE, DIFFERENT PROBLEMS

My last book was about the Brighton Downs, a landscape with very different problems from the

Brighton Line Weald. Over two thirds of the Brighton Downs are in public ownership, and all of the South Downs have a very strong cultural resonance, despite being stripped of their most attractive feature: their thyme-scented, unfenced, ancient sheep pastures. The central task there is not the containment of gross built development (except on the urban fringe) but of landscape restoration, to stitch back that lost flowery mantle, and stitch together the needs of wildlife with public recreation and sustainable pastoralism.

In the Brighton Line Weald, however, it is the dynamic of urban expansion which is the main threat. Projects like a second Gatwick runway, the North Horsham extension, and a second Brighton-London rail route, which link the Wealden economy ever closer with the London megalopolis, are symptoms of a huge thrust of regional hyper-development.

Yet both the Downs and the Brighton Line Weald have one major problem in common, which is that public usage and knowledge of these landscapes is extremely limited. Londoners and Brightonians, as well as Crawley and middle Sussex folk, do not use the Wealden landscape in large numbers. They do not penetrate the vast majority of its spaces, and therefore have no sense of 'ownership' of them. Those with deeper pockets may use its paid entry attractions, like the High Wealden gardens (Nymans, Wakehurst, etc) or war gaming, golf, and fishing businesses, and many families visit Tilgate Park from as far away as Brighton. Some will use Wealden footpaths and its few public woods and open spaces, like Buchan Country Park, Bedelands Nature Reserve, and Leechpool and Owlbeech Woods. Most of its landscape, though, has no right of public usage, and its woods, farm lanes and gateways bear a rich crop of 'Private Property Keep Out' signs.

If our collective connection with this countryside does not increase drastically, we cannot hope to build the broad urban-rural campaigning alliances necessary to preserve it from gross built development and the mass of incremental threats (such as fracking and industrial-scale solar arrays) that it faces.

ENDNOTES

1. Which is not to decry the wonderful landscapes in the rest of lowland England, from medieval survivals like the New Forest, to wetlands like the Norfolk Broads, the heathy relics of Breckland, and the salt marshes and estuaries of East Anglia. These places are, though, set within a matrix of devastated countryside monopolised by intensive arable tillage, in which most historic landscape features and wildlife habitat have been destroyed. Much of the midland and eastern counties are emptied of nature.
2. The distinction between 'Ancient Countryside' (enclosed piecemeal in medieval and earlier times) and 'Planned Countryside' (re-modelled in the 18th and 19th centuries by the parliamentary enclosures of the cooperatively organised medieval open field landscape) are neatly summarised in 'The History of the Countryside', particularly chapter one, by Oliver Rackham. J M Dent & Sons Ltd. (1986).
3. We scarcely hear, in these reactionary times, the argument made for more dispersed and equal patterns of settlement; for strict maximum sizes for any urban concentrations. We can point to the positive ways that Cambridge has developed its diaspora of villages around its new industries, or the positive aspects of dispersed settlement that the coal industry created, but we know that capitalism uses such potentially benign patterns for its own ends, not ours. The mining villages are wrecked by the destruction of the coal industry. The Cambridgeshire villages will be turned into a giant conurbation if capital can get its way, just as the small towns of the Black Country are now part of a sprawling 'Greater' Birmingham, or the mill towns of Lancashire and Cheshire are now conjoined to form Greater Manchester. It will take a more far reaching project than some reforms of the planning system, or regional governance, to manage our economy and settlement patterns in more rational ways.
4. Despite Salisbury Plain being preserved by army occupation from destruction by modern agriculture.
5. Such as, in Lowland England, the New Forest, the Norfolk Broads, Chichester Harbour, and the Norfolk and Suffolk coasts.
6. I write as a lifelong lover of the South Downs, and, for that matter, all our statutorily designated landscapes. I wish, though, for us to widen our sympathies still further.

SECTION 1
BACKSTORY

TIMELINE

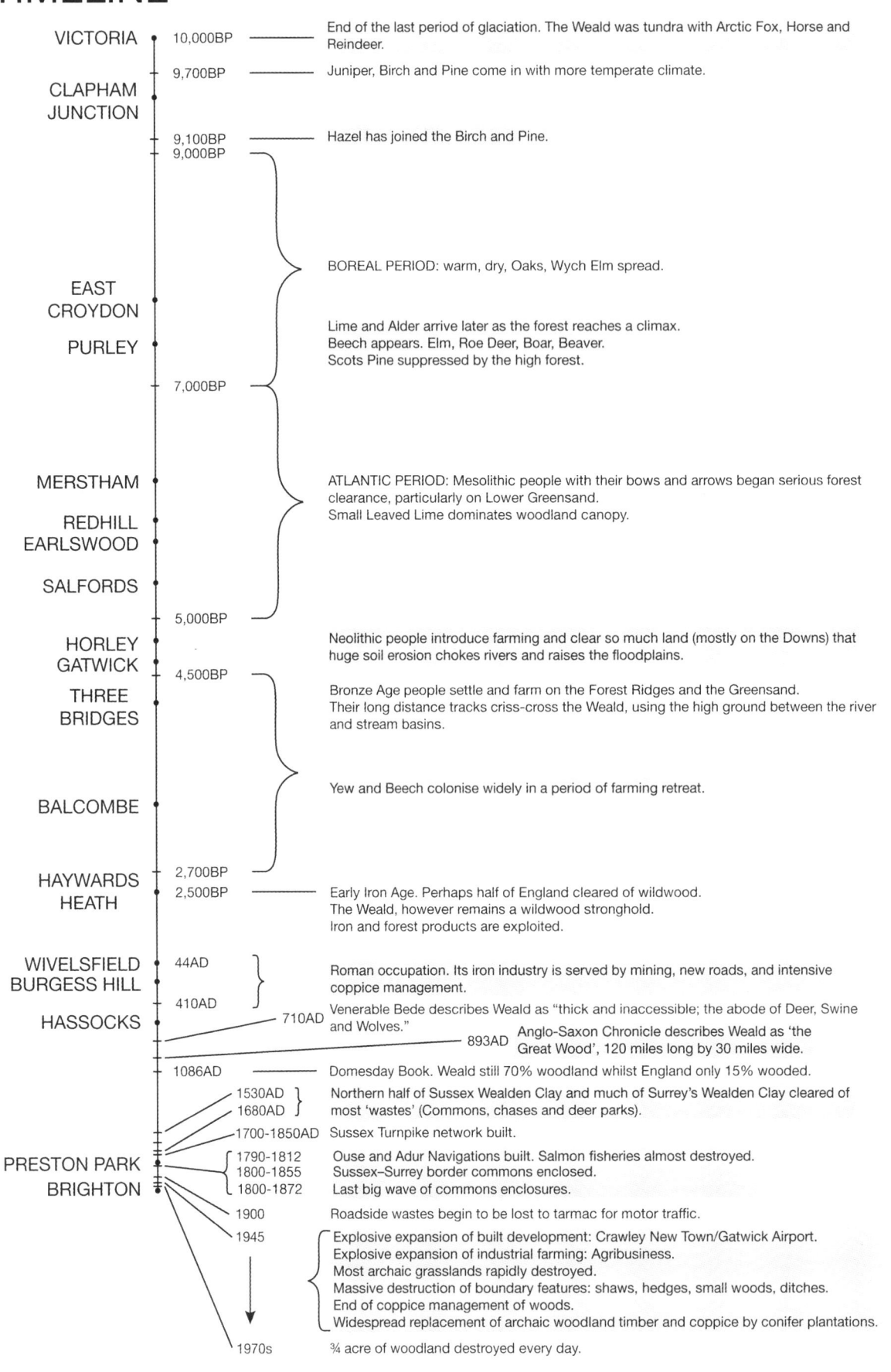

Station	Date	Event
VICTORIA	10,000BP	End of the last period of glaciation. The Weald was tundra with Arctic Fox, Horse and Reindeer.
	9,700BP	Juniper, Birch and Pine come in with more temperate climate.
CLAPHAM JUNCTION		
	9,100BP	Hazel has joined the Birch and Pine.
	9,000BP	BOREAL PERIOD: warm, dry, Oaks, Wych Elm spread.
EAST CROYDON		
PURLEY		Lime and Alder arrive later as the forest reaches a climax. Beech appears. Elm, Roe Deer, Boar, Beaver. Scots Pine suppressed by the high forest.
	7,000BP	
MERSTHAM		ATLANTIC PERIOD: Mesolithic people with their bows and arrows began serious forest clearance, particularly on Lower Greensand. Small Leaved Lime dominates woodland canopy.
REDHILL EARLSWOOD		
SALFORDS		
	5,000BP	
HORLEY GATWICK		Neolithic people introduce farming and clear so much land (mostly on the Downs) that huge soil erosion chokes rivers and raises the floodplains.
	4,500BP	
THREE BRIDGES		Bronze Age people settle and farm on the Forest Ridges and the Greensand. Their long distance tracks criss-cross the Weald, using the high ground between the river and stream basins.
BALCOMBE		Yew and Beech colonise widely in a period of farming retreat.
	2,700BP	
HAYWARDS HEATH	2,500BP	Early Iron Age. Perhaps half of England cleared of wildwood. The Weald, however remains a wildwood stronghold. Iron and forest products are exploited.
WIVELSFIELD BURGESS HILL	44AD	Roman occupation. Its iron industry is served by mining, new roads, and intensive coppice management.
	410AD	
HASSOCKS	710AD	Venerable Bede describes Weald as "thick and inaccessible; the abode of Deer, Swine and Wolves."
	893AD	Anglo-Saxon Chronicle describes Weald as 'the Great Wood', 120 miles long by 30 miles wide.
	1086AD	Domesday Book. Weald still 70% woodland whilst England only 15% wooded.
	1530AD / 1680AD	Northern half of Sussex Wealden Clay and much of Surrey's Wealden Clay cleared of most 'wastes' (Commons, chases and deer parks).
	1700-1850AD	Sussex Turnpike network built.
PRESTON PARK BRIGHTON	1790-1812	Ouse and Adur Navigations built. Salmon fisheries almost destroyed.
	1800-1855	Sussex–Surrey border commons enclosed.
	1800-1872	Last big wave of commons enclosures.
	1900	Roadside wastes begin to be lost to tarmac for motor traffic.
	1945	Explosive expansion of built development: Crawley New Town/Gatwick Airport. Explosive expansion of industrial farming: Agribusiness. Most archaic grasslands rapidly destroyed. Massive destruction of boundary features: shaws, hedges, small woods, ditches. End of coppice management of woods. Widespread replacement of archaic woodland timber and coppice by conifer plantations.
	1970s	¾ acre of woodland destroyed every day.

BACKSTORY / Chapter 1: The Wealden landscape's history

CHAPTER 1
The Wealden landscape's history

Jane and I know a bit about the earliest humans in our part of the Weald. It might only be a tiny bit, but it's large and personal to us, for she found an item of their lost property one February day whilst we were walking across a ploughed field near Barcombe. I think it is the most precious artefact that either of us have ever found on all our walkings, for it was likely made by another extinct species of ancient humans, the Heidelberg People,[1] *Homo heidelbergensis*, who lived in this countryside some half a million years ago.

We'd automatically gone into 'search mode' when we got to the field edge. She walked forward on one line, whilst I walked another, both scanning to our left and right. We didn't find much … but then Jane stooped and picked up a large flint object. By the time she brushed the earth off it was obvious it was very special. It was a bi-faced Old Stone Age (Palaeolithic) hand axe, convex, heavy, fitting neatly into the palm of her hand, and worked all over both surfaces. It was also peculiarly polished, even for flint, because of the effect of aeons of burial, with the actions around it of permafrost, water, tree and plant roots, worms and moles, and shifting soil and gravel. (That polish contrasted with the rough patina on the broken edge on one side, where a bit had been knocked off, maybe by a tractor).

Matthew Pope,[2] the archaeologist, told us that our flint tool could be anything from 600,000 to 60,000 years old, for those folk's technology was relatively unchanging over a huge period. In any case, when she made this tool our ancestral cousin likely lived in a world with several other species and subspecies of humans, and before the full development of the species we belong to.

At least three other bi-faced Palaeolithic hand axes have been found on the Ouse river terraces north of Lewes, and there is a scatter from all along the Downs and the river valleys through them and to the north. By far the biggest cluster of hand axes – 450 – was found at Boxgrove,[3] near Chichester, where the peopled land surface has been perfectly preserved on the buried seashore under the old cliff line, exposed in modern times by quarrying. Sussex back then, 500,000 years ago, was likely open grassland, heavily grazed, with Horse, Boar, Roe and Red Deer, alongside Elephant, Rhinoceros, Lion and Hyena.[4]

After the Ice Age interglacial Boxgrove episode, three more phases of glaciation and two more interglacials passed, before **the latest episode of glaciation finished in our area, a bit over 10,000 years ago**. At that time, when a milder climate returned, the Weald was a tundra of tall herbs and dwarf shrub heath, with beasts

Timeline
The left side depicts the Brighton-London Railway with its stations shown at their relative distances from each other. The right side depicts key episodes since the end of the Ice Age shown at their relative time intervals from each other.

Multi-purpose butchery tool. Jane's palaeolithic handaxe. Made by an earlier species of human.

like Horse, Reindeer and Arctic Fox. Fully developed humans, now just like us, but still with a late Palaeolithic culture, were present with that warming, too. A couple of their shouldered points[5] – largish flint projectile points for hafting onto spears – have been found, one at Old Faygate and one at Hawkins Bridge Pond in St Leonard's Forest.

WOODLAND ADVANCE AND RETREAT

As postglacial warming continued the woods began their overwhelming advance. They would still dominate our landscape now, but for us humans. At first, with the **return of temperate conditions by 9,700 BP**, Juniper, Birch and Pine came in. Were any of those Junipers the lineal ancestors of the bushes which still grew in St Leonards and Worth Forests at least till the 1930s? Hazel joined them by c. 9,100 BP, and with Birch and Pine came to dominate our woodland. A warm, dry **Boreal phase, from about 9,000 to 7,000 BP** saw the gradual spread of Pedunculate and Sessile Oaks and Wych Elm. Lime and Alder arrived later as the forest reached a climax.[6] Sussex became covered with woodlands of Oak, Lime, Elm and Alder, with Beech present but relatively uncommon. This expansion of woodland brought Elk, Roe Deer, Boar and Beaver. Scots Pine was marginalised in the south of Britain by the new high forest – and probably became extinct some centuries ago, only returning as a planted species from the 17th century.

ANCIENT ROADS AND WATERSHEDS

After the beginning of the warm and wet **Atlantic period, c. 7,000 BP**, the later Mesolithic people, with their bows and arrows, began the first serious forest clearance, particularly on the thinner soils of the Lower Greensand. They seem to have had a denser, more concentrated population than their forebears, particularly on and around the Downs and coast, and in the High Weald, perhaps

Ancient tracks are heavily aligned along interfluvial watershed ridges and other ridges.

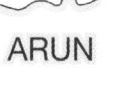 Watersheds and their interfluvial boundaries, mostly on ridges.

Some ancient roads and tracks, probably Iron Age, and maybe very much older. There are other routes currently being researched and written up by experts

 Some Roman roads. Others remain to be archaeologically verified – as does the road from Barcombe to Pevensey.

The South and North Downs and Surrey Hills

Historic County boundaries.

in response to the closing in of the Lime dominated woodland canopy.[7] At Henfield, at Fulking by Clapper's Lane, at Hassocks and at Streat,[8] all by or near to the Lower Greensand, these gatherer-hunters have left evidence of pits, much detritus of flint digging and working, and cooking (using heated fire-fractured flints as a means to heat water – 'potboilers').

Woodland clearance reached far greater intensity with the **Neolithic first farming culture**, though mostly on the chalk. Such clearance caused great soil erosion,[9] which choked Sussex rivers with alluvium and raised the floodplain. Those folk may have used the environment cyclically, travelling into the Low Weald as well as up into the High Weald, where they used the same shelters under the sandrocks as the Mesolithic people had before them.

In the **Bronze Age, from c. 4,500 to 2,700 BP**, forest clearance stepped up greatly, followed by a period of farming retreat and then re-advance. Though most of this clearance was on the Downs, there is ample evidence of a Bronze Age presence on the forest ridges, with a small scatter of round barrows in St Leonard's Forest, including the famous Money Mound (now gone) TQ 237 287. There was also a Bronze Age presence on the Lower Greensand of the Brighton Line Weald, with clusters of round barrows on Reigate Heath and Godstone in Surrey. Yew was an obvious beneficiary around 4,000 BP of the Bronze Age phase of farming retreat, for, like Beech, it seems better at secondary colonisation. Perhaps it was then that it first appeared on the forest ridges.[10]

By the **early Iron Age, c. 2,500 BP**, or even earlier, perhaps about half of England had been cleared of wildwood.[11] However, the Weald remained as one of a series of woodland strongholds. It was far from being unpeopled continuous waste though, and was integrated with the farmed Downland and coastal plain as a source of iron and forest products, as well as being farmed and grazed in many spots, particularly in the Low Weald. There were iron making bloomeries at Broadfield, Crawley, from the second century BC,[12] though the industry was mostly located to the east of our area. Long distance tracks criss-crossed the Weald along the ridges and watersheds, running both laterally and longitudinally. One crossed the Weald from the North Downs at Titsey, passed the hillfort at Dry Hill, south east of Lingfield, yomped over Ashdown, across Danehill and Scaynes Hill, down Ham Lane to Wivelsfield Green and on to Ditchling over its Common, then up the bostal onto the South Downs. Another passed along the watershed between the Adur and the Ouse, along the south side of the middle Sussex 'rift valley' through Warninglid, Slough Green, Whiteman's Green and Cuckfield, past Muster Green and on to Scaynes Hill. There were Iron Age hillforts at Philpots, just east of Wakehurst, and Dry Hill, east of Lingfield in the Brighton Line Weald, with others further east (Garden Hill, High Rocks, Saxonbury, Oldbury) and further west (Anstiebury, Holmbury, Hascombe, Piper's Copse).

THE ROMANS

The farming economy of the native people continued under the **Roman occupation from 44 AD.** The Romans planted their own people, both poor and rich, upon that pre-existing pattern, taking the best land under the Downs, expanding both farming and industrial output, and bringing in major new infrastructure. At least two Roman roads passed longtitudinally and one laterally, through this part of the Weald, serving different aspects of the economy.

The Roman Greensand Way from Stane Street at Pulborough to Barcombe (and on to Pevensey) served the farms and villas[13] on the good soils under the Downs, on both Upper and Lower Greensands. There is evidence of villas at Hurst Wickham, Danny, Clayton, and Plumpton, and scattered Roman remains, including a pottery kiln, have been found throughout this underhill area. The Greensand Way was lost for many centuries until its rediscovery by Margary in 1933,[14] but there is ample place name evidence for it. There is *Stret*ham where it crosses the Adur, *Wick* Farm, Albourne, Bas*twick,* Danny, Clayton *Wick*ham and Hurst *Wick*ham, *Streat, Wick*ham Barn and *Comps* Wood, Chiltington, Hewen*street* Farm and Bar*combe*. ('*Street*' was the name the Saxons gave to old roads with a made surface. '*Wick*', from Latin '*vicus*', often indicates a habitation name of Roman origin. '*Comp*' and (Bar)*'combe'* come from Latin '*camp*' for field).

The Portslade to London road passed through middle Sussex from Hassocks, where there was a major posting station, and through Low Wealden Surrey to the wind gap in the North Downs at Godstone. It ran more or less parallel to the Lewes to London Road to the east, which tracked from Lewes up over Ashdown, through Edenbridge to the North Downs. Both roads had the dual purposes of servicing the iron industry in the Weald and connecting the prosperous farmlands of the coastal plain and lower Downs with London. Barcombe may have acted as a sort of base camp for the Roman iron industry at the junction of two roads and the navigable Ouse. It is noteworthy that there is continuity between the church hamlet at Barcombe and the Roman villa, with the church building using some recycled building materials from the villa.

By the Roman period the dichotomy between the wooded Weald and the openness of the farmed coastal plain, the Downs, and the river valleys was sharp. In our time the flood plains of the Ouse and Adur river valleys are almost wholly denuded of ancient woodland, and it seems likely that we inherited this loss from those early times. Only in places like The Pells Holt at Offham, with its chest high Nettles, collapsed

'FELD' NAMES

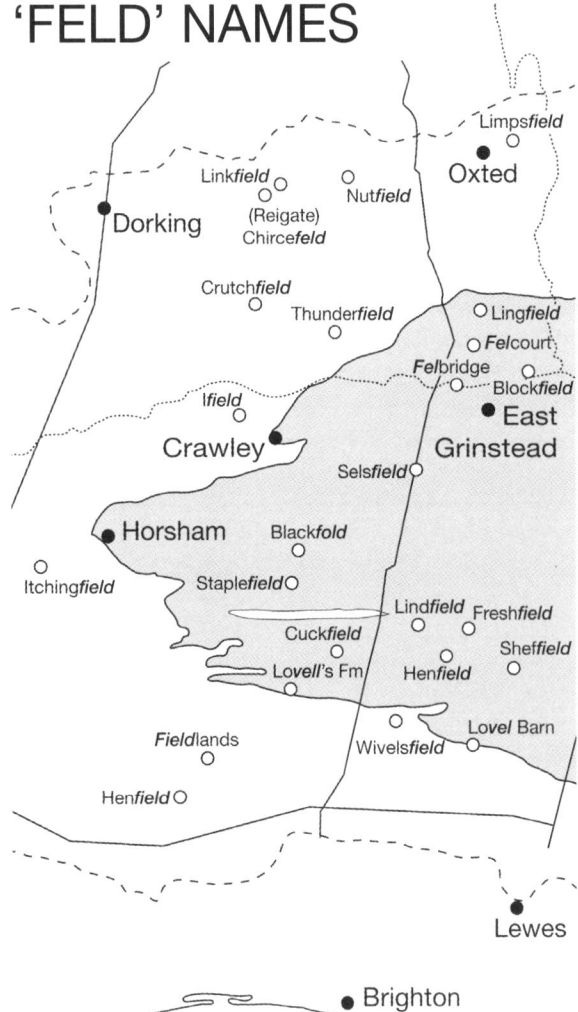

Permit Number CP18/021 Derived by British Geological Survey Material © UKRI 2018

© Crown copyright and database rights 2018. OS License number 100048229

The word *'feld'*, in its early usage, denoted unencumbered ground, that is, an area without trees, woods, hills, or buildings. The *feld* place-names on this map are of early origin, and mostly later came to denote the ancient settlements made upon them. They attest to early clearances of the forested Weald. Many seem to denote flat, open areas in the High Weald, on the Hastings Beds sands and clays. Were these early open areas particularly associated with iron industry activity – heightened during the Roman occupation – on the iron bearing Hastings Beds?

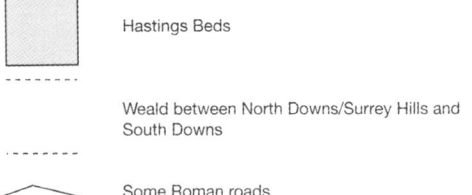

Willows, Blackcurrants and Hops … or Willow Shaw at Laughton, with its purple-tinted winter Alders, can we re-capture some of the lost prehistoric luxuriance of those soggy woods.

Rackham suggests[15] that if the output of the Roman military ironworks in the Weald was 550 tons a year for 120 years they would have utilised charcoal from 23,000 acres of coppice, and this calculation excludes all the other Roman and Romano-British ironworks. Roman period metallurgy may thus have influenced more woodland than medieval metallurgy, and may not have been surpassed even in the 17th century. South of Haywards Heath's Rocky Lane was an area known in medieval times as *Ise*woods (iron woods)[16] and the nearby area west of the Brighton Line is *Hease*lands (*hese*: brush, underwood) suggesting ancient coppice working, perhaps for iron foundry charcoal.

SAXON TIMES

The Venerable Bede described the Weald in 731 AD as "**thick and inaccessible, the abode of deer, swine and wolves**".[17] The Anglo Saxon Chronicle in 893 AD described it as *'se micla wudu'*, 'the great wood', and states that "**from east to west (it) is a hundred and twenty miles long or longer, and thirty miles wide**", a measurement which must have meant that its forest was continuous at its western end with those on the West Sussex and Hampshire Downs, the forests of Bere and Waltham, and the New Forest.[18]

At the time of the Domesday Book, 1086 AD, it is estimated that 70% of the Weald was woodland,[19] as opposed to 15% nationally. The Weald's woodland was far greater than that of the other most wooded parts of England, such as the Chilterns (Bucks 26%), around modern Birmingham (Worcester 40%; Stafford 32%, Warwick 19%), Essex (20%), Middlesex (30%), and Cheshire (27%). By contrast, the national figure meant that England as a whole was less wooded then than France is today.

However, the Weald had, even then, lost much forest. Centuries of Saxon assarting, after the clearances of the Romans and earlier prehistoric peoples, had already broken the continuity of the Low Weald's woods and reduced them to concentrations in Sussex and Surrey on the Gault Clay and the inward parts of the Wealden Clay. There were many farmed areas in the High Weald, too. By the Norman conquest, 1066 AD, settlement was well established right up to the southern boundary of St Leonard's Forest, north of Cowfold.[20]

The place names that the Saxon people had fixed on their new Wealden lands after the collapse of the Roman occupation c. 410 AD, included many indicating woodland, but also a fair number indicating large open areas: *'feld'*. There are many such *feld* names in the land around the old Portslade to London Roman Road: Wivels*field*, Cuck*field*, Lind*field*, Hen*field* (at Scaynes

MEDIEVAL ASSARTS

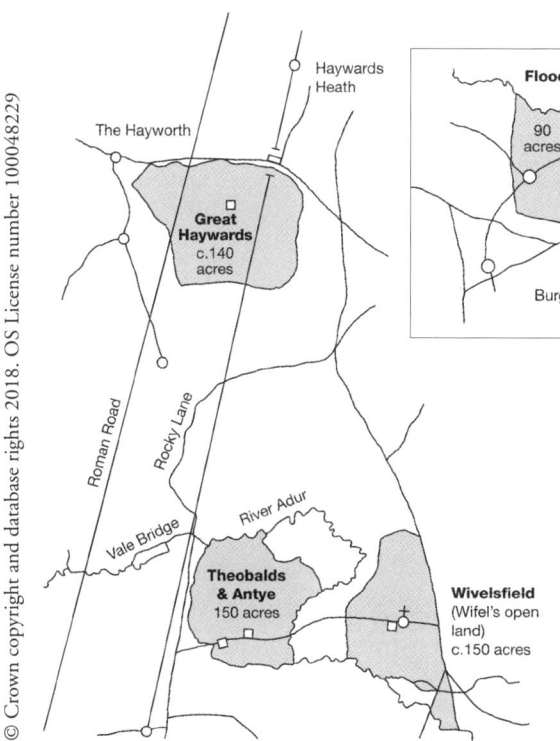
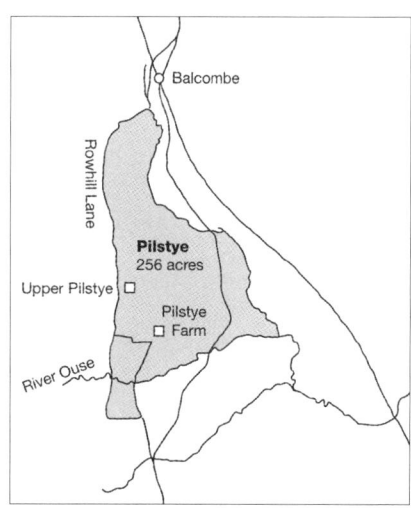

Sometimes singly, often as small groups of cooperating households, medieval settlers cleared ('assarted') areas of unenclosed forested land. Heather Warne's work has revealed several such assarted holdings near Haywards Heath and Burgess Hill.

Hill), *Feld*wick, Sels*field*, *Fel*bridge, Nut*field*, Ling*field*, Thunder*field*, Small*field*, and more.

ASSARTS

The scatter of *'fold'* (Saxon *'falod'*) place names in our area may indicate elements of an unplanned inward movement of settlers (though most *'fold'* names are found west of Horsham and north of Petworth). The place name means something like an enclosed stock or swine summer pasture, which later became an assarted farm or farm cluster. Cow*fold* is one such, now a village, with Woldring*fold* to its northwest and Dane*fold* to its west. There's Ash*fold* west of Handcross and Black*fold* to its east, Little Ash*fold* south of Staplefield, Ash*folds* in Rusper, and Kings*fold* in Albourne. It seems likely that the cattle and swine would be driven to these distant Wealden pastures in summer and returned after the harvest in the parent settlements.

*Horn*brook Farm, south of Horsham probably indicates that some of the *Horningas* people of Washington settled there, for Washington had *horninga dene* in its charter bounds. Due north of coastal *Somp*ing are *Sunt* Wood and *Sunt* Farm (now lost) near Maplehurst, which, with a second lost *Sunt* Farm in Shipley, were possible early settlements from there.

Land rising from the main river valleys in the Weald, especially the south facing slopes, was a target for early settlement. On the tops of the ridges agriculture petered out, leaving rough land. Settlers in the Wealden 'waste' may often have come as small groups of households,[21] sharing a plough or ploughs and the heavy tasks of woodland clearance. Such was Pilstye, TQ 207 284, just west of the Balcombe Viaduct, on a south facing slope down to meadow on the Ouse, with rough woodland to its north (*Row*hill). It had three cooperating households, though only one farm remains. Such was Theobalds and Antye, TQ 327 206, north east of Wivelsfield Station, part-bounded by the infant Adur. The two successor farmsteads of its early settlers still stand. By contrast, The Hayworth, later Great Hayworth, TQ 325 236, now split by the Brighton Line just south of Haywards Heath tunnel, appears to have been settled by just one family, though a second farm, Little Haywards, was created later. Its converted farmsteads and Reading Wood survive.

Highbrook, TQ 361 300, which used to be called Hammingden, on a ridge between Ardingly and West Hoathly, is an example of a medieval clustered settlement,[22] with the hall houses of four of its old farms surviving, including Hammingden (still a working farm) and Battens.

Early farms like Bishopstone Farm, TQ 285 222, south of Ansty, and Homewood Farm west of Bolney, TQ 245 227, (both held by the Bishop of Chichester) still display something of their founding division between a southern and south facing farmstead, and managed woodlands at their north end.

EARLY MEDIEVAL PLANNERS

Map derived from a pot pourri of different information sources. SORRY if you're confused!

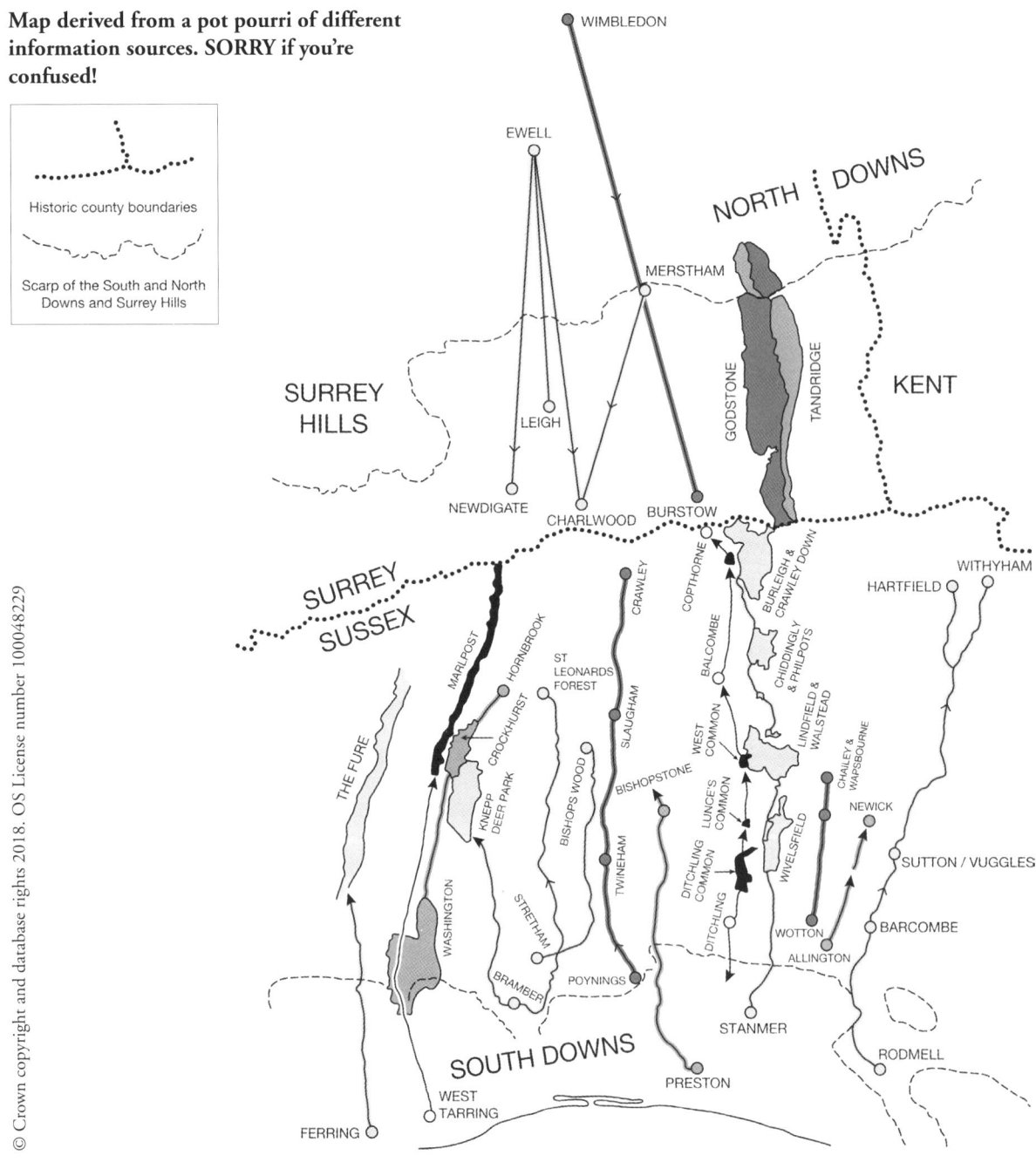

We tend to think of early medieval folk as having very narrow horizons. That is only half true. Their local economies exploited long distance, widespread resources. Peasants from West Tarring (Worthing) or Stanmer (Brighton) or Wimbledon (Surrey) may have had tasks that sent them right across the Weald as far as the Sussex-Surrey county boundary. This map shows the long reach of the rich manors of the North and Sussex Downs and coast to their outliers in the woods and pastures of the far distant Weald. The resultant outlier shapes were often bizarre, as with the long, worm-like shapes of The Fure and Marlpost outliers.

Some of these long-distant patterns are here represented symbolically, such as Wimbledon, Poynings and Rodmell. Stanmer's Wealden outliers are represented by what survived of them as a separate manor in 1830. Godstone and Tandridge are shown by their medieval parishes, not manors, but their linear shapes illustrate the same organising patterns of economy.

LARGE SCALE PLANNING

It would be a mistake, however, to underestimate the degree of large scale planning by the ruling class that went into this woodland clearance and land apportionment. There are detectable relics of the most extraordinary linear medieval manors,[23] some long owned by the church, and thus relatively static – indeed fossilised – organisationally. **Marlpost** was the Wealden part of the Archbishop of Canterbury's manor of West Tarring, now part of Worthing, gifted to him 941 AD. 8.5 mile long by only a little over 0.28 of a mile wide, the manor traverses Wealden Clay, Horsham Stone, woods, streams, the River Arun, sandstone, the old Horsham Common and the north Horsham Ridges to halt abruptly at the county boundary (thus proving that the county boundary was a fixed feature by the time the manor was organised). It can still be detected by hedgerows and lanes over much of its length, including through much of built-up Horsham, whose town centre 'Bishopric' area owes its development to the manor. Ancient Marlpost and *Court*land Woods, west of Southwater, were once part of the manorial desmesne, as the manorial *court* place name indicates.

Its boundaries seem as irrational and rigidly imposed as the boundaries of post colonial African states plonked down by their early colonial administrators in complete disregard of natural features or the dispositions of peoples. Two miles to its west there is an even more fantastic linear manor some 10.3 miles long by c. 0.7 wide, which was once **The Fure** Wealden outlier of the Bishop of Chichester's coastal Ferring manor (hence lovely *Bishop's* Wood, TQ 111 282, with its Wild Daffodils). Part of its alignment had been settled earlier (Row*fold*) and so its boundary wiggles round that assart. The manor's relentless march was only stopped at its north and south ends by pre-existing common land. It had another two linear manorial outliers to its east and west.

In Surrey we see the same pattern with the Surrey parish of Tandridge, which extended for seven miles to the Sussex border though only about three fields wide for much of its length, a pattern which may have owed something to the ancient trackway it embraced. Such manorial impositions were made easier by the flat landscape of the Wealden Clay.

The pattern elsewhere in the Brighton Line Weald may not be quite as rigid as those strips … but it wasn't far off. The Wealden outlier of Stanmer Manor marched almost due north of the Downland village right to the Surrey border. The manor must originally have formed a corridor nearly 14 miles long and between 0.5 miles to two miles wide from Wivelsfield Green, embracing Lindfield and Walstead, Hapstead Green (Ardingly), Philpots-Chiddingly, and Crawley Down. Alongside it westwards was the kingly parent manor of Ditchling, forming a similar corridor embracing much of Wivelsfield and Ardingly, with Worth Forest, broken only by the intrusion of Cuckfield, held by the manor of Plumpton. The manor of Ditchling, held in modern times by the Lords Abergavenny, collateral heirs of the Norman feudalists, only sold the manorial relics of Lunce's and Ditchling Commons in the last century!

These manors were each a sub-division of a former early Saxon *'regio',* that is, a territory of a petty king in the earliest, most chaotic Saxon settlement.[24] The Brighton Line Weald, between the Adur and Ouse, formed one 'regio' micro-kingdom, with Ditchling its capital. The area between the Adur and the Arun formed a micro-kingdom, based on a capital at Washington, with Burpham forming its *'burgh',* or fortress. From the Arun westwards was another 'regio', with Arundel as its burgh, and there was a possible further western micro-kingdom based on a capital at Fishbourne, with unknown further 'regios' in the east of Sussex.[25] Such 'regios' were similar to, but not the same as the administrative rapes that are recorded in Domesday Book,[26] 1086 AD.

Perhaps by c. 750 AD the county boundary had been fixed between the chiefs of the peoples of Sussex, Surrey and Kent. The Surrey-Sussex boundary marches along the *ridge tops,* and the Kent-Sussex boundary sticks to the *valley bottom streams,* but on the marshy Mole flatlands (modern Gatwick) and soggy moors, heaths and woods of Copthorne and Felbridge such boundary features are not so obvious.

DROVEWAYS

When my Mum was in her eighties and not up for more than the most minimal hobbling about, I took her pootling in my car up the long, quiet Low Wealden lanes, stopping whenever we saw something like a Bluebell bank, or heard a bird singing through the open windows, or found some lovely view, or cottage garden to admire. Sometimes we'd halt for a long time, the engine off, just listening to the peace, and talking as the fancy took us. The little used lanes were perfect for such very slow pootlings.

A lot of those lanes, tracking more or less north-south, have been travelled by folk for well over a thousand years, and perhaps back to the Dark Age, or Roman, even Iron Age, times. Near to the South and North Downs they were used by farmers working fields not far from their villages or tending sheep, but, deeper into the Weald, they were used by such villagers to reach their wood pasture outliers, herding their swine long distances to feast on the mast of Beech, acorns, fruits and fungi, and their cattle to browse the brush and the herbage of heath and meadow.

Such former droves are easily distinguished by their broadness, with a minimum width of 30 to 40 feet,[27] but often much wider, with high bordering hedgebanks. Most of them have lost their flowery grassland, cropped

MEDIEVAL DROVE ROADS

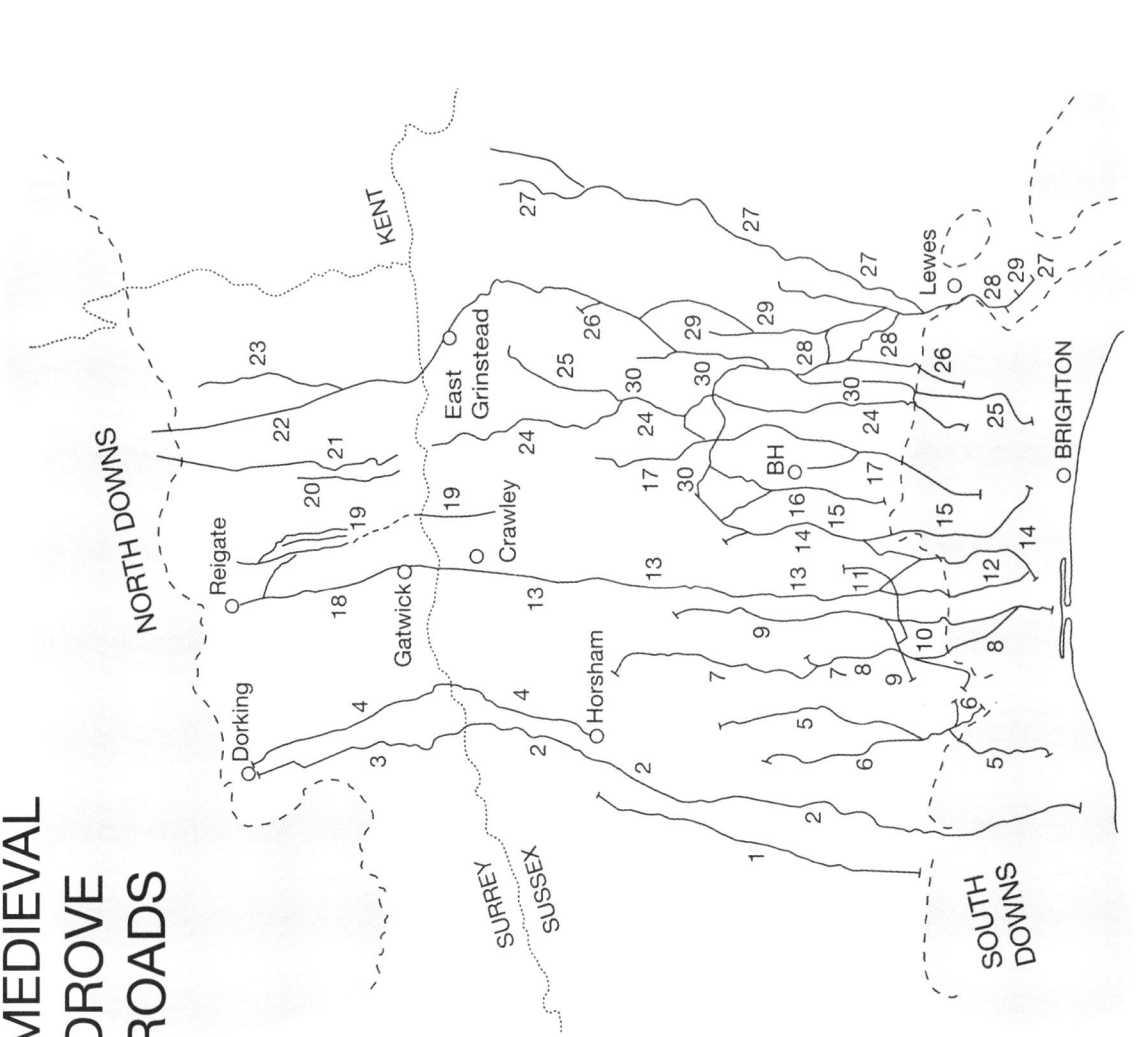

These roads and tracks are only a few examples of the routes along which peasants drove their livestock from the better land of the Downs and Wealden edges to forage in the inner forest, and along which they brought out their Wealden products of timber, minerals, hay, etc. If you look at old, large scale maps you will notice them running often parallel and north-south. Many other lost routes can be surmised from the pattern of surviving fragments.

Key
BH= Burgess Hill

1. Sullington to Broadbridge
2. West Tarring to Marlpost Woods and Horsham
3. Dorking to Holmwood and Capel
4. Dorking to Newdigate, Rusper and Horsham
5. Sompting to Sunt Farm, Copsale
6. Annington to Bassell's Farm, and Bramber to Knepp Castle
7. Upper Beeding to St Leonard's Forest
8. Kingston Buci to Shermanbury
9. Stretham Manor to Bishop's Wood, Warninglid
10. Southwick to Woodmancote
11. Stretham Manor to Albourne (Bishopshurst Manor)
12. Portslade to Perching, Fulking
13. Poynings to Twineham, Slaugham, and Crawley
14. Hangleton to Cuckfield
15. Preston to Bishopstone Farm
16. Clayton to St John's Common (Burgess Hill)
17. Ditchling south to Patcham, and north to Wivelsfield, West Lindfield, and Balcombe
18. Reigate to Horley
19. Reigate to Earlswood, Salfords, Horley, and Worth
20. Burstow to Burstow Park
21. Caterham to Bletchingley, Outwood, Smallfield, and Copthorne
22. Godstone to East Grinstead
23. Tandridge to Blindley Heath
24. Stanmer to Wivelsfield, Lindfield, and Crawley Down
25. Bevendean to Standen, East Grinstead
26. Balmer Farm, Falmer, to Birchgrove, Horsted Keynes
27. Rodmell to Barcombe, Newick, Hartfield and Withyham
28. Swanborough, Iford, to Home Wood, East Chiltington
29. Iford to Chailey and Wapsbourne (Sheffield Park) and Worth
30. Plumpton to Scaynes Hill, Cuckfield, and Highbrook (Hammingden)

© Crown copyright and database rights 2018. OS License number 100048229

28 BACKSTORY / Chapter 1: The Wealden landscape's history

till modern times by cottagers', farmers' and gipsies' horses, house cows and poultry, and mown by linesmens' sickles, or farmers looking for a supplementary hay crop. Their roadside waste has now mostly grown rank, or succeeded to thorn and woodland. Some of them have become fast modern roads.

The A2037 was once the drove from Upper Beeding, through Henfield and Cowfold north to St Leonard's Forest (coterminous with Lower Beeding). The stretch south of Cowfold has woodland waste on both sides. From Horn Lane (the old Roman road), Small Dole, the Bishop of Chichester's herds would have been driven up Blackstone Lane, due north up Wineham Lane, crossing three branches of the Adur, up Spronkett's Lane and Earwig Lane to his swine pastures at Bishop's Wood, TQ 240 260, west of Warninglid. Much of Wineham Lane's roadside waste has Bluebells and Anemones, forming an ancient woodland refugium in a landscape which has lost most of its old woods. The Bishops' workers from Hove and Preston would have trudged over the Downs past Poynings, High Cross, Twineham Place to their outlier at Homewood, Bolney, or through Hurstpierpoint and Goddard's Green to Bishopstone at Ansty. Ditchling Common Lane, Spatham Lane, Streat Lane, Plumpton Lane, and others in between them are all ancient droveways. The A275 main road from Lewes to Chailey, Sheffield Park and Danehill, was once a drovers and peasants trunk road, and it still has wide linear wastes along much of its length, mostly wooded, but some still grassy.

Though many of these droves are now motor roads, there are good stretches of green lane where their old character partially survives. Such is Shergold's Farm Green in Streat, TQ 356 165, a place of wild flowers and well tended hedges, with the possibility of hearing Nightingales near the railway line. North of Spatham Lane a green lane runs alongside delightful West Wood, TQ 343 192, till it reaches Wivelsfield. For over 1.5 miles from Blonk's Farm to Shipley, e.g. TQ 137 204, a green lane passes through re-wilded Knepp Estate land where you may see Barn Owl or hear Nightingales. It would have been one of the droves connecting Washington with its outliers at Crockhurst (by Southwater) and Horsham. West of Southwater, lovely Crookhorn Lane runs for a mile northwards, past ancient Crookhorn Farm TQ 139 258, between Netherwood and Dogbarking House.

In Surrey, Chithurst Lane is a quiet place of Bluebells, with the chance of seeing the rare herd of Dairy Shorthorns at Bysshe Court Farm, TQ 334 429. Green Lane, Tandridge, TQ 373 415, is 2.5 miles long, almost to Blindley Heath, passing several ancient Bluebell woods. Gail Lane-Green Lane, east of Salfords, forms a 1.5 mile linear ancient wood, TQ 287 459.

Probably the best surviving example locally of the generous wastes along the old droves lies on the west side of the Adur in Ashurst. It runs for two miles from Horsebridge Common to Bines Green. Most of Horsebridge Common and the roadside waste has succeeded to impenetrable thorn scrub and woodland, but Bines Green, TQ 186 173, is open, as it is at New Wharf Farm, Godsmark's Farm and a few other spots. The tragic neglect of Bines Green in recent decades, however, has turned it from rich archaic grassland to a rank and simplified mess. Twenty years ago I found Sneezewort, Pepper Saxifrage and Marsh Pennywort. I've seen none of them in recent years. It is another small scandal in an area full of people with money to spare. Intervention now would probably rescue and restore some of that interest.

THE LATER MEDIEVAL AND EARLY MODERN WEALD

The underhill manors (later parishes) below the South and North Downs were well settled by the time of the Norman Conquest, with extensive arable, often in common fields. It is noteworthy that these underhill manors-cum-parishes mostly claimed little more of the Downs than the nearby scarp slopes, implying that their focus was very much on the *Wealden* arable, not the relatively impoverished arable of the Downs. These manor-parishes formed long strips, which each had their own share of Down, springs and streams, Grey Chalk, Upper Greensand, Gault Clay, Lower Greensand and Wealden Clay, apportioned as arable, grazing, meadow or woodland as fertility and drainage dictated. In the early period the Surrey manor-parishes of Bletchingley, Godstone, Tandridge and Oxted stretched all the way to the Sussex border, and both Tandridge and Godstone still did until modern times.

Despite parish amalgamations the pattern of these underhill strip parishes can still be seen today. Their headquarters, where their churches were placed, form ribbons along the fertile Grey Chalk/Upper Greensand: *Edburton, Poynings, Newtimber (almost), Clayton, Westmeston, Plumpton*; or the Lower Greensand: *Henfield, Woodmancote, Albourne, Hurstpierpoint, Keymer, Ditchling, Streat, East Chiltington*. In Surrey, all but Gatton parish hog the Lower Greensand: *Dorking, Betchworth, Buckland, Reigate, Nutfield, Bletchingley, Godstone, Tandridge, and Oxted*.

These underhill parishes ate away at the lordly or commoned wastes[28] at their northern ends in the pre- and post-Domesday Low Weald. At Ditchling the farmers – probably the better-off – took in latitudinal strips of land for the plough – '*inholmes*' south of the present common, and their narrow hedged shapes remain today, TQ 335 165. They took in other land from the chase west of the common. At Streat a quarter of the common was ploughed up in 1258. At Plumpton they took in more 'inholmes' (see Inholmes Farm, TQ 363 174) north of the present railway line,

SAUSAGE-SHAPED FARMS AND MANORS

It is striking how the grand longtitudinal pattern of cross-Wealden medieval manors and parishes was often replicated down to the level of individual farms. Stanmer Hamlet (Wivelsfield) and Bishopshurst (Albourne) were thus once sub-manors of Stanmer and Stretham respectively. Homewood (Bolney), Blackstone, and Goffsland Farms were individual holdings.

STANMER HAMLET (WIVELSFIELD) c. 900 ACRES

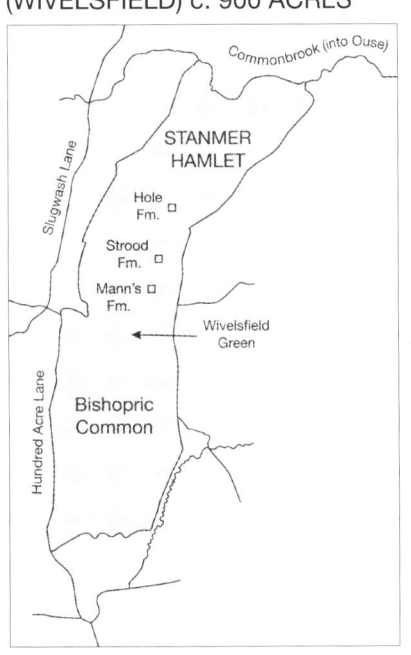

BLACKSTONE FARM (WOODMANCOTE)

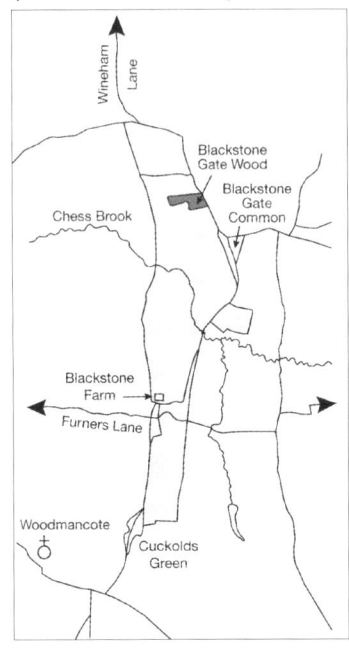

WOTTON MANOR (CHAILEY)

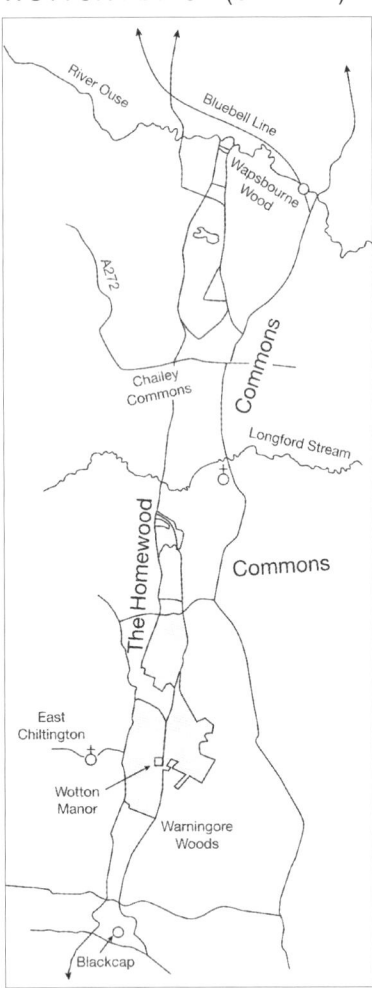

BISHOPSHURST, 1681 (ALBOURNE)

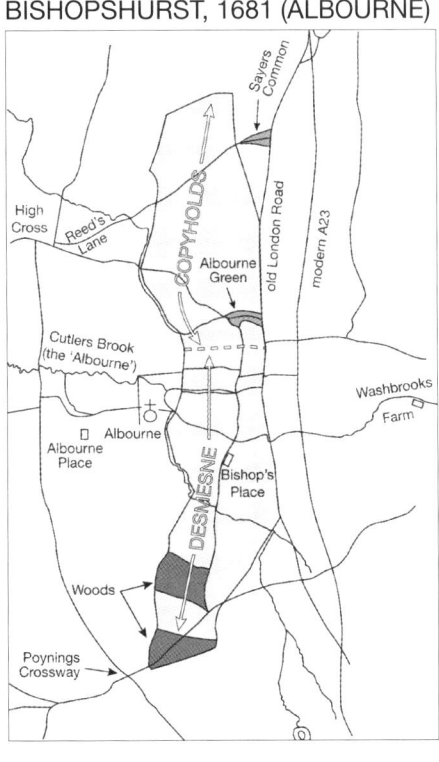

HOMEWOOD (BOLNEY)

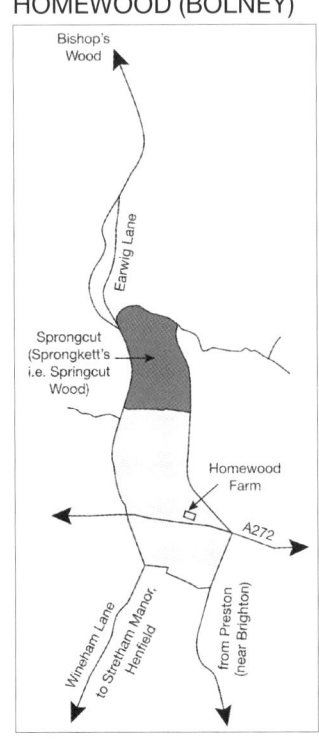

GOFFSLAND FARM (SHIPLEY)

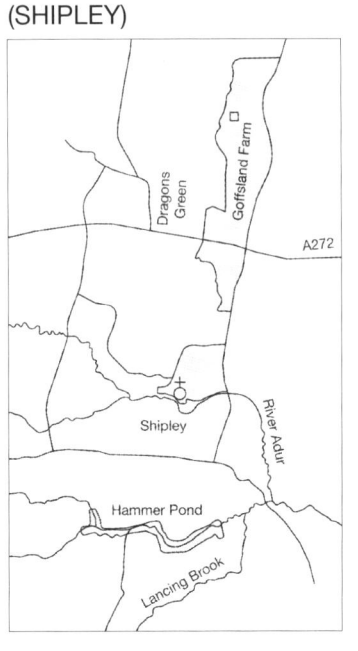

© Crown copyright and database rights 2018. OS License number 100048229

30 BACKSTORY / Chapter 1: The Wealden landscape's history

east and west of the drove, leaving a long and broad green – Plumpton Green – which survived until 1842. Elsewhere in the Low Weald other land was settled, such as Crockhurst, the large wooded outlier of Washington manor at Southwater, asserted in the first half of the 13th century.

However, by the late 13th century this colonisation ground to a halt. Part of the remaining unfarmed land lay in parks, chases, and desmesne (landlord's) woods, and the rest was within valued commoning economies. The extent of the present Ditchling Common (including the Country Park) has changed little since 1300. St Leonard's Forest, too, suffered little from new settlement in the late medieval period. A relatively static disposition of semi-natural land (wood pasture, enclosed woodland, heath, archaic pasture and moor) and farmed land in the Low Weald, survived for two centuries, reinforced hugely by the population crash after the Black Death plague epidemic of 1348–9 and its recurrences through the 14th and 15th centuries.

Subsequently, a new wave of clearance was stimulated by a number of factors: the recovery of population by the 16th century; the effects of the rise of the iron industry; the huge reorganisation of property ownership with the failure of the male line of the Warenne lords of Lewes Rape; and a similar great buying and selling caused by the confiscations of church lands in the 1530s Reformation. These advances of capitalist tenure and agriculture proceeded through the 16th and 17th centuries, creating the broad disposition of farmed land and woodland surviving today.

Near the start of that process in 1530 much of the northern half of the Wealden Clay north of Lewes had been in a semi-natural state, part common, part a kind of hunting ground known as a 'frank chase', part managed and enclosed desmesne woodland, and part enclosed pastures and meadows. About 600 acres of woodland owed its preservation mainly to Lewes Priory's conservative management. The commoners of Newick and Chailey grazed about 1500 acres. Much of this wide landscape had been kept semi-natural for centuries within what was known as the Forest of Cleres by the obsession of the Earls Warenne of Lewes Castle for hunting.[29]

MEDIEVAL PARISH OUTLIERS

The medieval administrative patterns of the Church often remained intact into modern times – fossilised through institutional inertia – despite reflecting patterns of feudal exploitation. These examples were all intact c. 1870.

VUGGLES FARM, A DETACHED RODMELL OUTLIER

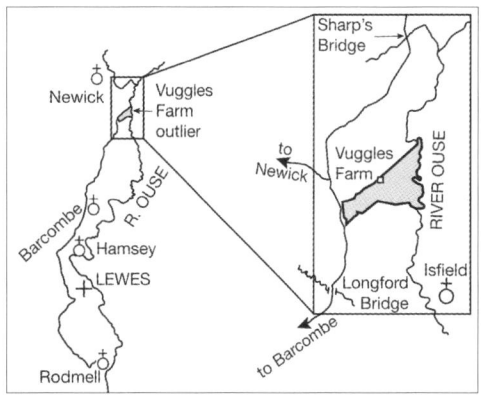

BROADBRIDGE, A DETACHED OUTLIER OF SULLINGTON

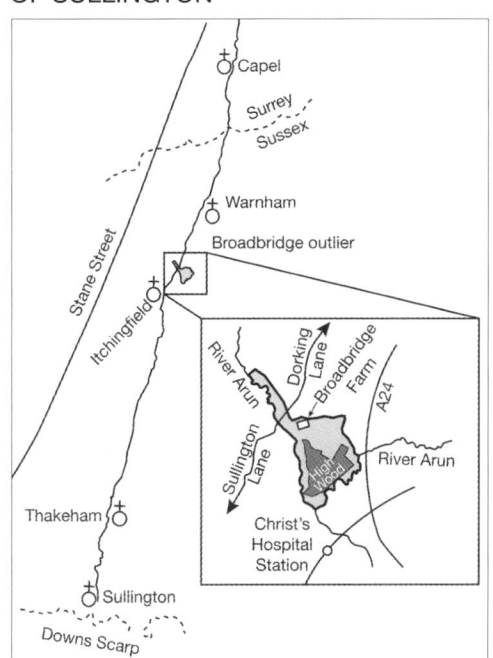

BLACKFOLD, ONCE A DETACHED OUTLIER OF SADDLESCOMBE, NEWTIMBER

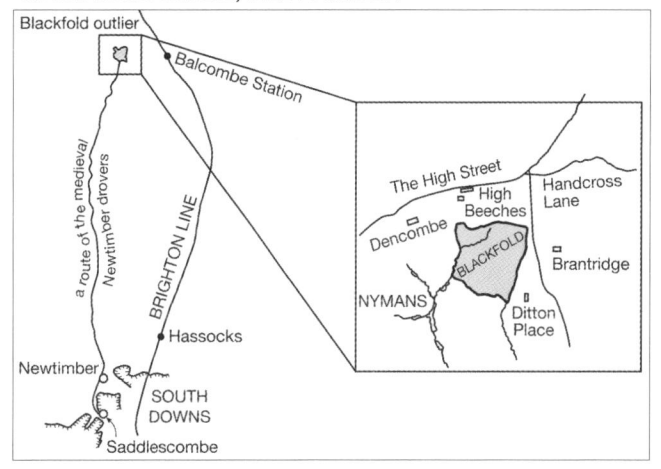

© Crown copyright and database rights 2018. OS License number 100048229

LOST MEDIEVAL DEER PARKS

DANNY GREAT PARK, DANNY LITTLE PARK AND POYNINGS

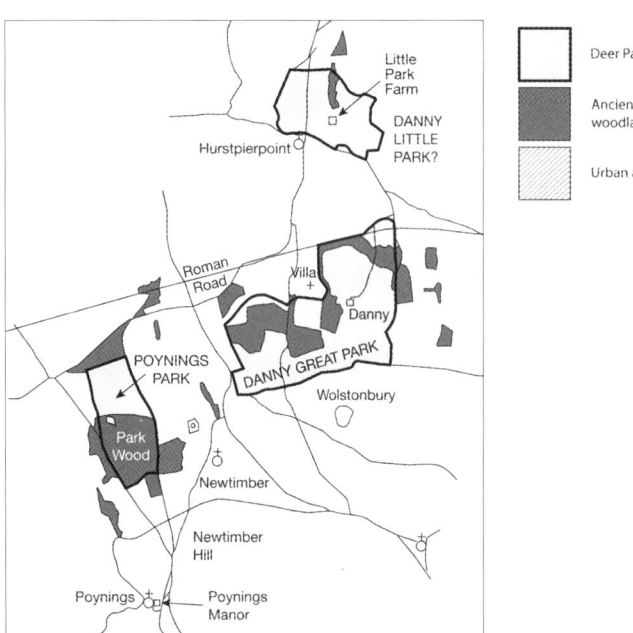

DITCHLING AND HAYLEY

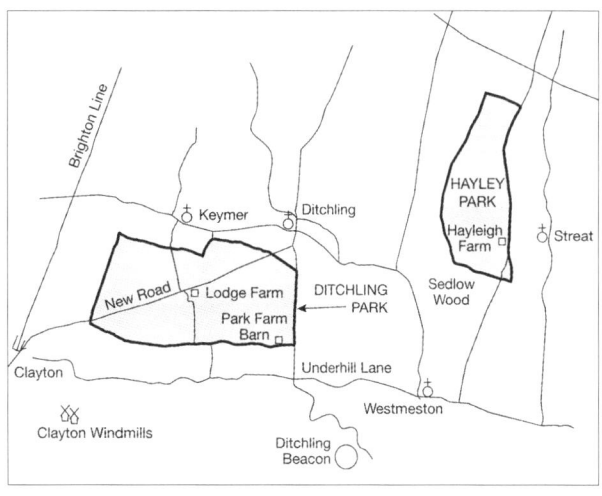

SLAUGHAM

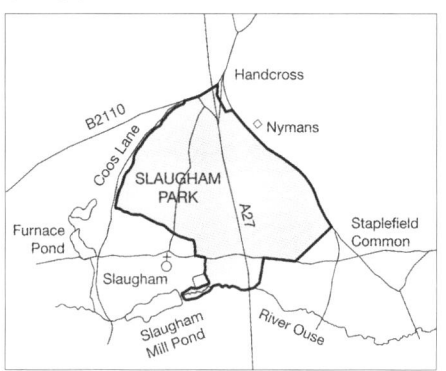

PADDOCKHURST

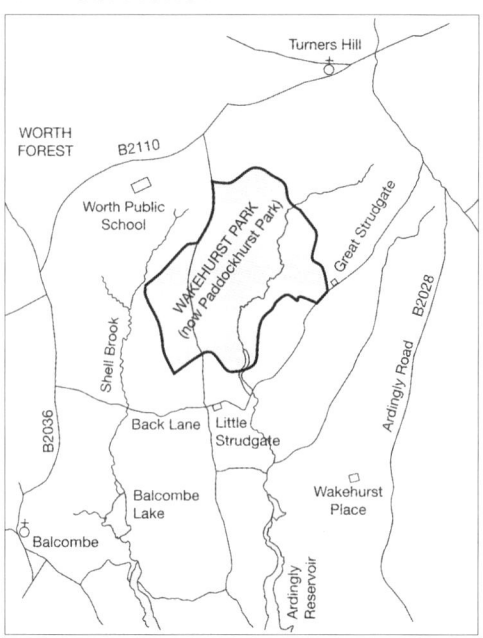

KNEPP

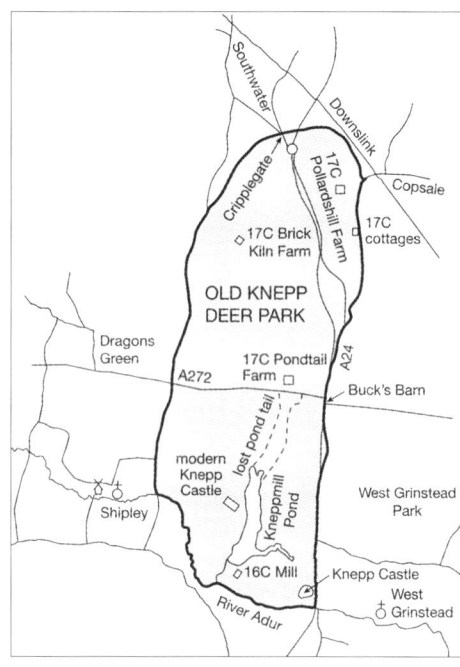

LAGHAM

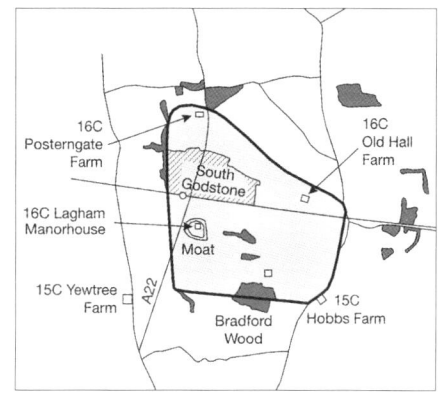

BACKSTORY / Chapter 1: The Wealden landscape's history

COMMONS, PARKS AND CHASES (LARGELY HEATH, MOOR, GRASS HEATH, PASTURE WOODLAND) BETWEEN HAYWARDS HEATH AND LEWES c. 1530

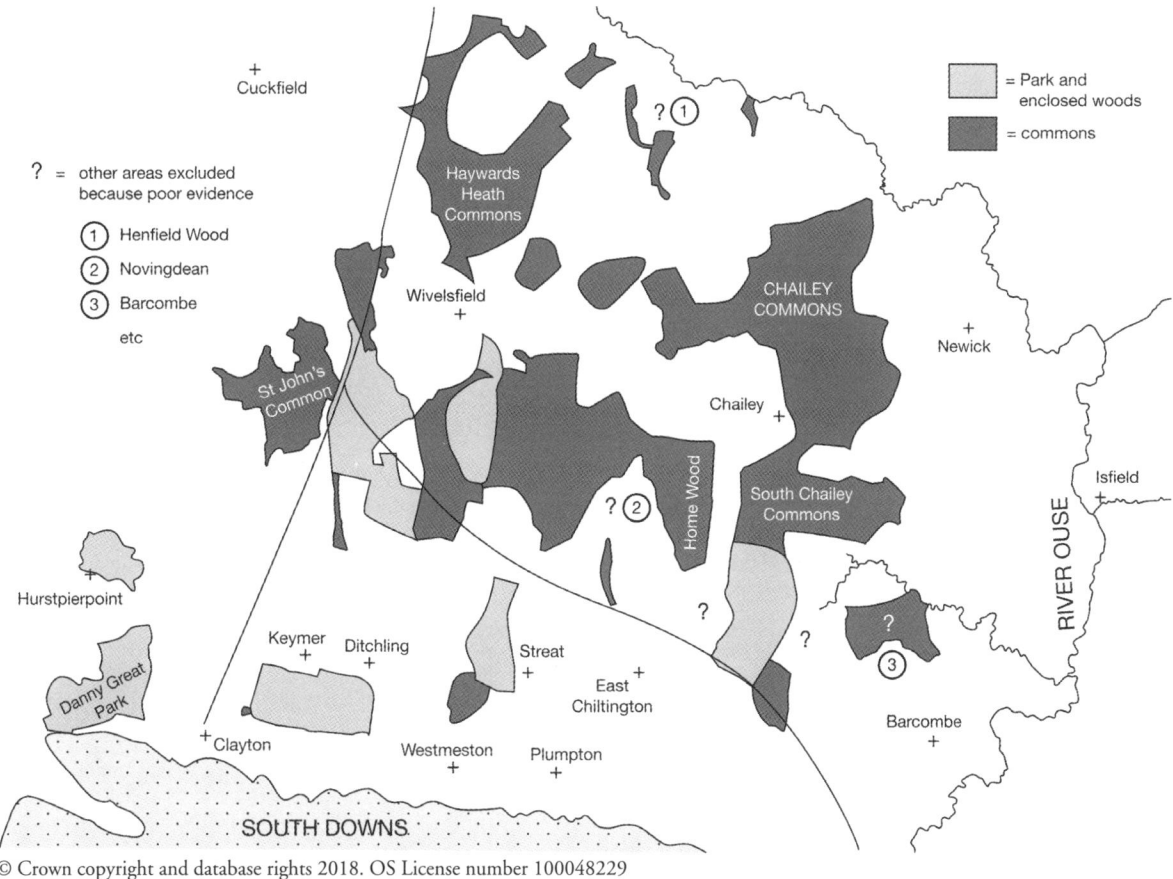

© Crown copyright and database rights 2018. OS License number 100048229

A huge area of semi-natural habitat survived at the end of the middle ages in this part of the northern Sussex Low Weald. **Indeed, this map greatly underestimates the true extent of semi-natural habitat, because it does not include many managed enclosed ancient woodlands (like Warningore and other Gault Clay woods), semi-natural meadow and floodplain grasslands, or other permanent enclosed pastures.** Some areas are excluded because of my poor boundary evidence, such as Henfield Wood (Scaynes Hill), Novingdean and Barcombe's commons, etc.

This map is mostly based on the work of Dr Peter Brandon in his superb 1963 unpublished PhD thesis (University of London) 'The Common Lands and Wastes of Sussex', with his kind permission.

This clearing of semi-natural woodland and heath was drastic, though often contested by the poor, against an alliance of rich commoners and lords, in its early stages. By 1680 at least 700 acres of woodland had been cleared, 3,000 acres of common enclosed, and 3,000 acres disparked in this landscape. *The Homewood, East Chiltington*, TQ 37 17, was cut over by speculators and left without mature timber. Only fragments survive today: Great Home Wood and Middle Home Wood. (Wet Home Wood was cleared in recent years). *Novingdean Common*, 40 acres next to Homewood, was lost after 1600. *Hayleigh Park* and *much of Sedlow Wood*, Westmeston, were cleared. (A fragment of Sedlow Wood survives). *Woods in Clayton, Keymer, and at Danny Park*, Hurstpierpoint, were cleared. By 1596 all 240 acres left of *Plumton Common* was enclosed and divided. Between 1595 and 1625 all of *Novington Common* was enclosed. On Allington Lane, *Beechwood Common*, 150 a., was enclosed by 1584. In 1574, the 246 acre *Barcombe Commons* were enclosed. Wivelsfield's common meadows at *The Breach* were enclosed by 1600, and its 300 acre *Bishopric Common* (south of Wivelsfield

Green) was enclosed soon after 1617. The *commons of Westmeston, Middleton and Streat manors* were enclosed between 1600 and 1684. *Chailey North Commons* lost 600 acres between 1622 and 1666. Three quarters of *Markstakes Common* was enclosed. The 500 acres or more remnants of *Shortfrith Chase* (where St George's Retreat is now, next to Ditchling Common) and *Frekebergh Chase* (south of Bedelands, Burgess Hill) were lost by 1600. *Cuckfield, Ditchling and Danny Parks* were converted to farmland and enclosed, managed woodland in the 16th century. *Bilsborough Common* (the present Woodmancote Moor) was gone by 1639.

More widely, the three square miles of Knepp Park was disparked and then broken up into farms after 1549. East Grinstead's Leigh Hothe was enclosed after 1600. St Leonard's Forest came to the Crown in 1563, and thereafter lost nearly all its magnificent woods. By 1609 2,500 acres had been let as farmland. Much of it was to return to heath, however, and by 1684, the Forest had become "a mere rabbit warren". (See Forests chapter).

In south east Surrey parallel processes were at work: *Hartswood,* south west of Reigate, disappeared, *Shellwood* in Leigh and *Ewood* in Newdigate shrank hugely. The woodlands were cleared from Crowhurst, which had been named after its wood, and the great *parks of Burstow and Bletchingley* were disparked. (See chapters 17 and 18).

THE LAST BIG ONSLAUGHT ON THE COMMONS AND WASTES

It is often thought that the 18th and 19th centuries were a relatively unchanging time in our Wealden countryside, before the onslaught of modern settlement and industrial farming. Indeed, the process of change was slow at the start of the eighteenth century, for the iron industry had collapsed, and in some areas, particularly in the Low Weald, the amount of common wastes still unenclosed was limited. Poor transport infrastructure hugely limited movement and carriage, particularly in the winter months, and on the rivers the situation had regressed from earlier improvements.

Later in the century things speeded up. The construction of the Ouse navigation right up to

Brookwood Farm, Ashurst: the house may be 400 years old, but the 'brook wood' after which it is named has long gone!

the Balcombe Viaduct (1790–1812), and the Adur Navigation (1808–1825) opened up trade. (See Rivers chapter). So did the expansion of turnpike trusts from 1749.[30] In the 18th century they brought engineered metalled roads: down to Horsham from London; down to Crawley, Cuckfield and Brighton; down to Brighton via Lindfield; and down to Lewes via East Grinstead. From 1800 to c. 1840 the network was consolidated with new east-west roads. A turnpike between Crawley and Horsham supplanted the ancient forest ridge route through Colgate. A new turnpike westwards from Cuckfield pioneered the alignment of the modern A272 and transgressed the age-old longtitudinal organisation of the landscape. A new turnpike running due south from Handcross split Slaugham's old deer park in two and pioneered the alignment of the modern A23 Brighton Road. The Cuckfield Road northwards from Hurstpierpoint was engineered, and the underhill lane from Ditchling to Offham was turnpiked, laying the basis for the B2116's modern speeding traffic.

The turnpikes were in turn supplanted by the railways. The Brighton Line opened first, in 1841, and by 1882 the rest of this area's Wealden railways had been constructed.

All this new infrastructure powered the grotesque expansion of the London metropolis and laid the basis for the new wave of clearances and colonisations of the majority of remaining wastes of the Brighton Line Weald.

The great triumph of local 18th century enclosure lay just outside our area at The Broyle, Ringmer, a huge medieval commoned deer park once owned by the Archbishops of Canterbury. At 2,020 acres it was a third the size of Ashdown Forest's commons. From

1767–71 it was carved up and allotted at the behest of the modernising plutocrat, Richard Trevor, Bishop of Durham and heir to Glynde Place.[31]

From Crawley to East Grinstead the chain of heathy commons were enclosed between c. 1800 and 1855. East Grinstead Common went soon after 1800; the remains of Hedgecourt Common was gone by 1810; Crawley Down was enclosed in 1848, and Copthorne Common in 1855.

From Crawley west to Horsham another set was lost. At the beginning of the process, Prestwood Common in Ifield was quietly enclosed in 1717, and at the end of the process Ifield Green and Langley Green were lost in 1855. Lowfield Heath, partly in Surrey, was enclosed in 1846. (See chapters 17 and 18 for details of the parallel Surrey enclosures). Horsham Common, a big purlieu common of St Leonard's Forest, was enclosed in 1812-13.

From 1820–40 Lindfield's West Common was lost. Keymer's share of St John's Common (Burgess Hill) together with Vale Bridge Common and Broad Street Green, totalling 450a., were enclosed in 1828. Blacklands Common, Henfield, went about the same time.

From 1840–60 the surveyors were busy. Bolney Common was enclosed in 1841, and so was Chailey's South Common and a big slice of its North Common, separating Lane End Common from the rest of North Common. Plumpton Green was lost in 1842. The Clayton portion of St John's Common and two thirds of Broadbridge Heath Common went in 1855. Walstead Common went in 1856.

After 1860 the last big formal enclosures took place. Haywards Heath was enclosed in 1862, Mannings Heath and Monk's Green, purlieu commons of St Leonard's Forest, were enclosed in 1871, and Jolesfield Common and Partridge Green were enclosed in 1872.

The smaller Greens and roadside wastes went at the end of a long process of attrition lasting centuries, often leaving nothing more than a place name, if that. Twineham Green lost its openness in the 19th century and is now just an elongated strip of roadside houses. Most of Dragon's Green, Shipley, went the same way. Cuckold's Green, at the south end of Blackstone Lane, Woodmancote, TQ 237 150, leaves only the slightest traces. It was lost in the early 19th century. Albourne Green at the north end of the village street was nibbled away by housing. Maplehurst Green, Barns Green (Itchingfield), West Green and Gossops Green in Crawley, Hapstead Green (Ardingly) and Wivelsfield Green have all been nibbled to extinction by houses and small enclosures. Small greens fronting clusters of ancient farms have lost their status and become ordinary small fields, like Strood Farm Green, Wivelsfield, TQ 355 204, Wootton Farm Green, TQ 380 150, East Chiltington, and Upper Streat Green, TQ 357/8 172.

Hatton's Green, once lawns at the edge of medieval Home Wood, East Chiltington, is just paddocks and cottages now.

The coming of motor transport has had a gigantic influence. Till the 20th century many Wealden roads had the character of linear greens. Since the car, however, roadside wastes have been inexorably squeezed by widening tarmac. Stone Cross Green (north of Lindfield), and Slough Green (west of Cuckfield) have been lost to roads and enclosure by neighbours, and this process *still goes on,* as greens and commons are managed as parts of adjacent householders' grounds, as at Bines Green and Horsebridge Common, Ashurst, or the old Blackhouse Common, near to the Sloop Inn, Freshfield Bridge.

ANCIENT COMMONS TO MODERN TOWNS

It is startling to notice how so many of the towns of the Brighton Line Weald are based greatly on commons enclosed in modern capitalist times – *Haywards Heath, Burgess Hill, Horley and Horsham*. That is true for many of the larger villages too, such as *Partridge Green, Mannings Heath, Broadbridge Heath, South Chailey, Plumpton Green, Crawley Down, Copthorne, Felbridge, Charlwood, Smallfield, Bolney, and Wivelsfield Green*.

Thus, these places swung from being the most economically backward (and thus biologically rich) in the Weald to the most heavily and intensively urbanised.

Partly this was due to the ease with which the new, fragmented post-enclosure patterns of land ownership could be exploited by speculative builders and business owners. The allotments which the old common rights holders acquired may not have been suitable in the long term for traditional farming, and may have been more valuable as building plots. On the site of the old St John's Common, and to some extent on Horsham Common, there was a great expansion of brick fields and potteries, as well as of villa building for well-off Londoners. South Chailey, too, saw an expansion of its brick field and others nearby.

Partly it was due to the petty politicking of big landowners. The Horsham Common enclosure was part-influenced by the Duke of Norfolk's desire to stop encroaching squatters who may acquire voting rights. The development of Haywards Heath was encouraged by the pushing eastwards of the new Brighton Line to its position adjacent to the Heath, because of landowner opposition to its more natural alignment with Cuckfield town.

Mostly, though, it was due to the proximity of the railway lines, which brought much middle class and working class immigration into the new railway settlements. As well as the Brighton Line towns, Partridge Green, Crawley Down and Plumpton Green were, or are, close to railway stations, and Smallfield,

ANCIENT COMMONS TO MODERN TOWNS

There is a close relationship between the footprint of some towns and historic commons enclosed in modern times. Some of my maps under-emphasise this closeness, for towns such as Burgess Hill, Haywards Heath, Horsham and Horley have greatly expanded from their old footprint on broken-up commons in recent decades

 Commons enclosed in modern times

 Current footprint of town

HAYWARDS HEATH

PLUMPTON GREEN

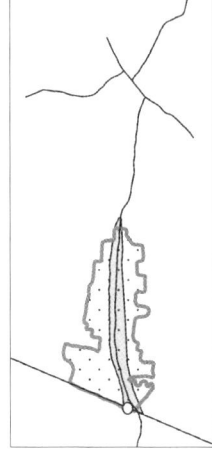

PARTRIDGE GREEN AND JOLESFIELD COMMON

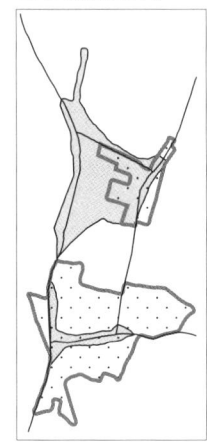

SOUTH CHAILEY

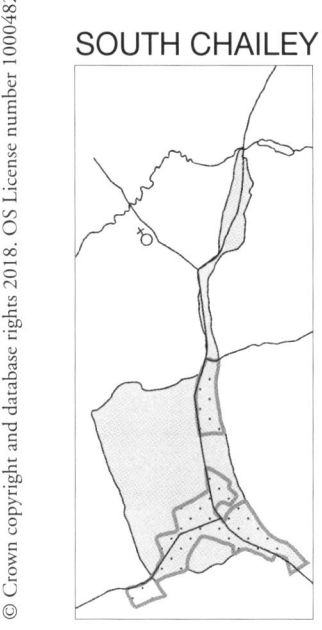

HORSHAM

© Crown copyright and database rights 2018. OS License number 100048229

36 BACKSTORY / Chapter 1: The Wealden landscape's history

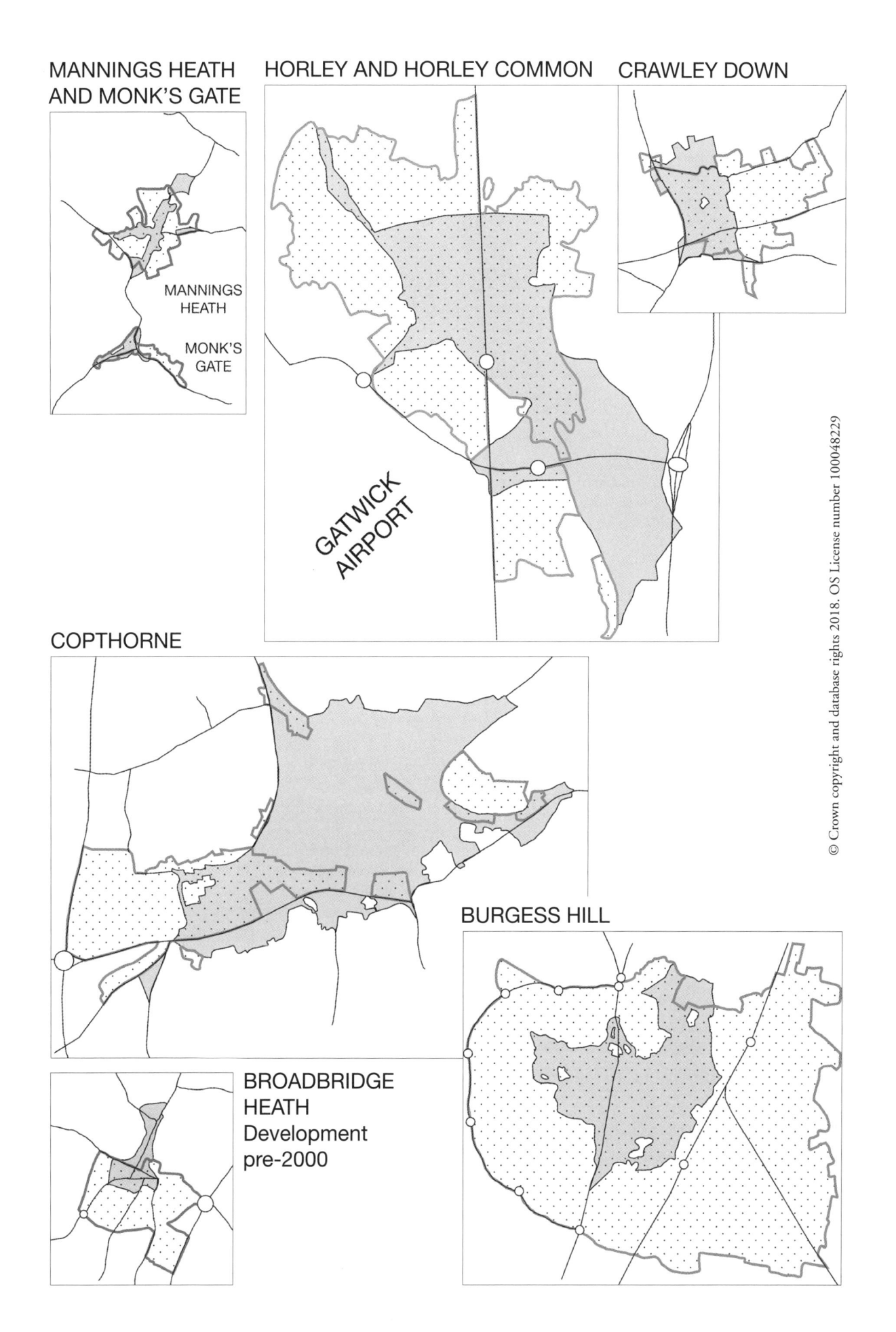

MANNINGS HEATH AND MONK'S GATE

MANNINGS HEATH

MONK'S GATE

HORLEY AND HORLEY COMMON

CRAWLEY DOWN

GATWICK AIRPORT

COPTHORNE

BURGESS HILL

BROADBRIDGE HEATH
Development pre-2000

© Crown copyright and database rights 2018. OS License number 100048229

BACKSTORY / Chapter 1: The Wealden landscape's history

Copthorne, Broadbridge Heath and Mannings Heath are within striking distances.

Some of this relationship between buildings and commons goes back to medieval times. Commons were places where homeless people could hope to squat and gain the retrospective approval of the manorial lord, or even his encouragement to settle. They were good places to erect windmills or even watermills (as at Slaugham and Vale Bridge Commons) for quarrying (sand, gravel, stone, iron ore, brick clay) for other craft activities (tanning, rope making on Godstone Green) or for services (shops, ale houses, smithing). Their edges were good places for the farmsteads of the poor, so that they could take advantage – legally or illegally – of rights of pasturage and wood, Bracken, peat, Gorse and turf gathering. The village of Horsted Keynes is clearly based on such piecemeal settlement, which eventually eliminated all of the common except its close pattern of interweaving tracks.

Paradoxically, part of the Victorian appeal of the Surrey stockbroker belt railway towns of Dorking, Reigate-Redhill, and Oxted relied on their close relationships to surviving airy commons, like those of the North Downs and Surrey Hills, and more closely, Holmwood and Redhill Commons, Reigate Heath and the 'chart' commons of the greensand east of Oxted – and this ensured their preservation.

CRAWLEY, GATWICK, MOTORWAYS

Crawley is the only example of a modern publicly planned new town in the Brighton Line Weald. It was built to address the problems of slum housing, urban sprawl, and class-based, socially divided development in Greater London. As part of its reform programme the 1945–50 Labour government passed the New Towns Act (1946) which planned 8 such towns, of which Crawley was the second to start building.

It was designed as a self-contained, balanced settlement with an autonomous economy based upon its own industry, and with its land in public ownership. It would counter the centrifocal drive of the capitalist economy towards an ever-spreading London megalopolis, which had swollen to double its size in the two inter-war decades. To this end its planners opposed the construction of a major regional airport serving London at Gatwick because of the way it would put pressure on the housing and labour supply and make Crawley a satellite of the London economy. However, the reassurances that the Crawley Development Corporation received from the Ministry of Town and Country Planning that Gatwick would not be developed were overturned within two months by government plans for a major international airport employing 3000 people within 10 years.[32]

An original Master Plan target for a Crawley population of 55,000 saw new housing districts built around the pre-war A23 Crawley Bypass, and linking the old town with the railway settlement at Three Bridges. This target was reached by 1959. Gatwick Airport, however, has proved an overwhelming influence, with its jobs rising to 15,000 in 1983 and over 20,000 in 2012. The original Master Plan boundaries have burst to the south west and the east, with new districts built at Broadfield (1972), Bewbush (1978), Ifield West (1979) and Maidenbower (1986). Now we are faced with new districts being built at 'Kilnwood Vale' towards Faygate, deeply eroding the 2.5 mile Strategic Gap between Crawley and Horsham, and at Tinsley Green, with the new Forge Wood district.

Crawley, Horley, and rural residents found their lives blighted by appalling aircraft noise, especially in the 1970s and '80s, and fought hard,[33] in tandem with national efforts, to reduce such pollution, achieving a real degree of success. However, they had to fight repeated proposals for a second runway at Gatwick. Faced with the constraint of the wooded limestone ridge of Stan Hill to the west and urban settlements to the east, airport planners proposed cutting a huge 'gorge' through the ridge, which campaigners fought off. They failed, however, in their long battle against a second Gatwick (North) Terminal in 1982, which eliminated what was left of the landscape of parkland and wood, as well as the old course of the River Mole, north of the runway.

The manufacturing businesses at Manor Royal industrial estate have been replaced by warehouses and airport services, and considerable office developments have taken place recently.[34] The villagers of Lowfield Heath have been driven out by aircraft noise pollution, their village demolished and only its church remaining, surrounded by a desert of warehouses, sheds and airport boxes.

Noise and air pollution, severance, and ratcheted up development pressures are also the consequence of the building of the M23 and the Reigate to Godstone section of the M25 from 1972–75, with the widening of the A23 south of the motorway, from Handcross to Warninglid, from 2011–14. These ghastly race-tracks, which clog to slow-moving car parks in some sections during rush hours and summer heat waves, have blighted wide corridors of Wealden countryside, turning parts of the best preserved wooded landscape in Britain into compromised, damaged shadows of what they were a century ago. The M23 motorway and the A264 ring road now form the southern and eastern boundary of Crawley, though for how long they will contain it is an open question.

Thus, Crawley New Town, a fine, planned solution to the desperate problems caused by capitalist development – destitution, homelessness, uneven development, and environmental destruction – is now being turned into its opposite: part of an out-of-control hyper-development on the point of fusing with the London megalopolis, and threatening to fuse with the Sussex coastal conurbation.

Capital has trumped social democratic planning, and the Wealden landscape is another of its numerous victims.

ENDNOTES

1. So called because a relic bone of it was first found by a worker near Heidelberg in 1908. He found a near complete mandible.
2. See 'The Earliest Occupation of Sussex: Recent Research and Future Objectives', pages 17–28, by Matthew Pope. In 'The Archaeology of Sussex to AD 2000', edited by David Rudling. Heritage Marketing & Publications Ltd (2003).
3. 'Fairweather Eden. Life in Britain half a million years ago as revealed by the excavations at Boxgrove', by Michael Pitts and Mark Roberts. Arrow (1998).
4. Page 21, Matthew Pope, in 'The Archaeology of Sussex to AD 2000', op cit.
5. 'Late Glacial and Post-Glacial Hunter-Gatherers in Sussex', pages 31–38, by Peter Holgate. In 'The Archaeology of Sussex to AD 2000', op cit.
6. 'A History of Sussex Wild Plants', page 15, by Ursula Smith and Eileen Howard. The Booth Museum of Natural History and Brighton Council (1997).
7. Peter Holgate, page 35, in 'The Archaeology of Sussex to AD 2000', op cit.
8. 'The Archaeology of Sussex', page 57, by E Cecil Curwen. Methuen (1937)
9. 'Taming the Wild: The First Farming Communities in Sussex', page 39, by Peter Drewett. In 'The Archaeology of Sussex to AD 2000', op cit.
10. 'The Flora of Sussex', page 534, edited by A H Wolley-Dod. The Chatford House Press (first edition 1937).
11. 'The History of the Countryside', page 72, by Oliver Rackham. J M Dent & Soins Ltd (1986).
12. 'The Wealden Iron Industry', page 28, by Jeremy Hodgkinson. The History Press (2008).
13. 'Roman Rural Settlement in Sussex: Continuity and Change', by David Rudling. Pages 111–140 in 'The Archaeology of Sussex to AD 2000', op cit.
14. 'A Roman Road from Barcombe Mills to the west, through Streat and Hassocks', by Ivan D Margary FSA. Sussex Archaeological Collections, Volume LXXVI, pages 6–34, (1935).
15. 'The History of the Countryside', page 74, by Oliver Rackham. J M Dent & Sons Ltd (1986). Rackham quotes from Dr Henry Cleere: 'Some operating parameters for Roman ironworks'. Bulletin of the Institute of Archaeology 13 (1976) pages 233–46.
16. See 'An Assessment of the early history of Hayworth and Trubwick in Haywards Heath', page 2, by Heather Warne, archivist and local historian, January 2009.
17. Quoted by Peter Brandon in "The Kent and Sussex Weald", page 9. Phillimore & Co. Ltd (2003).
18. Brandon, page 44, op cit.
19. Rackham, pages 76–8, op cit.
20. Heather Warne, pers comm.
21. 'Early hamlets of the mid-Sussex Weald', by Heather Warne, for the Wealden Settlement Study Circle, Oct. 2010, and '"Hayworth" and "Trobewyk"', by Heather Warne and Stuart Meier, including an Assessment of the early history of Hayworth and Trubwick in Haywards Heath', by Heather Warne. (2009). I am indebted to Heather Warne for her excellent suggestions on this section.
22. 'The Kent and Sussex Weald', page 87, by Peter Brandon. Phillimore (2003).
23. See the fascinating article 'Rethinking the early medieval settlement of woodlands: evidence from the western Sussex Weald', by Diana Chatwin and Mark Gardiner, pages 31–49 of 'Landscape History', Vol. 27 (2005), the journal of the Society for Landscape Studies.
24. The word 'regio' is related to the modern 'regions' and 'regal'. Heather Warne pers comm.
25. Heather Warne pers comm.
26. 'Economy and landscape change in post-Roman and early medieval Sussex, 450–1175', page 154–6, by Mark Gardiner. In 'The Archaeology of Sussex to AD 2000', edited by David Rudling. Heritage Marketing & Publications Ltd (2003).
27. 'The Sussex Landscape', page 74, by Peter Brandon. Hodder and Stoughton (1974)
28. The following account owes much to Peter Brandon's superb unpublished thesis "The Common Lands and Wastes of Sussex". Thesis submitted for the degree of Doctor of Philosophy in the University of London.
29. North Hall in East Chiltington, TQ 376 165, was called 'Cleeres' House in 1621, the last relic of this medieval chase.
30. See 'Growth of Communications 1720–1840', page 78–9, by John Farrant, in 'An Historical Atlas of Sussex', edited by Kim Leslie and Brian Short. Phillimore (1999).
31. 'The Broyle Enclosure, 1767–71', by John E. Kay, Sussex Archaeological Collections, pages 165–189, V. 138 (2000).
32. 'Crawley: Old Town, New Town', pages 35–37, edited by Fred Gray. Occasional Paper No.18, Centre for Continuing Education, University of Sussex (1983).
33. See the very readable and revealing history and part-autobiography by Brendon Sewill entitled 'Tangled Wings: Gatwick seen through green-tinted glasses'. The Aviation Environment Federation (2012).
34. 'Crawley New Town 1947–2000', by Charles Kay, pages 122–123 of 'An Historical Atlas of Sussex', op cit.

THE GEOLOGY OF THE MIDDLE WEALD

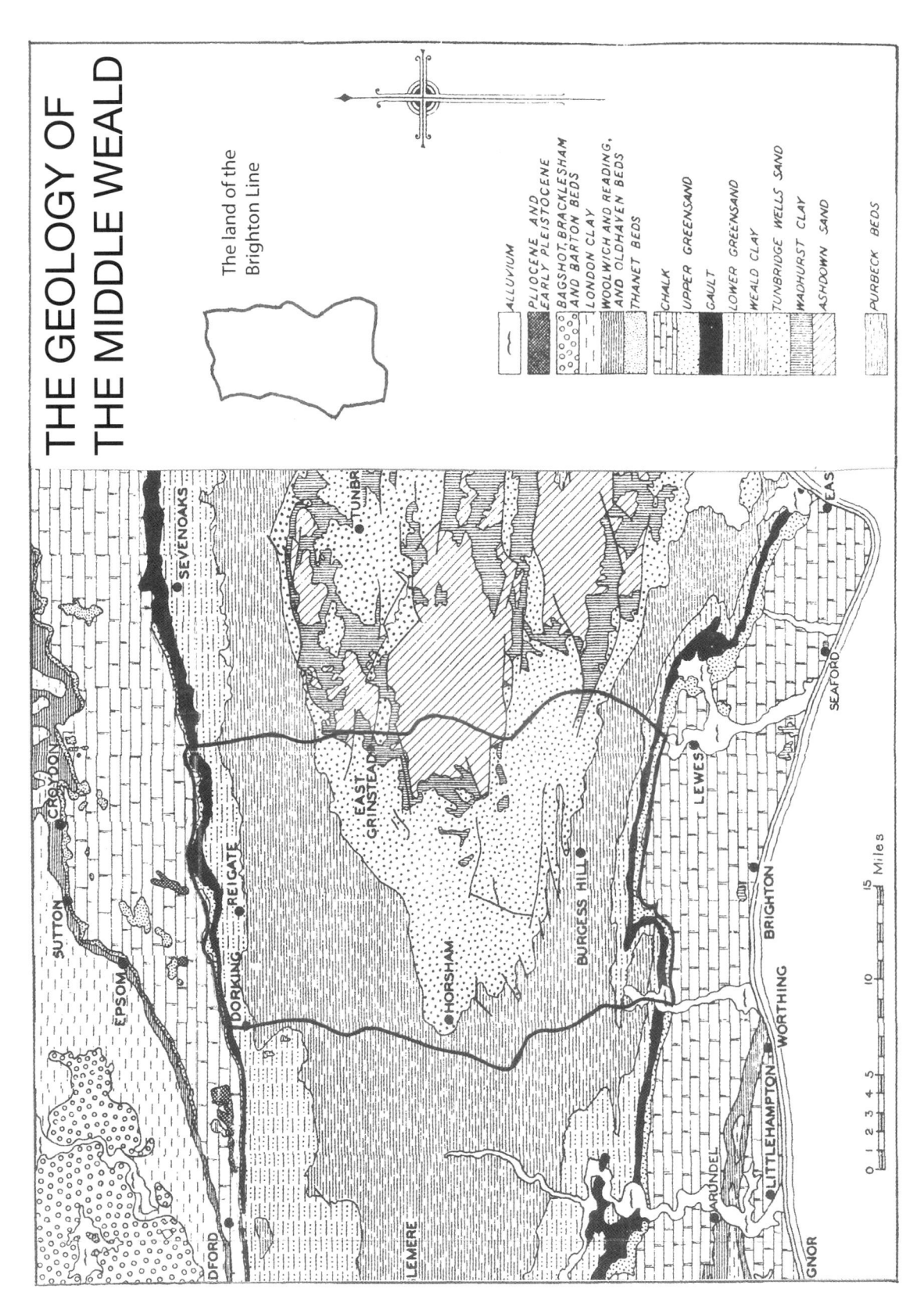

The land of the Brighton Line

- ALLUVIUM
- PLIOCENE AND EARLY PLEISTOCENE
- BAGSHOT, BRACKLESHAM AND BARTON BEDS
- LONDON CLAY
- WOOLWICH AND READING, AND OLDHAVEN BEDS
- THANET BEDS
- CHALK
- UPPER GREENSAND
- GAULT
- LOWER GREENSAND
- WEALD CLAY
- TUNBRIDGE WELLS SAND
- WADHURST CLAY
- ASHDOWN SAND
- PURBECK BEDS

From BGS Regional Geology, The Wealden District. Permit Number CP18/021 BGS © UKRI 2018. All rights reserved.

CHAPTER 2
Wealden earth history:

Dinosaurs, tropical swamps and seas, rift valleys, horsetails, tree ferns and quarries

Looking down from the North Downs Way or from Ditchling Beacon the Weald still appears as a land of woods and trees, its green mantle almost as uniform as the sea. Yet its landforms, its soils and geology are immensely varied – even from field to field and part-field to part-field. It is still a land of difference and variety, though capitalist farming and development ever more strongly drives to eliminate those differences.

THE PAST WORLD LIVES ON IN THE PRESENT

I was a bit cheeky really. I knocked on this farmhouse door because I'd read somewhere that the farmer had found an Iguanodon footprint in a stream bed on his farm. It was a lovely late spring day, with Chiffchaffs doing their drill, Moorhens sitting on their eggs amongst the reeds, and big dragon and damselflies patrolling.

The farmer was so nice. He didn't mind being cold-called, and brought out this big chunk of dusty sandstone. On it was printed a three toed dinosaur footprint. His great grandad had found it. He had another one he'd found himself only five years before, a bit smaller. His little toddler daughter peeked out at me from between his legs.

I was bowled over … as you'll see from my poem.

> **The Geology of the Middle Weald**
> The Land of the Brighton Line contains most, but not all, of the geological elements found in the Weald. It forms a 'sandwich'. The 'bread' is the separate Low Weald of Surrey and Sussex, with their Wealden Clay vales and Greensand-and-Gault Clay vales. The 'filling' is the High Weald, made up largely of Tunbridge Wells Sands, with Wadhurst Clay and Ashdown Sands to the east.

A dinosaur walked down this lane

A dinosaur walked down this lane –

This lane with hedgerows full of pink Dog Rose and springtime birdsong;
Chiffchaffs skulking, Toads a-rising in the pond,
and stripey Droneflies on the Dropwort umbels in the ditch.

It squelched across the little stream and left its dirt great footprints there.
Bigger than an elephant's foot,
with three great claws up-front; each one my hand's length long.

I know because the farmer showed me.

It's a famous place, this lane, for passing dinosaurs.

He brought it out the kitchen, this dirt great footprint thing.
Heaved it on the step; this lump of stone; this perfect cast.

It wasn't on its own, you know. It had its baby tagging on,
which left its footprint just as plain, a not-so-small Iguanodon.

Just passing through, they were, heading towards Capel.
Tromping 'cross the hedgerows here and walking 'cross the woods.
Nibbling the tops of trees and peering into chimneypots.

* * *

We took my grandson to walk along the Plumpton Mill Stream, and parked by East Chiltington church. I've known it for donkey's years and love its old Yew. I'd never noticed, though, what struck me so strongly that day. It is a fossil church … all its walls, nave, chancel and tower are made of Winklestone. It is a church made of fossils. Big winkle shells, *Viviparus*, stand proud of the stone, all reddish or grey, so like the water snail shells I've picked from riversides … which are, indeed, its close cousins of the same genus, though they live 135 million years later!

Across the Mill Stream, the Bevern Brook and the railway line, a long ribbon of Winklestone outcrops west-east from its Wealden Clay matrix. You can find old barn walls, cottages, hardcore on muddy paths and beneath stiles, flaggy outcrops in stream meanders under old pollard oaks, rubble piles in farmhouse yards, all made of this Winklestone – or Sussex Marble, or Laughton Stone, however you wish to call it – all the way from Ashington in the west to Laughton in the east.

* * *

Struggling along the steep, wet fields at the edge of a hangar north east of Bolney one autumn we walked onto a landslip, which had crashed into the wood below and turned it into a splintered tangle. Our progress slowed even further as we picked our way across cracked, bulging, slipping earth and the tangle of Bristly Oxtongue and young bushes which had colonised it. The slope's wet Grinstead Clay, had brought down the Cuckfield Stone above it, over the Ardingly Sandstone underneath, and onto the Wadhurst Clay in the gill … a slurried porridge of wet clay and rock.

It did not matter so much there. In Franklands Village, Haywards Heath, though, houses have been brought down by similar landslips.

THE FORMATION OF THE WEALD

The strata of the Weald are laid down one on top of another, stored like a pile of bedding in a blanket box, with the oldest at the bottom and the youngest at the top. However, after their deposition these layers were crunched up into a gigantic dome, with the North Downs on one flank and the South Downs on the other. There's been 65 million years of erosion since then, but we can still point to the paradox that the oldest strata of the Weald (exposed at the centre of the eroded dome) have been crumpled up to stand almost as high as the youngest (on the Downs at the edge). Thus, Crowborough Beacon, at the centre of the dome, is 787ft (240m) high and Ditchling Beacon, at its edge, is nearly the same height: 813ft (248m), despite the former being many millions of years older.

The Weald was formed in the last period of the era of the dinosaurs: the Cretaceous. The process of its deposition (for it is made up entirely of 'sedimentary' rocks deposited by water action) took about 42 million years … the whole first half of the Cretaceous period. (The oldest beds, indeed, pre-date the Cretaceous and go back to the late Jurassic, but those Purbeck beds do not outcrop in the middle Sussex Weald. You have to go to eastern Sussex, around Burwash, Battle and Brightling, to see signs of them).

The Weald was laid down in two stages: a *non-marine stage*, with a mixture of low ground and shallow waters lasting some 17 million years, and a later *marine stage* of some 25 million years. (Those marine conditions continued as the deposition of the Wealden clays and sands was replaced with the deposition of the Downland chalk).

The Wealden beds in their early stages, which were laid down in *non-marine* conditions, formed a gigantic shallow freshwater basin (which geologists call a 'graben') from eroded material brought down from three blocks of surrounding highlands: 'Londinia' to the north, 'Cornubia' to the west, and 'Armorica' to the south west. Sea only occasionally broke through a bit and made conditions brackish.

I remember a documentary once on TV about catching Anacondas in Lake Maracaibo, Venezuela. These experts sploshed around up to their waists and paddled in little boats around the very shallow lake that seemed to be choked with submerged greenery, looking for these monster snakes, which chilled out there, just under the surface. Geologists think that the non-marine Wealden basin was a bit like that … partly wet-but-shallow, with braided channels and lagoons, and partly muddy plain, sand bars and dunes … a place of big meadows of horsetails, with tree ferns, cycads and allied Bennettitales (now extinct) … and floating primitive flowering plants (a bit like modern water lilies or Water Crowfoot). There was plenty of mud-swamp, but not a lot of soil forming on the dry land, though ferns and fern-like plants formed a major component of the vegetation. There were conifers and their close relatives – and you can find their fossil cones – but modern trees of the Angiosperm (flowering plant) order hadn't been invented yet. There was enough greenery to make the herds of grazing Iguanodon happy, and there were enough Iguanodon to have attracted the attention of carnivorous dinosaurs. There were Pterosaurs in the air, and tank-like armoured dinosaurs such as Polacanthus and Stegosaurus left their bones for us to find. It was a place where crocodiles and turtles could make a good living, as well as heaps of shellfish, and the well-armoured fishes that fed upon them.

The 'Walking With Dinosaurs' team would have been chuffed to do a session there. You don't need to go to Dakota or Mongolia to look for dinosaur fossils. You can find them here, in homely Sussex and Surrey. Indeed, the first dinosaur ever discovered was found here, by

Mary Mantell in 1822 in Tilgate Forest. She collected the tooth of what later was named the Iguanodon (which means 'Iguana tooth'). The quarry where Gideon Mantell, her husband, found the first *in situ* Iguanodon fossils is still there, on the slope south of Whiteman's Green recreation ground, Cuckfield. It looks like a little Oak-Ash grove in the middle of a field (2012), but the trees cover the quarry and there are still clean Grinstead Stone exposures on the quarry floor, TQ 301 253.

Over the 42 million years of its existence an astonishing quantity of eroded clay and sand was brought down from the surrounding uplands into the Wealden basin. So much so that the basin sank along its edging fault lines, and the uplands were eroded out of existence, despite being periodically rejuvenated by 'uplift' (like new teeth growing under old).

The depth of the combined sediments of this non-marine phase of the Wealden basin is gigantic … roughly 2,670ft (890 m) … about the height of a respectable British mountain. Truly, the "mountains were laid low" to form these deposits … though the valley stayed as valley and didn't get "exhalted".[1]

Indeed, the Wealden basin was a remarkably stable place, in a way. It began about 142 million years ago, and its *non-marine phase* ended about 125 million years ago. Iguanodon were there near the beginning of that period … and they were still there near the end. They must have left a helluva lot of footprints in the mud and sand in that time. Horsetails, *Equisetites*, were pretty constant all the way through, too. We can often find them in their growth positions, held upright by the drifting sand and mud that both killed them and preserved them. After that came the *marine phase* of Wealden formation, through some 25 million years of deposition of the Greensands, with the Gault Clay sandwiched between their Upper and Lower formations. We don't look for land dinosaur bones and bits of fern and horsetail in those later sea floor deposits. Instead, we look for ammonites, belemnites and sea shells.

LET'S GET SOME ORDER HERE!!

It's probably easiest to look at the Weald's earth history in chronological order, working upwards through the deposits and through time.

Dinosaur forage. In situ fossil Horsetail, *Equisetites*, root (c. 130 million years old). Freshfield Quarry.

Modern Horsetails growing near to their fossil ancestors, Freshfield Quarry

The oldest strata are those making up the **Hastings Group** of beds (so-called because they outcrop wonderfully along the Hastings cliffs), and it is these that form the hills, valleys and gills of the **High Weald**, between Bolney and Crawley. They survive as this elevated landscape because they are largely made up of sandstones which can soak up rainfall like a sponge, rather than resisting it and thus getting eroded away by the force of running water, as happens with clays. They have a lot further to erode, anyway, to reduce them to the level of the surrounding Wealden Clay, because they were thrust up to the high centre of the Wealden dome.

Ashdown Sand

The earliest of the Hastings Beds was the Ashdown Sand, which forms a huge block centred on Ashdown Forest. It only comes as far west as Sharpthorne and Horsted Keynes. It was formed by very powerful erosion of the surrounding uplands, which covered the muddy

BACKSTORY / Chapter 2: Wealden earth history

SANDROCK OUTCROPS

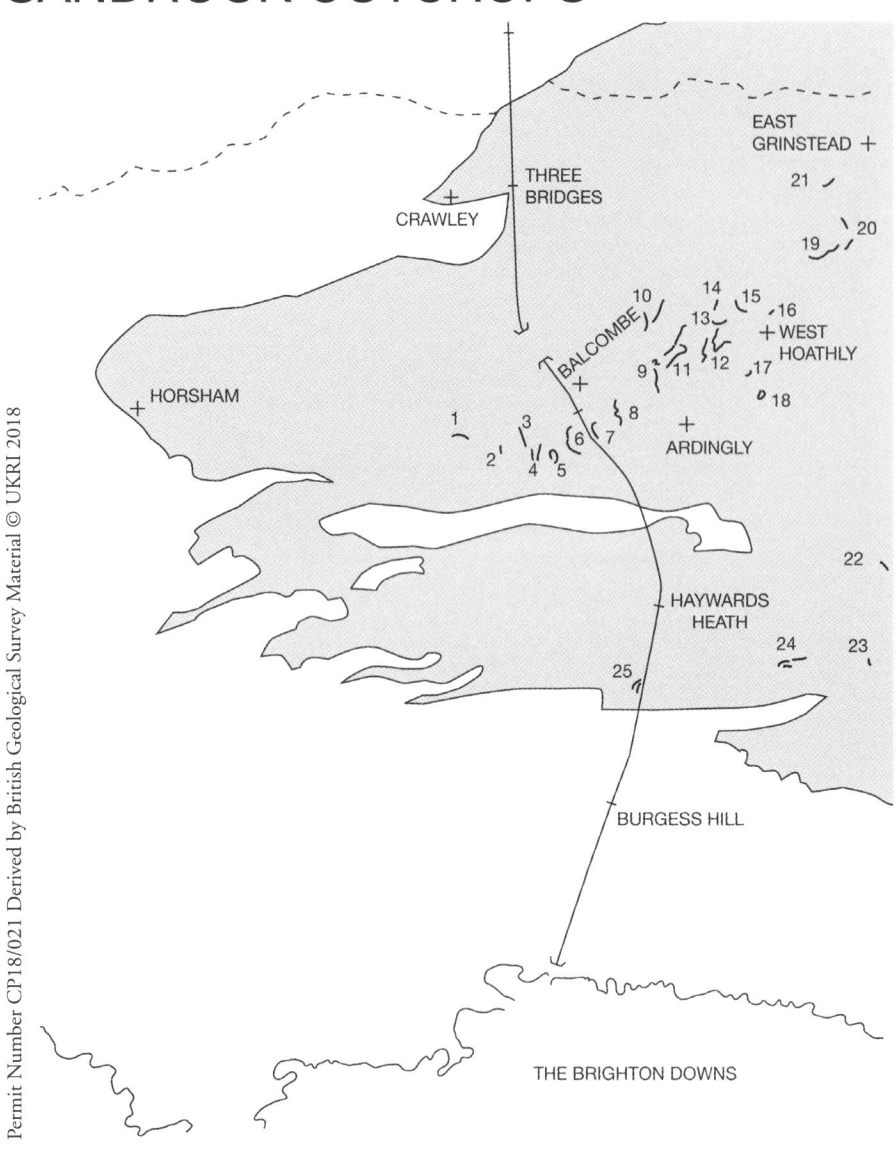

swamps with alluvial sands.[2] It is not very fossiliferous in our area (though its early Fairlight Clays sequence near Hastings has produced superb and famous plant fossils), but you can find ripple marks, sun cracks, rain pits and casts of footprints on the exposed surfaces.[3]

There's a big old wood we've been to a few times up towards Chelwood Common. It is airy and open, like a cathedral, with fine medium age Beech plumps, old outgrown Sessile Oak coppice, Bluebells, occasional Wild Daffodils, and Woodcock. Down in the stream bed there are broken slabs of fossiliferous Ashdown Sandstone covered in tiny carbonaceous plant fragments. They are mostly aligned in one direction, like iron filings, no doubt because the originating current laid them that way. Whether they are the debris of some flash fire, or just the unrecognisable detritus of rotting vegetation from those times, we could not tell. Who cares? It is wonderful to see remains of life, however modest, from the other end of eternity.

The Wadhurst Clay

The Wadhurst Clay was laid down next and tends to appear along the margins of the Ashdown Sand. In our area the Wadhurst Clay forms the countryside on either side of the Bluebell Line all the way north from Horsted Keynes to the

1. Nymans, TQ 271 295
2. Soles Copse, Staplefield, TQ 283 291
3. Northland Wood, TQ 289 293
4. Little Sion Wood, TQ 293 288
5. Coombehole Wood, TQ 289 299
6. Rowhill Wood, Pilstye, TQ 303 292
7. Stumble Wood, TQ 311 295
8. Balcombe Mill and Northlands Wood, TQ 318 301
9. Tilgate Wood, TQ 330 310
10. Paddockhurst Park, TQ 331 331
11. Wakehurst Valley, TQ 335 316
12. Chiddingly and Stonehurst Rocks, TQ 348 320
13. Chiddingly Farm Lane, TQ 349 329
14. Stonelands Farm, TQ 348 336
15. West Hoathly North Rocks, TQ 356 331
16. Shagswell Wood Rocks, TQ 364 332
17. Hook Farm, TQ 358 310
18. Whitestone House Rocks, TQ 362 306
19. Stone Farm and adjacent rocks, TQ 381 348
20. Standen and Old Standen Rocks, TQ 389 351 and TQ 388 357
21. Ridge Hill, TQ 372 359
22. Heaven Wood, TQ 400 256
23. Warr's Farm, TQ 394 228
24. Rock Wood and rocks west of A272, TQ 369 227
25. Rocky Lane, Haywards Heath, TQ 324 222

West Hoathly tunnel. Additionally, it forms the floor of the big south draining valleys between Balcombe and Horsted Keynes, including the proposed fracking site south of Balcombe, the Ardingly Reservoir, and the Wakehurst Place valleys. The clays are often dark grey and can be seen quite clearly in the lower, western of the two Freshfield Lane brick pits, TQ 382 266.

It is this clay that formed the main source of iron ore for the Sussex iron industry, and the most consistent ironstone horizon occurs near the base of the formation. Many of the Wadhurst Clay woods are pockmarked with mine (ore) pits. At West Hoathly, Streat and East Grinstead churches you can see iron grave slabs cast from these ores. Walking the gills and stream sides of the Weald you will readily notice the frequent orange ferruginous staining of their waters.[4] The Wadhurst Clay is by no means all argillaceous (clayey), and, as well as the clay ironstone, contains shelly limestone, beds of siltstone, sandstone and shales. The clays are good for fossils, with many finely preserved plant microfossils and small invertebrates like ostracods.

At both Freshfield Lower Pit and Sharpthorne Brick Pit the quarrying of the Wadhurst Clay reveals intact Horsetail, *Equisetites*, fossils with both upright stems and fat, winding roots *in situ*. At Freshfield's Lower Pit, the broken lumps of a quarried layer of tabular 'Tilgate Stone' revealed a rich assemblage of fossils on their undersides, including bits of freshwater turtle shell and armoured crocodile skin, sharks' teeth, fish scales, small limb bones of vertebrates (including pterosaurs) and fossil wood.

Deep in one gill wood, I came across a steep flush washing down over moss and mud. The moss felt hard, crinkly and rough. It was petrifying into tufa stone from the calcium laden clay run-off, just like the nick-nacks folk hang to petrify under waterfalls in Derbyshire. The moss was a rare species, miles from the nearest recorded site, which thrives in such places: Curled Hook-moss, *Palustriella commutatum var. commutatum*.

Tunbridge Wells Sand

The youngest of the components of the Hastings Group is the Tunbridge Wells Sand, which dominates our middle Sussex High Weald west-east from Horsham to Highbrook and West Hoathly, and north-south between Crawley and Bolney-Wivelsfield. Over large areas it forms poor acidic soils, but is varied by outcrops of often-calcareous Grinstead Clay on many valley sides. The Grinstead Clay is itself intersected by bands of Cuckfield Stone, or Tilgate Stone, as it used to be called. (Several distinct kinds of decent Wealden stone got called 'Tilgate Stone'.)

The Ardingly Sandstone sandrocks

Perhaps the most famous feature of the Tunbridge Wells Sand is the **sandrock outcrops**,[5] exposed on many an incised valley of the High Weald. They form bare, rounded cliffs, bluffs and crags up to 15m in height along the valleysides. At Wakehurst they extend for well over a mile, first on the west side of the Ardingly Brook in Tilgate Wood (where they are very small) and then dramatically along the east side in Bloomer's Valley.

They are formed from massive cross-bedded white quartzose sandstone[6] laid down by an episode of very vigorous upland denudation. They were probably exposed by heavy erosion during the last Ice Age, but they are very resistant to erosion from our current climate. However, that resistance depends upon them retaining the integrity of a thin-but-tough skin or rind that has developed over the soft inner sandstone. If that surface skin is broken by carving or climbing they can erode very easily. They have several sorts of odd sculptural weathering patterns upon their surfaces, such as 'honeycomb weathering' (with masses of circular hollows) or 'tortoise-shell weathering' (into polygonal networks of cracks), or erosion along the bedding planes, which give them the appearance of big cushions or woolsacks plonked on top of each other.

They are very often undercut by that bedding plane weathering, which made them very cosy as overhanging rock shelters for Mesolithic and Neolithic gatherer hunters. Sometimes whole blocks have shifted downslope, and wide cracks or 'gulls' open up between them and the main outcrops. The most famous of these blocks is Big-on-Little, at Chiddingly Rocks, which is a 400 to 500 ton block balanced in frozen pirouette on a wasp-waist join to its lower pedestal.

In middle Sussex we have found 34 sandrock outcrops in all, and 26 of them (76%) are in the parishes of Balcombe, Ardingly, West Hoathly and East Grinstead. The ones at Stone Farm, East Grinstead, TQ 348 324, are owned by the British Mountaineering Council and are heavily used for climbing, but the Chiddinglye Rocks are managed for their superb ferns, liverworts, mosses and lichen which survive from wildwood times.

Keep them safe. DO NOT climb or inscribe them, and respect ALL the ferns and the film of ancient, primitive vegetation which lives upon the rock surfaces.

Fossilling in the Tunbridge Wells Sand

Several summers ago I joined a party of geologists visiting two famous quarries in the Tunbridge Wells Sand. **Philpots Quarry**, TQ 354 322, exposing both the Ardingly Sandstone and its Grinstead Clay cap, vastly exceeded my expectations. I hadn't realised that Ardingly Sandstone was fossiliferous, but our explorations of it and the Grinstead Clay rubble showed otherwise. Some sandrock planes had extensive black carbonized plant remains from flash fires, together with non-carbonized brown fragments.

Fossil remains of an armoured fish, *Lepidotes*, from Philpots Quarry. The rats were gnawing it, so it was built into the wall for protection.

It was belting hot down in the quarry, almost as it would have been when the stones and clays were laid down, I thought. Looking at the grey Grinstead Clay I soon found some tiny fossil molluscs all varnished olive and only about 1cm across at most … only they weren't molluscs, but bivalvular crustaceans, called **conchostracans**, or **clam shrimps**. Next to them were much smaller and more evanescent bean shaped **ostracods**, in abundance. Conchostracans have a shell that grows with the animal, whilst ostracods shed and replace their shells.

Some of the others were working hard to lever off thin plates of sandstone, with good effect, revealing scatters of carbonized plant remains and at least one tiny **fern pinna**, complete with two rows of pinnules. It wasn't much more than a cm long, but what a sight!! 137 million years old, yet just like the living buckler ferns we admire today when we look at the mossy and fern covered sandrocks at nearby Chiddingly or Wakehurst.

One exposed slab had a tiny **cone**, again perhaps a cm long, with all its knobbly cone scales. Was this a cycad-type-thingy? One of us found a chunk of rock with thin brown lines crossing it, which Peter Austen (top Wealden fossil expert) judged to probably be **horsetail, *Equisetites***, stems.

David called out from the far side of the quarry track, where large lumps of Ardingly Sandstone were piled: "Hey, dinosaur footprint here!" I thought he was taking the mickey. There, though, on the side of a half sq m block was a large three-toed impressed **footprint of an adult Iguanodon**. We must all have passed it earlier on our walk-in, disguised under the shadowless nearly-noon sun.

Just before we left we went to see the big specimen ***Lepidotes*** **fish** that had been incorporated into the canteen wall to preserve it (because rats were gnawing off the 'lacquered' scales when it was stored on the floor). It was so impressive – circa 1ft x 8in – with chain mail type, umber coloured scales and armoured facial bones.

We then motored south to the huge **Freshfield Lane Pit**, TQ 385 263. This is a much bigger operation than the Philpots set-up, opening up clays and silts and crumbly sandstones, with great colour variety of oranges and yellows and steely gray clay.

Before he left us to our hunting, our guide rashly told us that he had not found any fossils in all the years that he had worked there. We took the long walk out across the pit, with the afternoon sun and our lunch both conspiring to induce lethargy. We chatted and walked on across the exposed rubble, when Peter Austen stopped and bent down to pick up a lump of purple/ochre stone about 3in x 2in … a **dinosaur vertebra**, lying in a slight gully, with all its labyrinthine 'crunchy' marrow and eroded processes/wings there to be seen. That was special.

We followed the little gully down, but didn't find any other bits of the beast. We did find a piece of **petrified wood** that almost looked like dinosaur bone … and some fossil **plant remains**, too, though none we could get close to identifying … but, hey, after a day like that, who'd complain?!

Knees and terraces

We've all had those pairs of well-worn jeans where the knees get ever thinner. Eventually, as we keep kneeling in them (which, as a gardener, I'm constantly doing) they fray right through and bits of our shiny knees peep out.

When we've been looking for sandrock outcrops we've often come across places where the geology is right, but no sandrock breaks the surface. The slope bulges out in the right place, like my knees in my jeans, but the thin layer of soil is not broken. Those are good sites to look for bits of unimproved old pasture, because the stone is too close to the surface for the plough, and the slope is too dangerous for tractors with back-mounted agri-chemical sprays to operate.

Sometimes just a teeny bit of smooth sandrock breaks through. At Tillinghurst, near Wakehurst, TQ 334 309, there was a smidgeon showing (2012), with nice archaic pasture plants around. At Stonelands Farm, south of Selsfield Common, there's a similar spot (2012), also with good old pasture herbs and fungi around the 'knee', TQ 348 333.

In a number of places the complicated layer cake of the Hastings Group means that valley slopes don't run smoothly down, but form several giant steps, or terraces, like a natural ziggurat, over the alternating layers of hard, resistant rock, and softer, more easily eroded rock or clay.

The slopes either side of Hammingden Lane and Hook Lane, south of West Hoathly, are like that. If you take the footpath eastwards from Highbrook church, TQ 362 301, the downslope terracing is very clear. First you descend gently across hard Ardingly Sandstone, then, at the transition to the softer part of the Lower Tunbridge Wells Sand the slope steepens perceptibly. The second, softer rock terrace is quickly crossed before the path steeply drops again across a band of chalk head onto the eroded gentler slope of the Wadhurst Clay, which fills the valley floor.

A similar terrace sequence can be seen east of Broxmead Lane, Cuckfield, TQ 283 245. The south facing slope drops sharply from a hard Ardingly Sandstone cap across softer sandstone, then the gentler slope of Wadhurst Clay, before crossing a fault and steepening again across sandstone to the gill.

Wealden Clay group

The gentle, lovely vale of the Low Weald is largely made up of the most immense accretions of mud brought down from the eroded hills of Cornubia, to the west, from about 136 to 125 million years ago.[7] These strata surround the Hastings Group hills. Their deposition was very much less energetic than that of the Hastings Group, but when the Wealden basin relapsed to mudswamp it did so for longer than ever before.[8] The mudstones and intersecting bands of sandstone, siltstone and limestone are estimated to be between about 400ft (140m) deep in Kent and around 1500ft (500m) near Guildford. It is only when I stood on the edge of the vast and bleak grey hole formed by Langhurstwood Quarry at Warnham and looked down at the pin sized figures working away at its base (2010) … and realising that those layers represented only a small part of the Wealden Clay sequence … that I got a real sense of the immensity of the time and the geological processes that went into the making of our soft countryside of little woods and fields and slow streams.

The Wealden Clay does not outcrop on the coast of middle Sussex, so its only good exposures are in the brick pits which are scattered across the Low Weald.

'Winklestone' in East Chiltington's 'fossil church'. Seams of it outcrop nearby.

In the area of this book, pits like Clockhouse at Capel, Smokejacks at Ockley, South Holmwood (all in Surrey); Chailey, Hamsey, Henfield, Southwater, Langhurstwood, and Keymer Tileworks, are household names to Wealden palaeontologists. There were many smaller pits, too, and a study of the old 1873 six inch to one mile Ordnance Survey map will reveal many such places, plus the place names of even earlier quarries. Burgess Hill was a town built upon the industry of brick and tile making and its pits.

Such pits – open air treasuries of fantastic quality – are rarely valued as they should be, though, and are land filled and often built upon, to realise value for their owners and meet the pressures of regional over-development.

Keymer Tileworks

After the enclosure of St John's Common, Burgess Hill's ground was pockmarked with new brick fields, and the grid of roads in the centre were lined with potteries, bringing "nauseous odours", "smoke", and "flames of fire".[9] Only the **Keymer Tileworks clay pit**, TQ 324 191, just east of Keymer Junction, survived till recently. I went there with a group of geologists in 2010 and 2013. We walked through the big old fashioned tile sheds, more like old barns than a modern factory, with big lumps of pugged clay and pallets of finished tiles. Leaving the gloom of the sheds for the sunlit clay workings was like entering a lost world. Within minutes we were gathering around trace fossils in white siltstone … maybe Ghost Shrimps, which back-filled their winding tunnels as they dug … at least 130 million years ago in the Wealden Clay. There were fossil Horsetail stems in the siltstone, too. Some areas were still being worked. Some areas looked like wilderness.

HORSHAM STONE PITS

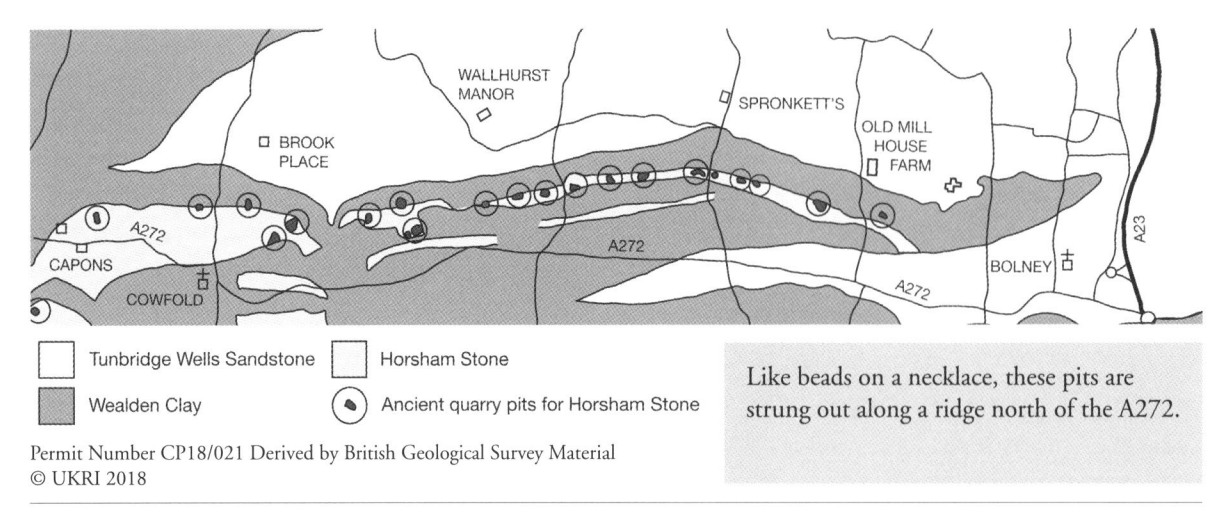

Like beads on a necklace, these pits are strung out along a ridge north of the A272.

Permit Number CP18/021 Derived by British Geological Survey Material © UKRI 2018

There were big cloudy ponds with large Reed beds, and rushy, damp ground. There were thickets, and glades, slopes and hillocks topped with Gorse, and wildflowery open ground with scattered Spiny Restharrow … a rare plant of old grasslands. The pit had been worked since 1875, so it would then have been surrounded by a much more wildlife-filled countryside, from which now-rare or scarce species, like Wood Horsetail and Marsh Ragwort, could hop over the fence. Skeins of Geese honked as they passed, and a party of House Martins dipped and swooped above us.

We found so much. I have some of my finds in front of me as I write: the vertebrae, the enamelled, diamond shaped scales (protecting like a coat of chain mail) and polished round crushing teeth of *Lepidotes,* the big armoured fish (up to a metre long) of the tropical shallows that lived by crunching molluscs for dinner. Someone called us over to see a piece of tiny crocodile jaw – teeth cavities and all – that he had found. The Weald was good for crocodiles of all shapes and sizes. 11 species have been found over the past 160 years.[10] We found turtle scutes (shell plates), other reptile and shark teeth and the fin spine of a *Hybodus* shark, bits of rib and bone and carbonised wood, Clam Shrimps, *Conchostracan sp.*, and many *Viviparus* winkle casts – the same shell that makes up the winklestone we find in old barn and church walls. I may have found a *theropod* dinosaur tooth. We even found coprolites – fossil turds, looking very like the human variety.

We found all this just by scrabbling and getting dirty knees and peering close, with magnifying glass and lens. My finds were commonplace to the experts, of course, though they were much too generous to say so. The extra value of the Tileworks pit lay in the ongoing series of discoveries of astonishing detail … about six species of small lizard, salamander and frog, the 'type' specimens of a primitive marsh dwelling flowering plant,[11] *Bevhalstia pebja*, extinct species of bug, the first Wealden fossils of fungus gnats and a pine-bark scale insect, cockroach, dragonfly, grasshopper, wasp, lacewing, caddis fly, and scorpion fly remains, microfossil stoneworts,[12] and on and on …

It's all gone now. In February 2010 outline planning permission was granted for building 475 homes on the site. In the Council's planning guidance document no mention was made that the site was designated as a RIGS (Regionally Important Geological and Geomorphological Site). *The RIGS network geologist was not even contacted before planning permission was granted.* Not that it would have made any difference, for the site was also an SNCI (Site of Nature Conservation Interest) and that *was* discussed. When I talked to a biologist surveying the site over 15 years ago he was so thrilled. "It's the best amphibian site in Sussex", he said. "It's got all five Sussex species in big numbers … masses of Palmate and Crested Newts". Many of the pools had species of native Mussels, *Anodonta sp.*, and so much more.

The site needed ongoing pump drainage to keep some of the exposures open, and its geological interest and wildlife depended upon disturbance to remain. The site was precious enough for that public cost, but shamefully not precious enough to survive the onslaught of hyper-development. Our children and grandchildren won't be looking for dinosaur bones there.

Horsham Stone

Stand amongst the fields, with their gnarled old hedge stools of Hornbeam, Ash and Holly, between Bull's Farm and Amiesmill Farm, south of Horsham, TQ 185 285. Look south and west to the **scarp of wooded hills that bound the lovely vale of the upper Arun**. It is a view of Claudian[13] beauty in the liquid light of a summer evening … from the southwards ridge of Home Wood and Sedgwick Park, westerly by Hard's Hill, and the Wellingtonias above Bourne Hill, to the slopes of Denne Park and Tower Hill.

BACKSTORY / Chapter 2: Wealden earth history

That is the **Horsham Stone scarp**, the high ground preserved by the age old resistance of that hard sandstone to the erosive force of the down-cutting Arun. In appearance the stone is similar to the Ardingly Sandrocks, but it is of a calcareous chemistry and thin-bedded.

Go anywhere amongst the villages and farms of the middle Sussex Weald and you will find houses, barns and churches roofed with heavy slabs of Horsham Stone. Such roofs are less steep than roofs of thatch, for the weight of the stonework dictated it so. You can still come across old barns which are collapsing under the weight of their roof loads, or with ridge piece and rafters bowing. The paths of many pre-modern buildings are paved with Horsham Stone slabs, often ripple-bedded, as at Shipley, Clayton and Warnham churches. At Warnham churchyard, too, there is a huge table slab of Horsham Stone four paces long by one and a half paces wide, and ripple-bedded.

There is a low ridge that runs for about two miles just north of the A272 between Cowfold eastwards to Old Mill House Farm, Bolney (e.g. TQ 225 230). All along the ridge top is a necklace of small, mostly flooded, old Horsham Stone pits that worked a long narrow outcrop. East of Deaks Lane, Cuckfield, there is another long necklace of Horsham Stone pits, TQ 28 27, on Hammer Hill, in Hammerhill Copse and Toll Shaw, that worked another narrow seam. At Long House, TQ 230 242, a mile south of Leonardslee, there is a tiny quarry on the wooded north slope that has a good Horsham Stone exposure.

The Christ's Hospital farm, TQ 150 288, is called Stammerham Farm, and Little Stammerham Farm lies a mile south west. They sit right on the centre of the Horsham Stone outcrop. 'Stammerham' means 'home of the stone masons', and memorialises those medieval workers and their quarries.

The Sussex Rift Valley

You're on the train yet again going back Brighton way … through the Balcombe Tunnel, then deep cuttings, with forest up above. Then the landscape opens, and … whoooohhh!! … out you go across that viaduct, way up above the countryside, with a long valley winding away to right and to left … and the feeble little upper Ouse river down below.

You have just passed across the Sussex Rift Valley. In that High Wealden sandstone countryside a seven mile long east-west section, a third to a half mile wide, has sunk between two fault lines: the Sidnye Farm Fault to the north and the Borde Hill fault to the south. Between those two fault lines a band of Wealden Clay countryside survives incongruously, with its big fields, low relief, and small woods. It is a slice of the Low Weald marooned in the High Weald.

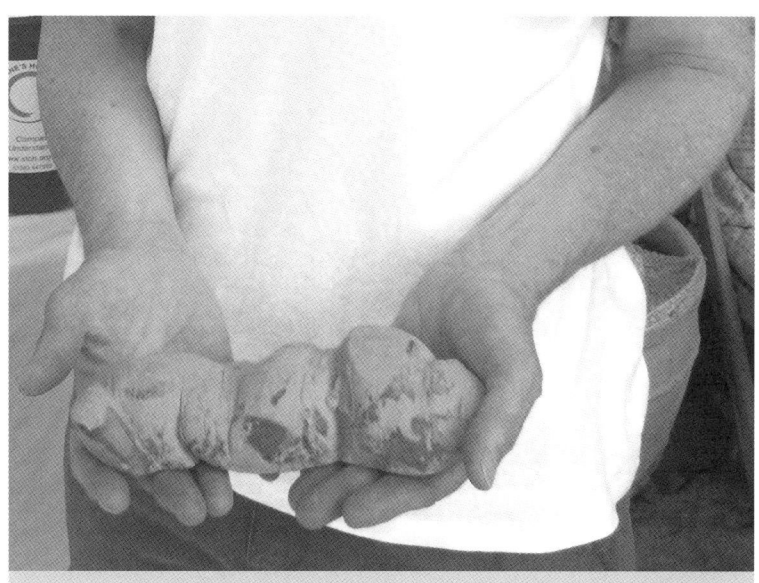

Dinosaur poo: a 'coprolite' fossil from the Horsham Stone Beds.

The Lower Greensand ridge

A long low greensand ridge tracks the line of the South Downs, keeping a distance of about 1 to 1.5 miles north of the chalk scarp. The greensand was laid down on top of the Wealden Clay in marine conditions after the barrier separating the Wealden basin from the sea was finally breached. In middle Sussex the greensand ridge has a mixture of fertile and infertile soils, all easily worked by the plough, and the ridge was an area of early settlement. It is marked by a line of medieval churches: Barcombe, East Chiltington, Ditchling, Keymer, Hurstpierpoint, Albourne, Woodmancote and Henfield. To the west south west of Wolstonbury Hill a subsidiary greensand ridge is marked by a series of farms or barns which are outliers of the main holdings along Underhill Lane: Poynings Grange, Perching Sands, Edburton Sands, Truleigh Sands and South Tottington Sands.

The Romans farmed there before the Saxons, and they built an east-west road which we call the Greensand Way all the way from Pulborough to Barcombe (and eastwards) along this ridge. The road still survives in fragments and in place names, and we can still see parts of its camber (or 'agger') at Randolphs Farm and Danny Park, Hurstpierpoint and at Hayleigh Farm, Westmeston.

The Folkestone Formation

The Folkestone Formation forms the southern slopes of the greensand ridge, and its marine sands have long been valued for building. These pure sands can show

BACKSTORY / Chapter 2: Wealden earth history

THE MIDDLE SUSSEX 'RIFT VALLEY'

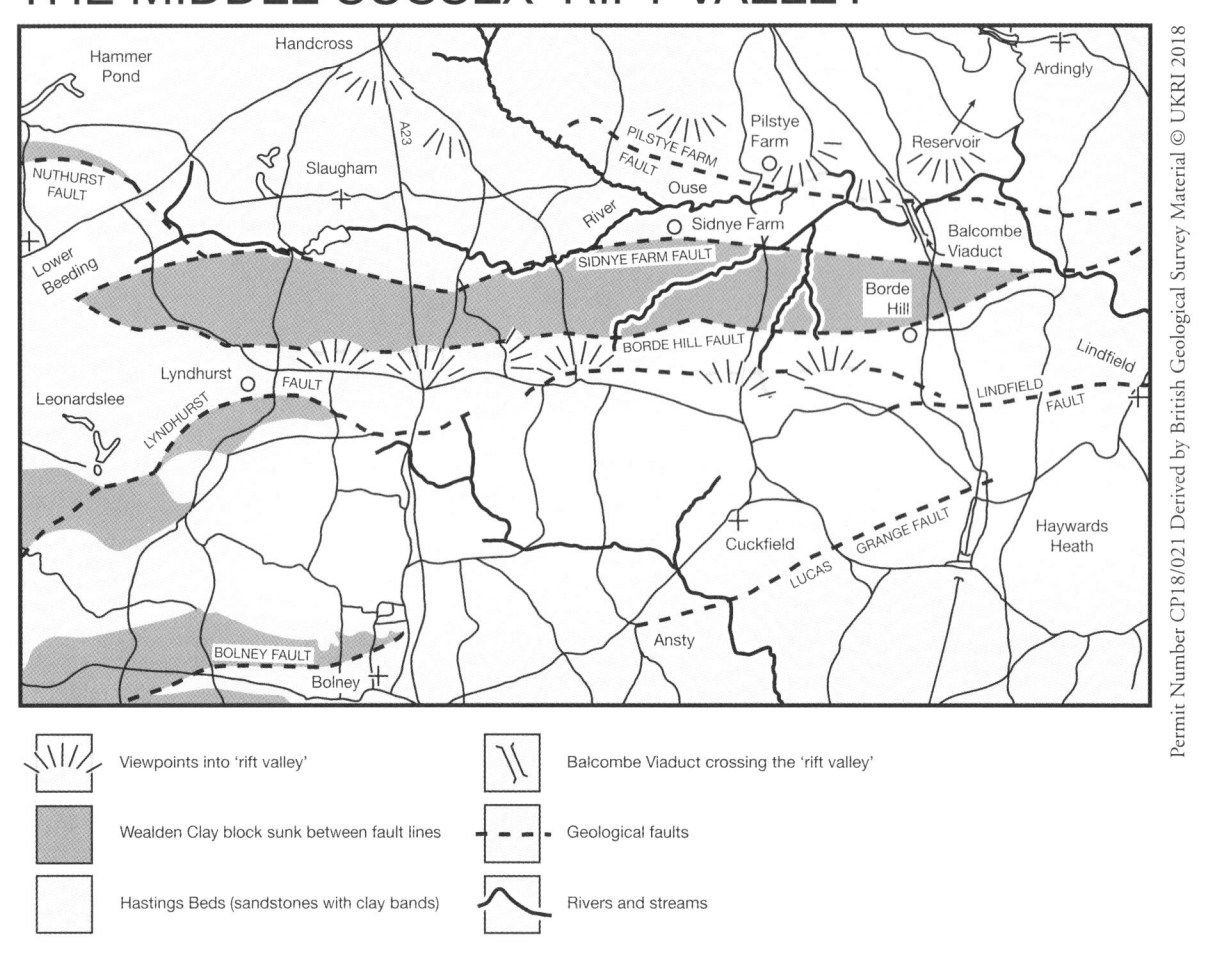

Map legend:
- Viewpoints into 'rift valley'
- Wealden Clay block sunk between fault lines
- Hastings Beds (sandstones with clay bands)
- Balcombe Viaduct crossing the 'rift valley'
- Geological faults
- Rivers and streams

Permit Number CP18/021 Derived by British Geological Survey Material © UKRI 2018

a beautiful range of colours from rose pink to warm orange-yellow, or even white ('silver sand').

The pits at Hassocks and Streat are now infilled and overgrown, but the Novington Sand Pit at East Chiltington, TQ 349 148, was worked till a few years ago. I moseyed to the pit one day and knocked on the portakabin door to bother the quarryman. We had such a good chat. He worked the pit solo. He had worked at the gypsum mines over at Netherfield and his family were miners. He came to East Chiltington after redundancy, utilising his mining skills, and commuted back and forth every day. He knew all about the fossils of the mines and their environs and gave me a good location for hunting them. Alas, neither the Novington Pit, nor the rest of the Folkestone Beds produce good fossils. We have to be content with its beautiful sands, shining gold in the summer evening light or glowing pink, orange and fawn from the low cliff of up-thrust strata. Once, as the grandson was digging and scuffling in the loose sand, he called out, "Look what I've found!" whilst he waved a grimy-but-intact ten pound note at us! No joke … it was well buried there … perhaps by the Psammead,[14] the sand fairy!!

The Gault Clay vale

Between the Lower Greensand ridge and the Downs there is a vale of sticky, heavy marine clay. From the South Downs Way you can see that it is marked by a ribbon of large woods. They start a few fields north of the Downs scarp, beyond Underhill Lane. Big woods like Tottington, Shaves and Park Woods, and Warningore Wood, all lie on those sticky clays. The prehistoric and medieval settlers weren't daft. They didn't waste much energy ploughing the Gault Clay.

The Small Dole Gault Clay pit, TQ 208 123, was known to generations of young fossillers from Brighton, Worthing and beyond, with its fabled luminous phosphatic nodules, its ammonites and other special things so keenly collected. All is buried or scheduled to be buried now, heaped way above the old land height with municipal waste.

You can find fossils on Gault Clay ploughland, and we've found several ammonite species and a bivalve (and a Neanderthal handaxe), but they seem harder to find that in the nearby Grey Chalk at the base of the Downs scarp.

50 BACKSTORY / Chapter 2: Wealden earth history

STICKY CLAYS AND FERTILE SANDS

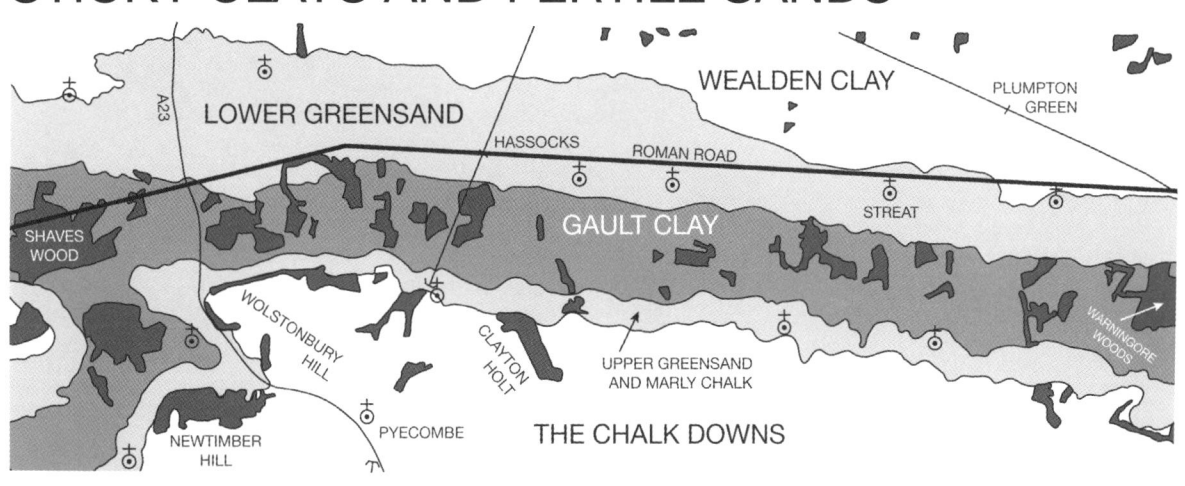

Permit Number CP18/021 Derived by British Geological Survey Material © UKRI 2018

The **Gault Clay** is heavy and sticky. Roman, Saxon and modern farmers thought twice before they cultivated it. That's why it has retained a far greater proportion of woodland than the land to its north and south. Most of its woodlands are ancient, and they have their own distinctive flora. The map shows only one medieval parish church on the Gault: Newtimber.

The **Upper Greensand and Marly, Grey Chalk** between the Gault Clay and the Downs, is, by contrast, mostly fertile and easily worked. Parts of it have probably been cultivated since prehistoric times. The Saxons heavily settled the spring line under the Downs, and the map shows four medieval parish churches marking that settlement.

The **Lower Greensand,** marked by a long ridge, **with the Folkestone Formation sands** along its southern part, are also easily worked and often fertile, sometimes exceptionally so. The Romans valued them highly and engineered a Roman road along them, which we now call the 'Greensand Way'. The Saxons valued them, too, and the map shows a necklace of six medieval churches along them, including Ditchling, which was an important royal manor, and possibly the capital of a Saxon micro-kingdom.

The **Wealden Clay,** to the north, was settled later and less densely than the lands to the south, but most of its woodland cover in this area is long lost. Only small, but often very wildlife-rich, woods survive. However, in other Wealden Clay areas greater woodland cover survives, for instance around Barcombe, Chailey, and Shipley.

The Upper Greensand and the West Melbury Marly Chalk

Just before the Downs, on either side of Underhill Lane, lie the big fertile fields of the Upper Greensand and the grey marly chalk.

The greensand is poor for fossils, though you can find well preserved bivalves and sponges and other marine species there. By contrast, the West Melbury chalk, the final fields before the chalk scarp, are packed with good fossils. A walk over the plough land after it has been tilled will turn up excellent ammonites, nautiloids and inoceramid bivalves. You could be on the beach at Bridport … It is that easy to pick up fossils, though they will often crumble, as the rock is soft and quickly damaged by frost action.

Chalk head

All over the Low Weald – the greensands, the Gault Clay and the Wealden Clay – you come across fields that are covered in Downland flints, both big angular chunks and much smaller pebbles and gravel. You find them miles away from the base of the Downs, in areas where the streams are small and gentle, and maybe even dried up in summertime. From every dimple and combe on the north face of the Downs fans of this 'chalk head' spread out around the pattern of small and larger streams that drain into the Ouse and Adur basins. You find these flints over Henfield Common. There are huge spreads around the North End Stream and the Bevern Brook that debouche into the Ouse, respectively south and north of Barcombe. There are big fans higher up the Ouse around Newick.

The bed of the Plumpton Mill Stream is all flint. A shingle bank a mile and half north of the Downs. We

BACKSTORY / Chapter 2: Wealden earth history

walked the stream side of the Bevern, nearly three miles from the Downs one spring, in hope of seeing the shoaling, rainbow-coated Minnows. The eroded stream bank, five or six foot high, showed a long band of pure Downland flint gravel hear its base, brought there by Ice Age torrents.

You find these flints, too, up in High Wealden gills, where you least expect them, way up around Balcombe and Wakehurst. How did they get there? Was it from the early erosion of the Wealden dome, so many millions of years ago?

They are proof of the huge erosive and disbursive energy of past climate and earth movements. We live on the back of a sleeping giant whose gargantuan power can flick us away like dust from the pelt of an ox.

Chalk Head (not mine): buried flints eroding out of the bank of the Bevern Stream. They were washed there in the Ice Age.

'Holloways'

The softer beds of Wealden sandstone, and occasionally of the clays, too, have been easily eroded downwards along their droves and tracks by the hard hooves of flocks and herds and the wooden and iron clad wheels of farmers' and traders' waggons. Eventually, they form 'hollow ways', shady cuttings sided by exposed rocks, ferns, and gnarled tree roots.

The youngest Wealden beds – of the grey chalk and Upper Greensand – around Underhill Lane, have such holloways, at Edburton, Beggars Lane (Newtimber), Clayton Street, Westmeston Place, and east of the Half Moon Inn at Plumpton.

The Lower Greensand ridge is cut deep by the old swine pasture droves at Streat, by the church, on Plumpton Lane between the Old Mill House and Upper Mill, at Oldlands Lane, Ditchling, TQ 323 154/5, and Langton Lane, Hurstpierpoint, TQ 272 167/8.

The Ardingly Sandstone is exposed along Rocky Lane, amongst Bluebells and Bracken, running up to High Bridge, just south of Haywards Heath, TQ 324 222/3. There are more such sandrock exposures at Founthill, south of Newick, TQ 421 200. You can see one at the top of Hermitage Lane, just before it meets East Grinstead's medieval Middle Row … and elsewhere.

Three lovely green lane holloways cut down through the Upper Tunbridge Wells Sand: Colwell Lane, TQ 345 222, and Ham Lane, TQ 357 217, both south of Haywards Heath, and Cockfield Lane, TQ 410 196, south of Newick. Pure delight all three.

There are many too, in the High Weald, such as so-steep Cob Lane, TQ 348 303, west of Ardingly, cutting through the Wadhurst Clay and the Lower Tunbridge Wells Sands.

ENDNOTES

1. The Bible, Book of Isaiah, Chapter 40, verse 4.
2. 'Wealden of the Weald: A new model', page 396, by P Allen. Proceedings of the Geological Association, Vol. 86 pages 389–436.
3. British Regional Geology: 'The Wealden District', page 24. British Geological Survey, R W Gallois BSc. London: HMSO (1965).
4. 'The Wealden District', page 26. Op cit.
5. 'Classic Landforms of the Weald' pages 25–34, by D A Robinson and R B G Williams. Landform Guides No. 4. The Geographical Association (1984).
6. 'The Wealden District', page 27. Op cit.
7. English Wealden fossils', Text-Fig. 2.1, page 8. Edited by David J. Batten. The Palaeontological Association (2011).
8. 'Wealden of the Weald', page 410. Op cit.
9. 'From Pyecombe to Cuckfield', page 65, by Mark Dudeney and Eileen Hallett. Mid Sussex Books (1999)
10. 'English Wealden fossils', page 305. Op cit.
11. 'English Wealden fossils', page 41. Op cit.
12. 'The Wealden of the Weald: short report of 1998 Field Meeting. Ed A. Jarzembowski and Jonathan D. Radley. Proceedings of the Geologists Association Vol. 112, pages 87–90.
    'The Stratigraphy, sedimentology and palaeontology of the Lower Weald Clay (Hauterivian) at Keymer Tileworks, West Sussex, southern England'. Elizabeth Cook and Andrew J. Ross. Proc.of the Geol. Assoc., Vol 107, pages 231–239.
13. Claude Lorrain was a 17th century French landscape painter with a superb ability to describe luminous distance, particularly at sunset. Check him out.
14. Go on, treat your kids … get "Five Children and It", by E Nesbit, for them … either the book or the DVD. The Psammead is 'It'.

ROCKS OF AGES

Two pieces (scutes) of freshwater turtle shell from Freshfield Quarry's Wadhurst Clay (with £1 coin)

Crushed fossil clams, *Cyrena species,* in a limestone chunk from the Wealden Clay at Kilnwood, between Crawley and Horsham

It's always worth peering at old farmyard walls. At Bower Farm, near Wivelsfield, the herringbone patterned masonry is made of Ironstone.

BACKSTORY / Chapter 2: Wealden earth history

"They had all things common (…) Neither was there any of them that lacked: for as many as were possessors of land or houses sold them, and brought the prices of the things that were sold (…) and distribution was made unto every man according as he had need" (The Bible, Acts of the Apostles 4: 32–35)

Many Wealden lanes have Daft Gates like this

Another super-posh status home going up: Greentrees Hall

CHAPTER 3
Landownership and farming

THE COLLAPSE OF SUSTAINABLE FARMING

When I first walked the Brighton Line Weald in a roughly systematic way, from 1963 to 1969, most of the farmsteads I passed along the lanes were part of working farms. There was mud, and cattle lowing from the yard, and often the crooning and crowing of hens and cockerels. There was the smell of musty hay and the sweetness of manure. Each farm had a waggon barn and a yard with open hovels on one side, and maybe an old raised-up granary. Mostly there would be a Dutch barn or two for stored hay and straw, a milking parlour, sheds, and a modern brick-built workshop and machinery store. Often, in Nettly or Brambly corners there would be discarded and crumbling wooden wheeled carts and waggons, and rusty wood-and-iron machinery from the last decades of the horse and the first decades of the tractor … old single or double share ploughs, tractors, seed drills, hay rakes, bailers, rollers … even the odd threshing machine.

The Weald was a working, food producing countryside, with a mixed economy of tillage crops, dairying and beef cattle, poultry, sheep and pigs, and orcharding. Of course, better-off and owning class people were socially dominant (as, in one way or another, they always had been) and their villas and detached houses lined the lanes, or were set back in their own acres of garden and mini-park. They were not, however, demographically dominant, except in the prettier villages, like Fulking or Lindfield, and the survival of village schools, shops, chapels and pubs reflected the continuing strong presence of working people. Indeed, the post-war Labourist settlement had brought good quality council estates to most villages and many hamlets.

Those were the last days of the small Wealden family farm. Many parishes now have as few as one or two, up to perhaps half a dozen, working, commercial, free standing farms, and a smatter of hobby farms and part-time smaller holdings amongst the leisure landscapes of the rich. That is a far cry from the twenty, thirty, forty or more farms that would have been characteristic of some Wealden parishes as late as the 1960s.

Traditional Sussex barn. Gallops Farm, Streat Lane.

Hovels such as this often hide ancient farm machinery, birds nests and owl houses

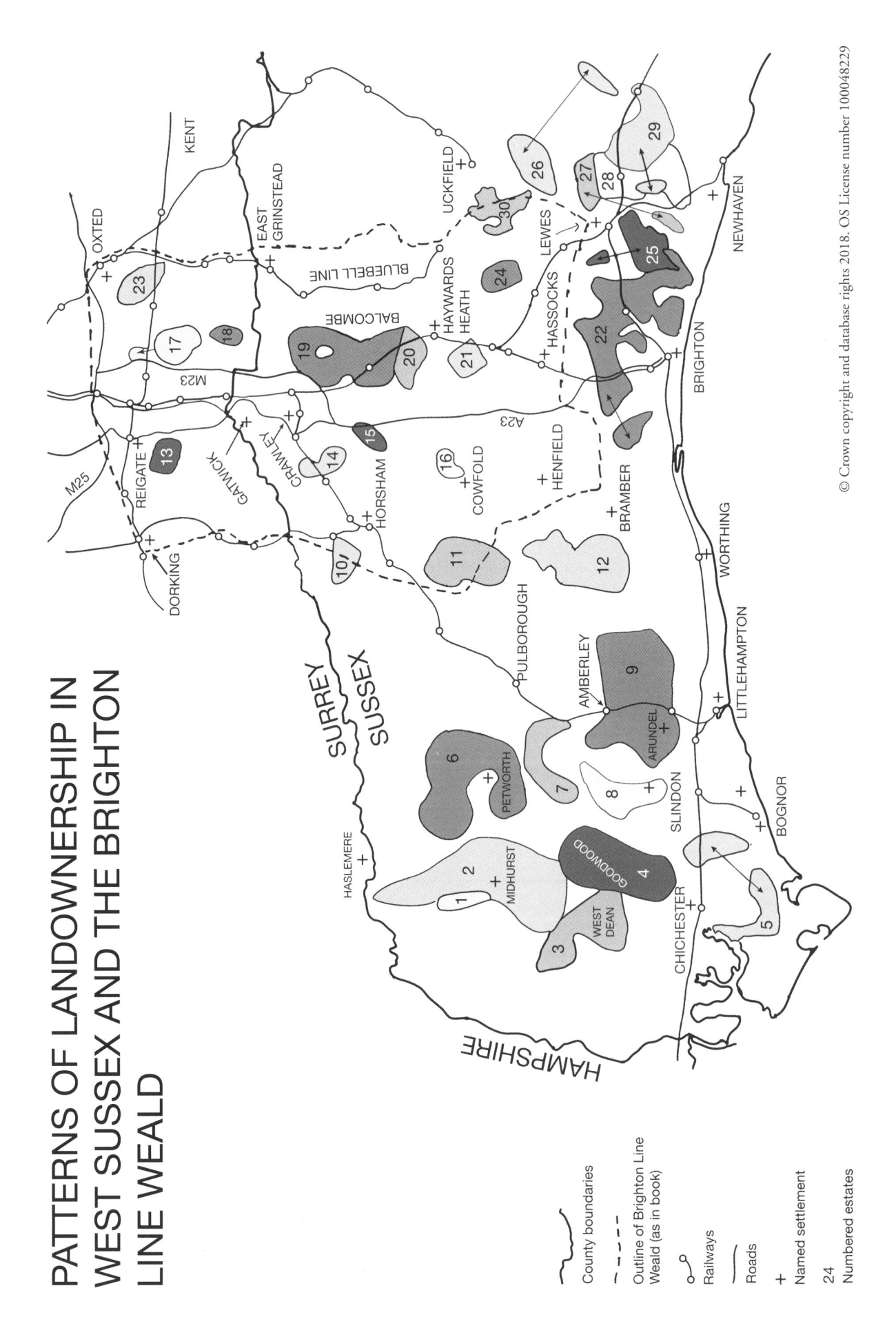

PATTERNS OF LANDOWNERSHIP IN WEST SUSSEX AND THE BRIGHTON LINE WEALD

56   **BACKSTORY** / Chapter 3: Landownership and farming

Patterns of landownership in West Sussex and the Brighton Line Weald

This map is based on information collected over several decades from many local people. It may therefore sometimes not be up to date. In any case, my information is far from complete. Many estates are omitted, because my intention is only to include sufficient to demonstrate *patterns* of landownership. The estates are represented only schematically, and these simplified drawings should not be taken as accurate in detail.

The South Downs and the West Sussex Weald and coastal plain are patterned with very large estates, often held by long standing gentry and titled families, but with a few large public and quasi-public estates held for conservation purposes.

The Brighton Line Weald, by contrast, is strongly patterned by medium sized estates, mostly owned by families whose wealth was created by modern capitalist activity, rather than traditional farming exploitation.

The category of medium sized rentier estates has now substantially blended with that of the larger surviving farm holdings.

Publicly owned holdings are more scattered and of smaller size than in the western Weald and on the South Downs.

List of mapped estates
1. Woolbeding Estate, National Trust
2. Cowdray Estate, Midhurst, Viscount Cowdray
3. West Dean Estate, Edward James Foundation
4. Goodwood Estate, Duke of Richmond
5. Church Commissioners Estates, nr. Chichester, Church of England
6. Leconfield Estate, Petworth, Lord Egremont
7. Barlavington Estate, Sir Sebastian Anstruther, Bt.
8. Slindon Estate, National Trust
9. Arundel Estate (18th Duke of Norfolk) and Angmering Park Estate (Trustees of the 16th Duke of Norfolk). *Heirs of 16th Duke of Norfolk*
10. Warnham Park Estate, Lucas family
11. Knepp Castle Estate (Sir Charles Burrell, Bt.) and Dragons Estate (other Burrell family members). *Heirs of Sir Walter Raymond Burrell, 8th Baronet*
12. Wiston Estate and Fair Oak Farm, Goring family. *Heirs of Rev. John Goring*
13. Bures Manor and Flanchford Estate, heirs of Charrington family
14. Holmbush Estate, Faygate, Calvert family
15. The Hyde Estate, Handcross
16. Long House Estate, nr. Cowfold
17. Harewoods and Sandhills Estates, nr. Redhill, National Trust
18. West Park Estate, Surrey County Council Smallholdings Estate
19. Paddockhurst Estate (now split into eight) and Balcombe Estate (Greenwood family). *Heirs of 1st Viscount Cowdray*
20. Borde Hill Estate, Haywards Heath, Stephenson Clarke family
21. Heaselands Estate, Haywards Heath, Sir Richard Kleinwort, Bt.
22. Brighton Downs Estate, Brighton and Hove City Council
23. Tandridge Estate, nr. Godstone, Knightwood Trust Farms (2014)
24. Hooke Estate, Chailey, Tillard family
25. Iford Estate (John Robinson) and Northease Farm (David Robinson). *Heirs of J. C. Robinson*
26. The Plashett and Pollards Estates, nr. Ringmer, Askew family and Charitable Trust
27. Glyndebourne Estate, Christie family
28. Glynde Estate, Viscount Hampden
29. Firle Estate, Viscount Gage
30. Sutton Hall Estate, Sclater family

To be sure, the Wealden soils are mostly no match for the prime (Grades One and Two) soils of the Sussex coastal plain or the Kent coast, but most of the Brighton Line Wealden soils are good to moderate – Grade Three in the Agricultural Land Classification. Only the Low Wealden ribbons of riverine flood plain, the High Wealden incised gill valleys, the poor sands of St Leonard's Forest, the River Mole flatlands, and the Rusper and Charlwood ridgelands descend to Grade Four, poor quality soils. There are too, bands of very good Grade Two tillage along the Sussex Lower Greensand ridge from Hurstpierpoint to Henfield, around Small Dole, along the underhill lane from Wolstonbury to Lewes, and along the Ouse flatlands from Offham to Barcombe.

Our Wealden soils may not be the tops. They are not Fenland soils, with their multiple cropping, or the Lincolnshire Wolds, ploughed end to end for two centuries, but they have produced good food for several millennia, on the basis of their own local inputs, sustaining their own communities and provisioning more distant regional communities.

The moderate nature of Wealden soils is not the driver for the collapse of its small farming economy. That collapse has three causes. The ***first*** is capitalist globalisation with its relentless search for low costs and high profits at the expense of poor peoples and the natural environment. Why would capital seek to preserve sustainable food production in the Weald when it could cheaply import foods from distant parts of the British Isles, or (in the past) its Empire, or from

MOVING THE GOALPOSTS

MAP 1. BLACKSTONE, WOODMANCOTE, c. TQ 23 16.

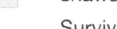

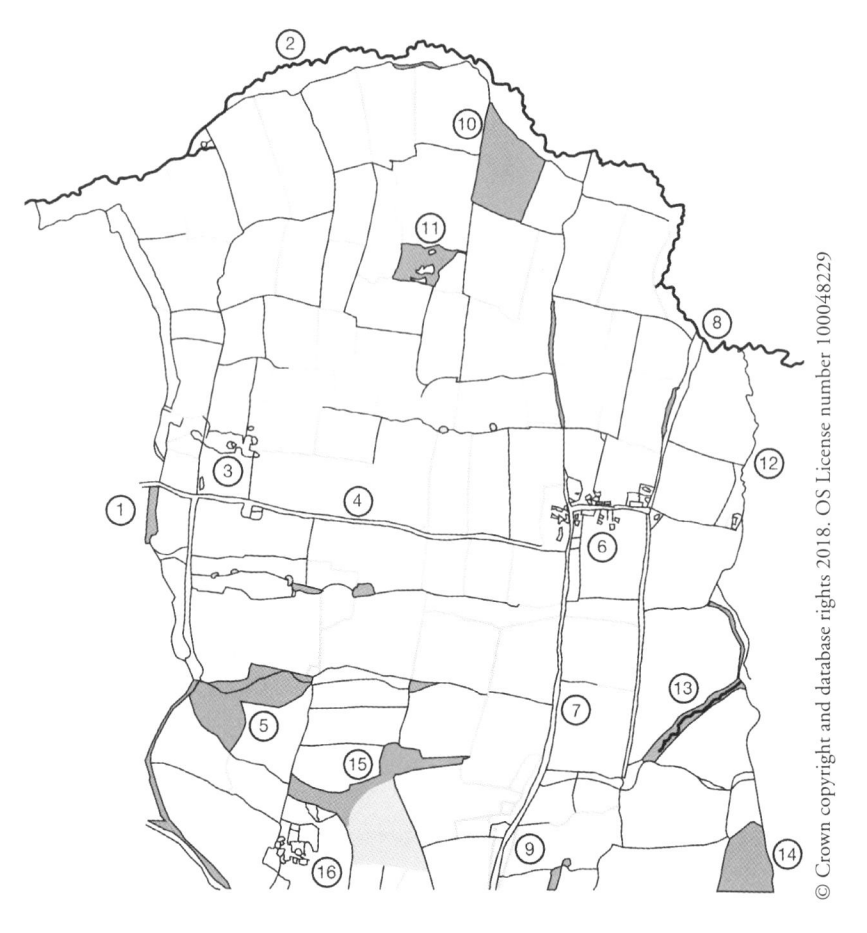

These two maps illustrate modern destruction of semi-natural landscape features – mostly hedges, shaws, fences and woods. They illustrate how Wealden countryside we now see as 'unspoilt' has, in fact, been substantially damaged. Very few of us have any knowledge of what we have lost. We are merely grateful to be out in the open, with green trees, long views, and big skies. Thus do landowners and farmers and their government sponsors destroy our heritage and escape our indignation.

Key to both maps

From 1873 6 inch to 1 mile O/S map, showing field boundaries and woods lost since that date. With the kind permission of the Ordnance Survey.

- Surviving old woods and shaws
- Destroyed old woods and shaws
- Surviving hedges and fences
- Destroyed hedges and fences
- Railways
- Roads
- Streams

1. Swan's Gill
2. Chess Brook
3. Bilsborough
4. Bilsborough Lane
5. The Alders
6. Blackstone
7. Blackstone Lane
8. Blackstone Bridge
9. Cuckold's Green
10. Woodhouse Wood
11. Woodhouse
12. Wick Farm Brook
13. Home Gill
14. West Wood
15. Woodmancote Wood
16. Woodmancote Place

© Crown copyright and database rights 2018. OS License number 100048229

Europe or other continents, and when it can guzzle cheap fossil fuels to power its giant machines, with their economies of scale? The ***second*** is the competitive scrabble for survival in the farming industry (as in any capitalist industry). That has made winners of those able to increase their farmed acreage drastically, eliminate waged labour and replace it with the most expensive capital equipment, and make clean production 'floors' ... giant fields without any impediments of steep contours, poor drainage, hedges and shaws ... and giant farm buildings which can accommodate modern livestock systems, or round which large farm vehicles can freely move. The ***third*** is that land in the Weald is valued as much, and often more, by well-off business leisure users from our towns, from the London megalopolis and farther afield, as by farming interests. The Weald now functions as a giant garden suburb, a dormitory and a retreat for capitalism's winners.

The Wealden countryside has divided into an intensive farming landscape and an owning class leisure landscape. Intensification and its ever-higher capital requirements drove out the great bulk of farm workers and all those farmers unable or unwilling to muster the resources for capitalist farming's new technologies. Derelict Wealden farmyards and barn yards are a familiar sight in the Brighton Line Weald, some only constructed a few decades ago during agriculture's post-war boom. Many of those with attractive vernacular farm buildings have now been converted to houses and neat gardens, and many others are now business centres. Many also have been converted to equestrian yards.

BACKSTORY / Chapter 3: Landownership and farming

MAP 2. FRESHFIELD AND COCKHAISE BROOK, SOUTH OF HORSTED KEYNES, c. TQ 38 25.

© Crown copyright and database rights 2018. OS License number 100048229

TYPES OF FARMING

The fate of **dairy farming** shows most sharply the fate of Wealden agriculture as a whole. Since the coming of the railways commercial milk production had been central to Wealden farming. Smallholders and mixed farmers as well as dedicated milk producers had milking herds, and a farmer could make a living from as little as 15 cows. Relatively low yield breeds like Shorthorns were common, as were specialist cream producing herds of Jerseys and Guernseys. Their cows lived long lives and, if required, had many calves. Militant action by dairy farmers against the milk distributors won the creation of the Milk Marketing Board in 1933, which rationalised distribution and maintained the price of liquid milk in the face of fluctuating demand, thus giving some stability to smaller producers. However, the drive to increase cows' production meant the highest performing herds outcompeted the small producers in a milk market that wasn't growing. With the move away from economic regulation[1] and the growth of large scale processors and the supermarkets from the 1960s onwards, the smaller producers were marginalised. Wave after wave of dairy farmers have been forced out of business, to such an extent that it is now possible with

1. East Mascalls
2. Cockhaise Farm
3. Cockhaise Mill
4. Treemans
5. Freshfield Quarry
6. Freshfield Crossway
7. Kidborough Farm
8. King's Wood
9. Town Place
10. Town Place Farm
11. Cockhaise Brook
12. Bluebell Line
13. River Ouse and Navigation

ease to list all the main commercial milk producers in the Brighton Line Weald, so few are they.

Imagine if men were able to demand that women produce five, six, or seven times the milk they naturally produce to feed their babies. Few things could sound more bizarre. Yet – now – that is what we ask of our dairy cows. On Wealden farms we see Friesian and Holstein cows plod through fields with their hugely enlarged udders swaying below them in a way that

BACKSTORY / Chapter 3: Landownership and farming

is painful to watch, leave alone suffer. Only the impediments of a corrugated landscape, with heritage designations and still relatively small fields and holdings, and a watchful public living close by, hold back some of the lunacies of dairy farming in other regions of Britain (with plans for herds of 8,000), or the USA (with herds of over 20,000).

At one extreme, in the Brighton Line Weald, we have at least (I think) two dairy farms with herds of 600–800 milking cows kept permanently indoors (zero grazing) and milked on an automatic circular turntable. If you had a choice, would you buy milk that came from cows kept like prisoners?

At the other extreme we have a local farmer with a long-standing herd of about 30 Guernseys who doesn't even market the milk (using it for the calves instead) because it makes more economic sense in her farm economy to breed the beasts for sale than to milk them.

Wealden dairy farming has been wrecked, despite the fact that small herds and low yielding cows are kinder and more environmentally friendly (having lower carbon emissions[2] and much lower artificial feed requirements, for instance) and despite the proximity of huge markets. Many of those farms that do survive are no better than any other agribusiness enterprise, with huge green-glowing super-fertilised grass fields, blankets of Nettles along every ditch, stream and hedge boundary, sprawling sheds, giant slurry lagoons and feed hoppers, concrete droves, and spreads of feed crops.

If you want to sense a sustainable way of dairying then check out **Plawhatch Community Farm**, with its herd of 40 Meuse-Rhine-Issel milkers and its friendly stockman … or pass by **Portmansford Farm**, Furner's Green, north of Sheffield Park, with its Guernseys and big old hedgerows … or **Bysshe Court Farm** only 3 mile east of Gatwick (but 100 miles away in spirit) with its rare Dairy Shorthorns … or **Aldhurst Farm**, Capel, which has kept most of its old hedges and copses.

Big commercial farms are now the norm in the Brighton Line Weald, with acreages from 300 to 1,000 or 1,500 being typical. The distinction between rentier landowners (gaining their income by simple parasitism from let farm and building rents) and commercial farmers has greatly dissolved. Throughout the post-war farming boom and up to the present, landlords have been taking more and more of their let farms in hand, and commercial farmers (often ex-tenants who initially bought their farms upon the break-up of the big estates) have greatly expanded their units. The Wealden part of the **Tandridge and Chelsham Estate** (between Oxted and Lingfield) amounted to 2,159 acres in 2010, managed in-hand from just two of its many erstwhile farms. **Felcourt Farm's** 600 acres between Lingfield and East Grinstead have been managed as a high-tech dairy farm for almost a century. **Weston's Farm,** on the Christ's Hospital School Estate, Horsham, has grown from 160 acres to 1,200 acres since 1989.

The big commercial farms can be identified by the size of their fields, the monotony of their cropping patterns, the large-scale singularity of their uses, and the coarseness and brutality of their management of landscape and wildlife features. Hedges, small woods, shaws, wet meadows and old barns will have been removed and large consolidated fields created, perhaps leaving a few 'lollipop' Oaks to mark the alignment of lost boundaries. Where hedges remain, large gaps have often been made for the easy ingress of big farm machinery. **North Barnes Farm**, east of Plumpton Green, is a particularly painful example, now converted back to intensive sheep pasturage.

Where the soils are better, big Wealden farms have large **arable** acreages, such as on the **Conyboro Estate**, at Cooksbridge, north of Lewes; the **Newick and Sutton Hall Estate**; at **Great Bentley Farm** on the Borde Hill Estate, north of Cuckfield; or **Weston's Farm**. The big farming company **Sentry Ltd.,** farm the mostly arable **West Grinstead Estate's** c. 2000 acres and **Lock Farm's** c. 650 acres near Partridge Green is largely arable.

There is no easy Low Weald and High Weald divide, despite the High Weald's supposed protected AONB (Area of Outstanding Natural Beauty) status. There are, thus, many damaged High Wealden intensive farming sub-landscapes, such as around **Grouse Road** in St Leonards Forest; **Cockhaise Farm** in Lindfield; the farmlands next to **Parish Lane**, Tilgate Forest; or **Broadhurst Manor**, Horsted Keynes.

Cattle rearing for beef remains of some importance, with many pedigree herds, particularly nowadays of the Sussex breed, and many more store cattle raised. It is possible for some hobby farmers to utilise graziers' cattle to keep their otherwise unutilised pastures in good heart. Other owners for whom farming is a second income or a hobby run their own herds, such as at **Tilgate Forest Lodge** with its pedigree Sussex cattle on its own land and on the adjacent Hyde Estate's ground (2012) ; or as was at **Goddenwick Farm**, Lindfield, before its conversion to xmas tree growing. Often farms which have had to give up dairying convert to beef cattle and other livestock, such as **Great House Farm** at Southwater (now threatened by housing development), **Townings Farm** at Chailey, or **Little Oddynes Farm**, Horsted Keynes.

Sheep farming has become more important than cattle, though the drainage and soils are not so suited to it. Some farms make it their chief business, as at **Upperstone Farm**, Chelwood Common (2013), **North Barnes Farm**, East Chiltington, and **Hammenden Farm**, Highbrook. Other farms have a flock alongside other income sources. Many hobby farmers have small sheep flocks, such as **Griffins Farm**, West Grinstead.

Ancient granary, Knepp north park: many of these ancient buildings are similarly decrepid.

Derelict intensive battery egg and broiler chicken sheds are a common feature of the Weald, particularly east of the Brighton Line landscape in the old **poultry farming** area centred on Heathfield. Long overdue statutory changes to the welfare regime and public anger at the industry's customary cruelties, have finally brought new growth in large scale free range and organic egg and chicken production. The big egg factories at Sayers Common are now gone, and there is a large free range enterprise at **Springles Farm**, near Barcombe, part of a cluster of free range farms including another at North Chailey and one in Ditchling's Common Lane (where there are at least two poultry farms). The old Kinswood Farm at Brooks Green has relocated to **Orchard Farm** to comply with the new standards. Such units at least provide relatively good numbers of local jobs in a generally depopulated farming industry. Modern commercial free range units are a world away from the old backyard, smallholding and small farm poultry production of the boom years of the Wealden poultry industry from c. 1850 to World War Two.[3] In those days the industry integrated local or on-farm grain and milk production for their feeds, and utilised the high levels of local woodland, hedgerow and orchard cover for their flocks. Now, free range units may seal off relatively large areas with two metre boundary fences.

Pig production has low visibility in this landscape, and there are few large scale producers. Pigs are often kept by hobbyists, or as farm attractions, and there are free range Tamworths on the Knepp rewilding project. Visiting the Townings Farm pigs has given the grandchildren much pleasure.

Orcharding and soft fruit production reached a large scale in some parts of the Brighton Line Weald in the later 19th century and the first half of the 20th century, though the industry was far bigger on the better soils of the coastal plain and the greensands to the west, and in Kent and the eastern Sussex Weald. One of my first jobs was apple picking on **Old Mill House Farm** at Bolney, and some of their orchards are still in production, whilst other parts are long derelict – and delightful in their wildness. The **Ashdown Land Company** at Broadhurst Manor, Horsted Keynes, had soft and orchard fruit on a large scale, with a packing station and on farm accommodation for pickers. There's almost no sign of that heritage there now. A few of the old fruit trees from the big **Furners Farm** orchards at Henfield are still standing. Small farm orchards still survive by many farmsteads in varying degrees of health. They are always worth looking for.

Small scale **horticulture** has massively contracted as a result of European competition and the giant economies of scale demanded by the supermarkets and other major retail outlets. **Clappers Lane, Fulking**, is no longer a place of market gardens and orchards, and the derelict glasshouses of **Ditchling Nurseries**, Beacon Road, below Ditchling Beacon, still sprout trees through their broken panes (2018) as they have done for many years.

Horse and pony keeping – horseyculture – has taken over much land in recent decades. Whole farmscapes are devoted to horse ownership, as on the Danehill smallholdings landscape east of Danehill; at High Hurst Manor, Maplehurst; around Tilburstowhill Farm, Godstone; and at Ifieldwood, Crawley. Some of these livery sub-landscapes are very posh, like the racing establishments at Elliotts, Copsale; or Cinder Farm, Newick … or at Hoe's and Baker's Farms, Shipley, with their nearby polo fields.

There are some **deer farms**, too, such as at Warnham Park and adjacent Bailing Hill Farm, at Woodmancote Place, at Maplehurst Farm, and at Newick Park.

Their spread is nothing like so explosive as the growth of **vineyards** though, with big sites at Plumpton College; at Ridgeview, below Ditchling Beacon; at Booker's Farm, Bolney; Court Gardens Farm, Ditchling; Mill Place at Kingscote, and many others. What deer farming and vineyards, intensive game bird rearing, free range poultry farms, private parks and landscape gardens – and hugely profitable solar arrays – have in common is tall security fences and CCTV cameras, and more policing of our access and usage. They intensify the hegemony of the rich, and often, by insulating the land from production which meets our workaday food needs, they drive up levels of food importation.

Giant food companies grab the land of poor farmers in Africa, Asia and Eastern Europe. Millions of hectares of tropical forest and bush are bulldozed, whilst good

BACKSTORY / Chapter 3: Landownership and farming

Wealden soils are wasted on non-essential premium products like sparkling wines and venison.

ALTERNATIVES??

Mixed, traditional farms are nearing extinction, though some smaller producers valiantly work to find a way of farming both sustainably and profitably. **Townings Farm**, Chailey, a tenancy of the Hooke Estate, is a fine example, with its small arable acreage, small piggery, hardy sheep and Longhorn cattle (used for the conservation grazing of adjacent Chailey Common) poultry and farm shop. At **Little Oddynes Farm**, Horsted Keynes, the footpath takes you through the cattle yard, where the sweet smells of hay and manure mingle. The cows and calves are shedding their winter coats as newly arrived Swallows sweep over the barns. The farmers said two Red Backed Shrikes spent a few days there just earlier – a tribute to the farm's conservative management. There is Cuckoo Flower still in some of the big top fields, and archaic marsh down on its brooks. **Daylands Farm**, too, just west of the Adur on the Wiston Estate, has been a superb example, with a small area of commercial nursery crops, as well as cattle, a fish pond and much educational work. Let's hope it continues. **Goffsland Farm**, a tenancy of the Knepp Estate, has beef cattle and sheep, B&B and a campsite, and most of its landscape features are intact. Farm shops, small camping sites and visitor activities are a life-line for many smaller producers.

The line between surviving traditional farms and **new, alternative farms** is indistinct. New organic growers took over **Ashurst Farm**, neighbouring Plumpton Race Course, in 1994. Till then, the on-farm dairy cows had been hand milked by the farm's old owners, and the land had received no artificial fertilisers since 1945, thus facilitating immediate organic status. The farm has a vegetable box scheme and employs much local labour. **The Laines Farm** south of Cuckfield supplies Infinity Foods, Brighton, again using much part-time labour. There are many other good, alternative small farming projects scattered through the Wealden landscape, mostly with little public profile.

The mother of all alternative farms is the community supported 200+ acre **Plawhatch Farm**, east of Sharpthorne (and its larger sister farm at Tablehurst, Forest Row, together with which they farm about 1500 acres). It combines traditional methods with reliance on planetary rhythms for the planting and harvesting of crops, producing unpasteurised milk, growing vegetables on 12 acres, with poultry houses around the farm, a small pig herd, and a sheep flock. They run a wholly integrated biodynamic system, exceeding organic standards. Their livestock numbers are small and sane: 30 ewes, 380 laying hens, a few pigs, and 35 milking cows. They retail their produce locally, with a busy farm shop, and generate a whole bunch of jobs, as well as providing apprenticeships and wider educational opportunities, and running a small care home. 'Good' inadequately describes the place!

Scattered across the landscape are a number of farms which have simply been left unfarmed and in various degrees of abandonment. **Roundabout Farm** at Copthorne, with its rich wildflower meadows and vastly outgrown hedges, is the best of them, vulnerable, declining, but a treasure house of past archaic grassland species (2017). **Amberley Farm** at Langley Green, Crawley, on the banks of the River Mole, has something of the same magical quality (now threatened by a second Gatwick runway). **Blanche's Farm** meadows, north of Partridge Green, are also minimally managed.

Farms with 'hope value' for development can often, too, have that 'preserved in aspic' quality: left by their owners in an unproductive and minimally managed state in anticipation of future planning permissions. **Langton Farm's** fields at Hurstpierpoint feel like that (2014) as do **Sunte House fields**, by the railway line on the north edge of Hayward's Heath; or **Weatherhill Common fields**, east of Horley. These places can be vastly under-valued for nature and public enjoyment.

Some farmers have opted to convert their businesses into paying country parks, with varying levels of sensitivity to local landscape character and wildlife. East End Farm, Ditchling, was a small dairy farm before the farmer carefully transformed it into **Stoneywish Nature Reserve**, a much loved country park with camping and many animals. **Washbrooks Family Farm** at nearby Hurstpierpoint has a high public profile. Gate House Farm at Newchapel, Horne, was transformed by its wildlife loving dairy farmer into the **British Wildlife Centre**, exhibiting many of our native mammals, owls and other raptors, and two of our three snakes. Local councils have also preserved farms for public recreation, such as the lovely **Bedelands Farm** at Burgess Hill, with its archaic flower meadows and Bluebell woods; or **Willoughby Fields** Local Nature Reserve at Langley Green, Crawley (threatened by the Gatwick second runway).

A range of rich owners who have gained or inherited wealth elsewhere, utilise the farms they have bought as private nature reserves, with varying degrees of empathy to public usage, from downright hostility to open-hearted delight in our presence. At the latter end is lovely **Knowlands Farm**, north of Barcombe Cross. **Hurstbarns Farm**, north west of Cooksbridge, has a friendly access regime too. The owner of **Shergolds Farm** at Streat has loved and preserved the farm's conservation features. At 200 acre **Tilgate Forest Lodge** the owners have managed a superb heathland restoration project, though it has no public profile. It is the same at **Northlands Farm**, North Horsham, with its superb archaic flower meadows (2012), and seems to be so, too, at the lovely archaic meadows of **Vixengrove Farm**,

Chailey. At Capel, the 86.5 acre Clarke's Green Farm, has, since 1992, become the **Dairy House Private Nature Reserve,** crossed by public footpaths.

All of those 'conservation farms', though, are dwarfed in size by the combined 'rewilding' project of the **Knepp and Dragons Estate**s between Dialpost, Shipley, and Southwater. Well over 3000 acres of erstwhile small Wealden farms are now bounded by 2m fencing and grazed at low intensity by herds of Fallow and Red Deer, Longhorn cattle, ponies and Tamworth pigs. The project was helped by the fact that a significant part of the Knepp Estate was already in hand (unencumbered by tenant farmers) and thus available for such an initiative. The gains for wildlife are obvious, with large numbers of Nightingales and Barn Owls, and Turtle Doves cooing amongst the leaves of summer trees. The premium food generated, though, is much the same as the premium food that was produced in Knepp's earlier medieval giant deer park for the feudal lordly class. It is not the commonplace vegetables, dairy products, cereals, meats, and fruit which our farmland needs to produce to help meet our needs and take the pressure off biologically superior poor world habitats of forest, wetland, bush, steppe and savannah. The 'Knepp Wildland's' contribution to wildlife may be great, but its contribution to the problem of marrying nature with sustainable food production is negative. The Barn Owls and Nightingales were at least as common in the old Wealden farmscape as they are in the Knepp 'wildlands'.

Private conservation estates rely on high market rents from residential and business property, non-means tested public agri-environmental subsidies, profits from game bird shoots and other expensive country pursuits and premium products, and profits generated from conventional external capitalist investments, to fund their conservation activities. They are not a progressive alternative model for managing nature. They are simply the other side of the coin from the devastated agri-business landscapes of the Sussex coastal plain and much of eastern England. On the better farmlands and in the City of London the rich extract their profits. In the Wealden countryside they spend and enjoy those profits …

PATTERNS OF LANDOWNERSHIP

Our Wealden countryside is not a democratic place. The pattern of landownership in the Brighton Line Weald clearly shows the dominant influence of big industrial and City capital, intermingled with left-overs from the days of feudal lordship, and a tangled farm ownership mosaic reflecting old patterns and drastic modern changes.

The descendants of the 1st Viscount Cowdray at Paddockhurst and Balcombe have inherited a 19th and early 20th century fortune first made globally in railways, oil, engineering and construction.[4] The Stephenson Clarkes of Borde Hill and Cinder Hill made their fortune as shipping magnates with a large bulk carrying fleet. The Kleinworts of Heaselands made their money from merchant banking. The Charringtons of Bures Manor made their fortune with the famous brewery. William Robinson of Gravetye made his fortune from modern gardening publishing. The first of the Powell Edwards of Novington Manor, near Plumpton, made his money in property, owning a section of Oxford Street.[5] The ancestors of the Monk Brettons of Conyboro made their fortune in law and Victorian politics.

To be sure, the Brighton Line landscape is now free of private landholdings of the grotesque size of those which lie on either side. To the west, there are the 18,750 acre Cowdray Estate at Midhurst, the 14,000 acre Leconfield Estate at Petworth, the 7,500 acre Duke of Norfolk's Estate, the 6,750 acre Angmering Park Estate of the Duke of Norfolk's cousins, and the 6,300 acre Wiston Estate. To the east, there are the circa 6,000 acre Glynde Estate, and the c. 7,000 acre Firle Estate. Those *latifundia* stretch for many miles.

Nonetheless, a walker going south from the Worth Way, over the M23 Crawley Bypass bridge, would scarcely leave land owned by descendants of the 1st Viscount Cowdray for six miles – all across Worth Forest, past Balcombe and the Ardingly Reservoir to the edge of Haywards Heath Golf Course. A walker going south from Marlpost Woods by Southwater, would not leave Burrell family land for nearly five miles – through Shipley and past Dial Post.

There are several major private estates of at least 3000[6] acres. The **Paddockhurst Estate**, now (2018) fragmented between multiple trustees, I am told, has a combined c. 6,000 acreage. It borders the

Balcombe Estate, of 3,500 acres, held by cousins of the Paddockhurst owners. The **Knepp Castle Estate** of c. 3,500 acres borders **the Dragons Estate** of maybe 1,600 acres held by relatives of the Knepp owner … and the family of the Knepp owner are related to the Balcombe Estate owners. In Surrey, the combined Weald and Downland footprint of the **Tandridge and Chelsham Estate** was 3,222 acres in 2010, but there have been sales since then.

Below that biggest rank are a series of large private estates of between 2,500 and 1,000 acres. Landed estates in the Brighton Line Weald are often of this rank in size terms, perhaps because their mercantile and industrial creators of the time of the industrial revolution were not primarily looking for farming profits, and could garner all the benefits of manorial lordly status on smaller areas. Two such estates wrap round the west side of Haywards Heath: the c. 1,000 acre **Heaselands Estate**, and the c. 2,000 acre **Borde Hill Estate**. Relatives of the Borde Hill owners have an estate at **Cinder Hill**, Horsted Keynes, which used to centre on Broadhurst Manor before that was separately sold. Between Barcombe and Newick is the c. 2,000 acre **Sutton Hall Estate**, and between South Chailey and Chailey Common is the c. 1,000 acre **Hooke Estate**, roughly the same size as the **Holmbush Estate**, between Faygate and Crawley. The **Warnham Park Estate** is perhaps 1,200 acres. Though the Hursts sold Horsham Park in the town centre in 1928, and The Nunnery in Rusper more recently, they still own c. 1,500 acres in the area, I was told. The **Conyboro Estate** covers perhaps 1,000 acres in a rough triangle bounded by Hamsey, Cooksbridge, Chiltington and Barcombe Mills. In Surrey the c. 1,600 acre **Bures Manor Estate**, Flanchford, is typical of this middling rank, and neighbours the 1,200 acre **Buckland Estate**, and the 1,100 acre **Betchworth Estate**.

There are a series of estates of between 500 and 1000 acres which nonetheless embrace very complex terrain and thus feel much larger. Such is **The Hyde Estate**, c. 850 acres, west of Hands Cross; the **Long House Estate**, now of perhaps 700 acres between Cowfold and Leonardslee; and the **Hurst Barns Estate**, South Chailey, c. 500 acres.

Many commercial farms easily compare in size with those more lordly estates. **Perching and Paythorne Farms**, part on the Brighton Downs and part in the Weald, cover c. 1,500 acres. The **Norris Farms Partnership** covers perhaps two miles of land at Ansty which was once part of the Cuckfield Park Estate. **More House Farm**, Wivelsfield, occupies a broken 2.5 mile strip of land going south from Haywards Heath.

Those estates in public ownership reflect these size categories because they are the result of the gifting or purchase of pre-existing private estates to public bodies. Thus, the c. 1000 acre **West Park** County Council smallholdings estate was purchased carte blanch by Surrey Council from the Palmer family (of biscuit firm Huntley and Palmers) in 1937. The total size of the Surrey CC smallholdings in the Surrey Low Weald must be about 2,000 acres, giving them a substantial potentially progressive role (2015). The National Trust is a large landowner in the Surrey Brighton Line Weald, having been gifted the **Harewoods Estate**, Outwood, c. 2,048 acres; **Sandhills**, Redhill, 430 acres; and the **Holmwood Commons**, 634 acres. In the Brighton Line Sussex Weald they just have **Nymans**, 601 acres, **Wakehurst**, 479 acres; and **Standen**, 58.5 acres. They possess no land in our bit of the Sussex Low Weald. The Forestry Commission controls some 1,625 acres in the Sussex High Weald: 610 acres in **St Leonard's Forest**; 372 acres in **Tilgate Forest**; and 643 acres at **Gravetye**. They own only **Highridge Wood**, Brockham, in our Surrey area, just over 100 acres.

The landed private Brighton Line estates must not be taken as the only holdings of their owners. Lord Hamilton of Dalzell's 1,100 acre **Betchworth Estate** by the River Mole is dwarfed by his 8,500 acre Apley Estate on the River Severn. The c. 150 acres owned by the Earl of Lytton at **Newbuildings**, Shipley (all that is left of a much larger estate once based at Crabbet Park, near Crawley) is dwarfed by the family's 850 acre Lillycombe Estate on Exmoor. The owner of the 350 acre **Great Ote Hall Estate** at Burgess Hill also has the 180 acre Randolph Farm, at Hurstpierpoint. The **Great House Farm Southwater Estate** is a mere outlier of the Chilton Estate, Bucks. **Mynthurst Farms** west of Horley are owned by a farming company based in Gloucestershire, and **Tandridge and Chelsham Farms** by a farming firm based in Nottinghamshire.

In the period after the First World War, from 1918 to 1922, about a quarter of all British land was sold as the 40 year long slump in agriculture resumed, and continuing agitation for democratic land reform put the wind up big landowners. Many big estates shed land or sold up altogether. The 1,400 acre Montefiore Estate at **Worth Park** was sold in 1915. Nearby, a big part of the Scawen Blunt estate at **Crabbet Park**, near Crawley, was sold in 1916. The Sergison family sold a large chunk of the **Cuckfield Park Estate** in 1919, and the rest was sold in 1968. The 2,200 acre **Tilgate Park Estate** was broken up in 1939. The 600 acre rump of the Eversfields' **Denne Park Estate** at Horsham (3,124 acres in 1875) was sold up in 1947. Part of the **Imberhorne Estate** at East Grinstead was sold for housing in 1953 and the family moved onto the remainder of their land at Tilkhurst. The Shiffner estate at **Coombe Place, Offham**, was broken up after 1950. In 1983, the Campions' erstwhile c. 2000 acre **Danny Park Estate** at Hurstpierpoint was broken up.

Most of the old feudal and early modern rentier landowning and titled families have gone, though those with modern capitalist fortunes have valued the

Big private landowners mostly prioritise recreational wild animal killing over free public access

old snobbery of titles enough to acquire them, too. Furthermore, 'new' monied landowners have meshed seamlessly with older landowning families in marriage and friendship ties, and landholding families have held fast to old local landowning continuities where those had worn very thin. The family that bought lovely **High Beeches Gardens**, Handcross in 1966, have thus traced a descent from the (Norman) de Poynings family of nearby Slaugham and Poynings. The Lambert (now Goad) family that bought the **South Park Estate**, Bletchingley, in 1875, can now trace a descent though 35 generations to Richard de Clare, who was given the land by William the Conqueror after 1066. There are still some Earls (the Earl of Limerick at Chiddinglye, near Wakehurst, the Earl of Albemarle at Hurst Barns, near Cooksbridge, and the Earl of Lytton at Newbuildings, but none of them are grand local landowners) the odd Lord (as at Betchworth, Dorking) and a smattering of Baronets[7] (Sir Richard Kleinwort, Sir Henry Aubrey Fletcher, Sir Charles Burrell and others).

Many of the modern wave of super-rich incomers buy only modest landholdings, like Lord Saatchi at Old Place Staplefield, or the new leaseholder (2012) of Gravetye Manor's house and garden (now a hotel) who made his fortune in hedge funds. Some still buy piles of land though, like Dr Jim Hay, the fortune maker who bought the 800 acre Birchgrove Estate once owned by Harold Macmillan.

Many farms have been bought up by rich leisure seekers. It is common for commercial farmers to sell off their old farmhouses with a plot of attached land, to realise their modern enhanced value. However, many farms are bought by the rich in their entirety, particularly in the more remote areas of the Low Weald and in the High Weald where farming is least profitable. In those areas the land ownership pattern can still bear a superficial resemblance to older patterns of farm tenure, though the reality is of swimming pools, tennis courts and livery paddocks; not chickens, granaries and milking parlours.

Long historical continuities of tenure do not imply any conservatism about land exploitation.[8] Old landowning families are not by any means traditionalist land managers, though they play on their long tenure to give themselves legitimacy. The Aubrey Fletcher dynasty and their forebears have owned an estate at Southwater since the 1730s and rented land there since the 15th century, but that does not stop them pushing for major housing development there. The Borde Hill Estate sold the land for the Penland Farm development on the edge of Haywards Heath. The Balcombe Estate host a fracking company on their land. The Heaselands Estate sold the woods and fields at Bolnore and Ashenground for a major housing development and bypass which broke up a woodland complex with at least 53 ancient woodland plant species. Under the Paddockhurst Estate

BACKSTORY / Chapter 3: Landownership and farming

the Worth Forest SSSI was so damaged by commercial forestry that the bulk of the portion that lay on their land was de-designated.

There have been many lost opportunities. The Crown Estate owned the c. 4000 acre Poynings Estate which covered many farms in the Weald and on the Downs at Fulking, Poynings and Pyecombe. The estate had never been sold since the Norman Conquest. It was sold to its tenant farmers in 1980–84. One of the purchasers now farms 1,500 acres. Yet, in public ownership, the estate could have been at the heart of the new South Downs National Park, driving forward sustainable farming and landscape restoration with much more autonomy from the commercial imperative. Few knew that it was for sale, and there was no campaign for its retention for conservation and public usage. Cuckfield folk succeeded in buying New England Wood from the wreckage of the broken-up Cuckfield Park Estate, but it was a mere 'precious fragment' amongst the rest of the estate's lovely landscape, in the place where the Iguanodon was first discovered. Both West and East Sussex County Councils sold off their Smallholdings Estates from the 1980s. Now, all the Wick Farm and Blackstone smallholdings near Albourne, and the Barcombe Mills smallholdings are sold. Many of their farming tenants have rightly benefited from this buy-out, but (like the sale of council housing) they may not be the ultimate beneficiaries, and more chances for new entrants without big money to try more sustainable ways of farming have been lost.

Beware the dreadful sign "Woodlands For Sale". There is a large and frightening market in fragmented woodland, as landowners realise that they can make big money by selling plots to aspirant wilderness seekers. Such fragmentation changes single 'Keep Out' signs at woodland entrances into obstacle courses of 'Private Property, No Public access' signs on multiple plots. At Tottington and Longlands Woods, Small Dole, local people have created a managed fragment of coppice wood, next to the industrial estate, which the public can freely walk and enjoy. The rest of the woods, however, have been sold off in plots and lost their regime of regular coppice management. Now the Nightingales have gone. In many of those woods that the Forestry Commission sold the public have lost their customary access. Now, many ex-Forestry Commission woods are only recognisable by their unmanaged conifers, unthinned, leaning, fallen, or standing dead, and their old tracks and gateways, now decaying and overgrown.

At the extreme end of this process of fragmentation is the sale of micro-plots to gullible members of the public for their investment value or as putative plots for mobile homes. Such was the fate of gorgeous Bones Meadow, by Bones Wood, Horne, with its many rare archaic pasture herbs. I fear for its survival.

Institutional landowners, such as churches, private schools, and charities, have taken tracts of land and big houses, particularly during the long agricultural depression of c. 1880 to 1940, with its low land prices. Cowfold Monastery has, I think, c. 240 acres. The St Julians (Anglican) Community at Coolham, now taken over by the Catholic diocese, had some 460 acres. Worth Abbey School has c. 400 acres, and St George's Retreat, Ditchling, c. 250 acres. Christ's Hospital School has a c. 1,200 acre estate. Great Walstead School, near Lindfield, has some 250 acres of Ouse riverside woods and meadows. Eton College owns North Barnes Farm, by Plumpton Green. The charitable Camelia Botnar Foundation has c. 550 acres (2012) based near Cowfold, and the charitable William Robinson Trust has the c. 643 acre Gravetye Estate, long leased to the Forestry Commission.

Getting information on patterns of landownership is difficult, and sometimes impossible. Using the Land Registry is costly, and, with the County Records Offices and local authorities, time-consuming and often frustrating, despite their superb workers. Local people are the best informants of course, but their information is sometimes shaky and contradictory. I know little about some categories of ownership, such as developers' land banks. We can walk this countryside for our whole lives, yet know very little about who owns it and their businesses. It is all very secret.

This matters greatly. Access to land is rationed by the possession of money. You do not gain land by having the skills to manage it sustainably and make it productive.

Common Treasury

Nature belongs not to any.

This much I know …

Not long or short,
Not old or young,
Not black or white,
Not friend or foe.

It is for **all** …

The trees, the streams,
The flowers, the corn,

This land is **ours** …

Not mine or yours

(*Written after a painful exchange with a Wealden landowner notorious for hostility to public access*)

You do not gain land by your local connections, or your love for it. Yet, if you are rich you can buy it or keep it, no matter how great your ignorance, selfishness and indifference to what and who is already there. If you are not rich you will likely be forbidden to use and even walk the land, except via statutory linear rights of way. Private landowners will not challenge the system which is destroying nature, countryside and sustainable food growing, for they mostly benefit from it. Their hegemony prevents us from seeing any alternative way of managing these resources – or even realising how threatened our common heritage is.

ENDNOTES

1. With the abolition of Retail Price Maintenance in 1964 (which had enabled producers to dictate minimum resale prices for their products), UK entry into the EU in 1973, the abolition of farm gate churn collection in 1979 (the death knell for many of the remaining smallholders), the introduction of milk quotas in 1984, the disbanding of the Milk Marketing Board in 1994, and the breaking up of Milk Marque, its successor, in 2000. See the excellent 'Dairy Miles' by Simon Fairlie, pages 48–57 of 'The Land' journal, issue 13, winter 2012–13.
2. 'Dairy Miles' by Simon Fairlie. Op cit.
3. " 'The Art and Craft of Chicken Cramming': Poultry in the Weald of Sussex 1850–1950, by Brian Short, in Vol 30, Issue 1 (1982) of the Agricultural History Review, published by the British Agricultural History Society.
4. Pearson Plc is now a global media, publishing and education company heavily criticised for its role in the expansion of global private education and education services.
5. 'Herry's Archives': The Powell Edwards Line (on line).
6. The estimates of acreage I give are from a variety of sources, informal and formal. Some are merely informed guesses. I welcome any corrections to my information.
7. Sort of hereditary 'Sirs' – hereditary knights. The title was re-invented by James 1st in 1611 for sale to raise cash.
8. The most howling example of this contradiction between tradition and desecration is the management of the Church Commissioners' estates on the Sussex coastal plain, where the church has held lands since Saxon times. Much of the farmland is an agribusiness desert with most of its old landscape features and wildlife long destroyed.

BIG FLOWS OF DEVELOPMENT

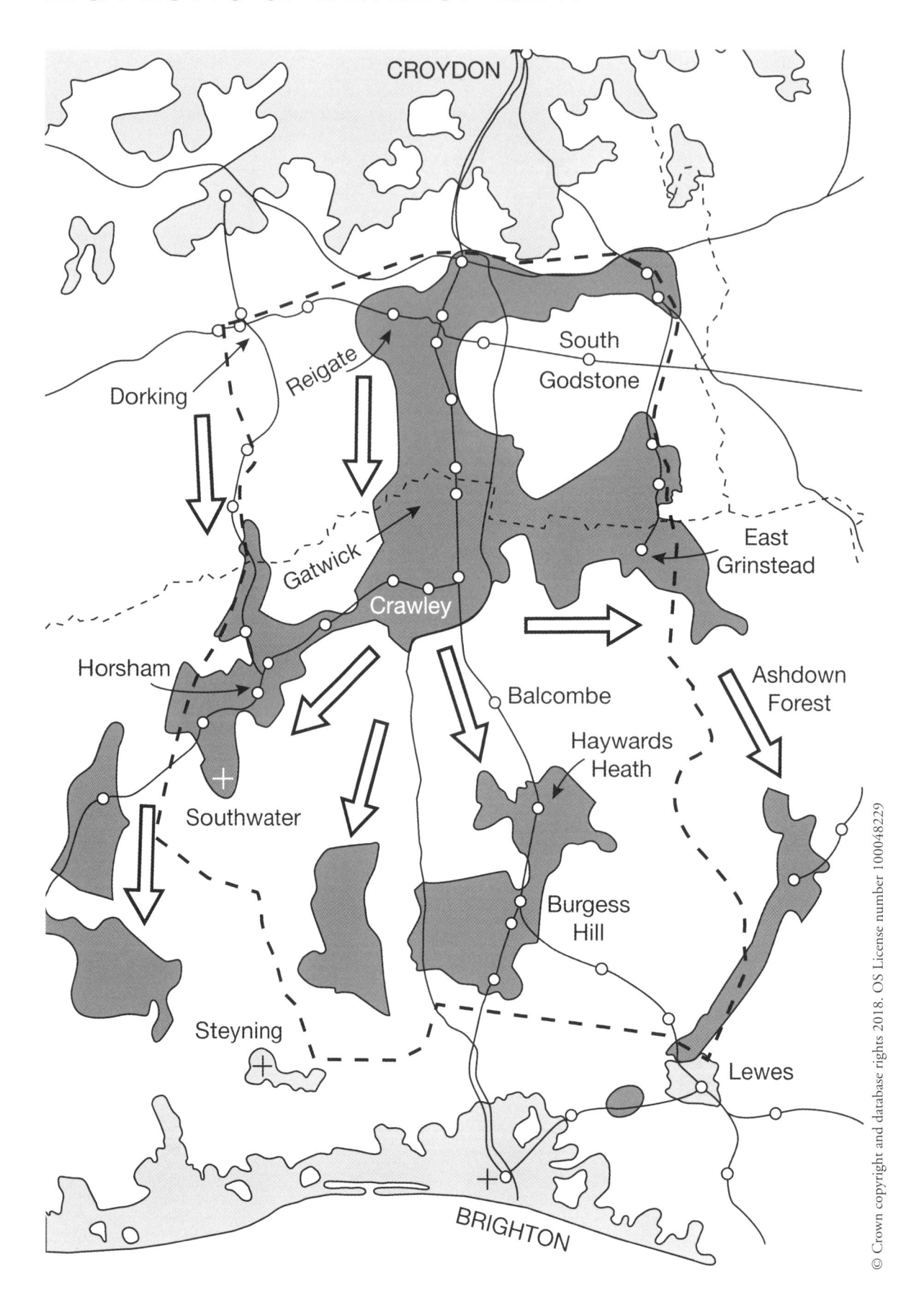

68 BACKSTORY / Chapter 4: The big threats

CHAPTER 4
The big threats

REGIONAL HYPER-DEVELOPMENT

From the North Downs to the South Downs the open Wealden countryside of the Land of the Brighton Line is disappearing fast – very fast. A great larva flow of urbanisation stretches for 26 miles south from the London megalopolis, over the rim of the North Downs and far into the Surrey-Sussex Weald, penetrating more than half way towards the South Downs. This huge conurbation is far advanced, embracing and coalescing Reigate to Horley to Gatwick to Crawley to Horsham to Southwater. This broad corridor of development stretches with ever-narrowing gaps between its constituent towns, which themselves sprawl to around three miles wide ... and growing wider.

That is only the strongest of several such waves of hyper-development, and new waves of development are in the offing in the minds of business predators, landowners and their governmental collaborators.

The whole waterland corridor of the River Ouse from Lewes via Offham, Hamsey, Barcombe Mills, Isfield and the River Uck to Uckfield is threatened by business plans to re-open the Uckfield to Brighton railway link, expanding the Uckfield Line to become a second Brighton Main Line. Its supporters include Green MP Caroline Lucas and Brighton Labour MP Lloyd Russell-Moyle, as well as Tories. This project threatens to bash through nationally important wetlands and riverine landscape, and smash through the South Downs to emerge by the A27 in the Lewes-Brighton corridor. This new infrastructure will drive a new corridor of hyper-development from Lewes, via Ringmer, Uckfield, Buxted, and Crowborough, into Kent and the London fringe.

A 14 mile corridor-conurbation is crystalizing from lunatic idea to incremental implementation, from Horsham to Billingshurst, and on to Pulborough-West Chiltington-Storrington and Ashington. Beyond the west of our area more sprawling urbanisation is threatened at Billingshurst, along the line of the A29 (Roman Stane Street) and the expansion of development between there and Christ's Hospital is mooted. Proposals for a new town at North Heath, between Billingshurst and Pulborough, have been knocked back ... but for how long?

For nine miles from the M23 at Crawley eastwards via Copthorne, Crawley Down, East Grinstead to Ashurst Wood and Forest Row, another corridor-

> **Big flows of development**
> This map shows the trajectory of new built development. It is based on the existing development footprint, plus both proposed and accepted major new developments (though I may have missed some).

- ▢ Existing London and coastal megacities.

- ▣ Areas of the Middle Weald subject to severe development pressures

- ⇒ Direction of flow of development pressures from the expanding economy of the London megalopolis

- - - - Brighton Line Weald

- ⁀ Key railways and roads

- ⁀⁀ Wealden county boundaries

Offham Marsh: will this piece of heaven soon be smashed by a new Brighton-London business rail link?

Thermos flask pouring essential cup of tea

**Gatwick monster.
The Noise of the End of the World. Picketts Wood.**

conurbation is well into formation, expanding around the chaos of century-old ribbon developments, plotlands and other speculator-homesteader past mistakes.

Development in Horley pushes towards the banks of the River Mole to the west and to the banks of the Burstow Stream to the north. Development proposals linked to Gatwick push east to the M23 irrespective of the negative decision made (and to be unmade?) on the Gatwick second runway proposal. The fragile and heavenly countryside of Langley Green is threatened by the bulldozer. The expansion of Gatwick Airport is already threatening dreadful increases in aircraft noise as new flight paths are suggested. If a new runway does come it will demand a huge increase in workforce and huge inward migration, driving more proposals for a second new town.

From Crawley to Horsham, developers, government and local officials, and councillors inch towards the destruction of the intervening countryside to create 'Crawsham' on the fields, meadows and small woods of Ifield; the slopes of Kilnwood with their wildwood relics; the flat lands of North Horsham with their streams, moated farmhouses and copses; and the slopes and ancient droves rising up to the Rusper Ridges.

From Horsham northwards to the Surrey border and on to Capel the six mile long landscape of the Vale of Boldings Brook that has meandered between cornfields, small farms, meadows, and woods for a thousand years and more is threatened, with the A24 road turned into more race track, and its valleysides covered in built development way beyond the financial reach of those who most need homes.

For three miles south of Horsham to Southwater a new beltway conurbation extends its grasp, lapping up to ancient woods, and ridiculing their survival over eight millennia and more; wrecking the fabric of hedges, fields and banks, ditches and streams that we inherit from far back in prehistory.

Now we can see why local and national planners more than thirty years ago took such care to shrink the protective boundaries of the new High Weald AONB (Area of Outstanding Natural Beauty) far back from the edges of Haywards Heath and Uckfield, Mannings Heath, Cowfold and Bolney; away from the bosky ridges of Rusper (at the same height as most of the St Leonards Forest ridgelands) and the forest lands south of Copthorne and Crawley Down.

It does not stop there. Developers and planners finger all of the Brighton Line Low Weald between Haywards Heath and Burgess Hill, threatening the Vale of the River Adur's landscape all the way from Hickstead, east to Ditchling Common. They covet the lands of the Heron Stream and all of the gap between Burgess Hill and Hurstpierpoint/Hassocks.

They spend big money on plans for a new town planted on the lovely flatlands and waterlands between Henfield, Cowfold and Burgess Hill, with their ancient droves, their little woods, and their tranquillity.

EXPLOSIVE MODERN TOWN GROWTH

The increase in the built-up area between c. 1870 and c. 1935 (65 years) is dwarfed by the increase between c. 1935 and 2015 (80 years). Future hyper-development regional pressures will be much greater. Gatwick, Crawley, and Southwater are almost wholly new developments, and Horsham is now approaching the pattern of development of a New Town.

Built development c.1870. From 1873 6 inch to 1 mile O/S map. With the kind permission of the Ordnance Survey.

Built development c.1935. Largely from 1935 & 1940 1 inch to 1 mile & 0.5 inch to 1 mile O/S maps (fully revised 1931 & 1933). With the kind permission of the Ordnance Survey.

Built development c.2015. Largely from 2012 1: 50,000 O/S Landranger Map 187 Edition C4, revised 1999, with selected change 2012, & Landranger Map 198, Edition E3, revised 2001, with selected change 2013.

GATWICK AND CRAWLEY

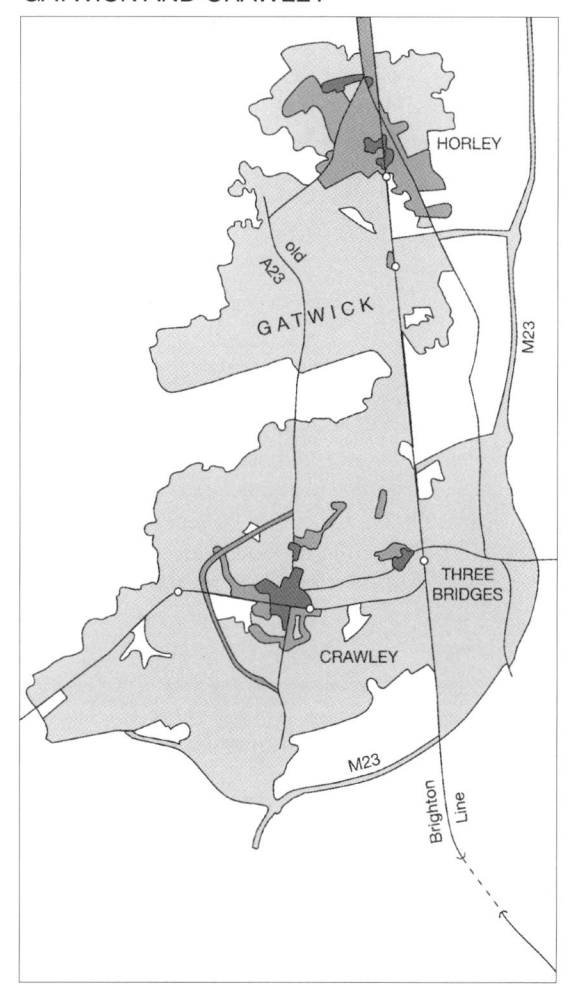

HORSHAM AND SOUTHWATER

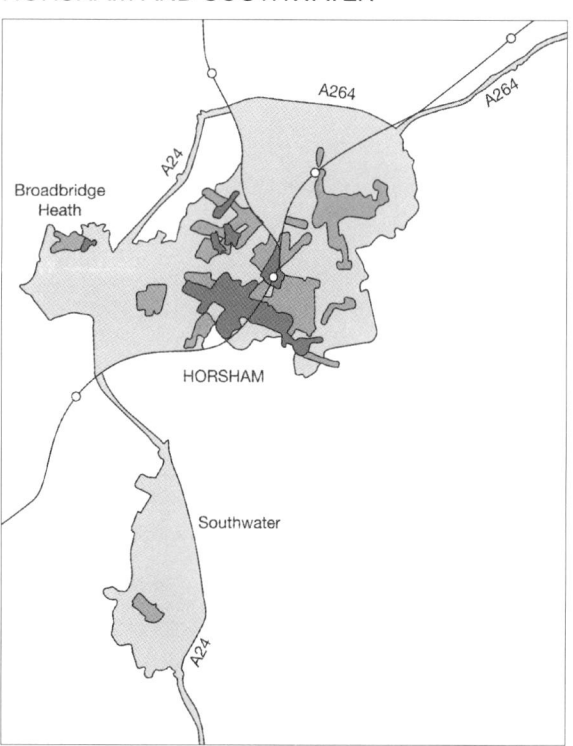

HAYWARDS HEATH AND BURGESS HILL

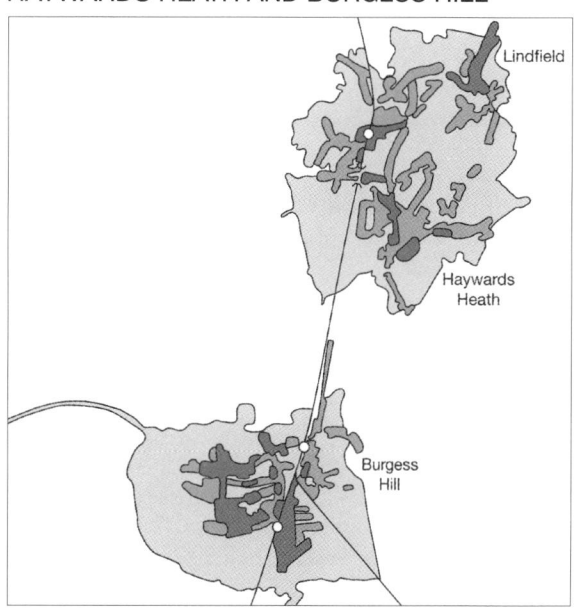

© Crown copyright and database rights 2018. OS License number 100048229

WEALDEN PLANNING PROTECTIONS

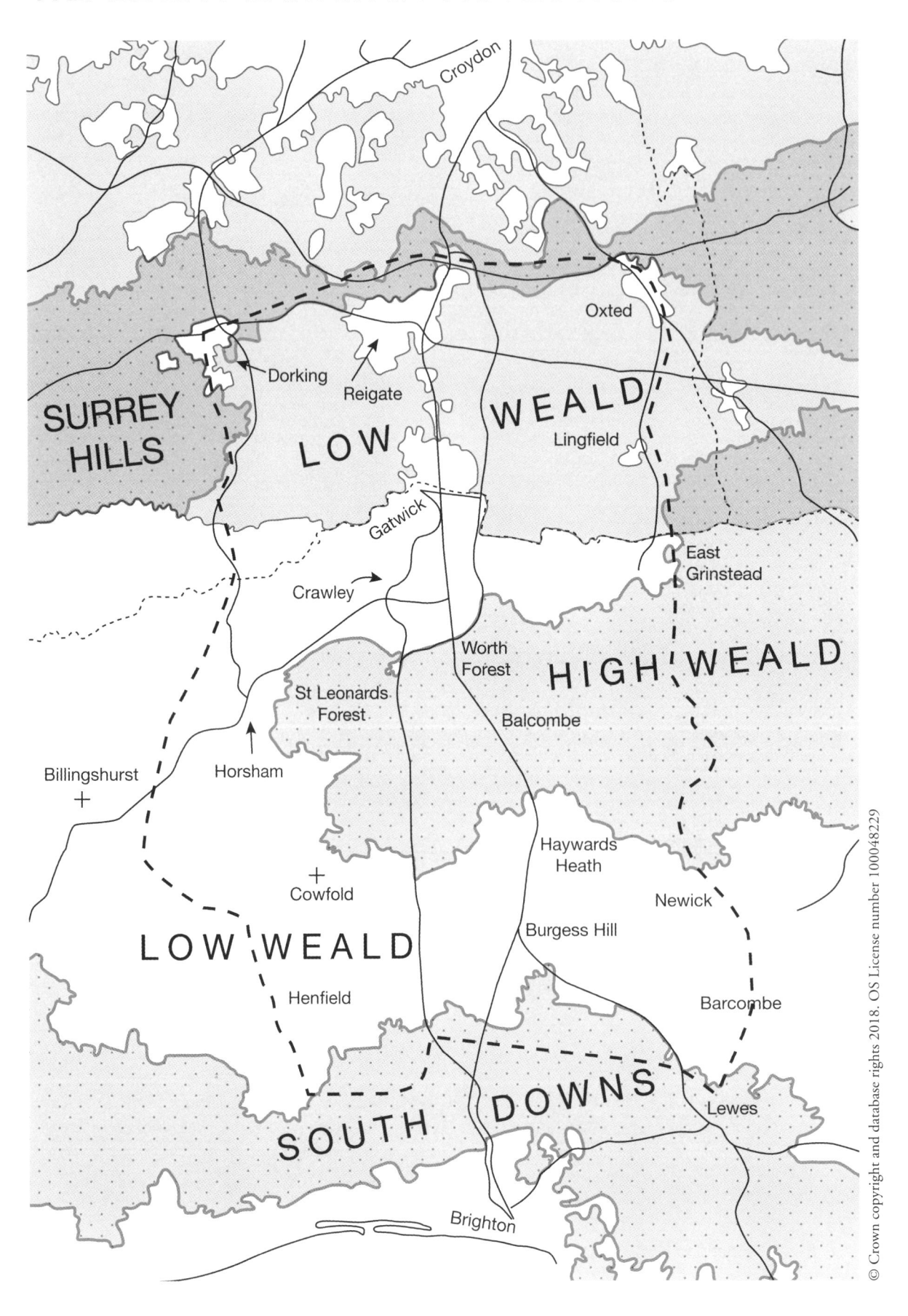

As the summer sun shines down on the South Downs Way our rambles there will be accompanied by the low growl of traffic from the townships of the Weald beyond – as they already are along the North Downs and the Pilgrim's Way above the roaring M25/M23; and as they already are on Newtimber Hill, Wolstonbury, and by Clayton Windmills above the A23; and Offham Down above the A275. We will look not upon "the wooded dim blue goodness of the Weald",[1] but upon thin screens of trees part-hiding the roofs of towns and office blocks. The universe of night time stars will everywhere be dimmed by the dull orange-black of an urban sky, and the great welcoming velvet blackness of the Wealden basin will be lost to the lights of conurbations and townships, and the ribbons of carriageway lighting.

Such has already been the fate of much of the Surrey North Downs, together with the Sussex Coastal Plain and the views we see of it from the Downs.

Such will be the fate of the Land of the Brighton Line … unless things change drastically and fundamentally.

UNEVEN DEVELOPMENT

This great wave of hyper-development is just one piece in a pattern of unequal development across the whole of the British Isles, across Europe and the globe. The de-industrialisation of parts of the midlands, the north and the west; the hyper development across the south east of Britain, parts of Germany and France; the part-collapse of the peripheral economies in the south and east of Europe, and to its west in Ireland, are just opposite sides of the same coin – aspects and phases in a *continuous history of geographic inequality and uneven development.*

All across the globe the story is the same. The imperialist countries of Europe, North America and Japan, with the rentier middle eastern oil dictatorships, leech off the poor countries of Africa, Latin America and Asia. They solve their food and mineral supply problems by huge land grabs and pillage of the relatively intact biological resources of those latter continents, whilst Wealden lands that have grown food crops for one, two, or three millennia are lost to built development and taken over for the leisure of the rich.

London expands to fill the entire Thames basin, explosively doubling in size in the 1920s and '30s and concentrating a population of nearly nine million, besides the non-residential labour of millions more. It is wider than the whole of the Brighton Line Weald and has a greater area than the whole of West Sussex.

The vast population movements of those forced out of their own disadvantaged, pillaged rural economies, and by climate change, and the expansion of dreadful regional wars, expand the mega-cities of the Pacific and Atlantic rims (like Mexico City, Sao Paulo, Mumbai, Lagos, Shanghai … and London) whilst the capitalists who depend upon migrants' cheap labour, foster division and strife against them.

Valiant pre- and post-war efforts[2] to contain this vast metropolitan expansion by the designation of Green Belt, which now covers nearly all Surrey's Brighton Line Weald, have not dealt with the underlying power of capitalism, which seeks to weaken and leap the constraints which ameliorative reforms placed upon it. The Surrey Hills Area of Outstanding Natural Beauty, designated in 1958, was trashed in the Surrey Low Weald by the building of the M25 in the early 1970s. The High Weald AONB, designated in 1983, is now threatened by the construction of a fronting urban edge along much of its north side.

Protective designations are not insuperable obstacles to capitalism's expansion. The Gatwick Diamond business association cheerfully delineates its area of operation irrespective of such statutory niceties as AONBs, embracing all of the Weald between Horsham and East Grinstead and away to the east. So does the larger 'Coast to Capital Local Enterprise Partnership'. If capitalists cannot exploit it, drill it, frack it, build on it, or land planes on it, they can still use it as a garden backdrop, an expensive wallpaper to provide lifestyle enticements to their investors. Plutocrats can fly in from the oil dictatorships, and from the ex-Stalinist states, invest their money and put security fences round their chosen chunks of our countryside.

> **Wealden planning protections**
> National Parks and AONBs are both meant to have the same level of statutory planning protection of their natural beauty. In fact, the level of planning protection both have is weak, narrow, and defensive. The same can be said for Green Belts.

- High Weald & Surrey Hills AONBs (Areas of Outstanding Natural Beauty) & South Downs National Park (which includes a large fraction of the Low Weald)
- London Green Belt
- Overlapping High Weald & Surrey Hills AONBs and London Green Belt
- Brighton Line Weald
- Modern county boundaries

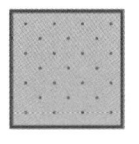

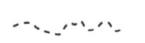

HOW TO DESTROY A STATUTORILY CONSERVED LANDSCAPE

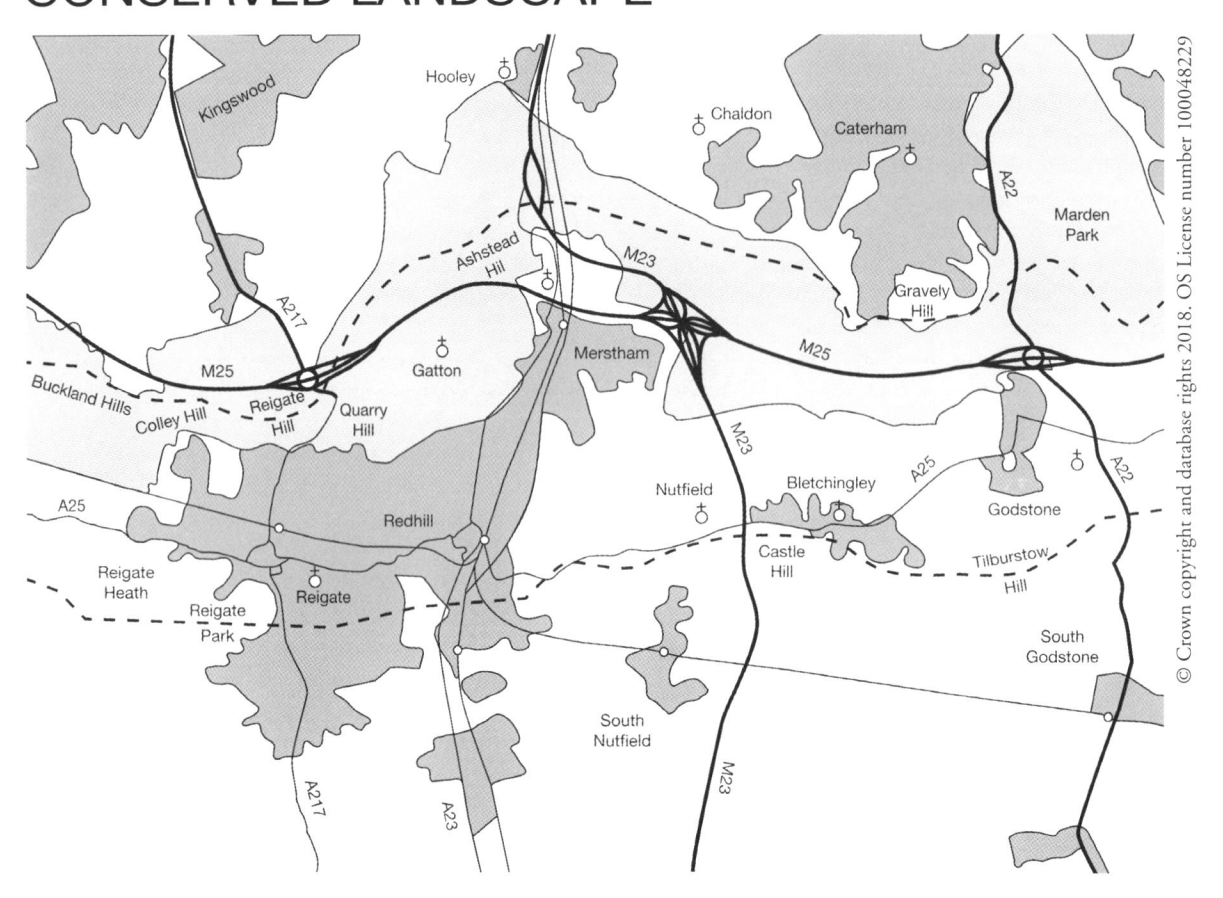

Designated in 1958, this part of the Surrey Hills AONB (Area of Outstanding Natural Beauty) was constrained by pre-existing sprawling built development to just a narrow belt around the scarp slope of the North Downs. With the coming of the M25, M23 and enlarged feeder roads (such as the A217 and A22) this part of the AONB has been split and split again, oppressed by horrendous traffic noise, and visually mangled. Capital's needs trumped our human needs for the joy of natural landscapes and the healing embrace of nature.

- Surrey Hills AONB (Area of Outstanding Natural Beauty)
- Main built-up areas
- Scarp slopes of the North Downs and the Greensand Ridge
- Medieval parish churches
- Motorways & dual carriageways
- Main roads
- Railways

VERTICAL AND HORIZONTAL INEQUALITY

Inequality is both *horizontal* (between regions and nations) and *vertical* (between classes: between rich and poor). Unequal geographical development is the very essence of capitalism, on the same level as the exploitation of labour by capital, and the two kinds of inequality intersect. Vital protective planning designations have weak social dimensions, and their resources of landscape, nature, and tranquillity are scooped up by the middle and owning classes. Golf courses, 'horseyculture', hobby farms, mini parks, field-sized private gardens, and Pheasant preserves claim land where food, wood and timber production once sat alongside public pleasures. We are asked to accept the 're-wilding' of thousands of acres of erstwhile farmed Wealden landscape, whilst watching global food companies destroy tropical bush and forest.

House prices in and near to our best landscapes jump to lunatic levels. In the Surrey Hills AONB in 2006 they averaged 50% above the region's average.[3] Wealthy Londoners take 8000 second homes in Sussex (2014), whilst ordinary Londoners are driven out of social housing and the private rented sector by sell-offs and extortionate rents.

Yet the majority of new Wealden homes are built to blatantly unaffordable private sale prices and unaffordable rents, not for social need.[4] If our food and clothing were similarly unaffordable the majority of us would starve and freeze … yet this hogging of new housing provision by the better-off is only weakly challenged. If there was rationality in patterns of house building and rural conservation policy ALL housing would be affordable to ALL on the basis of need, not wealth. Nothing else is sustainable or just.

Until 1980, with the coming of Thatcher's 'right to buy', council housing was available to a large fraction of rural working people and the poor, but such public housing is now largely gone (and 40% now in the hands of private landlords) and the 'right to buy' now threatens housing association rented housing too.

SENSE AND NONSENSE

The Weald is the **most wooded landscape in England**, and much of it is ancient woodland, linking us right back to the days of the wildwood. This woodedness gives it a public value – biological, cultural, recreational – of the greatest national importance.

The Weald lies in the most southerly, warmest part of the country, at the highest end of a graph line of biodiversity which sinks lower the more you go north from here. **Biodiversity is richer here than anywhere else in Britain.**

Yet, the **Sussex coast** was largely wrecked in a rush of development from 1890 to 1940, which pre-figured the trashing of the Mediterranean littoral from west to east after the post-war advent of cheap air travel. The **South Downs** were trashed by agribusiness plough-ups from 1945 onwards, and the **North Downs Brighton Line landscape** was trashed by London sprawl from 1918 to 1939.

Now the **Brighton Line Weald** awaits a similar fate. Is this rational? Whose interests does it serve? Who benefits from capitalist hyper-development? Who benefits from the slide of free market development to huge megalopoli in privileged regions, and the trashing and emptying of their super-exploited hinterlands?

Our Wealden villages, our ex-farms, our small towns are filled with the well-off, the beneficiaries of an unequal system. They do not want council housing. They do not want traveller sites. They do not want to see the problems of the London poor from which they have escaped.

War games. Boys toys. Holmbush Forest.

Our farms are abandoned to rich pleasure landscapes or giant farm combinations. As one surviving small farmer said to me: "There are no working class people round here now". Whole Wealden sub-landscapes are lost from food production, whilst 'horseyculture', polo fields, fishing lakes, solar arrays and vineyards proliferate. The world market brings us vegetables from Africa and the Mediterranean, whilst fields that grew greens, root crops, fruit and corn for one, two, or three thousand years, now grow haylage or amenity turf.

THIS MACHINE HAS NO 'OFF' BUTTON

Global warming stands co-equal with the mass extinction of wildlife species as the greatest environmental problems us humans face. Yet capitalism's requirement for continuous growth, competition and the pursuit of profit, are at the heart of its inability to address this crisis.

The result is that current use of energy and resources is far greater in the major economies than that required for the majority of us to attain a healthy and fulfilling quality of life. Ecosystems cannot sustain these levels of use and wastage of resources (land, biodiversity, soil, water, minerals, and energy). Such use must be drastically reduced. Production should be geared towards public use and not market-derived profit. The world economy should probably be, say, a quarter of the size that it is now (i.e. what it was in c. 1975) but with completely different production and economic priorities, and the energy supply system should be commensurately reduced.[5] (In 1975 primary energy resource use was about 40% of current use, but efficiency gains since then mean that such levels would not now be required). With a contraction in resources use of that order it may be possible to achieve a comfortable, sustainable living for all, at the same time as harmoniously conserving the natural world, which is our real home, our joy, and our greatest resource for self-actualisation.

Yet when capitalism addresses energy needs it disregards all such constraints of sustainability, seeking

BACKSTORY / Chapter 4: The big threats

to frack and drill in High Weald and Low, on the South Downs and in the forest lands, against the organised objections of the host communities, their fears of tainted water, of fossil fuel atmospheric pollution, and their fears of the loss of landscape and tranquillity.

Frackers have been faced in the Weald with a strong militant opposition, linking well-off rural residents with urban solidarity from Brighton, Worthing, London and many other towns and villages. Battles have been won, giving some protection to the South Downs National Park and the High Weald AONB, but such gains have now been partly rolled back by allowing fracking beneath them, providing the well heads are outside the protected landscape boundaries. Tory governmental strategists have even been prepared to trim the property rights of a part of their own class (anti-fracking landowners) to facilitate deep-well drilling below others landed property, in their bid to utilise this extreme energy resource, in the strategic interests of their class as a whole.

The resistance at Balcombe, Horse Hill and Leith Hill to fracking and conventional extraction has been stirring and exemplary, but such activism will need to be repeated and spread many times over for this danger to climate, landscape, health and communities to be seen off. There are oil wells at Brockham and South Godstone, too, as extractors pile on the pressure.

The effects of global warming will be expressed in many ways. Patterns of vegetation will change, for instance by threatening the conditions which give us our spectacular displays of woodland Bluebells.[6] Already we can see in some small and exposed ancient woods how Cow Parsley is taking over from Bluebells as the dominant spring flower. Newly arrived competitive species may win out over long-established vegetation communities. New waves of colonising invertebrates, fungi, and disease organisms will modify things in unpredictable ways that do not respect the protective measures we have taken to preserve particular wildlife communities. Our waterlands – rivers, brookland levels, streams, ponds, and wet ditches – are especially at threat. Waders and other over-wintering birds will retreat northwards and eastwards to their core areas. Snipe, Teal and Redshank are lost already as breeding species in our area and Lapwing have almost gone. What is left of wet acid pastures and wet heath are also at risk of total loss. Paradoxically, changing weather patterns may bring increasing floods over those same stressed areas, as well as over others that we would not normally associate with risks of flooding. In the longer term, sea level rise may mean that our floodplain Wealden lowlands will be threatened by the sea's ingress. Furthermore, displaced people from the coastal littoral and low lying floodplains will need rehousing on higher ground inland.

SOLVING NATURE'S PROBLEMS AT NATURE'S EXPENSE: SOLAR FARMS AND WIND TURBINES IN OPEN COUNTRY

88 years ago **"the Electricity Commission announced plans to erect pylons over the South Downs[7] in order to include Brighton in the national (electricity) grid. The opposition was so intense that the (Labour) Prime Minister, Ramsay Macdonald, intervened and instructed the Commission to do their utmost to avoid damaging such areas as the South Downs"**. That was in 1929.

Now, in 2018, proposals for industrial scale energy developments right across whole landscapes are met with vastly more confused responses from the environmental movement. Huge wind turbines, as tall as the tallest industrial chimneys, are dumped across our wildest landscapes, like the Cambrian Mountains, with many environmentalists supporting them. Solar arrays are dumped across our most tranquil and remote Low Wealden farmscapes, where at dusk the White Owl flits across the darkening field tussocks, or, at dawn, the mists cover the dew-sodden pastures to waist height, whilst the music of Nightingales singing from the Blackthorn brakes graces the silence with profound, enchanting beauty.

When that wing of the owning class that rightly acknowledges the coming catastrophe of human disruption of climate systems, seeks solutions to that crisis, it does so at the expense of other aspects of the natural world, such as our countryside. Driving forward large scale onshore wind and solar power, it proposes that we sacrifice landscape scale naturalness (of fields, hedges, trees, hills, vales, moors and mountains uninterrupted by major built features) as the cost of preserving relatively natural patterns of climate.

To date, we have largely succeeded in beating back the encroachent of **wind turbines** in the Weald, due largely to the protective mantle of the High Weald AONB, and the South Downs National Park, for wind turbines in the Low Weald would be hugely inter-visible with those two protected landscapes. We have not been entirely successful, for the three Polegate wind turbines horribly interrupt the naturalness of the view from Combe Hill and Wilmington Hill of the Hailsham Levels and wooded Low and High Weald. Glyndebourne wind turbine painfully intrudes on the naturalness of the Downs scarp, the Low Weald and the waterlands east of Mount Caburn. Furthermore, the cabling of the new Rampion wind farm off the Brighton coast, clips the species-rich grassland of Woodmancote Moor on its route north to the Bolney Substation, crossing streams and ancient field boundaries and gouging through archaic chalk grassland sites on the Downs.

With a changing political configuration we may well be faced with a major onslaught of landscape-disrupting Wealden wind turbines.

We are being defeated in holding back open country **solar farms**, and we face opponents amongst those we wish to see as our friends. Green Party MP Caroline Lucas has dismissed claims that solar farms (expansive arrays of large scale, ground mounted solar panels) are blighting our countryside[8] as "wildly overstated" because they "typically take up less than 5% of the land they are on". A similar argument could be used to justify the building of much modern housing, roads, intensive farms, and industrial buildings in high value landscapes, where the footprint of their built components is likewise a minority of the developments' total area.

The problem was sharply brought home to me on a winter's day on the Laughton Levels, a tranquil Low Wealden waterland east of Lewes. Far from main roads and their noise, and far from the Gatwick flight paths, this remote, largely treeless flatland of reedy brooks, winter-flooded fields with Rush and Reed Sweet Grass and the imprints of long-lost riverine meanders, is a refuge for large numbers of wintering waterfowl drawn south from their arctic summer breeding grounds. There are Snipe and Teal in large numbers, Shovellers, Wigeon, Greylag Geese, Swans, with huge numbers of Lapwing, Starlings and Rooks on the adjacent ploughland, and Barn Owls foraging the rougher fields. Watching one darkening afternoon I followed a large raptor which hunted sometimes like a low-flying Short Eared Owl, and sometimes soared high like a Buzzard. When I finally got close to her on a tussock field edged with brooks she was hovering, long and steady, like an overgrown, scruffy Kestrel, though her white tail showed her to be a Rough Legged Buzzard, a long way from her Scandinavian birth place, and its summer diet of tundra Lemmings. Yet behind her, covering most of the brookland at that point, was a new, shining, solar farm array – four fields full of it, a big chunk of her potential foraging ground – rubbing out all sense of the wildness of that place, all sense of the continuities across continents that that fine bird and that fine place represented. She had become, like me, a mere intruder.

The next morning I looked out of my kitchen window across the wide urban Brighton valley where I live. I looked at an array of roofs, mostly steep, tiled and slated, and some flat. Solar panels are still nigh as scarce here as Rough Legged Buzzards. Yet in my urban valley they would do much good and no harm, giving us our own energy sources.

Wealden solar farm projects have proliferated since 2011, sometimes on farms which have already been damaged by modern farming and are thus vulnerable to predatory development proposals, but often in places where the survival of thick ancient hedges and shaws and the absence of public rights of way is used to justify schemes by dint of their concealment from the public gaze and therefore their lack of public impact. This deception reminds one of the behaviour of landowners throughout the destructive decades of post-war farming industrialisation, when they commonly concealed their bulldozing of ancient woodland and its replacement with crops, or sterile conifers, by the retention of thin screens of the woods' aboriginal trees and bushes along the woods' edges.

High Wealden Solar Farm: CCTV, 2m fences, a major industrial installation in an 'Area of Outstanding NATURAL Beauty'

Wealden vineyard: where once we searched for microliths, fossils and wild flowers now there are 2m fences

Blanketting Australian Swamp Stonecrop where once rare Golden Dock flourished. Berwick Church Farm pond

On delightful mixed countryside on the Bentley estate, on open fields below the Downs scarp at Ringmer, and on a historic landscape next to lovely Pond Lye north west of Burgess Hill, new solar arrays are mooted or agreed. Such plans have been rejected at Flanchford and Mynthurst in the Surrey Low Weald, but accepted, for instance, at Twineham, Arlington, Ripe, Billingshurst, and – recently on appeal – at Priors Byne on the Western Adur. At one site I watched the bulldozers driving their new access road through an archaic brook meadow, where Pepper Saxifrage and other old meadow herbs grew, between sheltering hedges and infant streams.

AND THERE'S MUCH, MUCH MORE

Some of these issues will be noted in other chapters. **Invasive tree diseases** are a chilling peril to the Wealden landscape. Ash Die Back is now widely present in Sussex and has been present in Surrey for longer. Its effects will be utterly dreadful. The overwhelming dominance of Oak and the small overall numbers of key tree species in the Weald landscape mean that epidemics of tree disease amongst them will affect its whole vegetation structure and appearance, and threaten large numbers of dependent species. Sudden Oak Death, Acute and Chronic Oak Decline and newer perils like Oak Processionary Moth all threaten. English Elm has been eradicated as a timber tree in our farming landscape by Dutch Elm Disease, although it survives in our hedgerows as a suckering shrub. Wych Elm survives in our woods, but only rarely as a grown tree. A significant fraction of our wetland Alders are now affected by fungal Phytophthora Disease of Alder. Beech is also threatened by Phytophthora disease, as is Bilberry – an important indicative sub-shrub of some of our more acidic Wealden woods. Sweet Chestnut is threatened by Chestnut Blight, and Horse Chestnuts by Bleeding Canker and Conker Tree Leaf Miner moths. Pine is threatened by Red Needle Blight. Our appalling biosecurity, particularly in the gardening and landscaping sectors, has much to answer for.

Water pollution and water extraction in our rivers and streams are perennial and devastating problems. Such pollution is not just a problem of gross damage caused by accidents, chemical dumping or sewage plant breakdown, but of the background presence of damaging chemicals which sewage treatments do not reach, such as feminising hormone traces from contraceptives, and phthalates. Recent research on the River Arun has shown that the fertility of wild Roach is hugely affected by tiny traces of such 'gender-bending' drugs. Painkillers, antibiotics and other medications, as well as traces of natural human hormones (as well as the simulated preparations) are present in damaging quantities.

The River Mole suffered badly from gross pollution in the past. The Adur has been hard hit repeatedly, and so have large parts of the Ouse. When these pollution events occur they destroy most life-forms in their paths: fish, mussels, water snails, caddis, mayflies, dragon and damselflies. Indeed, riverflies (so important to our endemic Trout) are suffering long-term decline. For myself, I know of NO stretches of Brighton Line streams with abundant freshwater mussel populations (*Unio, Anodonta*). Yet a generation ago Duck Mussels could be so common in a Wealden stream that it was difficult not to tread on them, whereas now we are lucky to find single empty shells or live individuals.

Water extraction sees the headwaters of our Wealden streams retreat, and flows sink to such levels that they threaten fish and invertebrate assemblages. Housing development threatens any plan to conserve healthy river flows. Riparian landowners have a right to extract 20,000 litres from their watercourse a day … to water their horses or polytunnels, or fill the ponds of their fish farm. Such extractions threaten the flow of vulnerable winterbournes and chalk streams. The fry and parr of giant Sea Trout, which have used their nursery streams for millennia, may be killed in spring as their streams prematurely dry out and block their passage to deeper waters. Such is the vulnerability of rivers that some water ecologists suggest that we make the preservation of pristine ponds, separate from the drainage system, our priority, arguing that water extraction, drought and pollution will always keep our watercourses unhealthy for wildlife, to greater or lesser degrees. Yet the health of

THE DESTRUCTION OF THE VALE OF HOLMESDALE

© Crown copyright and database rights 2018. OS License number 100048229

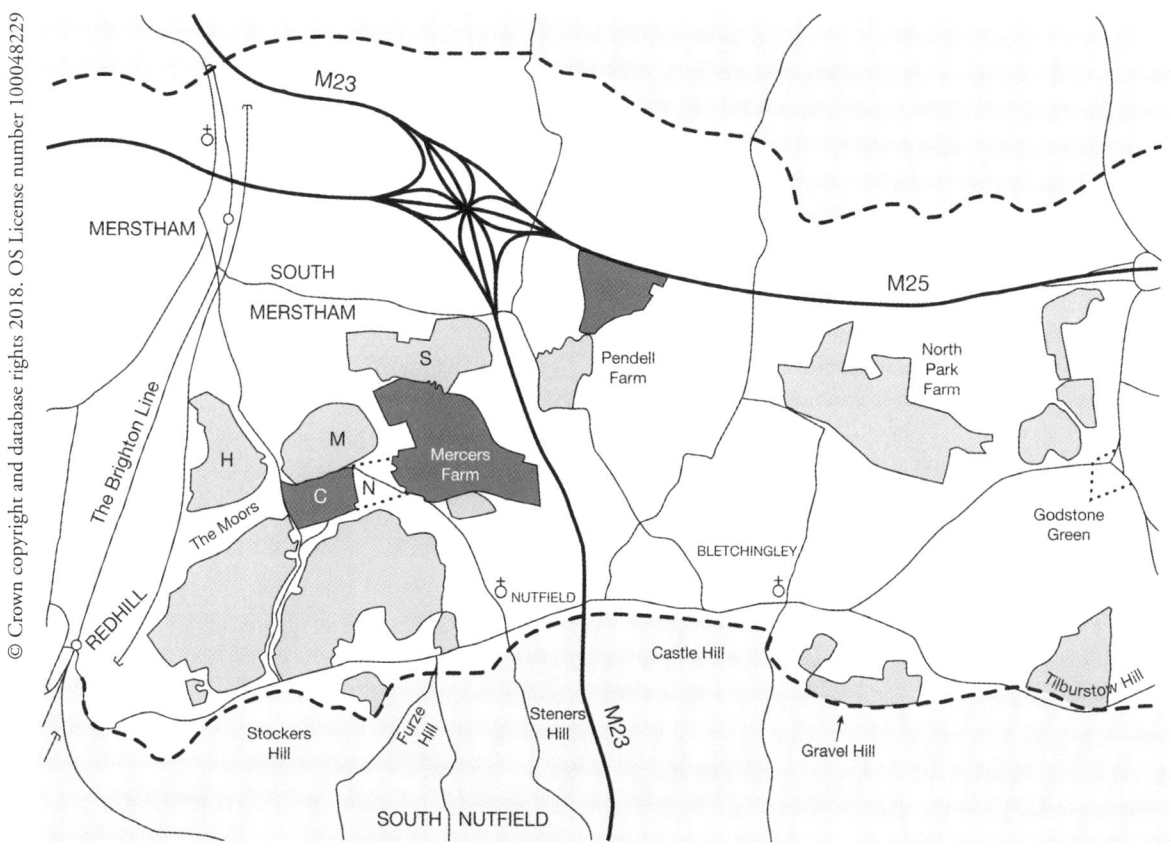

> The Vale's ancient and tranquil patchwork of damp meadows, sticky pastures, sandy fields, artisanal quarry pits, winding lanes, old farmsteads, smallish woods, and long views has been obliterated by landscape-scale mineral workings and the roar of the M25 and M23. Chaucer's company of pilgrims would not have been able to hear each other speak as they traversed this Vale on their way to Canterbury, if it was then as it is now.

- Fullers Earth, sand and gravel pits, past and present
- Proposed future minerals workings
- Scarp slopes of the North Downs and the Greensand Ridg
- Medieval parish churches
- Motorways
- Main roads and lanes
- Railways
- H = Holmethorpe Lagoons
- M = Mercers Country Park
- S = Speynes Mere
- N = Nutfield Marsh
- C = Chilmead

our farm ponds, threatened by pollution, encroaching vegetation, and the ingress of alien plants like Parrot's Feather and Australian Swamp Stonecrop, is as desperate as that of our streams and rivers. Indeed, **invasive aquatic species** threaten the survival of ALL our species-rich waterlands: rivers, streams, ponds and lakes. The monstrous destruction that Floating Pennywort has wrought over huge tranches of Pevensey Levels in the last decade or so is proof of that.

Quarrying (see Surrey chapters particularly) has destroyed the core pre-modern landscape and ecosystems of the Vale of Holmesdale east of Redhill, and what it hasn't yet destroyed has been mangled by golf courses and the awful noise pollution and severance of the M25/M23. To the west of Reigate quarrying has dried out and destroyed the rich moor and brookland ecosystems of Reigate Heath and Skimmington. Quarrying of the Wealden Clay, which has had such a huge impact on the wooded countryside of Langhurst Wood and Brookhurst in North Horsham, and, to a lesser extent in the Capel and Newdigate countryside, has largely stopped, but will

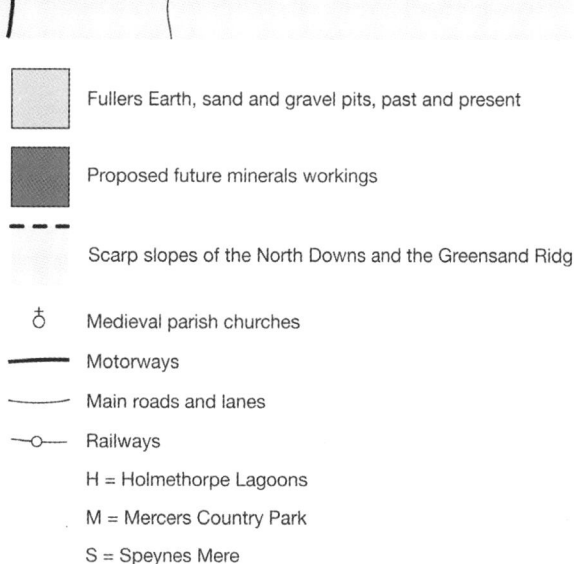

BACKSTORY / Chapter 4: The big threats

start again, as might more damaging proposals on the greensands.

Landfill and landraising will remain a threat. When East Sussex County Council recently fingered a series of sites for possible landfill they included several key Low Wealden areas, such as the Barkham spur on the Ouse between Gold Bridge and Sharpsbridge, the Glynde Reach and Firle Levels, and west Hellingly. What all such sites have in common is that they have been marginalised already: by agribusiness damage (Barkham spur); by an absence of public access and knowledge (Glynde and Firle Levels); or by noise pollution, motor sports and agribusiness (west Hellingly).

Roads building and traffic increase is a huge threat to tranquillity and public recreational usage, and causes massive severance to the free movement of wildlife. The enlargement of the A23 from Handcross to Warninglid was a disaster, but the A24 Worthing-Horsham-London main road faces drastic enlargement north and south of Horsham, and more schemes for the enlargement of the A264 between East Grinstead and the M23 are threatened, with an expansion of Gatwick.

Intensive farming still threatens in those areas where agriculture has not already been abandoned. Relict archaic grasslands are the worst hit, with some vegetation communities and individual grassland species now at risk of total local loss (see 'Meadows' chapter). Hedges continue to be lost, whether by direct removal or by destructive management (too frequent and drastic cutting, and grazing through and beneath them) and shaws are hollowed out by grazing encroachment and shrub layer clearance and 'tidying'.

Many modern farming income streams are inimical to a countryside of multiple uses that can accommodate both public enjoyment and food production. Vineyards, deer farming, large scale free-range poultry and egg production, and solar farm arrays require two-metre exclusion fences and CCTV cameras pointing their glass eyes at us, damaging the public's free usage. In this they ratchet up the traditional exclusions which we faced from orcharding and soft fruit production, (now much reduced). Local Wealden geology has thankfully so far militated against development of large-scale free-range pig production (such as blights many chalky and sandy localities around the country) or the industrial scale horticultural glass-houses and plastic sheeting of tender salad crops that disfigure parts of the Sussex coastal plain.

It feels as though every Wealden Bluebell wood is also a free-range Pheasant farm. The sound of them clattering away is vastly more common than the sound of Nightingale, Willow Warbler, Cuckoo or Turtle Dove.
Game bird shooting brings a gigantic biomass of reared Pheasants, with their release pens and their clutter of shacks and decayed caravans, bowsers, proliferating feed-hoppers, game cover and feed crops, 'vermin' traps, re-surfaced rides, dumped straw … and the ever-present danger of gamekeepers' intrusive questionings and forbiddings. The temporary decline of keeping and high-end shooting brought by the recession has been a small bonus to the bulk of countryside visitors.

Yet gamekeepers are people with high levels of countryside management skills, versatile, independent and often interested in wildlife and the old countryside. Many of them would make good and useful countryside workers conserving our landscape and wildlife and encouraging wider public usage. Their skills are wasted in shunting the public away from enjoyment of our heritage, and in organising the cruel and useless mass shooting of semi-tame 'wood chickens' by the rich.

SOLUTIONS AND THE ALLIES WE NEED FOR THEM

Our local and single issue campaigns may stop some particularly outrageous developments and save a few threatened high value sites, but they do not challenge the wider threats to the Brighton Line Weald. For that, *we need to link our efforts to a much broader alternative project which unites us in much wider alliances.* Most of us live in our towns and cities and are deeply alienated from our countryside and nature. We rarely go there and are unaware of its potential to enrich our lives. Yet we have the collective power to stymie the forces that work to destroy nature. Our interest in this is not compromised by possession of private wealth or landownership, which always makes nature a secondary consideration to profit and business advantage.

It was the broad labour movement of the early 20th century which mounted the first major systemic challenge to regional inequalities, to the spread of mega-cities, and to the destruction of nature and the countryside, with its achievements in the 1945–51 reformist Labour government. Those achievements were only partial and are now being rolled back … but they were real, nonetheless.

If the Brighton Line Weald and other threatened landscapes and ecosystems are to be saved it will be as part of the revival of a new alternative project for a world free of the imperative to eternally expand production, a world free of poverty and inequality, consumerism, exploitation, and wars against both people and nature.

It is long past time that we collectively recognise that those who seek to end the pillage of nature have common cause with those who seek to end the exploitation of people, the attacks on the poor and the destruction caused by war. The homeless on the London streets, the London council tenants evicted to make way for 'regeneration', and the London cleaners striking for a living wage are more fundamentally our allies than any number of local landowners or business people from whom we might seek favours.

ENDNOTES

1. From Kipling's lovely poem 'Sussex' (1902), published in 'Highways and Byways of Sussex' by E.V. Lucas (1904).
2. Such as the pre-war efforts by the London County Council, the effects of the Green Belt Act of 1938, and Labour's post war Town and Country Planning Act of 1947, and National Parks and Access to the Countryside Act (1949). Later, Duncan Sandys and other pro-conservation Tories were responsible for more ameliorative reforms.
3. Daily Mirror (11/06/12).
4. The proportion of required 'affordable' new homes in any development (2015) varies from council to council, and according to government advice, but it is nearly always a minority. (Furthermore, the government has recently relaxed the affordable housing obligation for small site developments). Tandridge, Mole Valley, Crawley, Horsham, and Lewes District Councils require 40% affordable housing (April 2015) on developments of over 15 homes (except for some smaller villages in Horsham, where it is 100%). Mid Sussex District Council requires 30% for developments of over 15 homes. Of course, much 'affordable' new housing isn't really affordable. You need a significant wage to afford most social rented homes nowadays, and the putative ceiling for social landlords' rents is now 80% of market rents, though many are now renting their properties at 100% market rents. Fortunately the stipulation that, in future, all social housing tenants with household incomes above a £30,000 ceiling will have to pay full market rents has been stymied for the time being.
5. Phil Ward. Private source (1/2/15).
6. 'Death Knell for Bluebells: Global Warming and British Plants'. Plantlife 1991
7. Page 81, 'Nature in Trust. The History of Nature Conservation in Britain', by John Sheail. Blackie (1976).
8. 'We should be supporting solar power', by Caroline Lucas MP. Opinion piece in The Argus (10.05.14).

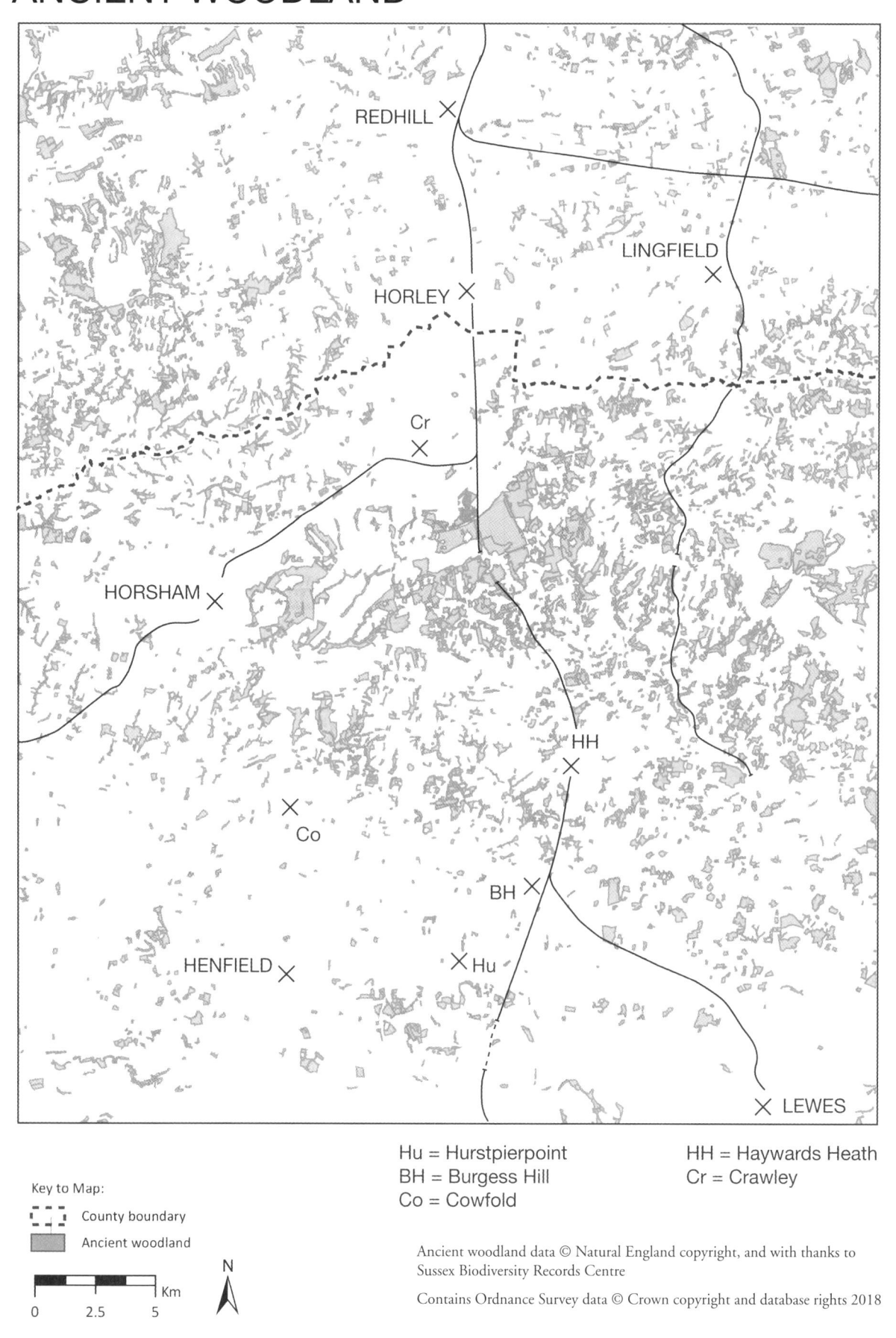

ANCIENT WOODLAND

Hu = Hurstpierpoint
BH = Burgess Hill
Co = Cowfold

HH = Haywards Heath
Cr = Crawley

Key to Map:
- - - County boundary
▨ Ancient woodland

0 — 2.5 — 5 Km

N

Ancient woodland data © Natural England copyright, and with thanks to Sussex Biodiversity Records Centre

Contains Ordnance Survey data © Crown copyright and database rights 2018

CHAPTER 5
Woods

From the heights of Box Hill and Ditchling Beacon woodland still seems to fill our great vale like a green rolling sea. It is its *woodland* that is the most special thing about the Weald. It defines its character as firmly as heather defines Dartmoor, or water defines the Norfolk Broads. The very word '*weald*' meant 'forest' to those Saxons who gave it that name.[1] Though the meaning of the terms '*wald*' and '*weald*' later extended to 'open high ground' (as in Cots*wolds* or Yorkshire *Wolds*) our own Weald never lost its link with woodland.

Much of it is **'ancient woodland'**, defined as woodland that has been in continuous existence at least since 1600 AD, and therefore quite likely to have been in existence long before that. About 35% of the High Weald is wooded. The south east of England[2] has more woodland than any other English region, and at 15% cover has twice the national average.[3] Surrey is the most wooded county (22.4% cover), with West Sussex (18.9%) and East Sussex (16.7%) following close behind. However, only 27% of Surrey woodland is ancient, in contrast to 65% of East Sussex woodland and 45% of West Sussex woodland.

You can mostly tell these ancient woods by their plants. Dense cover of Bluebells is a 'signature' of ancient woods, though not every wood with a Bluebell display is ancient, and some woods that do not have such a display are provenly ancient. There is a group of higher plants that are particularly faithful to ancient woodlands.[4] and the larger the number of these species present, the greater the likelihood that a wood will be ancient. In the south east region a working list of 100 such 'indicator species' can be used, with 20 present being a good total for any individual ancient wood. In the middle Sussex Weald Ashenground Woods (before parts of it were bulldozed for 'Bolnore Village') had 54 species, which would have given it 21st place on a list of 53 of the richest woods for these plants in most of the south east.[5] Wakehurst Woods is the only other wood in our area that is on that list. It appears at 50th place with 40 species.

These ancient woodland indicator plants include a suite of trees and shrubs such as Maple, Holly (if it occurs in the middle of a wood), Midland Thorn, Wych Elm, Sessile Oak, Crab Apple, Hornbeam, Wild Service, and Small Leaved Lime. As well as Bluebell, they also include such loved springtime plants as Primrose, Wood Anemone, Wild Daffodil, Early Dog Violet (but not the other violets), Ramsons, and Yellow Archangel (but beware the variegated invasive garden cultivar). Several mid Wealden orchids are indicative: Early Purple Orchis, Greater Butterfly Orchis, Bird's Nest Orchis, Broad Leaved and Violet Helleborines. There are also many less noticed plants: sedges such as Wood Sedge, grasses such as Creeping Soft Grass, and ferns such as Hard Fern and the two Shield Ferns.

On one or two springtime strolls through a wood you may total a good list of these indicator plants. My lists include: 25 for Tottington / Longlands Woods, Upper Beeding; 25 for Holmbush Wood, Woodmancote; 25 for Warningore Wood under Blackcap; 23 for West Wood, Woodmancote; 23 for Shaves Wood, Albourne; 19 for Down Coppice / Agmond's / Burtenshaw's Woods, Barcombe; and 17 for Woodhouse Wood, Blackstone. Smaller totals are frequent, such as 9 for Blackbrook Wood, Westmeston. They are much more likely, too,

> **Ancient woodland**
> Woodland which is likely to have been in continuous existence since AD 1600 (i.e. just over 400 years) is designated 'ancient woodland'. If it is that old it may well be very much older. Such woodland has a qualitatively richer assemblage of wildlife than more recent woodland. Woods with carpeting Bluebells are very often ancient woodland.

for single visits, or for smaller woods, such as 11 for Cottage Wood, Chailey; 12 for Long Wood, Novington; 10 for Folly Wood and 11 for Blunt's Wood, both near Cooksbridge. However, some small woods are exceptionally rich, like Plumpton Wood north of the agricultural college, with 20 recorded on a single visit.

'Secondary woodland' (post 1600 AD) may sometimes acquire great diversity in one or two centuries, especially if it incorporates or bounds smaller ancient woods. Before the 20th century new woodland was often planted as coppice with standards, or grew up naturally from abandoned land, so that the structure of a wood alone does not reveal its antiquity. A wood may well be composed of mature trees of native broad leaved species, like Oak, Ash, Hazel, but still be recent in origin. Thus, Holmwood Common near Dorking, with its fine Oaks and underwood has grown on neglected grazed common, and Ashen Plantation, Crowhurst, near Godstone, was largely fields in the 19th century. The woods south of Lambs Green, Rusper, TQ 225 364, and nearby Furze Field and Burnt Stubbs have that character.

Secondary woods were often planted or grew up to fill in gaps and consolidate existing ancient woodlands. In Edolphs Copse and Glover's Wood, Charlwood, newish woodland fills in all the gaps around a pattern of ancient shaws and relict woods. South Earlswood's woods, south of Redhill, TQ 272 472, have the same mixture of ancient and modern. Wealden gill woods were often consolidated like that, often at the expense of woodland and shaw removal on the plateau above. Thus, the long gill woodlands running south from West Hoathly and Turners Hill, and those east of Balcombe, sometimes have secondary upslope additions. Along the Sussex-Surrey border, the ridgelands' gill woods – Horsegills, Rusper House Gill, Cowix Gill, The Jordans, et al – have secondary woods between their ancient 'fingers', like webbing on a duck's foot.

Secondary woodlands are often revealed by their modern names, like *The Plantation*, east of Blackbrook Wood, Westmeston, Grantham's *Rough*, east of Chailey's Markstakes Common, Great *Rough* south west of Newick, or any of the woods named as *'furze fields'*.

Most of our middle Wealden woods have a history of **coppice management** for small wood, mostly with **standard trees** grown for timber amongst them. Most erstwhile coppiced woodland has long lain unmanaged, however, except for Pheasant shooting and landowners' amenity. It is rare, now, to see a traditionally managed coppice wood with standards, though a number are

Ancient woodland managed as it should be. A fine Oak harvested in Plashett Park Wood

being brought back into cycle for conservation purposes. Tottington and Longlands Woods in Upper Beeding used to be a superb example, but much of them were sold off piecemeal, and little coppicing is now done. River's Wood, just east of the Balcombe Viaduct, has a part which retains that coppiced character, TQ 333 277, with 'lollipop' Oaks regularly interspersed with the coppice shrub layer. Many coppice with standards woods retain their structure in a long-unmanaged form. Tilgate Wood, west of the Ardingly Brook at Wakehurst, exemplifies that *par excellence*, and its Oak standards have grown to magnificent dimensions. Henfield Wood, Scaynes Hill, TQ 366 242, has many fine over mature standards, too.

Sometimes re-coppicing fails, because uncontrolled numbers of deer eat out the inadequately protected regrowth and kill the old coppice stools. This has happened in the heart of lovely Great Home Wood between Wivelsfield Green and South Chailey.

The two world wars wreaked much havoc on our woods, for often the standards were clear felled and not regrown. After World War Two many landowners continued to take quick profits by **clearing the standing timber**, and you may often find yourself in coppice woods without standards, or with only small and scattered survivors. Warningore Wood, Oldpark Wood, Barcombe, and Wapsbourne Wood, west of Sheffield Park Station exemplify that.

The modern **bulldozing of whole woods and groups of woods** has been a far greater problem. *By the late 1970s three quarters of an acre of woodland was being lost in the Weald every day.* At that time came the traumatic destruction of ancient Balneath Wood, Chailey, whose clearance took two long years. It was one of many lost in that area since World War Two. East and west of the River Uck, north of Isfield, a densely wooded area was stripped nearly bare – losing Park Wood, Owlsbury Wood, large parts of Grove and Stroodland Woods, and Foxearth Wood (a bit further west). Woods north of Newick were lost, as they had earlier been lost to its west and south; and to the south of Bevern Bridge, Chailey. Gervaise Wood and others north of Cowfold Monastery were bulldozed. Wet Home Wood (part of the medieval Homewood), Gibbons Wood, and other small woods around Plumpton Green were cleared. Lagham Wood at South Godstone was built upon, and most of Poundhill Wood at South Park, Bletchingley, with others, was cleared. Ancient Home Wood at Turners Hill, part of the Saxon manor of Stanmer, was lost to mobile homes. At Cockhaise, at Wivelsfield Green, at Scaynes Hill, at Langhurst and Brookhurst in North Horsham, at Rusper, at Warninglid, at Itchingfield – indeed, in most places where you look – ancient woods have been cleared, and complex textures of shaw, hedge, and small wood have been reduced or wholly destroyed.

Since the 19th century many **new conifer woods** have been planted and **ancient woods replanted with conifers**, often transforming whole sub-landscapes. Large parts of Worth Forest were painfully damaged in this way,[6] mostly after 1945: Oldhouse Warren, Worthlodge, Cowdray and Monks Forests in the Paddockhurst Estate; Highbeeches and Brantridge Forests west of the Brighton line; and the Forestry Commission's Tilgate Forest. From Balcombe west to Brantridge Park the ancient woods have been turned into gloomy conifer farms: Brantridge Wood, Pond Wood, Northland Wood, much of Seyron Wood, as well as, to the east of Balcombe, the other Northlands Wood by Ardingly Reservoir, and much of Rivers's Wood, by the Balcombe Viaduct. The Gravetye Estate woods, north of West Hoathly, were horribly mauled in the Forestry Commission's past custody (they manage them better now), together with the woods to the north: Great Wildgoose and Holstein Woods.

Large parts of St Leonard's Forest were similarly damaged by conifer planting on old heath, wood pasture, and broad leaved woodland. I remember the old Holmbush Forest woods being bulldozed and coniferised in the early '60s, and the Forestry Commission made the same mischief to the south west. Large woods at the south end of St Leonard's around Free Chase were coniferised. West and east of Bolney, as far as Ansty, much woodland went the same way.

West of Southwater, those ancient survivors of medieval clearances, Marlpost and Madgeland Woods and their neighbours, were coniferised, as were those on the old Sedgwick Park Estate: Bushy Copse, Finche's and Home Woods. Wilding Wood at Chailey is a peculiarly horrible example. Park Wood in Poynings was mostly coniferised.

At South Park, Bletchingley; at the Harewood Estate, Outwood; at West Park, Horne, and elsewhere, superb small Surrey Low Wealden ancient woods were damaged by conifer replanting.

Particularly in the High Weald the old broad leaved woods already suffered from **invasive Rhodedendron**. Initially brought in by rich landowners for pleasure gardens and as cover for game birds, it is now so dense as to make even large woods frighteningly impenetrable, as at Plaw Wood (2012) south of Weir Wood Reservoir; and Wins Wood, west of Crawley Down. There has been good and concerted 'Rhodi' clearance in some places, as at Balcombe Forest east of the Balcombe Tunnel; at Monks Forest and Highbeeches Forest, south of Crawley and at Horsepasture Wood, Rowfant, TQ 318 369. Forestry Commission grants encourage that, to some extent.

New private amenity woods have been planted using native species by many large and small leisure landowners. There is a large new wood at Upper Soil Gill, south of Maplehurst, and a larger one at Upper Sheriff Farm, west of Horsted Keynes Station. Yet those fields grew crops to feed us till the agribusiness world market destroyed these farms.

BLUEBELL WOODS

After the funeral of my friend's dad I asked her what was the best memory she had of him. Their relationship had always been difficult. She thought for a few seconds, then said: *"when we were kids, him taking us to see the Bluebells in bloom in the woods"*.

Many years ago, another friend and I came down to the Weald to visit some big springtime woods. She had been brought up in Canada and lived for a long time in Greece. We bashed through some bushy place and came to a bank above a sunken dell. Below us was spread out a shining lake of Bluebells, a wash of lapis lazuli, tinted with sky. *She burst into tears.* Many of us will have felt that way too, when confronted by that all-surpassing beauty.

The glory of spring Bluebells is one wild thing which our islands can claim is of world significance. In our coppice woods[7] they are at their best, encouraged by the lack of competing vegetation in early spring, and completing their life cycle before the leaves of the trees emerge and bring summer shade to the woods.

The British Isles do not have much of nature that is superlative on a world scale. Our land mass was scraped clean to bare rock in the Ice Age. Nearly all that is here has re-entered the islands in the last 12,000 years, after the warmth returned, though the natural ingress of new species was blocked by the cutting of the land bridge with the continent about 8200 years BP. That left far too short a time for our wildlife to have diversified as it has in those regions where ecological continuity extends to many millions of years, like Greece or Spain or, far more, the tropical forests and coral reefs. Our Bluebell displays and our lower plant floras of the relatively unpolluted rainy west – mosses, liverworts and lichen – are much of the best our homeland can contribute globally.

It has sometimes struck me that the best Bluebell displays seem to occur in small Low Wealden woods. That is not a rule, for there are many superb High Wealden Bluebell woods, but it has some truth for me. Wortleford Wood sticks in my mind. It is on the bank of the Western Adur, west of Burgess Hill, TQ 278 211. It is too small to have many ancient woodland plants (12), but Bluebells cover almost 100% of its floor, with the density of a tufted carpet. Woodhouse Wood on the Chess Brook at Blackstone is another, slightly larger and richer in species, TQ 237 170. Then there is glorious Bell Copse, TQ 235 465, at Leigh, south west of Reigate, and Collendean Copse, TQ 247 447, 1.5 miles south east. Some fragments of Bluebell wood are miniscule. There's a fragment in a hedge corner at Curds Farm, Barcombe, TQ 410 150. It can be no more than half an acre, but it has dense Bluebells, with Holly and Maple. The line of the Roman Road runs close. It is an odd survivor.

All those previous examples are on the Wealden Clay geology. On the Tunbridge Wells Sand I think of tiny Broomy Wood at Bineham, TQ 384 97, north west of old Chailey church, another place with a display dense enough to form a carpet … or there's Sugworth Wood, squeezed between the Brighton Line and Haywards Heath Golf Course, on the Grinstead Clay and Cuckfield Stone. The wood is a local gem, somewhat mauled by trail bike riders, but its Bluebell display is magical.

Go and find your own examples. Most of our hidden Wealden ancient woods have this glorious spectacle.

The better off can make their trips to see the African game parks … and go whale watching … and see the birds of Gambia … but it is necessary to *ration* those big travels. Each and every plane journey, roaring over our small homes below, burning the fossil fuels and powering global warming, adds bit by bit to what threatens the lives of multitudes of poorer folk around the globe. Better first to discover, claim, protect and love the treasures on our doorsteps. We don't have to *ration* our delight in Bluebell woods.

Wood Anemones, Windflower, can form just as dominant a carpet in early springtime, before the Bluebells open. Some woods are best described as 'Windflower woods', though Bluebells may be abundant in them, too. I think of the Spithurst woods west of St Bartholomew's Church, north Barcombe: Oldpark Wood, TQ 419 179, and little Church Wood. Pure delight! Butcher's and Bonny's Woods, south of Hassocks Station, and parts of Plashett Wood, north of Ringmer, have superb displays, too, TQ 460 155.

On damp stream and river banks and winter flooded hollows, **Ramsons (Wild Garlic)** may cover large areas, scenting the air before you find it. Its shoots are pushing free of the mud even at New Year, and, if you pinch a fragment off, their heavy scent is evident even then. Deanoak Brook Wood, Mynthurst, Leigh, TQ 226/7 446/7, is almost wholly a 'Ramsons wood'. It is overwhelmingly dominant. River Wood, on the south bank of the Bevern Stream just east of Bevern Bridge, TQ 398 162/3, has good cover of it too.

In a few places **Wild Daffodils** dominate. In the 'Daffodil Forest', west of Handcross, TQ 249 297, the woods around the drive down to The Hyde are a carpet of early spring yellow. The display in the preserved part of Ashenground Woods, west of Ashenground Bridge, Haywards Heath, TQ 325 230, is treasured by local folk.

GILL WOODLANDS AND THE WILDWOOD

The word 'gill' (or 'ghyll')[8] is found only in the Weald and the English northwest, and refers to the deep clefts – mini ravines – carved there by aeons of busy tumbling streams. The steep Wealden linear woods that line the gills are the nearest we can get in darkest Sussex and Surrey to the primeval wildwood. The Weald is a redoubt for these ecosystems, which long ago disappeared from most of lowland England and retreated to the Atlantic west.

"To the gills, to the gills!!" … I scramble down some precipitous slope, tangled with overturned coppice stools and Bramble tentacles, where crumbling soil and flushing spring water make every footfall dodgy. Mostly it's worth the extra effort and care needed. In those small Wealden ravines many relict plants of the wildwood have their hideouts: like Small Leaved Lime; Coralroot Bittercress, with its pink tops and purplish bulbils; and Hay Scented Buckler Fern. You will find many lower plants there that are rare away from these steep humid woodlands, like Shining Hookeria and Water Earwort mosses, and Flagellate Feather Moss. The tiny oceanic and near-endemic English Chrysalis and Plaited Snails have their last known south eastern home in these gills. The sandrock bluffs, which are a gill feature where Ardingly Sandstone outcrops, are the main stronghold of oceanic bryophytes (mosses and liverworts) in the south east.

These Wealden gills are marked out by their humid microclimates, deep soil horizons and geological diversity, cutting through the large formations of Tunbridge Wells and Ashdown Sands and Wadhurst Clays, as well as the more particular variations of clays and sands within those formations. The Wadhurst Clays can frequently be calcareous, and hold big fossil mollusc bands outcropping on stream banks. There are often flushed areas with spring lines above clay bands, and there can be mires and small peat formations on the valley bottom pans, with their soggy Alderfields.

A Wealden gill. The nearest we'll get to the wildwood

Gills are common in the Weald. There are more than 1200 of them. In the rest of Britain and Europe there are clusters in the West Midlands (called 'dingles'); some in the Ardennes, Luxemburg; the Vosges; the Boullonais (a few); West Normandy; and Brittany … and that's it.

Most Wealden gills – over 1000 – are in the High Weald. There is a strong system of long gills in St Leonards' Forest (both east of Horsham and south of Mannings Heath, down to Cowfold and Bolney) and in Worth Forest. Much of the landscape around Balcombe, Ardingly, and south of West Hoathly and Turners Hill, is deeply incised by very long, south draining gills.

There are gills, too, in the Low Weald – more than we'd think. One large cluster lies in the North Horsham and Rusper Ridgelands along the Sussex-Surrey border, up to Charlwood. Another cluster lies south of Horsham around the Denne-Sedgwick scarp. Both clusters are based on the Paludina Limestone plateaus, whose hard resistant rocks above softer rocks are deeply incised. In Surrey there are more gill woodlands on the sandy sub-scarps of the Low Weald at South Park, Bletchingley; on the dip slope north of Outwood; and between Charlwood and Leigh.

Even in the small Lower Greensand exposures of our area there are a few. One cuts down through the Lower Greensand south of Furners Lane, marking the Henfield-Woodmancote parish boundary, TQ 226/7 160. One cuts through the Lower Greensand east of Perching Sands Farm and north of Fullingmill Bridge, Fulking, TQ 2438 125.

Exploitation must always have been light, perhaps confined to pasture woodland grazing within parks and forests, or light coppice working and timber extraction. Their woody cover is likely to be closer than most woods to the natural patterns of tree and shrub distribution, because they have not been subject to the same waves of woodland reorganisation (which have, through history, particularly favoured Hazel, Ash, English Oak, Hornbeam, and Sweet Chestnut … and conifers in modern times). In many gills there have been ponds powering iron forges and furnaces, and later industrial and agricultural milling. Many are gone now. Some remain, and new amenity ponds and fishing ponds are being made on a large scale.

Few gill woodlands are well known. Probably the best used is Sheepwash Gill, TQ 208 303, in the Forestry Commission's part of St Leonard's Forest. A footpath runs above its west bank, yet some parts are wild, humid and tangled. There are crossing points where children can paddle. The gills in Nyman's Cow Wood and Carroty Wood, e.g. TQ 269 296, have paths close by. The Wakehurst Estate embraces superb SSSI gills to the north, west and south of the main gardens.

Other good examples are (from west to east) … *Nuthurst Farm Gill, south of Horsham, TQ 188 262; Horse Gill, Rusper, TQ 195 372; Cook's Copse Gill, TQ 196 269; Glover's Wood Gill, Charlwood, e.g. TQ 225 405; The Glen, Bolney, TQ 243 247; Birchangar Gill, TQ 292 318; Stanford Brook Gill, both west and east of the Brighton Line, e.g. TQ 292 332; Monks Forest Gill with Sedgy Gill to the south, Balcombe, TQ 302 324; Copyhold Gill, Heaselands, Cuckfield, TQ 309 231; Paddockhurst Park Gill, Ardingly, TQ 332 334; Cob Brook Gill, Ardingly, TQ 349 300; Hook Gill, West Hoathly, TQ 361 310; and Furze Wood Gill, South Park, Bletchingley, TQ 348 488.*

WEALDEN WOODLAND'S TREES AND SHRUBS

As you familiarise yourself with the woods and trees of the Weald you begin to notice patterns in woody vegetation.[9] In the High Weald, Sweet Chestnut is the dominant coppice species in many woods, and Birch is abundant. Beech is often present as a timber or specimen tree. In the Low Weald, Hazel and Hornbeam form the major coppice species, under Oak and Ash. The Oak you find is nearly always Pedunculate Oak. You get an eye for spotting the scarce Sessile Oak too, but its patterns of occurrence are difficult to fathom, and hybrids are common. Sometimes Holly is abundant and makes walking across a wood a prickly affair. Some woods have obvious dominants. Other woods form mosaics of plant communities. Single Pines and other exotics appear at random in otherwise natural looking woods, planted on past whims of rich owners. Then there are the range of scarcer trees and shrubs you scan

GILL WOODLAND

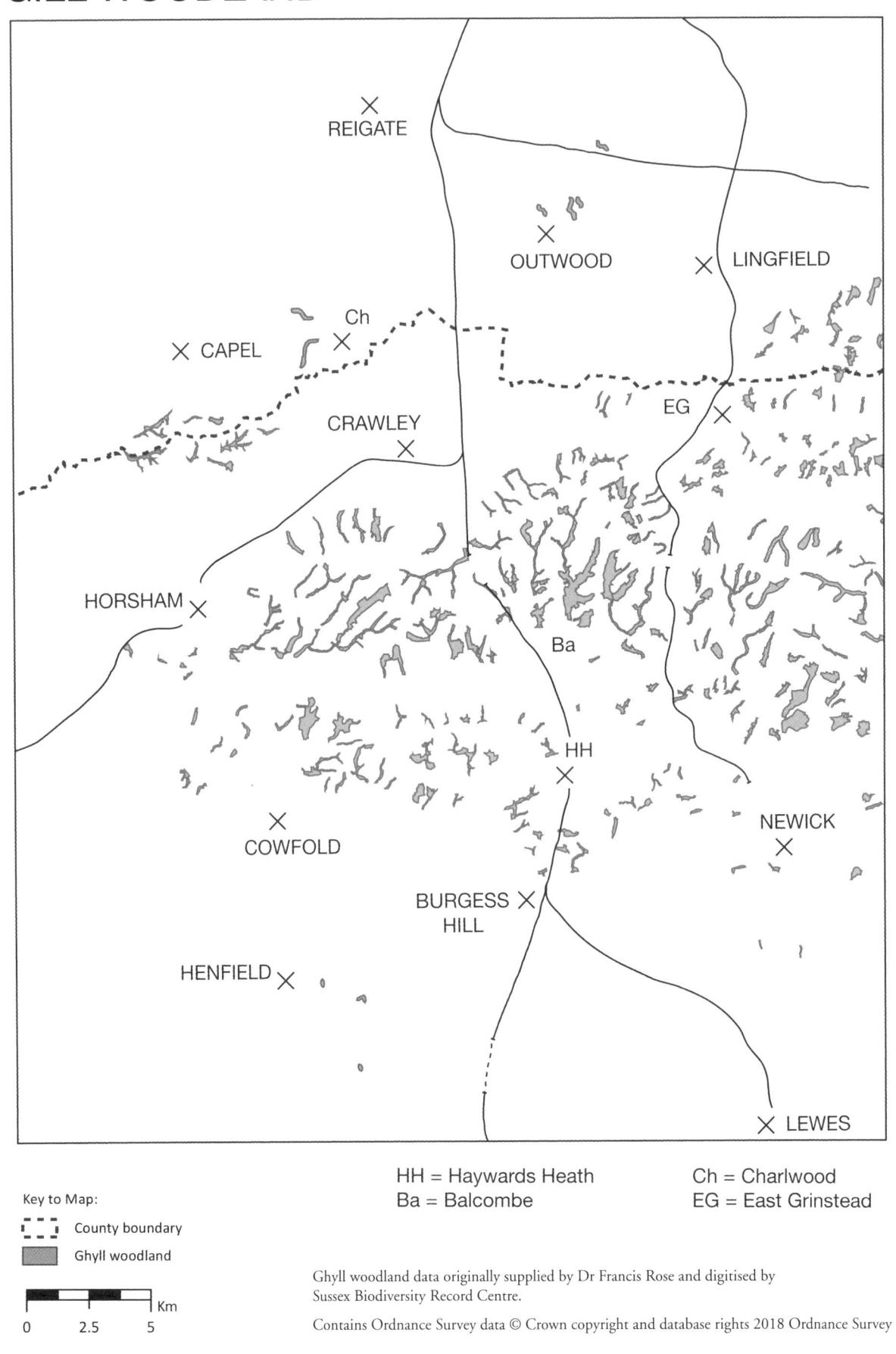

Key to Map:
- County boundary
- Ghyll woodland

0 — 2.5 — 5 Km

HH = Haywards Heath
Ba = Balcombe
Ch = Charlwood
EG = East Grinstead

Ghyll woodland data originally supplied by Dr Francis Rose and digitised by Sussex Biodiversity Record Centre.

Contains Ordnance Survey data © Crown copyright and database rights 2018 Ordnance Survey

for: Maple, Spindle, Guelder Rose and Field Rose, Midland Thorn, Wild Service and Wych Elm mostly in the Low Weald; Rowan and Alder Buckthorn in the more acidic parts of the High Weald. Downy Birch and Sessile Oak are also more common there.

Patterns of management can be discerned, which often used the natural distribution patterns of woody species, as well as local geologies, as the basis of their choices. Different coppice and timber species were managed for, at different times and for different purposes.

Oak is the 'Sussex weed', and by far the most important tree in our Wealden landscape. It is almost a monoculture in many areas. That is both its strength and its *weakness*, for if Sudden Oak Death, Oak Decline, and Oak Processionary Moth do their worst, and if future perils are allowed ingress as casually as many current tree pathogens have been, then the Weald will be left naked – in far worse desolation than was our farming landscape after Dutch Elm Disease had done its worst.

Pedunculate, or English Oak is everywhere. It is difficult to know how natural its present Wealden abundance and distribution is, for its huge production of acorns (and therefore usefulness for pastoralists' cattle and swine pannage), its preference for colonisation of open ground (and therefore its malleability in the landscape), together with the great premium for its timber and even small wood products, mean that it would everywhere have been encouraged. It is a stocky tree, with twisted angled branches, useful for the many idiosyncratic timbers needed in construction.

When I was a painter I tried to learn my technique for painting Oaks from pictures by Gainsborough and his ilk … the way they bunched their depiction of leaves in convenient blobs of varying detail, dependent on distance. Now I know they were mostly painting English Oak, for **Sessile Oak** doesn't seem to have that leaf bunching. Its leaves are more evenly distributed on straighter limbs, tending to an even, upward lift on a cleaner, often taller bole. It is much rarer than English Oak in the Weald, though it dominates the ancient woods of upland Britain. It is less versatile as timber and produces less acorns, but those are minor deficits for such grand trees. The finest Sessile Oak I know is a veteran maiden on Ragget's Lane, Cuckfield, TQ 280 233/4. It reaches to the sky (they can be taller than English Oaks) from a sturdy bole over three spans girth!

We think of Oak as the 'standards' component of 'coppice with standards' woods, but there was much Oak coppice in the past, when it was used as charcoal for the iron industry and other firings, and its bark for tanning. You can find small groves of outgrown Oak coppice in many Wealden woods of our area, sometimes just a few stools. Occasionally more substantial areas survive. Layhouse Wood, west of Rowfant, is almost all outgrown Oak coppice, much (all?) of it Sessile Oak, and there is more nearby around what's left of Bashford Wood on Copthorne Golf Course. The two fragments of Freeks Farm Wood, with Big Wood at Bedelands, Burgess Hill, have much old Sessile Oak coppice, too. Cuttinglye Wood, by The Monastery, Crawley Down, TQ 344 384, has much Sessile Oak coppice in a locally rare type of woodland usually found in the west and north of Britain … with Bilberry and Ling Heather, alongside Beech, Rowan, Birch and much Holly (and Rhodedendron).

Nowadays, much old coppice with standards has grown over to 'high forest', and mature Oaks are the climax trees that crown it, as in Tilgate Wood on the Wakehurst Estate. Not far away, the Oaks on the abandoned holloway of Shill Lane, TQ 324 301, cut by Ardingly Reservoir, form a linear high forest fragment of great character.

Ash is Oak's companion, its complement, and its opposite. Though far less muscle-bound than Oak, and often far less long-lived, it has a nimbleness which Oak cannot match, being an able coloniser, which can wood-up a field in just a decade or so. Its leafy canopy is a matter of lacework, not blanketting. It is a bringer of light to woods, not dimness. Grass can still grow beneath. It can reach up high, clean and straight limbed, like Beech, or it can spread wide limbs, like English Oak. It can make gnarled pollard boles and live for centuries – magnificent giants of three spans and more trunk girth – and give us small wood poles as rapidly as Hazel or Willow, growing up to 6ft a year. We can enjoy its shade whilst still enjoying the sun's warmth and light. For sure, it cannot make the final size of ancient Oaks, Sweet Chestnut or Beech, but it can make the coppice stool holes that Marsh Tits love to nest in, and the sweetness of its old trunks can bear a hoary cloak of lichen in many subtle colours and the greatest profusion. Its bark is a comfortable cushion to rest our backs on summer picnics. More like a pelt than Oak's crocodile skin.

The Weald is Ash country … especially the clay lands and milder Greensands of the Low Weald, and the Wadhurst Clay lands of the High Weald … but it can turn up anywhere. If we lose Ash in the Weald we lose much of its wardrobe and its character.

> **Gill woodland**
> These are woods found in deep clefts eroded by streams, mostly in the High Weald, with some in the Low Weald. Because gill woodlands are so difficult to access and exploit, it may well be that many of them are 'primary' woodland, that is, in continuous existence since the post-glacial return of the wildwood. They certainly shelter a suite of distinctive relict species (such as Small Leaved Lime, ferns, mosses, liverworts, and mini-beasts) which find it even harder to survive elsewhere.

Fine Ash-Hazel woodland. This was pasture 150 years ago!

On wetter soils it grows alongside Alder in an obvious contentment that surprises those of us used to it on the dry and skeletal soils of the Downs. It was sometimes planted. Mostly it seems to have got where it is on its own. The upper edges of our valley woods often have fringes of newer woodland dominated by Ash, with Primrose and Pendulous Sedge soon joining it. In ancient clay woods it forms an intimate coppice mixture with Hazel, sometimes dominating, sometimes scarce, sometimes on equal terms. It arrays in long lines along Low Wealden hedgerows, sometimes without Oak, sometimes paired up with it.

Ash Die Back is here in Sussex and Surrey with a vengeance, now. You may walk a stretch of river bank, a bushy slope, a derelict wood edge field, or a woodland ride, and find most of the young Ashes infected, their leafy branch tips drooping, browned, and crinkled. It will take the young trees first, but it will wear down and kill the fine timber, the gorgeous soaring maidens, and the ancient pollards over time.

The prospect of the loss of this fine tree and the landscapes it forms, is truly dreadful. It makes the words I write describing this so-familiar friend, and its place in our Wealden countryside, seem useless, redundant. I can barely bring myself to think of a future without it. We are on the edge of a disaster that those of us old enough to have watched the desolation caused by the loss of our Elm heritage hoped never to see repeated. If you did not see the Elm country before that loss, you will not mourn its passing. So the goal posts move. So it goes.

Maple often accompanies Ash, with Oak standards. It is often found in hedgerows, as both tree and laid bush. It likes best the same clay country as Wild Service Tree (see below) and its bark has the same flaked, chequered look. Like Wild Service too, you often detect its presence by the familiar pattern of its fallen leaves: neatly palmate and keeping their shape reliably all winter through. It is, though, a far commoner tree, and there are few parts of the Weald where you are without it. On the Paludina Limestone at Coltstaple, near Southwater, TQ 181 276, old Maples line a lost drove, and join with Ash, Hazel, Blackthorn, and Holly to form over half a mile of young scarp woods. It often grows in clusters. It is a common indicator species of ancient woods. It does not reach a great age, but the oldest, outgrown Maple hedgerow stools are very like old Hornbeam stools.

Hornbeam, being a warmth loving tree, was a late post-glacial returnee, just making it back into England before the opening up of the Channel could block its entry. It never naturally got beyond south east England (though people have scattered it much more widely). In fact, its advance seems to have ground to a halt right in the middle of Sussex. Thus, *to the west* of our area, Hazel is the dominant coppice species. *In the middle* of our area, there are advanced guards of Hornbeam in the mixed coppice of Newtimber Wood and Park Wood, Poynings. *In the east* of our area, Warningore Wood, between Plumpton and Cooksbridge, TQ 382 140, is solid Hornbeam coppice *par excellence.* Around Chailey and north Barcombe, the big woods – Great Home Wood, Knowlands Wood, Agmond's Wood/Down Coppice, Oldpark Wood, Church Copse, and others – all have abundant Hornbeam coppice. Now-destroyed Balneath Wood, South Chailey, was old Hornbeam coppice.

Such Hornbeam woods have a very distinctive character. The outgrown poles, the ancient stools, and the trunks of pollards are goblinesque, writhing, fluted, knotty and sinewy, like a skinny man or woman who has trained hard as a boxer, or an old man losing his body mass but keeping his fitness. They are the kind of trees that watch you from banks as you pass up darkening green lanes, or the trees which whisper their long memories to you. The smooth bark is marked by the interweaving territories of picture lichen, expanding, meeting, overwhelming and retreating in their so-slow struggles for light and space. The canopy, when it closes in late spring, is as dense and excluding as Beech, and the ground flora is often simplified, though the Bluebell displays can be spectacular. Its leaves are neat and comely, like upmarket Beech leaves, and its sprays of keys form a welcome late season dressing of the whole tree. This special character of Hornbeam makes it easy to forgive the way it can dominate and exclude the undershrub and herb layers when in monoculture.

It was mostly used for fuel wood, being little use as timber, but had much use for cogs and yokes, where hardness was extra important. *Yoke*hurst's name, TQ 383 168, East Chiltington, may commemorate such production. It is in an area of old Hornbeam woods, and the Saxon drove that passes by still has remnants of ancient Hornbeam coppice.

In the eastern parishes of this area, Hornbeam very frequently forms the boundary hedging of old woods. Mostly these hedges are long neglected, and their layered, outgrown stools reach great bulk and grotesquery. Its pollards are rare here, but can sometimes be found on wood banks or tracks, marking old coppice compartments.

Beech squeaked back into Britain at the same time as Hornbeam, just before the land link with the continent disappeared. It was not so fussy, however, being able to tolerate more acidic ground, especially when well drained, and it spread more widely, though as a small part of the tree community, not dominant. Its time came several thousand years later with people's clearance of the wildwood, and subsequent waves of farming advance and retreat. Where woods returned to exhausted land, Beech came back in great abundance.

It may have played a co-dominant role with Oak, in the sandy High Weald. *Buxshalls* in Lindfield, and *Buckwish* in Henfield, are both early 'Beech' place names, the former on sandstone, the latter next to greensand. St Leonard's Forest was described[10] in 1570 as well supplied with timber, especially Oak and *Beech*, of very great age and great length. Nowadays the best Beeches of the two forests survive as ancient pollards, commonest in Worth Forest and Paddockhurst Park, but with good numbers in St Leonard's too. 34% of the veteran trees of the Brighton Line Weald are Beech (2012). The tree was not used as timber in medieval times, being mostly a fuel wood and source of 'mast' (the fallen nuts) for wood pasturage, and for those purposes pollarding provided a better management. Beech was also coppiced. Mostly such coppice is found in small quantities and often it is easy to miss, for its young growth can easily be mistaken for Hornbeam. Nonetheless, it is quite frequent in coppice woods.

In the 18th century it came into new usage for both timber and ornament and was managed to grow tall maidens, often in groves, rising straight and clean-boled for great lengths to the crown high above. It is those elegant, columnar trees and the open cathedral-like spaces they make beneath which form the public image of this beloved species, and that perception has survived even the ravages of the 1987 and '90 gales, when these great poles crashed in huge numbers, whilst the ancient pollards proved somewhat more robust. Orlton's Copse, Rusper, TQ 221 387, and Cook's Copse, Nuthurst, TQ 198 269, both have these interior 'cathedral' spaces made by such Beeches.

Hazel is the 'workhorse' of so much of our Wealden coppice woodlands. Tough, pliant, long lived, growing and re-growing quickly, splittable and twistable, it was a pre-industrial equivalent of plastic. Flexible enough to use as binding, it could also form rigid, permeable sheets – wattles – which, plastered with daub, were the medieval equivalent of 'composition board'. Many Wealden timber framed houses still hide wattle and daub infill walling, centuries old. Outside, it formed moveable stock proof fencing – hurdles – essential to any shepherd till World War Two and after. Our hand tools, our utensils, our walking sticks were made of it, and some still are. Its foliage was browsed by cattle and cut for fodder. Its nuts provided a mainstay for Mesolithic gatherer hunters, and fed us through to modern times … until the import of larger varieties. Moreover, the modern depredations of Grey Squirrels have reduced the nut harvest hugely. Modern families seeking to go nutting will find meagre pickings. *Nuthurst,* by St Leonards's Forest, *Nutham,* by Southwater, *Nutknowle,* in Woodmancote, *Nutfield* and *Nutwood* near Redhill, and *Nutfold* at Capel, all testify to the importance to Saxons of nutting. Through about two post-glacial millennia (9000–7000 BP) Hazel co-dominated the landscape, before the increase in the big timber trees shrank its oligopoly, for it is intolerant of deep shade. The growth of coppicing in late prehistoric times halted and reversed its retreat. Always as underwood, never a big tree, Hazel remains a keystone species of Wealden woods.

Hazel is more frequent in the west of our area, where Hornbeam is more scattered and Sweet Chestnut not so suited, but it can be found throughout. The southern of the two Plumpton Woods, on the wet Gault Clay north of the College, TQ 355 145, is a Hazel coppice wood, with no Hornbeam present. The northern Plumpton Wood, however, on the Wealden Clay, TQ 365 185, has much Hornbeam coppice and far less Hazel. Small Dole's Tottington/Longlands Woods have fine Hazel coppice.

Hazel's 'lambs' tails' catkins, opening in January, are the first big marker of winter's retreat. Your children might like to hunt for the female flowers too, looking just like buds on the same twigs as the lamb's tails, but protruding tiny bright red styles, like the arms of unfurling miniature sea anemones. In Autumn, some of the ripe nuts have small bore holes, and when opened are full of frass. That might be the work of the quaint little Hazelnut Weevil, *Curculio nucum*, which you will find in summer, sometimes, dozing on the top of leaves. Her proboscis is like a long and gently curved drinking straw, or an insect elephant's trunk, with its two antennae perched half way along, like a pair of specs that have slipped down your nose. She uses this 'rostrum' to drill a hole in young nuts, so she can lay an egg inside.

A Beech clump in ancient high forest

If you are *very* lucky you may find Toothwort, *Lathraea squamaria*, growing in spring under Hazel stools on a bank or stream side. Its flowers look like discarded sets of false teeth, grubby pinkish white, and the plant has no trace of green, for it is parasitic on the trees above, and produces no chlorophyll of its own.

Sweet Chestnut was brought here by the Romans, and settled down pretty much like a native after they'd left, without being greatly exploited. The Weald, the Thames basin, much of the Midlands and the Essex coast seem to be its strongholds. From the 17th century onwards came its rediscovery. It was hugely planted in the 19th century as a coppice species, sometimes replacing older woodland vegetation, sometimes planted on open ground. It dominates Kent coppice woods as well as ours in the High Weald, being used for hop poles and as a fencing wood of choice, being more rot resistant in the ground than any other then used, bar Yew.[11] Its nuts, however, weren't commercially exploited, though very tasty, being smaller than strains nurtured for eating in the continental south. Most Chestnut coppice is now overstood, and its leaf fall forms dense mulch, inimical to pre-vernal woodland flowers like Bluebells. In the 20th century much Chestnut coppice at St Leonards and Worth Forests, and the high sandstone ridges was replaced by dense conifers, which are even worse for native wildlife. Much of Wapsbourne Wood at Sheffield Park is old Sweet Chestnut coppice, and its Bluebells survive well, thankfully, in parts. The finest Sweet Chestnut displays to be seen are the ancient pollards of old Betchworth Deer Park, Dorking, TQ 183 500, and the two Felbridge Chestnut Avenues, near East Grinstead, TQ 365 394/5.

Alder can form huge old coppice stools of several spans girth. There is a line of such Alder giants down Bull's Farm Gill, south of Horsham, TQ 181/2 283. Its roots form felted underwater shelves in streams, under which spider legged Beautiful Demoiselle larvae hide. Its catkins, painted soft purple, are a winter pleasure, but they do not open till early spring, when the fresh female cones make sort-of-flowers. Where water flushes over an Alderfield the ground in early spring may be spangled all over with Golden Saxifrage, and occasional tufts of Marsh Marigolds. The braided woodland stream under the Bluebell Line viaduct, just south of East Grinstead is like that, TQ 383 378. Where the peaty land dries out and shrinks, through land drainage or neighbouring quarrying, the Alder stools are left high and dry, more like short pollards than coppice stools, as at The Alders, Reigate Heath, TQ 229 500, and Heaven Wood, Danehill, c. TQ 400 260.

I don't know what's best ... billowing **Crab Apple's** spring blossom, topping off the Bluebells below, or its winter scatter of golden apples carpeting the ground right through till early spring. It's usual to find at least one tree in any ancient wood, even those of modest size, at least in the Low Weald. In Horleyland Wood, TQ 290 405, amongst the mess of Gatwick's sprawling car parks, there is a grove of Crabs with those everlasting apples. Near the banks of the Bevern, Chiltington, TQ 398 155/6, there is a thicket with several Crabs lining its edge like orchard trees. **Gean, Wild Cherry**, makes a similar show of blossom, and is commoner – a 'constant' of old Low Wealden woods. Its cherries are worth nibbling, and they fall in large numbers, but they're too sharp to gorge, and birds and animals take them quickly, so you need luck. It forms large clones, easily missed, but when noticed, they surprise with the extent of ground they cover. It's their bark you recognise first, not the leaves, which are forced high by competition for sky.

Midland Thorn, better named as **Woodland Thorn**, is a good marker of ancient woods on the Low Wealden clay. It is an inconspicuous shrub and flowers less freely than Hawthorn, but it does flower a week or so earlier than its relative, to better chime with the pre-vernal sunshine before the green canopy closes above. You will know it from its flowers, which have two styles forked from a common base, whereas Hawthorn has one; and from its leaves, which have three rounded lobes with many tiny edge serrations. Hawthorn leaves have more lobes with few and larger serrations. There are many confusing hybrids between the two, though.

I suspect **Wych Elm**[12] has survived Dutch Elm Disease a bit better than other Elm species, by dint of hiding deep in ancient woods, though it has as little natural immunity as the other Elms. It can make a fine tree, but that is very rare nowadays, and you mostly find it sprawling on thin limbs amongst other shrubs. My best memories are of finding it in old gill woods, with other wildwood refugees. It is a sexually reproducing true species, unlike its cousins from the English, East Anglian, and Cornish Elm aggregate species, which sucker vigorously and have mostly given up on sex. It came here under its own steam in the same post glacial period as the two Limes, and was once a co-dominant woodland tree across Ireland and parts of the west. It is still strong in Wales and Scotland. 'Wych' just means 'Elm', for the Saxons used both words for the group, with no indication that they meant *Wych* Elm specifically. Elms were trees of rich soils and of flood plains, but, like Black Poplar, they're now obliged to survive the extinction of those wet river woodlands.

To look across a Low Wealden farmland of **Field Elms** standing tall in receding hedgeline after line was one those sights of the countryside certain to bring a thrill. They stood so high, each one with its own distinctive irregular shape, bulging on this side or that, one great branch randomly above another till they topped off in a lofty dome … like thunderheads.[13] They were as stirring as the cawing of Rooks round a springtime rookery. The flatlands of the Low Weald, the Coastal Plain, and the last of the Downs where they met that plain, as well as in the Kennet Valley, are the open landscapes I remember it … before Dutch Elm Disease did its work 40–50 years ago. Our Field Elms (mostly **English Elm**, *Ulmus procera*) were not particularly woodland trees in Sussex, except in the hedges that surrounded Wealden woods, but they deserve commemoration as lost *timber* trees, though they survive as suckering shrubs in many Surrey and Sussex Wealden hedgerows. They reached great size in some old parks, too, like Danny and Firle, and carried their own distinctive epiphytes, like the lichen Eagle's Claws, *Anaptychia ciliaris*. You can sometimes find the tasty looking (but not edible) Wrinkled Peach fungus, *Rhodotus palmatus*, on dead Elms.

Small Leaved Lime,[14] known sometimes as **Pry**, seems to be particularly faithful to ancient gill woods. Of its 48 sites in this landscape that I know, 18 (37.5%) are gills or partly gill-like. It is in lovely Tickfold Gill, TQ 165 369, on the Sussex-Surrey County boundary. It is in Three Point Wood, Paddockhurst, TQ 334 343/4, on a ravine of cliff-like steepness. It survives in The Gill, south of Rowfant, TQ 327 362. There is a thicket on the banks of Stanford Brook in Brantridge Forest, TQ 283 323, that shines like a chandelier of hanging gold sovereigns in the autumn gloom. Damming of the pond downstream to bring flood relief to Crawley now brings the Lime within reach of periodic inundation. Can it survive? In Glover's Wood, Charlwood, TQ 225 406/7, it occurs in a gill which shelters many wildwood refugees. On a gill side in Great Wildgoose Wood, TQ 354 346/7, it has been spared the surrounding coniferisation.

Small Leaved Lime finds refuge along other watercourses that have preserved their free-formed alignments. The newly discovered linear ancient wood along the River Mole at Amberley Farm, Langley Green, e.g. TQ 260 392, has a scatter of outgrown Lime coppice and small trees, some on the old County boundary. All will be destroyed if a Gatwick second runway goes ahead. On the Maidenbower Estate, Crawley, TQ 292 355, the Council has preserved the old streamside woods and their Lime coppice stools. The natural wooded meanders of the Adur, upstream of Haven Bridge, east and west of the Downs Link, Copsale, e.g. TQ 178 235, shelter old stools.

Small Leaved Lime dominated the wildwood of lowland England in the warm and wet 'Atlantic' period around 6500 BP. It was put under pressure by the twin forces of climatic cooling, which stymied its production of fertile fruit, and organised woodland browsing by early pastoralists' and farmers' herds. Lime provides a very sweet 'bite' and would have been preferentially cut for fodder. It was still common enough to be used in Saxon place names, though I know of no surviving native Small Leaved Limes close to those places that take their ancient names from it. However, *Lindfield; Lentridge,* Plumpton Green; *Lyne* House, Newdigate; and *Lyne* House Farm, Lingfield, all come from '*Lind*' or '*Linden*'. *Bastwick*, south of Hurstpierpoint, and *Bashurst* (anciently '*Bashes*'[15]) in Itchingfield, are both possible '*bast*' names, that being the fibre that was made from stripped Lime bark.

Confined to its existing areas by its reproductive limitations, clearance and grazing pressure, its national distribution has now fragmented, though it is still strong in North Essex, parts of Lincolnshire, the Wye watershed, and elsewhere.

In our part of the Weald its presence is strongest in the ridgelands along the county border north of Horsham and St Leonards Forest; and in the ridgelands of Worth Forest, Balcombe, Turners Hill and West Hoathly. Scattered across the Low Weald, too, it probably remains to be recognised in a range of little visited small woods and wooded streams. Many of our Hornbeam, Oak and Hazel woods would once have been Lime woods.

You may very rarely find middle Wealden plateau woods with large areas of it, such as House Copse, TQ 226 358, at Faygate, and Brick Kiln and Rough Woods, near Worth Abbey. Other woods have large coppiced clones of it, such as Courtland Wood, Southwater, and Perry Wood, Salfords. Other plateau woods may have isolated old coppice stools, singly or in groups, such as High Wood, Broadbridge Heath; Knowlands Wood, Barcombe; and Collendean Copse, north west of Horley. Often it forms part of old field or wood hedges, such as around Standinghall Farm in Worthlodge Forest. Sometimes, nowadays, it forms part of 'natural' planting schemes, such as on the northern perimeter of Gatwick. When it occurs naturally it is nearly always found as grown out coppice, but the giant on the track just north of Worth Church is the biggest in Britain!

Wild Service Tree[16] is a rare old Wealden tree that you hunt for by looking at the ground. Amongst the leaf litter of any season its leaf shape is quite distinctive. Once found, you then scan shrubs and canopy to match leaf to parent. That can be difficult. In more open areas it can grow wide and tall, but mostly you find it squeezed amongst other shrubs and young trees, struggling to maintain its access to sunlight. Look, too, for its bright red autumn colours, which are easily missed … and for its May-time creamy white corymbs of blossom.

We'd been collecting its small brown fruits before, over the autumn, scuffling through leaves and sorting the shrunken from the plumped and promising. We knew they'd be inedible when collected, but they didn't get better with storage. Then, one November day of glorious autumn colours we found an old Service Tree on the boundary bank of a tiny ancient wood. Its fruits were fat, sweet, tart, appley, with hints of other fragrances. They had been 'bletted' by early frosts, and that's what was needed. *Now* I get why they were so loved by generations of country children; why they were collected and made into drinks sold in many a Wealden pub; and why, for so long the tree was classed with apples, pears, plums and cherries, as a standard fruit bearer for the table.

The fruits may also unlock part of the reason for the trees present rarity. Their edibility would have made them very attractive to foraging birds, rodents, Wild Boar, deer and Bears. The smaller creatures would have scoffed the lot, but the large herbivores would have trampled and rootled some of the fruits into the ground and thus secured their germination. Thus, when the Boar and their ilk were driven to extinction the Service Trees lost the midwives that had helped the birth of new generations.

That need for disturbed ground for reproduction may also account for the odd pattern of the tree's current distribution. I thought that there was a very close connection between the trees and ancient woodland, but it is more complicated than that. I've mapped 46 sites for Wild Service in the Weald of the Brighton Line. 26 (57%) of them are in field hedges, lane or track hedges, and shaws. Most of these features would have had ditches which were repeatedly cleaned and the diggings mounded under the hedges, thus mimicking the burying actions of the rootling Boars.

Nine (20%) of the Service Tree's sites were in gills, or the edges of wooded watercourses which would likely have had long ecological continuity, though they may not be recognised as ancient woodland – a bit like some ancient hedges which may once have been parts of woods. Clearly, Wild Service is far less tied to ancient gill woods than Small Leaved Lime. Seven (15%) of the Service Tree's sites were in ancient woodland. So, if we add the watercourse sites to the ancient woodland sites it shows that 35% of my Wild Service sites were in wooded areas of likely strong ecological continuity. The link with ancient woodland is thus there, but not in so straightforward a way as for Small Leaved Lime.

In Sussex and Surrey, Wild Service is closely tied to the clay lands of the Low Weald. It does not occur in Ireland or Scotland, and the Weald is its great British stronghold. It is strong too, in the Wye and Severn watersheds, in parts of Lincolnshire, Suffolk, and Herts. John Clare, the 'peasant poet', wrote of it in what's left of Rockingham Forest, Northants. There is a cluster of sites too on the footprint of the lost Forest of Arden, and on far western coasts.

The common Wealden name for it was 'checkers', or 'chequers'. That was probably not because of the chequered pattern of its mature bark, but because of the tree's connection with Wealden pubs, many of which have that name, for the ancient sign for a drinking house was a chequer board. Many of these pubs may have had Service Trees in their grounds, to utilise the fruit in their beer making, and the tree may have acquired the name by association. The Saxons knew it as *'syrfe'* and *'surf-treow'*,[17] and *'service'* is the plural of that. The Saxon *'f'* was pronounced as our 'v'.

There is a fine hedgerow veteran Wild Service Tree on the green lane at Lower Ridges, north of Burgess Hill, TQ 303/4 218. Around the site of the lost Capon's Cottage, Cowfold, TQ 207 234/5, and in the little shaws across the field to the north/NE are several Wild Service, one growing right next to an old wilding pear. Could it be that the Service had grown from an original graft on a pear stock?

ENDNOTES

1. 'The Landscape of Place Names'. Pages 253–257, by Margaret Gelling and Ann Cole, Shaun Tyas, Stamford (2000), and 'The Place Names of Sussex', pages 1–2, by A Mawer & FM Stenton, English Place Name Society (reprinted 2001).
2. Berks, Bucks, Oxon, Hants and Isle of Wight, Surrey, Sussex, Kent.
3. Regional Forestry Framework, Background information/research summary No 3. Forestry Commission SE England Conservancy, Alice Holt, Farnham, Surrey, GU10 41F.
4. 'Indicators of Ancient Woodland. The use of vascular plants in evaluating woods for nature conservation', by Francis Rose. British Wildlife, Vol. 10, No. 4, pages 241–251. (April 1999).
5. Rose, page 248, op cit. The counties in the list are Hants, Wilts, Berks, Bucks, Oxon, Sussex, Kent.
6. As a result, the Worth Forest and St Leonard's Forest SSSIs (Sites of Special Scientific Interest) were de-designated in large part.
7. In the west of Britain there is also a glorious Bluebell display in old damp meadows and on hedge banks, where Bracken unfurls in summer to protect the Bluebells from the competition of other plants.
8. I have extensively used an excellent paper: 'Gill Woodlands in the Weald', by Francis Rose and John M Patmore (June 1997). Peter Brandon's 'The Kent and Sussex Weald', Phillimore (2003) is also a very good source.
9. I have used the 'History of the British Flora', by Sir Harry Godwin, Cambridge Modern Classics (1975); 'A History of Sussex Wild Plants', by Ursula Smith and Eileen Howard, The Booth Museum of Natural History, Brighton (1996); and the 'Atlas of the British Flora', edited by F H Perring and S M Walters, Botanical Society of the British Isles (1990) extensively in this section.
10. See chapter: 'The Forests of St Leonard's and Worth'.
11. 'The History of the Countryside', pages 54–6, by Oliver Rackham. J M Dent & Sons (1976).
12. 'The History of the Countryside', op cit. Chapter 11 is all about Elms.
13. To quote Owen Johnson's beautiful phrase. 'Collins Tree Guide', Page 244, by Owen Johnson and David More. Harper Collins (2004).
14. 'Flora Britannica', by Richard Mabey, Sinclair-Stevenson (1996) is good on Small Leaved Lime, as is 'The History of the Countryside', by Oliver Rackham, J M Dent & Sons Ltd, (1996). Francis Rose's essay 'The Habitats and Vegetation of Sussex' is also good. The essay is in the 'Atlas of Sussex Mosses, Liverworts and Lichen', published by the Booth Museum of Natural History, Borough of Brighton (1991).
15. 'Barns Green and Itchingfield, Then and Now', page 3, by Mary Hallett. Fourbears Publishing (2012).
16. Dr Patrick Roper's little booklet: 'Chequer, Wild Service Tree', Sage Press (2004), packs in this tree's fascinating story. He has studied Service Trees for over 40 years, and led a national survey for them.
17. Dr Patrick Roper, op cit.

THE FOREST DISTRICT IN LATE SAXON TIMES, c. 1050 AD

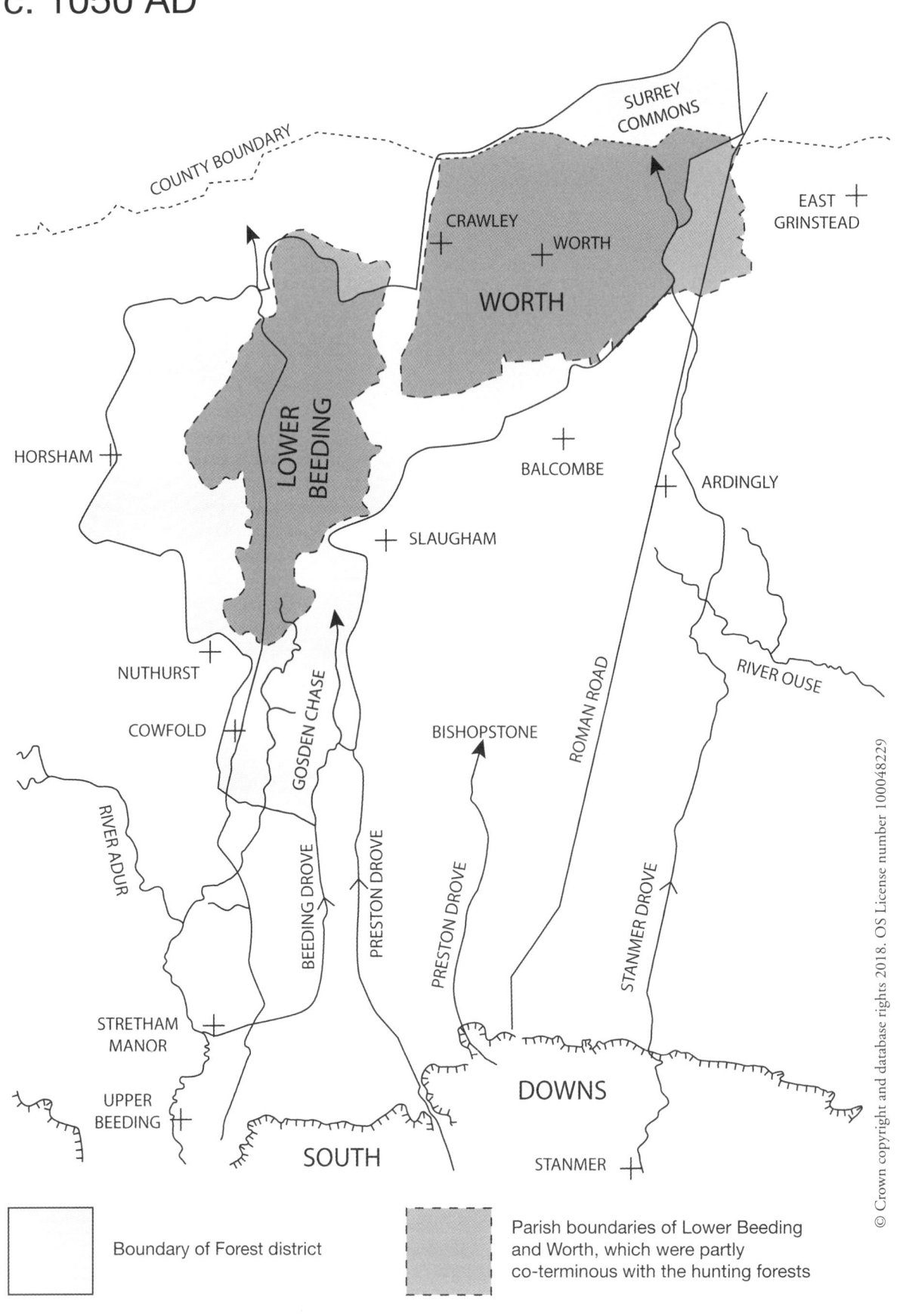

CHAPTER 6
The forests of St Leonard's and Worth

BIRDS OF PARADISE

There's a road that runs down the spine of St Leonard's Forest. It runs down the ridge between the Forest's two central valleys. It's called the 'Grouse Road'. The name has no traceable ancient lineage, though Grouse Gate appears on the 1795 Gardner and Gream map as a gate to the Great Warren, where its boundary crossed the Grouse Road.

We don't know whether this name refers to the **Black Grouse**, though it seems likely, for this bird would have graced all our Sussex forests and high wealden heathy ridges. We live, now, too late to see it, but we've missed it only by a matter of 160 years. Our forebears would also have known it as the Heath Cock, Black Cock or Black Game, but I'd like to call it the **British Bird of Paradise**.

> **The Forest district in late Saxon times, c. 1050 AD**
> The term 'forest' was a medieval legal term for areas set aside for the keeping and hunting of deer and other quarry animals, by feudal lords or royalty. Forests had unenclosed and unimproved 'wastes', as well as farmed land within them, and were subject to a special set of forest laws and courts. This map shows both the areas which probably had unenclosed forest vegetation (pasture woodlands, heath, mire and moor) or were subject to the hunting rights of the feudal lords. Thus, the Surrey boundary commons (like Copthorne) and Horsham Common would not have been within the hunting forests, but would have had similar vegetation to them and been continuous with them. Gosden Chase would have had extensive farming settlement, but would still have been subject to the hunting rights of the Bishop of Chichester, a feudal lord.

Imagine yourself back to the year 1750, or 1650, say.

You're up at dawn. The slopes of boggy heath stretch away from you on either side of the wide combe. A runnel of chilly water gurgles down its gill. Snow is still about, and the tussocks of moor grass and ling heather couldn't look bleaker. As the night gives way to wan light you hear it ... that weird cooing chorus ... rising ... there it goes ... to that snorting cackle.

Then you see one ... strutting and parading in the half light ... its lyre-shaped tail cocked and spread to display a pure white fan ... its wings spread. As the light comes the colours intensify ... a body of glossy purplish black, with bright red eyebrows sailing above ... its throat puffed out and shining. This is no ordinary bird. It's a plump and chicken-sized treasure in its full pride of courting power. There's a whole bunch of them here, waddling back and forth and launching and lashing at each other ...

You've seen gangs of mad March Hares a-boxing, but nothing beats this exotic dance-fight.

That's our British Bird of Paradise ... competing for the grey hens.

TAIL UP, HEAD DOWN: a Black Cock flaunting its courting finery.

And those 'leks', as these courting gatherings are called, would have been a familiar sight to foresters, cattle herders and wood cutters on St Leonard's and Worth Forests in medieval times, and to warreners of the 17th and 18th centuries.

As late as around 1840 a Mr Padwick of Horsham said that "his father shot as many as six brace in a morning at Combe Bottom, in St Leonard's Forest".[1] He must have been one of the last to see them in numbers. Looking back to the beginning of the 19th century the Rev. Edward Turner wrote of Ashdown Forest that "it was hardly possible to ride or walk about it in any direction without disturbing some of them", and we can be sure that it was the same at St Leonard's and Worth.

They were lost as a breeding species in all the Sussex forests in the 1850s, though stragglers were reported till about 1870.

Intensification of use exterminated the Black Grouse. At St Leonard's the waves of conversion to farmland in the 1800s and 1840s would have broken them, though the new planted woodlands may have given them temporary respite until the trees grew too thick and tall. At Worth Forest similar processes were at work.

Now, we have to yomp up to the far northern Pennines, moorland Wales or Scotland, if we want to see these birds.

Let us take the loss of this beautiful creature as an emblem for all that we have lost at St Leonard's and Worth Forests.

THE TRAGEDY OF OUR MID SUSSEX FORESTS

Many of us Sussex and London Line folk travel to Ashdown Forest, especially when we want to see the Heather and Gorse in bloom in high summer.

How many, though, would think of a trip to enjoy nature in St Leonard's or Worth Forests? ... *Only a sorry few* ... Yet those forests combined size equals that of Ashdown, and they directly neighbour the large towns of Crawley and Horsham.

Not that we *could* enjoy them as we do Ashdown nowadays, for the greatest part of them is fiercely private.

In the space of two hundred years their vast heathlands have been cut up and converted to poor quality farmland and dark conifer plantations. Their broad-leaved woodlands are being strangled by

The old forest: an outgrown Oak pollard

encroaching Rhododendron thickets. Everywhere there are high fenced, thick hedged, security gated mansions, villas, private gardens; and wired off, gated fishing ponds, pony ranches, golf courses, war gaming woodland and clay pigeon shoots; and game bird and deer shoots. This is a far, far cry from a countryside of wild nature, free and open to all. It has been asset stripped, super-exploited, neglected, re-exploited, enclosed, and re-enclosed for the benefit of the few.

IT WAS NOT ALWAYS SO

St Leonard's and Worth almost made it intact into modern times. They were the last surviving redoubts of near-natural landscape in mid Sussex. They made it right up to the time of the Tudor Queens Mary and Elizabeth, around 1560. We have missed their near-pristine wildness by just four and a half centuries ... not long in nature's lifespan.

Whilst the rest of the Weald was settled and assarted by Saxon folk, and their descendants under the Normans, the high, sandy ridges of Worth and St Leonard's were protected from such incursions by the Saxon micro-kingdoms of West, Middle, and East

Sussex, then by a united Sussex kingdom, and later by the kings of Wessex and the first kings of England. Their royalty valued these uplands for the hunt. Then, from the time of the Norman conquerors the ruling class had its own special venison based diet. These forests became their larders.

Woodland and open ground seem to have been in roughly equal proportions, at least in medieval times. There would have been a variety of woodland types, from vaulty tree-cathedrals of gigantic Beech and Oak, to light Birch and Hazel thickets, with Ash on the clays, and Alder fields on the boggy flats and gills. Large areas of dry and wet heath and grassy lawn, marsh, fen, bog and pool would have complemented them, dominating some ridges and flatlands, like Plummers Plain.

THE ANCIENT PEOPLES

Perhaps the large areas of open ground of the medieval forest were there much earlier, too. The **Mesolithic gatherer hunter people**, with their new bow, arrow, and microlith technology, have left their mark. Perhaps, indeed, it was them who were responsible for widening the primeval woodland glades into the open heaths and lawns of these sandy, easy-to-clear uplands. They seem to have played that role on the West Sussex heaths of the Rother Valley, at Iping and West Heath; on the greensands of the Brighton Line Weald; and more widely.[2] Their flint discards and lost microliths have been widely found across the forest ridges and on the surrounding Wealden Clay vales. Around the south eastern periphery of Worth Forest they used the sandrock outcrops to shelter their hunting camps. The first **farming peoples of the Neolithic,** who would also have been hunters, used those same sandrock shelters, and left their flint detritus and polished stone axes for us to find.

The **Bronze Age peoples** were certainly active in the two forests, and were probably responsible for much clearance, though their cropping would quickly have exhausted the thin soils and led to their retreat from intensive settlement into more sustainable pastoral exploitation. It could be for that reason that so few of their round barrows are to be found in the forests.

The **Money Mound**, northwest of Ashfold Crossways, was the best known round barrow, though no sign of it remains after its destructive excavation in 1961–2. It was sited on a ridge near an ancient east-west trackway, where the dazzling white silt used to cement its sandstone block construction would have made it doubly eye catching in an open, cleared landscape. It may well have been part of a barrow cluster, for earthen mounds were reported in the western adjoining field in modern times. It was used for the deposition of religious offerings in the Iron Age, and right through the Roman occupation, with 156 coins found (hence the name) covering a period from 69 AD right through to 388 AD, only a generation before the withdrawal of the legions.

There are two other known round barrows on the Black Hill ridge east of Colgate, again near an ancient east-west trackway.

For most of their routes these **ancient forest trackways** follow the watersheds between the headwaters of the five rivers which all cluster close together on these erstwhile royal forests. The ancient peoples chose those routes because they could keep dry shod on the high ground, and no doubt keep a good eye over the surrounding landscape.

The great majority of the lengths of these trackways are now motor roads. We drive our cars along the high ridges where for 10,000 years our ancestors walked either bare feet, or in clogs or leather-shod, alongside pony trains, perhaps on horse and donkey back, or beside rumbling ox wagons and sleds.

A **southern forest trackway** was the precursor to the modern east-west road which takes you all the way eastwards from Horsham along the forest ridge, and north across the Surrey clay vale to the North Downs. *It passes Mannings Heath onwards to Lower Beeding, then Handcross, along the High Street past the Cowdray Arms and Worth Abbey, then north from Turners Hill to Crawley Down and the Surrey border. From there you can still trace this watershed route – reduced to parish boundary, hedgeline and narrow lane – across the clay vale past Outwood Windmill and up onto the North Downs above Caterham.*

A **northern forest trackway** passes eastwards from Faygate to join the southern route at Whitely Hill, west of Worth Abbey. *It follows the Tower Road from Faygate to Colgate, then past Black Hill and Pease Pottage, along Parish Lane and the bridleway through Oldhouse Warren to Whitely Hill, by the Cowdray Arms.*

The course of the A23 London Road between Pease Pottage and Handcross also follows an ancient **north-south trackway** along the watershed between the upper Arun and Mole rivers.

THE MEDIEVAL FORESTS

In ecological terms,[3] the early forest district of medieval times (pre- and post-Norman Conquest) was of much greater extent than the later forests of the high middle ages (Chaucer's time) or the modern forests. Beyond the footprint of what later became the core parishes of Worth and Lower Beeding, the early medieval forest district would have encompassed large parts of Horsham and Nuthurst and parts of Cowfold, Slaugham, Crawley, Balcombe and Ardingly parishes. So scant was the extent of settlement in those early days, indeed, that Worth and Crawley received no direct mention in the Domesday Book of 1086. Not even Horsham or East Grinstead got in.

ST. LEONARD'S FOREST IN THE LATE MIDDLE AGES c. 1300–1500

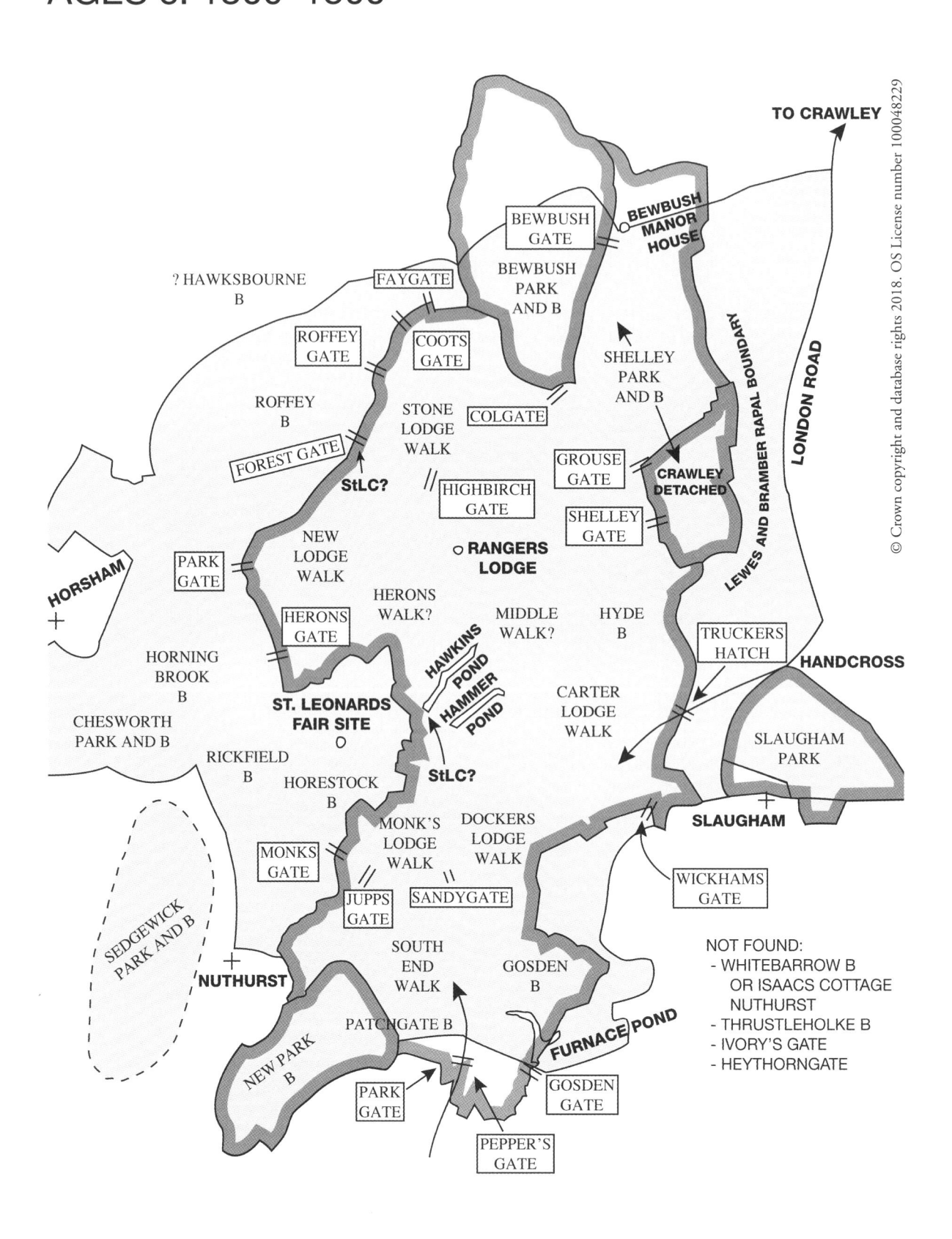

100 BACKSTORY / Chapter 6: The Forests of St Leonard's and Worth

We can reasonably guess that much of the still-wooded High Weald landscape north of the A272 between Cowfold and Bolney villages, north of Staplefield, and north of the infant Ouse as far east as Ardingly village, was ecologically similar to the core areas of hunting forest and chase.

On its northern side the forest district would likely have extended north of Horsham, and into Crawley's Bewbush district. Much of the bordering area of south Surrey, including Horley, Burstow, Copthorne, Felbridge and Hedgecourt, as far as Lingfield and East Grinstead may have been ecologically part of this forest district, too, although never incorporated in the formal forests.[4] In the time of the Saxon Kings of Sussex there may still have been Wolves and Wild Boar, as well as deer and lesser game to hunt.

The scanty records point to the main beasts of the post-Conquest forests being managed deer, cattle, swine, and horses. Horsham probably takes its name (meaning 'horse enclosure') from horse rearing in the forest district, and feral horses and ponies survived perhaps until the early 16th century. Cattle were traded at the big yearly fair of St Leonard's, which sold stock from as far afield as Wales.

The modern New Forest is the nearest we'll ever see to medieval Worth and St Leonard's, with wandering cattle and ponies half hidden in the ferny brakes, or tail-flicking the flies in Beech and Oaken summer shade.

Deer were still managed and harvested as the main purpose of St Leonard's and Worth until the mid 16th century, and they lingered on subsequently. It is probable that Roe, Red and introduced Fallow Deer were all conserved. Farmed swine exploited the pannage of Oak and Beech mast. Hare, Rabbit, Heron, Black Grouse, and Pheasant were no doubt taken by falcon, net and arrow, both in the forest and in its well-stocked purlieu parks.

FEUDAL PRESERVE, NOT COMMON

A dirty deal seems to have been done at the expense of the common people, probably early in Saxon Sussex. The High Wealden forests were partitioned between those managed primarily for royal hunting and those commoned by the peasantry. Ashdown was dedicated as the commoned forest. St Leonard's, Worth, and Waterdown (around present day Eridge Park) were dedicated primarily to the hunt and the preservation of game species.[5] Management for deer and other game still remained co-dominant at Ashdown, of course, but it existed alongside the legal rights of commoners to graze their cattle, horses and swine, take pannage of mast, and cut bracken, turf, and small wood.

In our twin forests, however, only limited rights of common were tolerated. Other manorial lords and proprietors were sold rights by the lords of the forests to pasturage and pannage for their stock on a long term basis. These were not legal rights of common, however, and quite unlike the rights of common which existed for all district tenants on the Wealden Kentish commons.[6]

We can see in this lack of common rights one reason why so little of the separate identity of Worth and St Leonard's survives today. It is not the only reason, of course, for most forests, heaths and pastures that *were* heavily commoned have also long been lost to enclosure. We cannot avoid the reality, however, that our sister Forest of Ashdown survived in great part because of the centuries of fierce resistance by its commoners to enclosure.

Only those parts of our twin forests in settled areas of the purlieu parishes away from the forest core had common rights attached to them. Thus, Horsham Common's usage separated very early from the adjoining hunting forest, and the same must have been true for Crawley Down and the commons along the Surrey-Sussex border, like Copthorne and Frog Wood. Balcombe Down, though, was not commoned, being desmesne (lordly) land. Its centuries-long usage as wood pasture – into modern times – accounts for its extraordinary surviving assemblage of giant pollard oak and beech veterans, lopped in the same way as the commoners of Epping Forest and the New Forest managed their pollards.

To this day the relics of this division between purlieu forest commons and core hunting forest survives in the scatter of commons fragments circling Worth and St Leonard's … Staplefield Common; Slaugham Common and Green; Ifield Wood Common; and the post-enclosure fragments of Mannings Heath recreation ground; Copthorne Common and Frogbit Heath.

St. Leonard's Forest in the late Middle Ages
The 3 ponds are late 16th century, and are included only as landmarks.

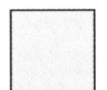

☐	Probable semi-natural forest & park vegetation: lawn, heath, covert & high forest
▣	Lower Beeding parish boundary, which was the likely Forest boundary, as well as the boundaries of Bewbush, Shelley, Slaugham, and New Parks
GATE	Gates and hatches of the Forest and its Bailiwicks, Wards and Walks
WALK	Forest 'Walks' in 1720. (Walks were management areas)
B	Bailiwicks (Also management areas – approximate locations)
StLC?	Two possible sites of St Leonard's Chapel
+	Medieval parish churches

CARVING UP THE LOOT

It is likely that the twin forests were managed as one under the united Sussex kingdom and the Wessex kings, but in later Saxon times Sussex was sub-divided up into north-south slices called 'rapes', which the Normans adopted and reshaped.[7] As a result, the huge unitary forest stretching from Horsham to East Grinstead was divided into western (St Leonards) and eastern (Worth) halves along the boundary between the rapes of Bramber and Lewes. Their Norman overlords were respectively the de Braose family, and the de Warenne family, both based at the castles of those places.

The feudal Bishops of Chichester had their share of the loot, too. They exercised hunting privileges over the district roughly south of Leonardslee's Furnace Pond, including eastern Cowfold and western Bolney parishes, as far south as the River Adur at Wyndham Bridge in Twineham. This was an area with much settled farmland. Their hunting 'forest' went by the name of Gosden Chase.

If you've been confused by the medley of 'forest' names that appear on the map where Worth Forest is – *Tilgate, Highbeeches, Brantridge, Balcombe, Monks, Cowdray, Worthlodge* – don't blame it on the Ordnance Survey. Blame it on all the greedy grabbing feudal and modern landlords. Worth was first divided three ways on the failure of the male de Warenne line in 1439. One of the three portions was later divided into two (and that's where the name Tilgate Forest comes in). In later centuries the rest was chopped up, sold, re-sold … and re-named.

THE FIRST GREAT DISASTER: PILLAGING THE WOODS

Two linked events in the middle of the 16th century brought the catastrophic destruction of the old high forest and thick 'covert' underwood managed for the wellbeing of the deer.

The first was the steep expansion of the iron industry in the Weald, using the vastly more efficient blast furnace technology. It guzzled as much as 100 times more wood fuel than the old methods.[8] The combined charcoal consumption of a blast furnace and secondary finery forge utilised about 4000 acres of coppice over a 15 year cycle. The new technology also needed new ponds and dams for a constant water supply, new roads and tracks, and a new scale of ore quarrying out on the forest plains and gill sides. By the 1570s there were two forges and furnaces in St Leonard's and 12 more within a ten mile radius. In Worth Forest the situation was the same at the height of the industry, with eight furnaces and forges within the old forest boundaries and many more within an 8 mile radius.

The second event was the reversion of St Leonard's Forest to the crown in 1562–3, which placed its administration with the Exchequer, and laid it open to the demands of courtiers and the iron masters for timber and wood.

Within a few years the woods were in dire trouble. Huge grants of timber were ceded without any regard to the long term sustainability of the resource. The wood and timber was taken at the convenience of the extractors, not where it made good forestry sense. The random extraction threatened the remaining trees and damaged the undergrowth. The keepers and rangers of the forest protested vigorously,[9] but the warrants for timber continued to be granted.

We know of one local hero – Roger Taverner, the Deputy Surveyor of Woods – who kept up "a long and eventually unsuccessful campaign" for perhaps 35 years or more "to preserve the southern landscape".[10] Around 1570 he produced a well-reasoned assessment of the resource after making a survey. His assessment gives a last glimpse of the old forest at the point of its passing. The trees grew in *"plumps"* together, preserved from overthrow *"by reason that the uttermost trees of the said plumps defend the wyndes from the innermost and the innermost trees growing thick do keep the uttermost from falling, by their nigh standing with them."* The forest was well supplied with desirable timber, especially Oak and Beech *"of a very great age and of a great length"*. One is reminded of 'old growth' forest, or the tall, straight boles of mature Sessile Oak. Taverner argued that if proper forestry methods could be enforced a continual supply of 500 loads a year for 100 years would ensure timber suitable for the navy and woodfuel for the iron furnaces.

Maybe Taverner's recommendations checked the flow of warrants for extraction for a while.[11] It did not last though. Wood fuel prices tripled between 1562 and 1591, and all of Taverner's action against the local timber predators did not stop the abuses and the supply of warrants for extraction. When a commission of inquiry was finally held in 1599 it was found that from 1579–98 some 75,016.5 cords of wood had been cut, leaving only 696 cords standing. The forest had been emptied of timber.

Though the production of coppice wood had stabilised by the 1650s, it was at half the level that Taverner had said would be sustainable if his plan had been acted upon … and by then the forest was a much diminished place.

The same pillage must have been happening in Worth Forest, too, but in 1560 it suffered an even greater trauma, for Queen Elizabeth authorised a great enclosing of the southern, eastern and northern parts of the forest. "This tract of upland waste", Peter Brandon wrote, "was enclosed and carved up into about 35 farms … amongst the very last to be won from heath and wood by small yeoman farmers".[12]

RABBITS AND BONNY BLOOMING HEATHER

For most of the 17th and 18th centuries the twin forests were dominated by heath, with some surviving woodlands, perhaps especially in the gills, and scatters, perhaps, of oak and beech pollard wood pasture. Most of the forests were managed for rabbit production in large warrens. Though there were various attempts at farming they came to little, and many of the small farms carved out in St Leonard's in the later 16th and early 17th centuries reverted to heath.

Worth Forest was covered with warrens – *Snashalls, Highbeech, Oldhouse, and, to the south east, Balcombe Warren and Wakehurst Warren (in what is now called Paddockhurst Park)*. Between Tilgate Forest Lodge and High Wood, long, almost parallel straight lines on the heath marked by heavy heather growth may signify possible 'pillow mounds'. The dense conifers of Worthlodge Forest and Oldhouse Warren hide better preserved old pillow mounds which the warreners constructed to shelter the tender bunnies, complete with ready-to-use dug out burrows. Some of these mounds are very large and elongated structures, like whale backs, ditched around, which you can pick your way along for good distances amongst the trees. Rabbits, for many centuries after their Norman introduction, were without the hardiness of their modern descendants, and needed the cosseting of artificial 'burys' to breed successfully. Only in the 18th century do they appear to have at last evolved the toughness to expand unaided to the plague proportions of Victorian, pre-myxamotosis times.

Around 1800, the centre of St Leonard's was dominated by two warrens, covering 3000 acres! Great Warren stretched for 2.5 miles south from Colgate to Hammerpond Lane. Warren Wood takes its name from it. Plummers Plain Warren stretched south from there. A further warren centring on present-day Holmbush Forest covered 1598 acres, and contained about 12,000 rabbits managed by several warreners. Its lodge perhaps stood on the site of the present day castellated Holmbush House. Pillow mounds do not seem to have been made in St Leonard's in the same numbers that are found at Worth, though the Forestry Commission Estate hides a number of them and there was one east of Colgate. The heath was fired periodically to encourage a fresh 'bite' of lawn growth for the rabbits.

"In 1794, St Leonard's Forest was said to yield only rabbits, which were sent to London in large numbers."[13] It was still good for British birds of paradise, too …

St Leonards Forest: the purple blooming heather, the Cotton Sedge, the ancient trees are lost to maize, hay and conifers.

THE SECOND GREAT DISASTER: DESTROYING THE HEATHS

From about 1800, three linked processes kicked in, which in combination destroyed the landscape of heaths that were the main surviving component of the medieval forest.

The first was clearance for poor quality farming. The 3000 acres of warren in the centre of St Leonard's were parcelled up and let, part-ploughed and cropped, in a campaign covering the first decade of the century. This was only partially successful, and much of this land reverted to heath as peace time corn prices fell after the Napoleonic wars. A second enclosure drive ensued in the 1840s, probably this time with under-drainage. New farmsteads and cottages were built, and a pattern of small fields and fence-lines created. This campaign transformed Plummers Plain, as well as the dissected plateau where the Great Warren had been, south of Colgate. Later improvements spread across the south and west of the forest, and consolidated the progress made earlier in Bewbush. By 1875, over 2000 acres of arable and 1259 acres of permanent grass had been won from the poor forest soils.[14]

In Worth, the Tilgate Forest land east of Pease Pottage along Parish Lane, to the south, and north to Tilgate Lodge, began to be cleared around 1800. By 1875 the slopes were cleared right down to Stanford Brook, and a horrible pattern of geometrical circular clearances had been made in the rest of Tilgate Forest – like a child's arbitrary doodling with a compass.

The second process was a huge afforestation, which seems as much driven by landlordly whim as by the needs of timber and wood supply. At St Leonard's much of the Buchan Hill and Holmbush estates were planted up. All the Hammer Hill slopes south of Carter's Lodge

THE FORESTS' COUP DE GRACE

WORTH FOREST'S SSSI

In 1954 the Nature Conservancy Council designated large areas of St Leonard's Forest and Worth Forest as SSSIs (Sites of Special Scientific Interest). These were the last major areas with surviving semi-natural broad-leaved pasture woodland, heath and moor. When these designations were reviewed in 1987 the NCC deleted most of those areas. The St Leonard's Forest SSSI's western areas had suffered extensive damage to their high forest and wood pastures by the Forestry Commission's coniferisation, and the eastern areas were damaged by modernising farmers and coniferising landowners. Worth Forest's SSSI was drastically damaged by coniferisation.

Worth Forest 1954 SSSI 423a / 171ha

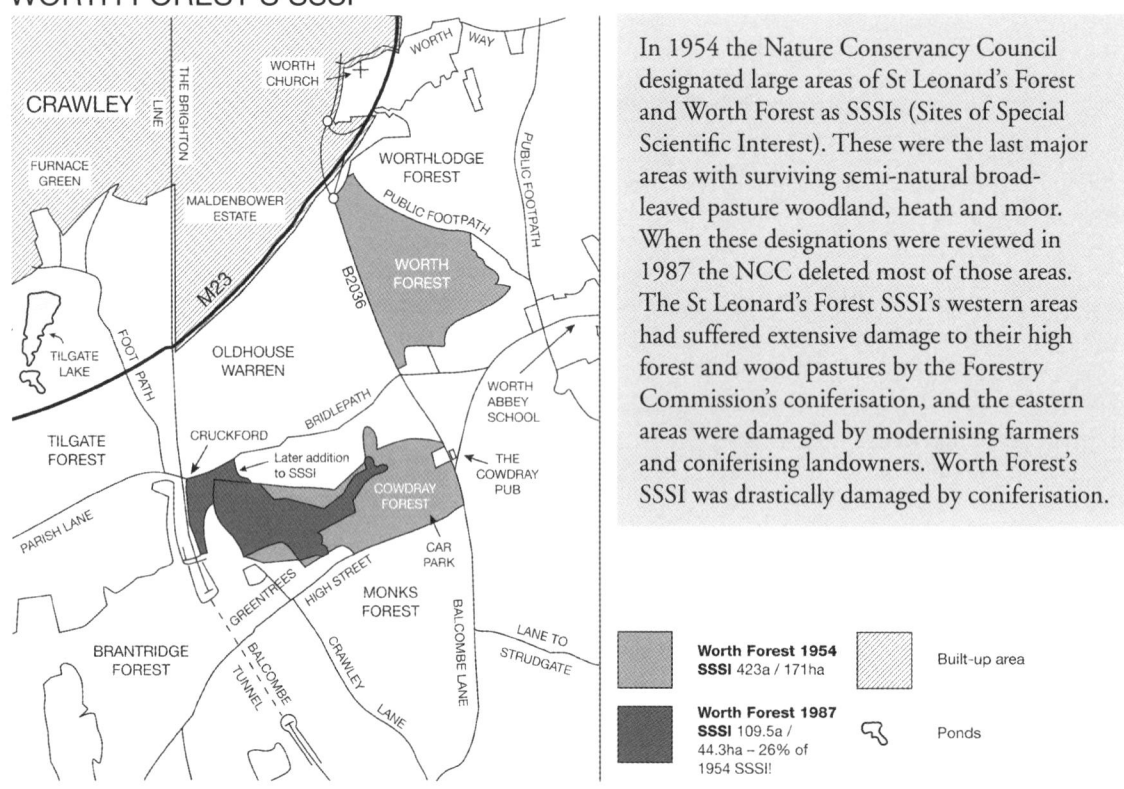

Worth Forest 1987 SSSI 109.5a / 44.3ha – 26% of 1954 SSSI!

Built-up area

Ponds

ST LEONARD'S FOREST'S SSSI

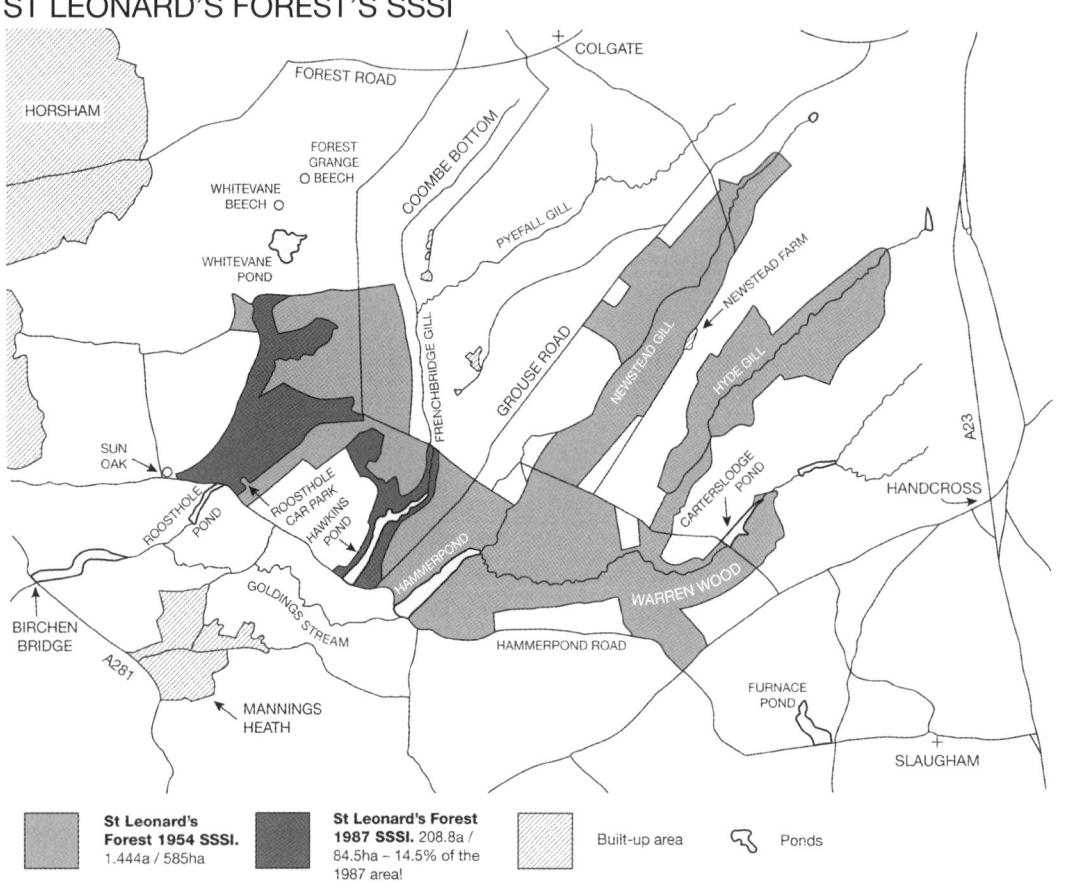

St Leonard's Forest 1954 SSSI. 1,444a / 585ha

St Leonard's Forest 1987 SSSI. 208.8a / 84.5ha – 14.5% of the 1987 area!

Built-up area

Ponds

104 BACKSTORY / Chapter 6: The Forests of St Leonard's and Worth

Gill, including Warren Wood and the ground around Hawkins and Hammer Ponds, were planted, as was much of the western forest around St Leonard's Park. The southern Forest between Lower Beeding village and Crabtree was also afforested.

In Worth Forest all the old warrens were planted, and by the time of the First Edition O/S map in 1875 the only substantial open areas of heath are shown on Balcombe Down, east of the Balcombe Tunnel. More heath must have survived than that, however, and in 1907 one writer[15] described "considerable heathland, beautiful though barren, as at Copthorne Common, Oldhouse Warren, and High Beeches Warren".

The third process was a massive gentrification of the landscape, as London profiteers spilled out onto these romantic uplands to realise their daft feudal fantasies. The process began in earnest around 1800, but was further ratchetted up by the coming of the Brighton Line. Bonkers mansion after bonkers mansion was built, and parks and ornamental gardens carved out. The list is huge. At St Leonard's we have had *Holmbush, Hollywood/Roffey Park, Buchan Hill (now Cottesmore School), Woodhurst, The Hyde, Coombe Wood, Forest Grange, St Leonard's Park, South Lodge, Leonardslee, Selehurst, Newells, Broadfield, Beedingwood, Beedinglee, Coolhurst, Ashfold, and a range of lesser imitations*. At Worth we have had *Tilgate, Handcross Park, Tilgate Forest Lodge, Nymans, Dencombe, High Beeches, Brantridge, Ditton Place, Paddockhurst, Crabbet Park, Worth Park, and Worth Hall.*

Their owners manicured, planted, sprayed, re-seeded, 'improved', neglected, and cultivated ad nauseum, decimating the archaic habitat as they went.

By 1909 only 281 acres of old heathland were left in St Leonard's … maybe less in Worth Forest.

MOPPING UP OPERATIONS

"Until the last century (and, indeed, in some parts as late as 1945 or 1950)" St Leonard's and Worth Forests were "one of the finest and most extensive ancient pasture-woodlands in England, outside the New Forest." So said the dynamic botanist Francis Rose, in 1991.[16] In 1954, the Nature Conservancy Council designated large southern areas of St Leonard's Forest as SSSI (Site of Special Scientific Interest) for their 'high forest' and heathland vegetation. Smaller parts of Worth Forest were designated, too.

It did not stop the process of attrition. Those last surviving St Leonard's heaths – on the slopes of Newstead Farm ridge – have been gone for perhaps fifty years now, (bar one fragment at The Steep) and ruthless coniferisation by the Forestry Commission and the Paddockhurst estate in the 1950s and '60s, eliminated all but postage-stamp-sized fragments of the extensive old Oak-Beech wood pasture around Scragged Oak Hill in St Leonard's, and eliminated the last Beech Fern population in our twin forests, which had clung on in Worth Forest.[17]

JUST MISSED …

The plants and small creatures that *almost* made it into our time make a tragic list.

In the 1930s **Juniper, Marsh Gentian,** and **Bog Asphodel** were still present in a number of places in both forests. **Small White Orchis** was still in St Leonard's then, according to Wolley-Dod,[18] as was **Heath Dog Violet. Crowberry** disappeared from there in the 19th century. **Royal Fern** is gone as a native species, killed off by habitat loss and fern collectors. The tiny grass-like **Pillwort** fern, disappeared from its last Worth Forest site in 1986, and was last seen at St Leonard's in, I think, the 1970s. Though the club-mosses have survived since the primeval Carboniferous swamps they didn't make it into our time on the forests (though Stag's-horn Club-moss was present recently at Leonardslee). In Victorian times three species – **Fir, Stag's-horn** and **Marsh Club-mosses** – were in St Leonard's and grew together at Starvemouse Plain, Tilgate. **Oblong-leaved Sundew** was present in both forests in Victorian times. Plants like **Intermediate Wintergreen** made it through till late Victorian times in St Leonard's, and **Yellow Centaury** was present at one site in St Leonard's and one in Worth Forest till a generation ago.

"By every account",[19] we are told, "Tilgate Forest was a legendary place for entomologists, and the chance of obtaining fabled insects enticed all of the great national collectors of the day … The heath", after the coming of the railway, "was undoubtedly then the foremost for lepidoptera in Sussex, and its destruction was another great tragedy". The **Kentish Glory** moth was the most sought after. It "flew commonly over the heather – occasionally in many hundreds". **High Brown** and **Marsh Fritillaries** and **Wood White** butterflies, with **Scarce Dagger, Purple-bordered Gold, Orange Upperwing, Anomalous, Small Grass Emerald, Dingy Mocha** and **Cloaked Pug** moths all flew there.

"St Leonard's was one of the last havens for **White-spotted Pinion** moth" and "**Kentish Glory, Alder Kitten** and **Purple-bordered Gold** there attracted many collectors during the final quarter of the 19th century … **Silver-studded Blue** butterfly just swarmed."

SO WHAT'S LEFT?

Exploring the Worth Forest woodlands south of Copthorne one September afternoon in 2009, I made my way through Bramble tangles to look at a fine veteran Beech pollard that had caught my eye on an earlier walk. I did not expect to do much more than pay my respects to this Methuselah. It had something to honour me with, though, for on its wide roots a huge and placid longhorn beetle waited. Though I had

The Sun Oak – brimming with health, though it was already a fine tree in Chaucer's time

never before seen this beast I knew straightway what it was, for it exceeded the Stag Beetle in size, though without its giant mandibles. It was a Tanner Longhorn, *Prionus coriarius*, and proved to be the first record for this old forest species in East Sussex for a hundred years! Its message for me was that these forests still, despite the 450 year onslaught upon them, have wonders and beauties to offer us and that they plead to us to fight for and defend.

Earlier that season, in late spring, we picked our way noisily across rotting pine brash and Purple Moor-grass tussocks in the Forestry Commission's St Leonard's woods not so far from the Lily Beds. We found a dryish spot to sit and have our picnic … and there, as we fussed and scuffed a decent place to sit, a brown Mistle Thrush sized bird lost patience with us and broke cover … up and away … a **Nightjar!** … the first I had seen in St Leonard's.

One midsummer dawn this year (2018) I switched off the car engine after parking on a forest lane long before sunrise, and through the open window a churring sound reached me across the ground mist covering the dewey wooded plain. That Nightjar's churring proved to come from over half a mile away! When I reached the bird, in the lower branches of a Scots Pine, its churring made such a din that if it had been outside my flat window I would have notified Environmental Health!!

There are Nightjars now in Owlbeech Woods, Buchan Hill, Brantridge and Highbeeches Forests, as well as St Leonard's Forestry Commission Estate[20] … The work of heathland restoration is bearing fruit.

The twin forests are special still.

They are special for their giant trees. Much more of the heritage of wood pasture still exists than is publicly or officially known, for most of its survivals are without formal public access; often hidden and in deep decline, for lack of life-preserving management.

Many folk will know the veteran beech glades of the Forestry Commission's woods, north of Roosthole car park. They are gorgeous, but they are not the finest survivors.

Some giants live in solitude, like the **Sun Oak,** which dates back to before Magna Carta, or the gnarled **Whitevane Beech,** amongst the drive-side Rhododendrons north of Whitevane Pond. But mostly the giant trees survive in ancient woods.

In Worth Forest, to the west and to the east of Balcombe Tunnel (in Monks Forest, at Greentrees and Cowdray Forest, across all of Oldhouse Warren and along upper Stanford Brook) is a fantastic assemblage of ancient Beech and Oak veteran trees, mostly pollards. I've noted 220 of them there, but there are more than that, for sure. There are giant five span Beech (over 30 feet in girth) and others of four span and more. Some must date back to the din of furnace hammers pounding, thumping, and drifting charcoal smoke above the canopy. Honeybees and Hornets nest in their holes. Woodpeckers and Nuthatches stack their 'apartments' one above the other, with Jackdaws at the top. Giant *Ganoderma* bracket fungi dust all the boles and roots and neighbour greenery in rust red spores.

In Coombe Bottom, St Leonard's, there are huge old beech pollards that once sheltered the Black Cock from off the heath in winter snows. At Paddockhurst (medieval Wakehurst Park) the giants cluster round the sandrock outcrops, across picturesque valley sides and plateau, and along ancient boundary banks. In Dabson's Gill, at The Hyde, and in Bashford Wood, the giants live.

Treebeard, the Ents, are living still.[21] They need our help again.

The twin forests are special for their ancient woods. In early April, the Wild Daffodils bloom in drifts across the bare woodland floor west of Balcombe Tunnel; around The Hyde and its west-flowing gills west of Handcross; and in Cowdray Forest too. There's Yaffle (Green Woodpecker) calling … and Nuthatch … and streamside mosses and liverworts still glistening bright with green life.

The banks of long gone Cruckford Furnace's broken pond bay are draped in hyacinth-scented Bluebells over a rubble of iron slag. They carpet too the slopes of Stanford Brook. Kingcups decorate the squelchy flats along the waterside. There's Orpine on the banks and foetid Blackcurrant. Marsh Tits feed amongst the broken Sallows, and Palmate Newts rest in flooded vehicle ruts. There's May and Rowan blossom, Wood Sorrel, Primrose, and gorgeous ferns – Broad Buckler, Hard, Scaly Male, Male, Lady, Soft Shield and Bracken. Everything bursts with life.

In Worthlodge Forest the Crab Apple is in glorious pinky white blossom. There's Windflower (Wood Anemone) and Wood Sorrel, Bluebell and Wood Spurge. Pignut swarms where a Grinstead Clay band outcrops. There's much Bilberry too. A Willow Warbler sings his heart out in plain view. I hear a Sparrowhawk yikkering long away through the Oaks. On a flooded slough not far from where the last Beech Fern throng once grew I see something very special … tiny candles glowing … yes, they have a kind of daytime luminosity … little white wax matches with glowing sun-yellow heads. These are Bog Beacons, *Mitrula paludosa* … the nearest I'll ever see to a will o'the wisp, marsh fire.

The huge Tanner Longhorn Beetle brought me a message…

A formidable nation of tiny folk is on the march along the edge of a bare sandy track partially shaded by overhanging heather in a glade amongst the woods of Buchan Country Park. The column of red-and-black Wood Ants, *Formica rufa*, hurries uphill many abreast, whilst their returning sisters teem downhill alongside. I follow the column, taking care not to disturb them. I keep walking … and walking … and still I do not reach the end point of their column … till it finally disappears amongst the trees and deeper heather, no doubt where the ant workers scamper up the trunks to milk their flocks of aphids for their honey-dew. You will find their wonderful domed thatched nests, two or three feet tall (and perhaps nine feet deep underground) in sunny parts of woods in St Leonards, Tilgate and Brantridge Forests; on Balcombe Down west of the Balcombe Tunnel; and in west Paddockhurst Park and The Warren, south of Worth Abbey. They live in 'nations' of several hundred thousands, each with many 'queens' who live long lives (sometimes as long as dogs or cats) in many federated ant 'castles' with populations of perhaps 50,000 each, surviving harsh winters and hot summers and foraging widely.[22]

The forests are special for their deep wooded gills. On a sunny day in late March we sprawl flat on the bank of Frenchman's Gill. The cool water is still, clean and clear. On the silt bottom some things are moving. Here, tiny 'sleeping bags', each made of micro-pieces of dead black leaf stuck together, are shifting slowly. Minute arms and the top of a tiny head are reaching forward from the front end of each sleeping bag, and pulling it forward. There, tiny tubes 1.5cm long made of multi-coloured dead leaf crazy-paving are on the move too … and over there, funny little tubes made of sand grains, curved like cow horns. The youth of three species of caddis fly are showing off their art and craft skills.

The forests are special for their open places: relict heath and lawn, and lush woodland ride. At Buchan

Curiously cleft ancient Beech pollard, Balcombe Down

Country Park, on the Forestry Commission's St Leonard's land, at Leonardslee deer park, and on rides, path sides and glades, the heathers bloom still.

On a hot afternoon in early September, we walk a rutted ride in Worth Forest amongst Moor-grass tussocks, bare mineral soil and short lawn. Tiny creeping flowers catch my eye. You need to kneel and peer through magnifying glass to see their beauty. Bog Pimpernel, and, even smaller Ivy-leaved Bellflower – sky blue. There's Trailing St John's-wort and starry Tormentil and Eyebright, Centaury and Dwarf Gorse too. Groundhoppers ping about. Jane beckons me over. She points. On a log a tiny tailess lizard lies, very dark. I see another, with a tail this time. We count a family of six baby lizards, basking together in the warmth.

On Greenbroom Hill, the Ling Heather grows tall, now. The Wood Ant workers stream out busily on all sides. This is not a place to picnic … but there, on the path is another creature … a tiny beetle, black-violet, with dainty white stripes and yellow-brown middle. It is an Ant Beetle, *Thanasimus formicarius*, running with the Wood Ants. Like the ants, they hunt, but for other tiny beetles, not for all-that-moves, as the ants do.

The forests are special for their dragons. Not the dragons of daft old stories, but real miniature 'dragons' whirring like helicopters across hot summer pond and mire. The northern edge of St Leonard's right into Crawley, and the valleys of the west, the middle and the south have many ponds, some very fine for dragonflies and damsels. The forest is a stronghold for them.

At Island Pond on the edge of Buchan Country Park conditions are perfect for them. There are weedy shallows, Bog-moss, *Sphagnum* mats, Bulrush, Marsh Bedstraw, Marsh St John's Wort and Marsh Pennywort. In July, mating Damsels dance in tandem. There are Emperors, Emeralds, and Four-spot Chasers whirring on patrol, checking, attacking, hovering.

Golden-ringed Dragonfly can be found in some of the St Leonard's south eastern valleys, and the twin forests have both Downy and Brilliant Emeralds, Common, Ruddy and Black Darters, and Black-tailed Skimmer.

The twin forests still have a distinct flora. Many characteristic species cluster there. The most famous of them is undoubtedly Lily of the Valley, and the Lily Beds of St Leonard's Forest have survived the depredations of the early decades of Forestry Commission management, and are now valued as they deserve to be. There's the Daffodil Forest (see chapter 14). Characteristic heathy species like Bilberry, Cross-leaved and Bell Heathers, Dwarf Gorse, Heath Milkwort and Harebell still cluster there, as do some scarce sedges. The diminutive Allseed, Chaffweed, and Bird's Foot (*not* the same as Bird's-foot Trefoil) may survive around Crawley and Tilgate Forest.

Bog Pondweed and damp loving plants like Water Purslane, Marsh Pennywort, Marsh Violet, Lesser Skullcap and Lemon Scented Fern, have quite distinctive geographical strongholds on the mid Sussex forests.

The twin forests are the best district I know for fungi in mid Sussex. It's got a lot to do with the kinds of trees. Mature Beech, and masses of Birch and Pine are all characteristic of the forests, and all three trees have the richest gill fungi assemblages we will normally find.

Sometimes the displays are spectacular. There is glistening Porcelain Fungus erupting from an old Beech's lightning struck bough. Amongst the carpet of leaves under its broad canopy we find tawny orange *Russulas* – the Geranium Brittlegill – and smell their apple-saucy fragrance. Other Brittlegills, too … the domes of Green Cracked Brittlegill, *Russula virescens*; flattened looking Hedgehog Fungus with spines instead of gills; Bay Bolete; Beechwood Sickener, looking all gorgeous and not at all sickening; White Saddle fungus looking all gnarled and witchy. By a steep sided stream, too small to be called a gill, there is an orange trail of Chanterelles growing from the mossy bank. We have a cup of tea under a beech and avoid sitting on the lovely Scarletina Bolete, with its lipstick red stem and pores.

On some steep slope covered in leaf mould we find a big troop of Fleecy Milkcap, each cap spanning a good six inches. There is Panthercap and False Deathcap everywhere amongst the light fern, Blusher too, Charcoal Brittlegill and all the old favourites … Purple Stocking Webcap all slimy and showy.

There are always surprises … always new things … little carpets of Wavy Capped Chanterelles … Parasitic Boletes piggy-backing Earthballs … troops of Dog

Stinkhorn and their tiny 'witch's egg' beginnings, big Purple Webcaps the size of plates.

The fungi of the fragments of surviving lawn and heath are the best too, though we have to look in forest churchyards and rides to find them. Only there are the conditions that they need mimicked. Instead of forest ponies we now have lawnmowers. Some forest churchyards are the richest for old grassland fungi in Sussex.

A PLEDGE

Let's neglect our twin forests no longer. Let's work to end the ruling class privilege which has dogged them for long over a thousand years. Let's pledge to make these erstwhile royal forests into people's forests.

Let's re-make that pledge every time we look through the train windows and glimpse the Oaks, the Bracken, the Bluebells, the Spruce and the Larch, as we speed by.

ENDNOTES

1. The Victoria County History of Sussex, Volume 1, Item 201.
2. See the excellent summary in: 'Holocene geoarchaeology and palaeo-environment; setting the scene', by Michael J Allen. Pages 5–20 of 'Archaeology of the Ouse Valley, Sussex, to AD 1500', Edited by Dudley Moore, Michael J Allen, and David Rudling, Archaeopress Archaeology (2016).
3. That is, in terms of their semi-natural vegetation cover. I see the medieval forest district as being characterised by a matrix of large, relatively lightly exploited woodlands, and open habitats, such as moor, mire and heath.
4. 'Horsham History', Vol. 1, page 59. Jeremy Knight. *A very readable mine of information.* These forests were more accurately called **'chases'**, in legal terms. **'Forests'** were areas that were royally owned and subject to forest law, whereas St Leonard's and Worth were mostly owned by feudal magnates after the Norman conquest, though St Leonard's, at least, was in its later history subject to forest law. We call them forests, now, because that is how they are commonly understood.
5. Heather Warne, pers comm.
6. Victoria County History of Sussex, Volume 6, Part 3, Lower Beeding, page 13–14. *This is a superb account.*
7. 'The Place Names of Sussex', pages 8–10, by A Mawer & FM Stenton, English Place Name Society (reprinted 2001).
8. 'The Wealden Iron Industry', by Jeremy Hodgkinson, History Press (2008). *A comprehensive introduction to the subject.*
9. 'Ecological destruction in the 16th century. The case of St Leonard's Forest', by Sybil M Jack. Sussex Archaeological Collections Vol. 133 (1995), page 241–7. *A superb and passionately argued account.*
10. Ibid.
11. Ibid.
12. 'The Sussex Landscape', by Peter Brandon, page 162. 'The Making of the English Landscape series'. Hodder and Stoughton (1974). Brandon listed Frog's Hole Farm (now converted into a nice pub on the Maidenbower estate, Crawley), Gibbshaven and Sandhill Farms (near Crawley Down), Standinghall Farm (sunk in the woods of Worthlodge Forest), and Spicers and Naylands Farms (looking south over the Ouse valley) as originating " in this spread of fields across the woodland glades and heaths". However, Heather Warne has argued convincingly (pers comm.) that these farms were NOT part of this 1560 enclosure, and that they had long been in existence at that time.
13. Quote from VCH, Vol 6, Part 3, Lower Beeding, page 15.
14. Ibid.
15. Heneage Legge, W., 1907. Forestry. In Page, W., (Ed.) VCH, Vol 2, pages 291–325. Quoted in Pratt (below – footnote xii)
16. 'The Habitats and Vegetation of Sussex', Francis Rose. From 'Atlas of Sussex Mosses, Liverworts and Lichen', by Rose, Stern, Matcham and Coppins (1991). The Booth Museum of Natural History.
17. Though the loss of the Beech Fern is also attributed to the clearance of the shade bearing gill woodland trees around it and the subsequent growth of Bramble.
18. 'The Flora of Sussex', Lieut. Colonel A. E. Wolley-Dod. (1937). *Most of my old records come from that superb Flora.*
19. 'A Complete History of the Butterflies and Moths of Sussex', Vol. 1, page 92. Colin R. Pratt. (2011). *A wonderful three volume masterpiece.*
20. There are Nightjars, too, on Red House, Pound, and Memorial Commons, which are all part of Chailey Common … and they are likely to be heard elsewhere, too, on those commons and in the Brighton Line Weald.
21. JRR Tolkien's tree people, who looked like gnarled veteran trees, in his Middle Earth fantasies.
22. 'The Ant World', by Derek Ragge Morley, Penguin Books (first published 1953). A superb read which will make you see ants with huge respect, not as useless pests.

THE RIVER ADUR CATCHMENT / THE SUSSEX OUSE CATCHMENT

CHAPTER 7
Rivers, streams, ponds and waterlands

RIVER MONSTERS

"We had a trout for supper, two feet two inches long from eye to fork, and six inches broad; it weighed ten and a half pounds. It was caught in the Albourne brook, near Trussell[1] House." Thus wrote Thomas Marchant, farmer, in the journal[2] he started in 1714. I know that stretch of stream: narrow, cutting low and overhung with herbage. It looks more like a ditch than a stream. How could a monster like that have been found there?

The Stanmer Saxon Charter of 765 AD lists **'Fish Wood'** (*'fischyrste'*), probably referring to the area south of Wivelsfield Green, a fragment of which survives in Lambourne Wood, hugging the tiny River Lambourne, TQ 356 186 – which is the smallest of streams. Lovely though it is, it seems incredible that the Saxons named it for its fish! You might as well call the Sahara 'Frog Land'.

South east of Barn's Green, Itchingfield, the Parson's Brook divides at Parson's Bridge and its lesser arm wanders east across the fields to disappear near Dogbarking House. Before it does though, it passes by **Trout Cottage** and under **Trout Lane**. Yet the stream is little more than a ditch, even in a wet autumn. Could it have been larger in the past, or are Trout plain suicidal?

Draining into a tributary of the Ouse, there's a tiny stream cut into a cleft that shrinks in hot summers to warm and often cloudy pools – big puddles, really – with only a trickle of running water between a few of them. One winter, after the rains had brought strength back to the stream, Sam[3] came upon two **Sea Trout** giants, so big that their backs rose out of the water. So big indeed that their length was greater than the little stream's width, and he worried that they wouldn't be able to turn in that narrow place, and when they did they had to wiggle and twist their muscle bound bodies. They had come to these shallows to nest and spawn.

Sam's story made me reconsider. Those tiny brooks I had dismissed as far too shrunken for these red and black speckled submarines may still be suitable, or nearly so, for hen and cock Trout nursery specifications – if pollution, water extraction, soil run off, weirs and other barriers do not spoil them.

One watcher always knows when the Sea Trout have returned to spawn in the stream that runs by her cottage, for her dogs bark in the night, alerted by the splashing of the Trout in their courting games and rivalries.

You may spot the Trout nests[4] in the riffles – the shallow gravelly areas – in the month before Christmas (but if you do spot them do NOT touch or tread on them, for that will cause damage). The 'redds' (nests) will show as mounds of clean, newly disturbed gravel, which might even rise proud of the surface as the spate water recedes. They can be as small as 20 inches across, but larger fish may make them much larger – and several hens can make a communal redd. Sometimes you may come across abandoned attempts, which just show as scrapes. The hen fish makes the redd by fanning the gravel rapidly with her tail to make a hollow depression. With the cock fish alongside her in the hollow, rubbing his flank against her, she lays her eggs and he releases a cloud of sperm just upstream. The hen then excavates further gravel to mound up over the eggs, which are buried up to four inches deep, to hatch some two to three months later.

The Sea Trout in the Rivers Ouse and Adur are larger and spawn over a month later than most other populations. Their numbers are small and vulnerable, though there are more of them than in any other river between Southampton and Whitby in Yorkshire.

I was tipped off by Sue that the Sea Trout were running the weir. She casually mentioned that they had seen a couple of 'Salmon' jumping when they had been picnicking there. I went at dusk … and saw nothing. I went again at dusk a few days later. I stood for half an hour under the trees, umbrella up in the heavy rain, and watched the foaming, roaring water tip over the weir. Then one jumped. *I saw it jump!!* Over the next 10 minutes they made five more leaps – some moderate sized beasts, maybe a foot long, and at least two big, heavy, deep bodied fish. None made it. One bounced off the stonework as it fell. Over 25 minutes the group made eight jumps. Then there were no more. It was almost dark when I left, deeply contented, deeply thrilled to have seen such wildness, not in Scotland, not in Alaska, but in my own soft, domesticated Sussex countryside.

Great Beast:
The corpse of the giant cock Sea Trout kelt

CHALK STREAMS BETWEEN THE RIVER ADUR AND THE RIVER OUSE

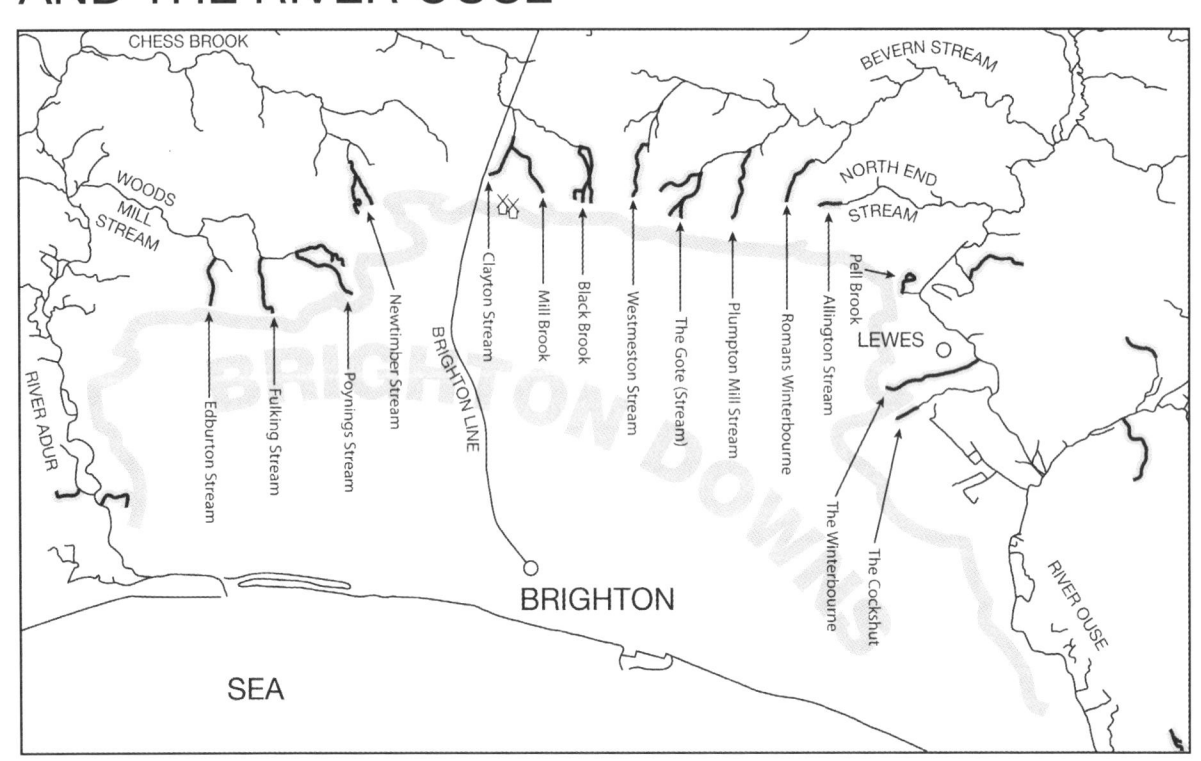

These streams arise from the spring line along the base of the Downs chalk scarp, and are fed by the chalk aquifer, which acts like a sponge. They are thus naturally clear, and tend to be protected from summer drying out (which is frequent on the clays of the Weald and on the 'winterbournes' of the chalk plateau). They also often run over gravels of flint washed from the Downs in Ice Age times and earlier.

This map's definition of chalk streams is quite tight. I tend to think more loosely of streams like the Bevern and Fulking Streams as 'chalk streams' all the way to their confluences with the Adur and Ouse main channels.

Contains Ordnance survey data © Crown copyright 2018 Ordnance Survey
Chalk streams data © Sussex Biodiversity Records Centre

Great Beast

On finding the corpse of a giant cock Sea Trout kelt,[5] 2.5ft. long, 6.5in. wide

We tracked the stream's edge through blackthorn brake,[6] and by muddy path,
Teetering on high banks, leaping the mud slides where deer slots[7] reveal their night-time fordings.

The dark of oaks and ashes conspires to make our way more dusk than day
And keeps us to the water's mirror light,

And there, within this gloom, the white-pale branch of you
Lies still – lies stiff below the spate ... a log beneath the surface,
Lodged up against a fallen oak.

I stop.
I see your line of mouth, your rounded eye ...

We haul your strong and slippery corpse and lay you on a bed of autumn leaves.
We gaze.
You wear your smartest courting suit, be-speckled head to tail in pink and black;
Your fins have tips of varnished Prussian blue and silver;
Your dainty teeth are strong white thorns;
Your fierce great kype[8] a battle sign.

I measure. We touch you, laugh, pose pictures with you, puzzle why your life has stopped ...

... So busy only yesterday, parrying your rivals,
Winning your fem; lying at her side in nest of stones
And emptying your twinned bodies.

* * *

... What was it like, old man,
To duck the bridges, shoot the sluices;
To dare the races, fight the spates;
To leap the weirs?

Is that where those scratches came, criss-crossing your white belly?
... Where your leap had failed; your body bounced off stone or scraped down concrete?

What was it like to feel the salty tang get stronger mile by mile;
To leave the river's mouth and break again to open sea?

What was it like
To hear ship motors up above;
To see the sea birds' bellies bob and dive against the sky;
To fear the spreading nets?

What was it like
To live in furious seas and roaring winter waves?

What perils did you pass, what terrors beset you from your gravelly birth?
... From spider-legged damsel larvae;
From lightning kingfisher's dive;
From heron's rapier beak;
From pike's torpedo rush;
And angler's jittering silver lure.

What was it like
To feel the lengthening of the days,
The urge for natal stream;
To pass again through river mouth
By dredgers, lights; by wharves,
And hear the roar and growl of cars and lorries?

* * *

Return you did, and then again, with others of your kind,
Up reedy narrows, between steep banks,
Up tunnels of trees, beating up trickles with scarce more flow
Than ditches – gravel bottomed drains where bramble draped above
And tangled fallen timber, poles and leaves threatened your way,

And there, with back scarce cloaked with water, you splashed in coupling frenzy,
Whilst dogs barked in cool night air to hear your noisy labours.

* * *

I lift you up and bear you to the bank, and tip your body down,
Where with great splash you hit the water one last time,
And, as the clouding clears, lie once again below the water's rush.

... And, that night, you filled my dreams with wonder
That you still made your journey back to Wealden wooded stream,
In face of all we do to kill your world.

Great beast, you touched our lives.

* * *

Great Diving Beetle mum

The Sea Trout were not the only giants. I chatted with the man who owns Shermanbury Place, on the Eastern Adur. He comes from a fishing family, and one of his Durham forebears invented the famous fly[9] called 'Greenwell's Glory', that was tested 160 years ago in the moorland streams brimming with Brown Trout. He suggested that Shermanbury took its name from the **Salmon** run that passed the place: *'Salmonesberie'* in the Domesday Book version. He seems to be wrong about the origin of the place name, but right about the past presence of those giants in the reedy river, making their way up to the headstream gravels. Mrs Merrifield[10] wrote of Salmon being taken in the Adur around 1864.

There's a spot called **Salmon Pool**, TQ 431 140, on the Ouse south of Barcombe Mills, and it's on the Ouse that the documentary evidence for these fish is strong. The Ouse Angling Preservation Society has been there since 1875, and their archives tell that the river "supported a significant Salmon[11] population, which persisted into the early 20th century, with possibly a small breeding population persisting until the mid 1970s". It seems that the navigation may earlier have eliminated most, if not all, the breeding Salmon, because the habitat the young fish needed in the main channel was destroyed by its canalisation, whereas the young Sea Trout could survive in the shallower tributaries. Mrs Merrifield[12] described the Salmon as only being present up to the first lock (at Hamsey). However, the collapse of the navigation and the decay of the locks may have allowed the Salmon to recolonise from c. 1870, till factors like the 1976 drought and a new weir at Buxted eliminated the last breeding group.[13] Salmon are still occasionally seen on the Ouse with the Trout, and a young fish was caught recently.

OTHER FISH AND WILDLIFE

Mrs Merrifield only listed *Pike, Chub, Roach, Perch, Gudgeon, Bullhead, Loach, River Lamprey, Eel, Minnow, Four and Ten Spined Sticklebacks, and Salmon and Trout*, on the upper Ouse and Adur (which additionally had *Bream*). She made no mention (as river fish) of Tench, Carp species, Barbel, Rudd, or even Dace.[14]

Our Sussex fish fauna is naturally depauperate, because of the Ice Age and post-Ice Age history of the British Isles. The carp and minnow family, *Cyprinidae*, have only 12 UK native species and a further seven introduced.[15] We have only two Loach species (one, in Sussex). Yet Iran,[16] a largely arid land, is home to 74 *Cyprinidae* and 21 Loach species!

Only[17] cold adapted species, such as Salmon, Trout, Bullhead and Eels would have survived in Sussex rivers in the final stages of the last glaciation. As the ice and cold retreated sea migrants such as Sticklebacks, Lampreys, and Shad would have recolonised. However, the southern route from the continent for would-be warm water colonists (the carp and minnow family, and others) would soon have been blocked by the opening up of the Channel, though species like Pike may have got to Sussex rivers first. Only the rivers of eastern England, such as the Trent, Great Ouse and Thames, remained connected to the continent, via the Dogger land bridge, till c. 8,200 BP. That accounts for the absence of such eastern England species as Silver Bream, Burbot, Barbel and Spined Loach as natives in our Sussex rivers. Some species, such as Roach and Perch, may early on have recolonised Sussex rivers from the Thames watershed (if they had not made it earlier from the south) as parts of our upper streams 'captured' parts of the Medway and Mole, and as transport by water birds and mammals would have mixed them up.

Since then, people have mixed things up much more, making our fish fauna one of the most modified groups of our wildlife. Common Carp was introduced to Britain in the 15th century. New stock and new species are brought in to our Sussex rivers and ponds, like Tench, different Carp species, Gudgeon, Bream, Rainbow Trout, Rudd and Barbel, some of which become self-sustaining, whilst other introductions die back, like Grayling, and others become pest species, like Wels and other Catfish, and Pumpkinseed.

Perhaps our tiddlers have the most natural pattern of distribution of our Sussex fishes. They, with the Sea Trout, are our true **wild fish**. You can find Minnow, Stone Loach, and Bullhead, in faster flowing, well-oxygenated conditions, both in the chalk streams under the Downs and in the High and Low Weald. You can find juvenile Eels, Three Spined and Nine Spined Sticklebacks in our weedy drains, derelict mill leats and farm ponds. You can find fish fry – including Dace and Minnow – in the shady pools of streams, around ox bow bends, in weedy areas, and everywhere the current is not strong. You may, with great luck and clear water, spot little Brook Lampreys on submerged sandy or clay banks, or the rarely-seen Sea Lamprey that migrates up river to spawn. The Brown or Brook Trout of our head streams, which do not migrate like their conspecific Sea Trout cousins, must also be partly, if not entirely, of natural origin in those places.

I never saw an **Otter** when I was roaming the Weald as a teenager in the '60s. I've never seen one since, and I doubt I ever will. They have scarcely re-colonised Sussex since their precipitous decline in the '50s, '60s and '70s, back to redoubts in the West Country, Wales and the north. On our Sussex rivers they were hunted by the Crowhurst Otterhounds, based on the Kent-Sussex border. Back in Henry Williamson's day the pack was taken down to North Devon to guest hunt with the hounds that hunted Tarka.[18] Across the country Otter hunting ended in 1977, and was made illegal in 1978. It was not hunting though, that rendered the Sussex Otters extinct, but organochlorine pesticide poisoning, assimilated via their favourite prey, the Eel, which has also fallen to only a tiny fraction of its past numbers. Otter hounds still draw the river banks, though it is Rats and Rabbits they mostly catch these days. **American Mink** have filled part of the niche left empty by the demise of the Otter, and you can see them if you walk quietly, on both the Adur and Ouse watersheds. Mink, in their turn, have been a major factor in the near extinction of the **Water Vole**, which now appears to have no major colonies in the Ouse or Adur watersheds, though it was so abundant in the 1950s that any walk along a stream, river or lakeside, rural or urban, would likely give you good views of them. I have not been quite so lucky in my sightings of **Water Shrews**, having seen them only four times, but beautiful they are in their black and white coats.

NATURE TAKES OVER: THE FLOODS AND THE BIRDS

In the deep winter of the year, the Adur brooks can flood with great sheets of water northwards from Bramber, between Henfield and Ashurst, to Shermanbury and Partridge Green. For a few weeks nature takes over, with some of the glorious abundance of the lost wild brooks. The only dry land is the thin levees of the river, with the swirling brown current between them and calm lakes behind on both sides, dotted with drowning thorn bushes and the tops of reeds and fence posts. Moles retreat to these banks, where they are as busy as ever. There's cracking ice all along the flood edges. Shape-shifting deceits of **Lapwing**, dense and high – 250 in one, maybe 300 in another – fly southwards towards dusk. **Starlings** move in small groups, fast, purposeful, joining into larger murmurations as they progress. We flush a solitary **Teal** from a stream side. Later, through binoculars, we watch a spring of perhaps 20 of them on the far landward edge of the flood.

Swaying in the wind: Reed Warblers nest woven onto the reeds

We sit and peer across the flood to its far side where the water meets green pastures, as the afternoon passes into dusk, and the mirror surface of the flood grows luminous with silvering sky. On those farm pastures big flocks of **Greylag** and **Canada Geese** sit, perhaps 70 birds, and a whiteness of perhaps 25 **Mute Swans** keeps a respectful distance, both from the Geese and from each other. Other families of Swans cruise on the flood, and on the bank, blood stained buff feathers and wing bones mark where a Fox caught a naive youngster. There are small companies of **Wigeon**, mostly resting, one **Shelduck**, a few Lapwing, and a solitary **Black Headed Gull**. Why was it there alone and not with the Gulls flying down river in 'v' shaped wedges – several hundred of them? I spot a chunky, dark **Brent Goose**, in dusk flight ... then a tight party of four more. All the way from Arctic Russia, they've come.

Far away to the west are two huge parliaments of **Rooks** – uncountable tiny pixels in moving clouds, like faint amoeba on the now-yellowing horizon – where we know the woods of north Wiston harbour huge numbers.

These crowds of wildfowl attract raptors to hunt and scavenge ... a **Red Kite** gliding low; a **Peregrine Falcon** swooping close to a small spring of Teal, but leaving be; a **Sparrowhawk** on leisurely patrol.

After the flood retreats the broken convolutions of fossil salting channels are picked out by the water they still hold, warning us where we should not tread. We pick our way across these rushy pastures, fringed by Reeds and Reed Sweet Grass, starting a **Snipe** from the muddy sewer edge. We see its white tummy, its absurdly long beak, hear its hoarse alarmed squeak. We spot three more of its companions. They've sought refuge with us from the deep frozen marshes of east Poland, or Russia. A **Little Egret** ignores us in its business, part hidden in a ditch. On a raised bank we find the still-warm body of a **Field Vole**, curled as though asleep. There's a **Barn Owl**

South of Gatwick: the bed of the River Mole. Will this ancient, secret place be destroyed by a second runway?

at work on the pastures near the river. Some young guys come by in a farm landrover, cheerful and friendly. They stop and pile out, taking their guns over towards a reedy pond. Ten minutes later shots ring out. The **Fieldfares**, the **Redwing**, the **Mallard** rush overhead, this way and that, as further echoing shots come from the far side of the river. Only the Owl behaves as though nothing has happened. She's still foraging forty minutes later – a white ghost crossing our path in the near pitch black.

Snipe no longer breed on our brooks, despite their frequency in winter of sometimes thirty and more at a time. Those winter sightings do not compensate for the lost spring thrill of Snipe zigzagging across the sky and tail-feather-drumming – *hoohoohoohoohoohoo* – as they tip in steep, repeated descent. Lapwings' spring time aerobatic tumbling and calling – *pooeeet, poowit, peueet* – can still occasionally be seen on our brooks, or on newly harrowed arables, never more than a few, often just singly. No longer, though, are they a familiar farmland bird of spring and summer, and every sighting now is special. Their nests are now rare indeed on both brook pastures and arables. That place where once I came across a clutch of four brown-buff, dark-blotched eggs nestled in lush grass near the Marsh Marigolds, is now improved, drained, levelled, and intensively grazed.

MORE WATER BIRDS

Kingfishers can still be sighted easily along both rivers, streams and larger waterbodies, but they have declined locally – and nationally by 26% in the fifteen years to 2010.[19] They patrol their lengths of water, piping shrilly, like little blue and orange missiles, and if they pass you once, they will likely pass you again coming back, if you stay close. They do not always appear to see where they are going, and we have had them fly straight at us, whizzing close by our heads. **Grey Wagtails** have become frequent breeding birds here only since Victorian times, and are characteristic, now, of pond bays and weirs, fast flowing High Wealden gills and wooded Low Wealden streams. **Yellow Wagtails** however, have disappeared from the middle Sussex Weald as breeding birds, though so emblematic of our brookland grazing pastures and arables in old times, following the herds, dancing up and down around their feet like fairy folk. They are now mostly noticed on migration.

Some birds that would not, in the past, have been especially associated with waterlands are now best found in these rough places. **Nightingales** are to be especially listened for in spring, each time you walk alongside Low Wealden streams cloaked densely with Blackthorn. What **Cuckoos** are left are to be listened for particularly where reed beds have best survived, for a clad of them specialises in parasitizing Reed Warblers. Barn Owls are often seen on our Low Wealden flood plains, foraging along vegetated ditches and over tussocky pastures.

Reed Warblers appear to have increased in recent decades. There is a necklace of sites along the Wealden Adur where they breed, as well as less often on the Ouse (but more so on Glynde Reach) and we hear them in odd watery places across the Weald. In the past **Sedge Warblers** were the commoner of the two, but are now rare in our part of the Weald. **Reed Buntings** are frequent in the right places, flitting from bush to bush along unmaintained ditches and tangled pond sides. **House Martins** and **Swallows** are to be seen in large flocks over sewage works, which are always to be found close to rivers and streams. **Sand Martin** is rarely seen. Does it still breeds in Surrey's Vale of Holmesdale sand pits? **Water Rail** breeds in the middle Sussex Weald, though it's heard far more than seen, but **Corn Crake** (Land Rail, Meadow Crake) has not bred in our wet meadows for perhaps seventy five years. Both **Great Crested Grebes** and **Little Grebes** can be found on our larger water bodies, and **Common Terns** breed on our bigger lakes and reservoirs.

I won't forget the sight of a mixed nesting colony of **Grey Herons, Little Egrets** and **Rooks** in a wood on the edge of one of our floodplains. Through the canopy we could see the spindly legs, snaking necks and huge wings of the birds and their fledglings on their untidy stick platforms, weirdly noisy with low cronks, barks, grunts and caws. They could have been pterodactyls. Mute Swans sail their family flotillas up our reedy rivers and make great *bouffants* of glorious white at their river bank nests.

The **Great White Crane**, *Grus primigenia*, survived into Romano-British times. **Pelicans** survived on our Sussex marshes until early Saxon times, and **Storks** survived till the middle Saxon period.[20] **Spoonbills**[21] bred in Sussex until the 16th–17th century, as did **Grey Cranes**, and **White Tailed Eagles** may still have bred in Sussex till circa 1780.

THE RIVER OUSE NAVIGATION

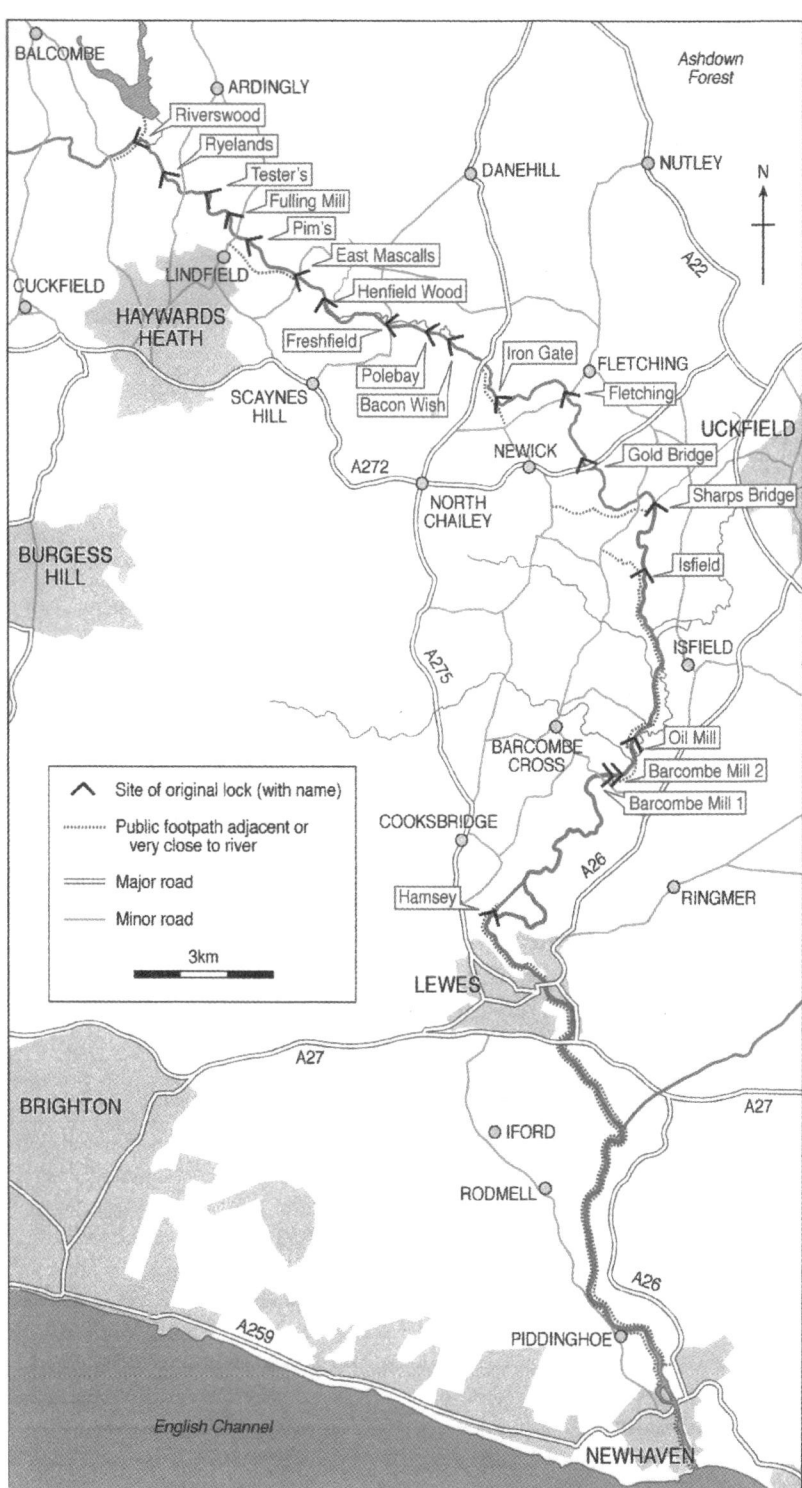

© With thanks to the Sussex Ouse Restoration Trust

Others have newly made their presence felt. **Mandarin Ducks** are now characteristic of our quieter, wooded Wealden reaches, streams and ponds, having first bred in 1971. Greylag and Canada Geese have become common over the last 60 years., and you can see **Barnacle Geese** honking overhead on their way

As much causeway as bridge: Mock Bridge, Shermanbury

More causeway than bridge: Wineham Bridge

More causeway than bridge: Sake Ride Bridge

back and forth to roost on Barcombe Reservoir.

Exploring the brooklands in summer you could find perhaps six species of damselflies with various kinds of sky blue colouration, some rare, some very common. You will also get to know the two Demoiselles – **Banded Demoiselle** on our sluggish Low Wealden streams and rivers, and **Beautiful Demoiselle**, sometimes with its cousin, sometimes on its own in shadier, clearer, faster waters. Amongst the commoner Darters, Skimmers, Chasers, and Hawker Dragonflies, you may come across the **Scarce Chaser**, *Libellula fulva*, confined to the Adur's flood plain.

RIVERS OR GIANT DRAIN PIPES?

Back in 2001 we took a long bus journey to eastern Poland. Passing through the flat countryside we crossed one or two big rivers. These still had what our own lowland rivers have lost. They were lazy. They sprawled. Their waters shallowed gradually to merge with the land. Broad zones spread away on either side – mud and algae, white beaches, marsh herbs, reeds, grazed meadows – with no engineered banks, or only ones set far back.

If only our Sussex rivers' still had all that! It's a fine walk up the Adur bank from Bramber northwards, but the river is hidden from the brooklands by high flood bunds. It is vaguely frightening – steep banked and fast moving, not to be toyed with – and if you fell in, no-one would hear your screams. In fact, it's a canal, a large engineered drain with moving tidal water, designed to get water off the land to the sea as fast as possible, and carry barge traffic to and fro. The barges have gone, but the drastic drainage engineering remains.

Till high medieval times the Adur would have been navigable by ocean going ships right up to Bramber, and a harbour existed close to Steyning Church in the 11th century, on a creek now reduced to the tiny Broadbourne and Tanyard Streams, that enter the river east of Kings Barn Farm. A wharf at Bramber might have been constructed close to St Mary's House for the import

Flood walkway, now disused: They used to be a common way of keeping your feet dry in winter floods

of materials for the castle construction, and Bramber[22] was still accessible to ships in the late 14th century. The muddy salt marshes of Bramber and Beeding were dotted with medieval salt works. Some of the 'saltern' waste mounds from the salt extraction still exist on the brooks just north of Bramber High Street, though those to its south have been destroyed. There is a larger cluster on the Beeding brooks just north of old Beeding parish church, e.g. TQ 191 114.

The settlements and place names attest to the Adur's history as a navigation route, and to its more distant history. On the levels south of Henfield, on the river's west bank, is the site of now lost *Heath* Farm, TQ 194 146. There was no heath. The name is a corruption of '*huth*', as in '*hyth*': river landing place. Still on the west bank, TQ 199 132, south of Stretham, is the site of lost *Scot*land Farm whose owners anciently paid 'scot', a tax for drainage purposes to the River Commissioners. On that bank too, is *Ea*ton's, once a hamlet with its own wharf, whose name indicates what Saxon folk called the old river: '*ea*' = river. By *Bine*ham Bridge (from *hop bine*: that plant of fenny places, fords and bridges) is New Inn Farm, TQ 191 153, now very old, once a bargees' and perhaps smugglers' hangout. Stretham, TQ 199 137, by the Roman road crossing, was no doubt also sited for its riverine resources.

How long is it since the old course of the Adur looped in a two mile ox bow around The Rye, TQ 201 151, picking up the Pokerlee Stream and the Woodsmill Stream before it resumed due south? It was aeons before the Saxon place namers were at work, for '*Rye*' means island ('*at ther ee*', that is: '*eg*') corroborating that the river, then as now, short-circuited its old loop to the west.

Under an Act[23] of 1807 (*"to cleanse, scour, enlarge, widen, deepen and render more straight … the said river"*) the Adur was canalised and the surrounding brooklands drained as far upstream as Bines Bridge, Ashurst, on the Western Adur, and Mock Bridge, Shermanbury, on the Eastern Adur, which both mark the limit of tidal reach. Under a further act of 1825 the stretch of river between Bines Bridge and Bay Bridge on the A24 by Knepp Castle, was also canalised and two locks constructed. One lock lay just west of West Grinstead Church, and one lay west of Partridge Green, south of Lock Bridge, TQ 179 184. Its lock chamber is still intact, though the gates and posts have gone. In winter spates the spillway roars with foaming flood water. There were wharves at Bay Bridge and Bines Bridge, now long gone, though their location can still be made out by the presence of bank and bushy ditch-stream, flowing over old masonry rubble. The navigation was abandoned in 1875 due to loss of trade to the new Shoreham-Horsham railway, but some goods were still brought to Bines Bridge c. 1890.[24]

The River Ouse Navigation was constructed at about the same period as the Adur, with the Upper Ouse Navigation Act being passed in 1800 and work on canalisation and the construction of its 19 locks[25] and other features being finished by 1812. It took in some 22 miles – much longer than the Adur navigation – as far north west as Upper Ryelands Bridge, TQ 324 279, by the Brighton Line's Balcombe Viaduct. Indeed, the navigation assisted its own demise, for its sloops and barges hauled the bricks used for the construction of the railway viaduct, opened in 1841. By 1868 all trade above Lewes had finished. Since then the river has reverted to its tidal state up to Barcombe Mills. The Anchor Inn, a mile upstream, and the Sloop Inn at Freshfield Bridge, both served the watermen of the navigation.

The upper reaches of the rivers beyond the navigations have not escaped radical engineering, partly for mill leats and impoundments, and partly for land drainage. Most of the streams of the Eastern Adur – *Cutlers Brook, the Herrings Stream, the Pook Bourne, the Chess Brook, Pokerlee Stream, Woodsmill River, Cowfold Stream et al* – have been much straightened, but stretches of low energy meanders still remain, as at Ote Hall and Antye, north east of Burgess Hill. On the Herrings Stream between Cobbs Mill and Hassocks there is a mixture of intact mill leats and lazy meanders. On the Western Adur, at Coolham, there are over a mile of meanders between Ashbrook Bridge and Slaughter Bridge. On the Ouse the two chalk streams – the North End and the Bevern Streams, and its daughter the Plumpton Mill Stream – all have straightened parts. However, the Longford Stream has some nice slow pool-and-riffle meanders, for instance east of

THE HERRINGS / HERON STREAM

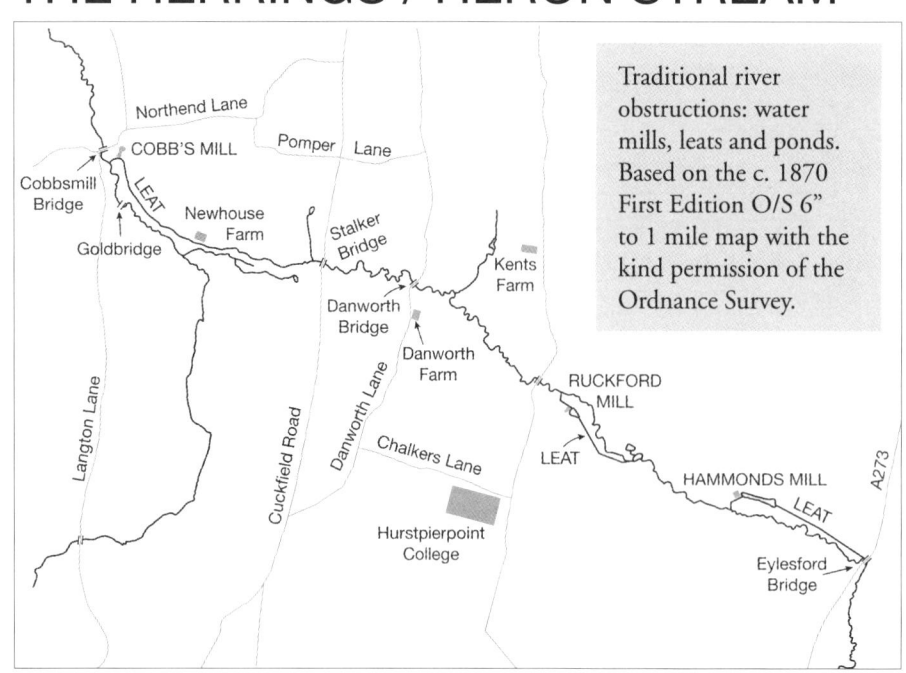

Traditional river obstructions: water mills, leats and ponds. Based on the c. 1870 First Edition O/S 6" to 1 mile map with the kind permission of the Ordnance Survey.

Cockfield Bridge, TQ 410 194, south of Townings Farm, TQ 375 196, and on the River Lambourne in Lambourne Wood (see above under 'River Monsters').

The most unmodified stretches are the head streams, near the Wealden sources of the rivers. The Cockhaise Brook seems only lightly modified along its whole five miles south from Sharpthorne to Great Walstead, Lindfield. In Paddockhurst Park, TQ 332 335, the Ardingly Brook feels like a Welsh mountain stream, bubbling over rocks and under mossy banks. West of Gaveston Hall, Maplehurst, is a beautiful wooded stretch of natural meanders, with gravels, tall banks and pools under tree roots, TQ 183 350. The streams north and east of Haven Bridge, TQ 173 234, and east of Tuckman's Farm, TQ 173 238, are similarly delightful.

The head streams of the River Arun in St Leonards Forest – *Alder, Sheepwash, Frenchbridge, Pyefall, Newstead, Hyde, Darkalley, and Dabson Gills* – are fast flowing, gravel bottomed, little engineered, and often with a taste of Wales or the west country, though modified by hammer and mill ponds in their lower reaches, and later on by landscaped ponds of the rich.

In recent years there have been efforts to restore the naturalness of sections of the engineered rivers. Just west of the Bluebell Line's Sheffield Park Station the old Ouse meanders are now restored, TQ 400 239. South of Kneppmill Pond, TQ 156 209, a canalised stretch of the River Adur west towards Capps Bridge has had its meanders and wet meadows restored. Perhaps, soon, it will again be suitable for the Tench, after which Tenchford, TQ 151 210, is presumably named, with the return of densely weedy, slow, sunny shallows. Between Woods Mill, the Sussex Wildlife Trust's base, and South Tottington Sands Farm, the Trust has restored the Woodsmill Stream's meanders, and already Sticklebacks enjoy the new weed growth, and Pea Mussels and water snails form part of a nice gravel.

WATER MILLS, LAKES AND RESERVOIRS

Many stretches of Wealden river were heavily modified for water mills, for corn, fulling (wool cleansing), oil, wire, buttons, iron working, et al. Aspects of their river engineering remain long after the mills have disappeared or been converted to new uses. There were multiple mills at Barcombe Mills since Domesday at least, and their braided leats and streams, impoundments and weirs survive. There were two mills on Poynings' tiny chalk stream south and north of the village. On the Woodsmill River there were at least three mills, one of which was close to Edburton church. The leat of Woods Mill runs for over a mile to just west of Edburton Sands. Between South Tottington Sands and Truleigh Sands it is thin, shallow, scarcely more than a weedy ditch, but still full of Freshwater Shrimps, *Gammarus*, and Fool's Water Cress. Between Goldbridge and Eylesford Bridge, on the Herrings Stream north of Hurstpierpoint, there were three watermills, and two thirds of a mile of good leat survives east of Cobb's Mill. In the mile of Plumpton Mill Stream below Plumpton Place there were three water mills. The pond of the Upper Mill is now a wonderful wilderness of soggy Alder carr and Marsh Marigolds, anachronistically called 'Reed Pond'.

Some of the best ponds are water mill and hammer ponds: *Kneppmill Pond, Warnham Pond, Pond Lye (Hurstpierpoint), Bolney ponds, Ifield Mill Pond, Furnace Pond (north of Crawley Down), Hammer Pond, Hawkins Pond, and the Leonardslee ponds in St Leonard's Forest.*

The Adur has escaped large scale modern reservoir construction, and so has the upper Arun, but the upper Medway has Weir Wood Reservoir, the upper Ouse has Ardingly Reservoir, and the lower Ouse has Barcombe Reservoir. It took a major fight to stop the gigantic proposed shallow water reservoir east of Barcombe at Plashett Park Farm, and it will take much vigilance and campaigning energy to see off further major landscape destroying reservoir building.

ACCESS TO OUR RIVERS AND STREAMS

Wealden rivers, streams, brooklands and ponds are not places where the public has much formal right of public access (though there is more informal access – some assumed; some granted). What legal rights we have probably derive greatly from the heavy river workers' footfall along the banks of the old canalised rivers, mill leats and streams. Given that most of our brooklands must have been common land historically, it is extraordinary that so few public rights remain there.

Both banks of the **Adur** have public footpaths going north to Eaton's Farm, Ashurst, and the east bank footpath continues on the Eastern Adur as far as Betley Bridge. However, most of the **Eastern Adur** is without river bank legal access. It might as well not exist as far as public rights to enjoy it go. Less than a mile of bank side to the east of Mock Bridge has a public footpath. The *Herrings Stream* has relatively good bankside access from Hickstead east to the A273, Eylesford Bridge. The *Pook Bourne*, the *Sake Ride Sewer*, the *Chess Brook*, two thirds of the *Pokerlee Stream* and most of the *Woodsmill River* are off-limits. Only the Woodsmill River west of Woods Mill, the Pokerlee Stream south of Henfield, and *Cutler's Brook* through Albourne to Hurstpierpoint, have good bankside access. The lovely *Cowfold Stream* is one of the least accessible of our middle Sussex streams, except for a small stretch north of Cowfold, and a stretch of forested headwater gill east of Leonardslee.

The **Western Adur** has much less access even than the Eastern, except for two disconnected stretches along the old navigation, totalling less than two miles between West Grinstead and Bines Bridge. Kneppmill Pond and the Daffodil-strewn banks along the stream through the old Knepp Park north end are without public access rights. So are the deep, wooded clefts of Rushett's Gill and Nuthurst Farm Gill, south and south east of Sedgewick Castle.

Most of the **St Leonard's Forest gills** have no public bank paths, though Forestry Commission access land embraces two of them, and bounds another.

The tidal **Ouse** from Lewes to Barcombe Mills is without legal right of access on its east bank, and only has public footpath on its west bank as far north as Hamsey. Northwards from Barcombe Mills one or t'other banks has public path for three miles to Vuggles Farm. Beyond that it has no statutory bank side access rights, apart from crossings, for four miles north to Rotherfield Wood, where it bounds old Sheffield Park. North of Sheffield Park Station the river bank has only small lengths of public footpath all the long way west to its source close to Lower Beeding. *Cockhaise Brook* and its tributary *Cob Brook* have no bank side access all the way north to the Selsfield/West Hoathly/Sharpthorne Ridge.

The *North End Stream* has one small stretch of public bank path along its entire length. The *Bevern Stream* has no bank side public paths at its east end, but several lovely bank paths north of Barcombe Cross. West of Holman's Bridge, then west again from Bevern Bridge, there are only crossings and short accessible bank lengths all the way west past Plumpton Green, Streat, and to the springs at Westmeston. The *Plumpton Mill Stream* has only a couple of little lengths of public bank footpath all the way to the Plumpton Place spring. The *Longford Stream* and its tributaries have only tiny amounts of public bank side footpath. The *Pellingford Brook* has no bank side public paths.

In Surrey, the situation is very similar along the Mole and the Eden and their tributaries.

The geography of our waterlands is a closed book to most of us, though we depend upon them for our water, our human waste disposal, our recreation and our delight.

WHOSE RIVERS, WHOSE PONDS?

The angling societies have the fishing rights along most of the main channels of the Ouse and the Adur, and many large and small ponds in addition. The head streams, by contrast, in High or Low Weald, are often controlled solely by the landowners.

The folk I've mostly chatted to on our river and stream banks are anglers … and they're a patient and friendly lot, happy to tell you what fish are in their stretch and what luck they have had. They tell you too of the kingfishers which nest in the steep bank, fish the large weir pool, and feed their brood, lined up like a dress parade along a branch. They tell you of the water birds and of the comings and goings of small creatures in the rivers' green tranquillity. One man, casting his

Henfield Brooks: springtime

lure into a pool, talked us through all the comings and goings of the Sea Trout, and his own perambulations along the river, casting only a few times in each spot. We bumped into him three times that afternoon. Another man told us of how he had fished the river for over 50 years. It is his greatest love, and he has lost two marriages to its pursuit!

On the **Adur**, the *Pulborough Angling Society* have the fishing rights to three miles of the river between Bramber and Stretham Manor. *Henfield and District Angling Society* have them from Stretham, where the Downslink crosses the river, north to The Fork, and then further along both the Eastern and Western Adurs. On the Western Adur they have the fishing rights directly north to Hatterell's Bridge and along the Honeybridge Stream to Honey Bridge. On the Eastern Adur they have rights to Betley Bridge and a bit beyond, then for half a mile east of Mock Bridge, and a half mile stretch west of Wineham Bridge (which they share with *Hassocks and District Angling Society*). They also have two sections of the Chess Brook, one by Little Betley, and one by Woolfly, NW and NE of Henfield respectively.

On the **Ouse,** there are three main fishing rights holders. The *Ouse Angling Preservation Society* has the fishing rights on the west bank nearly all the way from Hamsey Loop, north to Gold Bridge, Newick, apart from a half mile around White Bridge, and some excluded banks at Barcombe Mills. They share the northernmost eight miles, together with the lowest mile of the Longford Stream down to its confluence, with the *Copthorne and District Angling Society*. The OAPS also have the lowest section of the Bevern Stream from the first field upstream of Clapper's Bridge down to its confluence. Additionally, the *Lewes and the Isfield Angling Societies* share a half mile of the Ouse east bank south of Barcombe Mills, and the *Hassocks Angling Society* has over a mile of the east bank north and south of Hamsey Weir, TQ 414 125.

North and east of Haywards Heath the *Haywards Heath Angling Society* have the fishing on one or both of the banks from east of Lower Ryelands Bridge to Gold Bridge – a huge length.

Several of the big fishing clubs have the fishing of well known lakes and ponds. The *Copthorne DAS* has lovely Rowfant Mill Pond and the ponds east of Rowfant House. The *Horsham and District Angling Society* has several of the St Leonards Forest ponds, such as Roosthole, Birchenbridge, Island and Foxhole, but only a small stretch of the **Arun** south of Horsham. The *Slaugham Angling Club* has Carter's Lodge Pond and Furnace Pond at Slaugham Common, and the *Haywards Heath AS* has Valebridge Pond at Bedelands, Burgess Hill, as well as Slaugham Mill Pond and Balcombe Lake. The *Crawley Angling Society* has the Douster Pond at Buchan Park. Several organisations fish the Ardingly and Weir Wood Reservoirs.

There are also a plethora of commercial fishing businesses and syndicates stocking old ponds and creating numerous new ones, with little affinity for the old landscape, or the habitats and special plants, insects and other small animals that are usurped. There is nothing 'wild' or 'natural' about big stocked carp in chains of recently dug ponds, with car parking, mown lawns and walkways, fishing platforms, tackle shops, cafes, toilets, electric gates, buggies to transport your gear … and fish which are individually known and many times captured. It's a good way of separating the punters from their cash, though.

Although the angling club folk do not challenge you for strolling their banks, the commercial fisheries want your money, and rich landowners want their private ponds and streams to themselves.

The growth of this industry has been accompanied by an increase in serious fishery poaching activities, for re-sale and for food. Such poaching is often indiscriminate and can cause real harm to wildlife of nature conservation value, but is it any more irrational than the wholly artificial manipulation of fish stock, the manicured and artificial landscapes, the gates, fences, security and signboards that proclaim 'pay or stay away'? Is there any real difference between 'factory farming' and 'factory angling'? And aren't the millions of us who suffer the loss of wild nature from our lives being conned into accepting instead a vastly inferior commercial rip-off?

Izaak Walton Jnr.

ENDNOTES

1. Now 'Trusler's'.
2. Quoted in "Albourne to Ditchling: Along the Greensand Ridge", page 51, by Mark Dudeney and Eileen Hallett. Mid Sussex Books (2000).
3. *Pers com* 2014. Sam is a leading figure of the Ouse and Adur Rivers Trust (OARTS).
4. Information from OARTS, who run an excellent redds monitoring scheme with volunteers.
5. A kelt is a spent and emaciated Trout or Salmon after spawning. They may die after these exertions, or they may return to the sea and regain condition.
6. A brake is a thicket.
7. Slots are hoof prints, particularly of deer.
8. A kype is a hooked growth on the end of the lower jaw of the male adult Trout or Salmon which helps him ward off competitor males when courting.
9. Fishing 'flies' are fish hooks decorated to imitate Mayflies, Caddis or Stoneflies, the main summer invertebrate food of game fish like Trout, Grayling and Salmon, which they rise to snatch from the surface. They are made by tying bits of feather, hair, and wotnot to a fish hook.
10. 'A Sketch of the Natural History of Brighton and its Vicinity', page 161–2, edited by Mrs Merifield. H and C Treacher (1864).
11. *Pers com* Dave Brown, Scientific Director of OART (16/01/13).
12. 'A Sketch of the Natural History of Brighton and its Vicinity', page 161. Op cit.
13. Ouse Angling Preservation Society Newsletter, 2012–13 season. Dave Brown.
14. 'A Sketch of the Natural History of Brighton and its Vicinity', page 224, op cit.
15. 'Britain's Freshwater Fishes', by Mark Everard. Princeton Wild Guides (2013).
16. 'The Complete Fauna of Iran', by Eskandar Firouz. I.B. Tauris (2005).
17. These notes rely on chapter 8 of the superb new book 'Rivers', by Nigel Holmes and Paul Raven. British Wildlife Collection 3, British Wildlife Publishing (2014).
18. 'Tarka the Otter', Henry Williamson. Penguin Modern Classics (first published 1927).
19. 'The Birds of Sussex', page 375. Sussex Ornithological Society. BTO (2014). Much of the information on waterland birds is from this book and the SOS's other excellent publications.
20. Storrington = *'Storgeton'* (1086) = Stork's Farm. 'The Place Names of Sussex', op cit. Lost *Stor*wood Farm next to Oreham Common, Henfield, may also memorialise it.
21. This information is from a superb edition of 'Selborne Notes' in the West Sussex Gazette of 14/01/99 by Dr Andrew Allen: 'Interesting history of the Sussex marshes'.
22. 'British History Online': Bramber (1980), Steyning (1980), T P Hudson (editor). Victoria County History.
23. 'River Adur Navigation' Ref: IN/Adur. West Sussex Record Office.
24. 'British History Online': West Grinstead (1986), T P Hudson (editor). Victoria County History.
25. See the website of the Sussex Ouse Restoration Trust.

OLD MEADOW, HEATH AND PASTURE

CHAPTER 8
Archaic pasture, meadow, moor and heath

For me, old flowery pastures and meadows are the nearest places to paradise we have on earth.

Take a moment and try and free-associate what they mean to you. For myself, I think …

… Gardens … those pictures of the kingdom of god on Jehovah's Witness pamphlets … Timotei adverts (for the older of you) … children's story books … pastoral films where young lovers run through the flowers, disappear into the hay and make love … or eat a picnic!! … harmony, joy, peace …

They are nature at its most beautiful, innocent and unthreatening. They are a peak experience.

Pollen and other sub-fossil remains preserved in ancient lake deposits in East Anglia and elsewhere show that meadow-like plant communities comprising species we still see in meadows today, could have been

Old meadow, heath and pasture
If you think that this map shows little more than a scatter of tiny dots, like dust flecks on the page, then you are right. It's all I know that's left of these gorgeous places in this part of the Weald.

The map shows the whole range of surviving archaic open habitats, from heath to flower meadow, floodplain pastures, and the best roadside verges. The majority of what survives is damaged – often very badly. The majority is under-managed or badly managed. Much of it is derelict. Much, perhaps most, is threatened. Nearly all is vulnerable. Some will have been destroyed by the time this is published.

There will be many sites that I have missed, or misjudged. Please do tell me about them.

I list below some of the biggest and the best. Please don't blame me if they disappoint you. Their surviving special features are mostly seasonal, and often obscure, rare, or difficult to find or identify.

Many sites are very 'private', and you will have to make your own arrangements for access.

List of key sites
1. Reigate Heath SSSI
2. Wray Common, Reigate
3. Petridgewood Common, Redhill
4. Brown's Hill Meadows, Harewood Estate (Nat Trust)
5. Railway Meadow, Crowhurst (Mary's Meadow)
6. Misbrook Green, Capel
7. Stanhill Meadows, Charlwood
8. Broadbridge Pastures and Burstow Stream Church Meadows
9. Bones Wood Meadow, Horne
10. Blindley Heath SSSI
11. Northlands Farm Meadows, North Horsham
12. Langley Green Meadows
13. Copthorne Common Meadows
14. St Leonard's Forest Rides, Forestry Commission, Horsham
15. Buchan Country Park, Crawley
16. The Steep, Newstead Farm, St Leonard's Forest
17. High Beeches Garden Meadows, Handcross, Worth Forest
18. Tilgate Forest Lodge heathland
19. Worthlodge Forest pylon line ride grass heath
20. Parson's Brook Meadows, Landfall Farm
21. Sedgwick Park Meadows
22. Leonardslee Deer Park
23. Hapstead Farm and Brook House Pastures, Ardingly
24. Cockhaise Brook, Nobles Farm, and Oddynes Brooks, Horsted Keynes
25. Danehill and Chelwood Common Meadows
26. Twineham Place Brooks
27. Pond Lye Pastures, Hurstpierpoint
28. Bedelands Farm Meadows, Burgess Hill
29. Chailey North Commons
30. Ditchling Common, with St George's Retreat Meadows
31. Sedgebrook Farm Meadows and Bog
32. Roeheath Meadows, Cinder Hill, Chailey
33. Henfield Common and Woodmancote Moor
34. Longford Stream Brooks, west of Longford Bridge, Barcombe
35. Hillside Scout Camp Meadow, Small Dole, Upper Beeding
36. Poynings Stream Brooks and Marsh
37. Southmead Meadow, Ditchling
38. The Bluebell Line, Barcombe Cross to Knowlands Farm
39. Oil Mill Pasture, Barcombe Cross
40. The Pells Brooks, Offham

assembled more than 70,000 years ago, in previous warm inter-glacials.[1]

For Wealden farmers they were a major part of the reality of their farm economy ever since the big Saxon woodland clearances of Andredesweald … that is, for 1500 years … and back several thousand more years before that in some places, way back beyond the Bronze Age, and right up to the Second World War.

They formed part of a low-input, low-output agriculture, characterised by frequent movements of livestock, frequent movements of seed-rich hay, and frequent seed rain from slopes and hills to valleys and fallows. Horses, sheep and cattle would trek backwards and forwards every day, or from season to season, to places remote from the farmstead, and across different habitat types. Grasslands would be constantly renewed and cross-fertilised with new seed sources.[2]

Now, these places are so rare I doubt most people have even seen a traditional species-rich old meadow. The Wealden survivors are mere 'precious fragments' … museum pieces artificially kept alive to remind us of our lost heritage … or are they??

GONE? … OR JUST LOST?

A while back I got it really wrong. I assumed that we'd lost almost all the herb-rich pastures and meadows of the Weald, its small farms, road and path side wastes, little greens and commons … all except the few protected as nature reserves or by other benign non-commercial uses.

I hadn't looked hard enough. The patient is on life support … but she's not dead. There's hope yet.

And once we did start properly looking we kept on finding more and more. We hunted all through the summers and autumns … right on through the winters. And every time we went out purposely looking for old, lost meadows and pastures we found them … in places that are entirely off the radar of the official planning and nature conservation world. Mostly they are in a poor – often desperate – state … the last stage before total loss … but they *are* there.

One early April, we stumbled across **a little field just south of Balneath Lane**. It didn't seem that promising. Very rabbity, with a simple sward of few grasses and bits of Bird's Foot Trefoil, Barren Strawberry, Bugle, Pointed Spear Moss, *Calliergonella cuspidata*, and Ragwort. A scatter of young Spotted Orchids by the wood edge … but then … the dainty little leaves of Adder's Tongue Fern, *Ophioglossum vulgatum*, like fairy-sized Cuckoo Pint … then one fertile plant, with its little green tongue pointing upwards.

The swarm of this rare fern took up a significant part of the entire meadow (2011).

One sunny afternoon in mid June I skived off work and re-visited a place we'd crossed in late winter and thought to be promising … **just south of Barcombe Cross**, TQ 421/2 151/2. It had old anthills, lush gullies, and herb-rich, mottled turf. In just over two hours I clocked up 73 herbs and grasses, including 18 grasses, three rushes, three sedges and many special species. There was Betony, Heath Grass, Devil's Bit, Hairy and Oval Sedges. There was Quaking Grass and Yellow Oat Grass – both abundant on the Downs, but special in the Weald. On the yellow landing pad of an Ox Eye Daisy sat two mating Fairy Ring Longhorn Beetles, *Pseudovadonia livida,* (which seem to spend their juvenile lives in the 'roots' of Fairy Ring Champignon toadstools).

I've heard that Barcombe folk love this place, but I saw no management (2013). Fences were down, scrub was encroaching, part had been 'improved' and the only grazers were rabbits and deer.

One late August I went on a jaunt to explore the tangle of woods, shaws, gills and fields between Selsfield Common and Turners Hill. Just off the Roman road, I walked out of the cool woodland shade onto a **hillside meadow**, TQ 50 355, recently cut. That always makes things difficult for plant recording. No worries, though, for I quickly found a tiny patch of low-growing Lousewort flowers – always a good sign – and then masses of Bitter Vetch all over the hillside and Tormentil, Sneezewort, Devil's Bit, Purple Moor Grass, Tufted Hair Grass, Bird's Foot Trefoil, and on and on.

I had a lovely chat with the gamekeeper, who was tinkering with some fencing. He told me that the field had loads of orchids in season and that the farmer randomly cuts the field and depastures his cattle on it. Just what the place needs.

A fortnight before Christmas (2011) we went on an expedition to look at some places east and west of Haywards Heath. By late afternoon it was starting to drizzle, but we had one site still to visit. In near darkness we put our umbrellas up, fished out our LED lights, and left the footpath to check out **Bolney Cricket Ground**, TQ 263 228. Straightaway we started finding stuff. The rain started sheeting down … but … hey … there were big troops of King Crimson, Golden, Vermilion, Snowy, and Meadow Waxcap fungi, *Hygrocybe punicea, chlorophana, miniata, virginea, pratensis*, scattered across the grass like gaudy orchard windfalls. Up by the pavilion were big troops of Scarlet Hood, *H. coccinea* … and little tufts of Yellow Club, *Clavulinopsis helvola*, scarcely topping the height of the mown turf. As good as a New Forest lawn!! What a treat!!

WHAT THEY ARE LIKE

Surviving Wealden meadows and pastures in mid Sussex are either on soils which are neutral or acidic in chemistry. (In eastern Sussex there are some Wealden grasslands on calcareous soils, over the Jurassic Purbeck Limestones, but these do not occur in middle Sussex). Low Wealden old grasslands will mostly be on neutral soils (mostly Wealden or Gault Clays) whilst High Wealden grasslands will mostly be on more acidic sandstones, though some will be on clays. Acid and neutral grasslands have different vegetation communities, which can be recognised relatively easily, even though they have many overlapping species.

The most frequent type of unimproved neutral grassland in mid Sussex, such as you will find at the **Bedelands Local Nature Reserve** or **Sedgwick Park**, is characterised by flowers such as Ox Eye Daisy, Knapweed, Birds Foot Trefoil, Red Clover, Meadow Buttercup, Ribwort Plantain, Common Sorrel, Meadow Vetchling, and Creeping Cinquefoil. None of those species is rare, and you may get all of them on semi-improved grasslands, too (that is, grasslands that have received some agri-chemical inputs, but not enough to destroy all their naturally occurring species).

Flowers will take up a very significant proportion of the sward, relative to grasses … even its majority.

The key indicator species, which will suggest that a site is undamaged and possibly old, are the presence of Pepper Saxifrage and Dyer's Greenweed, and on some sites you may find Green-Winged Orchis. On short swards you may be lucky to find Adder's Tongue Fern, which seems to have some association with Green Winged Orchids. Rarely, too, you may find Spiny Restharrow. Yellow Rattle will be a feature of some sites, sometimes very prominently.[3]

As the soil becomes more acidic (but still neutral) you will find that Devil's Bit Scabious becomes more frequent, together with Betony, Burnet Saxifrage, Tormentil, and Common Dog Violet. Heath Grass becomes more frequent also, though rarely common, but this is a species of short swards, so it will not be seen on many of our unmanaged grasslands.[4]

When grasslands are left long-derelict they become much grassier, and dominated by tall, tussocky grasses that can't cope with grazing or mowing. The chief of these is False Oat Grass, though Cock's Foot and tall fescue grasses also become very common. On some sites the flowers of grazed or mown neutral grassland may survive for a long time, but eventually they will be overwhelmed by these tussocky tall grass species.[5]

On wet ground Tufted Hair Grass may dominate, with rush species and possibly sedge swarms, perhaps of Glaucous or Black Sedge, and the pond sedges.

Grasslands that have received some nutrient input will also become much grassier and lose many or most of their more delicate and sensitive archaic species. They may still retain much colour and interest, however, and can be restored over time, with care.

Acidic grasslands tend to be poorer in species, though they have their own specialities and can be very rich in fungi, mosses and lichen if grazed or mown. They are dominated by Common Bent Grass and Sheep's Fescue. Heath Bedstraw, Common Sorrel, Sweet Vernal Grass, Mouse Eared Hawkweed and Field Wood Rush are characteristic. Tormentil is often very common.

Bracken can be common in many neglected grassland communities, but it will only suppress lower growing flowers and grasses when it is left unmown.

FLOWERS OF ALL SORTS, AND A FERN

Cowslips are almost functionally extinct as a naturally occurring plant of wild origin in the Brighton Line Weald, though they were once so common as to be taken for granted. One old man told me that his mum used to gather huge quantities from a nearby brookside pasture to make Cowslip wine. That place was lost many years ago, and is now a boring grass ley. A few Cowslips do cling on nearby along a flowery woodland ride, but they will be gone soon.

I know only one surviving Cowslip meadow in the Brighton Line Weald, and in that lovely place they vibrantly colour parts of the sward. That site straddles the boundary between the Gault Clay and the Grey Chalk geology, giving it a favourable alkaline soil chemistry. It is only a mile from one of the best Cowslip displays on the South Downs scarp, and therefore not typical of the Weald.

Elsewhere, Cowslips survive in old Wealden grasslands only as a relict species, usually found in ones and twos, not mass flowerings, as they should be. A few tufts survive in an archaic meadow in the old north Knepp deer park, where they stand some chance, thanks to restoration efforts. A few tufts survive in a Danehill meadow opposite Little Bridge House (2012); in the Tickfold meadows (2014); the Sedgwick Park meadows; in Stanhill Court meadows by Edolph's Copse, Charlwood, Surrey; and, rarely, in scruffy field edges.

The safest sites, now, are non-agricultural, such as graveyards and other managed lawns. Thus, they are in High Beech Garden's meadows; St George's Retreat's lawns, Ditchling; Staplefield Churchyard; and Walstead Cemetery.

Dyers Greenweed, *Genista tinctoria*, is another glorious yellow thing. Where it thrives it forms large egg yolk yellow patches on clay and lightly acid pastures and heaths, around midsummer and July. Close up, its blooms look like little tongues of yellow flame. When it is really common its colour can be seen from some distance. It is a woody sub-shrub that is a blessing to both people and many small and special beasties. It is an ancient dye plant, which produces both a yellow and, when dipped in Woad or indigo, the 'Kendal Green', though its commercial use died out in the early 19th century. That past usage may account for some of its distribution pattern. It used to be very common in the Brighton Line Weald, and is still commoner there and in East Sussex than in the west of the county.

Ditchling Common is its headquarters in the Brighton Line Weald, both south of Folder's Lane East, and in the Country Park north of the pond. From the 19th century till the 1960s the Common was a happy hunting ground for a small group of specialist lepidopterists, because its Dyer's Greenweed hosted at least seven micro-moths which were wholly dependent on it, whilst the Greenweed's cousin, the **Needle Whin**, *Genista anglica*, hosted at least a couple more.[6] With names like the Large Gold Case Bearer, the Greenweed Leaf Miner, the Greenweed Flat Body, and the Petty Whin Case Bearer, they competed with many other insects, including leaf beetles, weevils, leaf mining and gall causing flies, true bugs and sawflies[7] which were also entirely dependent on the Greenweed for food and shelter.

Since then things have gone from bad to worse, with plough-ups of the common by rogue farmer-commoners, dreadful scrub encroachment, neglect of grazing and Bracken control in the Country Park, and over grazing on the commoners' common, all destroying the Greenweed's capacity to host this assemblage. In a recent visit one expert[8] found only a single one of these micro-moths: *Trifurcula beirnei*. The loss of another of the species, *Syncopacma vinella*, from the Common in 1990, marked its extinction in the British Isles. One after another these moth species went, in a heart breaking decline, with last dates seen in 1905, 1963, 1967, 1968, 1990, 1997, and 2005.

There are other local places with Dyer's Greenweed displays. The easiest to see is probably at Valebridge Common Field, TQ 321 210, in the Bedeland Local Nature Reserve, Burgess Hill. The derelict Gullege Meadow, TQ 361 381, on the Worth Way, also has a fine display in the middle (2012); as does Frenchlands Meadow, TQ 151 161/2, in the north Wiston woods; and the Bishopstone Lane meadows (2014) TQ 282 218/9, south of Ansty.

In the Surrey Low Weald, Dyer's Greenweed is a rarity. The best place to see it is at Bone's Meadow (2016) on the south side of Bone's Wood, Horne, TQ 345 424, where a public footpath gives access. There, the display makes dazzling pools of yellow. Bone's Meadow was fragmented into micro-plots in a get-rich-quick property scam.

In many meadows Greenweed is reduced to one or two plants, or small swarms encroached upon by scrub. It can still – rarely – be found along field hedge bottoms, and it occurs on a number of road verges, such as at the west end/north side of the Cuckfield Bypass, and on the Joles Farm verge at Maplehurst, TQ 188/9 238, but those are dangerous and neglected places. One of the nicest spots I've found it recently is on the tiny green at the crossroads by Little Strudgate Farm, TQ 325 321, amongst other archaic grassland flowers.

There is one other dye plant (producing a yellow, like the Greenweed) found in our part of the Weald that I have a special affection for: **Saw Wort**, *Serratula tinctoria*. I knew it first from its only South Downs site, north of Southwick, where it grows amongst Betony and Knapweed. Indeed, it looks like a more delicate version of Knapweed, with serrated edges to its leaves, hence its name. Again, probably the best place to see it growing happily is Ditchling Common, where it is frequent on the informal path sides alongside the Greenweed, amongst the Bracken north of the pond. It is happy on both clay and more sandy soils, but I've never seen it producing displays like the Greenweed … except (in a small way) on a verge of the Ifield Road, half a mile north of Ifieldwood Common, and half a mile west of the end of the Gatwick runway. There, opposite Birchfield, between TQ 239 398 and 399, the broad verge has large, dense clumps of it, where plane spotters stand and peer through gaps in the hedge at the monsters lifting off and roaring low overhead.

Saw Wort is on Blindley Heath in Surrey, at Gullege Meadow near Crawley Down, and on Chailey Common, for instance at Romany Ridge. It is rare now, on Henfield Common, and on the point of disappearing in a list of other verge, pasture, and meadow sites. It grows on the pub meadow behind the Plough Inn, north of Plumpton Green, but not in quantity (2013). It looks set to be reduced to a number of redoubts in conservation management, like Ashdown Forest and Ditchling and Chailey Commons.

In the past I thought of **Adder's Tongue Fern** as a *very* rare species – too rare to have much indicative value for old meadows. It is a tiny thing, not at all like a fern, more like a miniature Wild Arum plant with a green rather than brown 'tongue'. In the spring of 2012, however, I systematically searched for it on a range of Wealden archaic grassland sites … and found it there, in the most unlikely situations. Thus, on Streat Green it grew not only on the shortest sward, but on an area which was left to grow up to a yard high in summer! I found it on Ditchling Common on the bank of a shady woodland brook, as well as next to the busy car park. It was at Oreham Common; Bedelands Meadows; Merrifields pastures, Broxmead Lane; Gullege Meadow; and at Henfield, Sayers Common and Spithurst Churchyards; and many other places.

Little **Spring Sedge** behaves in a very similar fashion, growing happily in the shortest, most lawn-like archaic swards, as in old cricket pitches at Blindley Heath, Frogit Heath, and Henfield Common, as well as surviving in much longer swards managed for hay, like the Harewood Estate meadows, Outwood, or just derelict, like Tickfold Meadows. If you are able to recognise its presence, despite its small size, early flowering, and green-gold camouflage, then it becomes a welcome 'friend' in any search for surviving ancient grasslands.

I first took a fancy to **Meadow Thistle** (old fashionedly called **Marsh Plume Thistle**), *Cirsium dissectum*, as a result of spending some lovely times exploring Wharfedale and other parts of The Yorkshire Dales, where I had an elderly aunt. Along the lane side verges near the River Wharfe, in late spring, paraded this tall thistle with woolly stems and soft leaves, carmine-topped with big pompom flowers. It was the Melancholy Thistle, *Cirsium heterophyllum*. Later, I discovered that it had a sister species, our Meadow Thistle, alike in many ways but much smaller. They have exactly complementary distributions. The Meadow Thistle lives in Ireland and the south of England and Wales, and the Melancholy Thistle lives in upland northern England and Scotland.

The Meadow Thistle is a thing of beauty. It is beautiful enough for any garden, though it wouldn't survive in most of them. It touches me when it forms large, silver-tinged, bunny's ears swarms, with its oh-so-red pointillist blobs, in some wet meadow or marsh. It's not really prickly, and calling it a thistle gives quite the wrong impression.

It used to be common. In 1937, it was described[9] as "frequent and locally plentiful on damp heaths and boggy meadows" and "locally abundant on wet heaths." That's a joke, now!

It survives in only six places in Sussex, as far as I know. It grows (2016) beautifully and very happily near Henfield in a recently discovered location. It grows in an old boggy meadow near Chailey (where it has recently had 'rescue' management). It grows on Ditchling Common in the Country Park (where it also has recently had 'rescue' management) and on the 'commoners' common', to the south. It grows on Chailey Common (where, again, it has had 'rescue' management), and on a small well-managed pasture near Storrington (2011). It had about 10 sub-sites on Ashdown Forest till recent years, but may only be on two of them now, where it looks in poor condition. In south east Surrey its only site is on the very derelict Copthorne Meadows, where it just clings onto life. In Kent, it has long gone from its last site (on Ham Fen, where they nurture Beavers, but failed to nurture this beauty).

It's gone from *Beaks Marsh, Chailey Warren, Balcombe Marsh, Hooklands Farm (Shipley), Mill Place (East Grinstead), the Scrase Valley, Pond Lye, Station Pasture (Balcombe), Brookwood Meadow (Ashurst)* … despite all being recognised, designated sites, three in nature conservation management.

Lousewort, *Pedicularis sylvatica*, was so called because it grew on poor pasturage and was thought to be responsible for bringing down the flocks to poor condition and thus subject to attack by lice. Thus was

Pathetic clump of Great Tussock Sedge in an 'improved' pasture

the innocent plant reckoned as the cause, and not a mere signifier.[10] It is however, a very good indicator of archaic, wet, unimproved and acid pastures, and since those places are so rare, the plant has become so too, though it was described as "common" by Wolley-Dod in 1937. It is another very pretty thing, with its stumpy spike of pinky purple flowers. It can get mistaken for an orchid, and it does have that appearance, though its little fern-like pinnatifid leaves allow of no error. In May time it colours the marshy sward in places where it thrives. Its best site in the Brighton Line landscape is probably The Steep, near Newstead Farm in St Leonard's Forest, TQ 241/2 311/2. There it forms a major component in the 'tapestry', with Tormentil and Meadow Buttercup, over a wide area, in the second most colourful phase of the site's calendar, after the Wild Daffodil display. It is a hemi-parasite, like Yellow Rattle.

It has gone from a depressing litany of places, but is still healthy and happy on Woodmancote Moor, and was recently found on a hidden site in Ardingly, though it is on the point of extinction on Henfield Common and recently lost from Springfield Farm, St Leonard's Forest.

It has a more robust sister, called **Marsh Lousewort**, *P. palustris* – a gorgeous thing, which can be over a foot tall and likes sphagnum quaking bogs. I know it only from Oxfordshire and from Scotland and the Alps, but it used to occur on Henfield Common, at Ditchling, Newick, Rusper, and St Leonard's Forest.

It is odd to think of quaking bogs as a Brighton Line ecosystem. You think of them only on Ashdown Forest and the west Wealden heaths nowadays, where bog plants like **Bog Asphodel** and **Cotton Grass** are still easily seen. In the Weald of middle Sussex, Bog Asphodel is now only present on Chailey Common, and Cotton Grass is only found at Sedgebrook Farm near Chailey Common, in a woodland bog not at all like the moorland locations we now associate with it. It is lost from its other two local sites on Henfield's commons

ECO-WAR ON DITCHLING COMMON

Destroyed archaic vegetation

Destroyed archaic vegetation

Surviving archaic vegetation

Destroyed archaic vegetation

The Cease Fire Line (white lines): Ditchling Common. Agribusiness farmers were forced to halt their destruction – but too late for much of the Common.

Commons and Greens

Commons and greens have always been a major stronghold for natural Wealden grasslands. Despite the huge enclosures in modern times they still play this role. Little commons and greens like **Roeheath Common, Chailey**, **Scaynes Hill Common**, the **Streat Greens**, and two of the the **three Henfield commons** all hold aboriginal grasslands. **Horstead Keynes Green** looks like a boring bit of amenity turf, but is rich with old meadow fungi.

Ditchling Common is probably the best old Wealden grassland site in central Sussex. It is a miracle that anything survives there after all the abuse and neglect it has suffered over the past sixty years. Some of the consortium of commoners who used to own it, and still own the part south of Folders Lane East, ploughed up a large chunk in the '50s or '60s but were forced to return it to grazing by the public outcry. Since then they ruined about three quarters of the southern part by agri-chemical improvement (though in recent years the consortium's done much excellent work). And East Sussex County Council, who bought the northern part with the best intentions in 1974, and turned it into a country park, have, in practice, scarcely done better. They have never committed the resources the Common needs. Huge areas of the country park have been lost to Sallow, thorn scrub and young woodland, and large areas of what remains of the old grassland have been left without grazing and with inadequate mowing.

Rarities like the Tawny and Flea Sedges, *Carex hostiana* and *C. pulicaris*, have been lost, as has the Silver Studded Blue butterfly, *Plebejus argus*, and most of the special micro-moths that were the Common's pride and joy. The rare Meadow Thistle, *Cirsium dissectum*, teeters on the edge of extinction. One important patch had a farmer's hay bale dumped on it several years ago.

Despite all that, the place still retains a host of special species. I love the southern part best – that is, what's left of it after the farmer-commoners' depredations. It is the part which most retains the landscape and feeling of the old Common. Dyer's Greenweed is abundant and

and Balcombe Marsh. We had two insectivorous Sundew species in our area, where they would have been common in Worth and St Leonards Forests. Their old pejorative name was 'Red Rot', given for the same reason that Lousewort got its name. **Oblong Leaved Sundew** is now extinct in this book's area, though it was once on Henfield Common, but **Round Leaved Sundew** is still just present on Chailey Common, thanks to careful nursing. Once common **Marsh Cinquefoil**, or 'Water Strawberry', still survives in the Scrase Valley, at Woodmancote Moor, and Sedgebrook Marsh, and probably at a few other spots. **Wild Hop** is one plant whose association with wet and fenny places I was slow to recognise. Nowadays I think of it as a regular wetland indicator, growing profusely over bushes by streams, river bridges and causeways, as at Wortleford Bridge, Mock Bridge, Honeybridge, Pookbourne Bridge, on Broadmare and Chailey Commons, in the Pells Holt at Offham, and in Woolfly Marsh sedge fen.

WHAT'S LEFT AND WHAT'S GONE

What unimproved Wealden grassland and heath still exists is there because it has slipped through the fingers of intensive farming, or because it has non-commercial uses which offer it no threat (like old churchyards). Something about these surviving sites has kept them safe from destructive exploitation.

BALCOMBE MARSH POSTAGE STAMP

Petty Whin still clings on amongst the Tufted Hair Grass, Purple Moor Grass and Dwarf Gorse. In winter you might still surprise a Snipe or two from the wet ground.

Streat's two linear Greens are an exceptional survival of a once-commonplace Wealden landscape feature. Till the mid-nineteenth century the very similar neighbouring Plumpton Green survived as well, but no trace of that remains. Only the eastern and western 'arms' of Streat's Greens survive in their unimproved state.

More than two thirds of Streat Lane Green, the western arm, is still unimproved neutral grassland in the ownership of the parish council, who allow the residents to manage their adjacent portions. Pepper Saxifrage and Stone Parsley are scattered throughout. Where the sward is allowed to flower it is very colourful, with clovers and vetches, Knapweed, Fleabane, Ox Eye Daisy, Bird's Foot Trefoil, Meadowsweet, Agrimony, Burnet Saxifrage and Wild Carrot.

Shergolds Farm Green, the eastern arm, is a green lane that magics you right back to the medieval drovers' roads, meandering between thick hedgerows over uneven, damp or dry ground. Strawberry Clover was the thing that first caught my eye, with its fruits like frosted strawberries. It is common all along. There's Spiny Restharrow too, and scattered Pepper Saxifrage and Stone Parsley. At its southern end by the railway the Green crosses a brook with thick thorn on either side. Listen out for Nightingales in spring.

Some of those commons lost to enclosure have had morsels of their old vegetation preserved within their post-enclosure uses. Part of that heritage of the lost **Valebridge Common** survives within the Bedelands Local Nature Reserve at Burgess Hill. Valebridge Common Field and Furze Common Field are little pieces of heaven. In May time clouds of little Grass Rivulet moths rise up around you as you walk amongst the sea of Yellow Rattle (on which their caterpillars feed), Ox Eye Daisy, Dyers Greenweed, Spotted Orchids, plantains, clovers, vetches, and Eggs and Bacon. Adder's Tongue Fern just clings on. Tiny fragments of the vegetation of the old **Haywards Heath Common** (enclosed in 1862) have survived within Clare Park (Ling Heather and Tormentil) and the graveyard of St Wilfred's Church on the High Street (with a rich waxcap fungi assemblage). The legacy of **Walstead Common** survives within Walstead Cemetery one and a half centuries after its enclosure, with Ling and Bell Heather, Cowslip, Green Winged Orchis, and 21 waxcap species. A tiny part of **Mannings Heath Common**, also enclosed 150 years ago, survives under the guise of the Mannings Heath Recreation Ground and Cricket Club. There's a little piece of Chamomile lawn and enough heathy, mossy turf to support nine old meadow fungi, including a fragrant, honey-scented waxcap. The roadside verge along the southern edge of **Blackland Common,** Henfield, another Victorian enclosure, retained its flowery cover till recently, with Grass Vetchling, Perennial Flax, Perforate St John's Wort, False Fox Sedge and many different grasses. It is now just mown amenity lawn, ironically forming the entrance to the pay-to-visit 'Prairie Garden'.

Farm Fields

Remarkably, in two particular areas, one in the High Weald and one in the Low Weald, something of the ancient character of Wealden pastures and meadows survives across whole sub-landscapes.

The **Danehill Meadows** embrace a patchwork of tiny fields assarted from common pasturage, and surviving (2012) because they are too steep and too small to

To the left: banal modern pasture

To the right, in the nature reserve: archaic marsh, though very neglected

A postage-stamp-sized nature reserve in a sea of banal modern pasture. The Marsh Helleborine Orchis is gone.

BACKSTORY / Chapter 8: Archaic pasture, meadow, moor and heath

Rush pasture east of Clappers Lane, Poynings

cultivate or improve. They are within an area nearly two miles long by three quarters of a mile wide between Danehill and Chelwood Common, e.g. TQ 40 27, 41 27 and 41 28. Many have been lost, some are semi-improved, some very derelict, whilst a few are being restored and one or two are in near-pristine condition, with Chimney Sweeper moth, Heath Spotted Orchis, and other delights. Many of the meadows are managed for livery grazing, which is sometimes benign, but often brings its own insidious damage, with poached ground, over-grazing, paddockization, sheds and other clutter.

The **Langley Green and Amberley Farm Meadows, Crawley,** are embraced by hedges and shaws which have been 'preserved in aspic' for at least 150 years. They lie on the flat and tranquil flood plain of the infant River Mole, between Crawley and the edge of Gatwick Airport, and are threatened with destruction by the proposed second Gatwick runway. They are a mixture of rushy fields, with gullies, fossil meanders, and little overgrown farm ponds in their corners, and colourful flower meadows with vetches, trefoils, clovers, Knapweed and buttercups, Grass Vetchling, Spotted Orchis and Southern Marsh Orchis (2014). Some are grazed by horses, some cut for hay, one grazed by a lonely Belted Galloway cow, and others left unmanaged. In spring the hedges and shaws are alive with bird song and spangled with Stitchwort and Bluebells.

Elsewhere, a few significant clusters of farm fields have been preserved by their difficult terrain, or by sympathetic land managers. **Bedelands Farm**, just north of Burgess Hill, now a Local Nature Reserve, makes up the largest of these, with seven fields. Their variety is great, and can be traced back to all the nuances of history, drainage and soil type, some parts yellow with buttercups, others white with ox-eye daisy or darkened with rushes. **Stonelands** has a cluster of five unimproved and semi-improved pastures, east of the Ardingly Road, north of Wakehurst. The fields are on steep banks with hidden 'knees' of Ardingly Sandrock straining to bust out through the thin turf along the sill which tops the slopes … and they do, in one place (2014). A couple of the fields are derelict and colourful with Knapweed, Burnet Saxifrage and scattered Devil's Bit. The two northern fields, though, are cropped short and strewn with stars of Tormentil, Creeping Cinquefoil and Mouse Ear Hawkweed, whilst in autumn troops of Scarlet Hood and Golden Waxcap bejewel the steepest parts. **Batchellor's/Landfall Farm** south of Barns Green has (2014) a cluster of five flowery, colourful meadows, two of which are partly unimproved and the rest semi-improved. **Sedgewick Park** has three gorgeous large meadows between the mansion and the medieval castle site. The massed Yellow Rattle is a feature there, and in high summer it does indeed 'rattle' if you walk through it! There are a cluster of **six meadows south of Ditchling Common**, which are mostly semi-improved but with significant surviving interest, including unusual Oval Sedge fen by the brook (2012). At **Sedgebrook Farm**, south west of Chailey Common, seven fields remain unimproved and are managed for nature.

Other scattered farm fields survive in ones or two. At **The Pools**, TQ 223 145, just 12 minutes walk from Woods Mill at Henfield, there are two extraordinarily colourful derelict meadows. At dusk in July at the top of the north field a river of purple-red Betony flows away down the hillside. Only at a couple of other sites have I ever seen Betony in such glorious abundance. (Site in desperate condition, 2017). Almost a mile south of Copsale there is a tiny triangular meadow, part of the long-gone **Haven Farm,** alongside the embankment of the old Horsham Flyer railway (now the Downslink). Sitting in it munching cake and drinking tea we admired the sea of colour on every side, framed by wide blousy hedges – Yellow Rattle, Crosswort, Spotted Orchids, Betony, Lesser Stitchwort, Eggs and Bacon, Knapweed, clovers, bumbles, burnet and grass moths, crickets, froghoppers, grasshoppers, Harlequin Longhorn Beetles … it is indeed a haven. (Site in desperate condition, 2017).

North east of Crawley Down and west of **Gullege** farmstead there is another *shangri la* … a place so lovely I could happily just string superlatives together like a daisy chain. It is a long abandoned meadow on the edge of woodland surrounded by hedgerows, TQ 361 381/2. Everything is luxurious, abundant and alive. Dyers Greenweed makes a large egg yellow splash across the centre, and Saw Wort is still present in a couple of places. There are big old anthills, occasional Bitter Vetch, frequent Devil's Bit and Pepper Saxifrage, much Betony and some Sneezewort. A Fox cub wanders right up to me. Big flocks of Linnet and other finches twitter along, enjoying the abundant seed heads. Froglets hop. Jays screech. Woodies hum "take two cows, Taffy". I pick up a deer antler for the grandson. There's a boundary stream with Water Plantain and Water Mint. It has been derelict for many years and cannot last much longer (2011), with encroaching Blackthorn, Bracken, Sallow and Oak. The finer grassland is drowning under False Oat Grass, Creeping Thistle and Creeping Buttercup, and scrub and Hemlock Water Dropwort are taking over the old pond. How can we accept this blindness to such paradise gardens? Why do we collectively tolerate such loss?

The good people at **High Beeches Garden**, east of Handcross, have conserved two old forest meadows within the grounds. The gardens lie just on the boundary of the medieval Worth Forest, and indeed there are old oak pollards that mark that boundary. On one September visit we saw Pink Ballerina and Golden Waxcaps, *Hygrocybe calyptriformis* and *H. chlorophana*, pushing though the mossy turf. Nearby was a troop of Indigo Pinkgills, *Entoloma chalybaeum var. lazulinum*. There are Green Winged Orchids and Heath Spotted Orchids, Cowslip, Yellow Rattle, Ox Eye Daisy, and all sorts. We followed a gorgeous burly tachinid fly with a bright yellow and black abdomen, nectaring on Devil's Bit. Look carefully and you'll find tiny wefts of Ivy Leaved Bellflower in the turf. **Standinghall Meadows** are half-lost amongst tall forest trees between what remains of Standinghall Farmstead and the long footpath northwards from Worth Abbey, TQ 314 351. Spangled with summer rainbow colours, they are alive with bees and butterflies, like Heidi's Alpine home. Silver Washed Fritillaries race about and Brown Hawker dragons constantly patrol. A Roe Deer buck breaks cover. (Left uncut, December 2017).

Moor

'Moor' (from the Saxon *'mor'*) used to mean swampy, wild ground, and was a term used equally for small and large sites. A tiny marshy common or a wet and difficult field could be called a moor, as could a huge area of wet high ground (Ex*moor,* Dart*moor*) or low ground (Sedge*moor*). *Moor*hens and Purple *Moor* Grass inhabit the tiniest ponds and smallest fields. 'Moor' is an evocative term, conjuring up images of Snipe and the calls of wildfowl, silvery tussock grasses, rushes, sedges, Reed Buntings, and flashes of colour from Ragged Robin, Lousewort, Spearwort, Marsh Marigold, and orchids.

Lots of the 'moors' which appear on the map have now lost that vegetation, as with *Moor*fields Farm, west of Cuckfield, TQ 279 256, or *Mor*ley, at Shermanbury, TQ 206 198. A few, though, still have it, often in a battered and reduced state. **The Steep**, at Newstead Farm, St Leonard's Forest is one of the best examples of moor vegetation, with wet rushy gullies and soft, mossy turf, spangled with Bog Pimpernel and Tormentil. **Woodmancote Moor**, TQ 225 155, and **Henfield Common** have much of great beauty, with their Marsh and Heath Spotted Orchids. The **relict, moor east and west of Slugwash Lane, Wivelsfield, north east of More House Farm**, e.g. TQ 353 215/6 has a riot of Meadowsweet in its enclosures, and brooks scented with Water Mint and noisy with Marsh Frogs (2011). In Surrey, **The Moors** at Nutfield / South Merstham have now recovered some of their watery vegetation after years of quarrying, with their transformation as parts of the Nutfield Marsh Nature Reserve.

The one mile ribbon of wash land along the Cockhaise Brook between the Horsted Keynes sewage works, TQ 376 282, and Goddenwick Farm still has a bit of the character of 'moor'. (The northern fragments south of High Wood are now heavily drained, 2017). At **Goddenwick Farm** the lower part of one moor pasture is intact, TQ 363/4 283/4, with a Brackeny slope, full of flowers, as well as rushy gullies, beautiful stream side tall herbage, and a lovely damp plateau. All are nice, but the damp higher ground is particularly special. Big Marbled Orb Weaver Spiders, *Araneus marmoreus*, hang from their dewy webs. Tiny frogs hop out of the way. There are Carnation and Oval Sedges, *Carex punicea* and *C. ovalis*, Spearwort and Marsh Ragwort, and coneheads and grasshoppers ping about. Fairy clubs make a show in the autumn. There is a cluster of three unimproved pastures in the deep valley bottom just east of **Hapstead, Ardingly**. One field, TQ 351 294, has three deep rushy gullies, with Ragged Robin and Sneezewort, and Pignut on the drier knolls. The far slope is a sheer delight of points of colour … Lousewort, Pepper and Burnet Saxifrages, Betony and Knapweed, Marsh Ragwort, Square Stalked St John's Wort and bits of Zig Zag Clover and Ox Eye Daisy. (Ungrazed and deteriorating, 2016).

The webbing of **rides in Oldhouse Warren, Worth and Worthlodge Forests** serve to preserve linear remnants of ancient forest lawn and moor vegetation, with many tiny and special plants of acidic bare or waterlogged ground, short turf and moss. There are Ivy leaved Bellflower and Bog Pimpernel, Pale Sedge, Heath Grass, Lesser Skullcap, Lily of the Valley in one place, Heath Speedwell and Yellow Sedge, Centaury, Marsh Violet and *Sphagnum* bog mosses. (Damaged by a new network of hardcore-and-chalk rides, 2017). The **main east-west ride in Worthlodge Forest**, under the line of electricity pylons, has Eyebright and Heath Groundsel, Tormentil, Sneezewort, Corn Mint, Devil's Bit, Betony and Wood Sage. (Succeeding to scrub, with tree planting, 2016).

In Surrey, **Copthorne Common Meadows**, TQ 326 399, are classic damp and peaty moor, despite their dereliction – rushy, sedgy and tussocky. Two miles

Successful heathland restoration: Tilgate Forest Lodge (2011)

north west, the **Broadbridge Meadows**, TQ 309 419, next to the M23 have that same wild moor quality, and cattle still laze there, half hidden in the herbage, amongst the hoverflies and bees. The **Harewood Estate Meadows**, TQ 330 476, are even better managed, with mowing as well as cattle grazing, and can be very wet in winter. **Weirwood Reservoir pondtail**, TQ 377 344, is moor, too.

Heath

Heath, defined by its cover of ericaceous species – Ling, Cross Leaved Heather and Bell Heather – is now very rare in the Brighton Line Weald, though once abundant across much of the forest ridges, and very frequent on the High Wealden sands, as well as the Lower Greensand. Even the Wealden Clay had heath, as at **Ditchling Common**, though Ling Heather is now very rare on that Common, and was altogether lost to the view of its County Council managers till its recent re-discovery.

Chailey Common, with all three heathers in abundance, is our best example. Ericaceous vegetation occurs over about a mile there, from south to north. However, with the addition of Lane End Common and The Warren, with the heather and Bilberries of the Rotherfield and Little Rotherfield Woods, the heathy ride through Warr's Wood, under the pylons, and other bits and pieces, the Chailey heathland belt extends to some 2.5 miles SW to NE.

In **St Leonard's Forest** the best heath is in the old **deer park of Leonardslee**, TQ 226 258, where heathers have a scattered presence amongst grass heath, though new trees are encroaching on its open character. The **Forestry Commission**, in its modern wildlife friendly guise, is now restoring large areas of heath along ride sides, glades and intersections within its St Leonard's Forest estate, and this is bearing fruit in the return of such species as Nightjar. There is good heathland restoration at **Owlbeech Wood**, too, TQ 201/2 314. In the **Buchan Country Park**, Crawley, TQ 240 338, there are two major restored heathland sites amongst a matrix of conifer and broadleaved woodland and ponds.

In **Worth Forest** the best heath is in the superb restored site at **Tilgate Forest Lodge**, TQ 268 314, all the more remarkable for its wholly natural appearance after just a couple of decades of hard work removing impenetrable Rhodi jungle. **Paddockhurst Park** has heath by the drive at TQ 327 332, amongst other small sites. On the south edge of Copthorne village there are sad fragments of both derelict heath and over-managed heath on the common within **Copthorne Golf Course.**

In the Surrey part of the Brighton Line Weald heath is even closer to extinction, with **Reigate Heath** holding the only substantial area, and that in a fragmented sub-optimal form within the golf course there.

Churchyards and cemeteries

Churchyards and cemeteries are often the last local redoubts of old Wealden grasslands. Their regimes of tight mowing mimic the grazing of sheep, deer, cattle, geese or horses which many old grassland species depended upon.[11] Some of these sites are extraordinarily rich. Both **Slaugham and Danehill churchyards** have nationally important old meadow fungi assemblages, with twenty one recorded waxcap species each. At both of them I have seen the little flame-like tongues of Scarlet Caterpillar Fungi, *Cordyceps militaris*, peeping up through the grass. They belong to a group of fungi which specialise in parasitising over-wintering caterpillars which have buried themselves underground. In Tibet there is a major industry built around collecting these caterpillar fungi for traditional medicine. **Spithurst churchyard** has a famous display of Green Winged Orchids, and Spotted Orchids too. Its relaxed management gives it the appearance of a woodland edge meadow, with old anthills and tufts of Ling Heather. I counted four sedges on my last visit, and there are always new discoveries to be made. (Split into two and at risk, 2017). **Sayers Common Churchyard** is beautifully managed both for its old meadow flowers and grasses and for its superb old meadow fungi. **Tandridge Churchyard** in Surrey is another jewel, as is **Henfield Churchyard.**

Western Road Cemetery in Haywards Heath seems the most unlikely place to find wild things. It is managed in rigid sergeant major fashion, with frequent short-back-and-sides. The sound of mowing machines is ever present. Yet behind its old iron railings and gates there is an astonishing hide-out for the plants of old pastures and forest glades. Indeed, the cemetery is on the site of old Petland Wood and its shade is largely given by preserved oak standards from its woodland past. Once you "get your eye in" you will start to spot things. Amongst the damp grass you can spy Ivy Leaved Bellflower, and I found Bitter Vetch and rare Wood Horsetail on old graves. On a wetter area there is even sphagnum moss and Marsh Pennywort, and on drier areas Tormentil, Eyebright, Autumn Hawkbit, Ox Eye Daisy and even Ling Heather. I have yet to find Cow Wheat, Lousewort and Pill Sedge, but I have spotted 12 old meadow fungi on a couple of autumn visits.

Though medieval churchyards often have rich old grasslands, many of the best are also to be found around Victorian churches. Churches like **Turners Hill, Crawley Down, North Chailey, Lower Beeding, Colgate, Sayers Common, Staplefield, Spithurst, St Wilfred's (Haywards Heath), Highbrook,** and **Danehill,** are all Victorian. Their flora has either been directly enclosed from old grasslands, or has colonised from places nearby.

Cricket pitches

Naturally occurring Chamomile lawns are rare these days, but one place where you may find them is on old cricket grounds. A small area exists on sandy ground at **Mannings Heath cricket ground**, and larger areas on **Staplefield** and **Henfield cricket grounds**. Indeed, in season a car passenger can see the flowering Chamomile like a light snow fall at Henfield in the drive past along the adjacent road. (The majority of the Chamomile lawn destroyed, 2017). Chamomile used to be found too, on path sides at Chailey Common, but I can't find it now. It still occurs on both the cricket and football pitches at the north east end of **Reigate Heath**.

Those cricket pitches can be good too for a range of old meadow fungi, as well as for many low-growing mosses, herbs, woodrushes and grasses.

Verges

Many old Wealden drove roads and lanes retain wide verges that, in the past, would have been heavily grazed by farmers and by poor folk who lacked land of their own. It was a treat, till recently, to see chickens and ducks wandering on the roadside 'waste' outside Gallops Farm on Street Lane … but that sight is now vanishingly rare in our countryside. Though local authorities perform their duty to mow verges to retain sight lines and occasional parking for motorists, and walkways for pedestrians, they mostly do not collect the fallen hay, so that it forms mulch which, over time, suppresses the finer herbs and grasses. Neither do many landowners and councils rigorously cut back the encroaching thorn scrub that grows outwards from the old hedge lines to engulf the grassy verges. And so the rich flowery swards of the past have now gone from the vast majority of our verges. They have become as rare on these verges as they are on our farmlands.

Of course, many of us will know the roads and green lanes lined with Cow Parsley, Upright Hedge Parsley, Hogweed umbels, and Blackberries in late summer, but those frequent sights – lovely as they are – are a mark of the *decline* of the diversity of the old Wealden swards. They do not mark their health. Those few tall, rough herbs have taken over from a multitude of diverse grasses and herbs that characterised the older grasslands.

We are fortunate though, that council works departments in recent times have cooperated with naturalists to identify those places that still retain the old vegetation and manage them appropriately. If you look carefully, you can sometimes spot the labelled white posts that mark the beginning and ends of these 'notable verges'.

It was the egg yellow Dyers's Greenweed that had caught my eye several times as we passed in the car. I'll never tire of that sight. So, even though we got to **the roadside south of Joles Farm, south of Maplehurst**, at the end of a long jaunt, this was one place I wanted to give time to. Great splodges of yellow on both roadsides … and all the Turkish carpet colours the best verges can show off. Since then this verge has been neglected, and is in decline (2015). Walking back to Copsale in the long June evening we had another treat … the roadside banks at Steed Corner. Though there was no Dyers Greenweed, the list of plants we saw was even longer than at Joles Farm.

Like many surviving flowery verges the Joles Farm verges are not wide enough to allow walkers to really relax. The cars whoosh past too close and too fast. At **Malthouse Lane, west of Burgess Hill**, the traffic is much worse. The thorn has been allowed to encroach almost to the edge of the tarmac, and you take your life in your hands delaying there. A small tragedy, really, for the Dyer's Greenweed has gone and the Saw Wort, Betony and other special plants only cling on in shade. They will be gone, soon, if nothing changes in the management of the place.

Mallion's Lane, south of Staplefield, couldn't be more different, the narrow lane so quiet it would be safe for a child to walk there … Tall banks and deep

Imps' fingers … or tongues poking up from the underworld: Earthtongue fungi in a churchyard

hedgerows on both sides almost like a hollow way … Colour, colour, colour … the most beautiful tall herb community. I counted 73 herbs and grasses in a bit over an hour … orchids, vetches and vetchlings, Eggs and Bacon, native Goldenrod, Hedge Parsley, buttercups, mints, sedges, and clovers … lovely.

One **verge in St Leonard's Forest** was much visited just for one plant, Bastard Balm, *Melittis melissophyllum*, known there for over two centuries. A large-flowered member of the thyme family it is more usually seen on the warm and rainy Cornish coast's rough ground, and St Leonard's was its most easterly surviving English site. I've not seen it there on recent visits.

On **Stone Hill Road, south of East Grinstead** the roadside waste is wide enough to take you well out of harm's way. There's all sorts there – a tall hawkweed, lots of Cat's Ear, and plenty of Dyers Greenweed, Betony, Zig Zag Clover and Bitter Vetch, with abundant Meadow Vetchling, all in a matrix of Bent grass. The Moles are at home there, too.

WHERE TO HUNT FOR UNIMPROVED GRASSLANDS

Here are some tips for finding these lost places.

- They are often on **steep land** … too steep for machine cultivation and tractor access.

- They are often on **wet ground**. Brook side fields are a good place to look.

- They are often found in **parts of otherwise improved fields**, such as corners difficult for machinery or along the edges. Sometimes you can just find a linear strip of archaic vegetation along a hedgerow or field edge path.

- They may comprise **very small fields**, perhaps old farm closes near the farmstead, or small fields that have survived because they are in different ownership from the surrounding land.

- They are often **non-agricultural in usage**. Thus, land managed in ornamental parks, or for the amenity of some rich owner, land reserved for sports or public amenity usage, land banked for future development, or land over which the public may have access rights: all may be worth checking out.

- They are often **unmanaged and derelict**, with a rank, tall sward and invasive scrub and trees.

HOW TO TELL IF YOU'VE FOUND ONE

- By far the best sign is **floristic diversity.** Look for a wide show of different flowers, grasses, sedges and mosses. You don't have to be able to identify them, but counting them in a given area (like a rough square yard) can be very useful. When you get more confident you can start looking for **indicator species**, such as Bitter Vetch, Devil's Bit Scabious, Betony or Pepper Saxifrage. The presence of a number of them is a good sign of high value.

- The grass will be **duller shades of green** … olive, yellow, brown, or straw greens … rather than bright 'nitrogen' green (which indicates enrichment with fertilisers). It will be **patchy and vari-coloured**, rather than uniform.

- Good short swards will often be **mossy**.

- **Grassy anthills** are a very good sign, as are small surface variations … **dips, hollows, tumps, wet and dry patches.**

- The presence of **tussocks of rushes, sedges, or coarser grasses** can be a good sign.

- **Bright, colourful or varied fungi** are an excellent sign.

- **Dazzling displays of buttercups** (and not much else) can deceive beginners, for they mostly show that the field's been 'improved', but such fields are still well worth checking.

WHAT TO DO IF YOU FIND ONE

- **Find out who the owners are and make friends with them.** The easiest way is to knock on the door of the nearest house. It takes a bit of nerve, but folk are usually friendly and interested.

- **Tell the local authority ranger or the county ecologist** (via County Hall), and the Sussex Biodiversity Record Centre (SBRC) at Woods Mill.

- If the site looks as though it is suffering damage, or is in danger of any kind, then *act without delay.*

THE SITUATION IS DESPERATE

Since this chapter was first drafted seven years ago many of the sites I describe have deteriorated further or been destroyed. The situation for our Wealden archaic grasslands couldn't be more desperate.

We urgently need both a dedicated organisation locally and nationally, and a re-orientation by all environmentalists and wildlifers to the imperative of defending this public resource.

ENDNOTES

1. 'Meadows', page 94, by George Peterken. British Wildlife Publishing (2013). This is the definitive book on meadows, and is unlikely to be surpassed. Easy to read, with superb pictures and huge amounts of information, it is all the better for being written by a scientist who spent most of his working life studying and campaigning for ancient woods!
2. 'Ghosts in our grasslands', Andrew Jones, British Wildlife, Vol. 21, No. 5, June 2010, pps. 339–344.
3. This kind of neutral grassland is known as 'Knapweed-Crested Dog's Tail grassland, of the Meadow Vetchling sub-community': MG5a in the National Vegetation Classification (NVC).
4. This type of grassland is the Heath Grass sub-community, MG5c.
5. This derelict grassland, dominated by False Oat Grass, is known as the MG1, False Oat Grass vegetation community.
6. 'A Complete History of the Butterflies and Moths of Sussex', pages 80–81 and elsewhere, by Colin R. Pratt, FRES. Self published.
7. Factsheet on Dyer's Greenweed by Butterfly Conservation.
8. Tony Davis *pers. com.* 12/10/11.
9. 'The Flora of Sussex', page 250, by Lieut. Colonel A. H. Wolley-Dod. The Chatford House Press (1937 & 1970).
10. 'Wayside and Woodland Blossoms', page 37, Vol. 2, by Edward Step. Warne (1896)
11. Species diversity in old grasslands is dependent upon them being grazed or mown. Without such management the more robust, coarser grasses, rushes and sedges take over from the smaller (and often very pretty or wacky) herbs, mosses, lichen and other plants, in a process known as 'succession', which in our natural region will climax in woodland cover. Diverse, species-rich old grasslands aren't just interesting and beautiful, but serve as sustainable pasturage for farm livestock and horses, places for us to play sports on and ramble, and even places to bury our dead!

Balcombe Down giant Beech pollard:
Praise be to nature for dappled things (and thanks be to Gerard Manley Hopkins)

CHAPTER 9
Ancient Sussex giants:
The oldest and biggest trees

Some years ago I heard Ted Green, the doyen of ancient tree experts, give a talk.

Here's an 'idea bomb' he lobbed in … *There's more biodiversity in one ancient tree than in the whole of Sussex heathland.* He meant by that to include all that one tree's possible denizens … its *fungi, beetles, moulds, galls, flies, spiders, snails and slugs, slime moulds, lichen, mosses, liverworts, ferns, worms, ants, wasps, bees, moths, butterflies, birds, mammals, centipedes, millipedes, woodlice, pseudoscorpions and other littler things right down to viruses,* no doubt …

However controversial we still find his statement, we can all readily share his high valuation of these huge life forms.

When I talk about them I keep finding that I am tempted to use words like 'beast', 'monster', 'dinosaur', and call them 'she' or 'he' (rather than 'it') … pronouns you attach to large animals, not plants … for their degree of livingness seems so tangible … so animal-like. They have arms and trunks and legs; they stand, lean, give shelter, embrace, wave, murmur, sigh, groan, and roar to the wind. They grow in summer and sleep in winter, put on green clothing and cast it off.

… And I find myself showing respect … nattering to them … using soft words and praise to them … as though, indeed, they could hear me. They have a not-busy kindness, not-busy liveliness, a living stillness, which all of us can freely acknowledge.

* * *

Entering a young Hazel, Gean, Ash and Birch wood we quickly passed along a path into the presence of a huge forest Oak pollard in full, stretching, blooming summer health. A Buzzard called overhead. We sat down against its trunk to have a bite to eat and a cuppa. There before us we spotted a torn condom packet half hidden in the leaves. Some other folk had sought to celebrate this place. That was another act of veneration.

WHAT ARE 'ANCIENT' AND 'VETERAN' TREES AND HOW ARE THEY MEASURED?

The experts define **'ancient'** trees as being trees in old age. Their canopies may be shrunken. They will likely have very wide trunks, and be hollow.[1] They have much decaying wood, which forms an incredibly important habitat. **'Veteran'** trees will have some of the same features of wounds and decay, but will likely be of mature years, not in old age. **'Notable'** trees are those that stand out locally for their size. They will likely be in maturity, and may well be taller than ancient trees (just as old people shrink a bit compared to upstanding youngsters).

Trees come to those stages at different sizes and ages according to species. Pollarded Oaks can live a 1,000 years and reach six or more spans girth. Yews can live twice as long. Beech pollards can get to three, four, or even five spans girth, and perhaps reach 400–500 years old. I guess that Ash pollards will reach 300–400 years old. Birch is ancient at 150.[2]

We use simple rules to measure these giants, and a little digital camera to record them, as they specify in the Woodland Trust's 'Ancient Tree Hunt.' (For proper experts, tree measurement is more of a rigmarole). Oaks reach the veteran stage (loosely defined) at a bole girth (trunk circumference) of roughly 3 arm spans or 'hugs' at their narrowest point. Assuming an arm span of 6 foot, a three span veteran Oak measured by us has a girth of roughly 6ft x 3 = 18ft. Pretty huge. Beech and Ash reach veteran age at two spans, and Sweet Chestnut at four spans (because it grows much quicker). We assume veteran age for Birch, Maple, Gean and Wild Service at one span.

Roughly three span girth English Oak veterans may date back to the time of Cromwell or Charles 2nd, about

THE VETERAN AND ANCIENT TREES OF BALCOMBE DOWN AND PADDOCKHURST PARK, IN WORTH FOREST

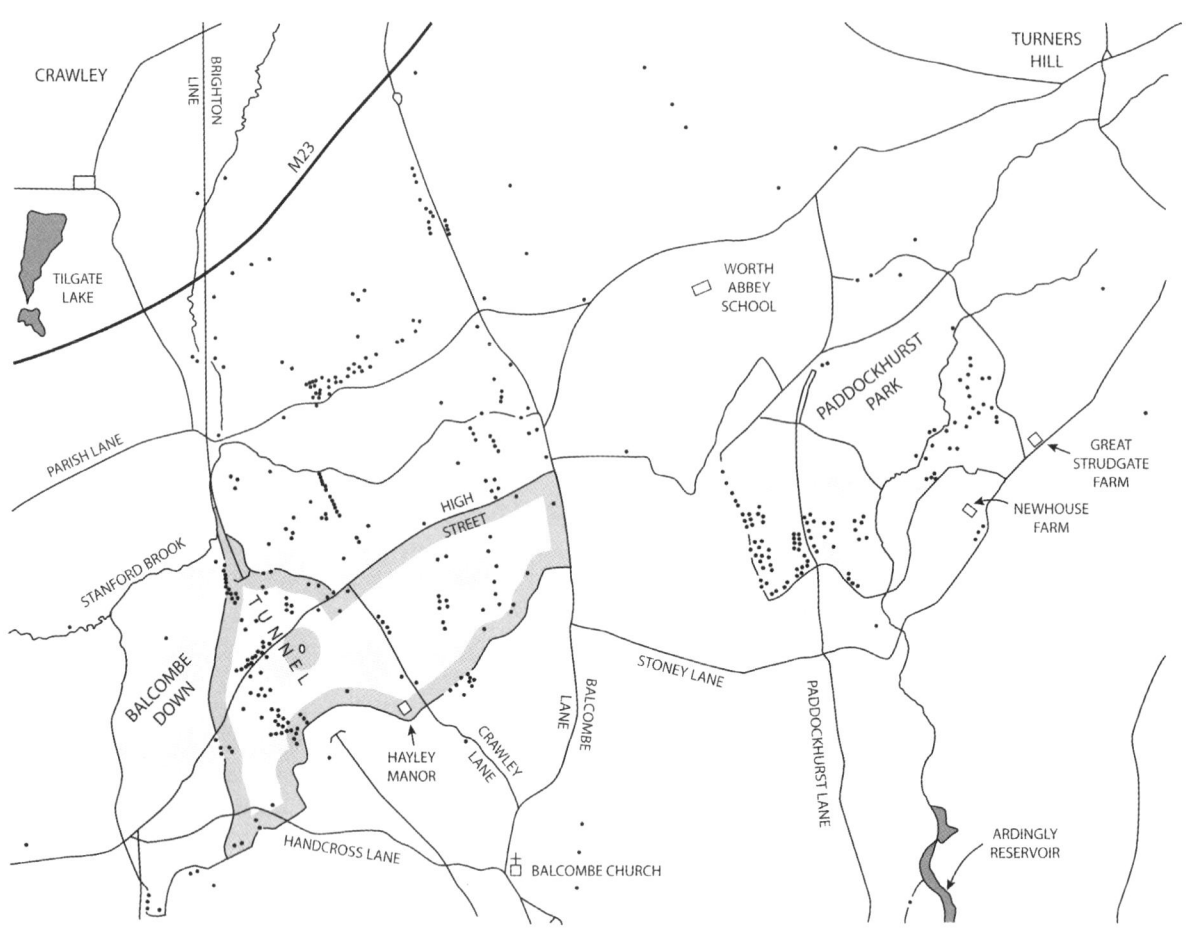

© Crown copyright and database rights 2018. OS License number 100048229

> These two sites – Paddockhurst, once an ancient deer park, and Balcombe Down, once desmesne manorial waste – hold a huge relict assemblage of old giant trees, mostly Beech, but with some Oak and a few Yew and other species, Most of the veterans are old pollards. The area I have mapped as Balcombe Down includes Monks Forest, Greentrees, and part of Cowdray and Brantridge Forests.

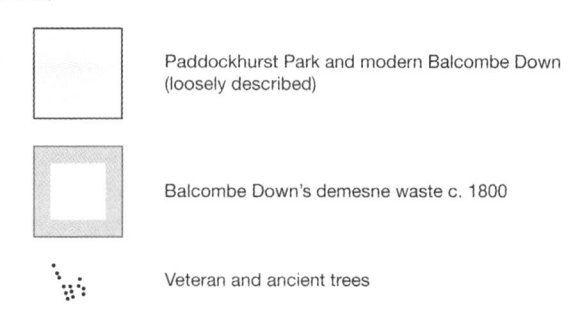

Paddockhurst Park and modern Balcombe Down (loosely described)

Balcombe Down's demesne waste c. 1800

Veteran and ancient trees

350 years old. Four span Oaks may date back over 600 years to the time of Owain Glyndwr's Welsh Revolt. (He died: 1415). Five span Oaks may take us roughly back to the 1086 Domesday Book, some 930 years ago.

THE WEALD IS FULL OF THEM

I first started noting these special trees systematically over 25 years ago, but in the last few years I've got really enthusiastic. I guessed that we'd found maybe 500 or 600 veterans in that period, but when I did the counting I realised that we'd recorded twice that ... 1075^3 just in the area covered by this book. There were 561 English Oaks and 377 Beech as well as Hornbeam, Ash and many rarer kinds amongst the 22 species we'd noted. My tatty maps are peppered with them. We found another eighteen just two days before my writing this.

They are very generally distributed across this countryside ... in hedgerows, by farmsteads and the sites

140   BACKSTORY / Chapter 9: Ancient Sussex Giants

of lost farmsteads, by manor houses, in woods and old parks, on commons, by watercourses, in churchyards, along ancient boundaries, and deep in shady gills. They occur across both the Low and High Weald. None of our old parishes are without them.

My early thought was that I was likely to find many more in the High Weald than the Low Weald, but that is not the real distinction. Many of our grandest giants – including the biggest native tree of all – are in the Low Weald.

There is though, a huge distinction between the numbers found within the footprint of our lost Saxon royal forests of Worth and St Leonards and their purlieu woods, and the numbers found across the rest of the middle Sussex Weald. About 44% of all the middle Sussex Weald veterans are found just in those two forests, and the old Forest of Worth has 31% alone. We can refine that Worth Forest figure further. The majority of its veterans are found just in one relatively small part: Balcombe Down.[4] There we have found 16%, that is 166, of all the book's veteran trees clustered, whereas the huge neighbouring erstwhile parish of old Worth, which included Turners Hill, Crawley Down and Copthorne village, well-endowed with ancient trees though it is, has a lesser total of 132.

Balcombe Down and the parts of Worth Forest near to it, still retain one of the best assemblages of ancient trees in the whole of Sussex – mostly hidden, mostly without formal public access, often neglected and endangered.

POLLARDS, WOOD PASTURE, COPPICE AND HEDGE STOOLS, MAIDENS AND BUNDLE PLANTINGS

Most of the veteran trees we've found have been **'pollards'**. That is, they are trees which have had their heads cut off,[5] and thus are paradoxically granted extra long life, maybe even twice their normal span. They were usually allowed to grow a trunk to just above the height at which grazing animals could graze them and then their young crowns were lopped, and the cut 'small wood' used for fuel and for all the construction tasks that farms and villages required. They had the advantage that cattle, deer, and other farmed animals could graze beneath them without damaging the wood growth. This combined system of grazing and wood growth was called **'wood pasturage'**, and it dominated the uncultivated tracts of the Weald until the later medieval clearances. Pollarding died out as a wood harvesting economy in the 18th and 19th centuries, though it survives as a way of managing street trees, like the limes in Lindfield village street.

When woods were enclosed against all grazing, trees could be safely cut at their base, and this **'coppicing'** method similarly extended the longevity of the trees. The woods themselves were hedged and banked around their boundaries, and the individual **'hedge stools'** often reach great ages. If they are then left to grow uncut they can also achieve giant sizes. On Low Wealden soils especially, neglected Ash and Hornbeam hedge stools can grow immense, as can Beech stools on the soils of the High Weald.

Naturally growing, un-polled **'maiden'** trees can also reach huge size and immense age, though they were rarely allowed to in medieval times, when available timber resources were turned quickly to human usage. In Tilgate Wood on the Wakehurst estate, the English Oaks on the steep slopes around the sandrock outcrops, TQ 330 310, have been allowed to grow fully into their mature stage. They contrast strongly with the much smaller maiden Oaks in places like Tottington Wood, TQ 217 122, or River Wood, TQ 330 279, which are near the commoner stage of traditional harvesting.

Occasionally, bundles of young tree whips were planted together and allowed to grow until they fused into one organism and reached immense collective size. When they do, it is often difficult to tell their origin. Way out on the Adur brooks, south east of Partridge Green, there is a huge **'bundle planted'** Oak marking the ancient parish boundary between West Grinstead and Shermanbury, TQ 201 181 (c. 2011). You can spot it in the bushy hedgeline, not because of any extra height, but just because of its dense, many-stemmed bulk. Just north of Slaugham Common and west of Coos Lane, within the bounds of Ashfold Park there is an immense bundle planted Beech, TQ 254 285. Its six arms (and one or two more have died) shoot up into the sky above a great sprawl of roots. There is a little natural 'stage' about 5ft up where children can stand and peer out between the multiple trunks. In the brook pasture on the south bank of the Adur east of Wortleford Bridge, TQ 283 210, there is a little impenetrable thicket, like a giant bush or small grove, sitting all on its own. It's made up entirely of Maple!

KINDS OF TREES AND THEIR DISTRIBUTIONS

The English Oak,[6] our 'Sussex Weed', provides clearly our most common veteran trees. They amount to 53% of those we've found. In the Low Weald they are overwhelmingly the most common. In Woodmancote 15 out of the 17 veterans we found were English Oak. In the High Weald, apart from the twin forests, they are also the most numerous. In Bolney, which is divided between Low and High Weald, all 8 veterans recorded were English Oak.

Veteran Sessile Oaks are much rarer, and we've only recorded five, I think, but that includes the magnificent giant in Pickwell Lane, TQ 280 234, and the fine specimen in the middle of Horsham Park, TQ 172 311, which marks the lost boundary of Horsham Common.

The Danny Old One: when she was young the local folk spoke Saxon and Norman-French

Beech veterans are the next commonest after English Oak, making about 34% of our veterans, and they are clustered on the High Weald sandstones of the Hastings Beds, where they are the majority species on the footprint of the twin forests. To a small extent Beech veterans also occur on the Wealden Clay, for instance at Markstakes Common, as well as along the Lower Greensand ridge of the Low Weald, for instance at Lodge Hill, Ditchling, TQ 324 154, and Little Park, Hurstpierpoint, TQ 284 165. They also occur along the base of the Downs, where the Wealden soils are at first very chalky, for instance along Church Lane, Newtimber, TQ 269 130.

We recorded 36 Ash veterans, but there are many more. They often form huge coppice and hedgerow stools, all full of holes. There is a cluster of at least four veterans in and around High Wood, TQ 147 299, in the crook of the River Arun south of Broadbridge Heath. There's a wizened old pollard in the upper gill south of Great Thorndean Farm, TQ 273 255, and huge hedgerow stools marking the edge of the Adur brooks, south of Great Betley Farm, north west of Henfield, TQ 198 168. At Brook Street, north of Cuckfield, is a soaring Ash maiden of three spans girth, TQ 306 264.

Hornbeam veterans are found particularly to the east, where they often survive as old coppice and hedgerow stools, but they are also found as pollards used to mark the edges of coppice compartments. The saddest and one of the most characterful of these is in the gill wood west of Freshfield Brickworks, TQ 385 267. It is extraordinarily gnarled and Rackhamesque, as only Hornbeam can be. Half its trunk has long broken away, and its knobbly surface is covered in writing lichen, *Graphis spp.* To its west, to its north, and to its south, much of the ancient Daffodil and Bluebell woods have been chainsawed, bulldozed, and incorporated into the quarry. There is another fine Hornbeam pollard marking a coup boundary deep in Orltons Copse, TQ 222 387, two miles west of Gatwick's runway, with roaring banshee planes overhead.

Maple veterans are scattered across the Low Weald in low numbers. There is a particular concentration on the Horsham Stone scarp between Denne Park and Sedgwick Park. A lost green lane, TQ 182 277, climbs the scarp north of Coltstaple Corner and disappears into the woods. Along its upper side it is lined with ancient Maples, Butcher's Broom, Spurge Laurel (the guardians of ancient tracks), Bluebells and Dogs Mercury.

Veteran Yew will be familiar to folk who visit churchyards, and we have a fair share of those giants, but they can also be found on old heaths, in hedgerows and by farmsteads. We have found occasional old Crack and White Willow pollards, often in a state of collapse. Small Leaved Lime, Wild Service, Alder and even Birch have good veteran survivors, and there are fair numbers of Sweet Chestnut, too.

THE BIGGEST OF ALL

Several of our biggest veterans are over five spans in girth, and a sprinkling are over four spans.

In the sandy field just north of Danny Lake, Hurstpierpoint, TQ 287 155, the biggest and perhaps the oldest of our middle Sussex veterans lives on: **the Danny Old One**. She is the grandest matriarch of a family of Oak matriarchs on a small fragment of the medieval Danny Park. I've known her since I was a teenager, and I'm sure she was stronger and more massive when we first saw her. She is nearing the end of her life and shrinking, but she still holds her presence.[7] She has huge bulbous roots and has a 32.5 feet girth just above them … That's nearly five and a half of our arm spans. She has four huge splaying limbs and a rusting Victorian brace between two of them (which seems to have killed one). The bark on the split limbs grows curling round to heal the exposed wood. Go see

The Greentrees Giant: The girth of this old friend is 5.4 spans

her before she fades further. You will be visiting a being that grew up with the Saxon talk of the woodsmen and parkers who walked beneath her, and the Norman-French of the medieval Pierrepoint lords, who rode by.

I have venerated **the Greentrees Giant** for many years. She has a massive presence. I can sit, happy and content, in her presence for hours. In spring her Beechen canopy spreads light and leafen shade and soft murmurings. In autumn her leaves turn copper, gold and russet. She lives on a woodland boundary bank, eastwards across a field from Greentrees Farm (now Place) on Balcombe Down, TQ 2977 3280. We've measured this ancient Beech pollard at 5.4 spans girth, a size which few British Beech reach. She is probably a bundle planting.

The Sun Oak, St Leonard's Forest, at just over five spans girth, is in vigorous, expansive health, despite her estimated 800 years. She's an English Oak pollard with a huge afro, braced, steady, and firmly founded. She stood against the '87 gale when all of neighbouring Coolhurst Wood was blown flat. She took her name from a next door pub, long gone, and it describes her nature perfectly: sunny and hopeful. She stands by the lodge gates to St Leonard's Park, east of Horsham, TQ 2027 299, easily approachable on the lane.

What must be an old bailiwick boundary bank crosses just north of Forest Grange in St Leonard's Forest, now marking the edge of the Forestry Commission estate. Upon it there is a line of giant Beech. They grow bigger as you walk west from Highbirch Gate, till you come to the biggest of all: **the Forest Grange Beech** ... an octopoid monster five spans in girth, with arms waving in all directions, TQ 210 319. She doesn't look like a pollard or a bundle planting ... more like a hedge stool that escaped its confinement four or five centuries ago. I climbed her bolling some years back and startled a Stock Dove from a scruffy hole. Woodpeckers make their homes there too.

There's a scatter of four span beasts in Worth Forest: around Brantridge, in Cowdray and Monk's Forests and Greentrees. The majority of them are senescent and on the point of collapse, or have recently collapsed ... or survive just as dead bollings. A couple or more of them look as though they may have been killed by traumatic surgery: cutting all their pollard arms and most of their crown base, too. There's an ancient 4.5 span Beech pollard, which may be a bundle planting, west of the north portal of the Balcombe Tunnel at TQ 2900 325. This ancient tree is also a time portal ... to the ancient forest. Its neighbour tree had a Hornet clan busy flying in and out of their trunk cavity home, whilst their sentinels watched from the entrance. Within a hollow bough of another neighbour was a group of Cave Entrance Spiders, *Meta merianae,* poised on their little orb webs.

The Small Leaved Lime just east of Worth Church, TQ 301 362, may be the biggest of its species in Britain.[8] It is not just massive – four and a third spans girth – but tall, as well. It is set back in the north hedge line off the Worth Way, so you could easily miss it.

There is a lost and grown-over green lane just north of Oreham Common, Henfield. (The modern footpath tracks the open ground just to its west). On that green lane just south of The Pools there is a humungous, bent over pollard Oak, TQ 222 145. Its limbs bend awkwardly groundwards. Its girth is 3.5 spans, but its *presence* is even greater. It lives on in the shade, vastly older than all that live round it. It lost one giant limb recently, which lies below it (2016).

It is possible that none of these trees is the oldest, though. For that we might have to look for something much less obvious, much less imposing, but with

BACKSTORY / Chapter 9: Ancient Sussex Giants

an even stronger link back to the days of the wildwood. Amongst the Bluebells and Primroses, Crab Apple and Gean, in the heart of Courtland Wood, TQ 150 272, just west of Southwater, you can make out coppice stools and upturned root plates of Small Leaved Lime growing in part-circles. There are several of them, but none of the circles are complete … they are semi-circles at best. One semi-circle measured 16 paces across and another part-circle 12 paces across. They are, maybe, the tree equivalent of toadstool fairy rings … circles of clonal growth from a long-gone centre. They could also, perhaps, have their origin in ancient coppice technique, whereby lime poles from the lost central stool were pinned down like the spokes of a bicycle wheel, to root and form new stools. Seems unlikely though, given the great size of the arcs. They must be centuries old, whichever theory is right … and Small Leaved Lime is a relict species of the wildwood. We know that, for sure.

Hunched, twisted, gnarled: an ancient Birch, Paddockhurst Park

COMMONS, GREENS AND OTHER 'WASTES'[9]

Middle Sussex is not a country of commons any longer, and those there are carry few veteran trees. Historically, though, the link between commons and wood pasturage was very strong, and all of our commons and maybe lots of our greens and wide green droves would have had pollard veterans a-plenty.

The southern boundary of Pound Common (part of Chailey North Common) has a fine three span pollard Oak hidden away amongst brush, TQ 375 203, where it abuts the fields of Townings Farm. Nearby Lane End Common has a three span Oak at TQ 405 2228, and others, too.

There's a fine 3.5 span Oak pollard on Ifieldwood Common, TQ 243 388, but I can find no others there to match it, though the common's name implies that it was always managed as wood pasturage.

Markstakes Common has a scatter of older, open grown Beeches amongst its mostly young trees. There is a good three-span-girth Beech by the footpath that tracks south of Furzeley Farm, TQ 396 182.

I've found a couple of lovely veterans on roadside manorial waste. There's a nice three span Oak pollard on the tiny wooded green at Town Littleworth Corner, TQ 409 183. We've listened to Cuckoos there and watched a Jackdaw at her nest hole high up the trunk. On Streat Green there is a fine three span Oak south of the railway, hidden on the east side boundary bank, TQ 351 164.

Balcombe Down was not a common, and was not a medieval park either, but it was 'waste' (in land use parlance). Its assemblage of 166 ancient pollard Beech and Oaks, scattered over about two sq km of high ridgeland at the northern end of the parish, must be the relics of its lost wood pasturage economy.

By comparison, Epping Forest, which was historically largely managed as wood pasture, had some areas with 130 pollards per acre and other parts with more than 500. The average number of pollard trees was probably around 300 per acre[10] … astonishing. That gives densities like a commercial osier bed.

It seems that what survives at Balcombe Down might only be a shadow of those that were there in its heyday. There are still enough though, for many of the denizens of ancient trees to survive – the gaudy click beetles, longhorn beetles, harlequin coloured 'old growth' craneflies, and bizarre fungi. No one's looked properly, to my knowledge. Time is running out for them …

PARKS

Things are better in what's left of our old manorial parks. These are great places for ancient trees, though only Leonardslee (a 19th century park) is managed unitarily as an enclosed and grazed ornamental park. Our park veteran tree assemblages are largely of English Oak, but Paddockhurst Park is blessed with the finest and wildest looking Beeches. Veterans of other rarer species can be found, too, such as Sedgwick Park's two good sized veteran Wild Service.

I would vote Paddockhurst and Denne Parks as the best of them.

Though Paddockhurst Park, TQ 32 33, has lost its open, wood pasture character, and is now largely a mixture of semi-natural woodland and plantation, it is almost as densely populated with veteran trees as nearby Balcombe Down, almost all of them Beech. They

One of the Danny Park Giants, Hurstpierpoint (NOW COLLAPSED, 2018)

stand guard along the Ardingly Sandstone outcrop that dominates the east side of the main valley. Many of them are over three spans girth and at least one is over four. Their gnarled and twisted roots embrace the crowns of the projecting rocks of 'Goblin Cliff'. There are good clusters of Beech pollards across the gentler western upper slopes of the valley, too, though their forms are more conventional there. Veteran Oaks are very scarce … just one or two. The old park continues west of Paddockhurst Lane, where there are lots of two to three span Beech pollards, some very fine. There are four good pollards (two Beech and two Oak) along the old western deer park pale too, a couple of which are of three spans girth. Like the rest of Worth Forest there are lingering continuities with the wildwood in the Park, though its ancient Small Leaved Lime stools may be gone.

Denne Park, TQ 16 29, is a very different place. Most of its veterans are English Oaks. I've counted thirteen with three or more spans girth, making them contemporary with the 17th century creation of the park, I think. There is a good cluster at the west end of the park, though a couple of them have been burnt, and only half the bole of another is upstanding (2012). More are clustered along the eastern slope and the line of the old Pedlar's Way drove. There are good Maples and old Hawthorns too … and an old Hornbeam.

Behind Park House at Denne are, or were (for I have not see them on my last visits) a couple of good three span Sweet Chestnut giants, TQ 170 290. Their location close to the manor house is typical for maiden and pollard veterans of this species. Several of those we have are humungous. There is a five span giant near Newick Park House, TQ 422 195, and another at Crabbett Park, Worth, TQ 304 372.[11]

Sedgwick Park, TQ 18 26, still has fine timber Oaks, though it no longer contains real giants. Conyboro has fine Oaks and a veteran Sycamore around the area of the old park and ornamental grounds. It has one three span Oak between Over's Farm and Curd's Farm, and another down on North End Stream. Others parks, like Shermanbury and Danny hold good clusters and scatters of notable, veteran and ancient trees. Knepp has the famous 3.5 span Castle Oak, TQ 152 217, by the house.

BROOKS AND GILLS

Despite their frequent sogginess the banks of our streams and rivers are great places to find veterans. Surprisingly, they are much more often Oak or outgrown Alder, Hornbeam or Ash stools, than the Willow pollards that our cultural memory first brings to mind. There is, however, a good cluster of White and Crack Willow veterans a mile north of Edburton church, around the confluence of the Edburton Stream and the Fulking Stream, including a huge three span girth pollard Crack Willow on the waterside (TQ 275 1303). We've counted seven (going as far east as old Catsland Farm on the stream side) but there could be more. It's a fine spot for Nightingales too.

At Brookhouse, East Chiltington, there is a 2.25 span pollarded native Black Poplar, *Populus nigra subsp. betulifolia*, by the barns.[12] It has been separated for 165 years from the banks of the Bevern Stream by the railway line. Native Black Poplar was a species of our lost flood plain woodlands (the kind of places Aurochs and Elk loved) and its scattered survivors have only just made it into the 21st century. It is still exceedingly rare in Sussex, though many have lately been planted.

Hidden away on the steep bank of Plumpton Mill Stream, half a mile SW of the race course, is a superb maiden English Oak, TQ 355 148. She is clean bolled to 10ft, with a girth of 3.66 spans, and great limbs straddling the stream. The banks are covered in Ramsons, Bluebells and Moschatel, and there are Bullhead, caddis and mayfly in the stream.

Just east of Blackstone a huge and gnomish Oak pollard is hidden away on the bank of Blackstone Stream, north of the footpath, TQ 245 163.

Gills are great places for old giants. They're safer hiding there than in many plateau landscapes. Sedgy Gill in Monk's Forest is a humid, jungley place of tangled Rhodedendron and old Oak and Beech pollards, one over four spans in girth with colourful slime moulds on its roots (2010). Birchangar Gill west of the Balcombe Tunnel is much more open … and packed with giants. Stanford Brook in Worth Forest, has a ribbon of English and Sessile Oak and Beech pollards all the way from Cowdray Forest down to the Maidenbower Estate, Crawley. Sheepwash Gill in St Leonard's Forest has some good notable trees too. The upper gill of Kerves Brook, TQ 182 282, below the Bourne Hill scarp, south of Horsham, has a primeval feel in parts. There's a veteran Wild Service tree, 1.4 spans girth, which can fruit prolifically. The gill has huge old Alder pollards up to 3.5 spans girth, lining the brook downstream.

FARMSTEADS LOST AND FOUND, AND MANORS

It is always worthwhile to look for veteran trees near farmsteads, where their chances of survival have been enhanced by the affection felt for them. They can still remain when all around has been bulldozed for giant sheds and concrete yards, or piled with rusting machinery and rubble.

There's a huge old Oak like that at Vuggle's Farm, near Sutton Hall. It stands south of the footpath, TQ 437 192. Behind More House Farm, Wivelsfield, TQ 341 207, there is an ancient matriarchal Oak in full vigour. You can just see her behind the buildings from the road.

Just east of Southwater, stands the lovely old farmhouse of Staker's Farm, TQ 167 261, tranquil for long centuries amongst fields and woods, but now cursed by the tinnitus of the A24 bypass right next door. Admire though, that huge and spreading Oak on its back lawn … it must be four spans girth, even. There's another of three spans at the front.

Just south of the ancient gentleman's farmhouse of Gullege, near East Grinstead, stands a magnificent three span Oak pollard on the hedge bank, TQ 365 383. It seems isolated now, but in past times it stood right by the busy crossing of prehistoric and medieval trackways.

Sometimes ancient trees remain when a farmstead has long gone. If you walk west from Jolesfield Common, north of Partridge Green, down the old hollow path through Hatterell's Wood and across the Adur at Hatterell's Bridge, you come to a destroyed landscape. Huge lengths of old hedgerow and small farms have been bulldozed. But there in front of you one tree stands out in a great ploughed field … an old Oak of three spans girth, TQ 175 197. It is the only trace left of Hatterell's farmstead.

There is a lovely place about a mile SW of Maplehurst, TQ 175 237. It is a low hilltop with an old hedged close upon its top, a couple of little overgrown ponds, and great Oaks all around. One of them is of four spans girth, and two more measure three spans. Both Jane and I had to climb the ladder into the crown of the largest. It is every child's dream. The place is the site of Haven's Farm, well named.

There's a place between Broxmead and Deak's Lanes, north of Ansty. It is just a nettley hollow with a hedge around and two modern barns. That is the site of Westup Farm. Behind the barns, on the eastern bank, is a gorgeous, muscley, bent old English Oak pollard of 3.5 spans girth. On the footpath below is another of over three spans.

Old Standen, by Weir Wood Reservoir, TQ 389 350, has a three span Sweet Chestnut on the bosky drove just before it meets the lost farm site. There are good Sweet Chestnut veterans close to gentry houses like Beechlands, just south of Newick, TQ 416/7 202; and at Bylsborough Farm, Henfield, TQ 299 163; and both Wapsbourne Farm and Ades, in Chailey parish. There was a big stand of fine veterans forming a short avenue at Carter's Lodge, St Leonard's Forest, but they are much reduced now, TQ 239 293.

Gentry houses hold many other exotics, now grown to fine proportions. Newtimber Place has a giant Turkey Oak, TQ 269 137, in its tiny park. Brook House, Highbrook, has two huge Hungarian Oaks of three and 2.5 spans, TQ 358 293, as well as two good English Limes, each over two spans girth.

LANDSCAPE CLUSTERS

Particular farm landscapes and small estates retain good numbers of veteran and notable trees.

The landscape west of Albourne Green (around TQ 25 16) has many fine old Oaks. So does the Hooke Estate, Chailey (around TQ 38 18), that also has Beech and Hornbeam veterans. The landscape east of Tulleys Wells Farm, Cooksbridge, TQ 39 13, has a scatter of notable Oaks. This farmscape was very badly damaged by hedgerow removal, but at least some of the Oaks were retained, and some of the hedgerows are being put back. Earwig Lane, TQ 242 242–9, Bolney – a lovely stretch of forest green lane – has good notable trees.

Harry's Wood, TQ 269 302, north of Nymans, and part of a larger SSSI, has many fine trees, including at least five Beech and Oak veterans, with several senescent trees in the deep and shady gill.

Old Ansty Wood, NE of Warninglid, now reduced to two fragments – Anne's Wood, TQ 253 262, and Anne's Wood East, TQ 258 263 – still holds at least five good veteran Beech amongst clusters of other fine trees, including oldish mature Sessile Oak.

CHURCHES

In this book's wider area, the two biggest churchyard giants are probably the Yews at Crowhurst and

Tandridge churches, Surrey. Crowhurst's Lych Gate Yew, TQ 390 474, is superb. It has a room inside its hollow bole accessed by a little wooden hobbit door, and is said to be 1700 years old, which would take its birth back to the time of Roman Britain. It was, so we hear, part of a group of six trees surrounding a long filled-in pond, and a place of pagan worship. The Tandridge Yew is gigantic. I measured it at five spans girth. It has a different character from the Crowhurst Yew … statelier and more imposing. There was a vivid yellow growth of Chicken of the Woods fungus on its bole when I last visited. Those trees resisted all that the late 20th century gales hurled at them, whilst all around was destruction.

We cannot quite meet that size and grandeur in middle Sussex churchyards, but we have our share of giants. The Slaugham Yew is probably the biggest, at 23ft girth (almost four span) and both Ardingly and East Chiltington have well-loved yews of 3.5 span. Both Ifield and Chailey parish churches also have Yews of over three span girth.

BOUNDARIES AND LINES

Old parish, manorial and property boundaries are places we should always look for veteran trees, for in the days before maps and literacy folk marked their territory visually, or lost it … and trees cannot be ignored.

At Lumberpits, SW of Wivelsfield Green, TQ 369 187, there is an Oak veteran hidden in a fence line, which stands almost at the meeting point of a cluster of ancient paths and parish boundaries, near where a causeway probably started out north across the flat Ouse marshland.

There is a line of six notable Oak maidens at Nunnery Farm, west of Rusper, TQ 188 361, which mark the boundary of the extraordinary elongated Saxon manor of West Tarring.[13]

The decaying giant Beeches along the medieval Shelley Deer Park boundary banks, in the woods around Shelley Plain, a mile north west of Handcross, are some of the most memorable survivors, but there are lots of goodly others, particularly in the old forests. At Truckers Hatch (the only 'hatch' name I know in St Leonard's Forest) there is a fine three span Oak standing just back from the road and rapal boundary, TQ 248 291.

At Greentrees Farm, on Balcombe Down, a line of giant Oak and Beech march down an earthen field bank to Stanford Gill, TQ 295 330. At the slope top, against the field, is the Greentrees Giant (see above). There are long lines of veterans, largely Beech, parallel with, and north of the Oldhouse Warren bridlepath, TQ 296 336; along the west side of the Balcombe Tunnel north entrance, TQ 289 325; and west of the Tunnel just north of High Street, TQ 291 320.

Ashfold Park at Slaugham has a remarkable feature. Along the old park pale, TQ 246 282, which may be partly the ancient boundary between Bramber and Lewes rapes, there is a long avenue of notable Beeches, fair numbers of which are of two spans and more girth. They are close planted, maybe often bundle planted, and they bend over … every one of them … like mourners (2011).

A superb line of 300 year old Sweet Chestnuts – The Felbridge Chestnuts – grace the north side of the Crawley Down Road, Felbridge, north west of East Grinstead, TQ 365 395, for nearly a third of a mile. There is a second more hidden, line just to the north. The Chestnuts were replenished with additional plantings on several occasions, and many of the trees have been lost, but they still have much visual power.

ENDNOTES

1. 'Ancient Tree Guide no.4: What are ancient, veteran and other trees of special interest?' by the Woodland Trust and the Ancient Tree Forum (c. 2002).
2. Ascertaining the age of trees is a very uncertain process when you can't count the rings in a cut trunk. I have found the following (in a superb report) to be very useful: 'Ready Reckoner for estimating the age of an oak tree', page 40, 'Wealden Ancient Tree Project 2007–2008'. Report compiled by Ali Wright, Wealden Ancient Tree Project Officer, (circa 2008).
3. The numbers in this chapter were compiled in 2012. Though they could be revised upwards somewhat now (2017), the patterns they reveal would be unlikely to change.
4. I define Balcombe Down as all the ridgeland at the north west end of Balcombe Parish (see maps), not the smaller area of desmesne land described as Balcombe Down on the c. 1800 map.
5. 'Poll' derives from the medieval word for head or head hair. Think of election 'polls' … counting of heads … or 'poll' tax … a headage tax … or 'polled' animals … that have had their horns or hair cut off.
6. Our survey is by no means complete and I am sure we have particularly under-recorded many of the smaller and shorter-lived tree species.
7. It is as though we are visiting the Queen Elizabeth Oak in Cowdray Park a century or more into the future when its long life is finally fading. That famous Oak is pictured on the front of Owen Johnson's marvellous 'The Sussex Tree Book'
8. Owen Johnson, op cit page 81.
9. 'Waste' was, and is, a term used to describe unimproved lands without intensive usages, and often even without commoning rights.
10. 'Epping Forest Through the Eye of a Naturalist', pages 18–21. Edited by M W Hanson. Essex Field Club (1992)
11. Owen Johnson op cit.
12. Sussex Biodiversity Record Centre. Record made by Frank Penfold (1998).
13. See chapter: 'The Wealden Landscape's History', 'Large Scale Planning' section.

Bishops' croziers – shiny springtime gold unfurling Scaly Male Fern

CHAPTER 10
More about wildlife

BIRDS

We scrambled down the tangled slope by the bridge to the muddy Sallow thicket on the stream bank. A dark, barrel chested, pigeon sized bird flew up and whirred away.

As we walked through the Sallow thicket along the stream side path I spotted it again, crouched dead still, just a few paces away in light cover. I stopped, and beckoned Jane. The **Woodcock** eyed us with her big beady black eye. We gawped back. Such a kaleidoscope of autumn colours … a miracle of woodland camouflage! A chequered pattern of russet and chestnut, fawn and creamy ochre, stippled in black, grey and white – like a stained glass window; like a luminous water colour, picked out by bold pen and ink work … the essence of autumn.

We have seen many wintering Woodcock in our Wealden woods over the years. Indeed, we see them most times we walk the woods at that time of year, flushing them from cover of Bramble, fern, or brush, usually on wet low ground, by gill sides, ditches, and mud pans. Often they do not fly far, and you don't know if your subsequent sightings are of the same bird. Often they sit tight till you are almost on them, so when they rise, you see their long straight beaks, their high foreheads and high set eyes, their broad wings and dark patterning. Often we spot them as they wing away over wooded valleys, or as they fly along a wood edge at dusk. Mostly we see them singly, but not always. We have seen some good 'falls' of Woodcock. (A 'fall' is their collective noun). Once, descending an open Brackeny, wooded gill, with gnarled, upturned, splintered Sweet Chestnut stools, we flushed a fall of five birds. Once we flushed four birds along a wooded sub-scarp. Other folk have seen much larger numbers.

We see them from November through to the beginning of April, and many of these winter migrants must come from eastern and northern Europe. As breeders they are rare birds now, in the middle Sussex and south east Surrey Weald, with Worth Forest and Chailey Common being likely places for them.[1] Only once have I seen a male bird 'roding' in this area – making its breeding season display flight circuit several times, just over canopy height along a scrubby ride.

In the bleak midwinter, with the clearest, coldest, luminescent sky turning watery sunset orange to the west, we tip-toed into an old weatherboarded barn out on a hillock in the midst of the flood plain. We just caught sight of the resident **Barn Owl** gliding away through the back entrance over the bushes and reeds. A Brown Rat skittered away. A little Jenny Wren hopped in silhouette in and out of the waggon doors, as we hunkered down against a stall for a snack and some hot tea. Across the concrete floor was a scatter of Ms Owl's pellets, some fresh, some old and hard. I collected five. At home, I picked them carefully apart and sorted the tiny bones from the matted fur that made up their bulk. Ms Owl had eaten eleven Field Voles, one Bank Vole and one Field Mouse! … just some of the community of small creatures that live and die out on the brooks, with the noise of honking skeins of geese coming in to land in the darkness, and occasional Lapwings' *peuwwhitting* calls back and forth.

Barn Owls have retreated, now, primarily to the Low Weald and its wet pastures and reedy, under-managed ditches, and rougher fields managed just for hay, amenity, or game birds. They will have to change their name to 'Box' Owl if things go on as they are, for many of their favoured barn nesting sites have been lost to demolition and residential conversion, and only the efforts to organise nest boxes by folk like Hurstpierpoint's Woodland Flora and Fauna Group, and sympathetic land managers, have partially replaced that resource. I can think of only a few old field barns in this area which are used for nesting by the birds. One of them is on the point of collapse and one more was recently demolished by the landowner.

Tawny Owls are much more common, and are especially noticeable in autumn and winter, when their hooting marks the coming of early dusk in wooded districts. In just eight winter weeks I counted 18 separate Tawnies on our walks, calling either singly or in pairs. We only saw the birds twice. **Little Owls** are now rare in central Sussex, though we occasionally surprise them from their fence post stands, or spot them silhouetted against the sky on a tree branch.

Speak to any older country person and they will tell you that **Cuckoos** used to be everywhere. A farmer friend tells me how they used to make such a din so close to the farmhouse, that he wished they'd stop interrupting his peace. I found a Wren's nest once, that I returned to often, soon realising that a Cuckoo baby had taken over. Gradually the Cuckoo grew, until, when fledged, it wore the little Wren's nest like a coat, with its big head poking out. It must eventually have bust free like Superman bursting out of his business suit.

Back in 2007, we noted 23 Cuckoos in this countryside, including males calling competitively above our heads in the woodland canopy, and others flying together. We saw one untidy looking juvenile as late as August, looking forlorn as it prepared for its big Africa trip. The decline I've recorded is not even, and my own pattern of wanderings changes from year to year, yet in 2013 we counted just eleven or twelve Cuckoos on eight occasions, once watching two females tracking down two calling males. That was a delight. They'd come off some reedy brooks, which seem to be their redoubt, where they parasitize Reed Warbler nests.

In 2014, in the Surrey Low Weald I heard them only seven times, but the number of birds I heard may have been just five … or just two, if one bird I heard was as mobile as they seem. In Sussex, places we returned to every year as dead certs for hearing them – like the north Barcombe or north Wiston woods – now seem to host only odd birds, not chasing, fast moving groups. That summer the three of us were out in the woods, and Jane and I were busy talking about summat or other. The grandson (then seven) called across to tell us about something he'd seen. We didn't respond … so he called out, "*cuckoo, cuckoo, cuckoo*". That got our attention. He knows those birds. Make sure your kids get to hear them too. They may be the very last generation that does.

On a note of hope, I recorded a likely thirteen Cuckoos in twelve separate areas in the spring of 2015. I was going everywhere, however, and targeting likely territory.

No Cuckoos No Cuckoos

"Shhhhh … Can you hear that? … Listen … "
Under Leith Hill … from Fulking Stream … in
    Warningore's deep wooded green …
Faint … off … but quite distinct …
The sound of spring.

* * *

No more.
The woods are empty now of call and counter call
Across the hursts and combes, the lanes and leys and
    brooks and bournes.

Springtime and Bluebells –
But now gone, that simple two note invitation to
Green mysteries of underwood and shaw,
Lush hedgerow, stream and meadow.

The chime that nature's clock has rung each spring
Since time long aeons past before our coming
Has stopped. Has stopped.

Like winter without Christmas,
Like soaps without signature tunes,
Like children without birthdays …

It marks an end that sinks my heart so low
That Bluebells heavy scent and all the song of evening
    Thrush
And tender freshness of new bursting leaf
Can't shift this heaviness.

We chatted with a man who has lived in his rented family cottage on a quiet track for all his eighty years and more. In his young days the **Nightingales** sung from the bush outside his kitchen door. Not any more. The pattern of Nightingales' decline parallels that of Barn Owls, and they have much retreated to the Low Wealden flatlands in our district, where you may hear them along the Blackthorn thickets that line streams and brook drains. If you are lucky you may hear several males in counterpoint, or so it sounds, even if the truth is that they are just plain rivals. Don't go looking to *see* them (as opposed to *hearing* them). They need to feel safe in their dense cover, if they are to breed. In any case, if you walk the quietest paths often enough you may just see one, with its handsome burnt sienna tail and back, and white-fawn chest. Once, walking a path amongst dense coppice regrowth, we heard a new sound like a distant motor, like some machine turning over, interspersed with a very high "*hui, hui, hui*". Then an agitated Nightingale appeared, right up close, circling us, calling and 'rattling'. We skedaddled as quick as we could, watching where we placed every footfall. If we'd walked on to her nest I'd never have forgiven myself.

They have now lost that core habitat of thick coppice regrowth, as almost all broad leaved woodland coppice is left unmanaged or purposively turned over to timber plantation. Six cock Nightingales sang in a dense thorny thicket which had developed in ancient woodland near Cowfold after it was flattened in the '87 and '90 gales. Now the landowner has cleared the thicket and all of them are gone. One old string of tiny, derelict wet meadows was a good place to hear them sing. Now the Sallow and thorn has been removed and the meadow cleared. Another stretch of tangled, derelict, orchard trees that they loved, set in dense Bramble is now much reduced by clearance.

Some birds you seem to have particular luck with. We came across **Spotted Flycatcher** nests several times a while back. They are a species in steep decline, though once familiar as a bird of mixed countryside and gardens. One spring we chanced on several **Marsh Tit** nests, two of them in the hollowed out stools of old Ash coppice, where they use small rot holes as entries. One was in the hollow top of a Victorian iron driveway bollard. They seem to love wet High Wealden woods, where they can be seen foraging through old thickets. **Willow Tit**, their sister species, has gone from Sussex in the last decade.

Wood Warblers are now gone, too, from their old breeding haunts in the High Wealden parts of our district. **Willow Warbler** has now largely retreated to the High Wealden Forests, though till recently so common that their song accompanied any walk in mixed countryside and leafy suburbs. Thankfully, **Chiffchaff, Blackcap, Garden Warbler**, and the **two Whitethroats** are still a reliable source of pleasure in spring time.

The bird books that we had in the '50s and '60s still portrayed fascinating birds like **Wryneck, Red Backed Shrike** and **Redstart**, as though any active child had a good chance of seeing them. They were out of date even then, but now only mobile birders with good binoculars will spot such species, either in the course of migration, or in special habitats like Ashdown Forest. In our ordinary Wealden countryside we have to be content with such beauties as **Nuthatch** and the **two larger woodpeckers; Treecreeper** and **Yellowhammer**, though even the latter, with such species as **Meadow** and **Tree Pipits,** are now always noteworthy, never just part-of-the-furniture.

Place names tell an interesting story, some of lost birds, some still common. There's *Partridge* Green; *Cran*mer (Crane) Barn and *Stor*wood (possibly Stork), both at Henfield; *Grouse* (Black Grouse) Road, St Leonard's Forest; and *Heron*shead (*earn*: Eagle, not Heron), Leigh. I know of three *Crow* names in our area: *Crawley, Crawley* Down and *Crow*hurst. There are two *Kite* names: *Kit's* Bridge and *Kitt's* Cottage. There are two possible *Owl* names: *Owls*bury and *Owls*beech. *Cuck*field is named for the *Cuckoo; Culver* Farm, for the *Dove; Gosden*, for the *Goose;* and *Gallybird* Hall for the *Woodpecker*, known as the *'galleybird'* in Sussex dialect.

MAMMALS AND REPTILES: LOST, HIDDEN, RETURNED

Till the time of the Saxons, our local Wealden woods and cleared lands had many more large wild animals, especially carnivores, than at present. **Wolf** survived into Saxon times and has left place name evidence. There's *Wool*borough (Wolves' hill) east of Salfords, Surrey and another in Crawley, Sussex; there's *Wool*fly (Wolves' clearing) north of Henfield, Sussex; there's *Wool*pack (Wolf pit) Farm at Fletching, which may be the same '*wulf*pytte' mentioned in Stanmer's eighth century Saxon charter; and there are Wolf pits in Ewhurst, Surrey ('*Wol*putte') and Bletchingley (*Wool*pits).

Wild Cat had retreated west to Wales and north to Yorkshire before 1800,[2] but probably appears in the place name *Cast*eye (*catt*: cat, *stig*: path) Balcombe, and maybe in *Catte*shall (hill of the wild cat?) Godalming.

Beaver may have survived in the Saxon Weald, though I know of no evidence. The place name *Bever*ley Brook, Wimbledon, indicates that it was still in the Thames basin at that time. **Wild Boar** was probably extinct as a genuinely wild animal in England around the end of the 13th century,[3] though sporadically kept or reintroduced in parks and forests since then. There were plenty of farmed swine, but not their wild cousins. Wild Boar are now common again in parts of East Sussex, and are reported now in our part of the Weald too.[4]

Polecat survived in numbers in Sussex till about 1800, and in Surrey till about 1850. They disappeared from both counties post-1880.[5] Now, though, they have returned,[6] with several records from the Henfield-Steyning-Storrington area in 2015. On midsummer night this year (2018) I drove through the darkness towards Lavington Common (where I once worked) to celebrate the dawn with the Nightjars and Wood Larks. Passing through deep woods at a pootling speed my headlights caught a Polecat in their glare. I braked hard. The Polecat did a little dance in front of the car, twirling round and jumping in the air, then dodged to the side and disappeared into the wood. That is the first time I have seen one live, though I have found a couple of road-kill animals in Wales and the west, and a dead Polecat-Ferret.

Pine Marten died out after 1800 in Surrey, and after 1850 in Sussex. It may just be that *Mer*stham, Surrey, is named for the Marten or Polecat (Saxon *'mearp'* = Marten). **Otter** dipped steeply to extinction in Sussex between 1957 and '77 and has scarcely returned. It's feral **Mink** we see in their place.

Seeing wild deer in the Weald in the 1950s and '60s was special. Now they are so common that we often don't remark on a sighting to each other if more noteworthy things are about. I often don't make a written note of them, just as I mostly don't note **Rabbits**. Our two native deer species, **Roe Deer** and **Red Deer**, were already scarce in 13th century southern England and virtually extinct outside protected areas in the 16th century.[7] The Red Deer of 13th century *Harts*wood, near Redhill, were managed, as were the Roe Deer after which *Rei*gate was named, perhaps from the 12th century. Large feral herds of **Fallow Deer** are now common in wooded areas of both High and Low Weald, eating out the shrub and herb layers and badly hitting song bird populations. They were the commonest kept beasts in medieval deer parks, after their post-Norman Conquest large scale introduction.[8]

Our walkings commonly take us through dusk and into night time, and **bats** are then our constant companions. We have no bat detector and do much guessing of species from flight patterns, size, habitat, and occasional closer scrutiny. They are found in richest diversity in structurally complex old Wealden countryside … where there are leafy green lanes and close-patterned hedgerows, ponds, woods, brook pastures and streams, old cottages and farm buildings. You can easily guess **Water Bats/Daubenton's**, foraging low over summer ponds and lakes, tiny **Pipistrelles** hunting round and round along wooded lanes, and the large **Serotines and Noctules**. I find the odd dead casualty on roadsides, and once found a **Brown Long Eared Bat** dead on the aisle carpet of a medieval church. We find bat droppings on church windowsills and even altars and hear their squeakings occasionally from church roof spaces. To sleep, breed and hibernate they use old churches, over-mature and veteran trees (with all their holes and cracks) and the roof spaces of old (and new) buildings … and old bridges, tunnels, ice houses, chalk 'dene holes' (where marl was quarried) and many other unregarded cavities. The ancient forest specialist **Bechstein's and Barbastrelle Bats** are now known to breed in the Brighton Line Weald, though I had long thought them to be vanishingly rare. The north edge of Tottington-Longlands Woods, Small Dole; Shermanbury Place and church; the Adur at Frylands; Streat Lane near the church; Markstakes Common and ridge; and Ditchling Common, have been some of the places whose bats have given us most pleasure in recent years … but those examples could be replicated dozens of times.

Mrs Mole, alias Mouldywarp, alias Mrs Wand, or Mrs Woont (sadly deceased)

We've come across the corpses of **Yellow Necked Mice**, and once one alive, in the ancient woodlands with which they are particularly associated. Only once have I seen a live **Mole**. We find their corpses often enough, though not the mole catcher's gibbets lined with them along fence wires, which I saw in my youth. Once I spotted a heaving Mole hill beneath which the excavating Mole stayed hidden. I squatted quietly close by and watched the hill rhythmically heave upwards for 20 minutes, but she never showed herself. We see live **Badger** very rarely in the Weald, though I saw them often on the Downs. Their corpses, though, litter busy Wealden roadsides and even quieter lanes. It is rare for us to see Wealden **Stoat** and **Weasel** alive, and it's long since I've seen them on gamekeepers' gibbets, but we do see their corpses lying on keepers' tunnel traps, where they are put to attract their mates to the same grisly end. They seem much reduced by game bird preservation. **Hedgehogs**, too, we rarely see, even as road casualties.

We see Wealden **Brown Hares** very occasionally, usually on arables, once recently as a road casualty. It can even be seen in woodland. It was not rare to see them in the Weald in the '60s. It is, now.

If we make an effort, visiting likely spots in season, we can still find **Grass Snakes** regularly. You may also find their shed skins around August time. Once

Young Grass Snake

I found a large shiny female beside the skin she had just sloughed, and I still proudly have the mounted 3ft 6ins shed skin. The snakes can be seen along wet and wooded ditches and gills, in frog-frequented brooklands, ponds, rough damp hedgelines, and probably in many larger woods and damper meadows. I have never seen **Adders** in the part of the Weald covered by this book, though they are on Ashdown Forest, of course, and in Worth and St Leonards Forests and other open heathy woodlands. I recently just missed seeing one of a good size on Chailey Common. I used to see them regularly on two West Sussex heaths I worked at, and recently we've seen them on west Wealden greensand heaths, and as near as Washington Common.

FUNGI

In a good season, with enough but not too much preliminary rain and sun, Wealden woods may show profuse and beautiful autumn fungal displays. Both Low Wealden clay woods and sandy high Wealden woods may have fungi in many colours and all shapes, on the bare ground, on dead and fallen trees, and in grassy openings. High Wealden woods on sand, particularly under Beech, Birch and Pine can be very productive. Yet ancient Low Wealden woods, particularly if they have varied geologies and mosaics of woody vegetation – Hornbeam, Hazel, Oaks, Ash, Beech, some conifers – can also be very diverse. Old Beech and Oaks in wood pasture have many rarities, and mature southern Beechwoods are the single richest fungal habitat.[9]

I would love to write about the best sites we have explored, to tell you of the spots we have found **Chanterelles, Horn of Plenty, Field Mushrooms, Giant Puffballs, Ceps and other boletes, Chicken of the Woods**, **morels** and other marvels. I won't, though, for if I did I would cause real harm. We don't collect! We leave alone almost all we find. Only if a species is plentiful and identification is needed may we take a specimen for later examination.

Fungi are having a seriously hard time. Air pollution and the destruction of habitats have vastly reduced the European biomass of larger fruiting fungi. To those threats is now added the rising tide of selfish fungal foraging … so I'm "keeping mum" about the names of sites.

Low Wealden woodland fungi

One autumn we made about four visits to a relatively dry Low Wealden wood, partly on raised ground and with some quite calcareous areas. It has a varied woody cover, with a conifer coup, Hazel and Hornbeam coppice, Birch and much else. We found so many bizarre life forms! Our prize find was a troop of rare **Barometer Earthstars**, that open like flowers when the air is humid or it rains, and curl closed their 'petals' when dry weather comes. There was a troop of **Fluted Birds' Nests**, each little 'nest' little over half a cm. wide and packed with tiny 'birds' eggs' (each filled with spores) which are splashed out of the nest when rain drops hit them. There was, too, a mat of **Cannonball / Shooting Star Fungi**, which shoot their tiny balls (packed with spores) from little cannon with star-shaped mouths … and much more: **Glazed Cups** on a mossy old Hornbeam stool, **Wavy Capped Chanterelles, Orange Peel Fungus, Dog Stinkhorn, Snakeskin Grisette, Scaly** and **Leopard Spotted Earthballs, Silky Piggyback** (parasitic on old **Blackening Brittlegills**), **Witches Butter, Twig Parachutes, Greasy Green Brittlegills, Golden Spindles, Death Cap, False Death Cap, Fly Agaric, Aniseed Funnelcaps, Jelly Rot, Panther Cap, Bay Boletes** and **Fiery Milkcaps.** We noted over 50 species on single visits. Experts would have listed far more. Tawny Owls kept us company as the light faded.

In another largely Hornbeam Low Wealden wood the season started early, in late August, with our finding of a rarity, **Lion Shield** – a yellow beauty – on a ride side. There were scattered **Hornbeam Milkcaps**, three

Giant Polypore – usually on rotten stumps. (This one fallen NOT picked)

High Wealden woodland fungi

In the High Weald a mixed area of sands and clays with many old Beech makes delightful autumn ramblings. There are **Chanterelles** scattered on banks (they like sandy ones) with **Penny Bun Boletes/Ceps** occasionally there too. There are **Trumpet Chanterelles** under Beech. There is **Wrinkled Club, Bruising Webcap** (a name which does no justice to this violet-purple-umber beauty). Also **Fragile, Birch, Stinking, Scarlet, Blackening, Charcoal Burner, and other Brittlegills**, with many **Milkcaps** and poisonous **Amanitas**.

In one forest area with a grove of old Beech above a bushy gill, we found so many pretty and strange things. There were **Oyster** and **Porcelain Fungi** on the broken Beech limbs of course, with **Geranium Brittlegill** and **Beechwood Sickener** underneath. There were **Ceps**. There was **Toothed Cup/Dentate Elf Cup, Woolly Fibrecap** (and yes, it is woolly), **Purple Stocking Webcap, Grey Knight, Piggyback Rosegill, Bay** and **Bovine Boletes, Stinkhorn** and **Dog Stinkhorn**. Yet when we crossed the gill to an area that looked similar, but had no old trees and had once been cultivated, there was the same volume of fungi, but none of the variety.

In another forest gill crowded with old Beech and Oaks, much Birch, conifers upslope, and Alder along the gill, there was a different fungal community. It had much **Woolly Milkcap**, some **Cauliflower Fungus, Alder Scalycap, Chanterelles, Green Cracked, Milk White,** and **Stinking Brittlegills, Wood Pinkgill, Burnt Knight, Fly Agaric,** and **Grey Coral** … so much of everything that you had to watch where to step.

Fungal foraging

One autumn Sunday we walked in a local Wealden forest to enjoy what was proving to be the best season for fungi for several years. At the edge of the car park lay a pile of discarded fungi, with a bruised and battered **Beefsteak Fungus** of huge dimensions, and an equally huge bolete, now broken into several pieces. Walking through the pines and spruces near to the car park there were plenty of brittlegills, *Russula spp.*, and smaller brown fungi, and some pretty caps of **Rosy Spike**, but the **Bovine Bolete** which normally accompanies that species was absent. Absent, that is, except for the tell-tale cut bases of its stalks. Everywhere through that pine wood were those sad little golden circles the size and colour, more or less, of pound coins. Cut, cut, cut, those collectors had gone. And that was to be the story everywhere in that part of the forest which was most easily accessible from the car park … and sometimes, too, in the more remote areas beyond the barbed wire and 'Keep Out, Private Woods' signs. Cut stalk bases everywhere, and little discarded piles of dropped **Blushers** and **Panthercaps** and pieces of **Ceps**, at frequent intervals along the rides and banks.

brittlegill species, **Brown Birch Bolete, Red Cracking Bolete**, and common species like **Weeping Widow, Clustered Toughshank** and **Common Funnel**. Things heated up at the beginning of October when we found several little troops of **Hare's Ear** and **Horn of Plenty**, with **Fluted Black Elfin Saddle** and nice things like **Lilac Fibrecap** and **Fruity Fibrecap** (sweetly fruity fragrant), **Stinking Earth Fan, Hazel** and **Suede Boletes**. By the beginning of November the Horn of Plenty had spread to cover much ground under Hazel and Hornbeam coppice, though the slugs had eaten the Hare's Ear. There were two Webcap species, **Butter** and **Parrot Waxcaps, Charcoal Burner, Ochre, Winecork, Geranium,** and **Beechwood Sickener Brittlegills** and **Curry Scented Milkcap** … and we flushed a Woodcock from the Brambles.

(Don't read into this account that every season in these places is so good. Some years seem dreadful, and in others the fungi appear very early, or late. Some years the fungi you find seem giants, but you may not see others of that size for years after. So be patient.)

There are good and robust reasons why the culture of fungi collecting did not really exist in this country until recent years. Poland, Germany, Sweden and Russia have such cultures because they are countries of woods and forests. They have far, far more than we do. The greatest biomass of macro fungi are to be found in such woods. Fungus collecting is a woodland phenomenon, largely, despite the delights to be found on old downland, heath and meadow. We did not collect in this country at least partly because there are relatively fewer good places to collect.

And it's not just the beauty of these things that foraging diminishes. They have a value far beyond the pleasure we get from looking or eating. Many other species depend upon them. For the hundreds of species of fungus flies and beetles, for the slugs and snails, for the small mammals, for other fascinating and often beautiful parasitic fungi and moulds, or for those species of weird half-animal slime moulds that move across the woodland hunting them, this annual fruiting is life sustaining stuff. We may plan to disburse our Ceps to our mates. Rich folk may love those expensive restaurant tastings of authentic 'wild food'. Those other small life forms just plan to stay alive.

Fungal foraging pleasures are simply not sustainable. For if we are to encourage – and we MUST – people to reconnect with nature and the countryside on a mass scale – all the many millions of us – then our common behavioural culture must be one of the most careful respect for that which we mutually enjoy. Not just every song bird nest and wild orchid, but every troop of beautiful boletes and hidden springtime morels must be respected.

MOTHS AND BUTTERFLIES

The story of the butterflies[10] of our coppiced woodlands is a sorry one. The two Pearl Bordered Fritillaries, with their exquisite orange-brown-and-black chequer board patternings, were an expected sight in any young springtime coppice, amongst the Bluebells, Bugle and Violets, till 40 years ago. **Small Pearl Bordered Fritillary** was extinct in West Sussex by 1997, and then extinct in East Sussex too. It was finally destroyed in famous Shave's Wood, Albourne, in 1983. **Pearl Bordered Fritillary** was last seen in our area in Plumpton Wood in 1982, in Shaves Wood in '83, and went from St Leonard's Forest a year or so later. There are reintroductions and more plans for their return.

High Brown Fritillary went extinct in West Sussex in 1986 and East Sussex in '87. It was lost from Shaves Wood in the early '50s and from Marlpost Wood and Pease Pottage in the '70s. **Marsh Fritillary**, which needs damp archaic pastures with Devil's Bit, was lost earlier still – in East Sussex in 1946 and West Sussex in 1975. The rough ground next to Shaves Wood in north Poynings and Albourne was famous for it, but it was gone there c. 1885. A 1960 reintroduction on Ditchling Common faltered on, with much bolstering by new stock, till c. 1991. The **Duke of Burgundy Fritillary**, though not a relative of the others, shares a similar beauty. It is gone from all the Weald, disappearing from its Shipley and Itchingfield sites in the '70s, to be finally extirpated at Shaves Wood in 1985.

We still have the big **Silver Washed Fritillary**, zooming up and down woodland rides in high summer and nectaring on tall herbs and Bramble. That's a blessing. **Purple Emperor** seems to be doing OK in our part of the Weald too, though its population fluctuates. It is in at least some of the woods on the Gault Clay under the South Downs, and is abundant at Knepp's rewilded area, Shipley.

Green Hairstreak can still be seen in hot Wealden glades and rides, and on fragments of archaic pasture. **Brown Hairstreak** is doing very well, and is very much a Low Wealden speciality. Much successful labour goes into searching for its eggs on Blackthorn twigs, whilst the butterfly is difficult to see. Both **Grizzled Skipper** and **Dingy Skipper** can still be seen in the same kind of places that Green Hairstreak likes. **Purple Hairstreak** is more elusive, being happiest on the canopy of Oaks, but they will come down to the ground, where we can see the glinting purple of their open wings. **Silver Studded Blue** is gone from our area now, I think. It's last site was at Chailey Common. Ashdown Forest is the nearest site for Brighton Line folk.

The biomass and diversity of moths has crashed in the post-war period. Large moths do not swarm like gnats round a lamplight as they would have done 60 years ago. To be sure, it's tempting to lull ourselves into complacency when we see several Hummingbird Hawk Moths nectaring on garden flowers, but if you want to see the exquisite **Bee Hawk Moths (Broad Bordered** and **Narrow Bordered)** don't expect them any longer in Brighton Line woods. It is no longer an everyday occurrence to find fat **Privet Hawk Moth** caterpillars on your garden hedge, or **Lappet**, looking like a crumbled leaf, in your moth trap. There are less hedges, less well managed, than there were, and **Small Eggar** is not to be found on most that survive. We can't blame the Cuckoo (which loves their juicy caterpillars) for they are disappearing just as fast.

I love taking my moth trap into local Wealden woods on my own in the summer. It's a 'definite' at midsummer, because it seems the perfect way of being in nature at that special time. I use a Heath Trap, which is portable and runs on a motorbike battery, so I can take all I need in a rucksack and shoulder bag: sheets to lay stuff out on, nets, books, torches, trap, jam jars, and a snack.

I visited one large Low Wealden mixed wood through two seasons, between March and September, always to the same spot in the wood, on a wide, flowery ride, with cut over coppice on one side and tall coppice and Oak standards on the other.

I aimed to arrive as the sun sank below the trees, so as to get settled down before dark. I had the whole night world to myself. A Weasel crossed the ride. The last of the birds went to bed and the bats took their places, with the Song Thrush last to stop singing. Once, a Cuckoo called in the deep dusk. A Fox with prey in its mouth appeared. A Toad squatted on the path. The orange moon rose. The stars came out. Tawny Owls hooted. Pairs of eyes glowed in the dark. Deer crashed away. As the season changed, different creatures joined the moths homing in on my trap. In late May big Cockchafers zinged in, and when I threw them clear they turned in mid-air like boomerangs, and zinged back. They got in my hair, they got in my clothes. I loved them all, and made great efforts not to harm them. Around midsummer, lots of male Glow Worms flew in. In high summer, soldier flies came by en masse … and big Caddis Flies. Big, gangly orange Ichneumon Wasps came later in the season. Once a Hornet crawled into the trap and went to sleep. If the air was damp, large slugs crawled on to my sheet and even up the moth trap. A Violet Ground Beetle (they are big) came by and sat up, staring at me from the edge of the sheet. Once, after midnight, on the edge of the wood, a Screech Owl let out a blood curdling scream, then flew close by at eye level.

Those sessions were a delight. There were impressive incomers – the rare **Clay Fan Foot** on two visits, and **Lappet** – but most of the pleasure was in the endless patternings of colour and shape, the beauty of small and living things. I could reliably identify about 80 species, and most of the micromoths went free without any attempt at identifying them. I didn't care. I loved those species made in emerald green, the better to hide in the greenwood: **Green Silver Lines, Green Oak Tortrix** and **Light Emerald**. There are many more I've seen like that in other woods and they always attract: **Large Emerald, Blotched Emerald, Common Emerald**. I loved the painterly moths: **Rosy Footman, Peacock Moth, Maiden's Blush,** and **Pink Barred Sallow**. I loved the ones of careful patterning: **Scorched Wing, Yellow Shell, Swallow Prominent, Feathered Gothic** … and the big jobs: **Swallow Tailed Moth**, the different **Yellow Underwings** and **Copper Underwing**, and those in subtlest disguise, like **Willow Beauty, Pale Oak Beauty,** and **Mottled Beauty**.

I'd pack up between midnight and 1.40 am around midsummer, and totter home, dead tired … and dead happy. Once I took a quick way and got lost in pitch black wet fields and ditches, with thick hedges and barbed wire. It took me a long time to find my way out. I look back on that now and smile. I'll get lost again, no doubt.

BEETLES

One sunny afternoon at the end of May the three of us wandered by a large wood stack in an old Low Wealden Hornbeam wood that was partially back in coppice cycle. Wood stacks are dangerous places and it doesn't do to play on them … but they are also full of wildlife, especially in late spring, and if they've been there a while. There were several **Wasp Beetles**, *Clytus arietus*, stop-and-starting across the logs in waspy fashion, which is how they dress too. If I was a bird I'd avoid 'em. There was a satiny **Cardinal Beetle** – right posh, first of the season; a **Lesser Stag Beetle**, a **Red Breasted Carrion Beetle**, a **Black Hairy Click Beetle**, *Hemicrepidius hirtus*, and a **Common Quaker Moth** caterpillar – bright green and flecked with yellow. All these pretty beasties were either on the bark or under the bark. They are all dead wood dependants. A couple of Lizards were basking together, very tame, and a Slow Worm slept under a bit of tarpaulin. A **Tree Bumblebee**, *Bombus hypnorum*, bumbled by, and a Song Thrush and Blackbird sang.

We wandered on into a flowery glade where a family was cooking sausages in a shack. The Spotted Orchids were full out. We sat on a log and had our own picnic. Then one of their kids started running after summat in the air. I snatched up my butterfly net and gave chase, too. In a flurry of leaping and rushing we netted two lovely male **Stag Beetles** as they helicoptered around. We placed them on a stump and admired them. They peered at us, arthropodily. When we'd let them go, we poked under some iron sheets and found a gorgeous Grass Snake and four more Slow Worms.

That's the Low Weald for you.

Look out for **Green Tiger Beetles**, *Cicindela campestris*, shiny metallic, fierce, with popping eyes and vicious jaws. They fly up in front of you, to settle again on hot early summer banks and paths. They can be tame (when not energised by the warmth of the sun) and will sit on your open hand and gawp at you quietly. They are no longer common. The family of Longhorn Beetles are large, colourful and easy to spot nectaring on flowers in late spring and summer, or resting on sunny woodland edges. Some species are very slow and can be picked up (gently), but others may drop to earth if you get too near without catching them. The biggest, **The Tanner**, *Prionus coriarius*, is a lumbering giant with a body that can be larger than a male Stag Beetle, but without the 'horns'. Their larvae live in old Oak and Beech, Birch and other trees. It's seen most in West Sussex, but I re-found it in East Sussex recently, in Worth Forest. Many Wealden Longhorn Beetles are wasp mimics, including the **Four Banded Longhorn**, *Leptura quadrifasciata*, the **Two Banded Longhorn**, *Rhagium bifasciatum*, and the **Harlequin Longhorn**, *Rutpela maculata*. With the **Variable Longhorn**, *Stenochorus meridianus,* they can reach some size in summer. The **Rust Pine Borer**,

Horse Leech from the Ouse Brooks. Don't worry – we put her back. They can't bite you, though we once found one in a flood pool eating an earthworm.

Arhopalus rusticus, is bigger still than the wasp mimics, but well camouflaged.

There are other large beetles that we come across in Brighton Line walks that can be easily admired. There are the ones with horns: like the **Rhinocerus Beetle**, *Sinodendrum cylindricum*, that you find on old logs, especially Beech, in late spring, sometimes in numbers; and the **Minotaur Beetle**, *Typhaeus typhoeus*, common in sandy woods and heaths. On paths you find their round burrow holes, but often the adults are there also, from winter through spring, and then again in early autumn. The male Rhinos have one horn and the male Minotaurs have two 'cow horns', and are almost as big as **Dor Beetle** species that you can find in similar places.

Turn over old mammal and bird carcases (and wash your hands in a stream after). You will find the most beautiful Carrion Beetles. The **Hairy Rove Beetle**, *Creophilus maxillosus*, is nearly an inch long and looks as though it is wearing a fur coat. It's got serious mandibles. Occasionally you will see a black and red **Sexton,** or **Burying Beetle**, *Nicophorus vespilloides*, flying round and round some spot that smells bad. It's homing in on a small carcass, and it can detect them from long distances. They team up to dig graves under little bodies, ease them down and cover them, making food for their babies.

ORCHIDS

There are a lot of Wealden orchids, though we especially associate the group with the Downs.[11]

Some of them live in woodland. My favourite is **Violet Helleborine**. In its subdued woodland colours and tall presence, it is a hiding, watchful, quiet flower. It is always a surprise, found in a silent, sun dappled wood under Hazel coppice, or a shady lane side, or dark gill woodland. Very rarely it appears as a ghost, a pink luminous presence, in a form entirely without chlorophyll. I have only seen that once. Of late I have found Violet Helleborine more frequently than **Broad Leaved Helleborine**, and I am not sure why. **Birds Nest Orchis** is also entirely without chlorophyll and therefore without green colouration. It is scattered across our Brighton Line woods in both High and Low Weald. **Greater Butterfly Orchis** is relatively widespread, but in low numbers, in our area's Low Wealden coppice woods. In early spring you may find just the two shiny, broad, opposite leaves. From its sweet fragrance, white flowers and long, nectar filled spur you can see that it is pollinated by night flying moths. **Lesser Butterfly Orchis** is much rarer.

Early Purple Orchis is a classic flower of Bluebell woods, sometimes in large swarms, with its prevernal companions. **Twayblade** is frequent all across the wooded Weald, and its two opposite leaves are also as much seen as its green flower spike.

Several other species prefer open ground. **Common Spotted Orchids** are a signature plant of Wealden archaic grasslands: meadows, woodland rides and glades, and lane side banks. **Heath Spotted Orchis**, with its pretty spotted 'pinafore' and fainter spotted leaves, is more common in the High Weald, but can be found in the Low Weald, too, such as on Ditchling Common, where it hybridises with Common Spotted Orchis. There are good numbers on one Lower Greensand 'moor', and new sites are easily found, such as in Danehill meadows. It is fairly wide-ranging, and appeared recently at a heathland restoration site in Worth Forest, and in a little isolated wet meadow at East Chiltington. The gorgeous **Southern Marsh Orchis** still holds its own where suitable habitat survives. The historic site on Henfield Common marsh is going strong, and it's appeared at a nearby site. I found it in 2014, in the lovely flower meadows along the banks of the infant River Mole, south of Gatwick. That site will be obliterated if the second runway is permitted. It popped-up recently in another old meadow under the Brighton Downs, and is in a lovely meadow on the banks of Ardingly Reservoir. The rarer **Early Marsh Orchis** is gone from the Brighton Line Weald, though still on Ashdown Forest.

Green Winged Orchis is the classic orchis of Low Wealden meadows, though it is also occasionally found in large troops on the Downs, as well as the High Weald and coastal plain. It can tolerate quite lawn-like management, provided its flowering and seeding are not interrupted. For that reason it occurs in a number of churchyards and cemeteries, such as Walstead Cemetery, Lindfield, and Danehill churchyard. Walk there with great care, in its season. **Fragrant Orchis** occurs chiefly on the Downs but also, rarely nowadays, in the Weald. Even **Bee Orchis** can turn up in the Weald, and we recently found it on a Horsted Keynes lane verge.

The faintly tropical looking **Marsh Helleborine** tells another sad story, for it must once have been frequent on Wealden wet clay lands, fens and marshes. I knew it in the mid '60s at Balcombe Marsh, where it flowered in numbers on the squelchy, shortish sward. Now the place (a mere vestige amongst improved pastures) is rank, neglected and jungly, and I can't imagine the orchis there. It used to be at Perching Sands Farm and Poynings, both under the Downs near the Devil's Dyke, but the orchis has long gone from there. It used also to be in wet meadows at The Nye, a mile north of Ditchling Beacon, but that was all hard grazed horse pastures the last time we looked.

The only place I've seen the minute green **Bog Orchis** was in a Cairngorms sphagnum bog, but it was once in St Leonards Forest and Balcombe, and elsewhere in heathy Sussex. It was last seen on Ashdown Forest in 1956. The **Small White Orchis** was once in St Leonards and Worth Forests and Horsted Keynes, as well as on Ashdown and elsewhere, but has been gone from Sussex at least since 1943.

OTHER PLANT 'SPECIALS'

One Wealden plant that catches my imagination is the **Wood Club Rush**, *Scirpus sylvatica*, though I'm not quite sure why. It grows over three feet high, and forms patches amongst the tall herbs of marshy meadows, pond and stream sides, and floodplain ditches. It has large, scruffy umbels of spikelets, which flop over as it expands. It needs regular hair brushing, really. Its flowers look rather diaphanous, and that makes it less visible, and no doubt means it is under-recorded. I think of it as a friendly, welcoming plant. It's widespread in the Brighton Line Weald, but not nearly as common as it used to be[12] one km sq dots would indicate. Its headquarters in the British Isles seems to be the Wealden basin, and it is absent from The Wash and The Broads and between the Yorkshire Wolds and Suffolk – exactly where you would think it would be most happy!! Did it fail to make it across from the continent via Doggerland? It must have got into Britain before the Channel opened up.

I think I like it because it occurs in the loveliest places … wet, soggy, humming with whirring, twinkling, hovering and flitting mini-beasts and full of lovely surprises … Kingcups, Ragged Robin, Water Forget Me Not, water beetles, and Moorhens' nests. It is an ancient woodland indicator species, too.

Sweet Woodruff, *Galium odorata,* is another plant with a funny distribution. Before I moved back to Sussex I'd grown used to seeing its dainty spring time neatness in woods across England and Wales. It was a surprise, then, when I realised how oddly absent it is in the Brighton Line Weald … except in the Rusper Ridgelands, and the wooded Low Weald west and north of Horsham. It likes old gill woodlands and is an ancient woodland indicator. It gets its name from its exceptional fragrance after drying – like new mown hay. I never pick it, though, for the sight of its beautiful little white flowers and neat green ruffs of leaves is much nicer than some dead, dry thing.

Part of the reason why Woodruff is so welcome is because it grows in those wildwood gills alongside **Coralroot**, *Cardamine bulbifera*, which has an even greater elfin elegance and delicate beauty. It is much rarer. I first knew it in the East Sussex Weald north of Hastings, visited on trips down from London, but it also grows in the ridgelands north of Horsham. Its flowers are pale pinky-lilac and could be mistaken for some variety of Ladies Smock, its cousin. However, you will soon find its brown-purple bulbils at the base of its upper leaves, by which it propagates vegetatively. It is a plant of Bluebell time, to be looked for on woodland stream and lane sides.

There is a cluster of rare plants which give a sense of connection to the deep wildwood past of the wet and warm Atlantic period[13] better than any others, and they live on the sandrock outcrops of our wooded gills: **Hay Scented Buckler Fern, Killarney Fern,** and **Tunbridge Filmy Fern.** All three have very similar distributions now, having been driven westwards to the Atlantic coasts by drying and cooling of the climate, where they have strongholds in Kerry, southern Argyll, Snowdonia, Devon and Cornwall and a few other western hideouts. However, the High Weald, in our deep and humid gills, our sandrock caves and mossy outcrops has provided refuges for these plants very similar to the rainy rocks and cliffs used by them in the west.

I know someone, who, like me, was a gardener for his living. He especially loves ferns and has a greenhouse full of them, as well as Wardian cases (sort of aquaria for ferns) of them in his living room. He loves filmy ferns, those plants of waterfalls and dripping cliffs with translucent leaves one cell thick, and has been to Madeira and the Azores where one of them, the Killarney Fern, *Trichomanes speciosum*, grows in luxuriant stands in the humid and frost free climate. Killarney Fern was not thought to be a Wealden species, till in 1992 it was detected near Hastings. Since then it has turned up at four sites in the Brighton Line

Weald. I have never seen it there and will not try, for it is much too vulnerable. I am content to have seen it in my friend's greenhouse. In any case, there is not much to see, for it appears in the Weald not as fine fronds washed by the mist of waterfalls, but as an insignificant moss-like mat of green-woolly filaments. You see, it sleeps in the Weald, like King Arthur in his cave, awaiting the return of the conditions that will allow it to flourish in glory once again. Like all ferns it has two alternating generations, one producing asexual spores from an upright and leafy plant, the other sexual generation huddled and lowly, like any smudge of moss, algae, or liverwort. The leafy 'sporophyte' needs great humidity, and such conditions are gone in the Weald, now. The mossy 'gametophyte' however, can tolerate dryer conditions and less light (indeed, near darkness), so it hangs on in deep cave and rock recesses where other plants cannot compete. I like to think of it there, waiting and waiting for the world to turn again in its favour.

Our other Wealden filmy fern has not been magicked into aeons of sleep like that. The Tunbridge Filmy Fern, *Hymenophyllum tunbridgense*, has been able to produce its fronds more openly on our sandrock outcrops. Those fronds though, are quite moss-like, at superficial inspection, and only the botanist would realise that what they are looking at is a mat of tiny fern fronds, like green reptilian scales or chain link armour, dull when dry and green-glowing when wet and happy. It grows in seven locations in the Brighton Line Weald, sometimes thriving, but sometimes in situations which threaten it with encroaching conifers and other shading vegetation.

Now it grows at one less site, for at Nymans woods, where I was first taken to see the fern, it was scraped clean off the rock face where it grew by some anti-social thief … may their bed fall in and their lover leave! It had survived some seven thousand years and more, whilst gatherer-hunter rock-shelter-makers came and went, through clearance of the wildwood, climate change, medieval swine pasturage, the coming and going of the iron industry, rock scrambling, exotic tree planting, Rhodi invasion, Victorian fern collectors, boisterous kids, the 1987 and '90 gales, and all the other changes that deep time brought its way … to be destroyed by some selfish idiot.

The Hay Scented Buckler Fern, *Dryopteris aemula*, is neat, light green, and smaller than the big-and-blowsy Broad Buckler Fern, which often occurs abundantly close by. Its pinnules (the serrated smallest units of its fronds) are concave on their upper sides, and have tiny white glands on their lower sides (and sometimes on their upper too). If the plant is dried it smells of new mown hay from the coumarin in those glands. It is commoner than the two filmy ferns, having been found in over a hundred Wealden sites, mostly in gills. That density of colonies[14] is amongst the largest in Europe, and western Ireland, Devon and Cornwall are the only other places where it is found in such profusion. It often grows in close company with the Tunbridge Filmy Fern.

Be careful how obsessive your searches are when walking the gills, or you will rightly get called a Buckler Fern bore. *Mea culpa.*

ENDNOTES

1. Woodcock breed in Ashdown Forest in reasonable numbers.
2. 'The History of British Mammals', page 176, by Derek Yalden. Poyser Natural History (1999).
3. Yalden, page 168, op cit.
4. 'Wilding, The Return of Nature to a British Farm', page 73, by Isabella Tree. Picador (2018).
5. Yalden, page 178, op cit.
6. 'Terrestrial Mammals', a report by Laurie Jackson, Sussex Mammal Recorder. Page 13 of 'Adastra, An annual review of wildlife recording in Sussex'. Sussex Biodiversity Record Centre (January 2016).
7. Yalden page 171, op cit.
8. Yalden page 153–7, op cit.
9. 'Britain's Ancient Woodland: Woodland Heritage', page 126, by Peter Marren. David and Charles, Newton Abbot, London (1990).
10. 'A Complete History of the Butterflies and Moths of Sussex', 3 Vols., by Colin R Pratt (2011). An unbeatable compendium and this account depends on it.
11. This section has greatly used: 'Wild Orchids of Sussex', by David Lang. Pomegranate Press (2001), and 'The Flora of Sussex', by Lieut Col. A H Wolley-Dod. The Chatford House Press (1970). First published 1937.
12. See 'The Flora of Sussex', by the Sussex Botanical Recording Society, Pisces Publications (2018)
13. 5000 to 7000 years before the present (BP).
14. 'Gill Woodlands in the Weald', by Francis Rose and John M Patmore (1997).

KEY TO THE AREA GUIDE SUB-LANDSCAPES

(Area numbers correspond to chapter numbers)

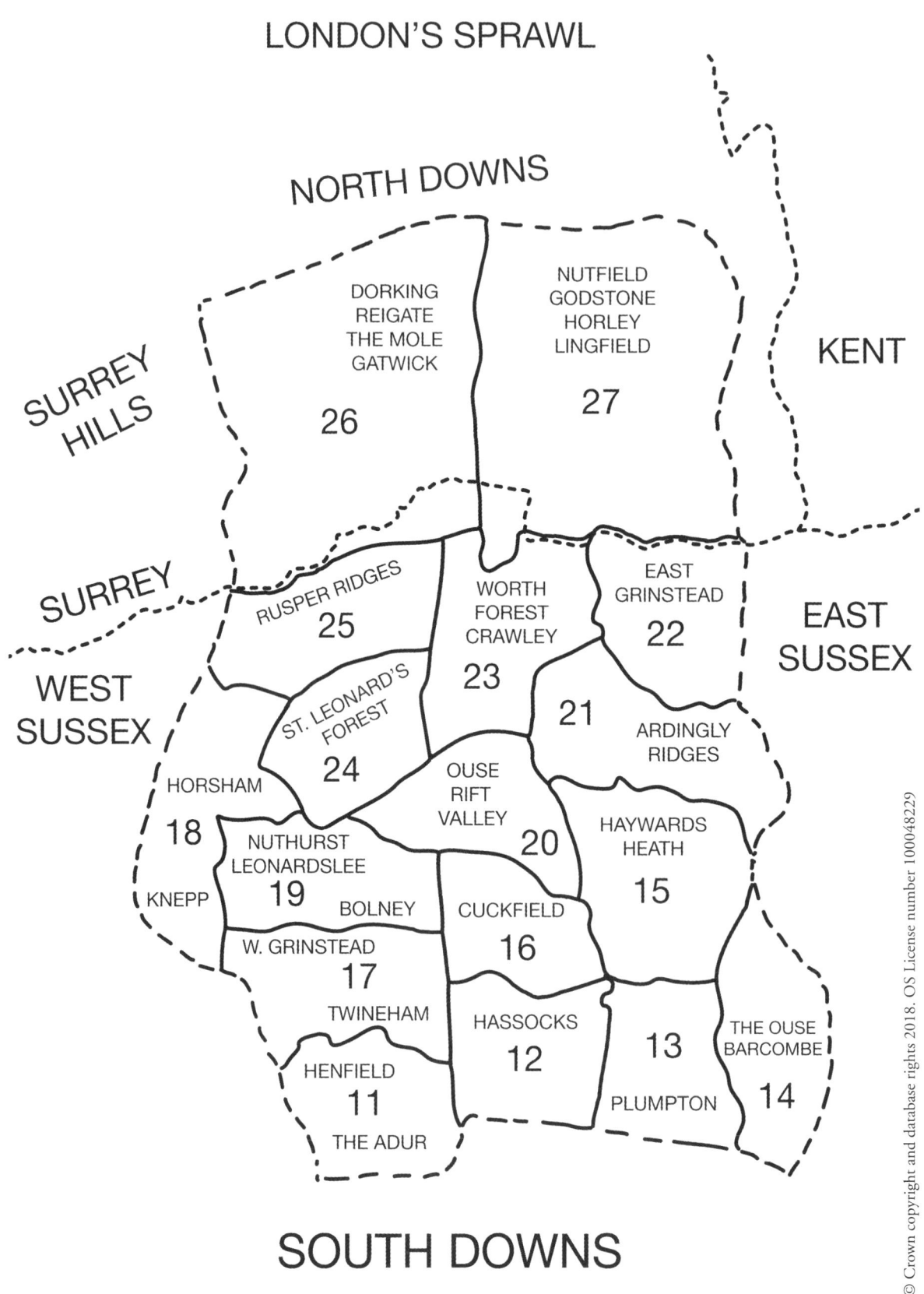

LONDON'S SPRAWL

NORTH DOWNS

SURREY HILLS

DORKING
REIGATE
THE MOLE
GATWICK
26

NUTFIELD
GODSTONE
HORLEY
LINGFIELD
27

KENT

SURREY

WEST SUSSEX

RUSPER RIDGES
25

WORTH
FOREST
CRAWLEY
23

EAST
GRINSTEAD
22

EAST SUSSEX

ST. LEONARD'S FOREST
24

21

ARDINGLY RIDGES

HORSHAM
18

KNEPP

NUTHURST
LEONARDSLEE
19

BOLNEY

OUSE
RIFT
VALLEY
20

HAYWARDS
HEATH
15

W. GRINSTEAD
17

CUCKFIELD
16

TWINEHAM

HENFIELD
11

THE ADUR

HASSOCKS
12

PLUMPTON
13

THE OUSE
BARCOMBE
14

SOUTH DOWNS

© Crown copyright and database rights 2018. OS License number 100048229

SECTION 2
AREA GUIDE

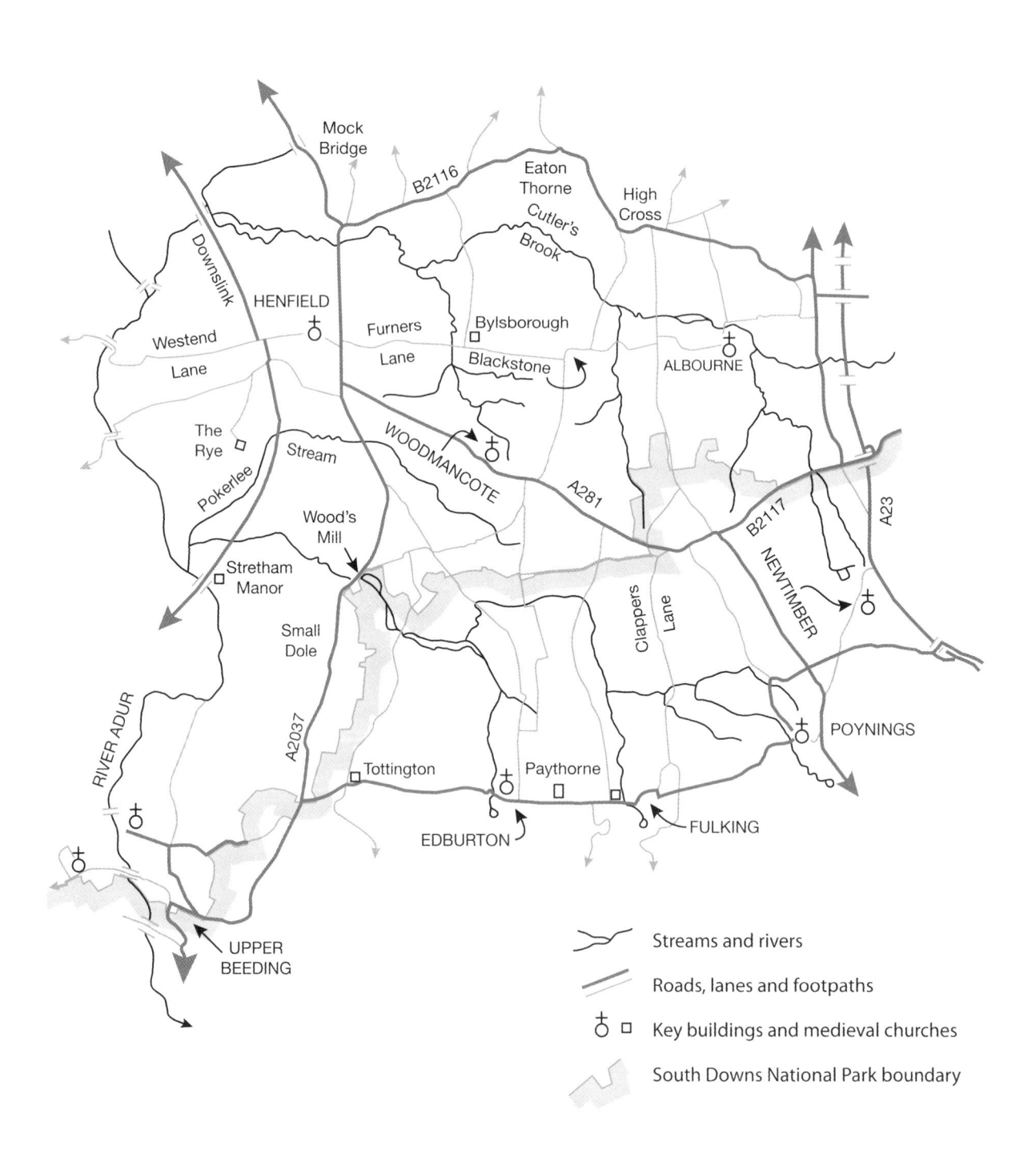

162 AREA GUIDE / Chapter 11: Henfield to Albourne and the Downs foot villages

CHAPTER 11
Henfield to Albourne and the Downs foot villages:
River, pasture, ploughland and woods

Subterranean primeval heavings rumpled this landscape, leaving a low east-west sandstone ridge from Henfield to Woodmancote, and doubling the exposure of heavy, glutinous Gault Clay.

The **sandstones** include both fertile and easily worked lands upon which the communities of Henfield, Bilsborough, Blackstone and Albourne were founded, and poor and marshy ground, upon which Henfield Common, The Moors, and The Alders woods sit. Along the spring line at the Downs foot, the fertile band of Upper Greensand and Grey Chalk attracted early farmers to build a string of hamlets and villages: Tottington, Truleigh, Edburton, Perching, Fulking, Poynings and Newtimber.

The sticky **Gault Clay** made even the most energetic farmers baulk at clearing their extensive woods, which still cluster north of Poynings and around Small Dole: ancient woodlands such as Horton, Tottington, Park, Shaves, and Holmbush.

Between and around the sandstones and the Gault Clay the **Wealden Clay** lands are dotted with farms, laced with streams, and still bear occasional small old woodlands of high quality.

This landscape is bounded on the west by the main channel of the River Adur and the broad floodplain pastures of Beeding, Horton and Henfield. In wet winters The Rye (from medieval "*ther ee*" = *eg:* island) is islanded again, keeping only just above the flood. North of Beeding the brookland waters are clear and calcareous, running from the Downland springline, and there can be a rich water snail and caddis fauna and many special plants. Most of these 'inundation pastures' are improved, though they often retain their estuarine saltmarsh gullies. Occasionally they still partially retain their archaic vegetation, such as east of Pound House Drove.

This landscape still has some of the best wildlife sites of the Low Weald. Around Oreham and its Common, Woods Mill and Woodsmill Stream, the Nightingales cling to one of their remaining Sussex redoubts. I stood on Oreham Common on my birthday in early May, whilst a Nightingale made bubbling music from a thorn thicket on one side and its rival responded with a long rattling motif from a thicket on the other. Not even the 'people carriers' chundering along Horn Lane could diminish my delight.

Henfield Common still boasts rich marshland and heathy grassland, though under-managed and in continuing decline. The archaic flowery grasslands of Oreham Common, The Moor, The Pools, and Hillside Scout Campsite are still partially intact. At Holmbush, Shaves, West, and Tottington Woods I have easily recorded over 20 ancient woodland indicator plants in single visits. Many of these woods suffer badly from inappropriate usage. At least they don't share the fate of Woodmancote Wood though, most of which was grubbed up, whilst what's left has been eaten and trampled by the bored captives of a new deer 'park'.

The ancient roads took their alignments from three factors. The most important locally was the presence of *good soils*. All along the northern outcrop of the Lower Greensand you can trace the lost east-west trunk road from the Eaton's Farm river crossing, eastwards along Westend Lane, past Henfield church, along Furner's Lane past Bilsborough, through Blackstone, past Albourne church, across Cutler's Brook, and on past Hurstpierpoint church. It is several centuries since it lost its importance (and became part-muddy footpath, green lane, minor road and suburban highway) but its route is still plain to see. The Henfield-Brighton Road, A281, tracks the southern arm of the fertile Lower Greensand ridge all the way east to Holmbush. Underhill Lane[1] (Edburton Road / The Street, etc) follows the fertile Upper Greensand bench all the way from Newtimber, through Poynings to Beeding. At some points it becomes a holloway, as by the 'Shepherd and Dog' pub at Fulking, and at Edburton. It crosses and runs parallel

GEOLOGY AND SETTLEMENT

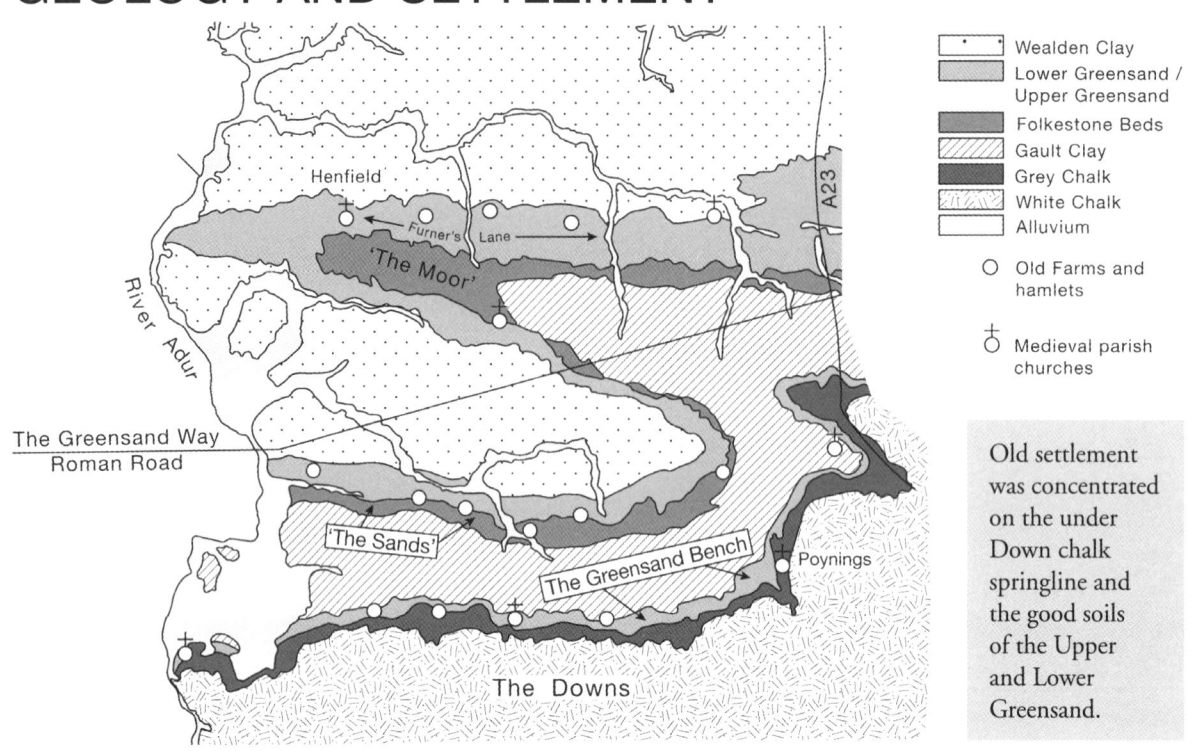

Map legend:
- Wealden Clay
- Lower Greensand / Upper Greensand
- Folkestone Beds
- Gault Clay
- Grey Chalk
- White Chalk
- Alluvium
- ○ Old Farms and hamlets
- ⌁ Medieval parish churches

Old settlement was concentrated on the under Down chalk springline and the good soils of the Upper and Lower Greensand.

Permit Number CP18/021 Derived by British Geological Survey Material © UKRI 2018

with a short section of the Roman secondary road from Portslade to Hassocks, TQ 266 122, just east of Poynings, under Newtimber Hill.

The second factor was the need to *keep dry shod* by following the watershed. Wheatsheaf Road along the northern boundary of this landscape follows the watershed between the Chess Brook and the Sake Ride Sewer. The Henfield-Brighton Road is a watershed route too.

The third factor is the *need to access wider economic resources*. The Roman trunk road now called the Greensand Way, links all the fertile scarp foot farmlands from Pulborough to Barcombe, and was engineered to a high standard. It thus straddled many of the minor streams which lesser routes avoided. It crossed the river just south of Stretham Manor and shot straight-as-an-arrow eastwards past Woods Mill, along Horn Lane, through Shaves Wood, and on to Hassocks and beyond. Sections of its 'agger' (raised camber) are still visible on, and next to, Oreham Common, and in Shaves Wood.

A network of north-south drove roads grid the landscape too. The drove from Poynings tracks northwards through Poynings Grange Farm and Poynings Crossways to High Cross, and though more difficult to detect thereafter, can be traced to the forest land from Slaugham to Crawley. Fulking, Perching, Truleigh and Tottington all had their droves, coming up from the coastal plain, down bostals cut deep into the Downland scarp, and tracking north to the High Weald.

Five of the seven parishes that make up this landscape have nucleated villages: Fulking, Poynings, Albourne, Henfield and Upper Beeding. Indeed, Albourne may have been a planned settlement[2] of the erstwhile episcopal manor of Bishopshurst, for the old houses in Albourne Street were all regularly laid out and held by the tenants of the manor. Henfield and Upper Beeding have been nucleated for the past two centuries, but were much less so for their earlier history. Henfield was built more than a mile and a half from its old political and economic hub at Stretham, down by the Roman crossing of the Adur. It is now a small town. Woodmancote and Newtimber have dispersed settlement patterns, and the latter has more of the character of a deserted village.

THE BEEDING AND HORTON BROOKS

These wet pastures are often at their wildest best in winter when the fossil salt marsh channels are flooded and the birds from the north make it their own. For nearly three hours into deep dusk one February afternoon I watched a pair of Short Eared Owls (I call them 'Moor Owls') forage back and forth over Horton brooks, resting on the tops of thorn bushes, then resuming their floating hunting flight. One of them flushed a Skylark, which rose straight up and into song. For a while one of them companionably sat watching a Barn Owl hunt over the ground in front of her. The Snipe stayed hidden deep in the rushes, but small parties of Reed Bunting and Yellowhammer continued through the nearby thorns. Geese honked their way overhead in the pinking dusk and a ragged 'dragon's tail' of several hundred noisy Rooks beat across the sky eastwards to their roost in the big woods of Tottington and Longlands.

On another February afternoon we flushed a party of six Snipe from the soggy rush brook. As they zig-zag-climbed, a Peregrine Falcon – streamlined and muscled – scudded past our sideways view and shot at one of them. It dodged. She followed. It rose. She rose above it … then stooped. It zigged. She missed. It zagged. She missed again … but stayed 'locked on'. We watched as the desperate Snipe – fighting for its life – dodged and dodged again – and the Peregrine – fighting for its dinner – kept up the chase till both had shrunk to tiny dots and disappeared far off. Never was there a better demonstration of why Snipe always fly so fast and zig-zag so confusingly. Millions of years of avoiding falcons have made them so. Later that same afternoon we saw a Merlin (the Peregrine's little cousin) hunting fast and low across the part-flooded brooks, scarce more than a foot or two above the rush and grass tussocks.

Most of the Beeding and Horton brooks are beautiful, though their specialness is fraying, particularly from the advancing edge of built-up Beeding, with its horse paddocks and tatty, sprawling buildings. To the west, on the New Brooks around Church Farm Drove, e.g. TQ 191 114, the Skylarks sing and the Yellowhammers wheeze in springtime, under a blue sky. The Blackthorn is gorgeous with white blossom and full of bird song. Yet ditches are choked with rotting Reeds and algae, and many are shallowing to the point of disappearance, whilst lines of outgrown bushes have taken over many that were water-filled. Below Beeding church the brooks are now ungrazed and rank (as they are – 2017 – north of Bramber's Street). By contrast, on the more traditional cattle grazed Horton brooks east of Pound House Drove, e.g. TQ 200 116, two Lapwings soar and swoop in their displays, and the view is unstopped by bush and tree way over to Horton Hall and Windmill Hill. The turf is mottled with sedge swarms, herbs and grasses, and the ditches are more often clean and deep, with mosaics of clear water and emergent water plants.

Neither the western or eastern brooks have been much levelled, so they have preserved the ancient indentations of the wandering salting channels. A number of 'saltern' mounds (the detritus of the medieval salt industry) survive towards the River Adur, e.g. TQ 192 114/5. They are doubly worth our

The Henfield Sea: winter floods

attention here, for south of Bramber the farmers have systematically destroyed most of the big saltern groups.

Two of the main drainage channels flowing westwards are the responsibility of the Environment Agency which keeps them clean and deep, and wages a good war on exotics like Parrotweed which threaten to choke them. This hyper-cleanliness, however, is not so good for the archaic water vegetation, or the beetles and bugs that depend upon it.

The brooks best ditches have to be hunted for, but when they are found they are pure delight. There's Ivy-leaved Duckweed, Water Horsetail, Starwort, Water Crowfoot, and Brooklime. My scoop net fills with a 'gravel' of many species of water snail, from the tiny Moss Bladder Snail, to Great Ramshorn Snail. I found nine species in one short section. Water Hoglice crawl about, with Damsel and Mayfly larvae, small water beetles, the cased larvae of China Mark moths, and loads of different cased caddis fly larvae. When I got home I picked one empty caddis fly case apart (*Limnephilus flavicornis*). Here's the recipe it used to build its fantastic little house: *Three Yellow Flag Iris seeds, one Contorted Ramshorn Snail shell, one Common Bithynia snail shell, lots of Rush fragments, several other leaf fragments, and a little twig.*

Upper Beeding church, TQ 192 111, has a heavy roof of Horsham slabs and a squat flint tower. There is much ashlar sandstone in the east and south chancel walls. Some of the blocks there, and in the long churchyard wall, have bits of carved moulding and decorated column capitals. Were they incorporated from the ruins of the Priory, or from the two long-demolished chapels? There are no ruins left of the Norman Priory which occupied the knoll to the north, where a handsome Georgian rectory, now called 'The Priory', replaced its last remains. The only mark of the connection between the church and its erstwhile

The Good Life: Henfield Brooks

monkish users is that The Priory garden still comes right up to the north and west walls of the church.

There are many people from Worthing, Brighton, Lewes and way beyond, now growing elderly, who have memories of **fossiling** as youngsters and adults **in Horton Clay Pit**, TQ 209 124. In the Gault Clay they found many marine creatures, especially molluscs – ammonites and belemnites, bivalves and gastropods – as well as the remains of higher creatures. The clay pit has been transformed into a giant flat-topped rubbish hill, and is now in the final stages of landscaping. Now, all that remains (2016) of these rich exposures, with their luminous phosphatic nodules, is a tiny one acre SSSI fragment at TQ 212 125. Soon that will be gone, too, for all the main agencies, with their purported conservation responsibilities, have agreed with the site owners that it should be buried …

One lovely part of the ancient waterside landscape is hidden behind the rubbish hill. About 40% of **Horton Wood** survives, TQ 207 125. It is a Maple-Oak-Hazel wood with Crab Apple and Midland Thorn and much Hawthorn. The Rookery is noisy in the canopy in springtime. There are Bluebells and Goldilocks Buttercup, Anemones and Early Purple Orchids. We counted 15 ancient woodland plants in one visit.

Henfield Brooks flood spectacularly in some winters. On Christmas Day 2012 and '13 (and in 2015) the waters lapped across the causeway to The Rye, TQ 203 153, and only the track's two side bunds broke the water. The ancient farmhouse was only kept dry by its new clay bund. West of Lashmars and Blundens Farms, TQ 195 163, the line of the Adur was only marked by its two parallel banks above the flood. Swans floated in front of Buckwish Farm's greenhouse. In the late afternoons ragged flocks of Rooks, Black Headed Gulls, Starlings and Lapwings flew southwards, the Rooks part-settling in the crowns of flooded trees.

We re-floated a washed-up pallet and tied some bailer twine to it. The grandson hopped on, and, with a steadying hand, we pulled him through the flood! *Pirates ahoy!!*

In spring the brooks are full of life. Marsh Frogs call on the Adur Brooks west of Lashmars, and you might hear Cuckoo or Lapwing, or see occasional Reed Bunting or Sparrowhawk. Little Egrets are often present. In summer there are scarce and handsome plants in the ditches, like Greater Water Parsnip, Tubular and Fine Leaved Water Dropworts, Arrowhead, and Flowering Rush.

Around the edges of the brooks a necklace of farmhouses were built centuries ago: Grays, Catsfold, The New Inn, TQ 191 153 (once serving the bargees who tied up at the Bineham Bridge wharf), Buckwish (medieval), Blackhouse, Brookside, and Pokerlee. Only Catsfold is still a working farm now. When the railway was built Brookside moved inland about 300 yards and Pokerlee eventually disappeared. Under the turf the two old farmstead and barn platforms can still be made out, and at **Pokerlee**, TQ 204/5 144/5, the farm pond and a little holloway leading down to the brooks survives. It is a lovely spot. One autumn I watched a Lesser Spotted Woodpecker foraging, and a Snipe rose from the meadows. Nearby, too, one spring, I surprised a Little Owl leaving its hole. The claw of an eaten songbird dangled out of the nest.

Further south, where the Downslink crosses the Adur, is the moated site, TQ 199 137, of the Bishops of Chichester's medieval **manor of Stretham**. To avoid constant floods the manor house was relocated in the high middle ages a few yards to the south, where the fine half-timbered building still stands. The manor court house was re-located again, to New Hall, TQ 208 132, in the 16th century.

The scatter of old farms and cottages on the **West End** ridge, e.g. TQ 199 156, shows that it has long been favoured for its fine and scarce (grade two) soils, and only now are the last of its nursery greenhouses being replaced by posh new houses … and more development is happening. We build on our own best soils and feed ourselves from the stolen soils of African farmers.

SOUTH OF HENFIELD

From all along the South Downs Way the **white Victorian terrace at Nep Town**, TQ 211 155, above the Spring Hill / Windmill Hill slopes, is an anchoring landmark. Six separate paths lead down the steep slopes to the **Dag Brooks**, erstwhile 'dole meadows', held in common and lotted in strips for the hay cut. When enclosure came they were divided and fenced permanently into thin strips or 'dags'. There are only five fences dividing them now, but there were once lots more. The stream side is wet and tangled and great for birds and insects (though with some recent clearance, 2017). Along the southern edge of the brooks runs the partially blocked Dag Brook Lane, with its Bluebells and Primroses.

Broadmare Common, at the Dag Brooks eastern end, TQ 16 150, has also always been a wet place ('broad *mere*'), and its many pools are old flooded brick pits. It was famed by botanists for the plants of muddy greens and ponds poached by commoners' cattle: Small Fleabane, *Pulicaria vulgaris*; Star Fruit, *Damasonium alisma*; Mudwort, *Limosella aquatic*a (all three nationally rare); and Lesser Marshwort, *Apium inundatum*. They're gone now, except the Marshwort, which is about to vanish under a blanket of Australian Swamp Stonecrop (2017). Local volunteers did heroic work some 25 years ago and later, clearing the pools for dragon and damsel flies and opening up the 'lawns', but the efforts have stalled. It is still lovely, with lots of Water Mint, Great Birds Foot Trefoil and Fleabane, Swan Mussels in the pond, Yellow Flag, Pussy Willow, Meadowsweet, occasional Marsh Woundwort, and even the scarce Meadow Brome, *Bromus commutatus*. The ponds need re-clearing, and the common needs fencing so that a few friendly, heavy footed cattle can open up the rank vegetation and help roll back the ever-encroaching carr scrub.

To the south is a quiet countryside of Oak-lined fields down to the Woodsmill Stream and New Hall.

HENFIELD AND HENFIELD COMMON

Henfield is an attractive and socially varied town, not gutted by any superstore, with some nice council estates around the old station and at Wantley. It has an extraordinary number of fine old houses, mostly timber framed, in two main loose clusters, one around the medieval church, TQ 212 161, and one along the High Street. South of the church is a maze of twittens, though most of the tiny fields they snaked around are now built up – except the Tannery Field, TQ 212 159. The church stands on the probable site of a founding church of 770 AD, built only ninety years after Wilfred's missionary binge to convert the pagan Saxons kings of Sussex – who had held out for paganism for nearly 80 years, whilst the other English petty kings were converted. It was likely a 'minster' church for a big 'parochia' (early mega-parish), taking in Woodmancote and Albourne, as befitted the ecclesiastical centre of the giant Stretham manor.

Ploughing up Henfield Common's Memorial Field (2017) to improve the football pitches, and destroying most of the Chamomile lawn, Spotted and Marsh Orchids, and much else.

At the southern end of the High Street the marsh, woods and pastures of **Henfield Common**, TQ 219 156, open up before us from Golden Square, at the Brighton Road turn off. It is a fascinating place, despite its continuing decline. In June and July the Southern Marsh Orchids of its central marsh and reed bed are superb, and make a kaleidoscope of hybrids with Spotted Orchids. In that central marshy area Ragged Robin, Bog Pimpernel, Marsh St John's Wort, Marsh Pennywort, Creeping Willow, several scarce Sedges, and Reed Bunting may be seen. You may see the pretty Bog Hoverfly, *Sericomyia silentis*, or a Lizard, or the gorgeous Three Lined Soldierfly, *Oxycera trilineata,* or the webs of the chubby Four Spot Orb Weaver Spiders, *Araneus quadratus.*

There are some surviving patches of Wild Chamomile (the tea and lawn kind), *Chamaemelum nobile*, on the cricket pitch between the square and the pavilion. In Sussex it is almost confined to a few old cricket pitches, greens and commons.

In late summer the grass can be tinted purple over perhaps half an acre by Devils Bit Scabious south of the marsh, and the scarce Saw Wort is to be found scattered there, too. In autumn, I found twelve colourful species of old meadow fungi, including seven Waxcap species and four Fairy Clubs. They grow on the heathy grassland on either side of the Brighton Road, and on the cricket pitch. Amongst them was a finger of Scarlet Caterpillar Fungus, *Cordyceps militaris.*

The Common's core character – now much faded and cloaked – is what used to be called a *moor*, and indeed, the wet fields to its east behind the Swains Farm Shop are still called *The Moors* by local people. It lies entirely on the infertile and poorly drained Folkestone Beds sandstone, and perhaps owes its survival to that poor productive potential. Three quarters of the special plants I've roughly recorded are lovers of marsh or wet ground, and a quarter are lovers of heath or grass heath.

ARCHAIC HEATH, MOOR, MEADOW AND MARSH AROUND HENFIELD

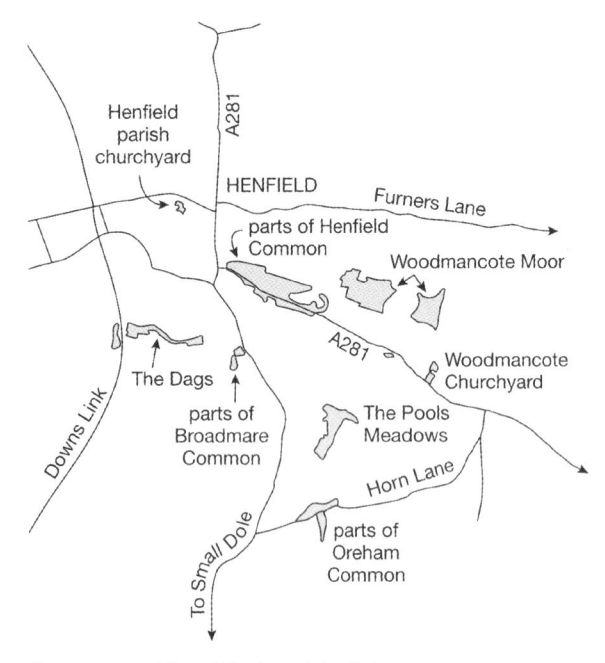

© Crown copyright and database rights 2018.
OS License number 100048229

The picture I have painted, however, is far too upbeat. The Common has already gone through one long wave of extinctions, and is now beginning another. The *first wave of extinctions* was of the most vulnerable marshy plants, and must have begun after a main drainage ditch was dug in 1886. Marsh Lousewort, which rivalled the Marsh Orchis in beauty, has long gone (and from the rest of Sussex too). All the extinct rarities I listed for Broadmare Common were lost too, from Henfield Common, which also lost Bogbean, Sundew, Marsh Cinquefoil, Bottle and White Sedges, Chaffweed, and Bog Myrtle (not seen since 1977).

The *second wave of extinctions* that has begun is of the heathy plants of the drier grasslands south of the marsh, which cannot tolerate the minimalist mowing regime. Needle or Petty Whin is reduced to one small patch at Henfield, and is half choked by the 'thatch' of surrounding grass. (It may be lost now: 2018). It is a scarce sub-shrub (with fierce spines) of *grazed* commons, but is killed by indiscriminate mowing and competitive rank grassland. Ling Heather and Lousewort, Dwarf Gorse and Mat Grass may be gone soon, too, as will some of the colourful Waxcap fungi, which are already much rarer than they should be: species like the Honey Waxcap and the Scarlet Waxcap, or the Moor Club. These species cannot fruit in rank grassland, such as that south of the marsh and south of the Brighton Road, and may have disappeared from much of the cricket pitch, though there is no need for them to be lost, as the experience of other species-rich cricket pitches in Sussex proves.

In the spring of 2017 further disaster struck, as the Common's Parish and District Council managers destroyed the majority of the glorious Chamomile lawn and all of the recovering marsh vegetation of the Memorial Field, damp football pitches which had been constructed on the marsh 70 years ago. The only patch of scarce Adders Tongue Fern on the Common, Marsh Pennywort, Heath and Southern Marsh Orchis were sprayed with herbicide and ploughed to destruction to improve the sports fields, though cricket and football had co-existed with wildlife on the Common for over two centuries.

We need a sea change if anything of the significance of Henfield Common's wildlife heritage is to survive. The open marshy and heathy parts of the Common must be managed more boldly and traditionally to halt and reverse the second extinction wave. That means *re-wetting* the marsh and *grazing* as well as mowing. As commoners, Mr White's family of Holdean Farm grazed cattle on the common till forced to stop in 1948 by the rise in motor traffic and the lack of conservation fencing. The Common's wildlife is the product of many centuries of such grazing and mowing. The cattle must be brought back. The choking reeds must be pushed back and the ancient marsh restored.

AROUND OREHAM

The name 'Oreham' sums up this countryside's qualities. '**Ora**' means '*flat topped hill*' and '**hamm**' means (roughly) '*watery land*' … and this is a countryside of low hills and valley streams, arable, pasture (some archaic) and some ancient woodland. The Pokerlee Stream separates the fertile Greensand ridge's large arable fields from the Wealden Clay of Oreham.

At the heart of this area is lovely **Oreham Common**, TQ 222 139. It straddles Horn Lane, whose one mile long more-or-less-straight course is the longest section of the Greensand Way Roman road still functioning as a road. Part of the Roman camber is still visible – raised and dry – crossing the open ground south of Horn Lane, and just east of Oreham Common lane. It seems likely that the Common was open ground when the Romans used their road, for woods weren't liked along major roads for fear of bandits. *That suggests that the Common's archaic flowery grassland may have an ecological continuity way back to Roman times!* Its rich flora includes Sneezewort, Pepper Saxifrage, much Adders's Tongue Fern, and Spotted Orchids, and I listed fifteen grasses one season amongst 86 herbaceous species. Some species (like Dyers Greenweed,[3] Betony and Devils Bit) seem oddly absent, though. Have parts been damaged in the past, perhaps in the World Wars, as well as suffering from the long absence of grazing?

There has been some good recent scrub clearance on the south part of the Common, which was losing its remaining grassland. (Over half the tiny common is woodland – some long established – or scrub.) Volunteers used to put in much effort clearing around the western pond for dragonflies, but it is now shaded and dank with trees and scrub (2017). Even the thorn thickets needed by the Nightingales must be cyclically brashed, or the birds will go. Like Henfield's other two commons, Oreham receives some care, but not enough to prevent the slow loss of its rich heritage. *Fence, bring back the cattle, brash and renew the scrub, mow more, restore the ponds … and traffic calm!!*

An ancient south-north green lane forms the eastern boundary of the Common, north of which it is wooded-over, but still traceable to The Pools, Eastout, Bylsborough and onwards, though its walkability is part-lost and the footpath diverted into adjacent fields.

Next to the green lane was a little farm, of which only the yard pond survives, called **Stor**wood, TQ 224 141, whose name may refer to the Stork, a bird extinct in Britain since mid Anglo Saxon times.[4] Storwood's location (near the Adur wetlands) is similar to *Stor*rington[5] (near the Arun Wild Brooks) and '*Storg*elond', (at Wartling, next to Pevensey Levels). It seems the Sussex marshes may have been a last stronghold for these birds.

The footpath over Horton Golf Club's little three field course (with its old hedges still intact!) passes **Rough Piece**, TQ 220 142/3, a Bluebell wood, with Anemones, Orchids, Maple, Hazel and Hawthorn under Oak and Ash. The footpath goes on past **The Pools**, where a gap in the hedge reveals the sight of a massive, gnarled Oak of 3.5 spans girth on the green lane bank, TQ 222 145. Beyond that is a real jewel … two derelict archaic pastures, **North and South Hedgecocks**, TQ 223 145, and below them a flowery meadow, **Pond Croft**, TQ 224 146/7. In July, the Betony on North Hedgecocks forms a river of purple-red down the hillside. Amongst the rank grass there is much scarce Zig Zag Clover, and a damp rushey area has much Sneezewort.

Bush Crickets and Green Veined White butterflies jig about. Species like Heath Grass, Spring and Oval Sedges, Devils Bit and Pignut cling on, though the hedges grow inwards and small bushes now threaten to turn the meadow into scrub and woodland (2016). One New Years Day we sat and watched a Barn Owl foraging, as dusk turned to night. It caught a vole and flapped up into an Oak to have its dinner. At dusk in summer the Roe Deer come out to graze in Pond Croft. That meadow is even more colourful than Hedgecocks, though without the rarities. There's lots of Ox Eye Daisy, Birds Foot Trefoil and Buttercups, and I admired a White Crab Spider, well camouflaged on a White Clover head.

In this landscape of Nightingales you may notice a couple of 'nightingale' place names on your O/S Explorer map, including **Nightingale Hall and a little wood next to it**, TQ 219 149. The wood and its birds have gone – grubbed up, and now horse pasture. In springtime forlorn Bluebells still come up all over the field to tell of its woodland past …

WOODS MILL, TOTTINGTON WOODS, 'THE SANDS' AND UNDERHILL LANE

One calm late Maytime evening, after listening to the Nightingales at Oreham Common, we walked the fields to **Woods Mill's** meadows and mill pond, TQ 218 136. A Cuckoo called … soft and loud … perhaps the one we'd heard on several previous visits. A Barn Owl hunted over the mead, like a big white feather floating in the dusk. Whitethroat and Song Thrush sang from the mill leat bushes. By the mill pond we sat as quiet as we could (for my little grandson was with us) as two more Nightingales sang from the scrub across the pond … and a Reed Warbler joined in. Nearby, a Kestrel hovered.

The old water mill, mill pond, leat, flood meadows and Bluebell woodland at the Sussex Wildlife Trust's headquarters, are all a delight. The Trust own only about 45% of ancient Hoe Wood. About 40% was bulldozed for housing and the rest is private.

As Scouts we enjoyed lots of weekends in the early '60s at the **Hillside Scout Camp**, TQ 212 121. Once I found Green Winged Orchis growing in the field where we played. The top half of that field (the GW Orchis spot) has now been re-seeded and ruined, but the southern 40% has been managed to conserve its archaic meadow herbage. In May, Spotted Orchids bloom en masse, and there's Quaking Grass, Twayblade, lots of Bugle, Adders Tongue Fern, much Glaucous Sedge, Agrimony, and Knapweed. Burnet Companion moth, Small Heath and Small Copper butterflies flit about.

The sticky clay woods of the Gault are all rich in wildlife. Years back, I got up for the dawn chorus in **Tottington/Longland Woods**, TQ 217 122. The warblers were in full song, with a Cuckoo far off, and a

Edburton's medieval Clergy House? By the church

CARR WOOD, MARSH AND ARCHAIC MEADOW AROUND FULKING

Nightingale singing softly from young Hazel coppice. There were Silver Washed Fritillary caterpillars, Cardinal Beetles and longhorn moths and beetles. I counted 23 ancient woodland plants, including that classic of the Gault: Thin Spiked Wood Sedge. The wood's Hazel used to be regularly coppiced under a uniform canopy of Oak maidens. Now, it has been sold off in lots, and that continuity of management broken. Sadly, the warblers and Nightingales have dwindled. The northern edge of the wood is a fine spot for bat watching. One warm, still, midsummer evening we counted about five species, including possible Noctule, Serotine, Brown Long Eared, and a Pipistrelle species. The bats wait to emerge until the noisy Rooks, and the Martins and Swallows have gone to sleep.

Flacketts Wood, TQ 223 125, is a fragment of its former size. What is left is hollowed out by cattle grazing. The woodland flowers are partly replaced by grass. **North and South Furze Fields**, TQ 229 123, have gathered many old woodland species in the two centuries since they were left to grow into woodland. Early Purple Orchids are abundant. **Perching Hovel Wood**, TQ 239 119, is too wet for many woodland fungi, but Scarlet Elf Cup appears now and then, and I've found Elastic Saddle, *Helvella elastica*, and Willow Shield, *Pluteus salicinus*. The wood is mostly outgrown Ash coppice stools. What will it become when Ash Die Back hits it?

Where the light soils of **'the sands'** – the Lower Greensand – are ploughed, plants like Bugloss, *Anchusa arvensis*, Sticky Mouse Ear, Thale Cress, and Field Pansy grow, and the Glossy Ant Spider *Micaria pulicaria*, (which pretends to be an ant) loves it. Of the line of farms on this fertile outcrop only **South Tottington Sands** and **Poynings Grange** are still working farms. **Edburton Sands barns and brooks**, TQ 233 124, on the Edburton Stream, are a wild place of derelict brook meadows, Sedge and Reed, *Phragmites*, fen, Willow carr, and fine Oaks on the dry banks. The fen has Ragged Robin, Greater Tussock Sedge, Wood Club Rush, Common Sedge, and both Lesser and Greater Pond Sedges. Nightingales, Warblers, Cuckoo and Song Thrush all make music. Downstream, and along the Fulking Stream towards Catsland Farm, are perhaps seven veteran Crack and White Willows. Swallows, Swifts and Martins forage over the brook ponds near Oreham Manor, TQ 228 131. The footpath crosses the west end of a nice brook meadow, TQ 230 133, with Oval and Hairy Sedge, Knapweed and Ox Eye Daisy.

Just east of **Perching Sands Farm** the Fulking Stream meets the Poynings Stream at **Fullingmill Bridge**, TQ 2439 1253, and cuts north through the Lower Greensand ridge to form a short rocky gill. The public footpath crosses the bridge above a rocky waterfall which crashes to a shady pool below. It is a lovely spot. You may see Grey Wagtail. There is a grand veteran Oak perched on the steep bank above the east side of the pool, and a little Willow carr wood nearby. Beyond the gill to the north the Stream slows, and there are Black Tailed Skimmers and Demoiselles, TQ 243 128.

In springtime, the little path that leads to **Edburton's church**, TQ 232 114, is lined with daffodils, which, 55 and more years ago, my mum loved for us to walk over the Downs from Hangleton to see. Founded, so they say, by King Alfred's granddaughter Eadburh some years after 900 AD, and rebuilt at the time of transition from the Norman era to Early English (circa 1200 AD) the church is a cool and lovely place, and feels quite like an old barn. A couple of its bells have been rung for 500 years. Next to the church is a tiny thatched, timber framed house that may have been the clergy house before the Reformation.

Along **Underhill Lane (Edburton Road)** six Domesday manors were positioned either at points where chalk springs flow from the base of the Downs (Fulking, Edburton and Perching), or where such springs probably flowed in medieval times when the chalk aquifer held more water (Tottington, Truleigh, Paythorne). 50+ years ago all six were still working farms. Perching Manor Farm's huge old waggon barn was filled with straw and machinery, and ducks swam in the muddy pond. Aburton (the dialect spelling of Edburton) Farm was a dusty place of chickens and lowing cows. Tottington Farm was a bit more genteel, and as boys my brother and I got invited in for tea, in return for weeding the patio and tidying the tack room. Now, Aburton Farm has been gutted and poshed up; Perching's barns have been converted to homes, and big new farm sheds built at a tasteful distance (and the duck pond is now hidden behind a new hedge and has a strictly "do-not-touch" air); Truleigh Manor has a small industrial estate; and Tottington is a hotel / restaurant (closed 2018) though the modern farm is still adjacent. Most of the rich arable land between Underhill Lane and the Downs foot, which had grown fine crops probably for several millennia, now grows no food except grass for bored horses. However, on those still-ploughed scarp foot Grey Chalk fields good fossils – ammonites and nautiloids – are exposed.

Though only two of Fulking's original chalk streams still flow – the Edburton Stream, flowing by Edburton church, and the Fulking Stream, flowing by the Shepherd and Dog – they are fine places, clear and cool. Both were used as sheep washes in the old days.

Fulking's old houses, TQ 247 114, are a plum pudding of different types: one or two of local greensand, some timber framed (like the Shepherd and Dog, under its stucco), some flint, some brick, one or two thatched, even one with a corrugated iron extension. It is mostly a posh place, and has been for several generations, though with some council-built homes. **Clappers Lane**, going north from Fulking, must have been an old swine pasture drove, but much of it has been narrowed over the centuries, except to the north, where Bluebells mantle the banks. It takes its name from the early plank (clapper) bridge across the Poynings Stream, TQ 250 125. Just north of the bridge over the Poynings Stream and to the east of the Lane is a fine little marsh in a gully, TQ 250 128, with Great Tussock Sedge, some Carnation and Black Sedge, Ragged Robin, Water Figwort, loads of Common Blue and some Green Veined White butterflies.

A tiny bridge over a tiny chalk stream: Locks Green, Newtimber

Poynings, TQ 264 120, has a superb cruciform baronial church, of circa 1390. An identical twin with Alfriston church – without the spire – it has a huge internal space which feels like a mosque. It was built by the Poynings family, whose mansion next door has crumbled into a solitary stump of masonry in Manor Farmhouse garden. The gardens of a private mansion with a fence-too-tall-to-see-over (but now collapsing, 2016) still dominate the central village space and fragment the village into three parts. The Poynings Stream – another chalk stream – is attractive, north and north west of the village, though obstructed in several places.

The wide moat of lovely **Newtimber Place**, TQ 268 137, is fed by clear chalk spring water. The gardens are superb in springtime, with a white bridge over the moat like the one in the TV 'Night Garden'. *Hello Igglepiggle!*

THE POYNINGS CROSSWAYS WOODS

Around the remains of the lost Poynings Common, centred on Poynings Crossways, TQ 255 141, are a cluster of ancient woods, all on the Gault Clay except Stonestaples on the Wealden Clay. They are exceptionally botanically rich, and were long famous to lepidopterists for their moths and butterflies, such as Wood White, Black Veined White[6] (now extinct in Britain), and Duke of Burgundy Fritillary. The Shaves Wood 'Dukes' were finally exterminated in 1985 by the bulldozing of their last Wealden home in middle Sussex for pasture. Even now, there is anger in the voice of my friend when he repeats the story of this species' wanton destruction there.

At **Shaves Wood**, TQ 255 145, I've counted 23 ancient woodland indicator plants at one go. Though heavily coniferised, it is not uniformly so, and the ground flora survives well in many areas. **Pondtail Wood**, TQ 261 144, next door, is similarly rich in parts, and has a mixture of intact Hazel coppice with very tall, clean Oak standards at its east end, and heavy pine planting elsewhere. Recently, much of it was sold and the new owner bulldozed part of the centre of the wood and laid hard core upon it, despite the binding legal requirements for permission for such felling. Demonstrators marched to the site, and several intrepid campaigners worked all one night to lift some of the hard core and dump it at the site entrance. There is now a new owner who is committed to the wood's restoration (2018). By my count **Holmbush Wood**, (*not* Plantation), TQ 247 143, has more ancient woodland plants than any of these woods. It retains its old coppice with standards structure of Hazel under Oak and Ash, with a stream flowing through it. There is a population of the scarce and fairy-like Giant Lacewing, *Osmylus fulvicephalus*. It was, however (2007) owned by an off-road motor cycling club, who have churned up a dense mesh of muddy tracks through the Bluebells. **West Wood**, TQ 242 149, is almost as rich as Holmbush, and less damaged, though its coppice was largely unmanaged and many of its Oaks were thin poles, when I last looked (2007). It has/had Butterfly Orchis, along with classic clay woods plants like Wood Millet and Midland Thorn. **East Wood**, TQ 249 151, has much old Hornbeam coppice, though a small 'farm' and a 'Country Club, Hotel and Spa' have been plonked in it.

In medieval times **Park Wood**, TQ 262 135, formed part of the de Poynings family deer park, and may have been much more open. After disparking it was likely managed as coppice with standards till the last century, when much of it was coniferised, particularly with Cypress. The northern section partly retains its Hornbeam coppice structure, over plentiful Bluebells, though as an official scout camp site it gets a hammering. **Newtimber Wood**, TQ 266 134, is still intact Hazel and Hornbeam coppice with fine Oaks and Ash. Both woods are botanically rich. The ancient deer park bank forms a prominent boundary between the two woods.

Stonestaple Wood, TQ 252 135, must once have been joined to the other woods, but the intervening ground to its east is fertile Lower Greensand, and so was grubbed and ploughed centuries ago. *Staple* meant 'post' and the stone post may have been a marker, perhaps of the old Poynings Common boundary, or to mark the road. The wood is rich in fungi, often colourful, and has big old Hornbeam stools under an Ash canopy, over Anemones, Primroses, Bluebells and Orchids. It is heavily used for war gaming, with its clutter and heavy trampling, and when I last looked (2007) the trees were white to head height … presumably something to do with paint ball stain.

ALBOURNE, BLACKSTONE AND WOODMANCOTE

Church Lane, Albourne takes you down past some good veteran Oaks, past the old school, over the stream (which floods in winter) to the **tiny church**, TQ 256 161, and grand rectory, which has yellow Winter Aconites and Snowdrops on the lawn in January. In the crook of the Lane, to its south, TQ 258/9 163, is a lovely spot – a sheltered tangle of tiny fields and streams, squelchy plats, dry banks and slopes, bushes and mature Oaks, where Cutler's Brook meets two other streams. Cutler's Brook's earlier name was the '*Alor* (Alder*)* burna (bourne)' of the parish name.

To the north and west of Church Lane the Low Wealden countryside of hedges and Oaks is relatively well preserved. To the south, the 'Singing Hills Golf Course' is horrible, and the farmed fields on the fertile greensand are large. **Albourne Street**, TQ 264 165, has a series of very fine old houses, often timber framed, at its south end. Truslers Hill Lane used to be lined by a series of County Council smallholdings, but they are all sold now. On the brook south west of Truslers Hill Farm is a massively muscled goblinish Oak, TQ 245 162, which once marked a barnyard. West across the fields is the lovely hamlet of **Blackstone**, TQ 240 161, with many ancient houses and barns, in a still largely farmed landscape. To its north, Blackstone Lane widens to a linear green for much of its length to Blackstone Gate, though the little triangular common at the Gate was enclosed perhaps 150 years ago.

Along the Brook (which Little Egrets and other water birds haunt) west of Blackstone Bridge is **Woodhouse Wood**, remote and quiet, TQ 237 170, with carpeting Bluebells and a fine stand of Oak maidens. The bumbles and beetles and nibbling caterpillars were busy when I was there one early May. A Banded Demoiselle flew in from the brook. Most special, though, was to find a Cotton Wool Gall, *Andricus quercusramuli*, on Oak, its metallic green gall wasps scarcely 2mm long.

In early medieval times this was a lonely countryside of commons, marshes and woods (Mor*ley*, Wool*fly*, Want*ley*), with wolves still about (*Woolfly*) and paths needing many markers as they tracked across house-less wastes for long distances. Perhaps that is a reason why so many *boundary mark names* seem to survive here even on our modern maps? The most evocative is **Eaton Thorn**, TQ 238 181, (a half-timbered 'gingerbread' house), which may be a corruption of '*Heathen Thorn*'. It lies about two miles due north of '*Wodesmansthorne*', the old alternative name for Woodmancote, and just over four miles due north along the swine pasture drove from **Paythorne** (*Paga's thorn*). The Saxons commonly noted thorn bushes as boundary marks. Then there are the crosses (**High Cross** and **Terry's Cross**) and the stones (**Stonestaple** and **Blackstone**) and the bushes (**Holmbush**) …

Just north of Furners's Lane is **Bylsborough**, TQ 229 162, once an ancient hamlet, now reduced to a posh house, outbuildings and an old cottage. In front of the big house is a giant Sweet Chestnut pollard.

Woodmancote church, TQ 231 149, has some fossil winklestone in its south wall. It outcrops in a band in the Pokerlee Stream valley, just to the south. **Woodmancote Place**, next door, TQ 231 151, and its surrounding outbuildings, are of many periods, right back to Chaucerian times. It has, with the other big farmhouse conversions nearby (like Eastout and Kentons) security gates and/or CCTV cameras pointing at your mug.

Between Woodmancote Place and Henfield Common, is a low plain with some fine unimproved wet rush pastures known as **The Moors**, TQ 225/6 155. They have much Gorse and Birch in the fence lines and Bog Pondweed in two ditches. The pony grazed western fields behind the Swains Farm Shop hold the largest, best managed population of the rare and lovely Meadow Thistle in Sussex, with a fine display of Heath Spotted Orchis, Lousewort, Tormentil, Ragged Robin, Marsh Pennywort and at least six sedges. **The Alders** woods, TQ 229 154/5, are mostly wet carr, but are carpeted by Bluebells on the northern rising ground … and are known locally as the "Bluebell Wood". On the east side of The Alders is a small but lovely **marsh** TQ 230 154, with Heath Spotted Orchis, Marsh Cinquefoil, Narrow Buckler Fern and Water Purslane (now far advanced to a mess of Bramble and young saplings, 2018). The Rampion Wind Farm cable route smashes along its eastern edge. The adjacent deer farm has wreaked havoc with the remains of ancient Woodmancote Wood, TQ 233 152, whose bare floor has become poached mud (2018). You can see what's been lost by looking at the lush Bluebell carpet that survives just outside the deer farm fence.

NORTH OF HENFIELD

A medieval deer park dominated the landscape from Henfield north to the Chess Brook. It was disparked in the 1640s, but Parsonage Farm marks its old Lodge, and **Parsonage Wood**, TQ 209 172, is a surviving relic of its 'vert'. It still feels oddly like wood pasture, open and raggedy edged, with its patchily distributed Bluebells, Primroses and Anemones, and lots of mature thorn. Good for birds. Its Crab Apple was at bud burst when I last passed by. East of the A281 there's a nice morsel of sedge fen – **Woolfly Marsh** – on the north side of the Chess Brook, TQ 221 173/4. I've seen a wisp of 15 Snipe there in February, and Cuckoos like it in springtime. Are they there still?

There's been ripping out of hedgerows roundabout, but the meadows along Chess Brook and the Adur are lovely, and Barn Owls especially like the scruffier bits, for instance west of **Bottings Farm**, TQ 209 180 – an ancient place, but poshed up and sealed off. **Little Betley**, TQ 203 171, is also ancient and timber framed. West of **Stonepit Lane** in the hedge along the edge of the flood plain, TQ 198 169, are three huge outgrown Ash coppice stools.

All the higher ground west, north and east of Henfield is threatened by housing development.

ENDNOTES

1. Forgive me, but I call the whole length of the lane running under the Downs 'Underhill Lane' because that is what it is, though sections have the local names 'Edburton Road' and 'The Street'.
2. 'Albourne: Economic History', page 2. British History Online: Victoria County History. 'A History of the County of Sussex', Volume Six, Part Three. (1987).
3. Even though a 'Dyers Field' was marked next to, and just north of, the Common on the 1845 Henfield Tithe Redemption map.
4. West Sussex Gazette, 'Selborne Notes: Interesting history of the Sussex marshes', by Dr Andrew Allen. 14/1/99.
5. 'The Place Names of Sussex, Parts 1 and 2'. Mawer and Stenton. English Place-Name Society (Reprinted 2001).
6. 'A Complete History of the Butterflies and Moths of Sussex', Vol. 1, page 42, by Colin R Pratt FRES. Published by Colin R Pratt (2001)

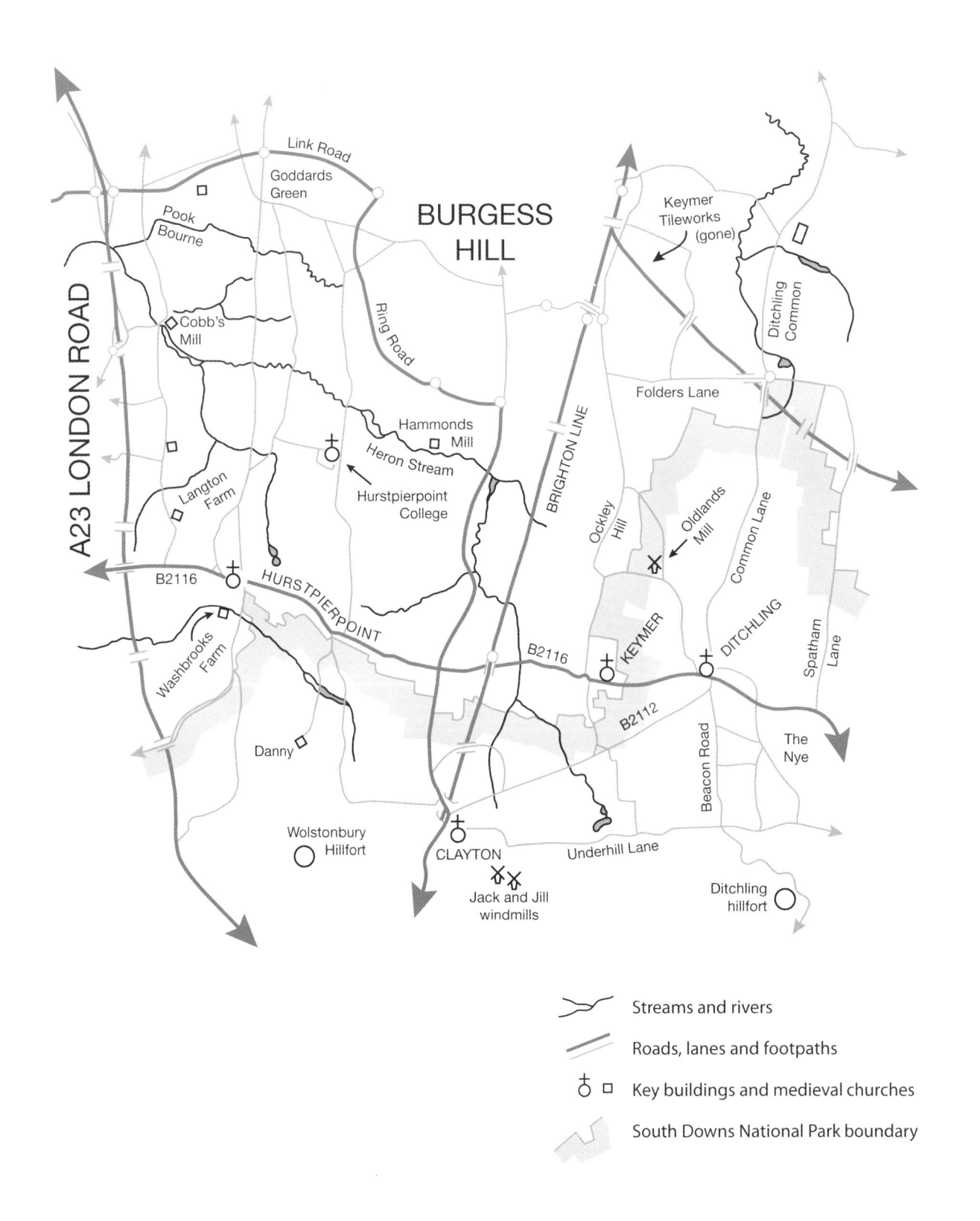

© Crown copyright and database rights 2018. OS License number 100048229

CHAPTER 12
Ditchling, Clayton and Hurstpierpoint:
A common, mills, fords and small woods

This is a countryside with much built development and much more threatened. It is at the sharp end of capitalist development. Its natural and historic cultural assets are ignored, or minimised, in the face of this wave of regional over-development.

Ditchling Common is the very best of these assets, with an extraordinary assemblage of the wildlife of damp Wealden Clay grasslands, which clings on despite a till-recent history of brutal damage by a few farmer-commoners, and consistent under-resourcing by East Sussex County Council.

At Keymer Tileworks Clay Pit, searchers on hands and knees found the teeth of miniature crocodiles and the scales of swampland fish. That is all now lost to housing development.

On the Gault Clay, south of Hurstpierpoint and Hassocks, are a cluster of ancient woods centred on the Elizabethan mansion of Danny, which have mostly escaped coniferisation and heavy recreational damage. They are damp places, with lovely spring wildflower displays. East of Hassocks, the Gault has only a few surviving ancient woods, but it is crossed by several chalk streams, at least one of which is bosky and of high value.

The greensand ridge from Hurstpierpoint to Ditchling, is tracked by both the modern B2116 road, and the Roman Greensand Way whose camber is still visible at Randolphs Farm, TQ 278 158, at Danny's Sandy Field, TQ 288 156, and at Lodge Hill, Ditchling, TQ 324 154, and the fields to its west.

The southern slopes of this ridge, south of Hurstpierpoint, hold clusters of fine veteran trees mostly Oak. Two of the biggest of these Oaks are over four span girths, and three over three spans. At a slight distance southwards of those trees sits the real Methuselah, the oldest and grandest English Oak in Sussex, which still measures over five spans in girth, though its bole is now split into several fragments.

The *hill woodland* after which *Hurst*pierpoint was named (Saxon *'hurst'* means 'large hill wood') may have been on the shadier, northern side of the greensand ridge, for the sunny south side is partially on the fertile Lower Greensand (at Wanbarrow, Washbrooks, Tott Farm, and Bedlam Street) and would have been an area of early farming settlement. On the ridge's northern side, however, the less fertile Wealden Clay comes almost to the ridge top and would not have been preferentially cleared. Indeed, the '*hurst*' woodland may have formed the core of Little, or Hurst Park, one of the two manorial parks of the Norman Pierpoint family. That Park survived until about 400 years ago (circa 1610), but there is still a sliver of ancient woodland north of Little Park ponds, that may be the last surviving smidgeon of the ancient *hurst* after which the village is named. Next to it is Edger*ley* Farm, whose '*ley*' name corroborates the close presence of ancient woodland.

Though there has been recent damage to the few surviving archaic pastures of farmed land, for instance at the Nye, south of Ditchling, and west of Spatham Lane, at least one superb old mead survives south of Ditchling, and there is a cluster of partial survivals just south of Ditchling Common, and some small sites west of Burgess Hill and Hurstpierpoint.

Meandering tributary streams of the Adur flow north from the Downs foot spring line and across the Wealden Clay plain westwards. Just east of Hassocks Station, as the Keymer Road kinks to the right after the old school, TQ 307 155, the Millbrook Stream passes under the road at the Roman Road's ancient fording point, which till modern times, was known as Spital*ford*,. It is almost unnoticeable in the modern street scene. The braided streams of the wet plain generated such '*ford*' names: Eyles*ford* and Ruck*ford* on the Heron Stream, and Shal*ford* on the Pook Bourne. There were watermills hereabouts, including three on the Heron Stream, at least two of which – Cobb's Mill and Hammond's Mill –

Why was this megalithic sarsen built into Ditchling churchyard wall?

its squat, late medieval flint church to a new Victorian building. Its spire is visible all across the middle Sussex Low Weald.

THE DANNY WOODS

These woods are mostly ancient. **Stalkers,** TQ 272 149, **Randolph's Copse,** TQ 274 145, and **Foxhole Shaw**, TQ 279 145, are rich and interesting at all times of year, despite the noise of the London Road. As boys in the early '60s I remember our duffle bags being searched there by the gamekeeper. Once, we stood still to watch a Weasel dive down a small mammal hole in a glade. She popped up again a minute or so later from a different hole. I've counted 20 ancient woodland flowers in Randolph's Copse, including Butterfly and Early Purple Orchids, Ramsons and Guelder Rose. There's also Ragged Robin and Betony. There were White Admiral and Silver Washed Fritillary butterflies on the rides a few years ago and they're probably still there. There were orange Waxcaps, *Hygrocybe sp.*, on the narrowing rides of Foxhole Shaw.

Old Wood, TQ 282 147, next to Danny, has been damaged by the whims of past big house owners, with heavy planting of non-local species, including lots of Horse Chestnut and both Large Leaved and Common Lime. Does this Large Leaved Lime cast doubt over the provenance of the supposedly ancient Large Leaved Lime coppice stool under Wolstonbury, due south of Little Danny, TQ 284 142? However, Thin Spiked Wood Sedge, *Carex strigosa*, the marker plant of these old Gault woods, has been found at Old House. There's much Privet.

Randolph's Farmstead is a nice group of buildings, and the farmhouse has a timber framed fifteenth century core. The camber of the Roman Road, just inside the pasture from the Brighton Road, TQ 278 154, is exceptionally pronounced. The mansion of **Danny,** TQ 284 148, is a huge splash of late Elizabethan extravagance in this wooded countryside. It is built of warm brick with a sunny and lovely Queen Anne south face, and an E-faced eastern front with mullioned stone windows rising to the full height of the building and flooding the Great Hall behind in morning light. The warmongers co-responsible for the blood bath of World War One – Lloyd George and his gang – here cooked

were operational until modern times. One mill leat still runs clear and swift.

In Saxon and early Norman times, the manorial headquarters huddled on the good lands under the Downs and on the greensand ridge, whilst the settlers pioneered northwards into the Wealden fastnesses.

Ditchling was a royal manor of King Alfred, and before that of the Saxon Kings of Sussex. It embraced both Clayton, Keymer and Wivelsfield. In the starting centuries of the Saxon settlement it was probably the capital of the middle of several Sussex '*regio*', or micro-kingdoms, and controlled the area between the Adur and the Ouse. Its church occupies a knoll at the crossways of the south-north watershed between the catchments of the Adur and the Ouse, and the east-west Roman Greensand Way. A huge Sarsen boulder bulges out of the rubble retaining south wall of its churchyard. South of it, Ditchling Beacon is the highest point on the eastern Downs, and three ancient trackways descend the Beacon northwards to cross the Weald. Oldlands Mill, TQ 321 163, sits on the watershed droveway, and an ancient linear common – Broad Street Green – marked its path northwards till its enclosure in 1829.

Hurstpierpoint also, was a giant manor taking up all the land in a giant parish, with large outliers way to the north in Bolney, Twineham, Slaugham, Worth and across to Ardingly and West Hoathly. Keymer and Clayton additionally, held lands way northwards to Haywards Heath and onwards to the Surrey border.

The Norman church of Clayton has a cycle of the very finest Saxo-Norman wall paintings, probably done between about 1080 and 1120, at the time of the stone church's construction. Keymer's apsidal church marks its early and powerful feudal patronage. Hurstpierpoint lost

up the terms for the 1918 armistice … which presaged even more misery.

There were twin Parks at Hurstpierpoint through the later Middle Ages, Little Park north of the Greensand ridge and **Danny, or Great Park**, TQ 285 152, to its south. Danny Park was made by enclosing existing woodland in the early 13th century. It remained a special place right up till the 1970s, particularly for its many ancient Elms, which formed an avenue northwards from the house. They had been known from the days of Borrer, the dynamic local botanist of the early nineteenth century, for their flora of Elm dependant lichen, but the trees succumbed to Dutch Elm Disease. Now the best ancient trees are clustered in **Sandy Field**, TQ 288 155, which was part of the original Park. These English Oaks make a magnificent display, and words do no justice to the fading magnificence of the Danny Old One, TQ 287 155. There used to be a colony of Bee Wolves, *Philanthus triangulum*, mining the sandy lane side soil a decade ago, but their population surge seems since to have contracted greatly. These big solitary wasps, like military helicopter freighters, bring in their paralysed Honeybee prey, slung under their 'fuselages' …

Danny Lake and **Pondtail Wood**, **TQ 288 153,** that embraces it have always been favourite places for quiet contemplation, with Bluebells, Anemones and Primroses and strong Oak trunks to rest a weary back against on the pond side. On the west side of **New Way Lane**, TQ 288/9 150/1, the old Park shaw has two old Common Lime stools … just down the lane from the site of 'Little Bastwicke', a cottage marked on the 1873 First Edition OS map. 'Bast' is the old name for the fibrous and useful bark of Lime, but is this name a Victorian fancy, or is it further evidence of the ancient provenance of the Danny and Wolstonbury Large Leaved Limes, or for the past local presence of Small Leaved Lime? **The Gill**, TQ 289 150, is a good coppiced Ash wood east of the lane.

THE CLAYTON AND HASSOCKS WOODS

These lovely woods sit north of the Clayton Tunnel, and are split by the Brighton Line and the A273 Burgess Hill Road. **Butcher's Wood**, TQ 303 149, is the only one of the Gault woods in quasi-public ownership – by the Woodland Trust – and even there its northern section was shaved off for house-building

Oldlands Mill, heroically restored in recent times

and its western side separated by the railway line. Windflowers – Wood Anemones – are as common there as Bluebells. It is largely a Hazel wood under Oak maidens, but there is a small Hornbeam grove at the south end. There is good re-coppicing work, though the shrub layer is poor in some areas, but the song birds, the Treecreepers and Nuthatches clearly benefit from the added structural complexity, though the many walkers have created a mess of very muddy wide paths. **Lag Wood**, TQ 302 146, southwards across a pleasant little meadow, is an even wetter wood, as the name implies ('lag' = brook meadow). Indeed, the best part is down by the south boundary brook, where Hornbeam is co-dominant with Hazel and Ash. There is Wood Sorrel and Meadowsweet, Blackcurrant and Spindle, and little Early Dog Violet, Kingcups and Ladies Smock. A Giant Cranefly, *Tipula major*, jits along the stream, looking for places to drop her eggs …

The railway side footpath to Clayton Church has Pepper Saxifrage, Nettle-leaved Bellflower, St John's Wort, Marjoram and Basil clinging on for a few final years before extinction (2011).

'I'm the king of the castle!' Lodge Hill, Ditchling (see church in trees). A royal manor in King Alfred's time.

Bonny's Wood, TQ 299 147, too, is an Anemone wood, and has also seen more (semi-private) human usage in recent times. It is a bit more of a mess (c. 2012) with a muddy working clearing in the centre, with trailers and much mud. **Ockenden Wood,** TQ 297 148, seems to suffer from the worst of the road noise. It, too, has its builders' clutter and its inevitable tree house, but also much quite dense young coppice growth. It, too, is a Bluebell-Anemone wood, under Hazel, but with few maiden Oaks. It is great to see attempts being made in these woods to put them back into coppice cycle.

FROM CLAYTON TO DITCHLING ALONG UNDERHILL LANE

Clayton Church, TQ 299 139, is very special indeed. It looks a humble stone structure, scarcely bigger than a domestic building, with tiny windows, late medieval timber porch, no tower, and just a stumpy chancel. It is distinguished externally only by its relative height, which itself is a mark of its Saxon origin. I have always loved its cycle of Norman mural paintings, done in true fresco, with their elegant, elongated simplicity of figuration and modest earthy palette.

I am not so relaxed as I was about the meaning of these paintings, however. They show the Last Judgement ... the separation of 'good' and 'bad' folk for eternity, with a very human Christ judging us to bliss or damnation. It is very disturbing. My attitude was turned by seeing the medieval Judgement cycle in little Chaldon church on the Surrey Downs. It is a depiction of pornographic torture, an instrument of the harshest social control, no more, no less. It revolted me. And Clayton church is not so humble, either. It was a grand piece of feudal architecture for its time, like a smaller version of baronial Worth church, which indeed, lies exactly north of Clayton, up the droveways. It had the same side twin '*porticus*' (like mini transepts) and has the same fine Roman chancel arch. They were vile times, those times of feudal Christianity. What is startling to realise is that *ideological* control (as opposed to naked force) was as important to the feudal ruling class as it is to the capitalist class in our times. Those manorial lords invested in their stone church building as they did in their own homes (which were often just of wood). Their grand churches legitimated their rule, just as grand shopping malls now legitimate capitalist rule.

The **chalk stream that runs down behind Spring Lane**, e.g. TQ 303 141, under the New Road, B2112, and on to Spitalford, is bright and clean. South of New Road it makes a clear pond, once a sheepwash. North of the road it winds through Yellow Flag and Hemlock Water Dropwort. We found some fine Three Spine Sticklebacks, including several breeding males with show-off red tummies. There are some old houses in Spring Lane's detached hamlet of Clayton, including a fine timber framed cottage on the corner with Underhill Lane.

North of Keymer Down and just below Underhill Lane, a chalk stream rises from **Whitelands Reservoir**, a turquoise pool behind spiked railings topped with barbed wire (2013). From there **Millbrook Shaw stream,** TQ 314 141, bubbles fast over a gravel bed, with Bullhead, abundant Orb Shell cockles, and Freshwater Shrimps. The shaw is filled in spring with the sound of tumbling water and Rooks. It has Golden Saxifrage, Wild Garlic, Anemones and Bluebell.

Eastwards across Beacon Road is **Jointer Copse**, TQ 327 144, a wet Gault wood of young Hazel coppice under old Ash stools, with Goldilocks Buttercup, Redcurrant, Meadowsweet and Angelica to complement the Bluebells and Ramsons, Anemones, Midland Thorn and Early Dog Violet. On the east side of the Copse two ancient lanes, Nye Lane and Wellcroft Lane cross each other, making a delightful tangle of stream, gullies, small pits, wooded banks, and over-mature Oaks. Around this crossways are three fields designated as **The Nye SNCI** (Site of Nature Conservation Interest), TQ 330 145, for they were home to rare Marsh Helleborine orchis once, and had much other damp-loving fen meadow stuff, like Sneezewort and Pepper Saxifrage. Perhaps some of that floristic interest survives west of the Lane, but they are hard-grazed horse paddocks now (2013).

South of The Nye, the archaic **Southmead meadow**, TQ 333 140, on Wellcroft Lane, provides a perfect antidote to that depressing destruction. Its traditional management was taken over by the folk who bought it in the early sixties, and they have continued its regime of summer hay cut and aftermath sheep grazing ever since. It is a gem. In springtime drifts of Cowslips cover large parts, and, later on, there is abundant Yellow Rattle, Ribwort Plantain, Knapweed, Ox Eye Daisy and Meadow Barley. Adders Tongue Fern is very common. The mead lies half on the Gault, but the chalky influence is strong, with Nettle Leaved Bellflower under the hedge. I have never seen Cowslips so abundant on a Wealden site. It is an extraordinary survival, and a tribute to its owner's loving care (2013).

FROM DITCHLING TO BURGESS HILL

Ditchling has retained its historic integrity thanks to the fierce defence by its past residents, who have thwarted a bypass scheme and various built developments. Little fields come close in to the heart of the village, which is nonetheless oppressed by through traffic. The church is mostly thirteenth century, but over-restored. Its large churchyard has big patches of tiny black Earthtongues, *Trichoglossum sp.,* on the mossy grass in late autumn. To the south of the church **Wings Place** is a fine Tudor-and-older timber framed pile. Down East End Lane is the **Unitarian Chapel** of 1740, full of polished woodwork, and standing in its own crowded graveyard. There are many brave dissenters in Ditchling's past. Above the village to the west is **Lodge Hill**, TQ 324 155, where Mesolithic folk left their flint debris. The terrace of the Roman Greensand Way passes across its south flank. Though damaged in the past, the Hill's sandy pasture had much Sheep's Sorrel and Sheep's Fescue (or did till recently) in similar fashion to Sandy Field, Danny, which the Roman Road also crosses.

The old drove going north from Lodge Hill passes the lovingly restored **Oldlands Mill**, TQ 321 162, a landmark visible from the South Downs Way. It then forks left and meets Ockley Hill at the north end of ancient **Ockley Wood**, TQ 317 169, tiny-but-lovely, with its Bluebells and Anemones. East of Broad Hill and south of Wellhouse Farm are a number of little ancient

A long radical tradition: Ditchling's Unitarian Chapel (1740)

woodland fragments, and semi-improved and derelict pasture fragments in a still-farmed landscape with a modern vineyard.

East of Ditchling Common Lane, the fields are small, and to the north, seen on the map, look like bacon slices – east-west strips piled on top of each other, e.g. TQ 334 165. That is because they were formed from the old strip-cultivated common fields, or (northwards) were taken in directly from the 'waste'. These **Ditchling assarts** have occasionally partially escaped improvement, and small parts are almost unimproved, though various enterprises – failed and successful – have made heavy inroads. Grass Snakes like this damp countryside. We saw two on one walk a few years back, and another in **Stoneywish Nature Reserve**, TQ 332 153 (the friendly country park based on the old East End Farm). The field corners have Oval and Spiked Sedges or False Fox Sedge, and there are rushy parts, with Fleabane and Meadowsweet in the ditches, Meadow Vetchling and the like.

The best 'assart' meadows are at the north end, though some have been damaged and others do not seem safe from damage. One small meadow next to the brook forms a sedge fen, TQ 335 168, dominated by Oval Sedge, with Tufted Hair Grass, Ragged Robin, and Spearwort (2011). In summer, it is alive with butterflies: Green Veined White, Marbled White and Meadow Browns. Next to it a drier meadow has some Betony and there's a bit of Heath Grass. It has clouds of Burnet Moths and Ichneumon Flies of many colours, Grass Moths, Grasshoppers, Bumbles and Skippers.

DITCHLING COMMON AND AROUND

Ditchling Common, e.g. TQ 335 183, is one of the most precious jewels in the crown of the Low Weald, but it is dulled and crusted and no longer shines. Only

DITCHLING COMMON: HOW TO DEGRADE A NATIONALLY IMPORTANT WILDLIFE SITE

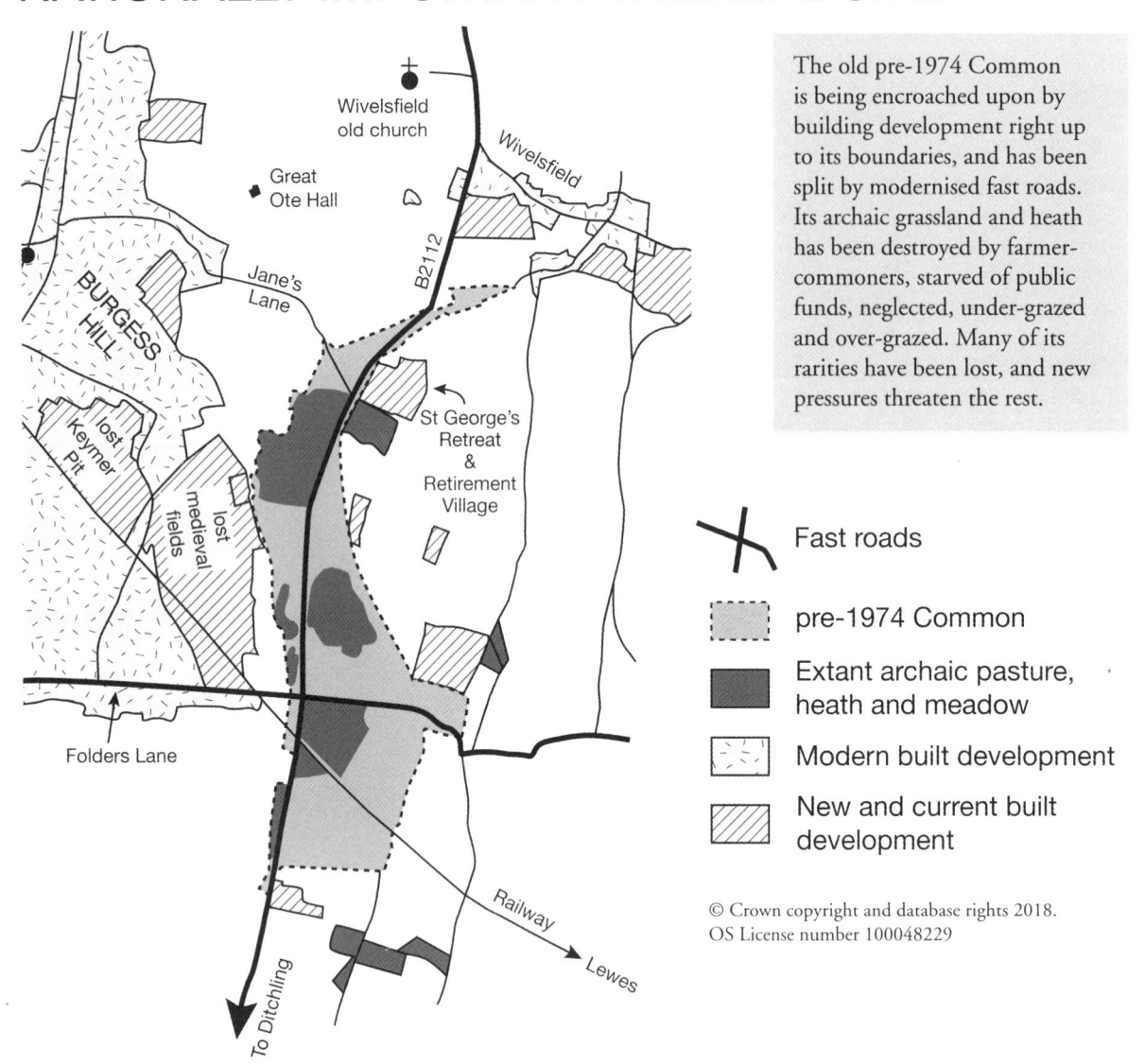

The old pre-1974 Common is being encroached upon by building development right up to its boundaries, and has been split by modernised fast roads. Its archaic grassland and heath has been destroyed by farmer-commoners, starved of public funds, neglected, under-grazed and over-grazed. Many of its rarities have been lost, and new pressures threaten the rest.

Map legend:
- Fast roads
- pre-1974 Common
- Extant archaic pasture, heath and meadow
- Modern built development
- New and current built development

© Crown copyright and database rights 2018. OS License number 100048229

a serious increase in resources and dedication will return some of its lost glory. The old photographs show a unified, open expanse of marshy grassland, gated at both ends, grazed by peaceful cattle – and a refuge to all manner of rare and special creatures and plants.

It is a refuge still … but an unsafe one. The Common is now split into two. The ***northern half*** was bought from the commoners (who collectively owned it) in 1974 by East Sussex County Council, de-designated as common land, and designated as a **Country Park**. It was never properly resourced though, by the Council leadership, and Bracken, scrub and poor-quality woodland has greatly taken over from the airy tapestry of heathy flowers. The dedicated staff and volunteers have worked hard to stem this tide, but the trashing of countryside services by the Council and its government part-funders, and the threat to European agri-environmental funding continues …

The ***southern half***, south of Folders Lane East, is managed by the Commoners Association, and there you can still see great egg yellow sheets of Dyers Greenweed in early summer. Cattle grazing and scrub control are systematic and regular. Yet three quarters of that **'commoners' Common'** was ploughed and fertilised by a couple of farmer-commoners in the early seventies (as well as the 'Hope Farm field' in what later became the Country Park). What survives is only a fragment of what was there 40 years ago. A ragged 'cease fire line' – plain to see – runs north-south across the commoners' common at the point where the advance of the farmer-destroyers was halted by the legal action and campaigning of the other commoners and local people. Death threats were made to one leading activist. *To its* *west*, the old vegetation is still intact: a mosaic of Tufted Hair Grass and Purple Moor Grass, Tormentil and Dyers Greenweed, with low clumps of Dwarf and European Gorses, some thorn scrub, and a few super-special 'lawns' of rare Marsh Plume / Meadow Thistle, *Cirsium dissectum*, with accompanying Least Willow, *Salix repens*, Spring, Carnation and Glaucous Sedges, *Carex caryophyllea, panicea and flacca*, and Quaking Grass. Grizzled Skipper flits about. *To the east of the 'cease fire line', and south of the railway line*, there is a boring sheet of improved hay meadow grasses …

On both the commoners' Common and the Country Park, the closely related sub-shrubs Dyers Greenweed and Petty Whin were host to dependant populations of at least seven rare micro-moths, which were the chief fame of the Common to lepidopterists. Only one has been found again recently. Perhaps more survive, but the over-grazing of the southern Common and the lack of grazing and loss of grassland to scrub on the northern Common are not good signs.

The Country Park is well known for its spring time display of Bluebells, which are sheltered by Bracken in much the same way that the leafy tree canopy protects them in woodland (2014). Deservedly loved though it is, that display is not the Common's real claim to 'specialness', and why it was designated an SSSI (Site of Special Scientific Interest). In the whole of the middle Sussex Low Weald, it is *here* that the old clay land community of lovely herbs and sub-shrubs, grasses and sedges, on the spectrum from marsh to dry slope, is at its most complete. We can still see Petty Whin, Meadow Thistle, Bitter Vetch, Saw Wort, Dyers Greenweed, Heath Bedstraw, Tormentil, Betony and Devils Bit along the path sides, as pretty as any flower border. Heath Spotted and Common Spotted Orchids are aplenty, and in a kaleidoscope of hybrids. Wild Columbine flowers at one of its few truly native sites, and Ling Heather clings on. Though some of the most famous rarities seem now lost (like Tawny and Flea Sedges, Starfruit at the pond, and Silver Studded Blue, Marsh and Small Pearl Bordered Fritillary butterflies) there are still Narrow Buckler and Adders Tongue Ferns, lots of Pignut, and little Heath Milkwort, and in springtime, Emperor Moths rush up and down in the early evening sunshine.

The commoners' common is the only part of the historic Common where its old landscape-scale openness survives. On the marshy winter grassland, Snipe are still visitors. In the red sunset of late summer one, sometimes two, large Serotine Bats forage so close that their dark fur, rounded ears, their noses, faces and tails are plain to see! Skylarks still sing in the heavens. One autumn, a lost Red Deer hind attached herself to the herd of bullocks that have the run of the common. Their easy acceptance seemed to give her confidence.

Now, further drastic attrition of the ancient common's landscape is underway, as a major housing development replaces (2016) the ancient landscape that erstwhile separated the common from Burgess Hill, destroying the **medieval patchwork of tiny irregular fields with their rich outgrown hedges west of Pollards, Freckborough and Hope Farms**, e.g. TQ 328 186. That landscape was a place of great specialness in its own right, for its higgledy-piggledy field pattern was a relic of its medieval enclosure from Freckborough Chase. The development is justified by extolling the benefit the Common will receive from money given in compensation for this landscape loss and encroachment, but no such money can compensate. Urban and urban fringe commons are subject to a qualitatively greater range of human pressures than more distanced places, and the push to downgrade the management needs of the nationally important wildlife assemblage and capitulate to the interests of particular users – like dog walkers – will be hugely ratcheted up. This must be one of the most irresponsible housing proposals in the whole of middle Sussex.

St Georges Retreat and its Catholic care home and 250 acre farmed estate, run down the eastern boundary of Ditchling Common. Recently they built a big retirement village in their extensive grounds, thus squeezing the common with just that bit more urban hinterland. However, the Retreat has preserved one extraordinary resource: a **set of four unimproved brook meadows** on either side of a stream just inside their entrance from the Haywards Heath Road, TQ 336 192. In spring these meadows have one of the best displays of Green Winged Orchids in Sussex, with occasional Cowslips and Spring Sedge. In early summer the other herbs and grasses of archaic clay meadows flower … more orchids, Ox Eye Daisy, Yellow Oat Grass, Common Cat's Ear. The meadow is mown too often, (like a garden lawn, not a traditional meadow) so the taller plants of old meadows, like Pepper Saxifrage, struggle to set seed, and the many ornamental trees further squeeze the high value herbaceous areas, but the meadows survival is still a tribute to the Order's management (2013).

THE POOK BOURNE AND GODDARDS GREEN WOODS

All the area south of Goddard's Green was threatened by a proposal for a massive new settlement of over 3000 homes. Local people fought it off, but now the area north of the Link Road is targeted for an even bigger development (called the 'northern arc').

West of Burgess Hill the **Pook Bourne** (Saxon for '*Goblin Stream*') e.g. TQ 275 199, makes a shallow meandering valley between small ancient woods. It is the best of our English countryside … but for the noise of the London Road and the Burgess Hill Link Road. The lush brook meadows have escaped 'improvement' in some spots. There is Gipsywort and Corn Mint,

Sticklebacks, Damselflies and House Martins: Cobb's Mill Leat, Hurstpierpoint

Spearwort and Reed Canary Grass. On a bank on the south side, TQ 274 199, stands the best Wild Service tree in Hurstpierpoint parish, with Pepper Saxifrage in the turf. A shallow pond has Spike Rush, *Eleocharis palustris*, (and much invasive Himalayan Balsam). Till it was flattened in the winter of 2011/12, old **Pookbourne Barn** still stood, TQ 273 199, sheltering its roosting Barn Owl. Wild Hop clambers all over the bushes by **Pook Bourne Bridge**, TQ 273 198, as is its wont.

Great Wood, TQ 281 198, is a beautiful full-on Bluebell wood, with Anemones, under a good coppice with standards structure. On the south side of the Bourne is a **part-ancient, part-plantation wood**, TQ 279 198. The secondary part has a ground cover of Dog's Mercury and the ancient part has Bluebells and Anemones. South of Shalford, TQ 284 197, are two more little ancient woods, **Hungerfields Wood**, in the crook of Northends Lane, TQ 280 191, and **Northend Copse**, TQ 285 181, a Bluebell wood under Oak and Hazel, with at least one Wild Service tree. To the east, **Parson's Withes**, TQ 292 197, in the angle between Gatehouse and Pangdean Lanes, has a varied flora and much thorn, both Midland Thorn and Hawthorn and their hybrids.

Just north of the Bourne, TQ 274 200, there is a nice **fragment of old meadow**, with a colourful tapestry of flowers, including much Pepper Saxifrage and Sneezewort. Just west of the Burgess Hill Ring Road are **several derelict fields,** some in Council ownership. They could become fine places, with management, otherwise they look set to succeed to scrub thickets. The **verges of Malthouse Lane** as it turns east to join the Ring Road TQ 292 193, were rich in archaic flowers, but encroaching scrub had left only the Water Dock, Betony and Saw Wort surviving, in an enfeebled condition in 2012.

THE HERON STREAM AND NORTH HURSTPIERPOINT

The walk along the **Heron Stream** from Cobb's Mill, TQ 274 189, east to Eylesford Bridge (on the A273) reveals a waterland geography separate from the geography of motor roads and settlements. It passes many bridges and lost fordings – Cobbsmill *Bridge*, Gold *Bridge* (as in Marsh Mari*gold*, Kingcups), Stalker *Bridge*, Danworthbrook *Bridge*, Ruck*ford* and Eyles*ford Bridge*. For two thirds of a mile from Cobb's Mill to Stalker Bridge (where the Cuckfield Road crosses) you can walk alongside the running mill leat, with its sticklebacks, Emperor Dragons, Grey Wagtails, Banded

182 AREA GUIDE / Chapter 12: Ditchling, Clayton and Hurstpierpoint

Demoiselles, rustling trees, and twittering House Martins. Upstream of Ruckford and Hammond's Mills the leats no longer function, but can still be made out. East of Ruckford Mill there is a lovely wooded lily pond, TQ 2960 179, where frogs plop noisily into clear water, with much Hornwort and Curled Pondweed. Between Ruckford Mill and Locks Manor are two well managed archaic flower meadows, e.g. TQ 293 180/1. Between Danworth and Kent's Farms we saw several Trout in meanders, in clear water over gravel. In some places the little brook meadows survive. At other points they have been incorporated into larger fields.

To the west of Hurstpierpoint **Langton Lane** has pleasantly little traffic, and wide roadside wastes dominated by tall herbs in summer, busy with nectaring hoverflies and bees. At its southern end it forms a shady holloway through the Greensand ridge. Langton Farmstead has been sold away from the farm, but **Langton Farm fields**, TQ 275 171, largely retain their old webbing of shaws and hedges (2011). The farm seems mothballed (for future development?) but, for the moment, it is a lovely spot. A small **archaic brook meadow** just survives, TQ 275 174, with several sedges, Sneezewort, Marsh Ragwort and Devils Bit. There are Common Green Grasshoppers and Wasp Spiders (which presumably lunch on them). A tangle of Nettle, Creeping Thistle, Bramble, Bindweed and Tufted Hair Grass advances year on year. Soon the meadow will be gone, at this rate.

North of Langton Farm, where more hedgerows have been ripped out, an old meadow survived (2011) within the grounds of **Knowles Tooth,** TQ 275 178. Does it still? It has a handsome veteran oak at its middle, graced with a tree house, and the meadow is crowded with butterflies, Burnet Moths and grasshoppers, before its summer cut.

On the northern edge of Hurstpierpoint there are two ancient woods. **Tilleys Copse**, TQ 283 173, is a Bluebell wood, with Crab, Wych Elm, Gean, Midland Thorn and Hornbeam. **The Wilderness**, just to the south, TQ 279 169, is a damper place.

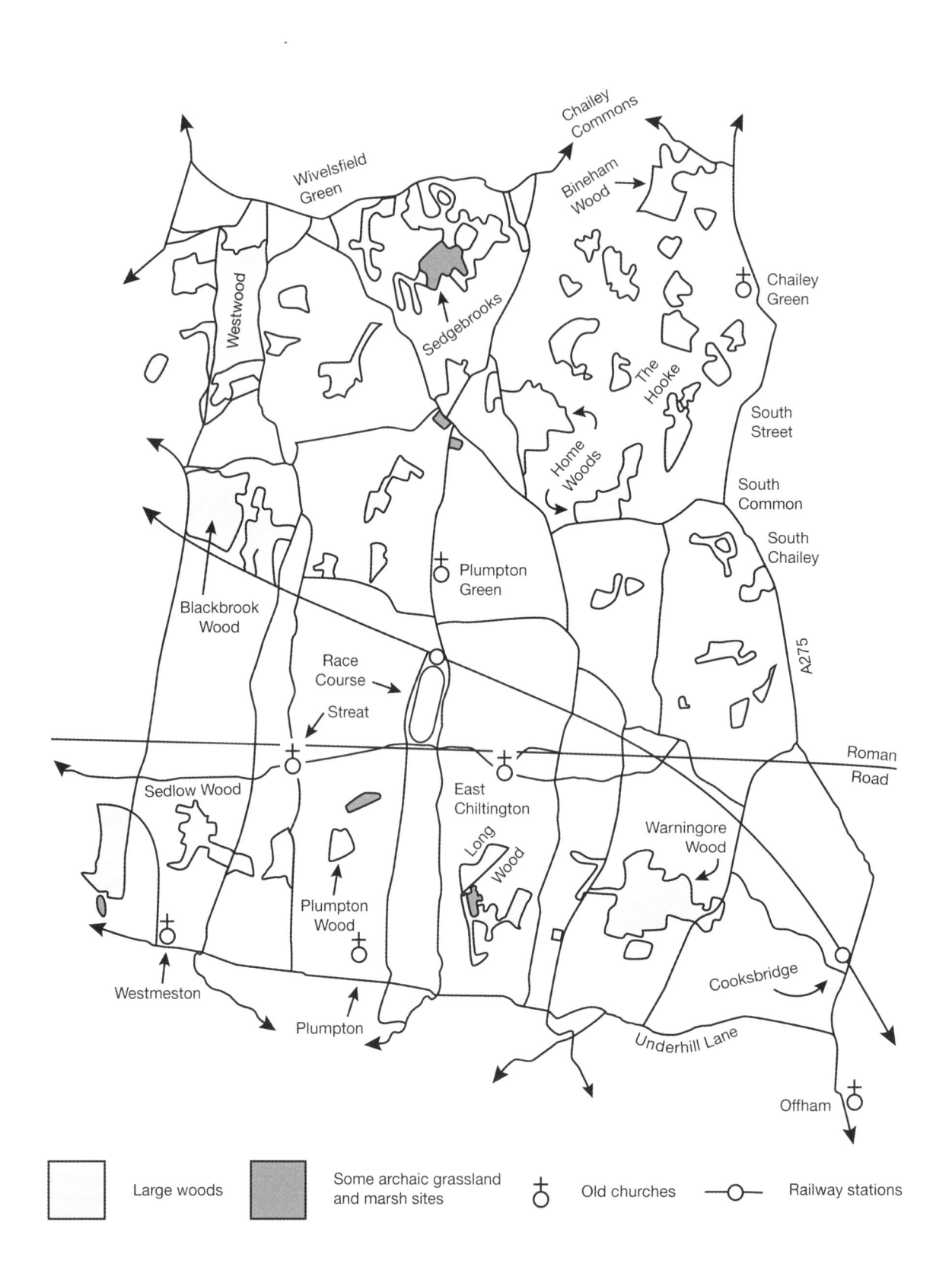

AREA GUIDE / Chapter 13: Westmeston to Wivelsfield Green

CHAPTER 13
Westmeston to Wivelsfield Green and Plumpton to South Chailey

In this landscape we begin to get to wood after wood! There are far more of them east of Burgess Hill than to the west.

On the Wealden Clay there are major clusters of ancient woodland. West Wood and Blackbrook Wood take up much of the northern third of Westmeston parish. South of Wivelsfield Green are some fragments of old woodland on the footprint of 'the Bishoprick', the medieval Stanmer wealden common – places like Lashmar and Cottage Woods. There are substantial fragments of medieval Home Wood, broken up in the early seventeenth century, though they suffered further losses to make a D Day Landing Ground, and to feed the maw of greedy modern farming. Between Chailey Common and South Chailey are the many medium sized woods of the Hooke Estate and its neighbours.

On the Gault Clay there is one big wood (Warningore Wood) and a chain of smallish woods from Westmeston (Sedlow Wood) to Novington (Long Wood).

Only the fertile greensands are open and unwooded: the (lower) greensand ridge on which Streat and East Chiltington churches sit, and the (upper) greensand bench along which Underhill Lane runs,.

In the Middle Ages this was a land of big commons, hunting chases and parks from Burgess Hill to Chailey, and it was only in the sixteenth and early seventeenth centuries that they were largely eradicated. The long linear Streat and Plumpton Greens, which had funnelled into those northern commons, long survived their destruction. Important parts of the Streat Greens and their archaic vegetation still survive, but Plumpton Green was enclosed in the nineteenth century, as was Chailey South Common, the last of this landscape's big clay commons.

However, Sedgebrook Marsh and Longridge meadows, and ancient woods such as Great Home Wood cling on to parts of the archaic vegetation of those lost wildlands.

The North End Stream, the Bevern Stream and the Longford Stream flow eastwards to join the main channel of the River Ouse. The Bevern is fed by the clear chalky waters of Plumpton Mill Stream arising at moated Plumpton Place.

THE GAULT CLAY WOODS AND UNDERHILL LANE

Warningore Wood, TQ 382 140, has given me much pleasure over the years. I'd stop the car on Allington Lane (that passes through the eastern part of the wood) and my old Mum and I would sit with the windows rolled down amidst the Bluebells, breathing in their heady scent. One April, I was in the wood by 5.00 am for the dawn chorus. Garden and Willow Warblers, Blackcap and Chiffchaff had all returned, and a Cuckoo called far off, but the chief delight was the noisy music of ordinary birds: Blackbird and Wood Pigeon, Tits and Song Thrush, Yaffle and Great Spotted Woodpecker.

The wood is outgrown Hornbeam coppice, with no standards, but there is woody variety enough, with Wych Elm, Wild Service, Crab, Spindle, Guelder Rose and Aspen, and I have counted 25 ancient woodland plants, including Early Purple and Butterfly Orchids.

The wide rides had a rich herbaceous vegetation of old Wealden plants like Ragged Robin, but many of them have now had chalk rubble dumped along them in long white scars – visible even from the South Downs Way – and much harm has been done. The wood was a candidate SSSI. If that designation had been completed it would have had some protection from such damage.

Long Wood, TQ 367 142, at Novington; **Brocks Wood**, TQ 349 143, on Streat Lane; and **Sedlow Wood**, TQ 342 146, a half mile north of Westmeston church, are all lovely and species-rich woods, and different from each other. Sedlow Wood is a tangled and wild Ash

Warningore's ancient north-south drove. Did Simon de Montfort's army trudge down here on their way to the Battle of Lewes? (1264)

wood. Brocks Wood is a Bluebell wood with a stream. Long Wood has Laurel thickets.

If its small size is taken into account the best of these Gault woods has to be **Plumpton Wood**, TQ 355 145, north of Plumpton College, and owned by them. Its Bluebells thickly carpet. It is largely Hazel coppice with Oak and Ash standards, but with remarkably varied vegetation. I counted 22 ancient woodland plants in one visit. It has large damp areas with Ramsons, Redcurrant, and even Alder Buckthorn. It has a fine, sunny western edge, which is the old parish boundary with Streat. The boundary bank has big Oaks, a big old Ash, a Gean swarm, Wild Service and Pignut.

There is an old book[1] of 1946 describing a walk along **Underhill Lane from Lewes to Clayton**, with beautiful drawings. Three of them show people walking down the Lane … Not the *verge*, but in the *roadway*. On most of it I wouldn't even cycle, now! Only the length from Clayton to Westmeston, is still safe enough for walkers.

Both **Westmeston and old Plumpton churches** are basically Norman (the naves), with later chancel and south aisle at Westmeston, and later tower and chancel at Plumpton. Their small size demonstrates how exceptional building in stone was in those times. Both of them had paintings of the Lewes Group[2] of Frescoes (with Clayton, Coombes and Hardham), though those at Westmeston, TQ 338 136, were not preserved after they were uncovered in 1862. Parts of the paintings at Plumpton, TQ 356 134, on the north wall of the nave, do survive and have recently been restored. Extraordinarily, it is thought that the wooden bell hanging frame may date back to 1040. The stone tower may have been built around the original wooden tower and its bell hanging. Plumpton church is forlorn amongst the ever-expanding college buildings. New planted trees in front will further obscure our views of it from the Downs and the Lane. The churchyard is rank, though if it was regularly mown who knows what plants and old meadow fungi may pop up?

The **Plumpton Agricultural College** has a large estate and many projects. Neighbouring it on its east is the moated **Plumpton Place** (16th and 17th century and 20th century Lutyens), which was on sale for £8 million in 2010. Six bedrooms, five bathrooms and no bedroom tax for the likes of them. The college uses its big 17th century threshing barn, though. **Plumptonplace Watermill**, TQ 361 136, to the north, still has its mill wheel, and its gravel bedded chalk stream has frequent Bullhead and freshwater shrimps, orb shell cockles, and pond snails.

EAST CHILTINGTON TO BEVERN BRIDGE

East Chiltington and Chiltington are remarkable for their long stretches

The catslide roof of Westmeston's tiny church. Horsham slabs and tiles.

186 AREA GUIDE / Chapter 13: Westmeston to Wivelsfield Green

EAST CHILTINGTON WILDFLOWER VERGES

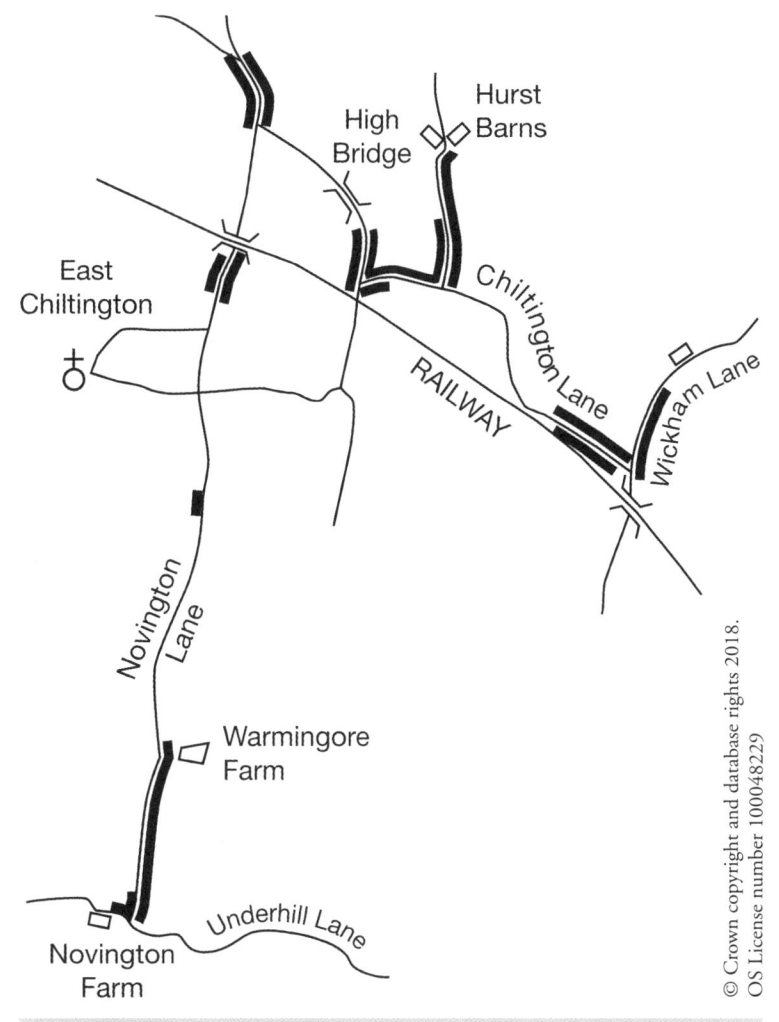

of relatively intact flowery lane sides. There are also several small archaic meadows, one of which is of superb quality, and lovingly cared for, with a big display of Southern Marsh Orchis, Marsh Marigold, Ragged Robin, Heath Spotted Orchis, and both Black and Carnation Sedges.

Novington Lane could change its name to 'Meadow Cranesbill Lane', for there are at least five spots where it flowers in July along the two miles between the tiny green at the junction with Underhill Lane, TQ 371 130, and North Hall, TQ 376 162. Experts suspect that Meadow Cranesbill is not a native Sussex herb,[3] because two species of weevil associated with it across the main parts of its range, in middle and northern England, are absent from it here. It was first recorded[4] in Sussex at "the side of (a) copse near Plumpton" in 1805, so these nearby Novington plants may be the oldest Sussex denizens. Nearly 40% of Novington Lane's length is still colourful with wild flowers. The best stretch is just south of Warningore Farm, TQ 374 136, where there is much Spotted Orchis and Ox Eye Daisy, Birds Foot Trefoil, Hoary Ragwort and Meadowsweet. Just south of **High Bridge**, e.g. TQ 380 155, and along **Chiltington and Wickham Lanes** are good flowery stretches, too, though they are under-managed and cut too late, if at all.

Just south of the railway bridge that crosses Novington Lane is **Brookhouse Farm**, TQ 375 155. Across the yard from the Lane stands a native Black Poplar veteran, bent and hollow, divided but still freely sprouting, that once – like the farmstead – stood on the edge of the Bevern brooks, now blocked from view by the railway embankment. One late May evening, as we walked under the railway bridge by the Blackthorn thicket, we heard a duo singing ... a harmony, a rivalry of Nightingale and Blackbird. At first the Nightingale softly copied the Blackbird's song ... The Blackbird strongest, dominating the music ... Then less so ... Then it gave up ... and only the Nightingale sang ... tentative, experimental, deeply throaty and liquid, with warbles and trills ... and strong spaces between phrases. Then, distantly and faintly, a Cuckoo joined in from far off. The residents of Brookhouse had an upper window open. I hope someone inside was listening with us ...

> These lanes are blessed with wide grassy verges, which often have good displays of common wildflowers. Some of them are well managed (as between Warningore Farm and Underhill Lane) with orchids and Meadow Cranesbill. Others need better management and have lost some interest.

sharing the magic. As we made shift to go a sports car roared past.

East Chiltington church, TQ 369 151, was once the chapel of a detached part of Westmeston parish ... hence Chapel Lane and Farm. It has one of the largest Yew trees in Sussex, and its walls are made of fossil winklestone. Plumpton Mill Stream and its feeder streams that flow around the hill upon which the church sits, are clear and gravelly and Bullhead love them. The farmlands there and north of Warningore retain perhaps half of their old field pattern. **Stantons and Chapel Farms** at East Chiltington, and **Whitehouse and Wootton Farms** north of Warningore, have big old farmhouses and threshing barns, for they tilled the good

Plumpton Place Water Mill and its gravel-bedded chalk stream

greensands. The latter two are sited on the edge of a small green,[5] where the footpaths criss-cross.

Between Long Wood and Stanton's Farm is the now disused **Novington Sandpit**, TQ 368 145. Tufted Duck, Little Grebe, Canada Geese, and gangs of Coot and Mallard like the pools there. In February Coltsfoot spangles the fawn-and-pink sands, and fat mating Toads swim in amplexus in the chilly shallows. The western pool is heavily invaded with Australian Swamp Stonecrop, but the pools still have nice pondweeds and pond snails, and the air is buzzing with mayflies, dragons and damsels in summer.

North of the railway line and the hamlet of Chiltington, is the **vale of the Bevern Stream** and its little woods. Both Comps Wood and Wickham Wood have a likely Latin lineage to their names, for the Roman Greensand Way passes two fields to the south. '*Comp*' (as in *campus*, a field) often indicates land around a Roman settlement and *Wick*ham (as in *vicus*) indicates just such a small Roman settlement.[6]

Little **Wickham Wood**, TQ 393 158, has carpeting Ramsons throughout, as **Comps Wood**, TQ 390 156, also does in its wetter bits, though it is primarily a Bluebell wood of Hazel coppice, under Ash and Oak. We were well equipped with wellies and jam jars – my grandson and I – one sunny June day, as we lowered ourselves down the woodland bank and splashed up the gravel-bedded stream. I was David Attenborough on an Amazon tributary (minus canoe) seeing the edges of the jungle in a way no dark woodland path can show. My five year old companion knew the pools were 'spawning pools' because he'd seen it in his dinosaur films. Big mayflies – shining adult 'spinners', 'greendrakes' – dip, dipped their tails into the water … dropping their eggs … then rested on the greenery … and were up and away … jigging in clouds above the bushes. A Giant Lacewing, *Osmylus fulvicephalus*, rested on a Dropwort umbel. We had some sword fights (rotten sticks,

actually) and managed to stay upright and dry(ish). Beautiful Demoiselles and Large Red Damselflies played in every sunny spot along the stream. There were Duck Mussels (though we found no live ones) and Welshman's Button Caddis Flies, *Sericostoma personatum*, and lots of (scarce) Copse/Orchard Snails, *Arianta arbustorum*. I found a beautiful Lime Longhorn Beetle, *Stenostola dubia*, resting on an overhanging leaf … but no Lime was present in the wood. Only the next day was the puzzle solved when we found a line of Limes at Hurst Barns, just across the fields. House Martins played above us, and a couple of Skylarks sung above the field. (NOTE: in late 2016 the Plumpton Mill Stream and the whole of the Bevern Stream below it were polluted by a huge volume of slurry from Plumpton College Dairy Unit. All the fish in the affected streams were killed. The streams may take many years to recover).

West of Cooksbridge the farmland around **Tulleys Wells**, TQ 39 13, had many hedgerows ripped out, but several of them have now been replanted. There is a scatter of fine isolated old Oaks.

HOMEWOOD AND 'THE HURSTS'

The footprint of the **lost medieval Homewood** begins at the north end of Novington Lane, and a cluster of names attest to it: Middle, Wet, and Great Home Woods, and Great Homewood Farm. Hattons Green and Homewoodgate Farm must have marked its western edge. At 300 acres, it was an important desmesne wood of the Priory of St Pancras at Lewes, but was lost to the church, its commoners dispossessed, and its woodland part-cleared and converted to farmland before 1650. Though the Explorer Map still marks **Wet Home Wood's** existence, it was bulldozed several decades ago, and only tiny bits along its boundaries survive. **Great Home Wood**, TQ 372 182, had drifts of Wild Daffodils at its northern end, though they seem very scarce now. The large amount of coppiced Oak present is unusual, alongside a mixture of Ash and Birch poles and old Hornbeam coppice, with Ash and Oak standards and a coup of Pine at the south end. The ground cover is part Anemone and Bluebell and part bare. The coppice that was cut some years ago does not seem to have been protected from deer, and their browsing seems to have turned whole areas of old coppice stools into dead mossy stumps, so that the wood is becoming painfully open. Nightingales or Warblers would not find it a hospitable place. **Lumberpit Lane**, the wood's west boundary drove to Hatton Green, is very rich, with Wild Daffodil, Sessile Oak and Butchers Broom, old flooded pits and braided tracks. **Middle Home Wood**, TQ 378 174, is a Bluebell wood under Hornbeam, Hazel and Oak, with a gentle valley stream at its centre and a derelict unimproved pasture along its north side, which a footpath crosses.

The old **Wootton manorial drove** runs from Wootton Farm northwards, TQ 380 152, to cross the Bevern Stream. Thereafter, its disused greenway can still be traced through the shaw around the west slopes of the hill, TQ 382 159, where we finally saw a Cuckoo (which had been calling for ages) land on the nearby phone wires. On top of the hill, and on top of the next hill to the north, sit two '*hurst*' farms. **Hurst Barns**, TQ 383 160, has a handsome 18th / 19th century farmhouse, cottages, an old threshing barn and wooden (converted) granary, and old **Yokehurst Farmhouse**, TQ 383 168, is of the 15th century. It may be that small fragments of the two medieval '*hursts*' (large woods on hills) survive. **Sawpit Wood**, TQ 383 163, on the drove north of Hurst Barns, may be one, with its Wild Daffodils, scented Sweet Violets and Bluebells. Little **Hurters Wood**, TQ 379 166, south west of Yokehurst may be another.

East of Hurst Barns is nice-and-scruffy **Woodbrooks Farm**, TQ 392 163, with its old field pattern still intact, tall thick hedgerows, and some good Oaks. It's now used for free range horse grazing. There's a dying Wellingtonia by the farmstead that shows some past farmer had aspirations. **Hovel Wood**, TQ 389 162, next door, is a Bluebell wood under over-stood Hornbeam coppice, with young Oaks.

Behind what used to be the Swan Pub in South Chailey are several pleasing woods. **Swan Wood** itself, TQ 393 168, is Oak with Hazel and Bluebells – quite Brambly – twinned with an Ash wood, to its south west. Just north, alongside the playing fields of Chailey Secondary School, is a classic old Hornbeam coppice wood over Bluebells, TQ 388 171.

PLUMPTON GREEN AND STREAT GREENS AND AROUND

The surviving pattern of this countryside is very old, though more intact in Streat parish than Plumpton. Names like *Riddens* Farm and Wood, and *Inholmes* Farm both indicate very ancient enclosures from the wild, as does the presence of Wild Service tree in the hedgerows. *Lent*ridge (*lime, linden*) Farm's name takes us back even further, to when Small Leaved Lime was far commoner. I can't find it in the area now.

Plumpton Green really was a green till its 1842 enclosure – over three quarters of a mile long and quite wide in the middle. Now, I know of only one tiny place where its archaic vegetation survives: the **churchyard of All Saints Church**, TQ 362/3 168, which was carved out of the manorial 'waste'. The little front churchyard has lots of Common Spotted Orchids amongst Ox Eye

WHAT'S LEFT OF HOME WOOD

Great and Middle Home Woods are all that is left of the c. 300 acre medieval Home Wood, once held by St Pancras Priory, Lewes, and subject to some rights of common. Wet Home Wood was only destroyed a few decades ago and still appears on some maps.

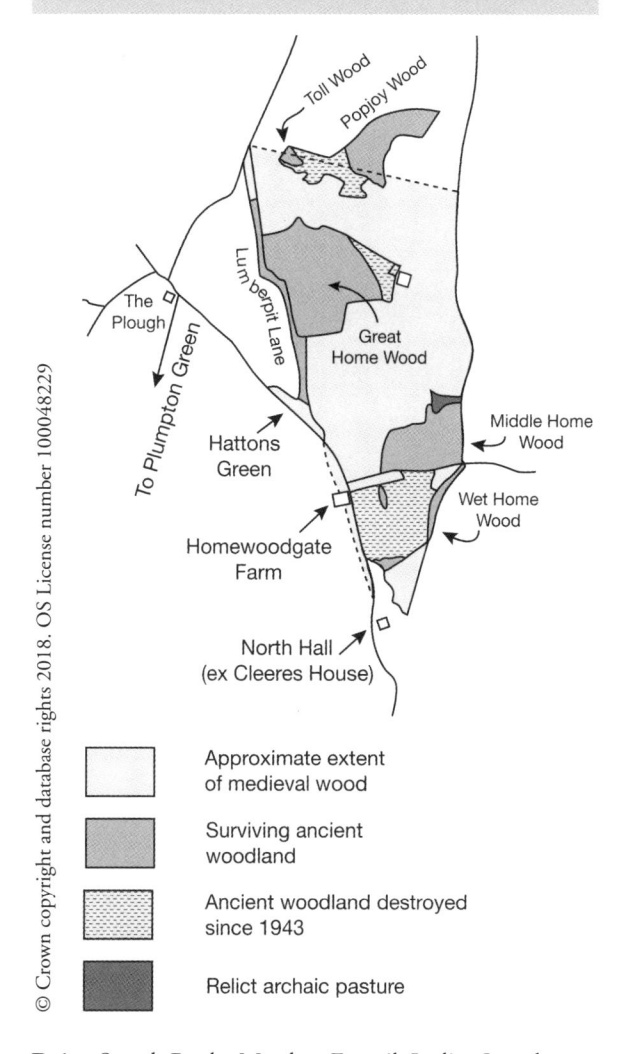

© Crown copyright and database rights 2018. OS License number 100048229

- Approximate extent of medieval wood
- Surviving ancient woodland
- Ancient woodland destroyed since 1943
- Relict archaic pasture

Daisy, Sorrel, Bugle, Meadow Foxtail, Ladies Smock and Thale Cress. The larger yard at the back is also unimproved, but often unkempt, and may have lost some value.

Streat Greens, however, are partially intact – an extraordinary survival – and the western and eastern arms retain much of their archaic grassland. (See Meadows chapter). Though most of the greens are no longer registered common, their boundaries still exist. The western arm, **Streat Lane Green**, TQ 352 167, is owned by the parish council and managed by the residents backing on to each section. Parts are managed sensitively, others are over-mown like suburban lawns, and the flowers and grasses get no chance to set seed or

STREAT AND PLUMPTON GREENS

☐ Footprint of Greens before partial enclosure (Total enclosure at Plumpton Green)

▓ Surviving archaic flowery grassland

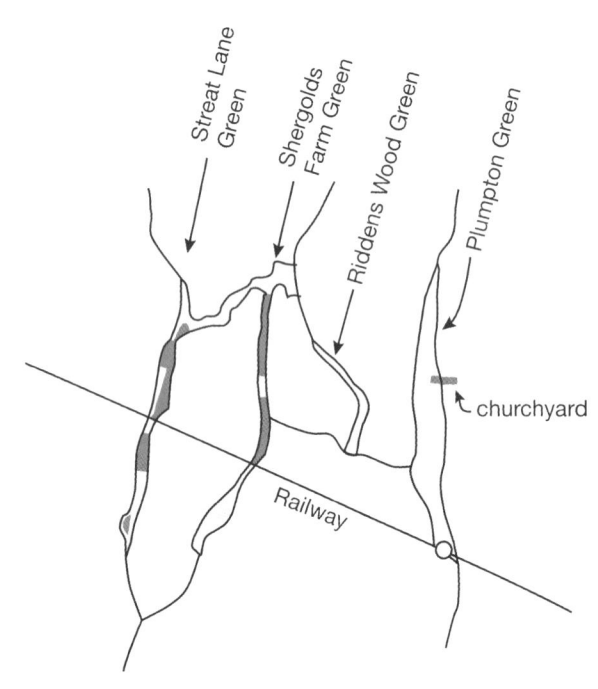

Using the c. 1870 1st Edition OS 6 inches to 1 mile map with the kind permission of the Ordnance Survey.

attract butterflies and bees (2016). Some parts are lost to thick thorn scrub, making it difficult to envisage the green as a unitary habitat. Enough survives, though, to give hope that it could regain more of its past richness. In the spring of 2012 I hunted the length of the Green for Adder's Tongue Fern, knowing it was an exceptional year for its appearance. I found it in five locations, including both over-managed and under-managed areas. The eastern arm, **Shergold's Farm Green**, TQ 356 165, is more appropriately managed and gives a better impression of the past, with Strawberry Clover, Spiny Restharrow, and much Stone Parsley.

Before its nineteenth century enclosure there was a third arm to Streat Green which tracked south through **Riddens Wood**, TQ 358 170, down to Riddens Farm, by the railway line. The braided paths can still be made out in the wood. It used to be called 'Chinese Wood', for there was a chinese 'temple' there. Though that is gone, it explains the presence of Bamboo and other exotics in the wood, alongside Sessile Oak, Gean and Hornbeam. The Wild Service tree on the western boundary, one early November, had fruits that had been 'bletted' by frost, and were sweet, tart and appley. **Dean's Wood**,

TQ 353/4 169, on the western side of Shergold's Farm, is similarly lovely, with many of the same woody species.

For nearly two miles north of the Downs, **Streat Lane** is narrow and winding with sheltering nutty hedgerows, and is sufficiently traffic free to make walking possible – *with care*. Tiny **Streat church**, TQ 350 151, commands grand views from the greensand ridge. It has two cast iron grave slabs in its aisle, commemorating 18th century folk from a Wadhurst iron masters family. **Streat Place**, next to the church, is a huge Jacobean mansion of flint, with stone details and a Horsham stone roof. It is incongruous in this modest place, and, indeed, was let as a farmhouse for a long time. On Streat Lane the **Blackberry Wood Campsite**, TQ 351 147, is enchanted and eccentric, with an American diner, a gipsy caravan, a London bus, and streamside with fallen trees across and tree swings ...

North of the church and west of the Lane, a footpath bisects one of a cluster of unimproved meadows, TQ 349 157, that has Sneezewort, Pepper Saxifrage, Ox Eye Daisy and lots of Marbled White butterflies (2013).

For many centuries it was forgotten that **Streat** owed its name to the nearby presence of the **Roman road**, which was rediscovered less than a century ago. Its remains are difficult to detect as it crosses Streat parish, but westwards down the hill across the Westmeston boundary, the raised agger of the road can be seen running right along the north side of an east-west hedgerow, TQ 343 153. When we last visited the field was fallow, and there was a very obvious vegetation change marking the agger. On top of it the vegetation was *taller* (feral Oats and Sow Thistle) and below the agger it was *shorter* (Dock and Black Grass).

The ridge track that was the Roman road passes **Ashurst Farm**, TQ 360 153 – a brave organic undertaking with its own box scheme. To the west, the Farm's brookside has a colossal maiden Oak, TQ 355 148, in the peak of health, 3.66 span girth, with a clean bole to 10ft and huge limbs straddling the stream, which is clean and clear, with Bullhead and Caddis, and banks carpeted with Violets, Bluebells and Ramsons. The tussocky brook meadows, TQ 356 148, have thick hedgerows, and a relict marshy flora, with Pepper Saxifrage.

WOODS, STREAMS AND WORKING FARMS: BETWEEN CHAILEY NORTH COMMON AND SOUTH COMMON

There is a cluster of working farms in this landscape – Townings, Bower, Great Homewood and Broomfields – and much of it is part of the Hooke Estate. Nearly all of its woods are ancient. **Southam Wood** is the only major exception, for it was part of the heathy South Common until its enclosure in 1841, and must have been planted up subsequently. Just inside the wood, where the footpaths fork, east of Southam Farmhouse

WATERLANDS

The hidden geography of streams, ponds, bridges, and watery place names

(Tudor, timber framed, modernised) is an ancient Hornbeam we dubbed 'The Octopus', TQ 384 181, its many tendrils writhing and wrapping around each other. Colourful **Southam Meadow**, TQ 384 182, by the public footpath, has Spotted Orchids and many old herbs. At the north end of the wood, east of the footpath is a veteran Beech with '1945 Audrey and Bill' carved on the bole next to two hearts pierced with an arrow …

Rabbit Wood, TQ 389 186, is a classic Chailey Oak-Birch-Hornbeam-Bluebell wood, with lovely glades and very tall, clean, straight boled Oaks. **Long Wood**, TQ 385 189, is an Oak-Hazel-Bluebell wood with much Birch. The Longford Stream divides it from **Eels Ash Wood**, TQ 385 193, which has had much coppicing and clearance work since the gales a quarter century ago. Just upstream is **Cottage Wood**, TQ 380 194, very damp on the streamside with an Alderfield, Marsh Marigolds and Ramsons in plenty. In spring the Owl Midges swarm. They are NOT biting or harmful, and when looked at closely do look like fluffy, miniscule Owls! On the Longford Stream west of Chailey Green and church is **Chailey Moat**, TQ 388 194, once the Rectory, part Tudor / part Georgian, probably medieval in origin, now even posher, with a new lake dwarfing the moat.

Some nice corners of rough tall herbage survive along the Longford Streamside and wood edge. The **drained ponds between Long Wood and Cottage Wood,** have become a wonderful **marshy area**, TQ 381 192, with frogs, dragons and damsels and scarce wetland plants, like Cyperus Sedge, Wood Club Rush and Lesser Marshwort. The sunny woodside nearby has Silver-washed Fritillary butterflies and Harlequin Longhorn beetles. My grandson found a just-dead Mole and carried it round with delight … soft as a velvet cushion.

As the ground rises towards Chailey North Common, the Wealden Clay gives way to Tunbridge Wells Sand and the woods subtly change, becoming drier and more acidic. Thus, in **Townings Wood**, TQ 377 196, there is Ling Heather and Heath Bedstraw in the open areas, and much Gorse, Downy and Silver Birch. **Bineham Wood**, TQ 384 202, is big and varied, with several senescent Beech pollards. The southern half is coppice, with carpeting Bluebells, and an ancient laid Hornbeam hedge, now much gnarled and twisted, that goes all round the boundary bank. One September, the Blackthorn hedges in the field west of the wood yielded a harvest of Sloes so great that the branches bent low under their weight, and the hedge took on a purple haze. You could pull off a fat bunch of 'grapes' with one hand, and imagine yourself in some southern vineyard …

© Crown copyright and database rights 2018. OS License number 100048229

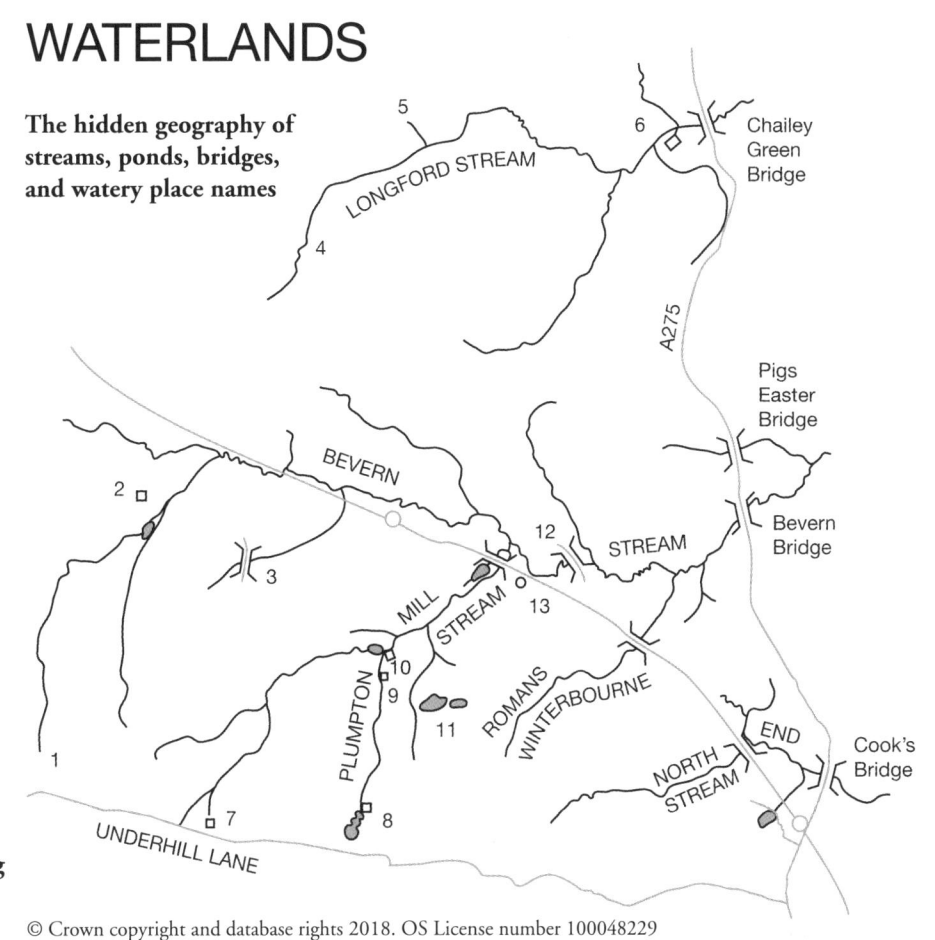

1. *Well*croft Shaw
2. Black*brook* Farm (Why black?)
3. *Duck's* Bridge
4. Lam*bourne* Wood
5. *Sedgebrook*
6. Chailey *Moat*
7. The *Gote* ('the stream')
8. Plumptonplace *Mill*
9. Upper *Mill*
10. Plumpton *Mill*
11. Novington Pit *Ponds*
12. High *Bridge*
13. *Brook*house

MARSH AND AIRFIELD

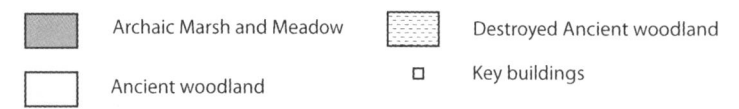

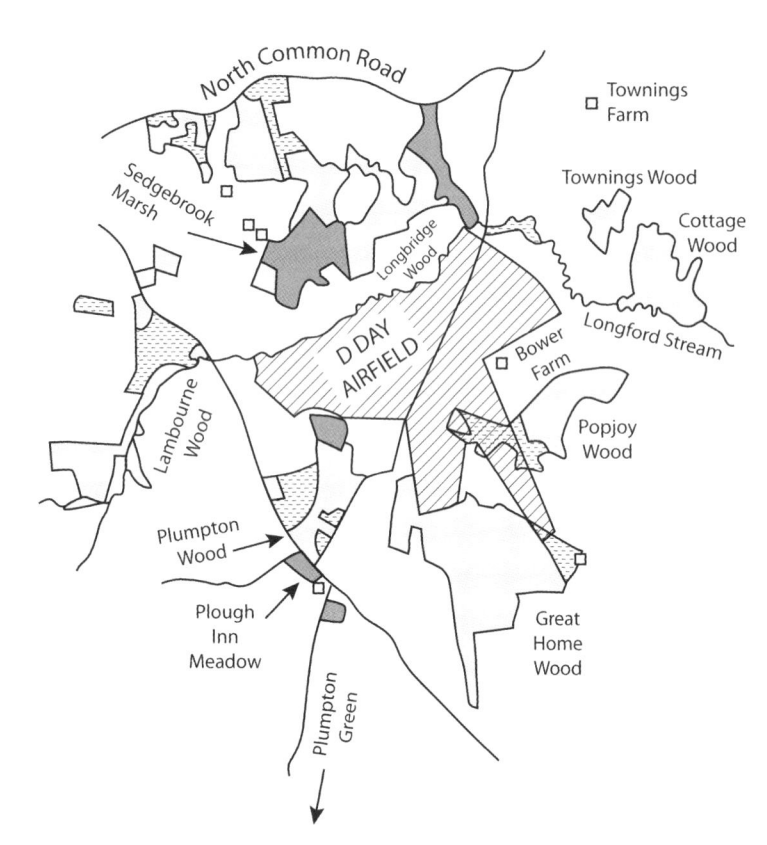

▨ Archaic Marsh and Meadow
▨ Destroyed Ancient woodland
☐ Ancient woodland
▫ Key buildings

© Crown copyright and database rights 2018. OS License number 100048229

There is little archaic grassland in this area. The large **graveyard of the parish church of St Peter's at Chailey Green**, TQ 392 193, (with its two fine Yews) is unimproved and an SNCI, but the parts nearest the church are mown too often, and the southern extension was in poor condition the last time we looked. At least one relict wet meadow, just north west of The Hooke – part of an SNCI,[7] TQ 380 189 – has been lost only recently, though a smidgeon survives amongst scrub at its northern end. On Townings Farm there are several fields which look as though they have been 'improved' only lightly, without the usual thoroughness. The pasture along the west side of Bineham Wood is one of those, where tiny patches of Tormentil and other old herbs survive. The woodland rides are the last redoubt for these old grassland species, but straw has been laid for the Pheasants on rides in several of these woods, and can only harm that relict vegetation.

Townings Farm, TQ 377 201, has an old fashioned air, with a good farm shop, some very attractive pigs, poultry and sheep, and fine vernacular farm buildings. **Bower Farm**, TQ 373 190, to the south, has a dairy herd and some good buildings, including, like Townings, an outhouse with herringbone ironstone walls. The layout of the Second World War D Day airfield just managed to avoid destroying the farmstead, but one runway did bulldoze right through the woods just to the south. Though most of little **Toll Wood**, TQ 371 188, was destroyed, the bulk of **Popjoy Wood**, TQ 375 188, survives: a Bluebell wood, flat and wet in winter, with fine Oaks, Primroses, and lots of Ramsons at the south eastern end.

From the west side of Mott Wood, part of the old Wotton Manor drove runs northwards, with a **line of grand Oak veterans** on it and nearby, e.g. TQ 380 190, three of which are over three spans girth and several more approaching that.

MARSH AND WET WOODS: SEDGEBROOK, LONGRIDGE WOOD, AND UPPER LONGFORD STREAM

From both ends – north and south – the shady lane descends the slopes till the landscape opens out, flat as a tabletop, wide as the eye can see, almost bare of hedge and tree, rimmed by distant woods. **'Bower Farm moor'** (my made-up name[8]) e.g. TQ 370 192, must have been the soggiest of places in distant times – marsh, fen, carr, bog, mire – with the Longford Stream meandering across it. From the south and the north the lanes and boundaries funnelled into the single lane (the Plumpton Road) that crossed the 'moor', and must have been a causeway. What hedgerows existed were removed by the RAF, clearing the ground in 1942/3 for the Chailey Advanced Landing Ground, largely manned by Polish exile Spitfire squadrons, which supported the Normandy D Day landings in June 1944.

Nitrogen green dairy pastures are what we see from the road now, but behind the rim of trees to the north and north west the most remarkable relics of ancient wildland cling on. **Sedgebrook Farm's fields** (the clue is in the name), TQ 363 194, are the centre of a series of wet woods, damp meadows and carr that extend east to **Godleys Green**, TQ 371 198. **Sedgebrook Marsh** is a place of treasures. In late spring the Cotton Grass and Marsh Cinquefoil covers many square metres of quaking bog amongst the carr. The smell of Water Mint is everywhere. There's Angelica and Marsh Pennywort, Purple Moor Grass tussocks, Sharp Flowered Rush, Black Sedge and Bog Stitchwort. In late May, a southern meadow has swarms of Meadow/Marsh Plume Thistle with soft shaving brush carmine flowers on white-woolly stems, and there's Ladies Smock, Spotted Orchis, Creeping Willow and Spring Sedge. The higher and drier meadow in July, is yellow with Great Birds Foot Trefoil, and Bush Crickets, Cone Heads, Marsh and Meadow Grasshoppers, and 'bloodsucker' Soldier Beetles are everywhere. Clambering over the wood bank from a wood of Hornbeam and Bluebells into a derelict meadow of tumbled, broken Sallow we see an expanse of glinting, glistening mud pierced by the swarming spikes of Water Horsetail like a little glimpse of the Carboniferous, seeping into a bright orange iron stained stream. The rushy meadows have Sneezewort, of course, and there are clumps of Narrow Buckler Fern in the shadier places.

East Chiltington's 'fossil church' (looking very fortress-like). Much of the walls are made of *Viviparus* water snail fossils compacted to form 'winklestone'.

The quaking bog is the sole surviving middle Sussex site for Cotton Grass, and one of perhaps three surviving middle Sussex sites for Marsh Cinquefoil. Expanding Sallow carr has taken over nearly all of the wetter ground (2013). Grazing and mowing are difficult to arrange on the meadows, but some mowing has been reinstated recently, so the Meadow Thistle (reduced to three middle Sussex sites) now has better prospects, for it has been lost from parts of the marsh it was present on 25 years ago.

This is a disorientating area, and the boundary between the marsh and **Longbridge Wood**, TQ 366 195, is difficult to detect. The southern part of the wood, flat and wet, has a 'wildwood' feel, and there are marshy plants like Meadowsweet and Yellow Flag, Water Mint and Ragged Robin. Some areas have lovely glades with much Bracken and very fine Bluebells. There are large areas of Birch, and its coppice is mostly Hazel, with some Hornbeam. On a sunny day in early May, Maiden's Blush and Peacock[9] moths showed themselves on the woodland edge, and, whilst we had cake and tea, a magical Concealer Moth, *Alabonia geoffrella*, settled next to us – tiny, but dressed like a Tudor prince at the 'Field of the Cloth of Gold'.

Between the eastern side of Longridge Wood and Godleys Green there is a narrow **strip of five little rushy meadows** (2014). Four of them have had some 'improvement', but one to the north west, TQ 368 200, has escaped such treatment, perhaps because its little stream makes it damper than the others. There's lots of Marsh Thistle, but the Rushes dominate – Soft, Jointed, Sharp Flowered – though the flowers of shorter pastures, like Tormentil and Devils Bit, just cling on. It has the wood on one side and a strip of Sallow carr on the other … and it can't have changed much since it was first assarted. **Godleys Green** itself was open and heathy 60 years ago, but is now all woodland.

The verges of the Plumpton Road on the south side of the 'Bower Farm moor' are flowery and colourful, TQ 369 189, and a walk up the rising ground brings us to **Plumpton Wood**, TQ 365 185. This is the second wood of that name in the parish (see this chapter) and this one is as outstanding for the Wealden Clay as the southern one is for the Gault, though about 40% has been cleared in modern times and houses and gardens have bitten chunks out of it. There is Wych Elm and Wild Service, Spurge Laurel and Midland Thorn, and in recent times Green Hellebore, Birds Nest Orchis, and Greater Butterfly Orchis have been recorded (2011).

At the Plumpton Green–South Road crossroads is the **Plough Inn**, and behind the inn is an archaic meadow used as a campsite by the pub. It is a lovely place, and the pub is commendably (2015) trying to manage it with its old flowery sward in mind. There are lots of Ox Eye Daisy, Knapweed, Fleabane, and even bits of Saw Wort and Gorse. In the autumn there are old meadow fungi like Cedarwood Waxcap and Fairy Club. In Worcestershire there are many pubs that have (or had) old meadows attached to them, but the Plough is special, for this is not a strong Sussex tradition. The pub was originally sited down by 'Bower Farm moor' but was re-located to the crossroads when the airfield was built. The airmen's monument is by the pub.

BLACKBROOK WOOD, WEST WOOD AND THE BISHOPRICK

At the northern end of Westmeston parish, Blackbrook Wood, West Wood and Purchase Wood (just over the Ditchling boundary) make a block big enough to get delightfully lost in. Though they are all on the Wealden Clay, their geology, relief and history are nuanced enough to give them considerable internal variety.

Bounding West Wood, **Hundred Acre Lane**, part of an ancient south-north drove, TQ 347 189, tracks the watershed between the Adur and Ouse catchments for over a mile south from Wivelsfield Green.

West Wood, TQ 345 194, grows on the site of Westmeston Common, and must have been consolidated as woodland after the common's enclosure in 1672. Its northern end is on a steep slope which has many large shallow pits and roughly north/south braided tracks. These may be ancient ore diggings in the band of ironstone which outcrops along the slope, and perhaps clay pits for some nearby brick works. (There is a little Kiln Wood just across Hundred Acre Lane to the east, TQ 352 196). The field layer on the slope is almost bare. The wood is largely Hornbeam coppice and Oak, over a mixture of Bluebells and Anemones, but there's Gean and Midland Thorn, Silver Birch and Maple as well. The wide green lane along its western boundary separates it from Purchase Wood, and there are Wild Service trees in both woods in that area. The green lane with its braided tracks is one of the most varied features of the wood. **Purchase Wood**, TQ 341 194, is ancient, but is open and mown on its south side where the graveyard of the nuns from St George's Retreat is located. The southern end of the West Wood block, separated by a woodbank, has a different character, and feels far more remote. The part called **Bushycommon Wood**, TQ 344 188, may have a different history to West Wood, and was perhaps enclosed later. There are few paths and Bluebells form a continuous carpet. Some years ago, in early May, we found its Hornbeam coppice seriously defoliated by small caterpillars that rested up in silk retreats under the leaves.

The narrow field along the southern boundary of the wood, TQ 345 186, closely coincides with a thin sandstone band, and this may have provided enough of an incentive to assart and plough that strip.

The green lane passes southwards by bank and shaw, fields and cottages, and over a little stream before crossing Middleton Common[10] Lane to lovely **Blackbrook Wood**, TQ 343 174. Two bands of Sussex marble/winklestone outcrop there in wandering lines, one across the middle of the wood where the ground rises to a small hill, and one across the south east corner, and they may partially explain the limey flora of some parts. Most of the wood has youngish Oak standards over both Hazel and abundant Hornbeam, and some of the Hornbeam coppice stools are very large and old. There are areas which have been recently coppiced, areas long over-stood, dry well-drained parts, soggy parts, and a block of planted conifers to the south west. The old waste of the manor along Spatham Lane, to the north west, has grown into woodland superficially indistinguishable from the rest of the wood. The best area may be in the south east, where Ash, Oak, Birch, Gean, Maple and Hazel are intermingled. Butterfly Orchis is recorded from the wood, though I've not seen it. It has many special species. **The Plantation and Oldhouse Copse** to the east, TQ 346 171, are also rich and varied.

Between The Plantation and Streat Lane Green the ancient **Middleton drove**, TQ 349 169 (which continues northwards to become Hundred Acre Lane, and thence deeper into the Weald) was almost as wide as the Streat Greens, though wooded. It was largely bulldozed in recent years and is now just a path and fence line with some forlorn surviving Bluebells. **Gallops Farm**, TQ 350 176, has retained most of its pattern of little fields and hedgerows. The farmhouse is part-ancient and timber farmed, the barn is tiny and weather boarded, and the geese and chickens foraged on the lane side waste till recently.

South of Wivelsfield Green is a patchwork of smallish woods and fields on the site of '**The Bishoprick**', e.g. TQ 35 19, the lost Stanmer and Wivelsfield Common enclosed in 1626–30.[11] There is a delightful smallholding, TQ 349 193/4, on the green lane south of Coldharbour Farm with friendly pigs and other livestock (2012). **Lashmar Wood**, TQ 350 193, though halved in size in modern times, is a Bluebell-and-Anemone wood with a large old Hornbeam boundary hedge. What is left of **Mercers's Wood**, TQ 357 192, and little **South Wallers Wood**, TQ 354 189, are also rich Bluebell woods, colourful in spring.

The best of these woods are probably **Cottage Wood**, TQ 355 185, and **Lambourne Wood**, TQ 356 187, which run together. All is lusher there, down by the **Lambourne brook**, and the Bluebells bloom after they are gone on drier ground. It is another Hornbeam wood, and there's Hedge Garlic, Goldilocks Buttercup and Early Purple Orchids (2010). Cottage and Lambourne Woods are likely relics of the *'fischhyrstes'* – 'Fish Wood' – of the Saxon Stanmer charter.[12]

The veteran Black Poplar at Brookhouse, East Chiltington

ENDNOTES

1. 'A Sussex Highway', by Ruth Cobb. The Epworth Press (1946).
2. The painting of these frescoes was supervised by Lewes Priory, which had rapidly become a major power in Sussex after its post-Norman Conquest foundation, c. 1081.
3. *Pers. comm.* Peter Hodge, Sussex coleopterist (beetle expert).
4. 'The Flora of Sussex', page 94, edited by Lieut. Colonel A. H. Wolley-Dodd. Bristol, The Chatsford House Press (1937. Reprinted 1970).
5. The green was not registered as a 'town or village green' and is no longer managed as such.
6. 'Signposts to the Past', pages 69–80, by Margaret Gelling. Phillimore (1978).
7. 'SNCI' stands for 'Site of Nature Conservation Interest'. These local authority designated sites are now called 'Local Wildlife Sites' (LWS).
8. Though Bower Farm Green did survive along the Lane till perhaps three centuries ago. The place name is in the Chailey Tithe Redemption Award of circa 1840. The *'bur'* in *Bower* Farm, by the way, simply means cottage, which is all we would expect in this bleak landscape, rather than bower's modern meaning of a poetic garden.
9. Peacock moth, not Peacock Butterfly!
10. Middleton Common was enclosed in 1684, twelve years after neighbouring Westmeston Common.
11. 'Wivelsfield. A History of a Wealden Parish', chapter 6, pages 112–117, edited by Heather Warne. Pier Point Publishing & Wivelsfield History Study Group (1994).
12. 'Wivelsfield. A History of a Wealden Parish', chapter 1, pages 5–10, by Heather Warne. *Op cit.*

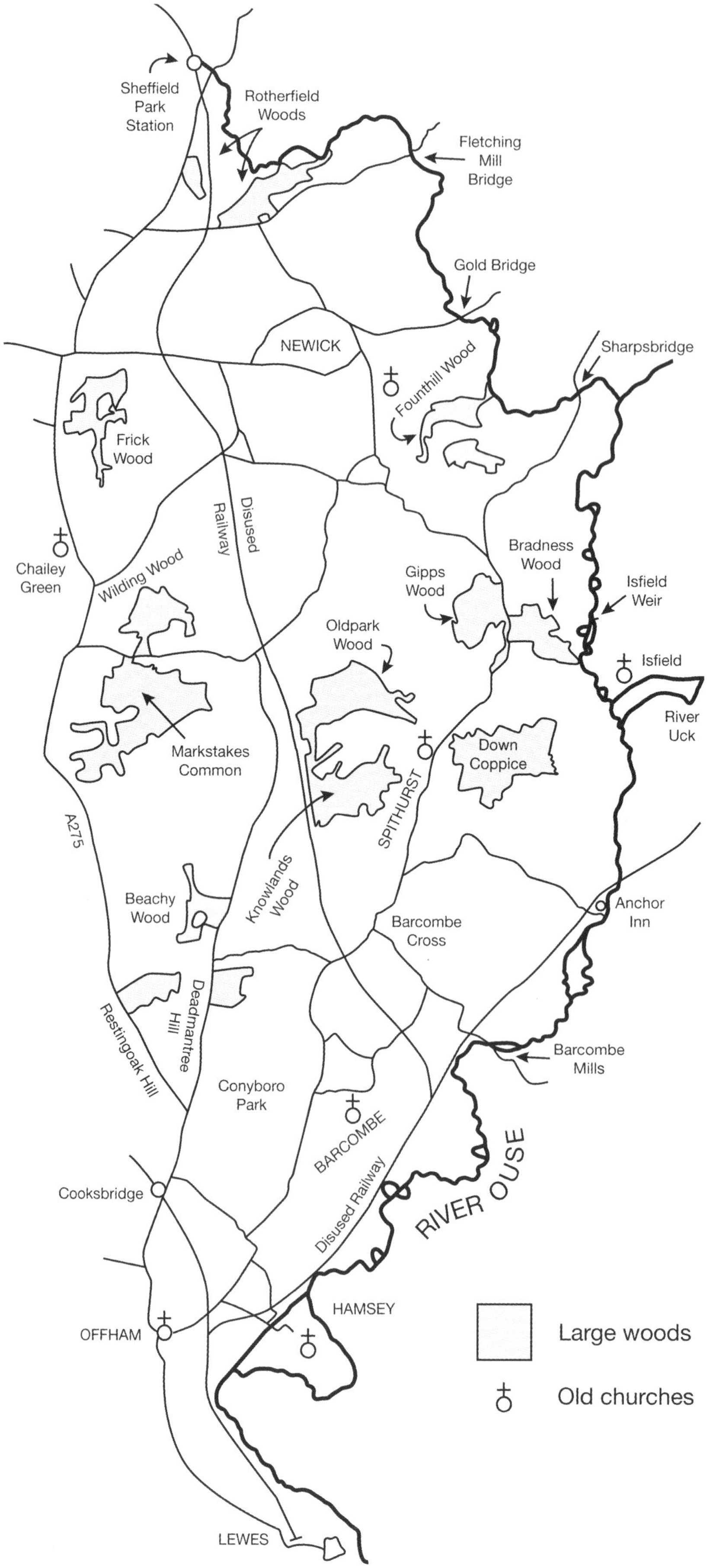
Sheffield Park Station
Rotherfield Woods
Fletching Mill Bridge
Gold Bridge
NEWICK
Founthill Wood
Sharpsbridge
Frick Wood
Disused Railway
Chailey Green
Wilding Wood
Bradness Wood
Gipps Wood
Isfield Weir
Oldpark Wood
Isfield
Markstakes Common
River Uck
Down Coppice
SPITHURST
A275
Knowlands Wood
Beachy Wood
Anchor Inn
Barcombe Cross
Deadmantree Hill
Restingoak Hill
Barcombe Mills
Conyboro Park
BARCOMBE
RIVER OUSE
Cooksbridge
Disused Railway
HAMSEY
OFFHAM
LEWES
Large woods
Old churches

CHAPTER 14
Along the River Ouse:
Hamsey, Barcombe and Newick

"BARCOMBE MILLS!! BARCOMBE MILLS!!", the station master would shout.

Every few weeks from 1959, through most of the sixties, our family took the train via Lewes to Edenbridge to visit our grandparents there. From Brighton and Lewes the train was crowded at weekends with anglers – men and boys, baskets and fishing rods, wellies and waterproofs. At Barcombe Mills the train half-emptied. Returning in the sunny evening on a sleepy and empty train we'd stop again at Barcombe Mills. "Shift up, shift up", we'd have to do, as the anglers, weary but still lively, packed back aboard.

It was a lovely line ... trundling dozily beside the river up the Vale of the Ouse and the Uck, across wet brookland pastures, rumbling over their fingered tributaries onwards to Uckfield and beyond. It closed between Lewes and Uckfield in 1969. Its re-opening cannot be good, however, whilst capitalism continues, for it would only ratchet up the over-development of the already over-developed south east region (particularly the London megalopolis) and do great new damage both to the South Downs (with a huge tunnelling project) and to the Low Weald.

The Ouse and its brooks bound the whole east side of this landscape, and its three tributaries divide it into four blocks: the Hamsey block, the Barcombe block, the Spithurst block, and the Newick block. They are divided from each other by the North End stream, the Bevern Stream and the Longford Stream. In winter and rainy weather before the early 19th century, these blocks became "different islands[1] absolutely cut off from each other".

There are two contrasting landscape types. To the south and south east, a large swathe with richer soils is entirely without ancient woodland. In this open area even the Gault Clay is without such woodland, though it had a relict common at Hamsey till modern times. This swathe takes up all of Hamsey, old Barcombe and the riverine lands north to Isfield. Its superficial deposits of Alluvium, River Terrace Deposits and Chalk Head, over Lower Chalk, Gault, Lower Greensand, or Wealden Clay, can grow fine crops.

To the north, the landscape is much wilder, with large blocks of ancient woodland, such as those centred on Markstakes Common and Down Coppice. Historically, it was a hotchpotch of no less than seven manorial outliers – probably relics of ancient swine pasture 'denns'[2] – including those of Rodmell, Houndean, Warningore and Allington (apart from the three Barcombe manors).[3] There are no sizeable villages in the three miles from Barcombe Cross north to Newick, and the hamlet and lane of Spithurst, known in 1296 as *'Splytherst'* – 'split-wood' – did indeed split two giant *'hursts'*, of which, on the west side, Knowlands, Oldpark, The Butletts, Spithurst Wood, and Slutgarden Woods are relics, as are, on the east side, Burtenshaw's, Agmond's and Down Coppice Woods. All those woods are on the Wealden Clay.

Going north, the acidic Hastings Beds, with their sands, hard sandrocks and clays, begin towards the Longford Stream and form all the Newick block. They give a subtly different character to its woods. Rotherfield and Little Rotherfield Woods, just south of Sheffield Park Station, have heathy Bilberry and Cow Wheat, Devils Bit, Tormentil ... and big Wood Ant nests. Frick Wood, south west of Newick, is also quite heathy, with abundant Birch, and Ling Heather and Gorse on the rides. These Newick woods remain frequent, but without the sheer size of the Wealden Clay woods.

There are stretches of sunken lane – holloway – where the Ardingly Sandrock outcrops, along the Chailey Lane ridge south of Newick: at Cornwell's Bank; the north end of Cockfield Lane; Mackerells west of Gipps Farm, near Founthill; and at the northern end of Ridgeland Lane.

GEOLOGY AND SETTLEMENT

Map legend:

- Below this line there is no ancient woodland
- Hastings Beds; sands, clays, silts
- Wealden Clays; **both heavy and light**
- Lower Greensand; **good tillage**
- Gault Clay; **heavy and sticky**
- Grey Chalk; **good tillage**
- Alluvium and river terrace deposits; **good tillage, if drained**
- Old churches

The Ouse floodplain and better soils have been cultivated since prehistoric times, and have lost all ancient woods. The more remote section of the Wealden Clay retains some large woods. The complex Hastings Beds have more mixed patterns.

Permit Number CP18/021 Derived by British Geological Survey Material © UKRI 2018. © Crown copyright and database rights 2018. OS License number 100048229

This Newick block retained its western commons – part of the giant Chailey Commons complex – right up till 1620–66, when Roeheath and Cinder Commons were almost all enclosed … But not entirely, for little Roeheath (more a green than a common) still survives, its archaic heathy and old meadow vegetation clinging on, just up Cinder Hill from the Five Bells pub near Chailey Green. So, too, does Lane End Common, part of the Chailey Common nature reserve, though now separated from most of the reserve by enclosed land.

Together with Markstakes Common, and the little greens at Chailey and Newick, that is all the common land that survives in this landscape.

The river and brooks are still grand places to see Kingfishers, leaping Trout, Banded and Beautiful Demoiselles, and banks colourful with Greater Yellowcress, Hemp Agrimony, and (sadly) Himalayan Balsam aplenty in high summer. Yellowhammers love the bushy streamsides. Pied Wagtails like the gravels and clay banks, and Grey Wagtails, the weirs and pond bays. The main Ouse channel and several tributaries are Sea Trout runs and their upper reaches are nursery areas for them.

Long gone, though – 30 years and more – are the passes of countless silvery Elvers[4] (young Eels) rising up the weirs, as at Isfield. There has been much pollution and many major incidents, and Southern Water has been both polluter – prosecuted and fined – and prosecutor of other polluters. Nitrates, phosphates and deadly trace chemicals from farming and sewage are major threats, with low flows from extraction and droughting summers.

This landscape was the scene of a major nature conservation disaster of the early '80s, when a local farmer bought and then destroyed the wonderful ancient wood of Balneath. Its destruction took his workers two years, left nothing but fields of indifferent quality, and destroyed woodland "teeming" with wildlife.[5] The exceptional quality even of the cosmetic fragments that were left bears sad witness to what was lost.

As is par for the course, it is open habitats – archaic meadows and pastures, heath and fen – which have taken the heaviest punishment from capitalist farming and development. Three tiny-but-colourful old meadows still survive around Spithurst, including the old 'St Bartz' churchyard. The Longford Stream has/had a series of exceptional relics: Beaks Farm Marsh; the marshy brooks west of Longford Bridge and south of Gipps Wood; and the north side meadow at Cockfield Bridge. There are fine archaic pasture fields north of Vixengrove Farm on Cinder Hill's north slope, and south of Mongers Farm, Barcombe Cross.

At the southern end of this landscape, the Pells Marsh is wonderfully primeval, though the railway line runs just a few yards away, and the nearby lane sides of The Drove are colourful with the tall herbs of chalky soil: Bellflower, Scabious, Pyramidal Orchis and much more in summer. It is threatened, though, by the proposed second Brighton Main Line (BML2) which may smash through the wooded chalk escarpment and march across the brooks.

Heathland, once so common here, is pretty much gone except at Lane End Common and The Warren just to its south, though some rides and glades still have a heathy character.

OFFHAM AND HAMSEY UP TO THE NORTH END STREAM

Once, near the bank of the **Pellbrook Cut**, TQ 404 120, we heard the scream of a distressed Rabbit on the edge of a Reed thicket, where we found a Mink about to deliver the death bite to the cowering beast. Pontius Pilate-like, I asked my friends' two boys what we should do …

"Thumbs up, we chase off the Mink. Thumbs down, we let it eat its dinner".

No hesitation from the boys. It was thumbs down from the bloodthirsty pair. My friend and I looked at each other … and couldn't handle it.

"Sorry, I'm letting it go", I said, and chased off the Mink. The stunned Rabbit lolloped into cover …

That place and **The Pells and Offham Marsh**, TQ 404 117, are such old fashioned country. Till forty years ago, experiencing wildlife like theirs would have been normal to a country upbringing for many children. Now, their rarity makes them part of a nationally important SSSI.

I know them intimately only from the time, in 1997, when they were threatened, and the farmer, with permission from English Nature, began to plough up the marshes for Flax. A brave band of activists occupied the site. This was a two pronged fight, for the farmer was also ploughing much of Offham Down's archaic flowery turf.

We won that struggle, and in the course of it we learnt much about the wildlife of its brooks and marsh.

In the Pellbrook Cut and other brooks there are scarce Water Violet, Arrowhead, Frogbit and Water Dropworts. The clear chalky spring water brings an abundant Water Snail fauna, which the rare Great Silver Diving Beetle, *Hydrophilus piceus*, larvae love to crunch (very noisily). The fierce Great Diving Beetle, *Dytiscus marginalis*, larvae no doubt take many unlucky Marsh Frog, Newt and Toad tadpoles, too. It was for its huge Common Toad population that the Marsh was first designated an SSSI. They migrated in huge numbers every spring down from the overhanging woods. (Not any more though). Once, a young Eel crossed the path in front of me up in those woods. It's not often that we see Eels these days, leave alone when they go slither-about on land. There are Water Scorpions, Water Measurers, Water Spiders (with underwater silken diving bells), Water Crickets, Whirligig Beetles, shining Reed Beetles, *Donacia sp.*, and lovely Leeches and Flatworms of many kinds.

The Pells, north of the Pellhouse Cut, has an old Willow holt with Wild Hop and Blackcurrant amongst its robust carpet of Nettles. The marsh to its east is about one third sedge fen, one third horsetail Fen, and one third Meadowsweet fen. The newish pools have nice dragons and damsels, and Amphibious Bistort, *Polygonum amphibium*. Reed Warblers, Whitethroat and Chiffchaff love the place.

On the east side of the railway line, the tilled ground rising from the marsh to The Drove and beyond is on the Grey Chalk and Gault, which bring many fossils and iron pyrites nodules. The grandson filled his pockets till they bulged with the nodules. They reminded him of the musket balls that the Irontown people had shot the boar god Nago with, in their onslaught on the forest and its gods.[6] We found a fine fossil Brachiopod once. The ancient peoples loved this rich wetland edge place, and, many years back, we found a possible fragment of a Palaeolithic axe head, scrapers and a possible unfinished arrowhead there.

As kids, leaning out of the train carriage window just before you whooshed through the Hamsey cutting, you'd glimpse the lonely **brookland church of Old St Peter, Hamsey**, TQ 414 121 (now a parish chapel of ease) perched above you on its promontory. Its replacement by the 'new' church at Offham in 1860 served to remove the threat of unsympathetic restoration from it. Squat and solid, it has a Norman nave and chancel and buttressed Perpendicular tower. It is some years since I've been inside it, but I haven't forgotten its musky antiquity. Its "uncomfortable pews[7] have been uncomfortable since the days of Queen Elizabeth". A medieval manor house companioned the church, but has long disappeared. Nearby **Hamsey Place Farm**'s fine vernacular buildings have now lost their chickens, manure and mud.

River Ouse pastoral idyll. Flatlands are more lovely than corrugated lands! (Debate)

This Domesday manor's 200 acres of meadow was of similar extent to that of modern Hamsey. However, the nineteenth century parish lost much of its wildness with the 1812 opening of the Upper Ouse Navigation. Its **Hamsey Cut** and lock bypassed the Hamsey loop. The **Chalkpit Cut** took barges from Offham chalk pit to the river, and two railway lines were built across the brooks. Nearly all the meadowland is now improved or cultivated, but the **east bank of the Hamsey Cut,** TQ 09 120, retains some archaic meadow vegetation, with the rare Corky Fruited Water Dropwort, *Oenanthe pimpinelloides*, and other colourful flowers (2011).

BARCOMBE, FROM THE NORTH END STREAM TO THE BEVERN STREAM

With Hamsey, this is a landscape of enlarged fields, much arable, and isolated old cottages and farms. The best of it is its **winding lanes**, gently rising and falling, often between banks, flowery verges and ditches, good old hedges and trees, and with grand views of the Downs. They are rightly loved by cyclists.

At **Barcombe Mills**, TQ 432 148, up to the last century, there were oil mills and a button factory, and the Domesday Book recorded 3.5 (!) mills present in Barcombe back in 1086. The heavily braided Ouse, there, with its tiny tree-shaded lanes, weirs, pools, and little bridges is partly the heritage of that millennium of milling.

Barcombe Cross, TQ 420 158, was just one of the dispersed hamlets that formed the pattern of settlement in the parish, but has formed its busy hub since 1882, when the railway station opened close by on the new Bluebell Line. It has good council and housing association estates and recreation ground. **Mongers Farmhouse**, TQ 420 155, (17th century) and a few cottages survive from the pre-modern settlement.

The bushy **Bevern Stream** meanders attractively from **Clappers Bridge**, TQ 422 161, eastwards past **Red Bridge** and **Beam Bridge**, and, under the lost railway line, to the Ouse. The countryside is much mauled by modern farming. The **big pond at Red Bridge**, TQ 426 159, on Camoys Court Farm, was enlarged for crop irrigation perhaps 40 years ago. **Banks Farm**, TQ 431 162, overlooking the Stream, has an odd flint barn built to imitate a chapel and an even odder castellated folly, with towers.

Our perception of **old Barcombe, where the parish church is,** TQ 418 143, has changed much since two major excavations. The first is the excavation of its Roman villa and surrounding buildings, south of the church, TQ 419 142, from 1999 onwards. The second is the more recent excavation of the Wellingham Roman defended settlement just across the Ouse at Bridge Farm, TQ 431 144, which corroborates the importance of the Roman presence here. It may be that old Barcombe's landscape is in continuity with that of the Roman period. The place name 'Bar*combe*' (Saxon '*Berecampe*', meaning 'barley land') contains the Latin loan word 'campus',[8] a field. The villa lay near the crossroads of the Roman Greensand Way, the Roman road to Pevensey via Arlington, and the Malling (Lewes) to London Roman road. It may have thrived upon industrial activity associated with the iron industry in the Wealden forest to the north.[9] It was abandoned around 300 AD, and was much robbed by later Saxon settlers. The **medieval church,** with its fine shingled, broached spire, may incorporate some materials robbed from the villa (though this is not visible in the restored church).

Court Farm, next door, (poshed up) has a 14th and 15th century core and an ancient horse gin, perhaps used for threshing, by the church path.

A footpath takes you from Church Road across cow pasture and into **Camoiscourt Shaw**, TQ 419 153, a woodland gill (with Bluebells and birdsong) along which the derelict Bluebell Line ran. Above the Gill on the north side is the remarkable **Oil Mill Pasture**, TQ 422 152, with its old anthills, wet rushy gullies, and bushy slopes. Though much neglected (2013) it still has a range of archaic meadow plants, from the acid grassland Tormentil, Heath Grass and Devils Bit, through classic neutral grassland Ox Eye Daisy and Pignut, to alkaline loving Quaking Grass, Yellow Oat Grass and Ladies Bedstraw.

We camped with the Scouts in **Conyboro Park**, TQ 406 142, Cooksbridge, in the early sixties for some Jamboree to meet the Chief Scout. (Too much smartening up; too little play). The Park and its woods are still nice now, particularly on its south side, with some good veteran trees. The section of the **North End Stream** to the south, TQ 405 137, is even better, with a bankside Bluebell wood, and another a bit to the east at TQ 410 136.

Roman travellers of the Greensand Way on top of **Resting Oak Hill** and **Deadmantree Hill**, TQ 405 152, looked north across rough, forested country in the **vale of the Bevern Stream** between **Bevern Bridge**, TQ 395 162, and Barcombe Cross. Old Stone Age folk lived here, for we found a Palaeolithic hand axe on ploughland – maybe half a million years old. A large common survived until Tudor times, and a bunch of "common" field names around **Birdshole Lane**, TQ 412 159, commemorate it.

The farmed land now has large, tamed fields, but a fine cluster of ancient woods remains. **Beachy Wood**, TQ 404 161, is the best of them, and the gill wood along its western stream is the best of the best, with Wild Service, Sessile Oak and Crab Apple. The main flattish part of the wood is dignified, shady, and silent but for the tops of the tall Oaks sighing in the breeze. **Folly Wood**, TQ 399 153, has wall-to-wall Bluebells under Hazel coppice, with a bit of Hornbeam and much Scots Pine at the east and west ends. The Bluebells of **Blunt's Wood**, TQ 06 153, are just as abundant, though there has been much replanting with conifers and Beech amongst the older coppice shrubs. **Bird's Hole Wood**, TQ 410 158, is half Bluebells and half Bramble, as befits a wood that is partially ancient and partially descended from rough common. It is Hazel coppice under Ash and tall, fine Oaks that had nice Oak Apples when we made a May visit. We once had a memorably damp picnic in drizzling rain sitting amongst sprawling Ramsons under a large umbrella in **River Wood**, TQ 398 162, with the Bevern Stream running by.

Nightingales and coconut-scented Gorse: Chailey Brick Pit

South of Bevern Bridge is the site of the old **Hamsey Brickworks**, TQ 398 160, which worked the Wealden Clay until the late 1980s. After working ceased an almost complete fossil of the bony fish *Leptolepis brodiei* was found there, looking like a partially eaten fish dinner (130 million years old!). The northern part of the landfilled quarry is now a pond that has Tufted Duck and Great Crested Grebe, May Flies dancing above it – and Swallows feeding on them. There's flaming Gorse between the edge of the pond and **Kiln Wood**, TQ 399 160, which betrays its industrial past with its many wet vwith Bluebell hyper-dominant. Lovely.

SOUTH CHAILEY AND SPITHURST: BETWEEN THE BEVERN STREAM AND LONGFORD STREAM

Here are some of the largest ancient woods of the middle Sussex Wealden Clay. It is tranquil countryside, with few motor roads.

To the east of **South Chailey** the woods bear the imprint of centuries of quarrying and brick and pottery production. **Chailey Brickworks,** now the Ibstock brickworks, TQ 390 176, is one of the oldest factories in Europe, in continuous production for over 300 years. The **deep pit**, TQ 394 176, with its blue flooded lake, and Gorse around its rim, is largely made up of bluish-grey Upper Wealden Clay mudstones, with a bold pink stratum. There's not been much fossilling there, though folk have found trace fossils made perhaps by crustaceans, bands of fossil wood, insect and fish fossils, the early flowering plant *Bevhalstia*,[10] and a large, scale-laden fossil turd (coprolite)! All around its crumbling

ANCIENT WOODLAND LOSS IN MODERN TIMES

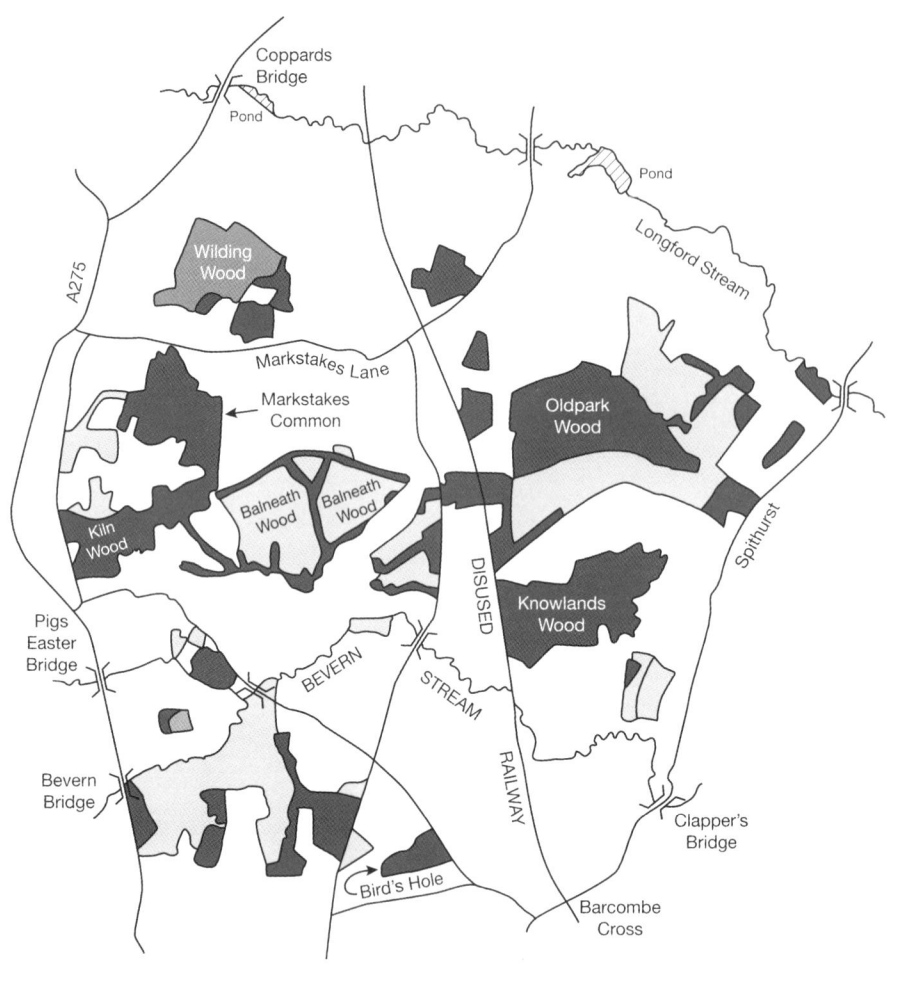

Map legend:
- Ancient woodland destroyed over the past two centuries. Balneath Wood and others have been lost in recent decades
- Ancient woodland damaged by conifer painting
- Surviving intact ancient woodland

© Crown copyright and database rights 2018. OS License number 100048229

The boundary of **Markstakes Common**, TQ 398 178, with Starvecrow Wood is vague, and the southern high ground of the Common is also much pitted and rumpled. A seam of red marker clay outcrops there. Is that what the quarry workers were after? It is a wooded common, but it used to be wood pasture – a much more open mixture of trees and heath. Most of the Common's trees are young, and its woodland ground flora meagre, but there is a scatter of good veteran trees of several species, including old open-grown Beech, mixed with Hornbeam, Holly, Hazel, Yew and Oak. The southern high ground used to have more Ling heath, grass heath, and even a few patches of lichen heath amongst the Bracken, but they seem much reduced now. There is more open Bracken down the slope to the north. The common receives loving management, but – as so often – we can only regret that this did not start 50 years ago. Many of its plants of grazed heath, like the rare Heath Dog Violet, Lousewort, Heath Cudweed, Sheep's Fescue and Sheep's Sorrel seem to be gone, though others, like Saw Wort and Heath Milkwort cling on. In recent surveys, too, folk have found or re-found special wetland plants like Bog Pondweed, Marsh Pennywort, Ragged Robin and Wild Hop, as well as Dormice, Adder, Grass Snake, and Great Crested and Palmate Newts.[11]

Wooded **Balneath Lane**, TQ 405 178, tracks the ridge eastwards from South Chailey to the Town Littleworth Road, with grand views north and south. At its western end, where it passes between the buildings of flowery banks and surrounding lanes, when the Gorse thickets flame yellow in spring, the Nightingales sing their courting music.

Kiln Wood, TQ 394 173, on the pit's southern edge, has Sessile Oak poles, old Hornbeam coppice, and Gean. It has a small council estate within its embrace, and an old work yard with a rusty collection of vehicles and tractors and even a traction engine (2012). **Starvecrow Wood**, TQ 398 176, on the pit's eastern side, has an open structure, and humps and hollows everywhere, with some old knotty Hornbeam.

the Brickworks, it is called **Caveridge Lane**. Could that be the ancient name (*Cafa's Ridge*) for the whole ridge?

All the land *north of the ridge* was part of Markstakes Common till 400 years ago, and **Dodson's Rough and Grantham's Rough**, TQ 4034 159, retain many of the common's archaic wood and rough ground flowers. One October, whilst looking for fungi, we picnicked at dusk on the sheltered field edge crook of the Roughs, overlooking Markstakes Lane. The Bats were out in numbers – little Pipistrelles, but also a medium sized species with a slow and low flight, partially under trees and partially in the open. Maybe they were part of the very rare 'old forest' Bechstein's Bat colony recently discovered on Markstakes Common?

To the *south of the ridge* lay the lovely **Balneath Wood**, TQ 403 174, destroyed in the two years 1980–81 in a monumental act of folly. The farmer-landowner was persuaded to leave the woodland gill and boundaries intact, for cosmetic reasons and for game, so I was told, and we counted 16 ancient woodland species there in just two short spring walks, with lots of Midland Thorn, Wild Service in two places, a big Aspen swarm and Crab Apple in blossom. It was largely a Hornbeam wood, fuelling the brickwork's kilns, and, where fragments of the wood survive, their old stools survive. Tragic.

Wildings Wood, TQ 400 187, north of Markstakes Lane, is another disaster area. Though ancient, it was coniferised wall-to-wall and only a thin strip of old woodland survives along some edges. It is dark and dead underneath, though a big herd of Fallow Deer take shelter there.

A tiny wooded Green lies at the junction of Town Littleworth Lane and Markstakes Lane, TQ 409 183, where we have several times stopped to listen to Cuckoos. It has an ancient pollard Oak, screened by the trees, and once we watched a Jackdaw stuffing its nest hole there with a bit of black cloth and a stick! West of Town Littleworth Lane is, or perhaps was, a **little meadow**, TQ 411 175, with much Adders Tongue Fern and Spotted Orchis in spring.

The **Bevern Stream** from **Holman's Bridge**, TQ 410 169, west to **Springles Bridge**, TQ 401 166, is delightful, with gravel banks, Minnows, Bullhead, Cased Caddis, Water Moss, *Fontinalis antipyretica*, Duck Mussels, River Limpets, Mayflies, Stoneflies and Mandarin Ducks (at least, before Plumpton College's heavy stream pollution of 2016).

A thin strip of colour stretches for a mile north of Barcombe Cross along **the disused Bluebell Line**, e.g. TQ 414 169. Expelled from their old homes in the surrounding pastures, meadows and common wastes, all the wildflowers of ancient open places have found a refuge there. At the southern end there's Upright Hedge Parsley, Meadowsweet and Agrimony, vetches, thistles and Teazel, Wild Carrot, Corn Mint, and Pepper Saxifrage, animated with butterflies, beetles and bugs.

The line crosses the Bevern Stream by a sleeper bridge, and northwards the embankment herbage is lower, more open and grassier, e.g. TQ 414 169. We passed a patch of sprawling Dodder (a rare parasitic herb), a few tufts of Dyers Greenweed and a large patch of Spiny Restharrow. Picnicking in the sun we noticed Small Copper, Burnet Companion, Dingy Skipper and Orange Tip butterflies, and groundhoppers pinging away. A Cuckoo called. There were several orchid species, and Zigzag Clover, Milkwort, and Spring Sedge. Guelder Rose was in flower. We were told Adders are occasionally seen.

North of the bordering green shade of Knowlands Wood the line's ground gets damper and there's Ragged Robin, Marsh Bedstraw and False Fox Sedge.

Now (winter 2017–18) nearly all this rich open vegetation is lost to a linear thicket of tall encroaching saplings, bramble and thorn, and the path has narrowed to single file. If only the linesmen who worked every day to keep the railway banks open (and free of grass fires from the steam engine cinders) were still working there!

Knowlands Farm and Wood, TQ 419 170, are places where visitors are made to feel welcome. No spending is expected at any farm shop, or to view the Bluebells. No gamekeepers challenge you.

In the deep cold of January 2009 we took the nearly two year old grandson in his buggy to see the farm. There was a heavy hoar frost and ice in the tractor ruts. Everyone was out on the iced-up farm pond … the owner's family, lots of teenagers, and three little four year olds … playing a fast-moving game of ice hockey. We stood and watched and told ourselves it was far too dangerous. Then we got braver. We took his hands and ventured gingerly onto the ice … tottering round happily as the light faded. *That's* a memory to treasure …

The Wood has Grass Snake and occasional Adder. There are three sites for Small Leaved Lime and two for Wild Service. There's Alder Buckthorn and Aspen, and Stag Beetles. There's Purple Hairsteak and White Admiral, and the owners would like to see Purple Emperor restored.[12] The rides are wide and sunny and there's a big glade spangled with violets in spring. It is an Oak-Hornbeam wood with Anemones and Bluebells co-dominant. There is active coppice management, and Willow and Garden Warblers, Blackcap, Chiffchaff and even Nightingales sing heartily in the coppice re-growth. There are Swan Mussels in the farm pond and Kingfishers bring their young.

Only the pastures of Church Farm separate Knowlands Wood from **Oldpark Wood**, TQ 418 179. It is also Oak-Hornbeam coppice with standards, though less open. Wood Anemone is overwhelmingly dominant in April. A large part of the wood to the south was grubbed perhaps 200 years ago, and nearly 100 acres to the north was destroyed only about fifty years ago, when

THE LONGFORD STREAM

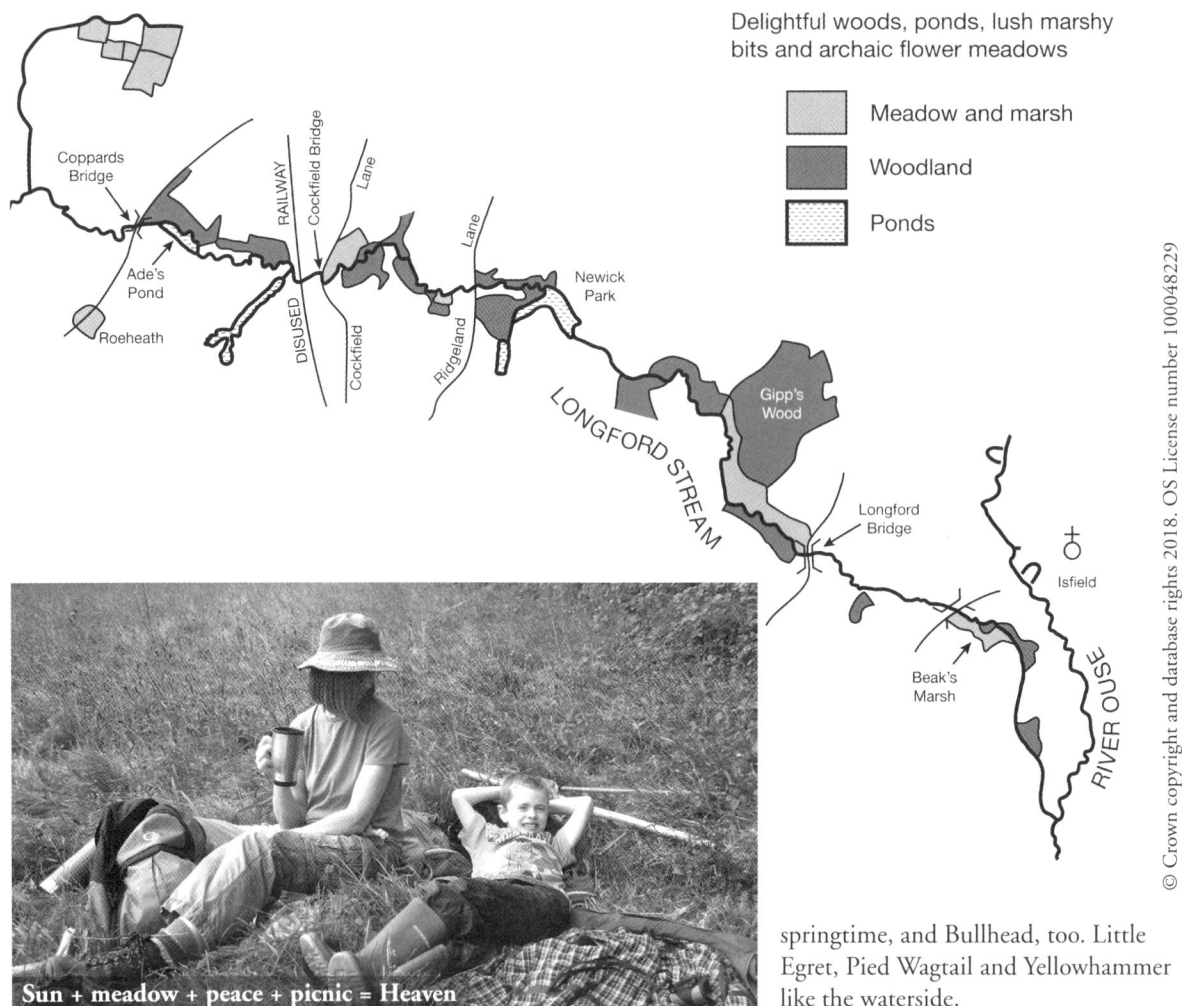

Delightful woods, ponds, lush marshy bits and archaic flower meadows

Sun + meadow + peace + picnic = Heaven

little **Spithurst Wood**, TQ 425 175, was separated from Oldpark Wood, too.

The little Victorian church and **churchyard of St Bartholomew's, now St Bartz**, TQ 426 174/5, is embraced on two sides by the wood, and the lovely churchyard wildflower meadow has the character of a woodland glade, with Anemones, Bluebells and Goldenrod mixed in with Devils Bit and Betony, Ling Heather, Pepper Saxifrage, Bitter Vetch and Tormentil – and lots of Birds Foot Trefoil, Mouse Ear Hawkweed and Red Clover. (The graveyard has been split into two: 2017). On the other side of the road from St Bartz, squeezed between back gardens and Down Coppice, is little **Whitegate Meadow**, TQ 427 174, with a spectacular display of Green Winged Orchids.

The **Bevern Stream** from **Clappers Bridge**, TQ 422 161, to Holman's Bridge, is exceptionally lovely. Marsh Frogs plop into the water as you approach. Cattle come down to the water to drink and the stream is gravelly along many stretches. Some spots are newly stocked with Water Crowfoot. There are Minnows in springtime, and Bullhead, too. Little Egret, Pied Wagtail and Yellowhammer like the waterside.

Across the Lane from St Bartz is the big wood named in parts: **Down Coppice, Agmond's Wood and Burtenshaw's Wood**, TQ 43 17. Generations of folk, from both far and near, have strolled these woodlands and their flowery rides and glades. In sunny spots, such as clay banks, there are Green Tiger Beetles, and the big pond has Tadpoles crowding its shallows, TQ 430 174, whilst its lawn is pretty with Betony and Tormentil in summer and Primroses, Anemones and Bugle in spring. It's a very varied wood, with areas of Larch and scented pine, maturing Oak, Sweet Chestnut coppice (rare on the Wealden Clay), much old Hornbeam and some Hazel coppice, part of which is still cut.

Across the pasture north of the wood, the **banks of the Longford Stream** are fierce with nettles, as we have come to expect from the highly enriched pastures of modern dairy farms. Just east of Dallas Lane, though, **Beak's Marsh**, TQ, 439 177, partly retains its archaic fen and damp meadow vegetation. There is a large area of Greater Pond Sedge, *Carex riparia*, which Roe Deer hide in, and there are Lizards, and Whitethroat and

Drowsy meadow afternoon

Goldfinch in the edging scrub. Sadly, lack of grazing, inadequate mowing and failure to remove the arisings has rendered extinct the flagship species of the site, Meadow Thistle, *Cirsium dissectum*, and other old meadow species seem doomed. Trees have now been planted across the erstwhile grazed species-rich open parts of the site (2017). The Roman road to London passed across the eastern part of the marsh. Did its travellers get wet feet?

Between Agmond's Wood and the Ouse are several good small woods, two of which are ancient Bluebell woods. There is much arable, with rich grass on the brooks. **Blunt's Lane**, an attractive brook edge green lane, takes you to the **White Bridge** river crossing, TQ 444 173. The **Anchor Inn**, TQ 442 160, on the riverside, once served the bargees of the lost Ouse Navigation. There are row boats for hire. Just north of the lane to the Anchor Inn is **Scobells Farm**, with its 17th and 18th century farmhouse. The farm meadow to its north west has a bank, TQ 426 166, with lovingly managed old meadow vegetation, old anthills, Spiny Restharrow, Dyers Greenweed and Heath Grass.

NEWICK, NORTH TO SHEFFIELD BRIDGE FROM THE LONGFORD STREAM

The line of the Longford Stream north west of Longford Bridge, e.g. TQ 428 185, for two thirds of a mile towards Newick Park, is a magic place of colour and variety … swamp, tall herbage, steep nettley river bank, Ardingly Sandrock riffles (and deep and dodgy mud), Bluebell Wood, hedgerows, Yellow Flag fen, hot bee-busy banks and pasture, soggy froggy stream sides, red-ochre iron smears in shining mud, and warbler song. Some years ago, we spent a perfect early May afternoon there. Red and Black Froghoppers, *Cercopis vulnerata*, were out. The grandson found a bright red Cardinal Beetle on a stump, and I pieced together the colourful husks of a Longhorn Beetle some mouse had crunched on. Blackcaps made bubbling song. A Cuckoo called. The smell of Water Mint was with us in the fen, and the narcotic scent of May blossom on Gipp's Wood's lea. This is good countryside for playing "We're Going on a Bear Hunt!"[13] As we picnicked on the bank, drifts of Sallow fluff sailed solemnly towards us like asteroids voyaging through the cosmos. The Stream has Bullhead and Stone Loach. At the southern end it is old pasture and swamp, and at the northern end it is Alder carr of the richest kind, with Red Campion and Meadowsweet amongst the Kingcups and Water Dropwort … from meadow to jungle in a short walk. (Sadly, part of the Kingcup marsh has recently been planted up with willows).

The part of old Newick Park south of the Longford Stream, e.g. TQ 423 189, is bosky and Brackeny, with old Holly brakes and oldish Beeches. There is a line of Hornbeam maidens along the stream bank. Years back we found many broken Duck Mussels scattered along the mud and gravel banks for a long stretch. What killed them? … stream management work? … or Mink, perhaps? We found a whitened Cormorant skull there once. The **Lower Park Pond**, TQ 419 192, is bleak and 'managed'. A new Red Deer farm with two metre fencing now covers the eastern Park, and its denizens browse every leaf and shoot they can reach. **Newick Park House** sits at the head of a wooded gill tangled with Rhodedendrons, which descends to the Longford Stream, sometimes around open dells which they brighten with their blossom. There are wild Daffodils on the grassy slope under the House, several old Sweet Chestnuts, and a good burry Oak by the Drive. The old walled garden has fine Rhubarb beds (2014). **West of the Park as far as Ridgeland Lane is wet Alder carr**, TQ 417 193, with much Golden Saxifrage and Marsh Marigold (Kingcups). Ash is abundant in the swamp, showing that this versatile tree is as much at home in soggy ground as it is on the dry Downs. We watched a white Goose sitting on her nest in the swamp one April, much like Jemina Puddleduck, whilst her partner hissed at us from the stream.

The banks of the Longford Stream for a mile between Ridgeland Bridge, TQ 416 193, **and Coppard's Bridge**, TQ 400 196, are nearly all wooded, sometimes with sheets of Bluebells, sometimes with Ramsons, and sometimes with swamp Alders. However, the north bank of the Stream between Cockfield Bridge and Cockfield House has a lovely **brook meadow**, TQ 410 194, heavily sprinkled all over with Anemones in early spring. There's much Pignut and Spring Sedge and a few Daffodils by the Stream (2015). Once, at **Cockfield Bridge**, TQ 408 193, we froze as we realised that we were surrounded by many tiny 'fingernail Frogs' (that's how big they were) hopping away.

The Ash woodland, e.g. TQ 405 195, **between Ade's Pond and the wooded embankment of the disused Bluebell Line** is packed with ancient woodland herbs, and the shallow stream, east of the Pond, runs over gravel, with a couple of little weirs and mini-falls.

Cockfield Lane, also known as Pack Pony Lane, TQ 409 190, was a lovely green holloway, with muddy bits the little grandson loved, and fallen rotten boughs to hunt for beetles in. At the northern end there are slab exposures of Ardingly Sandrock. It was a great place for him to explore and feel free. Now it has been hard-surfaced with an industrial aggregate for bikes and horses, and wild nature has been engineered away. Better to traffic-calm the nearby tarmac lanes than hard-surface this green one.

The two miles of **Ouse brooks from Oaktree Wood,** TQ 441 180, **opposite Isfield church, north to Sharpsbridge**, TQ 439 207, are tranquil cow pastures, woods, and wilded meanders – places of lush vegetation, duck, Moorhen and Kingfisher. There is a project[14] to restore some of the brook meadows east of Vuggles and Bunce's Farms, e.g. TQ 440 191. Some of their archaic vegetation – for these were Cowslip meadows – still survives on the ditch banks. The east side of the river and its nearby ditches north from **Isfield Weir**, TQ 440 186, to Rocky Wood has Dame's Violet, *Hesperis matronalis*, and Hemlock, *Conium maculatum*, scattered along it.

The old **Isfield Lock**[15] (currently being restored) **and weir** are much loved. The waters thunder down the weir to a sheltered pool, whilst above, the embayed river is still enough for water lilies. The **woods around Sutton Hall** are lovely and ancient, with magnificent Bluebells in places, old Oaks and Hornbeams and several ponds. **Gipps Wood**, TQ 430 188, west of the lane, is coniferised to the north, but still open, pine-scented and airy, with old coppice on the lower ground.

Just south of the confluence with the Shortbridge Stream, are two scruffy meadows, TQ 444 205, where, on one late May afternoon of sun and blue sky, we came across a most extraordinary tree. It *hummed*, quietly but audibly, as we approached, from the vast choir of drone flies nectaring on its blossom, whilst Song Thrush, Robin and Blackcap made harmonies … *"the Humming May Tree"*.

There are several good woods in the **hilly country between Broomlye**, TQ 431 198, **and Newick**. Some of the slopes are steep where the underlying Ardingly Sandrock offers more than usual resistance to erosion. The **Sharp's Hanger river cliff** is a real scramble, TQ 435 204/5. **Broomlye Wood**, TQ 429 201, is Hornbeam coppice, with lots of old wooded pits (2012). **Founthill Farmhouse**, TQ 420 202, is Tudor, with unusually elaborate timber framing. The 'fount' bit of the name means well, or spring. Along the valley to the west are the **landscaped grounds of Beechlands**, TQ 417 202, with a line of huge Sweet Chestnut pollards, three alive and two dead, and a quarried Sandrock outcrop, now made into ponds and rock garden, with Wild Daffodils on the slope to the east. **Beechlands** and, just to the south, **Ridgelands Farms** may have been a very early assart from the Wealden forest.[16] The owners of Beechlands donated **Mill Wood**, TQ 412 204 – half ancient and half secondary – to the Woodland Trust. **Tilehouse Farm**, TQ 409 203, has an ancient, mouldering pre-war railway carriage that you pass on the footpath – the sort that plotlanders used to live in.

The mile-wide **country between Cornwell's Bank and North Chailey** was common until the 17th century, and there are hints of that in the landscape still. '**Frick**' **Wood** probably means '*frith*' or 'rough' wood, and '**Roeheath**' means 'rough' heath. There are several **archaic meadows** surviving, one with Anemones all over in April, a few Cowslips, and a Gorse thicket, TQ 400/1 204. A wooded gill winds down to meet the Longford Stream, often streaked orange with iron traces … and indeed the early iron industry is the origin of the name '*Cinders*' **Hill**. The little common known as **Roeheath**, TQ 397 191, on the roadsides south of Longford Stream, still has Heath Grass, Heath Bedstraw, Tormentil, Spring Sedge and Minotaur Beetles on one *over-mown* side, and Ox Eye Daisy and Spotted Orchids on the other, *under-mown* side.

Newick was not a nucleated village – few Wealden villages were – but the houses clustered around **Newick Green**, TQ 418 213, have grown into a large settlement since the Second World War. Its **medieval church**, TQ 421 208, still stands in isolation to the south. Its stone was probably quarried from the sandrock down near Founthill. The nave is part-11th century, the chancel 13th century, the porch 14th century, and the tower 15th century. The churchyard is unimproved, with Green Winged Orchis, Ox Eye Daisy, Cuckoo Flower, and good old meadow fungi.

Much of the countryside between Newick and Fletching has been wrecked in modern times by the destruction of woodland and hedgerows. One extraordinary survival is the **north verge of the A272**, TQ 424/5 213, **west of Goldbridge**, famous for its purple-red Betony display in July. We counted 50 herb species in one short visit in 2014. (It has become more overgrown since then). The fragments of old common waste along **Redgill Lane**, TQ 404 217, and at **Fletching Common**, TQ 412 217, have lost their archaic heathy vegetation, but are still attractive. Much better than that was a fragment of damp heath called **The Warren**, TQ 401 218, separated for centuries from the rest of Chailey Commons. When we last went there it was a wretched mess of rank Purple Moor Grass and scrub, but I am told[17] that Marsh Gentian is just surviving, and new management by the Sussex Wildlife Trust, who own it but have had awful access problems, is now in hand …

Lane End Common, TQ 403 223, was separated from the bulk of the Chailey Commons in the nineteenth century. Its heathy and bosky spaces are now fenced and grazed by mild and delightful park cattle, and its blooming Gorse and the red haze of massed Birch twiglets, cheers the chilliness of late winter.

Between Lane End Common and the Ouse are several good woods, all with different characters. **Little Rotherfield Wood**, TQ 403 227, has much Oak coppice over a bare woodland floor, but there is Common Cow Wheat. **Rotherfield Wood**, TQ 409 224, was heavily coniferised by the Forestry Commission, but its heathy character was not eliminated, and large areas of Bilberry survive along the east-west ride, with Rowan and Hard Fern. **Great Wet Wood**, TQ 413 226, to its east, is lovely down by the edge of the brooks, with Bluebells and Ramsons, Redcurrant and Kingcup. The Ouse brooks are tranquil pastures. Those on the Sheffield Park side of the river are currently being restored by the National Trust and its partners in the River Ouse Project. I'm sure the Kingfishers approve.

Lane End Common, Little Rotherfield and Rotherfield Woods share a fine and healthy population of Wood Ants, with many trails and nests, some of great size. The *'little people'* have been known there for many years.

ENDNOTES

1. 'Contrasting Communities: Anglican Ecclesiastical Development in Barcombe and Hamsey in the Nineteenth Century', SAC 147 (2009), pages 169–92, by Pam Combes, quoting Robert Allen, Rector of Barcombe 1826–77.
2. Seasonal settlements in the Wealden forest where folk from around the coastal plain and the downs, to the south, brought their pigs and cattle in autumn for the 'mast' of nuts, berries and fungi.
3. 'Contrasting Communities …' Op cit, page 188 and footnote 79.
4. Jim Smith (the famous 'Jim the fish'), retired Ouse water bailiff extraordinaire, *pers. comm.*, 11.04.11.
5. Chris Yarrow, Wilderness Wood, Hadlow Down, *pers. com.*, 16.04.11
6. From the Japanese anime film 'Princess Mononoke'.
7. 'The Kings England: Sussex', page 94, by Arthur Mee. Hodder and Stoughton (1964).
8. 'Signposts to the Past', pages 76–79, by Margaret Gelling. Phillimore and Co. Ltd. (2010).
9. 'Barcombe Roman Villa', an excellent summary report online by David Rudling, Chris Butler and Rob Wallace. Chris Butler Archaeological Services.
10. 'English Wealden Fossils', page 44, Edited by David J. Batten. The Palaeontological Association (2011).
11. 'Friends of Markstakes Common Annual Reports', 2010–2012
12. Mr and Mrs Lear, *pers comm.*
13. The title of Michael Rosen and Helen Oxenbury's magical book, originally published in 1989.
14. 'The River Ouse Project' started by the Centre For Continuing Education, University of Sussex. Margaret Pilkington, Will Pilfold, Nick Steer, and others.
15. Now being restored by the Sussex Ouse Restoration Trust.
16. Old maps indicate that the ridge top lane, Cornwell's Bank, used to curve *round* the old Beechlands Farm, meaning the farm was older than the lane. The site, on well-drained south facing land, is typical of early assarts.
17. Graeme Lyons, Sussex Wildlife Trust ecologist, *pers comm.* (2012).

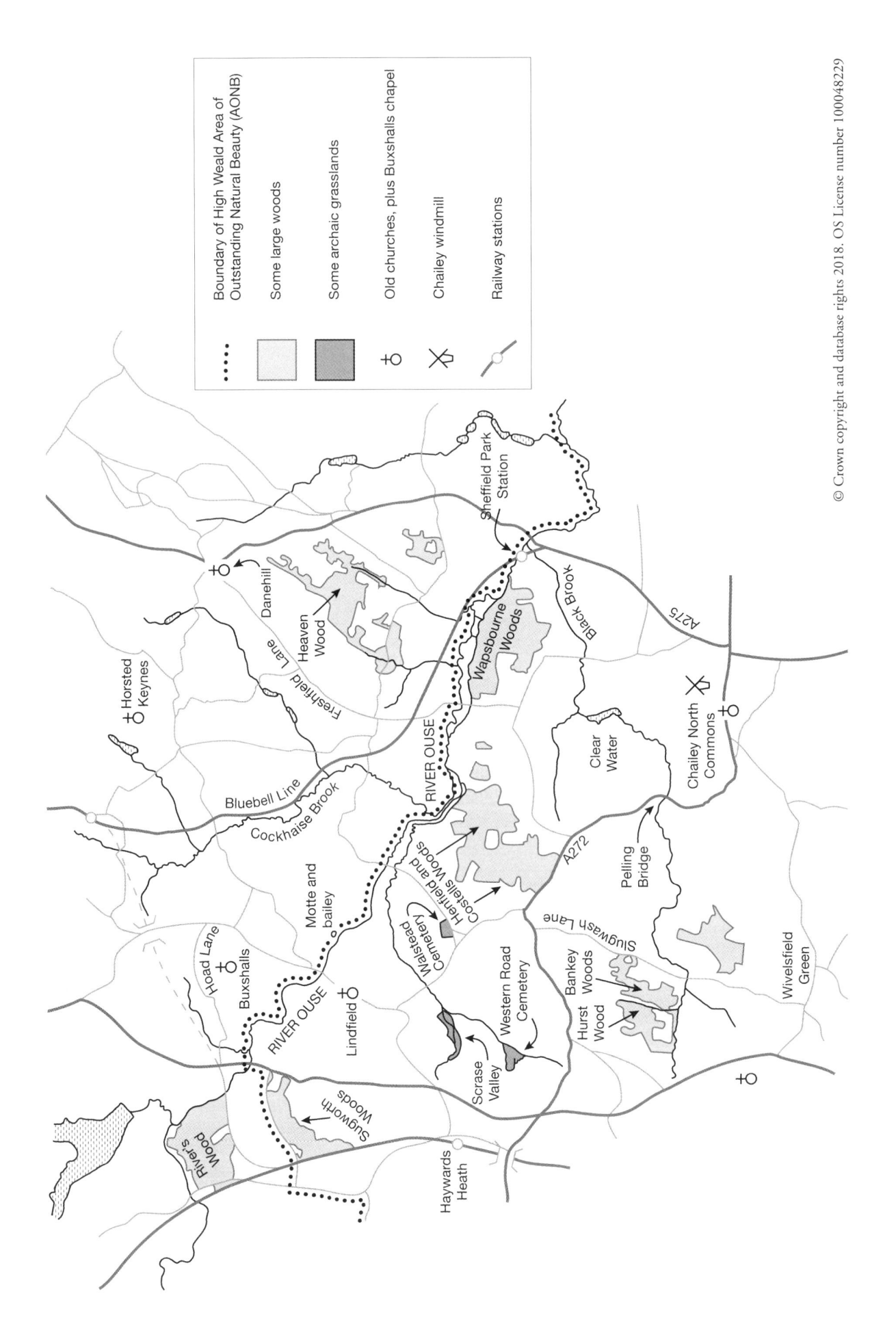

AREA GUIDE / Chapter 15: Haywards Heath to Chailey Common

CHAPTER 15
Haywards Heath to Chailey Common and the Bluebell Line

The Bluebell Line was well-named, for the original five miles of preserved railway[1] between Sheffield Park and Horsted Keynes pass amongst many hyacinth scented Bluebell woods of the Upper Ouse and Cockhaise Brook. It is delightful to stand in all that blueness, as the distant steam whistle marks an oncoming train, chundering above us on a flowery embankment, or marked only by the puff, puff of steam and smoke and the tip of its funnel as it passes, hidden in a cutting.

This is mostly a High Wealden sandstone countryside of hills and valleys, descending gently to the clay vale south of Haywards Heath. Only the area north of the Ouse, however, is protected within the AONB (Area of Outstanding Natural Beauty).

Haywards Heath was indeed mostly heath and big old woods till the Brighton Line came. There are still smidgeons of those places in the town. Superb extensive heath does still survive at Chailey Common, however, with glorious displays of purple heathers in high summer, and many rarities, such as Marsh Gentian, Meadow Thistle, Sundew, Bog Asphodel and Nightjars.

The River Ouse winds across the middle of the area. Indeed, this upper part of the Ouse was known as the 'Midwyn' or 'middle winding river', perhaps because it lay on the boundary between East and West Sussex, or perhaps because it was the river of the middle kingdom of the micro-kingdoms of Sussex. Lindfield Bridge is still sometimes called by its old name of Midwyn Bridge. Large tranquil woods – Wapsbourne, Henfield and River's – come down to meet the Ouse. Along the Cockhaise Brook, north of Keysford Bridge, unimproved rushy meadows survive.

Many lanes are too dangerous, now, to walk comfortably, but there are still a few fine green lanes, such as Ham Lane and Colwell Lane north of Wivelsfield, Hoad Lane north of Lindfield, and Wyatt's Lane south of Horsted Keynes.

Most of the area, away from Chailey Common, retains only a scattered few morsels of archaic pasture, meadow, and moor, but there is one outstanding exception, for, east of Danehill, there is an extraordinary cluster of tiny unimproved fields – ancient piecemeal enclosures from the old Danehill Common – now mostly managed (if at all) by horse grazing. There, special things like the Chimney Sweeper moth, Cowslips and Heath Spotted Orchis still live on.

CHAILEY COMMONS

We always seem to see something special when we visit the Chailey Commons. Nature gave one pal more than she bargained for when she answered its call and went off behind a bush. She reappeared to tell us that she'd shared the spot with a large Adder, which had slid off unhurriedly. We first went to the commons over 50 years ago, after I'd read about Garth Christian's efforts to save the Marsh Gentians. We found them then, their trumpets full of tiny stars, like looking down a telescope at the darkening sky. They are still there, though much reduced.

One September I went to the boggiest parts, amongst treacherous Moor Grass tussocks, to find the rare Strawberry Spiders, *Araneus alsine*. They were there, bless 'em … fat little red tummies all flecked, like the pips on strawberries, hiding in their curled-up-birch-leaf retreats. There are many other fine insects and spiders, too.

One of our best ever trips there was also on a September day. The whole sunny moor (part of **Romany Ridge Common**) was full of life … black Hebridean sheep, Lizards, a large Grass Snake, big Southern Hawkers whizzing by. We spotted some Sundew in its wire cage. (Yes, it really needs that emergency care). Fortune really shone on me, for amongst low cut Birch I found an old Yellowhammer's nest. Good thing I bothered to look in it, for there was one broken egg shell still there. Now, you may not think that so special,

SURVIVING HEATH AND ARCHAIC GRASSLAND AROUND CHAILEY NORTH COMMONS

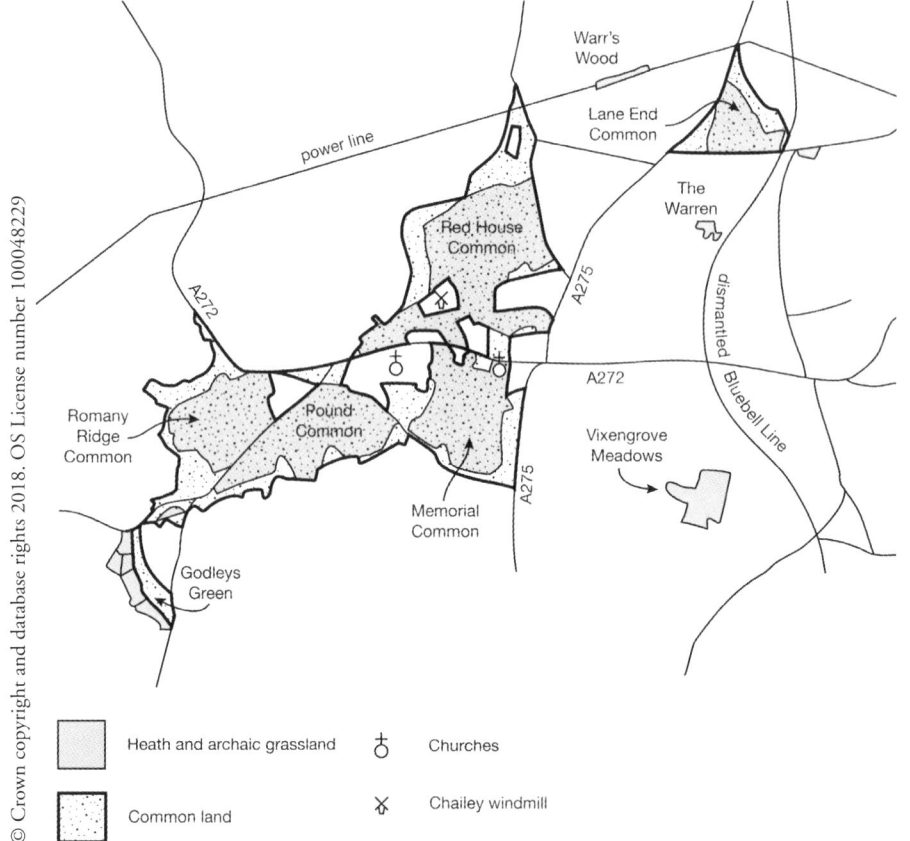

years without commoners' grazing has hugely increased the Bracken, scrub and woodland at the expense of the young heather and New Forest-type 'lawns' that Chamomile enjoys. The latter's gone from Chailey Common, now.

My delight at being on the Common always used to be mixed with that horrible sinking feeling that all that was special there was disappearing. I don't feel that now, for finally the battle to fence and graze the Common, and thus conserve its ancient heathland, has been won. Now you may see White Park Cattle, ponies, or heath sheep munching on the rank grass and young Bramble and trampling the Bracken. During the campaign to get the commons fenced, I noticed that many of the posters opposing the fencing were posted on the tall, visually excluding fences, gates and hedges of the poshest perimeter houses. Clearly they didn't want their own properties opened up to the gaze of the vulgar. For them, what was sauce for the goose wasn't also sauce for the gander.

The commons are now a place of hope … despite no longer even having a dedicated ranger and the County Council funding stripped to the bone … and this in a countryside full of the well-off, the rich and the super-rich!!

The Common is made up five sub-commons and is still in multiple ownership. It is much smaller than it was historically. The most recent enclosure was of the stretch between **Red House Common** and **Lane End Common** in the nineteenth century. One small part of that enclosure still retains its heathland. If you walk from Lane End Common through **Warr's Wood** you will find there a long sliver of heathland underneath the power lines, TQ 395 225, with Lousewort, Ling Heather, Purple Moor Grass and Heath Grass, Tormentil and Heath Speedwell.

but I'd always wanted to see one, being an ex-painter, for Yellowhammers are also called Scribble Buntings … and that egg showed why. It was like a Jackson Pollock action painting … with an under-layer of dribbled whites and white-pink-purple blobs, and an over-layer of dribbled lines of purple and purple-brown-black. Close by (I do not kid) was an abandoned Goldcrest's nest … tiny and perfect … a woollen cup lined with horse hair and thistledown and 'plastered' with Oakmoss lichen, *Evernia prunastri*, and Gorse sprigs and pods. The whole thing was only three inches across.

Paths are good places to look … and in spring Small Bloody Nosed Beetles walk them, too. I counted 11 on one small section recently. You often find Minotaur Beetles there too – dead or alive – and even if you don't you will still see the neat round tunnel entrances to their deep-down nests. I have found Purse Web Spider and Black Headed Velvet Ant, *Myrmosa atra*, on paths. (They are only pretending to be ants. They are tiny solitary wasps, really).

Paths are good because they are trampled and worn and that exposes bare sand and gives burrowing bees and wasps and finer herbs and grasses a chance, for the sixty

Red House Common, Chailey: overlooking the vale of the Pellingford Brook

CLEAR WATER, GREAT WOOD, AND THE FARMS FROM PELLING BRIDGE TO BLACKBROOK BRIDGE

One January day, there was a deep frost. **Clear Water**[2] lake, TQ 383 224, was mostly under thin and crinkled ice. There was no sound. Almost no sign of birds. It was several degrees colder there, than on the surrounding hills. Only the southern part of the lake near the reed beds was still open water. A plain-chocolate-coloured Mink paddled slowly across, low in the water, leaving wide, expanding ripples. A Great Spotted Woodpecker sounded its alarm from the tip-top of a dead Larch.

Later, on the cusp of February and March, the Alder grove on the west side of the lake was busy. Little parties of Redpoll were feeding-up on the Alder cones … and there were one or two Siskin. High in the tree tops I saw a Redwing gang … and there was a Cormorant in another tree top over the lake. A couple of Great Spotted Woodpeckers were tap-tapping up a trunk … and a Tree Creeper … and parties of Great and Long Tailed Tits, Chaffinch, the odd Robin – a Heron, too. It was all happening.

Great Wood, TQ 380 225, along the west side of the lake, is large, ancient, and varied, with big stands of outgrown Hornbeam coppice and close-grown Oak maidens on the plateau, Sweet Chestnut coppice on the north slopes and elsewhere, large areas of Birch, and much Holly. There's a flooded pit where Cuckfield Stone must have been quarried.

West and north of the wood, around and beyond the burgeoning vineyard, there are pits and diggings, some flooded, which must have been for the stone … or maybe sometimes for brick clay. The sandrock is exposed in **Rock Wood**, TQ 372/3 228 as a low, broken platform. Rock Wood is ancient on the west side of its gill, with lots of Bluebells and Wild Daffodils, and secondary on the east side, with carpeting Bracken and Rhodi clumps.

The old farms are mostly sited on the high ground overlooking the little **vale of the Pellingford Brook** (aka **Black Brook – Blackbrook Bridge**: TQ 391 229). To the *north* of the Brook, along Nash and Butterbox Lanes and eastwards, there's Nash, Butterbox, Massetts, Sennotts and Wapsbourne Farms, all with farmhouses built in the seventeenth century 'great rebuilding', or earlier. To the *south* of the Brook on the slopes rising to Chailey Common, there's Teagues, Bush, and Warr's Farms, all timber framed and from the seventeenth century, and Leylands, Vale and Great Noven, all of which are also old.

Some of the land is managed primarily for agriculture, as at **Butterbox Farm**,[3] run on organic lines, with Dexters and Sussex Cattle, Portland and Romney Sheep, and its own meat box scheme. It's big money that must have bought many of these farms and farmsteads for life style owners, though, not the skills to produce the food and manage the landscape we all need. **Warr's Farm**, TQ 392/3 226, is lovely, with a cock-eyed 'gingerbread' range of cottages, lots of old tiled barns, Swallows nesting in the stables, sheep in the fields (and game cover crops), and the whistles and "chuff-chuff" of the Bluebell Line the only sound in all the tranquility. **Lindfield Farm**, too, TQ 388 228, had a fine herd of tiny Dexter cattle in calf grazing when we last visited … and Shetland ponies, ducks and chickens round the farmstead.

HAYWARDS HEATH'S *RUS IN URBE*[4]

It must have been a wild place two hundred years ago. Hayward's Heath common was of the same rough size and long shape as Ditchling Common, with Lindfield's commons close by to its north and the continuous bulk of Petland and Frankland's Woods to its east. The County Lunatic Asylum, later St Francis Hospital, which still dominates the skyline from the south like some Victorian Versailles, was built in 1859 on the southern edge of the common so that the patients could benefit from bracing walks on the windy heath. Just three years later, however, in 1862, the heath was enclosed. Now it is those rich enough to buy flats in the posh Hospital conversion[5] – 'Southdowns Park' – that enjoy those views.

One good relic of the old heath survives right in the middle of the town: **St Wilfred's Churchyard** on South Road, TQ 330 238, which was enclosed and adapted directly from the heath. It retains many of the fungi of the lost heath's archaic lawns, all colourful in shiny scarlets, egg yellows and creams when the fungi season is good. **Clare Park**, TQ 332 243, was also a direct intake from the heath, and till recent years Ling Heather, Tormentil and Haircap Moss, *Polytrichum sp.*, survived on some of its banks. Perhaps they still do.

The **Western Road Cemetery**, TQ 340 238, is at first glance typical of its kind: a place of heavily manicured lawns, dense with ornamental gravestones amongst specimen trees. That is deceptive however, for the full panoply of the flowers and lower plants of the rides and marshy places in the lost Petland and Franklands Woods, hides out there. There's Marsh Pennywort, Sphagnum moss and Indigo Pinkgill, *Entoloma chalybaeum, var. lazulinum*, under Sallow. There's Ling Heather, Ivy Leaved Bellflower, Sneezewort, Eyebright, Dog Lichen, *Peltigera sp.*, Ox Eye Daisy, Heath Speedwell and Heath Bedstraw. There's Wood Horsetail and Bitter Vetch on the platform graves. Just don't bother going to the fenced off 'Nature Reserve' by the north side stream. It is a rank place of Stinging Nettles, Japanese Knotweed and Himalayan Balsam … testament to what we lose if we just 'leave nature alone' (2012).

Just over a third of a mile northwards is the **Scrase Valley Nature Reserve**, TQ 345 245, a much loved series of marshy meadows, Sallow thickets and woods around the **Scrase Stream**, running towards the Ouse. There are some huge old Oaks by the stream, and Hazel coppice with Bluebells. The Reserve still has Marsh Cinquefoil and other lovely things, like Kingcups, Spotted Orchids and Meadowsweet and several good sedges, though it has long lost its Meadow Thistle. It needs grazing and traditional hay making, if more of its special identity is not to be lost. Neighbouring the Nature Reserve is **Oathall Community College** with its own three field **College Farm**, TQ 339 248/9, complete with cattle, pigs, chickens, a Farm Shop, old Oaks and the Stream running by.

On the north side of Haywards Heath, towards the railway line, there is an old green lane, running north from **Wickham Farm** and **Sunte House**, TQ 332 255. Its abundant Holly makes its holloway very dark. Perhaps the Holly originally formed its hedging? Wickham Farm is a fine old timber framed place with a giant Oak on its east boundary. To the north, the fields are much used by local people, despite notices saying 'Private Property Keep Out'. Are they banked as future development land. To the west, the Bluebell woods along the railway line – **Sugworth** and **Highgrove Woods,** and **Staves Copse** – are superb and varied, mostly ancient, sometimes dense, sometimes open, sometimes wet, both north and south facing, and with lovely old Hornbeam glades. We counted 21 ancient woodland plants in one walk through them (2012). Staves Copse, TQ 330 260, has been moonscaped for skate boarding …

The **Haywards Golf Course** is an antiseptic place, full of exotic garden trees. Grass cuttings are dumped in many of the woodland fragments, which suffer from their proximity to the course.

WALSTEAD AND SCAYNES HILL

Henfield Wood,[6] TQ 366 242, with **Costells** and **Nashgill Woods**, forms a large block stretching for a mile between the A272 and the banks of the Ouse. Its southern part is mostly owned by the Woodland Trust. Parts of the wood on the ridge of the Sussex Ouse Valley Way are secondary, with bare field layers, but the bulk is ancient. There are fine Sweet Chestnuts and burry Oaks. A chain of little ponds drops towards the Ouse. They have clean water, with crowfoot, water lilies, and Broad Leaved Pondweed. Most of the block is sandy, with large areas of young Birch and Bracken, but Nashgill Wood is on clay and has a lusher character, carpeted with Bluebells and Anemones. Across a field to the east lies **Home Wood**, with much old Holly and coppiced Beech. It feels like old wood pasture. How much of this woodland block was commoned till recent centuries? What's left of **Scaynes Hill Common**, TQ 370 234/5, used to be called Henfield Common and feels like a typical edge green of a woodland common,[7] such as you still find in the New Forest. It retains an archaic acid grassland flora.

Henfield Wood meets the Ouse as a river cliff, TQ 372 245, rich with old woodland plants. The Ouse, there, has three parallel channels, relics of the Ouse Navigation. It is a jungly place. The brooks westwards towards East Mascalls Bridge are semi-derelict, but lovely, with Blackthorn thickets on the ox-bows and old Oaks.

North of Home Wood is a big **sewage works**, TQ 378 244, which attracts spectacular flocks of Martins and Swallows in spring, when the noise of Rooks vies with the swooshing of water and the works machinery.

Walstead Cemetery, TQ 357 246, retains the old archaic grassland of the long-enclosed Walstead Common. In springtime you may find Green Winged Orchis and Cowslip, and in autumn wonderful displays of old meadow fungi, including species like Moor Club and King Crimson, *Hygrocybe punicea*. The open country to the west, between Snowdrop Lane and

Lindfield, is currently being eroded by big new housing developments.

NORTH OF WIVELSFIELD GREEN

Slugwash Lane bisects this area, (TQ 350 216). Forget slugs and snails. It means 'muddy hollow of the wet meadows',[8] and this was an area whose greatest asset was its rich meadowlands. Indeed, it may well be that the cross-Wealden Iron Age track that passes through Scaynes Hill, down *Ham* Lane and Slugwash Lane and on to Ditchling, transected these meadow lands (Saxon *'hamms'*) so as to facilitate transport of the hay crop to the Downland mother parishes. Slugwash Lane forms a wooded holloway north of Townings Place. Bats flit about in numbers there in the summer dusk.

To the east and to the west of the Lane along an infant Ouse tributary, are places which retain some of the ancient vegetation of these lost, lush meadows (2011).[9] To the east, **The Moor brooks**, TQ 353 215/6 and **The Ham brooks**, are semi-improved horse pastures, but the ditches are often choked with colourful herbs: Gipsywort, Water Mint, Spearwort, Marsh Ragwort, Yellow Loosestrife, et al, and a derelict meadow fenced out of grazing is thick with Meadowsweet, Angelica, Lesser Pond Sedge and other tall herbs. Marsh Frogs are noisy, till they hear folk approach. To the west, a lovely derelict meadow, part of **The Breach**, TQ 347 217, is dominated by Meadowsweet, with a wide range of relict archaic meadow plants, including Ragged Robin, Greater Pond Sedge, Marsh Ragwort,and Tufted Hair Grass. It is often Rushy, with much Fleabane and small amounts of Devil's Bit and Sneezewort. Barn Owls haunt the brooks when all is quiet.

Hurst and Bankey Woods, TQ 348 221, and **Cains Wood**, TQ 355 230, are lovely places. On one memorable dawn walk in late February, I surprised Woodcock in the brackeny glades of Bankey Wood with its green haze of young Bluebell shoots. Both **Colwell Lane**, TQ 345 223, and **Ham Lane**, TQ 356 212, are greenways, often sunken, with superb lines of outgrown Hornbeam hedging stools. Around Ham Lane, **Wilderness, Ham** and **Strood Woods,** though often soggy, have been much coniferised, but small fragments of ancient Oak-Hazel-Bluebell woodland survive to their east on these old Stanmer manorial lands.

Across the Awbrook vale northwards, there has been much bulldozing of ancient woods post-1945: Eastland, Lead, and Gibbs Woods, the southern half of Anchor Wood and most of Holford Wood. **Anchor Wood**, TQ 367 227, still has Wild Daffodils in its south eastern corner though, and they bloom all along the streamside shaw as far as the A272. The shaw has sandrock outcrops too, though they are of Cuckfield Stone, not Ardingly Sandstone. The ancient (Iron Age, at least) **Abrook Lane**, TQ 362 223, is the northwards continuation of Ham Lane. It climbs over the hill north of Awbrook Old Farm, one field east of the modern Sussex Border Path. Now closed and deserted, it has become a linear wood, with outgrown hedge stools and a vestigial path. It must be full of ghosts.

Awbrook Old Farmhouse (15th–16th century, timber framed, TQ 360 221) is nice but sealed from our eyes. **Clevewater Farmstead**, TQ 338 217, is also ancient, with fine barns, Horsham slab roofs and stone farmhouse front. Its name indicates that it marks the watershed between the Adur and the Ouse.

FROM THE OUSE AND THE BLUEBELL LINE TO DANEHILL

This is high country, with a dense lacework of ancient woods, intermingled with secondary woods planted or left to grow over from derelict fields. Some parts retain their medieval mesh of small fields (as just south of Danehill); others have suffered from destruction of their old hedges and shaws (as on Town Place Farm). Almost no archaic grasslands survive except for one or two semi-improved pastures by the Ouse (as TQ 394/5 242).

Looking south from Ketches Lane (eg from near Town Place, TQ 386 255) we see some 2.25 miles of ancient woodland along the southern slopes of the Ouse valley – Henfield, Nashgill, Home, Pegden, Hammer, Cole and Wapsbourne Woods … a view that was substantially shared by Saxon folk … huge 'hursts' with a patchwork of small farms carved from them. **Kings Wood**, north and south of Ketches Lane, TQ 391 254, has abundant Bluebell and Anemone under Hornbeam and Sweet Chestnut coppice, some Oak coppice, and large areas of Birch. The gill sides north of the Lane have Pignut, Redcurrant and Hard Fern. **Coneyborough Wood**, TQ 398 245, is even richer, with a big interior open space of young Birch, Bracken and Broom. There are many Gean / Wild Cherry clones.

North of Ketches Lane, the open land around **Northlands, Butchers Barn and Cowstocks** eg TQ 399 267, is mostly a leisure landscape of livery grazing, with poshed-up ancient farmsteads. The secondary parts of Northlands and Cowstocks Woods are mostly Birch, with relatively bare field layers. The ancient parts have abundant Bluebells, old Hornbeam, Chestnut and occasionally Hazel coppice with Oak standards, and old Hornbeam perimeter hedges.

Heaven Wood, TQ 399 258, is big, varied, tranquil, full of pits, small ponds and wet patches. Its large Alderfield has Triffid-like Alder coppice stools on stilts. I wouldn't like to meet them on a dark night. There are fine Oaks, naturalised Solomon's Seal, and masses of Anemones.

Best of all there is a goblinesque Ardingly Sandrock outcrop along the south eastern boundary, mossy and ferny, forming a mini-canyon down which the southern

"I ain't dead yet!" – knotted, gnarled, weathered and ALIVE! … A Freshfield Hornbeam pollard

gill brook debouches. Badgers have obviously been here for aeons, judging by the size of their sett.

Slider's Lane has several smallholdings along it. **Pound and Circle Woods**, eg TQ 404 249, are Bluebell woods under columnar outgrown coppice and maiden Ashes, streaked with orange algae. Gorgeous.

FROM HORSTED KEYNES TO FRESHFIELD LANE

The linear **village green at Horsted Keynes**, TQ 384 281/2, bordered with pubs, the working men's club and cottages, is all that is left of the common there. The squatters' cotts and closes along the lost common's criss-crossing tracks, coalesced centuries ago to form the present village. The Green's trim suburban look is only recent though. Within living memory it was rougher and more workaday, and in a good autumn season you can still find the troops of little waxcap fungi that betray its ancient continuity. I found seven species in one visit, and there are more.

It is the woods to the south that are most special: tranquil, mostly ancient, and little managed (except for Pheasants). There are Wild Daffodils here and there and much old Hornbeam and Sweet Chestnut over Bluebells and Anemones. Paid-for leisure pursuits dominate. A new fishing pond – inevitably – has been dug by the Danehill Brook, north of Down Wood, and a cross-country horse trail with jumps winds through the woods and bland 'improved' meadows south of Valley Holme.

The lovely greenway of **Wyatts Lane / Bonfire Lane** drops south into the valley from the Green, and where the road twists there are two old **flower meadows** surviving (2012), TQ 386 277, now home to one or two Saddleback pigs. **Little Plantation,** TQ 386/7 273, east of the Lane, is delightful, with Daffodils along its northern boundary. **Wyatts Farmhouse,** and **Hole House** down by Danehill Brook, are ancient (17th century, timber framed) and picturesque. **Latchetts**, on the southern slope, is a fancy 'cottage ornee', with huge grounds.

West of Latchetts, the Danehill Brook runs through an erstwhile wooded valley between the main quarry of the huge **Freshfield Lane Brickworks** and its new extension on the opposite valley slope, TQ 383 266. In 2009, this was a nightmare place. The big standard Oaks and old coppice stools of East Wood and Four Acre Wood, lay flattened amidst the tracks of quarry bulldozers and the marks of chainsaws. In the valley bottom between this carnage, a gnarled Hornbeam pollard – so ancient that only half its bole remained – still stood (and still does, 2016) on a boundary bank, its smooth bark covered in the delicate hieroglyphs of writing lichen, *Graphis spp.* Along the marshy flat by the gill shone the yellows of Wild Daffodil, Kingcup and Primrose, and the golden croziers of Scaly Male Fern … as though that spring was just another like the thousands that had passed before …

The Brickworks quarry, despite all its destructiveness does reveal to us the secrets of our deep past. Lovely warm yellow sandstones all veined orange; friable shaley stones, muds, and clays with lots of ironstone laminations and pyrites bands; and cross sections of Grinstead Stone and Ardingly Sandstone – and big exposures of fossiliferous Wadhurst Clay across the Brook.

Just to the south, the **verges at the junction of Monteswood Lane and Treeman's Lane,** TQ 391 256, are rich and colourful. We counted 67 flowering plants there in one August visit.

AROUND THE ARDINGLY BRANCH LINE

The **Ardingly Branch Line** to Horsted Keynes closed in 1963 after 80 years of operation, but track is still in-place as far as Ardingly Station (now used as an aggregates depot) and the Victorian station office is intact. The Bluebell Line has plans to re-open this link to the Brighton Line. The branch line crosses the upper Ouse at the site of the old **Riverswood Lock**, TQ 336 275, on the Navigation, and the river bank between the Lock and **Lower Ryelands Bridge**, TQ 340 272, is a lovely spot.

Rivers Wood, TQ 330 279, is grand, ancient, and varied, covering the slopes of a low hill right down – on its north and east sides – to the Ouse. The river isn't the origin of its name, however, which means 'steep slopes': Saxon *'yfre'*. The wood has areas of old fashioned, managed coppice (Hazel, some Chestnut) with fine Oak standards, and large areas of conifers (Pine, Cypress, Hemlock, Spruce and Larch) often with carpeting Bluebells. There are fine Beeches scattered through the northern parts. In its tranquil centre is a grown over stone pit with a pond, TQ 333 277. The old river brooks and ox bow bends east of Rivers Wood are now under Poplars and Sycamores, but the brooks to the south of the wood are a mixture of small woods and fields.

The **vale of the upper Ouse**, north of the Wood, is bounded to the west by the **Ouse Valley Viaduct** and to the east, by the sprawling campus of **Ardingly College**. It is a palimpsest of little woods and hedgerows, and fine old Oaks overlooking Alder-lined meadows. **Alder Wood**, TQ 326 284, has the gold sovereigns of Marsh Marigold, and Bluebells on dryer ground. The **hanging wood** to the east, TQ 330 284, is a 'happy wood' … a sunny, south facing, tranquil 'nut wood' … with trampled paths in all directions from the Badger sett. Big trees have fallen down the steep slope, exposing their root plates. A Robin does a confusing imitation of a Nightingale and a Cuckoo calls. There's a fine veteran Ash maiden, and an ancient Maple pollard fragment.

The east side **road verge just south of Ardingly Station**, TQ 340 274 is rich and colourful. We've easily counted 45 herbs and grasses in summer. Eastwards, a permissive path takes you from **Avins Farm** across a humid gill, TQ 344 277/8, with Whirligig Beetles, Water Boatmen and Drone Flies. **Bursteye Meadow**, lies hidden in the woods just south of the disused railway line, TQ 347 280. It is tiny, wonderful and colourful, with big anthills, Dyer's Greenweed, Betony, Carnation Sedge, Sneezewort, Quaking Grass and Devil's Bit (2011). Across the valley to the south **Hillhouse Farm** is its antithesis, a hyper-modern intensive dairy farm with its indoor herd milked on an automatic turntable, so I'm told.

Eastwards again, **Hoad Lane,** TQ 354 279, passes through half a mile of varied woodland: Eightacre, Whiteways and Hoad Woods. It has a fine old Beech grove by the sunken way (same map ref.) whose shady banks have nice mosses and liverworts with Halloween names like White Earwort and Creeping Fingerwort (*Diplophyllum albicans* and *Lepidozia reptans*) … It's all a little bit 'Legend of Sleepy Hollow' …

LINDFIELD AND NORTH EAST TO HORSTED KEYNES STATION

Lindfield's ancient village street was built broad and long to accommodate its high medieval market. It is

Dean's Water Mill and Pond, Lindfield, on the Ouse

lined with Limes, which commemorate the origin of its name.[10] Nairn and Pevsner describe it[11] as "without any doubt the finest village street in East Sussex", and it packs in the ancient buildings – over 40 timber framed, alternated with Georgian brick buildings because the older houses were so generously spaced that the Georgians could infill.[12] The church is also of those high medieval times of prosperity (before the Black Death and after the recovery from it). Its shingled broach spire is its finest feature.

Lindfield's **West Common** was enclosed in the early 19th century, though **Lindfield (Town) Common** escaped enclosure, perhaps because its middle classes used it recreationally … for its cricket club was already old (founded in 1747) at the time West Common was lost. It is a fine recreation ground, but lost its ancient vegetation probably between the 1920s and '50s.[13] One of Lindfield's commons is still intact, though: **Town Wood**, TQ 343 262, a Bluebell wood with Anemones and much Sweet Chestnut coppice.

Just north of the church the land drops down into the Ouse 'rift valley'. **Spring Lane** takes you through **Fullingmill Farm**, (beef cattle, polytunnels) TQ 348 266, to the river. The farm has (2012) an old fashioned 'farmer's museum' nailed to the house wall – gin traps and old iron implements. The lane to the farm cuts through the embankment of the **never-completed Ouse Valley Branch Line** of 1866, which joined the London Line south of **Skew Bridge**, TQ 325 273. Across the river is a lovely **marshy woodland,** TQ 349 268. Squelching through tussocks, I caught my first Grass Snake there 54 years ago, whilst exploring away from our scout camp site in neighbouring Buxshalls Park. Its Alderfield smells of mint, with tiny velvety owl midges (moth flies), Marsh Valerian, Ramsons, Yellow Flag, and Golden Saxifrage … and some little thickets of Bamboo and Japanese Knotweed.

To the north of **Buxshalls** is a **redundant stone quarry**, TQ 352 274, higgledy piggledy with huge Ardingly Sandstone blocks. A little gravel path winds into the quarry dell from its south end, past huge trees lying crashed and rotting on its slopes, to a grassy plat in its midst where stands a **deserted stone chapel**, with honey bees nesting in its roof line and scattered rhododendrons in gorgeous flower.

To the east of **Lindfield / Midwyn Bridge**, TQ 352 262, the Ouse glides between rough meadows past the weatherboarded 19th century **Dean's Water Mill** and its eyot (river island). What's left of **Paxhill Park** overlooks the River, with some nice trees and the stone, part-ancient-part-Victorian, mansion, with tower and pinnacles, garden terrace and balustrade … very romantic … or 'Hammer House of Horror' … take your pick! The **motte and bailey castle**,[14] TQ 356 261, below Nunnery Wood, is the nicest spot, with old Oaks. It feels very like the motte and bailey at Isfield, on the eastern arm of the Ouse, and it probably functioned – and was abandoned – much like it, too.

The countryside around **Plummerden Lane**, TQ 366 266, and **East Mascalls,** (a lovely Elizabethan timber framed manor house, TQ 366 256) is a bit bleak, having lost lots of old field boundaries and old Montes Wood, and acquired a golf course and (inevitably) a vineyard. There are some newish woods though (like **Skein Winders**) and restored bits of hedgerow. **Cockhaise Farm** has two battered giant Oak pollards and a huge Oak maiden where the farm green used to be, TQ 373 258. To the north of the farmstead the **Cockhaise Brook woods**, e.g. TQ 370 265, by the Bluebell Line, are lovely (2012), but heavily managed for ducks and pheasants – in many thousands – with piles of feeding grain dumped on the tracks, and new ponds everywhere. If you came from a country of hunger, or even a local food bank, you'd be utterly disgusted.

The stretch of the old Ouse Navigation (now the main river channel) either side of **East Mascalls Bridge**, TQ 363 255, still has big Barbel, lots of big Chub and Dace, and occasional Brown Trout and Eels.

STONE CROSS AND WOODSLAND CROSS TO COCKHAISE BROOK

The stone cross and little green at **Stone Cross**, TQ, 357 274, are gone, now, as they are, too, at **Woodsland Cross** to the east, at the end of **Stonecross Lane**, TQ 362 271, but the Lane verges are still colourful with Fleabane and vetches. The **flowery north bank of Keysford Lane**, e.g. TQ 364 274, north

COCKHAISE BROOK ARCHAIC MEADOWS, HORSTED KEYNES

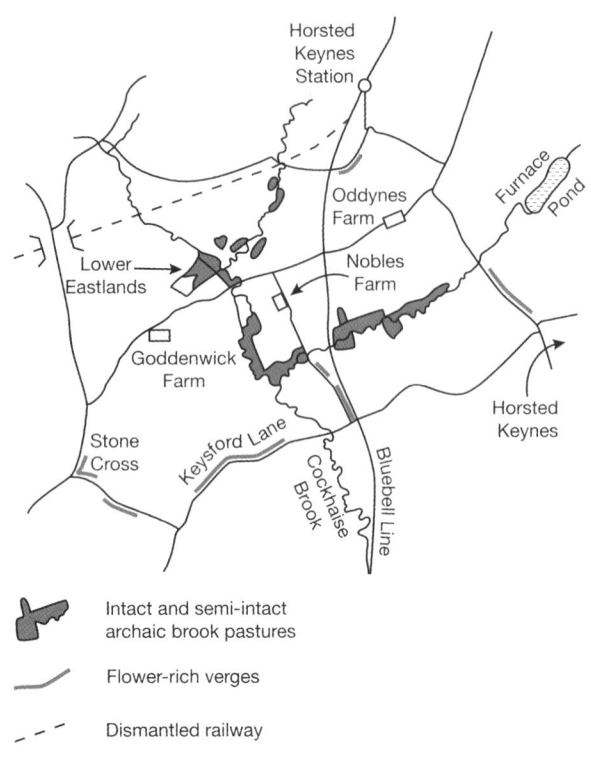

© Crown copyright and database rights 2018.
OS License number 100048229

of Woodsland Cross, is good, with Goldenrod and Hawkweed, Betony, Wood Sage, Bracken, Knapweed and Devil's Bit, Grey and Glaucous Sedges, though it is increasingly overshaded. But watch out, for there is no verge to retreat to from the traffic.

North of these lanes, the countryside around **Goddard's and Goddenwick Farms** has retained most of its old hedges, woods and shaws. Little **Hillyshaw Wood**, TQ 362 279, is the best of the woods – a gorgeous sea of Bluebells under tall, straight Oaks, with veteran Gean and Pear/Apple, on a slope down to a stream with Golden Saxifrage. The fine russet herd of Sussex cattle on Goddenwick's has sadly now gone (2017) and many of its fields are planted with xmas trees. However, the east half of one old pasture, **Lower Eastlands**, TQ 363 283, has miraculously retained its archaic herbage. Its dry knoll has much Burnet Saxifrage, Tormentil and Mouse Ear Hawkweed, with Spring Sedge. Its rushy, wet gullies have Ragged Robin, Tufted Forget Me Not, Smooth Stalked and Star Sedges. (The latter may now be gone, 2016). The wet plateau has Carnation and Oval Sedges, and Marsh Ragwort, with Marbled Orb Weaver spider and Long Winged Conehead bush cricket. On misty autumn days the wet grass shines with Golden Waxcap, Apricot and Yellow

Clubs and Golden Spindles old meadow fungi. It is a precious fragment of past plenty.

THE UPPER COCKHAISE BROOK MEADOWS AND AROUND

Around the junctions of the upper Cockhaise Brook, the lower Furnace Brook and High Wood Brook, a remarkable cluster of archaic wet rush meadows survives. Flocks of Swifts, House Martins and Swallows can be seen hunting low and high for the tiny flies that prosper in all that marshy productivity. Though the drier upper ground is improved, the wet flats still have a heavy cover of rushes, hiding many special species.

The old Ouse Navigation: Wapsbourne Wood

On the **High Wood and Osier Platt meadows**, e.g. TQ 366 284, many species have 'meadow' or 'marsh' in their name: *Meadow*sweet, *Meadow* Barley, *Meadow* Foxtail, *Meadow* Fescue, *Meadow* Buttercup, *Meadow* Vetchling, *Meadow* Brown, *Meadow* Grass, and *Marsh* Marigold, *Marsh* Bedstraw, *Marsh* Thistle and *Marsh* Foxtail. There are Spotted Orchids, six kinds of sedge including Wood Club Rush, and many other pretty things. (Sadly now heavily drained, it is reported, and with new fencing: 2017).

The **Cockhaise Brook meadows**, e.g. TQ 366 280, are more overgrown, with rough, wet grassland bounded by woods, which come down to the stream in places. In Eastlands Wood, TQ 361 285, there is the rare Touch-me-not Balsam, *Impatiens noli-tangere,* which may have washed down the Cob Brook from Stonehurst, near Wakehurst. It grows with Himalayan Balsam.

The **Oddynes Farm meadows**, e.g. TQ 371 281, on the Furnace Brook east of the Bluebell Line have Ladies Smock, Kingcup and Spearwort amongst the rushes. Two of them stand out. One is a little **Wood Club Rush meadow**, TQ 372/3 281, in the river woodland by Parson's Wood. In June it is steamy and lush. The Club Rush is threatened by invasive Hemlock Water Dropwort. The other is the gorgeous **railway marsh** right next to the railway embankment, TQ 370 280, which has Bogbean (just), Marsh Pennywort, Bog Stitchwort, (not so) Common Valerian, Ragged Robin, Spotted Orchids, Wood Club Rush, Marsh Ragwort, Devil's Bit, Purple Moor Grass … and shiny insects as beautiful as the rainforest, like the Mint Leaf Beetle, *Chrysolina menthastri*, Beautiful Demoiselle, and Hornets … all amongst Yellow Flag, Angelica, Hemlock Water Dropwort, Water Mint and Water Forget Me Not, Water Figwort, Reed Mace, Codlins and Cream, much tussocky Soft Rush, and shady Alder and Sallow.

It is a worrying place though, for the best and wettest part of the marsh has been fenced *out* of cattle grazing and is growing rank and tall, with invasive Sallow and Alder (2017). The Bogbean and other special plants can't survive if that isn't changed.

On the west side of the railway line **the drive from Nobles Farm to Keysford Lane**, e.g. TQ 370 277, has many Wild Strawberries, and Pepper Saxifrage, Betony, Ox Eye Daisy, Dyers Greenweed, Yellow Oat Grass and Zig Zag Clover.

If you look northwards from around **Parson's Wood**, TQ 376 280, the view takes in the three spires of Highbrook, West Hoathly and Horsted Keynes churches. Lovely.

WAPSBOURNE WOOD, THE SLOOP, AND AROUND

Wapsbourne Wood, TQ 395 238, is a great place to get lost in. It goes on and on, and if the children run fast then you'll have to keep up to avoid losing them to the witch in the gingerbread house. Try using a breadcrumb trail (or these days a biscuit trail). This wood has big stands of Hornbeam (with many dead overstood poles) and Sweet Chestnut coppice and higgledy-piggledy toppled old stools, few standards, little Bracken glades, banks and dells, and flushes of Bluebells. On the north side, it runs down to the Ouse and the old canal, which is deep and wide, with Ramsons along its banks and Scarlet Elf Cup. The Ouse greatly meanders here, with steep, deep banks and sometimes gravelly shallows.

DANEHILL MEADOWS

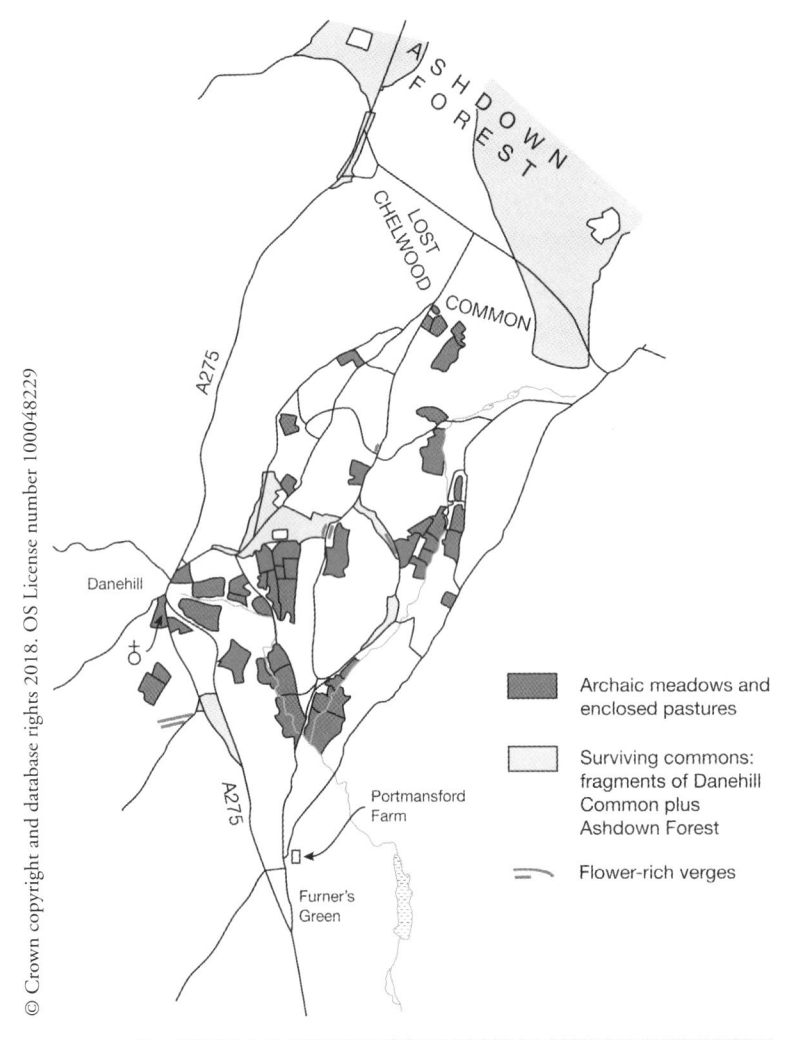

This is a remarkable surviving assemblage (2012). Some are well managed, some are being restored, many are poorly managed and over-grazed, others are derelict, or 'improved'.

There seem to be no freshwater mussels, though, and few emergent plants. Odd … witchery perhaps? … or the influence of the sewage works upstream?

400 year old **Wapsbourne Farmhouse**, TQ 399 233, is described in its listed building citation as "probably the most interesting house in Chailey parish" … a fine L shaped, timber framed, three storey job, with diamond shaped leaded panes in its casement windows, and big brick chimney stacks. Good enough to be somewhere in Cheshire or the Kentish Weald. The name means 'bourne path' *(werpel)* and perhaps referred to the partly lost track from Wapsbourne Gate and Farm westwards to the defunct **Hunt's Gate crossroads**, still marked by a huge veteran Oak pollard, TQ 391 234, hidden in the hedge where the footpath turns off from Butterbox Lane.

To its west, Wapsbourne Wood is contiguous with **Cole Wood** (with dark Larch plantings) and **Hammer Wood** (much Scots Pine), and beyond that you come to the **Sloop pub**, once much used by the bargees of the old Ouse Navigation. If you walk up the lane across the Ouse, you will notice an old raised narrow wooden walkway along the lane side, constructed to keep folks' feet dry when winter flooding drowned the road surface. These walkways – great for kids – could be seen by many lowland river crossing lanes till recent decades, but most of them are decayed and lost in vegetation nowadays.

There was a **Tudor iron forge and its pond** four centuries ago, north of Hammer Wood, with another north of Sheffield Park Station.

DANEHILL MEADOWS

Between Danehill village and the edge of Ashdown Forest lies an area of tiny fields and smallholdings nibbled out over the centuries from the fabric of old Danehill Common, a purlieu common of Ashdown Forest.[15] Fragmented ownership, the rumpled landscape and poor soils, have served to preserve not just this pattern of fields, bits of common and woods, but much of their rich archaic grassland too. It is an extraordinary collective survival (2012). I call this area the **Danehill Meadows**, e.g. TQ 408 278.

To get a flavour of it, the best place to start is **Danehill Churchyard**, TQ 403 274. It is beautifully kept, much like a local traditional meadow. In late spring you can see hosts of Green Winged Orchids and Ox Eye Daisy amongst many other scarce plants, and in a good autumn there can be a colourful display of waxcap fungi. Indeed, the churchyard is nationally important for that group.

At least two of this area's surviving hay meadows have the rare Chimney Sweeper moth – all sooty black with fine white forewing edges – which feeds on Pignut. In Sussex, it is now in a shrinking redoubt based on Ashdown Forest. These meadows have Pale Sedge, Cowslip, Heath Spotted Orchis, Devil's Bit, and Pepper Saxifrage. Just south east and down the slope from Danehill Church is a steep pasture of humps and rushy gullies, TQ 406 272, with Pale, Black, Oval, Spring and Carnation Sedges – all scarce species. In the valley bottom below Dane Wood, TQ 409 269, is a lush meadow bisected by a stream, which has a large hybrid swarm of Heath x Common Spotted Orchis, with Pignut and Cowslip.

A few of the meadows are in fine condition, and on at least one holding they are being actively restored. Others are neglected and grown over to Bracken, scrub, and wood. Many are being damaged by heavy horse grazing, with all the mess of paddock fencing and sheds, or hard conventional sheep grazing … or even, still, by agro-chemical improvement.

The unique qualities of this area need public recognition, and owners and managers need advice, help, praise and restraint if these qualities are to survive.

Over the past century the surviving bits of **Danehill Common** (e.g. the main bit north east of the village school, TQ 409 280) have grown over to a species-poor mixture of Holly, Birch, Oak and much Bracken. Their archaic open vegetation can now only be found on rare morsels of lane verge, such as those west of Danehill Lodge, TQ 411 279, where Cow Wheat, Bitter Vetch, Hawkweed, Betony, Sanicle and Spotted Orchis, give a flavour of what the lost common was like. Some brave person was depasturing a small flock of sheep on the waste of the manor by Tanyard Farm in 2012. That shows how quiet these lanes remain.

The lanes and green lanes of the Danehill Meadow area converge southwards on the tiny hamlet of **Portmansford and Furner's Green**, TQ 409 261/2.

It is a magic place … with its scruffy, miscroscopic green, duck pond and farm yard, overlooked by four ancient cottages. It is a place straight out of Tunnicliffe's countryside of the 1950s – all muddy and rough, with Snowdrops in the green lane below the farmhouse, grown-tall hedges, greeny-black ducks, goats, Swallows in the barn, lots of bats, and chickens. Best by far, though, is a fine herd of Guernsey cattle and calves in the pastures. What beautiful animals! The story of the farm in recent decades is a moving one of both sadness and hope … of fields sold lot-by-lot to stay afloat, of the sale of the brook pastures (now the Tanyard Fishery) and of the struggle to make traditional low-intensity farming pay. It was all nearly lost … but the young people who were blessed by the late farmer's generosity are surviving and making it work (2015). May they prosper!

Just south east of Furner's Green is **Beachy Wood**, TQ 412 256/7. Its western plateau part is replanted with Scots Pine, but its long eastern edge hides a dramatic Ardingly Sandrock cliff and gill. There is a 24ft tall sheer rock face, which must make a waterfall in winter. It is crowned by a big two span broken Beech and its writhing roots. A twinkling stream runs southwards through the brook pastures below, e.g. TQ 415 254, passing between banks of Bluebells and over a stony bed with big lumps of slag from the iron furnace that was upstream at **Sheffield Mill Farm and Pond**, 400 years ago.

ENDNOTES

1. The Bluebell Line between Barcombe and East Grinstead was finally closed by British Rail in 1958. However, the five mile section between Sheffield Park and Horsted Keynes was reopened as a heritage line in 1960, and now extends and connects again with the wider rail system at East Grinstead.
2. Clear Water was created in 1935 by the farmer at Butterbox Farm, Reggie Mason. See: butterboxfarm.co.uk
3. See: butterboxfarm.co.uk.
4. The Latin means 'countryside in the town', but sounds better.
5. St Francis Hospital closed in 1998.
6. Both Sussex Henfields derive their names from the Saxon 'hean' (high) 'felde' (open ground). Scaynes Hill's old name was 'Henfield', and the 'feld' bit indicates that parts may have been less wooded in Saxon times.
7. A mile to the north east was Blackhouse Common, TQ 384 242, between Freshfield Bridge and Freshfield Place, which shared with Scaynes Common that character of an edge green of a woodland common. Its last fragments, along the eastern roadside south of The Sloop pub, were only enclosed in recent decades, though a bit still has the status of common.
8. Slough (Saxon: 'sloh') of the wet meadows (modern Sussex dialect 'wish'; Saxon 'wisc').
9. 'Wivelsfield: the history of a Wealden parish', pages 16 and 110 et al. Edited by Heather Warne. Pier point publishing & WHSG (1994).
10. 'Linda-feld': Saxon for 'lime tree'd open land'.
11. 'The Buildings of England. Sussex', page 561, by Ian Nairn and Nikolaus Pevsner. Penguin (1965).
12. Nairn and Pevsner, page 562, op cit.
13. It was still a "fine common of geese" in 1904. "Highways and Byways in Sussex", page 219, by E. V. Lucas. Macmillan and Co. Ltd. (1912). It was still grazed in 1919. *Pers comm.* Richard Bryant and the Lindfield History Project Group, via Dr Margaret Pilkington.
14. A form of early Norman castle, with a raised hillock (motte) which would have had a defensible retreat behind a stockade built upon it, and a bailey (stockaded yard) below as the main and first line of defence.
15. Medieval forests (and sometimes chases, too) were often surrounded by commons free from forest law, known as 'purlieu commons'.

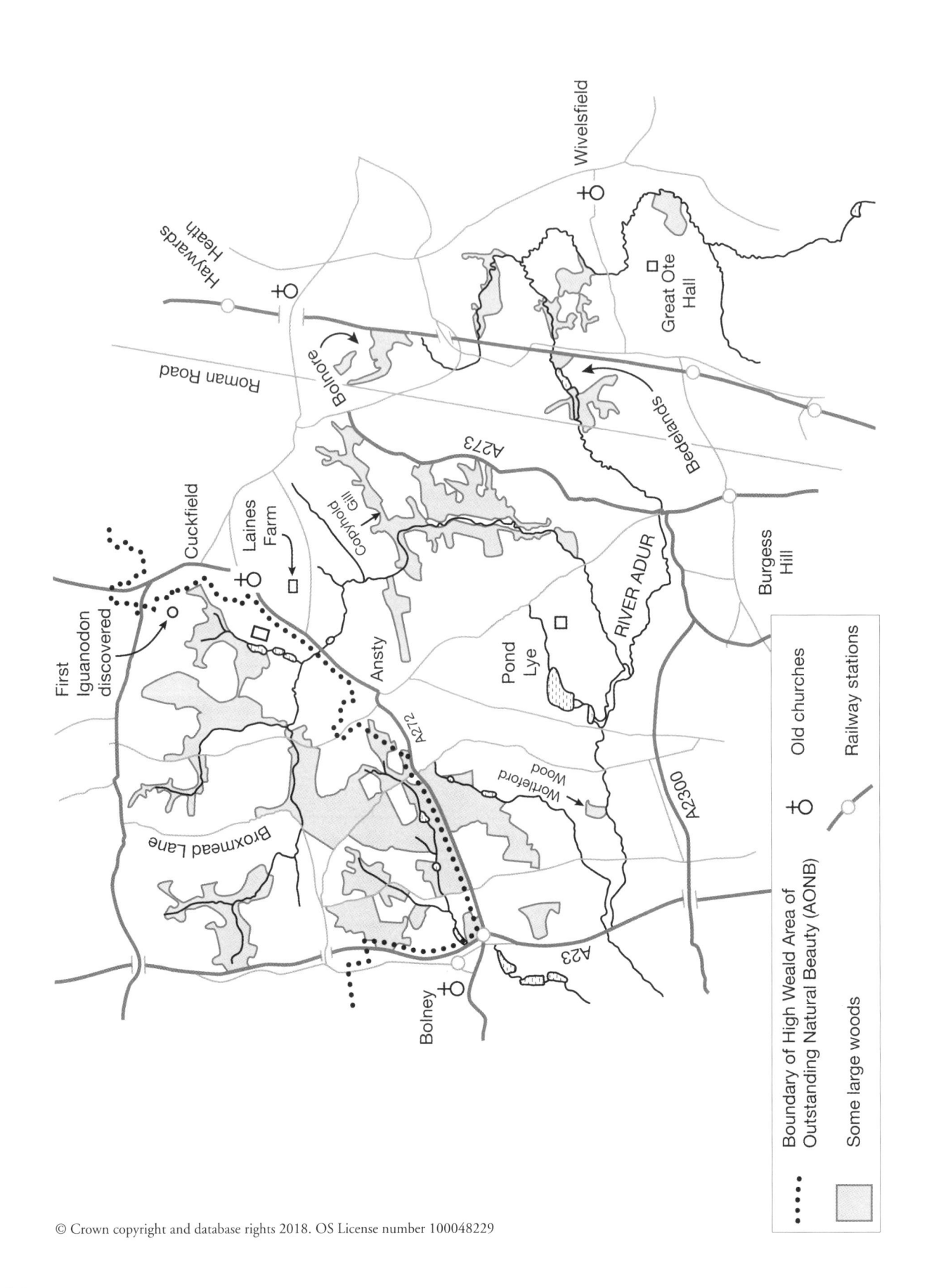

© Crown copyright and database rights 2018. OS License number 100048229

220   AREA GUIDE / Chapter 16: Between Haywards Heath and Burgess Hill

CHAPTER 16
Between Haywards Heath and Burgess Hill:
Ansty, Heaselands, Ashenground and Bedelands

It was my birthday. The beginning of May. Sunny and the sky clear. I worked shifts in Haywards Heath, and for the past year I had been in the habit of spending time before or after my shifts in Ashenground Woods, on the partly-cleared site of the proposed Bolnore Village development. I wandered across the open ground of chainsawed ancient woodland between the cleared line of the future ring road and the preserved rump of Ashenground/Catt's Wood. The gentle slope was a stretching marvel of blueness … that blue-with-a-hint-of-mauve that marks out native Bluebells. The bulldozers had not killed that yet. A Willow Warbler was making music.

"What a birthday treat!" I thought, "even if I am one of the last to ever see it". It is gone now, of course.

On a midwinter day, the little streams between Stairbridge and Bishopstone Lanes were in coffee-coloured spate after rains, and it took long legs to stretch across them without getting wet feet. Here, the din of the London Road lessened slightly. A mixed flock of Redwing and Fieldfare rose above the outgrown thorn hedges and invading saplings of three hidden fields on the edge of the wet Wealden Clay, just before it rises to the sands of Foxashes wood. Tattered stands of dried Fleabane and Marsh Thistle, rush and tussock grass, Knapweed, Angelica and Bracken testified to long abandoned archaic pastures. Golden Crab Apples lay under a hedge, still unbledded and hard. A neglected, but still magical place.

Many of the treasures of this countryside have that provisional, insecure character. You want to enjoy them all the more for the thought that they may not long remain. Huge housing developments are proposed in the gap between Haywards Heath and Burgess Hill, surrounding the Bedelands Farm meadows and woods nature reserve, and sprawling northwards from the line of the A2300 Burgess Hill–A23 Link Road (the 'Northern Arc').

The southern third of this countryside is Low Wealden, gently undulating, with many brooks and much wetness, old hedgelines, and little ancient woods. The northern two thirds is High Wealden, rising ground, with bigger woods and deeper, steeper valleys. The AONB (Area of Outstanding Natural Beauty) boundary rides roughshod over the natural boundary between these landscapes, leaving half the High Wealden part unprotected, east of the line of the A272/B2036 road from Bolney Crossways to Cuckfield, and ignoring altogether the loveliness of the Low Weald.

Copyhold Gill, near Heaselands, dark and jungle-ferny, and Freeks Woods, where the pack horse trains splashed across the Romans' fording of the Adur, are as fine as the best protected places in the Weald, yet lie in a landscape without statutory protection. Bedelands' superb flower meadows deserve better than to be threatened by looming built development on all sides.

There are so many fine places. Pond Lye, with its sedge and reed beds, water birds, Sallow carr and ancient meadows, was an easy cycle from Hove on my dad's old bike, back in the mid-sixties, though the traffic has destroyed the quiet pleasure of those lanes, now. The Adur brooks retain a high level of naturalness, with lush vegetation, busy with wildlife, all the four miles eastwards from Rice Bridge on the London Road, under Stair Bridge, Wortleford Bridge, Fairplace Bridge, Vale Bridge, and on past Clearwaters Farm.

The gills, wooded pits and hanging woods to the east and west of Broxmead Lane, are superb but little known. There is a cluster of archaic meadows there, too. The broad woodlands around Buncton Lane and Pickwell's Lane have old pits, plains and steep slopes, glades … and modern shacks in one place.

Just east of the Brighton Line is the peculiar plotlands landscape north of Antye and Theobalds, with its lacework of little woods and fields and half

BEDELANDS: ANCIENT WOODS AND MEADOWS

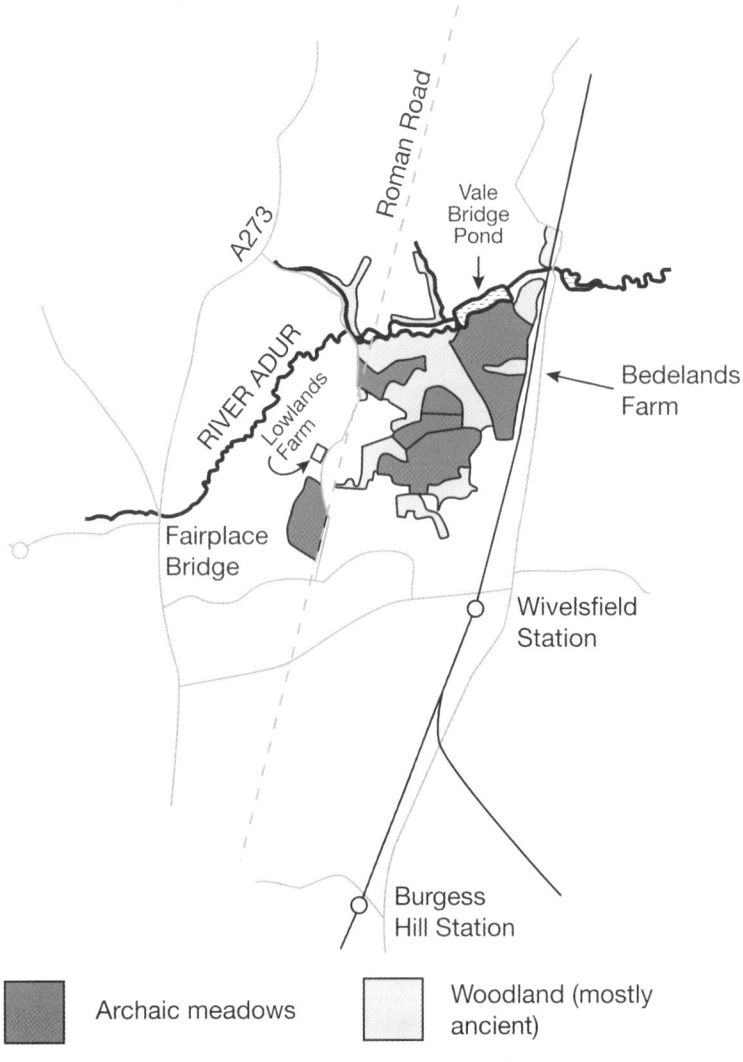

soldier beetles, dung beetles, ichneumon wasps, mining bees, damsels, cuckoo bees, earwigs, Black and Red Bugs ... all cast under a spell by cloud and springtime chill.

It is a rain foresty, mint perfumed place, brimming with beautiful, unassuming, tiny life forms amongst Yellow Flag, Dock and Buttercup, with Wren and Blackcap in song.

Bedelands and Freek's Farm's meadows, lags (wet meadows), ancient woods, riverine hangars and glades have magic ... most of all where the **Roman road fords the young Adur,** TQ 316 211. It is just as the Romans would have known it, though the only emperors to be seen are Emperor Dragonflies, with red and blue damsels, and Beautiful and Banded Demoiselles. Heavy, May-scented Wild Service blossoms overhang the almost-stilled little river that is guarded by steep, wooded clay banks above grassy riverside plats. It only lacks Wild Boar prints in the streamside wallows, though gangly Herons hidden by Guelder Rose, Nettle and Bramble, still flap up through the canopy from their waterside vigil. Many-coloured Bullocks grazed the south side buttercup meadows on my last visit.

In **Freek Farm Wood**, TQ 316 210, overlooking the fording, the Wild Service Tree is the most frequent I remember seeing it, clustered along the bank top. All around in the wood are very tall Sessile Oak poles. I am used to seeing Sessile Oak woods in the High Weald ... but here? ... in the Wealden clay vale? The wood has been managed for its Oaks, though there are remnants of struggling coppice of Hazel, Hornbeam and Holly. It is a shady, tranquil wood of Bluebell and Anemone with many other old woodland plants, like Field Rose on the boundary with **Freeks Farm meadow**, TQ 316 209, which is archaic and colourful, and has Grizzled Skipper (2013).

Big Wood, Watford Wood, Long Wood, and Leylands Wood, all on the neighbouring Local Nature Reserve, have many of the qualities of Freek Farm's woods, but benefit from the management of the District Council and the Friends of Burgess Hill Green Circle. The Bluebells of Big Wood are a wonder.

Freek's Lane is the direct descendant of the ramrod straight Roman road, but 1,800 years of traffic have led it to weave in more relaxed fashion between huge old hidden houses, with old Wivelsfield and the Ote Hall countryside to the east and south.

BEDELANDS AND FREEK'S LANE'S MEADOWS AND WOODS

We squelched through the black mud and chest-high Water Hemlock of the **eastern pondtail of Valebridge Pond**, TQ 322 212/3, almost under the **Valebridge viaduct**, on a typical May day (2013), cool, under a grey sky. The chill acted like an enchantment. All the zoo of bright and prettily patterned arthropody life seemed asleep, comatose, on flower heads, on leaves, under leaves, and in the crooks of stems. *Cardinal Beetles (both species), longhorn beetles (3 species), longhorn moths, ladybirds, sawflies, scorpion flies, snail killing flies, craneflies, hoverflies, empid flies, butterflies (Green Hairstreak, Green Veined White, Common Blue), shiny leaf beetles, Noble Flower Beetles, Angle Shade moths,* oak trees and rich hedgerows colourful with woodland flowers. The tractor ruts are some of the deepest I have squelched through, especially by the crumbling **Freek's Farm**, and deep along the farm woodland tracks and across the meadows. They prompt no complaint from me. I feel blessed to have spent time there, and angry that anyone should even think of building on any of this complex, rich and ancient landscape (2013). The farmstead, TQ 314 205, marked the edge of St John's Common, till enclosure came.

The glory of **Bedelands LNR (Local Nature Reserve),** e.g. TQ 320 210, is its archaic flower meadows. There are seven of them, each with a different history and character. Buttercup and Ox Eye Daisy dominate visually, the Ox Eyes bending like worshippers towards the sun. Yellow Rattle is abundant over much of the meadows, and hosts the scarce Grass Rivulet moths, which jig around like dust on sunny days in late May. Bedelands is their greatest Sussex stronghold.[1]

Watford Meadow feels like a medieval assart from Andredesweald.[2] **Wet Meadow** (with its boardwalk) has Ragged Robin and Sneezewort in addition to the commoner old meadow flowers, and the **Old Arable** is plainly a Buttercup meadow, though Ribwort Plantain, Knapweed and Yellow Rattle vie with them.

The three eastern meadows were part of Valebridge Common till enclosure, and that history is reflected in the abundance of Dyers Greenweed on **Valebridge Common Field**, and in the name of its twin: ***Furze* Common Field** (though Furze now seems to have gone from there).

There are many small 'beasties' to enjoy. The Wasp Beetle, Clytus arietus, seems to be particularly common. Bumble Bees are everywhere, with Burnet Companion moth and Common Blue butterfly. The flowers of May time host many beautiful spiders, like the Yellow Crab Spider, Misumena vatia, and other Crab Spiders, Xysticus spp., the Cucumber Green Spider, Araniella cucurbitana (often near hedges) and a host of others.

EAST OF THE BRIGHTON LINE: OLD WIVELSFIELD, ANCIENT TRACKS, PLOTLANDS

Old Wivelsfield parish church, TQ 338 207, sits high on the Long Ridge's ancient east-west trackway that runs eastwards from Bedelands, past Theobalds, Antye, Lunces, and on beyond More Farm. There, its original course has been lost. The Yew on the north side of the church (with only half of its trunk surviving) is

Every lane was a green lane. Now they're a rarity! Cow Lane, Wivelsfield.

probably the oldest thing on the site, perhaps marking a pre-Christian holy place. The church's dedication to St John the Baptist, whose midsummer (24th June) saints day was marked by hilltop bonfires,[3] may represent continuity with the pagan solstice celebrations. The narrow north door is Saxo-Norman.

West of the church, beyond the stream valley lies the 'hamlet' of **Theobalds and Antye**, TQ 325 206, two farms that have developed separately, but which probably originated in the Saxon period as a single defended settlement on high ground. Their field pattern, even today, reflects their origin as an early cooperative farming community. Antye has at its core a timber framed hall house of circa 1400, and Theobalds is of the 16th and 18th century, with a Horsham slab roof perhaps quarried on the farm (just as the sandstone rubble of Wivelsfield church may have been quarried from adjacent Lunce's Common[4]). The farms were sold off field by field as plotlands by the Otehall Estate in 1920, and the Valebridge Road and Janes Lane frontages 'ribbon developed'. For all that, their countryside still retains a patchwork of tiny ancient woods and fields. A lovely Hornbeam-hedged green lane tracks north from Antye past **Tilebarn Wood**, TQ 330 210, (Hornbeam coppice with Bluebells and Holly) and across the infant Adur to Fox Hill.

To the south, beyond a screen of woodland, is the grand, timber framed Tudor mansion of **Great Ote Hall,** TQ 331 202, as good as the timber manor houses of the Cheshire plain, so fine is it.

North of **Clearwaters Farm** the Wealden Clay gives way to sandstones, and the ground rises beyond ancient **Kiln Wood**, TQ 329 219, to meet painful new built development on the south edge of Haywards Heath,

Great Ote Hall: as good as the timber manor houses of the Cheshire plain

further squeezing the strategic gap between the mid Sussex towns.

WEST OF THE BRIGHTON LINE: HEASELANDS, ASHENGROUND, AND CUCKFIELD

There is dense cover of woods in this area, mostly ancient, some new. Many of the woods on the Heaselands estate have been heavily replanted, with lots of ornamentals too, but the hangars to the north and west of **Hease**lands, TQ 311 228, feel wild and natural. 'Hese' is Saxon for brush or underwood, and these woods could have been coppiced for iron furnaces since Roman times or earlier. If you face north on the bridge where Copyhold Lane crosses the little river, TQ 302 230, you look towards the site of a **Tudor iron making forge**, TQ 302 235, next to Mackrell's, a timbered cottage perhaps as old as the forge. If you face south, the broken pond bay of its twin **iron making furnace**, TQ 303 230 is nearby. Old Furnace Cottage, Furnace Wood and Cinder Bank are adjacent.

Below, and east of the lost Furnace, e.g. TQ 305 229, the **Furnace stream gill** narrows like a Welsh mountain ravine: steamy, damp, green, moss-and-fern-draped. The stream riffles over a shingle of furnace slag and sandstone and noisily pounds over several mini-waterfalls. There are winklestone fossils. Rotten logs and collapsed trees and banks make soggy and dodgy 'bridges' across the stream, with exposed wet clay and broken sandstone smears. There's Violet Helleborine orchis in the brush, and both large thallose and tiny liverworts and mosses.

Further east, a tributary of the Furnace stream flows down **Copyhold Gill** to meet it, e.g. TQ 309 231. It is a wonderfully long, deep, dark, sandrocky place, with fine Oaks – tall and straight – that host woodpeckers' nests with noisy fledglings. It is a place of ferns … abundant Male, Scaly Male, Soft Shield, Narrow Buckler, Broad Buckler, Hard Fern and Hart's Tongue. It has Shining Hookeria (far from its High Wealden strongholds) and St Winifred's Mosses by the water. Rhodedendron is very tangled and extensive in its western hangars, as we might expect near the pleasure grounds of a mansion.

The Saxons imagined goblins in this countryside, for the name *Pook* **Ryde** still lingers for one of the little woods, TQ 300 229, west of Old Furnace Cottage.

Southwards, the **flood brooks of the Furnace stream west of Great Wood and Hookhouse Farm,** e.g. TQ 306 217, are partly bushed up and partly topped to cut back the tall herb growth. There is Marsh Valerian and Ramsons amongst the Nettles. The sun reaches in and attracts rich animal life, including lightly flitting Giant Lacewing, *Osmylus fulvicephalus*.

The majority of the old hedges in this area are intact, though there's a lot of arable land. There are many old timber-framed-and-tile-hung cottages and farmsteads: West Riddens, Ansty Place, Lodge Farm, Mackrells, Upper and Lowers Ridges, Little Burchetts, and Lye's. At an old cottage amongst the woods we counted four rooftop CCTV cameras, two big 'keep off'-type notices on a gate, and the Hound of the Baskervilles (I think it was) in a pen. Oh! … the simplicity of country life!

Walking across **Ashenground Bridge**, TQ 327 230, from the suburbs of Haywards Heath into the greenwood, used to be like stepping through the back of the wardrobe. Deer would stare, then step away from the path. Bold and unaware, a Water Shrew ran to and fro, up, down and along the stream bank, swam, both on the surface and under the surface. For more than five timeless minutes I was privy to its life. So much life … drifts of Wild Daffodils in March, Bluebells a bit later. Bumble Bee nests, Field Mice, Pygmy Shrews, Bank Voles, Palmate Newts in flooded vehicle ruts. Orpine on the site of a cottage garden reclaimed by woods for centuries, a Grass Snake by a tree stump, a Giant Ichneumon Wasp[5] like a little black snake, wiggling across the top of a pine log on Pierce's Wood's cleared ground, Yellow Legged Clearwing moths resting on a cut oak stump from which they had freshly emerged (they are another harmless stinging wasp mimic, like the Giant Ichneumon), big Pine Borer Longhorn beetles[6] on the trunks, too.

Where housing estates and roads now stand we sat on summer nights whilst Glow Worm males pinged into our moth trap, with Peppered Moths, Emeralds, Green Oak Tortrix, Ruby Tigers, Rosy Footmen, Coxcomb Prominents, Lobster Moths, and all the rest … and on summer days I stalked Green Tiger Beetles and iridescent jewel wasps, and got to see Tree Pipits.

Over several years the astonishing diversity of woodland plants became clear, and by the end of my time there I had amassed a list of 54 ancient woodland indicator plants, putting the woods on a par with the best and most protected sites in the country.

However, this quality did not save the complex. I mourn the bulldozing of so much of **Ashenground Woods,** sold for development by the Heaselands Estate (and now re-named 'Bolnore Village'). The woods' defence was hard fought for many years, and the parts that remain are a tribute to its defenders.[7]

Cuckfield's church spire, TQ 303 244, on rising ground overlooking the vale, is a landmark for many miles.[8] The church is a great barn of a place with an enormous Horsham stone roof and fine carved ceilings, bulling-up a medieval town which was both a big market and a baronial hunting centre of the de Warenne lords of Lewes Rape. They had two deer parks there, one on the slopes south of the town (crossed now by the Cuckfield bypass). It was disparked in the 16th century. Timber framed **Lodge Farm**, TQ 305 235, probably originated as a deer park lodge, maybe in the late 15th century.

The best part of the town is the ancient huddled quarter by the church, but the whole town is full of venerable buildings … though it has an empty, lost, tweedy feel. Labour voters must feel as lonely as modern Cuckoos in the place, though Cuckoos were once so abundant that the town was named after them.[9]

The **museum**, in the High Street, holds much, including local dinosaur fossils and rare books … and friendly, helpful staff.

After the partition of the estates of the failed de Warenne male line, and the disparking of their deer parks, a member of the new class of plutocratic iron masters built **Cuckfield Park mansion**, TQ 298 244, in 1580, to the west of the church. He may have used stones that remained from the old hunting lodge of the de Warenne's, which stood near the church's south wall.[10] The nicest bit of the mansion is its brick gatehouse with four octagonal turrets … very 'knights of the round table'. **Cuckfield Park**, around the house, sadly has no ancient trees left, I think. The best of it is **New England**

Heaselands Forge: waterfalls are a rarity in the Weald.

Wood, TQ 298 249, north of the house, an ancient woodland nature reserve around a gill.

The **north verge at the western end of the Cuckfield bypass**, TQ 297/8 239, has colourful archaic meadow vegetation, with much Dyers Greenweed (2012). Between the bypass and the church is the long-established **Laines Organic Farm**.

THE CLAY VALE: LONDON ROAD (A23) TO HARVEST HILL AND PAINS FLAT (B2036)

Despite the appalling noise pollution near to the A23, this countryside remains lovely.

Lovell's[11] **Farmstead**, TQ 274 223, has tall chimneys, ancient barns of herringboned ironstone and ashlar (Cuckfield Stone?), an ancient Oak, little ponds … and chickens. Behind it are large woods. **Foxashes** wood, TQ 280 224, is ancient, with much Sweet Chestnut coppice, some recently cut. The richest part is along the eastern boundary stream. **Chaites Wood**, TQ 275 219, is mostly secondary, but nice.

North of **Stair Bridge**, TQ 273 209, **Stairbridge Lane** has at least two working farms (Stairbridge and Field Place) and often wide, grassy, mown verges. **Chaites Farmstead**, TQ 269 214, has a range of good Victorian and early 20th century outbuildings, including granary and threshing barn of sandstone, and big tiled roofs. **Wantley Wood,** TQ 268 218, is ancient (Oak-Hazel, with Bluebells) and well managed, with major efforts to control Rhodi infestation.

Little **Wortleford**[12] **Wood**, TQ 278 212, running down to the clay banks of the Adur, is emblematic of the best of the Low Weald. Bluebells are almost 100% dominant, under Oak and Hazel, with large Hornbeam coups and Crab Apple. Cuckoos call, distant and near. On the meadow banks of the Adur, east and west of the Wood, Demoiselle Agrions (of both species) cluster in dormitories in the reed beds as the vernal evening cools. **Wortleford Bridge**, TQ 282 210, in Maytime has Wild

'NORTHERN ARC' WOODS AND ANCIENT MEADOWS

The 'Northern Arc' is a projected major development zone in the lovely Vale of the River Adur.

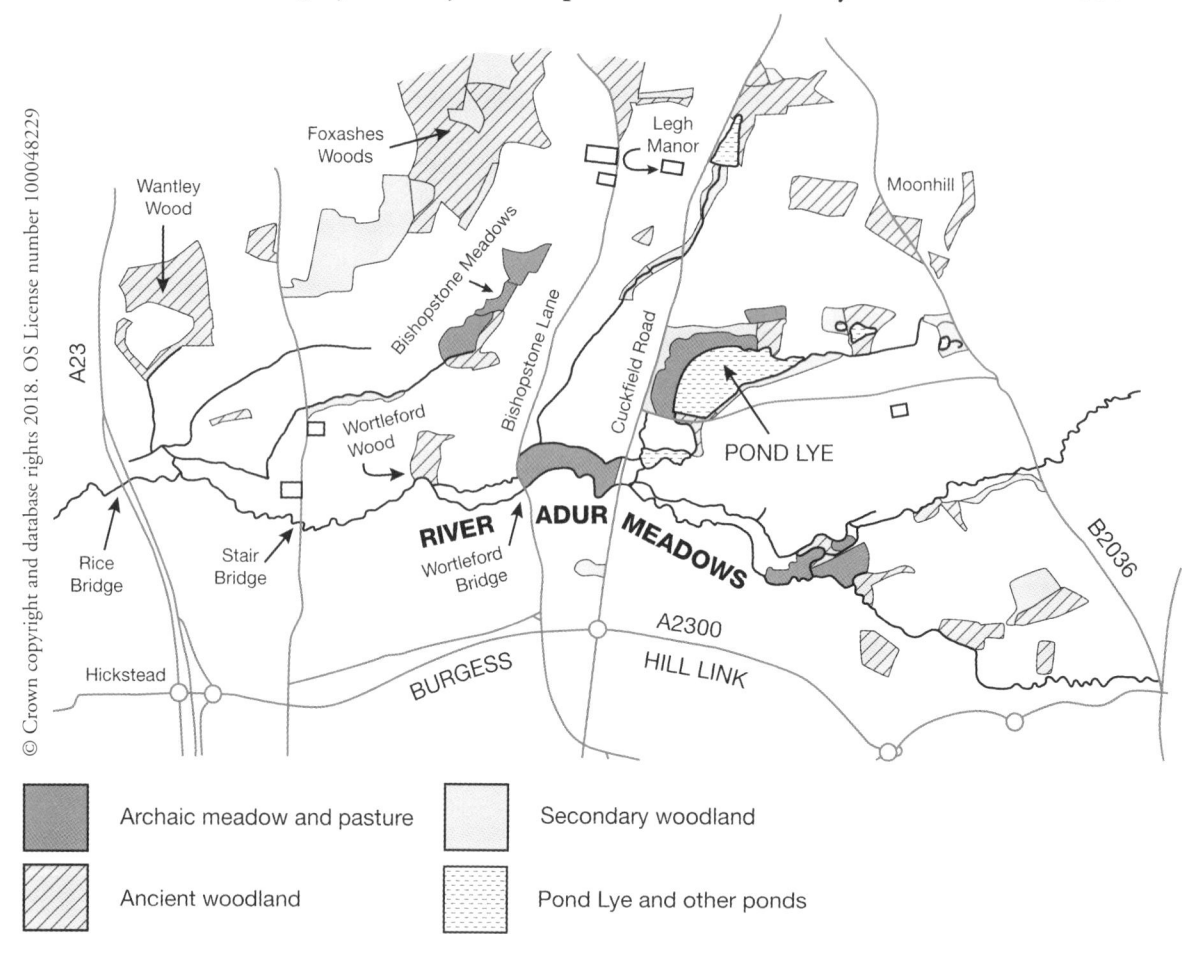

- Archaic meadow and pasture
- Ancient woodland
- Secondary woodland
- Pond Lye and other ponds

Hop sprawling over the bushes, frothing Cow Parsley, rampant Dog Rose, Sallow cotton from the bushes by the gurgling weir, and rich insect life. There's only a slight smell from the large sewage works upstream. The meadow to the east, TQ 284 211, is flowery and colourful.

There are Glow Worms on the sometimes meandering, sometimes sunken **Bishopstone Lane**. **Hilders Farm and Bishopstone Farm**, form a huddle,[13] TQ 285 223, with a cluster of good old buildings: weatherboarded and rubblestone barns, Lodge Cottage, and little timber framed Hilders[14] Farmhouse. **Three meadows** to the south west, TQ 280 216, retain their archaic vegetation (2014) with Dyers Greenweed, Sneezewort. Trailing Tormentil, Pepper Saxifrage, and Betony, though little managed and succeeding to scrub and woodland. Close by **Legh Manor and Barn**, TQ 288 222, also form a fine old group, though much poshed up. The Manor used to belong to the Sussex Archaeological Society, open to the public. Not any more.

Reed Warblers are noisily busy in spring at **Pond Lye**, TQ 289 214. It is a delight, thanks to its benign management[15] and the heroic work of conservation volunteers on its derelict meadows, though they desperately need the help of grazing cattle. The wet southern meadows are rushy, with Pepper Saxifrage, and the northern, drier meadows have much Betony and Devil's Bit (and Ragwort) and still had Spiny Restharrow in 2011. There is scarce Bladder Sedge fen amongst the sallow carr. A wonderful rough place, with flocks of Goldfinch in winter, and big flocks of Martins over the pond in summer. One Christmas afternoon, we sat on the pond bay with ginger chocolate biscuits and hot tea, entertained by a pair of Kingfishers. On hot summer days the yellow ant queens (four of five times the size of their consorts and workers) arise in clouds from their anthill cities. At dusk in winter armies of birds – Fieldfares, Rooks, Starlings and Wood Pigeons – come in to roost in the fringing woods. It could be the 1950s …

North of St Paul's Catholic College and the Burgess Hill Link Road (A2300) there's a **spur of higher** ground, between two branches of the **Adur**, TQ 294 207/8, partly clothed in old shaws, full of Bluebells. It is lightly grazed by Sussex bullocks and horses (2013). There are mossy old anthills, Broom along the wood edge, and Quaking Grass on the south slope. There's frogspawn on the flooded lower ground by the Adur, which forms a wiggly green ribbon of lushness, between young willows. In autumn the mists rise up over the spur, and the cobwebs on the grass are spangled with dew. West of the spur, north of the sewage works, the brooks are wild and unkempt, TQ 289 209, with big Nettle swarms, but the Martins and Swallows hunt above, and the shaws are a mass of Bluebells, with gnarled old Hornbeam and Ash.

North and south of **Paynes Place**, TQ 296 213, the hedgerows, small woods, brooklands, pits and ponds are mostly still intact.

All this is mortally threatened by the Northern Arc development proposals. A new solar array now crowds Pond Lye (an erstwhile candidate SSSI) on its south side.

PICKWELLS, HORSMANHOAD AND BROXMEAD: DEEP WOODS AND GILLS

'Deep' is a word that springs to mind to describe this area … deep woods, deep gills, the deep past. It is a good countryside to get mildly lost in. Its oldest place names evoke untamed qualities: Moorfields Farm; Horsmanhoad and Hoadsherf (hoad = 'heath'); Barnsnape (probably 'steep boggy land'); Thorndean ('thorny swine pasture')' Pookchurch Pit, TQ 279 248/9 (puca = 'goblin'); Broxmead ('brocc smeagel'[16] = Badger hole); and Raggetts ('ra geat' = Roe Deer gate).

You enter big woods with running streams the moment you enter **Buncton Lane or Pickwells Lane**, e.g. TQ 271 224. Only the noise of the London Road anchors you in present time. Many of these woods are modified by modern conifer plantings, but some are in the process of restoration, and there are large new woods connecting fragmented ancient woods. There are Wild Daffodils here and there, other worldly Scarlet Elf Cup in wet spots just after Snowdrop time, and Violet Helleborine orchis under summer's shady canopy.

Walking up **Pickwell's Lane** I look forward to seeing an old friend, the Sessile Oak giant on the east side bank, with its massive clean bole, shooting upwards, TQ 280 233. Sessile Oak is a feature of these woods, with a grove in the south east corner of **Long Wood**, TQ 281 239, by the footpath and the field edge. In **Raggetts Wood** it is new planted. **Westup Wood**,

Dead Badger on *Brox*mead Lane: named for its Badgers perhaps a millennium ago (*brocc smeagel* = Badger hole). The name gives them no protection now.

TQ 286 239, has Sessile Oak too, as has **Pickwells Shaw**, TQ 282 232, with Wild Service Tree. There are big wooded pits on Long Wood's north slope, probably dug for Grinstead Stone. Old **Hoadsherf Farm,** TQ 285 236, has the quality of an assart, scooped out of the forest. Does it still have its flock of white Geese grazing the stubble? A new vineyard (2015) crowds the footpath along the wood edge to its north, with its 2m fencing, stopping our hunts along the tilled land for flint artefacts.

The **Black Forest**, TQ 281 236, is modern conifer planting, now with much Birch, but old caravans, huts, chalet, earth moving, and builders' materials, make an ugly mess (2012).

Up **Deaks Lane**, across the valley northwards from Westup Wood is the site of lost **Westup Farm**, TQ 285 247, now just rusty straw and cattle barns, but behind them on the vertical bank is a muscly, bent monster of a tree: an English Oak pollard all of 3.5 spans in girth. On the clay bands of these slopes, the old hedges are glorious in autumn colours: red, orange and egg yellow Maple, with Spindle, Hazel, Dogwood, Ash and Dog Rose. A short distance north again, Deaks Lane bridges a gill stream. On the east side **Hook Wood**, TQ 287 251/2, and on the west side **Wyllies Wood**, have been brutally coniferised, and the dark, bare ground runs right to the water's edge. However, west of Wyllies Wood the gill turns north, with intact ancient woodland, spectacularly steep mini-ravines, waterfalls and tumbled trees, TQ 283 252.

At the top of Deaks Lane, near **Henmead**, it's all very posh big houses with daft gates … "a non-community with silly big gates," as Jane said.

Along the high watershed ridge tracked by **Sloughgreen Lane** (between the basins of the Ouse and the Adur) I know of only one surviving fragment of its old moorland vegetation, in a **hidden meadow just south of Pitts Head Crossroads**, TQ 268 258. It has probably succeeded to thicket, now, but the Devils Bit, Sneezewort and Tormentil survived in 2011. On its tussocky grassland, I learnt that all three autumn spiders, the Marbled Orb Weaver, the Four Spot Orb Weaver, and the Garden Orb Weaver, are efficient catchers of Bumblebees … of several species.

Between Broxmead Lane and the London Road, a winding valley is cloaked with the intact ancient woodland of **The Hanger**, e.g. TQ 272 249: a place of English Oak, Ash, Birch and Gean, over abundant old coppice Hazel. For nearly a mile its shady gill stream, with big fleshy liverworts, runs through this wood. New woods have been added to it in places, such as where **Little Thorndean Farm** once stood, TQ 273 251, now marked only by a little quarry: a hollow where the well once was, the remains of an outgrown Ash hedge … and a wonderful Oak pollard in blooming health, with the broadest sheltering canopy. We found flint flakes and broken microliths in the ploughland adjacent.

On the west side of the gill stream a landslip, TQ 272 245, recently brought Wadhurst Clay and sandstone crashing into The Hanger, splintering trees into an inpenetrable tangle.

The little **Merryfields**[17] **valley** north of Broxmead Lane, has a cluster of three archaic grasslands, two on the south side of the stream and one on the north. The pasture that the footpath descends from the Lane, TQ 275/6 241/2, was ploughed as recently as thirty years ago, but now has much Adders Tongue Fern, with Common Spotted Orchis. To its east, a tiny pasture now cared for in the grounds of Merrybrook, TQ 278 241, has Heath Spotted Orchis, Ragged Robin and Devil's Bit. There are Stock Doves in tree holes, Grass Snakes, and Bullhead in stream pools.

The best site, though, is an **isolated meadow** on the north side of the stream, TQ 277 242. On a sunny, early June day (2012) it was full of small and busy creatures … often with lovely names … like the Green Gem, *Microchrysa flavicornis,* the Broad Centurion, *Chloromyia Formosa,* and the Common Orange Legionnaire, *Beris vallata* – all Soldierflies – and Black Snipefly, *Chrysopilus cristatus,* with golden hair on its thorax. There's Common Blue, Small Copper and Dingy Skipper butterflies, damsels and lacewings, Linnet and Lark, Thrush and Blackbird song. Though it was mostly left uncut it still retains Dyers Greenweed (just one clump), but Ox Eye Daisy, Common Spotted Orchis and Pepper Saxifrage are widespread, and Spring Sedge and Zigzag Clover cling on, with Common Valerian down by the stream. It is a small piece of heaven. Trail bikes had done some damage. It's been grazed more recently (2016).

ENDNOTES

1. *Pers comm.* Colin R. Pratt, County Recorder of Butterflies and Moths. (2011).
2. The late Saxon and Norman name for the Wealden forest.
3. And still is, in many countries, such as those of Scandinavia, where midsummer fires burn on many a hill and mountain. The church is also now dedicated to St Peter.
4. 'Wivelsfield, The History of a Wealden Parish', edited by Heather Warne. Pier Point Publishing & Wivelsfield History Study Group (1994).
5. *Rhyssa persuasoria,* or an allied species. They call them Sabre Wasps too, though the long swords coming out of their behinds are ovipositors, not weapons. They drill down through the wood to reach and lay their eggs in the grubs of another large stinging wasp mimic, the Horntail, *Urocerus gigas,* a Sawfly wasp glimpsed occasionally amongst Pierce's Wood's pines.
6. Better known as Dusky Longhorn beetles, *Arhopalus rusticus,* big jobs an inch long that may have spread southwards from their original redoubt in the Caledonian Pine Forest.
7. Like the late Roy Horobin, of the Friends of Haywards Heath, and Tony Whitbread, then Chief Executive of the Sussex Wildlife Trust. I am proud to have paid my part in the later stages, too.
8. The spire was burnt in 1980 and rebuilt on a new steel frame.
9. Cuckfield was 'Kukufeld', 'Cucufeld', 'Kukefeld' in the half century after the 1066 Norman conquest.
10. 'A history of the parish of Cuckfield', page 77. Cooper (1912).
11. The name 'Lovel' presumably from 'hlot feld': open land divided by lot – commoned land.
12. Wortleford is not named after a flower, but from the Saxon personal name 'Wyrtel'.
13. Could these twin farms be another example of an erstwhile medieval, co-farmed, assarted holding? The Lane bends around them in a long arc, implying that the holding pre-dated its delineation.
14. The name 'Hilders' can be traced back to 1296 and probably refers to the person who lived here, on this slope, or 'hylde' (Saxon).
15. It is leased by the Sussex Piscatorial Society and the meadows are managed by the Woodland Flora and Fauna Group of Hurstpierpoint and Sayers Common, who both deserve our thanks.
16. Smeagel (meaning 'burrow') was modified to Smeagol by Tolkien to name the creature later called Gollum.
17. Merryfields may be merry, but the 'merry' bit probably comes from the fields' proximity to the (Cuckfield parish) boundary = (ge)maere (Saxon).

Pond Lye: a place of foraging birds, water birds, woodland birds, wintering birds and roosting birds

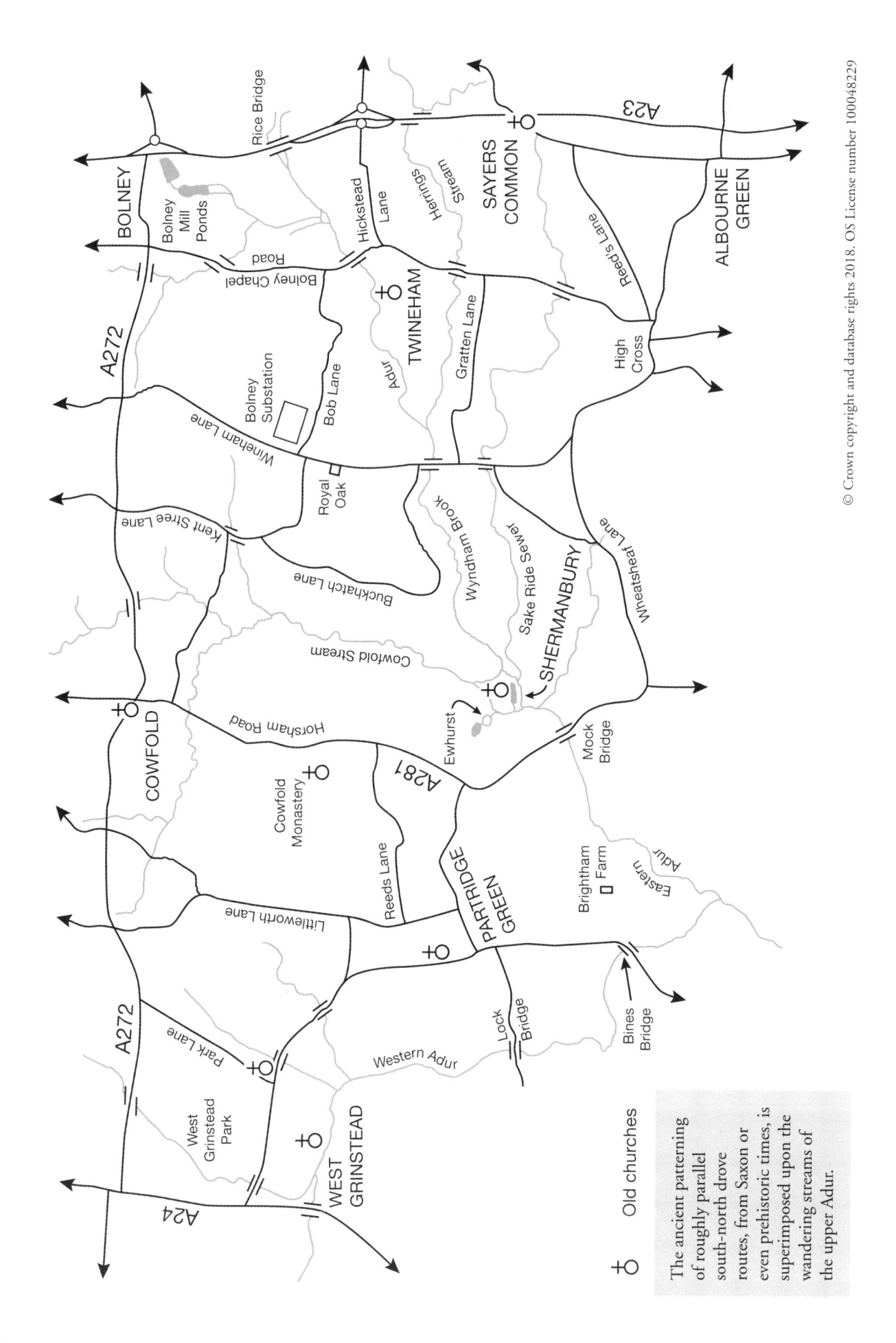

230 **AREA GUIDE** / Chapter 17: West Grinstead to Twineham: Nightingale country

CHAPTER 17
Nightingales, waterlands and droves – the heart of the Low Weald:
West Grinstead to Twineham; Cowfold to Shermanbury

Tender indeed is the night,[1] under the darkening sky, in peace, in silence, save for the Nightingale.[2] These brooks, these thickets, these unregarded ancient hedges, broken willows, and tangled corners are now their heartland, their redoubt, in their relentless retreat.

Nightingale

Day's warmth, with cool of dusk … and liquid, bubbling music.

I half sit, half lie in this small grassy glade.
Big thickets of bramble, blackthorn-topped, enclose me, bounded by scrub oak and birch.
By my elbows stand a company of bugle – blue-mauve candles shining in the fading light.
There's noise of planes, though happily far off.
A distant cuckoo that has circled me all evening calls, now faint.
A wakened magpie family squeak and re-settle.
A cock pheasant coughs. Whitethroats jingle.

The sky is dove-grey and cream, shot by sinking sun;
The trees and bushes are freshest, spring leaf-green;
The half moon takes the old sun's light,
And, like an old bar heater, it begins to glow …

… Whilst, filling all this place, you weave the loveliest sounds …
Refined by golden evening light and gently sighing trees.
Full, even when soft; clear-voiced in every note;
Buzzing, zitting, making melody …
… Fluting wet-throated lyrics,
Slip slap trills and arabesque warblings,
Rattling … reflective … bold …
Teazing, wheezing out long tip-toe riffs …
Then staccato calls that cannot be ignored …

The music of night silence, dawn's loud chorus, evening peace.

Distant thrush and blackbird harmonise with your song, pause, then cease,
And leave the world to you.

Few things in wild nature have so moved me as this hour,
And my mind, seeking analogy, turns insistent back to human love.
I sense this moment as intensely, with all my heart and body,
As when I lie beside my love, in each other's arms.

I am all, every bit of me, here with you, little brown bird,
As you pour forth your passion.

It is not me you call for,
But your music breaks the wall between your failing world and mine.

Nightingale Country: Cowfold Stream's brooks

Frylands Farm on the Adur brooks at Wineham

We have had such delightful times along these rivers and streams. Before sunrise in April, mist lies over the dew-soaked brooks and the bird chorus fills the air. There is Song Thrush on every side … Blackbirds … Chiffchaff … a drum section of courting woodpeckers, the loudest Wrens, the melodies of warblers and Robins. In the thicker cover, first one, then another … and another Nightingale sings up. Pairs and small parties of Canada Geese and Greylags honk by, and Rooks are already noisy. The Milkmaids, Cuckoo Flower in the taller grass cease to stand out so luminously white, as dawn light strengthens. Under the wood edge, below the pussy willow catkins, the Kingcups shine glorious yellow in the first warm sun. When I get home my head is filled with a quiet tinnitus of bird music … soft crowdings of song … quiet cuckoo calls. They remain there all day, and into the next day too … an unasked-for choral gift that brightens all I do.

On a mild October afternoon we settle on a picnic spot beside the near-still waters of the Adur, above the steep bank, with Bulrush nearby, not far from Frylands Farm. A herd of shorthorns and their calves – some blue, some fawn – wander the brook over the river. Night comes early at this season, and by six the western sky has turned apricot, with a pencil silver moon. The bats start to emerge. One large, long-winged, flies over the tall poplars rimming the brooks … a Serotine? Three or four medium sized bats begin patrolling above the river and making steep dives down to its surface. As they turn to dive their neat white breasts flash clear. Smaller, dark bats, sometimes three together, join in the river beat, enjoying these last harvests of river flies before the onset of winter cold. A Tawny Owl calls.

This flat waterland geography of the Adur's fingered streams is a land of '*hamms*', that word that the Saxons used to denote long, reedy brooks and meadows, wetlands hemmed in by higher ground, or land hemmed in by marsh.[3] Places like Twine*ham*, Bright*ham*, Sake*ham*, Wynd*ham* (now Wine*ham*), and Chest*ham*. It embraces the lands between the Western and Eastern arms of the Adur, and it embraces the confluence of the Eastern Adur and the Herrings (or Heron) Stream, all of the Sake Ride Sewer,[4] and much of the Cowfold Stream.

There is another forgotten geography too, that stripes this landscape in long south-north parallels: the geography of the drove roads. Probably early medieval, maybe some earlier still, these were the wide ways whereby the cultivators of the rich lands of the coastal plain, the Downs, and the under-down spring line, brought their swine for the autumn pannage (nut harvest) in the Wealden woods, and their cattle for the lush bite of the meadowlands. Some of these droves are plain to see. The Horsham Road, A281, was one of them. So was Wineham Lane, and Kent Street, Littleworth Lane and Bolney Chapel Road. Others have faded greatly into the landscape, though hedgelines and old boundaries mark them out, like that going north from High Cross through Twineham Place, and on to Spronketts Wood north of the A272.

Though trees are everywhere, this is a landscape with only a light dusting of small ancient woods: none large. Our maps show more names that denote old woodland clearance (*Reeds* Farm and Lane, *Inholmes* Farm, *Riddens* Farm, Sake *Ride* and Ship*rods* Farm)[5] than names that denote ancient woodlands (Cow*fold*, Oaken*dene*, Ew*hurst*). In fact, the flora of ancient woodland has often retreated to the hedges and shaws along the swine pasture droves, which in ecological terms, have some of the 'refugia' function that the gills play in the High Weald. Wild Service tree survives at two sites at least along Bolney Chapel Road, and one on Littleworth Lane, whilst Bluebells, Anemones and Midland Thorn grace Wineham Lane's banks.

Commons and greens here have withered to extinction. The last were eliminated through the nineteenth century. Jolesfield Common and Partridge Green, the largest survivors, were enclosed in 1872, and

232 AREA GUIDE / Chapter 17: West Grinstead to Twineham: Nightingale country the last bit of Blacklands Common had gone by 1845. The Royal Oak green on Wineham Lane went about 1800. It is now a caravan site. Only Sayers Common survives as a public space, though it is not registered common or green, and is now enclosed by hedges. It is only along the wide verges of the swine pasture droves that the old wastes survive, sometimes as mown grassland, sometimes as tall herbage, and sometimes as wood or thorn thicket.

However, over the last two centuries a series of new woods have been planted, many quite recently, whilst others have grown up from old furze fields, or from land left derelict. Some of these secondary woods now form quite large clusters, such as around Shermanbury and Ewhurst: Waymarks Wood, TQ 202 198, the Buckhatch Lane woods, TQ 226 206, the Shiprods Farm woods, TQ 222 185, or Furzefield Wood, TQ 185 220. Some of the older secondary woods have acquired many ancient woodland species, and have been managed on traditional lines, like Bugshole Copse, TQ 242 224, or Eastlands Wood, TQ 216 222. They are wholly delightful, and difficult to distinguish from ancient woodland.

From all along the South Downs Way, and from higher ground all over the Wealden plain, the 203ft spire of St Hugh's Monastery at Cowfold stands out. It is to the Low Weald, what Chichester Cathedral spire is to the western Sussex Downs and coastal plain.

The area south west of Cowfold, as far south as the monastery, has suffered greviously from the bulldozing of small woods, hedgerows and old farm sites. Other areas have suffered to lesser extents. West Grinstead Park lost its huge lawn pastures, probably during the Second World War. However, round Twineham's Hooker's Farm, the large fields have been present for at least 150 years and there are more fence lines now than there were then!

Some areas have preserved the ancient Low Wealden farmscapes of small fields with rich, full hedgerows, as around Well Land Farm, north of Littleworth, TQ 186 214, Cratemans Farm, by Cowfold Stream, TQ 218 210, and Frylands Farm, TQ 231 197. Blanches Farm, north of Partridge Green, TQ 196 200, is the most delightful of these, for it is a patchwork of old shaws and tiny pastures, most of which are only semi-improved and one unimproved.

In this area, four of the medieval churches (Shermanbury, Cowfold, West Grinstead, and Twineham) list their old parish farms on the backs of their pews, or on portions of the churchyard fencing, providing an accessible base-line for marking the agricultural collapse and drastic inter-class change in this countryside.

SHERMANBURY AND EWHURST MANOR

The Saxon settlers at Shermanbury chose a perfect defensive location, and at Christmas 2012 this was demonstrated again, as it must have been many times over the past ten centuries and more. **Shermanbury's manor house and church** on their knoll, TQ 214 188, surrounded on all sides by the Adur and the Cowfold Streams, became an island for 10 days, cut off by floods, with the park drive under three foot of water. Christmas church services had to be cancelled.

Shermanbury's Saxon name indicates its past function: the *burh* or defended stronghold of the *scir man* – shire man, perhaps the sheriff, but maybe some other official or steward.[6] Perhaps the *burh* was the stronghold of one of the Saxon longitudinal divisions of the county?[7] The abrupt slopes of the hillock used to be joined to the higher land to the east, but a second channel of the Cowfold Stream was cut through that peninsular long ago, making it an island. On that eastern side too, you can see the remains of an ancient bank and ditch[8] defending the peninsular *burh*. To the south of the 18th century Place (which replaced the earlier manor house) is a reedy mill pond, whose peace is only broken by the calls of water birds. To the west, where the old Cowfold Stream joins the Adur, are the footings, races, and wharf of the water mill that long clacked and rumbled there.

It is sad that the medieval church of Shermanbury is now locked, but the friendly church warden will show you round if you enquire. Its wildflower-rich graveyard is untouched by burials since it was declared full in 1888. Inside, each pew is marked with the name of the farms and houses to which it was allocated: Perrymans, Sakeham, Vadgers, Pooks, and so on. I counted 26 names, but not a single one of their respective farms is now farmed by its resident farmer, and just four let their land for farming by neighbouring farmers. The rest must be managed for leisure in its various forms. Frylands Farm was the last to be broken up and sold, in 2015.

Scattered about the knoll, and towards Ewhurst, are eight fine veteran Oaks, one over four spans girth. Sitting towards dusk in front of the graveyard looking north over those scruffy pastures one snowy February day, we watched a Barn Owl quartering the higher ground, quite oblivious to the two men working nearby.

Much is wild around the Place and its outbuildings and Park. The drive is cratered with potholes (2016). Its light-touch management, however, offers much more space for nature than over-busy tidying and modernisation. The wintering Snipe upon the brooks love it.

Neighbouring **Ewhurst Manor's** stone gatehouse and porter's lodge (of circa 1300) guarding its moat – still with water – look straight out of some Arthurian romance, but the poshed-up and much-extended manor house blows away any medievalist imaginings, TQ 211 189.

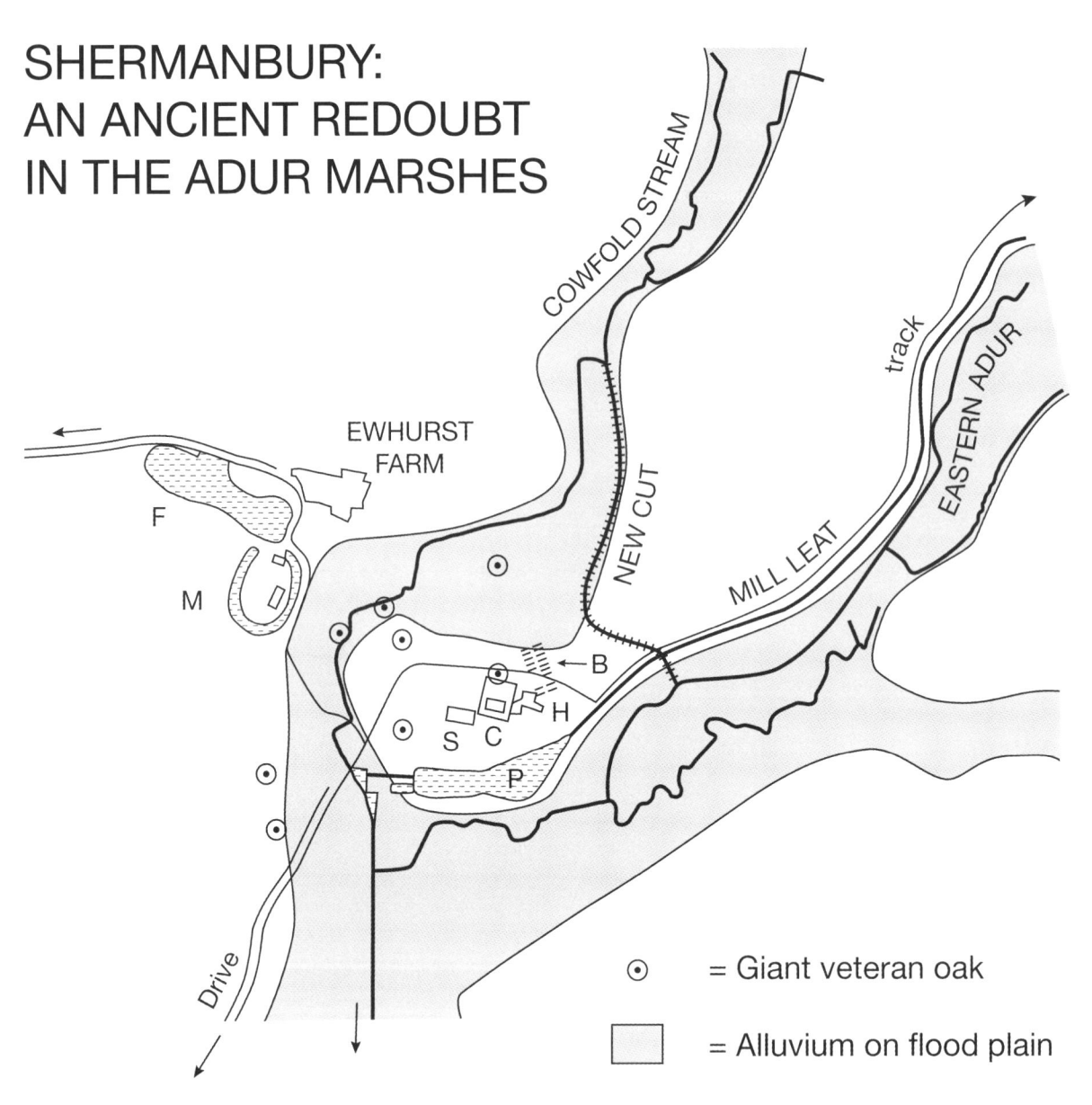

SHERMANBURY: AN ANCIENT REDOUBT IN THE ADUR MARSHES

⊙ = Giant veteran oak

▢ = Alluvium on flood plain

Ordnance Survey old map bases used with the kind permission of the Ordnance Survey.

Shermanbury was a Saxon 'burh', or fortified place, perhaps even an older 'promontory fort'. It was protected on three sides by the Cowfold Stream and the Eastern Adur (Wyndham Brook) at their confluence. It was protected on its eastern side by a bank and ditch, which is still visible in part. A modern cut, through which flows the re-directed Cowfold Stream, now severs the spur from the high ground to its east, thus making Shermanbury a kind of island.

The manorial cluster of big house, church, and home farm survive, and were joined some time before 1611 by a water mill, whose overgrown reedy pond survives, though the mill buildings are gone. There are wonderful giant Oaks. Nightingales sing of summer in the bushy thickets. Barn Owls hunt on the rough pastures. Water birds call, and bats of many species flit by in the dusk.

Ewhurst Manor rivalled Shermanbury from close by, though it is not mentioned in the Domesday Book. Its moat is still in water, and it has a grand medieval stone gatehouse.

Table of places
F – Fish pond, feeding Ewhurst Manor's moat
M – Ewhurst Manor's moat, medieval gatehouse, and part-Tudor house
S – Shermanbury Place (18th and 19th century)
C – Medieval parish church of St Giles
H – Home Farm
P – Mill Pond
B – The burh's ancient bank and ditch

THE COWFOLD STREAM VALLEY FROM SHERMANBURY AND EWHURST TO COWFOLD

In early April the Blackthorn hedges round the old brook meadows billow snowy white amongst the still-grey branches and twigs of other trees and shrubs. The Nightingales sing from the thickest of them. They sing a quiet song, these earliest arrivals. Some meadows which are rough and ungrazed are easy walking at this time, with Pond Sedge, Meadowsweet and Milkmaids, before the Hemlock Water Dropwort takes over. *By St George's Day, 23rd April,* there's a bevy of cock Nightingales in full voice. They're not the only singers. I'm getting used to the presence of a Mistle Thrush pair here, and the song of the Skylark from the Shermanbury ploughland comes from far-off. As I walk by Crateman's farmstead I realise that I can hear the brookland Nightingales – three or four of them – from way across two fields, and there are more close to me. The first pair of Swallows has arrived. Though this is Ash Country, the Buzzards have chosen a fine Oak along the brooks for their high nest. *By the 9th June,* I expect the Nightingales to be silent, but they are there still, some eight of them in voice, interspersing their song with alarm calls as I walk by, or stand admiring the fine hay crop, with so many different grasses mingling with Knapweed, Eggs and Bacon, Sorrel and the smell of Water Mint. By this time both the Blackthorn and the white May blossom are over, but the 'Pink May' Hawthorn variety of these local hedges is still in full bloom. A Grass Snake slithers into cover, as I close a gate behind me. I scramble down to the Stream to see what's there: caddis and stonefly, Freshwater Shrimps, Pea and Orb Shells, and dainty leeches. All around me in the thicket the Nightingales sing. I'm in a kind of heaven.

This is the heart of the area developers want for their Mayfield new town.

Some brook pastures are now horse-grazed, as are many fields around the **farms to the east of the Stream: Furzefield, Park, Pooks, Moatfield, Lower Barn and Lidford.** These are not working farms, though all of them are centuries old, with much timber framing. Most of the valley woods are secondary (but lovely), though small bits of ancient woodland survive, often along stream sides, with old Hornbeam stools, Bluebells and Primroses on the drier areas, and Alder and Ash on the wetter ground. I've had some fun in years gone by, looking for colourful slime moulds there on rotting logs.

Most of the land between Wineham Lane and Cowfold Monastery, south to Wineham Bridge, was part of the Bishop of Chichester's Gosden Chase in Norman times, and the big deer parks of Ewhurst and Shermanbury were carved from it. They were disparked in the seventeenth century, and now only the place names *Buckhatch* Lane and *Buckbridge Wood, Park* Farm and the site of *Horsepark* Barn, TQ 216 195, commemorate them.

On the west side of the Cowfold Stream, there are many Blackthorn hedges with Hawthorn and Oak, and they are often left tall, making good, dense

Blackthorn, Barn Owls, Nightingales: The upper Cowfold Stream

windbreaks. **Crateman's Farm** fields, TQ 218 210, are mostly left only partly 'improved', with many surviving archaic meadow herbs. It has a lovely vernacular tile-hung farmhouse, hovels and barns and much weather boarding. There's Wild Service tree in the hedge to the west. **Eastlands Farm,** TQ 218 221, has a superb hall house of circa 1374: Chaucer's time. It was a barn for centuries, and has now been sensitively re-converted to a posh house. Lovely but neutered, for it was built for chickens and wood smoke. **Eastlands Wood,** TQ 216 222, has abundant Bluebells under Oak, Ash, Hazel, much Hawthorn, frequent Maple, and some Midland Thorn. It is a treasure for neighbouring Cowfold residents.

KENT STREET, THE RIDGE, BUGSHOLE COPSE AND WINEHAM LANE

Around Kent Street and Kings Lane, there are many old timber framed farmhouses and cottages, though there seem to be no working farms. West of Kent Street, there are tiny fields with hedges thick with fine old oaks, many around two spans in girth. There's a characterful and burry Oak pollard, TQ 228 217, north of Kings Lane. One April day we sat on the edge of the pit in **Taintfield**

THE WATERLANDS

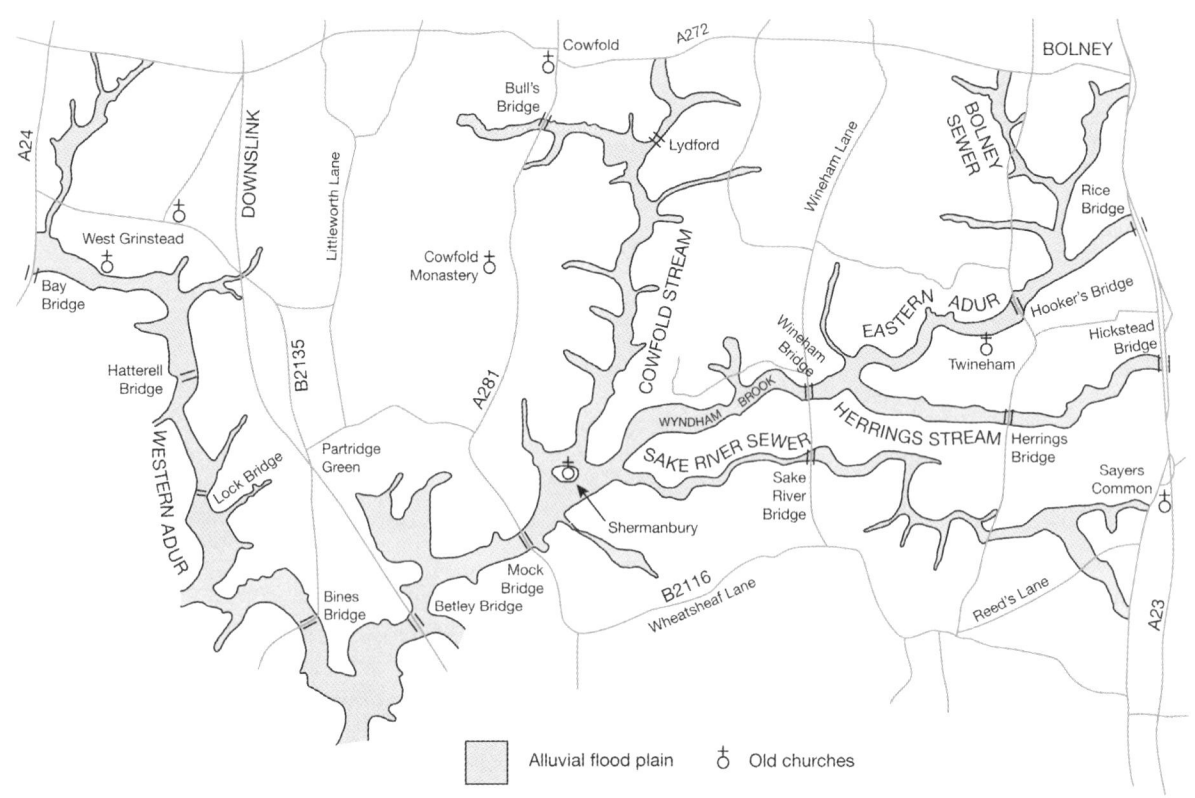

© Crown copyright and database rights 2018. OS License number 100048229

> The flood plain of the Eastern and Western Adur is central to the character of this gentle, tranquil, flat landscape. Its wet pastures and glinting water have piping Kingfishers and wintering Snipe, Ducks, Geese and Swans. It is all threatened by proposals for a new town to serve the over-developing regional economy.

Wood, TQ 228 220, and watched a Spotted Flycatcher darting out over the pond: back and forth. The main part of the wood is a sheet of Bluebells in spring, with lots of Primroses, but the thicket of thorn and Birch has been mostly cleared, now, and most of its Nightingales have gone.

From Taintfield Wood eastwards to Coombe House, TQ 248 214, across both Kentstreet and Wineham Lanes, there is a low ridge marking an outcrop of Horsham Stone, and many of the wooded pits are old stone quarries. The ridge is topped by the modern **Eastridge and Westridge Farms, and Eastridge Place**, with many horsey paddocks.

Wineham Lane, as it cuts through the ridge, widens to perhaps three times the width of a normal two lane roadway. It is colourful with ancient woodland wild flowers. At its northern end is **Bugshole Copse**, TQ 242 224. It is a wet wood, more so at its northern end, and when I last visited, in early spring, Scarlet Elf Cup fungus was all over the wood. Anemone and Bluebell share dominance with Dogs Mercury, and Pendulous Sedge is frequent. There's Midland Thorn and Early Dog Violet under managed Hazel coppice, with Oak, Ash, Sallow and much Birch. Gean and Holly are on its Wineham Lane wood bank.

TWINEHAM, BOLNEY MILL PONDS AND HICKSTEAD

Around **Twineham** is a level, open countryside of meandering lush streams and large fields, a bit like the best of old Norfolk in the well-timbered Weald. Along the streams, the sounds of Reed Warblers and Yellowhammers do their best to compete with the low roar of the London Road. A large Tawny Owl, of that kind which is largely grey, has made it its home (2016) and hunts along the thick hedgerows and low scrub much as a Barn Owl would.

Farms like **Twineham Place** have big spreads of modern industrial-scale shedding, whilst the derelict battery egg production sheds of **Whiteoaks Farm,** TQ 260 180, on Reeds Lane, covered several acres. They are now replaced by a 'tastefully' landscaped industrial estate. There is still a fair amount of cultivated ground and farmed land, relative to much of the Low Weald.

Twineham church, TQ 252 199, is a homely delight of local brick, the first of that material in mid Sussex, circa 1516.[9] It likely replaced a wooden church. Does

Twineham Church: Sussex's oldest brick church

that mean the beams and frames of some old local houses include recycled timbers from that earlier church? Inside, some of the aisle slabs are of fossil winklestone, for a Sussex marble band outcrops roughly along, but just south of, Gratten Lane. The pulpit and squire's pew have the finest carving: the former Jacobean, the latter Elizabethan. There's a Householder's Pew with old farm names gilded upon it.

From **Hooker's Bridge,** TQ 255 203, along the little Adur west to its **confluence with the Herrings Stream,** TQ 240 196, and back east to **Herrings Bridge,** TQ 254 193, the dragons and damsels dart and flit: Emperors, Chasers, gorgeous Banded Agrion, and many more. At the confluence the Reed and Greater Pond Sedge beds are extensive, and the discordant grating of bands of Reed Warblers – with Reed Bunting flocks – is on every side.

In spring, the Primroses are plentiful along **Gratten Lane,** e.g. TQ 245 192, with long views in all directions. At **Bob's Lane,** TQ 246 205, a pair of Barn Owls foraged the fields, hedgelines and wood edges. To the north of the lane, amongst Oak shaws and pastures, is the giant **Bolney electrical substation,** TQ 240 210, and its lines of pylons, now added to by the underground Rampion wind farm cables from the Channel, off the Brighton coast. There are lots of century-old red brick villas and timber framed cottages, both on the lanes and across the fields.

Just south of the A272 from Bolney, are the two exquisite **mill ponds,** TQ 264 221, of the lost Bolney Mill, surrounded by **Church and Pond Woods**, with their carpeting Bluebells. If only the London Road tinnitus would stop for one moment! Garston Farm (posh), Brookland Farm (working), TQ 254 218, Coombe House, Dawes Farm, Red House, Partridge Farm, and Purvey's Cottages are all ancient, with much timber framing. The **wood at Purvey's Pit,** TQ 249 219, is ancient and lovely, with Early Dog Violet, Sweet Woodruff, orchids, Primroses and Bluebells. Just west, TQ 247 219, the field appears to show old 'ridge and furrow'[10] cultivation preserved under pasture and visible in the slanted sunshine of late afternoon.

At **Hickstead,** the Herrings Stream cuts between the Show Jumping Course and Hickstead Place. West of the Course, the Stream passes a **wooded medieval moated site**, TQ 262 195, and several fine old Oaks ... precious fragments in a mess of road noise, show jumping clutter, and too-much-money.

SAYERS COMMON

Sayers Common Wood and Coombe Wood, e.g. TQ 267 180, sandwiched between the old and the new London Roads, are well-loved ancient Bluebell woods, large by the standards of this countryside ... but noisy. **Sayers Common church**, TQ 269 186, built in 1880, has a lovely wildflowery churchyard, with Ox Eye Daisy, Spring Sedge and Adder's Tongue Fern. We could not find the Green Winged Orchis that used to be there. Even on a frosty mid-December day, though, we were able to find five old meadow fungi, including the rare Straw Club, *Clavaria straminea* ... and my later lookings showed that there are many more.

Just west of the church, along the north edge of Furze Field wood, are **derelict brook meadows**, TQ 263 185, beautiful and rich in wildlife, but rapidly losing value (2012). We found a baby Roe fawn nestled amongst the Tufted Hair Grass and Dropwort next to the brook that divides the meadow. This tangle of coarse vegetation is squeezing out the Betony and Sneezewort, the Pepper Saxifrage, Devil's Bit, Tormentil and Spotted Orchis that still cling on around the edges. South of Furze Field is a **damp meadow** wholly dominated by Tufted Hair Grass, with some Spotted Orchids, TQ 262 182.

The countryside around the **ex-Priory, Stuccles and New House Farms**, TQ 263 189, has Oaks, Oaks, and more Oaks, and in July the Purple Hairstreaks can be seen flitting and sunning in their canopies.

CHESTHAM, SAKEHAM, BLACKLANDS

Chestham, TQ 214 179, was once a hamlet. Now only one of the old cottages survives, near the big posh house. There are good old Oaks in the park and one of them facing the footpath has CCTV cameras posted on it, and a notice saying 'beware dogs running free'. There's a rich crop of similar notices littering the place. At least neighbouring **Nymans** is still a working stock farm. The modern secondary broad-leaved woods – **Marl Wood, Eight Acre Shaw, Fir Tree Wood** – are all good places, as are the open brooklands along the south bank of the Wyndham Brook (the Eastern Adur). The **farm houses at Sakeham, Shiprods, Abbeylands and Nymans** are fine old listed buildings.

Along Wineham Lane the **twin bridges at Wyndham Pool,** TQ 236 195, **and Sake Ride,** TQ 236 189, are raised on meandering causeways. Over 2 decades ago, with my friend and her two boys, we collected reeds, rushes and twigs from the brook sides and made a small masted boat each, like Viking ships. In the long evening we went out to the little Adur, placed a tiny bit of firelighter on each boat and set them afloat and aflame to drift downstream in the dusk till their lights were extinguished in the gathering dark.

THE WATERLANDS FROM MOCK BRIDGE TO WEST GRINSTEAD

It rained solidly all day. Only stir-craziness and habit made us don our heaviest rain gear and come to **Bines Bridge**, TQ 189 175. We squelched our way along the upstream bank. Not far along, a big silent bird sat hunched on the branch of a nearby Oak … a Tawny Owl … getting some shelter under the tree canopy. We edged our way towards it … stayed silent … edged a bit more … stayed still … shunted forward … till we were just a few paces under the bird. Magic.

Way back before Beeching's closures, the low chundering of the Horsham Flyer's diesel engine used to turn to loud drumming as the train crossed **Betley Bridge** TQ 200 174, over the Adur. It gets lonelier now, on the flat lands where the two main arms of the river diverge. Towards **Brightham Farm**, TQ 194 178, there's little sign that the railway ever existed, amongst the bleak modern fields. Barn Owls still forage the rougher parts towards **Mock Bridge**, TQ 210 182, though, and faithful Swans with large families still claim the river as their own.

Bines Bridge is an anglers spot, and the fishers spread out along the banks north and south. These river reaches are gentle and often still. There is Tench, Bream, Carp, Pike and Roach, and, especially after dawn, Kingfishers pass. Mink are frequent. There's Banded Demoiselle, Black Tailed Skimmer and Scarce Chaser dragons and damsels. The Chaser is a rare beast nationally, and only found in Sussex on the Arun and the Adur. There's Amphibious Bistort near **Hookshile Bridge**, TQ 177 192, and we've listened to a pair of Turtle Doves purring near Lock Bridge.

Sitting on Adur's bank, near **Pinlands Farm** one January dusk, we watched pellucid sky and mirror river's pink streaks, be-taken by a flooding orange glow. The pinprick silver dot of the Evening Star, over Chanctonbury, grew large as darkness fell. In silence a Kestrel mobbed a sleepy Buzzard, till it fled. A pair of Barn Owls floated back and forth across wet tussocks, their whiteness fading as the darkness grew.

The river up to West Grinstead was navigable through the 19th century. There was a towpath, and locks south of **Lock Bridge**, TQ 179 184. Cattle graze the brooks. There has been much destruction of the old landscape on the higher ground to east and west however, and Whitenwick House, Hookstile's Barn, Cottages and hedges are all long gone.

The woods are still intact. **Hatterell's Wood**, TQ 179 199, and **Sandpit Copse**, TQ 178 208, are ancient and lovely, cloaking the slopes overlooking the river pastures.

West Grinstead Church, TQ 170 206, could only be of the Sussex Weald, with its heavy slab roof, and its muddle of aisles, extensions, monuments and furniture: Saxon, Norman, Early English and onwards. Its woodwork is a marvel: late medieval waggon vaultings, spire, and big porch; and pews, pulpit and screen from Tudor to Victorian in age. Its pews are all labelled with the farm and house names of the parish – at least 62, for this is a big parish. Less than 10, I think, are still working farms. Some are gone completely. Most are posh homes for 'life-style' owners.

A little footbridge takes you over the river southwards, though this was once an important crossing. The big **Glebe Farm**, just to the east, is a fine four-century-old brick building with slab roof, now much poshed-up.

WEST GRINSTEAD PARK TO LITTLEWORTH LANE

West Grinstead Park is a shadow of its ancient self, and its deer grazed pastures succumbed to the plough before I first visited, some 55 years ago. It still holds many delights, however. The old manor house moat and stews (fish ponds) survive, TQ 171 216, with scatters of ancient Oaks, and clumps of trees festooned with Mistletoe. The Rooks float back and forth in their ragged springtime battalions, and gangs of winter Fieldfare hurry from copse to covert and clump. Both old and newer mansions are gone, but by the site of the lost mansion is a huge doubled Oak veteran, TQ 176 219. The brooks, TQ 162 222, and ancient **Park Covert** are good.

Park Farm, TQ 168 224, was a plutocrat's stud, and its architecture of display is horrible. There are giant electronic ornamental gates on the main lane, which is a public footpath, but walkers must use a stile (2014).

Along Park Lane, on the Park's east side, is the very old fashioned **Griffin's Farm**, TQ 179 216, with a fine flock of ewes and their lambs in the little yard and hovel, next to a traditional weather boarded Sussex barn. To its east, its little hidden brook pastures and ancient shaw are graced by Snowdrops and Wild Daffodils.

The **Priest's House**, TQ 176 211, at the southern end of Park Lane, next to the catholic church, has an extraordinary history as a catholic safe house during the fierce religious persecutions of the 16th to 19th centuries. The catholic Caryll family, who owned West Grinstead Park till 1754, fostered a strong recusant[11] community, whilst being efficient exploiters – ironmasters, forest destroyers, state functionaries, and landlords.

Eastwards to Littleworth Lane the old farm landscape is relatively intact, and its farms have fine vernacular buildings. Well Land, a working farm, is the best of them. Both **Furzefield Wood and Moon Wood**, TQ 190 220, have greatly expanded from their ancient cores over the past two centuries.

THE MONASTERY, NORTH TO COWFOLD

At a distance **St Hugh's Charterhouse** spire, TQ 206 206, dominates this whole countryside, like Salisbury or Chichester Cathedrals. *In middle view* it is like the "outskirts of (…) Bethune[12] or Arras" in France. *Seen close-by* the monks' housing is like a prison, or the backs of Balham tenements.[13] The order came here to escape the anti-clericalism of the French republic, at the missionary prompting of the nearby catholic community at West Grinstead. Built from 1876–83 on a gigantic scale, with a cloister the best part of a kilometre long, it is a reminder of how tiny groups of people can shoehorn in gigantic architectural statements: like a 220ft wind turbine on the South Downs, or Dungeness Nuclear Power Station … or the Three Gorges Dam on the Yangtze, for that matter. Half empty now, it could make fine college buildings, or, better still, an alternative farming community.

Much of the landscape northwards has been damaged by agribusiness: Gervaise, Grovelands and Poundlane Woods are all gone, with their farms, barns, hedges and shaws. Still, old **Mockford**, TQ 200 208, and **Gervaise Cottage**, TQ 207 222, amongst the fields, testify to what has been lost. Much of the land has been returned to grass, and the cows in the fields south west of Cowfold, with the stumpy church tower in the background, are a nice reminder of the naming of the village.

Cowfold seems to have a greater social mix than most Wealden villages, with a central park, shops and school. Its centre is badly damaged by the A272 cross roads, but next door, the church and its large churchyard form a tranquil counter-point, with old cottages facing in towards it, like a tiny cathedral close. The church is of fine local ashlar, with a Horsham slab roof and ripplestone flag paths. It has not altered for nearly 400 years. Each portion of the (much decayed) churchyard fencing has a 'church mark' naming the local farm to which responsibility for its upkeep was allocated. There are 33 named farms.

PARTRIDGE GREEN TO PARKMINSTER WOOD

Few signs of **Jolesfield Common**, enclosed in 1872, remain today. As in many such late enclosures, the organisers felt obliged to make minor provision for the lost public amenities of ordinary local folk. They plonked a recreation ground right in the middle of the old common, with fields all around it. Walking by one wet winter day we had to splash through six inches of water to approach the playing field, TQ 188/9 200, along a footpath. It's got nice allotments next to it, though. Only the straight roads give obvious evidence of the lost common. The old Green Man pub (behind the present pub) hosted bull baiting almost up to its 1835 abolition.

Reeds Lane takes you through the old fields and shaws of **Blanche's Farm**, TQ 196 200, where the semi-improved pastures display occasional Waxcap fungi, and Skippers and Marbled White flit amongst the commoner old pasture flowers. The shaws and hedges have Hazel, Field Rose, Crab, Holly, young Ash, Oak and occasional Maple, with Bluebells and Primroses.

Wymarks Wood, TQ 203 188, just to the east, is mostly modern, but rich in wildlife for all that. There's Ragged Robin and old woodland flowers, and we watched nectaring Silver-Washed Fritillaries, Treecreepers, and a very agitated Sparrowhawk that behaved as though its nest had been disturbed.

The very best of this area is **Parkminster Wood**, TQ 207/8 201. It is a classic Hazel coppice Bluebell wood with very tall Oak standards good enough for the masts of HMS Victory! All the Low Wealden 'specials' are there – a mature Wild Service tree, with many small poles, Maple, Midland Thorn, Wood Spurge, et al. Ancient and lovely.

ENDNOTES

1. From line 35 of Keats' unsurpassable 'Ode to a Nightingale'.
2. Heard on 13th May, from 8.00pm to 8.50pm, in Twineham's countryside, at the centre of the Low Wealden area targetted for a New Town, where many landowners have signed developers' options, we are told.
3. 'The Landscape of Place Names', page 46, by Margaret Gelling and Ann Cole. Shaun Tyas, Stamford (2000).
4. 'Sewer' just means flood plain brook, or drain. Its excretory usage is modern.
5. 'The Place-Names of Sussex, Parts One and Two, by Mawer and Stenton. English Place-Name Society (reprinted 2001).
6. 'The Place-Names of Sussex, Parts One and Two, page 212, op cit.
7. These divisions prefigured the Norman 'Rapes', but were not the same as them. Perhaps the *burh* was a stronghold marking an early division between East and West Sussex, taking the Adur as the natural divide between the two?' Heather Warne, pers comm.
8. 'An introductory History and Guide to St Giles' Church, Shermanbury, West Sussex', compiled by Colonel Richard Puttnam CBE TD DL (2007). An excellent read.
9. 'The Church of St Peter Twineham' parish guide.
10. Old parallel ridges and furrows of medieval and early modern ploughing preserved under cover of pasture.
11. Recusants were Catholics who refused to conform to the Church of England in the times of religious persecution.
12. 'The Buildings of England: Sussex', p. 317, by Ian Nairn & Nikolaus Pevsner. Penguin (1965).
13. That you see from the Brighton Line as it passes into central London.

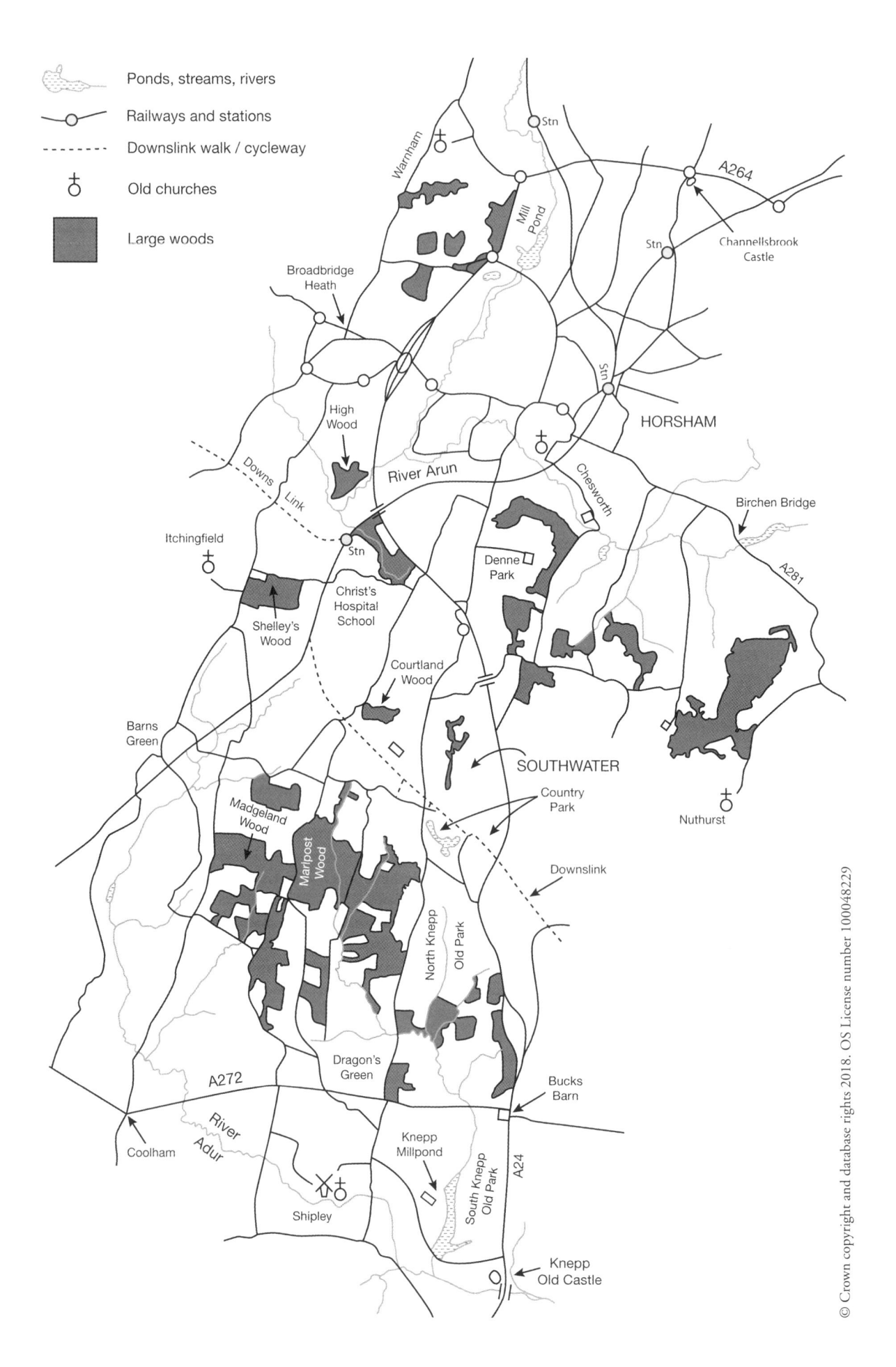

240 AREA GUIDE / Chapter 18: Horsham, Warnham, Shipley, Southwater and Knepp

CHAPTER 18
Horsham, Warnham, Shipley Woods, Southwater and Knepp

Sixty years ago this area was remote, old fashioned and deep-Wealden in character. Since then it has come to face the full onslaught of regional over-development. The modern A24 and A264 north Horsham bypass have galvanised the beltway development of Broadridge Heath and Southwater and the great expansion of Horsham. The narrow leafy lanes, the patchwork of woods and cattle pastures, the village shop and blacksmiths at Barns Green, will soon seem as anachronistic as a pony trap or horse plough team, if this trend is unchallenged at a systemic level.

This was a landscape of small farms and small fields separated by thick woodland belts known as 'shaws' or 'rews'. In some areas this character is still apparent, such as around Dragon's Green, Brook's Green and Barn's Green (all of which have long lost their greens).

In medieval times, however, its Wealden forest was assarted so effectively that only a few largish ancient woods survive. The biggest of these are Marlpost and Madgeland Woods, south west of Southwater, with the smaller Blinks and Middle Woods narrowly joined to them. Modern woodland creation has now stitched these old fragments together again and expanded them to the south, around Newbuildings Place, to make a block almost double the size of its ancient core.

Some of these woods connect us to the deepest past. Courtland Wood, next to the proposed housing development west of Southwater, has several gigantic Small Leaved Lime coppice clones, which must be the oldest life forms most of us could ever meet. High Wood, next to Broadbridge Heath's new 'Wickhurst Green' housing development, has at least 29 ancient woodland plants, including Small Leaved Lime.

To the west of Horsham the best countryside is being reduced to 'precious fragments': Warnham Millpond, High Wood, Parthings, Sparrow Wood, Shelley Wood and Sharpenhurst ... the more obvious in their quality, the more their surroundings are damaged by the loss of hedgerows and linear woods, and new urbanisation.

Christ's Hospital school was plonked down on the middle of it with all the sense of entitlement that Victorian public schools could muster ... built like an ersatz Oxbridge college, with a major landholding roundabout.

South of The Causeway and old St Mary's Church Horsham, a short walk into open country brings you to Denne Park. This four hundred year old deer park (now without its deer) is rich in ancient trees.

The vale of the young River Arun runs east from Denne Park, past Chesworth Farm, Amiesmill Bridge and Whites Bridge, to the boundary of St Leonard's Forest at Birchen Bridge. This vale was once enclosed in two big medieval deer parks, Chesworth and Sedgwick, which were disparked before Denne Park was created. The vale is edged on its south side by a ragged and romantic wooded scarp from Tower Hill eastwards by Denne Park, Bourne Hill and Hard's Hill to Bushy Copse, capped by bands of hard Horsham Stone.

The River Adur forms the south boundary of this chapter's area, and the lovely church and hamlet of Shipley sits on its north bank. The pattern of roads was – and still is – dominated by the south-north drove roads made originally by the southern manors to access their northern wood pasture outliers in the Weald. Most all the river crossings of the Adur would first have been fords, where now they are bridged. Tench*ford*, however, preserves the memory of fording, and Kings Bridge (close by Shipley's King's Windmill) preserves the character of an ancient ford, as the track widens out and dissolves into mud and gentler river banks (though it is crossed nowadays by a wooden footbridge).

The contrasts are extreme ... a thatched scout hut ... a factory farm ... medieval farmhouses and shaws ... polo fields ... gated communities ... Bluebell-and-

Daffodil woods … ribbon development … lanes older than the English language … advancing housing estates.

After the Norman conquest the de Braose barons of the Rape of Bramber carved out a giant deer and hunting park based on a castellated lodge at Knepp. It was disparked in late Tudor times. Nonetheless, two adjacent landowners have re-enclosed the majority of the lost park as a 'rewilding' experiment, though it produced useful crops for perhaps a thousand years. Kneppmill Pond is superb and little known.

None of this area's loveliness is protected by AONB (Area of Outstanding Natural Beauty) designation.

SHIPLEY

From family walks to **Shipley**, TQ 144 218, in the early 1960s, one memory stands out … our mum reverentially showing us the Shipley Reliquary[1] in its little niche in the north wall of the **church** nave. There it sat, all colour in the shadows: blue and red enamel and gilt, with child-like images of Jesus on the cross, little winged angels and saints, and jewel-like studs … a thing of such antiquity and beauty. It may have been part of the treasures of the Knights Templar,[2] who built this church by an ancient droveway crossing of the Adur. It was stolen in 1976 and has never been heard of since.

The large and robust church was built about 1130, and has fine Norman carved mouldings on its west door and chancel arches. Its stonework displays the earth history of the clay Weald. Its long south wall is made of beautifully laid Horsham Stone. Its other walls have Wealden rubblestone, including occasional ironstone and flint. Its graveyard paving slabs are of Horsham ripplestone. Within the south porch the paving includes Small Paludina and Large Paludina fossil limestone slabs, with what looks like an old river mooring post of cast iron (for this was an ironmaking district), and its quoins, window jambs and door surrounds are of a good freestone.

Near the church stands **King's Windmill**, visible for miles, made in 1876 and still with all its machinery. We visited it many times from the sixties onwards, scrambling up the narrow ladders and teetering out onto the gallery. Its owner closed it to the public in 2009.

The quiet reaches of the **Adur** from **Capp's, King's and Ashbrook Bridges**, and on to St Julian's Lake at Coolham are a delight, with reedy edges, water birds, Arrowhead and Flowering Rush, Purple Loosestrife and Stone Parsley. Schools of little fish flick by when the water is clear. The canalised stretch from **Bay Bridge**, by Knepp Castle, to Capp's Bridge has just had some of its lost meanders put back to re-wet the flood plain and slow up the river's flow. Old farm houses, like **Church Farm South** and **Church Farm North** are often ancient and timber built. Although much of the land is still farmed, there are polo pitches west of Ashbrook's Bridge.

The ancient **lanes around the church hamlet** are quiet enough to walk, often with wide grassy and flowery verges and sudden 90 degree turns. Some of them are green lanes, like lovely **Boar Lane**, TQ 141 226, **Kingsbridge Lane**, TQ 142 216, and **Greenstreet Lane**, TQ 148 227. The best of the verges is on **Smithers Hill Lane**, TQ 137 227, north of Butterstocks Farm, where we counted 70 herbs and grasses, with the rare Corky Fruited Water Dropwort, Betony, Stone Parsley, Crosswort, Corn Mint, Pepper Saxifrage and Creeping Soft Grass.

OLD KNEPP PARK, NORTH AND SOUTH

Old **Knepp Park** had the characteristic elongated shape of a dark age swine pasture *denne*, probably taken over *en bloc* by the Lords of Bramber as a deer preserve and hunting park, from a distant coast-wise farming settlement. It was about a mile wide by nearly three miles long. Its boundary banks can still be traced in many spots around its northern half, and, often, there are patches of bristly Butcher's Broom upon them, a common 'signature' of such old boundaries. The Park was thoroughly parcelled up into farms at its Tudor disparking, and at least five of the farmhouses and cottages within its boundary are now between 300 and 500 years old. Nearly all its ancient woodland *vert*[3] was cleared, though it is now, again, quite wooded, as a result of modern estate plantings. At the same time old hedgerows have been removed, so that parts in the middle of the Park, especially just north of the A272 (which bisects the Park), are quite bare, with 'lollipop' oaks.

After a start in 2001, nearly all the Park (except for the sliver stranded on the east side of the A24) is now enclosed behind 2m high perimeter deer fences in a large rewilding project, and most internal wire fences have been removed. Deer, Longhorn cattle and Tamworth pigs roam freely (though, in the case of the deer, less freely than they do elsewhere in the Weald).

Towards the end of March, a necklace of Wild Daffodils blooms along the wooded stream from **Hartsgravel Bridge**, TQ 152 236, eastwards across the north Park, through **Constable's Furze**, TQ 161 240. They form a glorious sheet at the northern end of **Constable's Furzefield**, TQ 160 238, and in the adjacent gill. There, on the ride, with the sun in the west shining through the Birch lattice, whilst Bumblebee queens drone, the air is full of the coconut scent of flowering Gorse, and any step must be taken with care to avoid nodding Daffodil blooms. Only the relentless noise and murderous chainsaw din of motor bikes racing on the A24 tarnishes this paradise garden.

In a neck of woodland a small meadow, **Crab Tree Platt**, TQ 160 240, has been recently restored by the estate (after a little nudge from me). It still has a few Cowslips (2014), Zig Zag Clover, Betony, Agrimony and woodland Primrose, Bluebell and Bugle, though it has lost its Dyers Greenweed and Sneezewort.

Hartsgravel Wood, TQ 153 237, is the largest of the Park's ancient woods, and the best of it is by the Daffodil stream along its southern boundary, and in **Alder Copse**, TQ 157 235, where there are Anemones, Ladies Smock, and sheets of Ramsons. Silver Washed Fritillaries patrol the wood edges and rides.

Brick Kiln Farm, TQ 157 242, has a fine old farmhouse and granary (near collapse, 2012).

The **southern half of Knepp Park** is dominated by the over-half-mile-long **Kneppmill Pond**, TQ 158 215, with its wildlife-rich tawny edging reed beds, with Bulrush, Yellow Flag and noisy water birds. It used to be twice that length, right up to Pondtail Farm, but the northern half long ago silted to carr and tall fen … now being dredged and restored (2017–8). It once powered an Elizabethan iron furnace, though little sign of that survives. **Kneppmill House**, below the pond bay, is of 16th century date however, and therefore contemporary with the working furnace.

Knepp Mill Pond used to be the largest freshwater body in Sussex

All that is left of the castellated 11th century hunting lodge known as **Knepp Castle**, TQ 163 208/9, is a dog's tooth of thick masonry on a knoll – *cnaep* – just west of the A24. It wouldn't have been more than a few hours ride in summer (about 6.5 miles as the crow flies) from the home castle at Bramber. The **Adur south of the Castle mound** (between TQ 156 209 and TQ 162 207) is a delight of colour and interest in high summer, with many water plants, damsels, and much fish fry. Huge Swan Mussel shells lie stranded in mud just below the dried outlet of the Kneppmill Pond.

The other place known as **'Knepp Castle'** is the sprawling pseudo-gothic castellated stucco mansion overlooking the Pond. It was first built two centuries ago (started in 1809) but was burnt down in 1904, with the loss of priceless paintings, and subsequently rebuilt. Just by its outbuildings is the **Castle Oak**, TQ 154 217, which was already old when the mansion was first built.

DRAGONS GREEN AND THE SHIPLEY WOODS

The Shipley woods feel very remote in places, with winding lanes, rough tracks, narrow paths, and lonely farms and cottages, like Crookhorn, Trawlers and Madgeland Farms. They are centred on the ancient woodlands of Marlpost and Madgeland. Both of these, like Blinks and Middle Woods, were much damaged by large scale planting of conifers, which have now largely been cleared. The old broadleaves are returning. There are very few ancient trees in the complex, though there are at least three good old Oaks on the drive east of **Goffsland Farm**, TQ 150/1 237, and three close to **Trawler's Farm**, TQ 145 246/7, an ancient 'teapot hall' with pentice[4] roof coming right down on both sides, and Wild Daffodils on its drove.

Madgeland Wood, TQ 133 257, has a rim of old Hazel coppice left along its western edge. Hazel was probably the main coppice species both there and in **Marlpost Wood**, TQ 143 255. Both woods can feel quite heathy,[5] with much Gorse amongst their young growth, and herbs such as Devil's Bit, Tormentil, Heath Speedwell and Eyebright along their rides. Birch and Sallow are abundant. Wild Service and Wych Elm are rare. The woods' young growth and developed ride system make them very sunny in high summer, and in July there are parties of White Admiral and Silver Washed Fritillary, Ringlet, Comma, Large Skipper and Meadow Brown. One balmy April day the two gills on each side, and to the south, of **Middle Wood**, e.g. TQ 147 250, were sweet with the scent of Crab blossom above Early Purple Orchids and Bluebells. A big crowd of Green Longhorn Moths danced above the crown of a Sallow, rising, then settling, then rising again, glinting silvery and green-blue iridescent, their long white 'whiskers' waving up and down with their rhythm.

The new woods established over the last century often embrace ancient shaws around their edges or through them, which have a richer herbaceous vegetation. Many of these secondary woods feel quite mature, though their lack of ancient woodland species, like Bluebell, is a sure sign of their relative youth. There are big, youngish woods east and west of **Newbuildings Place**, TQ 140 243, a fine brick manor house of 1683, with Dutch-type gables. In **Newbuildings Plantation**, to the west, is the table tomb (very mournful and sylvan in a Yew-lined ride, TQ 138 245) of Wilfred Scawen Blunt, the Victorian poet, orientalist and anti-imperialist. I'd respect the bloke more if he'd given up his own large estate and bank balance.

A 2.5 mile walk southwards from **Dogbarking House and Cottages**, TQ 140 266, down **Crookhorn (green) Lane**, then down **Oldhouse Lane** and **Baker's Lane** to **Dragon's Green** passes through secondary woodland for half its distance. Yet the tree-lined hedges and shaws along the lane have many ancient woodland species. In spring, there are Wild Daffodils in at least three spots along Oldhouse and Baker's Lanes, and in summer you can find Wild Service on the drove by **Crookhorn Farm**, TQ 138 258 – a timber framed, part-medieval, Handsel and Gretel-type place, with a flower-edged pond in front. **Abrahams Well**, in the woods on Oldhouse Lane, TQ 135 243, has crystal clear spring water rippling up, and a fine sandstone top. Draught horses and passing travellers could rest up on a shady lay-by opposite. **Dragons Green**, TQ 143 232, has a nice range of houses, from tiny gingerbread-house crooked cottages to handsome ex-council houses, with big old Oaks in their front gardens which mark the edge of the lost Green. One fine new house has two superbly kept gipsy waggons, all painted up. A real treat!

To the south west of the woods is the posh-polo-pitch country around **Hoe's and Baker's Farms,** all neat and monied and over-tidy. The **thatched scout hut** is memorable, TQ 138 235: the only one of its kind in the country.

BARNS GREEN, SOUTHWATER, CHRIST'S HOSPITAL, AND IN BETWEEN

Around **Brooks Green**, TQ 127 249, north to **Barns Green**, TQ 125 268, is a funny mixture of little fields and old shaws, bits of ribbon development, livery paddocks and rough grazing. **Sunrise Farm**, TQ 126 253, off Emms Lane, is a smallholding still worked by the family who once had all of Courtland Farm till they had to sell most of it off, back in the 1920s. It has a fascinating stash of old farm tractors and other scrap farm machinery. **Trout Cottage** (now just The Cottage, I think) TQ 132 264, is on a little brook no bigger nowadays than a ditch! Did it give its name to **Trout Lane**?

Landfall Farm, TQ 125 261, has six flower-rich meadows, a superb survival (2014), with all the original hedgerows. They are all colourful, with abundant Knapweed and all the old common meadow species, like Meadow Vetchling, Fleabane, Red Clover, Large Birds Foot Trefoil and Sorrel. The biggest of them have received some measure of improvement, for they lack rarities, but two little fields at the north end have wholly intact, unimproved areas, with Betony, Bitter Vetch, Devils Bit, Sneezewort, and Burnet Saxifrage. There has been some dumping on one of them, and it is now very rank.

Back in the early sixties when I regularly took the Horsham Flyer train to **Southwater**[6] it was a quiet country place of brick pits, a bit of ribbon development, and some small housing estates. Now, with the A24 bypass, its built up area is nearly two miles long by a mile wide. At least its ancient woodland **gill** is preserved, TQ 159 266. Ancient farmsteads like **Easteds**,

"You can tell them by their width": ancient swine pasture drove near Shipley.

TQ 164 264, are stranded in urban development, and lovely **Stakers**, TQ 167 261, is marooned next to the roaring bypass. The **Country Park,** TQ 158 257, based on the clay pits, is much loved and a great place for a stop if you're cycling or walking the Downs Link.

Now we are threatened with a major expansion of over 500 houses to the west of Southwater, partly on **Great House Farm**, TQ 152 268, part of the Aubrey Fletcher estate (an absentee landlord). The farm tenant's family have no right to block this development or buy their farm, though they've worked this land for 191 years, since 1825 – five generations. (Yet council tenants can claim a right to buy, despite the fact that their homes are the valuable property of the whole community. Why, therefore, should not the farm tenants be able to do so?). The farmhouse may be more than 500 years old.

Close to the **Bax Castle pub** there are giants of immense age hiding in **Courtlands Wood**, TQ 150 272. These coppice stools of Small Leaved Lime have grown so big that they have hollowed out in the centre, like huge fairy rings, and can now only be detected as separate stools or root plates forming parts of circles, one of 16 paces diameter, one of 12 paces. They are true survivors from the wildwood. It is a Bluebell wood, with Gean, Midland Thorn, Maple and Crab Apple.

To the west, beyond the Arun Valley Railway, **Sharpenhurst Hill** rises, TQ 138 281, with superb views. **Shelley's Wood**, TQ 138 286, north of the Hill, is mostly ancient, with spectacular Bluebells and Anemones under Hazel coppice, some Oak standards and coppice, and much Bracken. The middle part is secondary, and has lots of Violet Helleborine Orchis, though deer seem to nibble off the majority of spikes.

West of the Wood, down a little lane, is **Itchingfield Church**, TQ 131 289, one of my favourite spots, with a little stream and wooded gill running right by the churchyard. It has a fifteenth century timber tower, like those across the Surrey border at Newdigate, Burstow and Horley. In the churchyard is a tiny 'black and white' Priest's House, part of it built around 1500. It shows just how small medieval homes were.

To the north of Itchingfield and Sharpenhurst the countryside around **Westons Farm** (part of the Christ's Hospital estate) and **Fulfords Farm** has been damaged by much hedge and shaw removal.

Sometimes when you caught the Horsham Flyer at Shoreham or Horsham, there would be **Christ's Hospital** schoolboys waiting with battered trunks on the platform, dressed in wacky Tudor gear – ankle length

Itchingfield churchyard's tiny Priest House

belted woollen blue coats, yellow socks, knee breeches, and 'parson's bands' at their neck (like barristers). When Christ's Hospital School, TQ 148 285, parachuted into the Weald in 1897 from its erstwhile City of London home, they bought 1200 acres of countryside, a lot of which they still own. The school and grounds cover half a square mile. Alright for some …

Just north and south of the railway, by **Christ's Hospital station**, is an ancient woodland cluster around a sharp 'U' bend in the River Arun. **Sparrow's Wood** forms the southern part, TQ 150 292. It is a tranquil, sun-dappled wood, with abundant fine Oak maidens over Hazel coppice, centred on a deep gill and its silent stream lined with Alders. On a promontory north of the river is **High Wood**, TQ 147 298, a superb ancient woodland survival. It also marks a peculiar historical survival, for with **Broadbridge Farm and Mill**, it formed a Wealden outlier of the parish and manor of Sullington, under the Downs south of Storrington, for at least 650 and probably a thousand years, up to 1878. A drove road takes a nearly-straight route NNE from Storrington all the way to the (broad) bridge, west of the wood. The best parts of High Wood are the steep river cliff slopes and the tip of the promontory, where Small Leaved Lime stools intertwine with Wych Elm, and there is Wood Melic and Wood Millet, Broom, and overstood Hornbeam coppice mingled with Gean. The plateau is pitted with old shallow diggings and even a pond, which mark past quarrying for Horsham Stone. It is an Ash-Oak-Holly-Hornbeam-Hazel-Bluebell wood. Indeed, nine of the 29 ancient woodland indicator plants I know of there are woody species. Below the steep slopes the disused mill leet runs, and has its own cluster of damp loving species. The river around the Wood has Arrowhead, Yellow Water Lily and Purple Loosestrife, Branched Bur Reed and abundant Banded Agrion. We thought we saw a Water Vole, and much low vegetation had been nibbled back.

DENNE PARK, HORSHAM: SOME VETERAN AND NOTABLE TREES

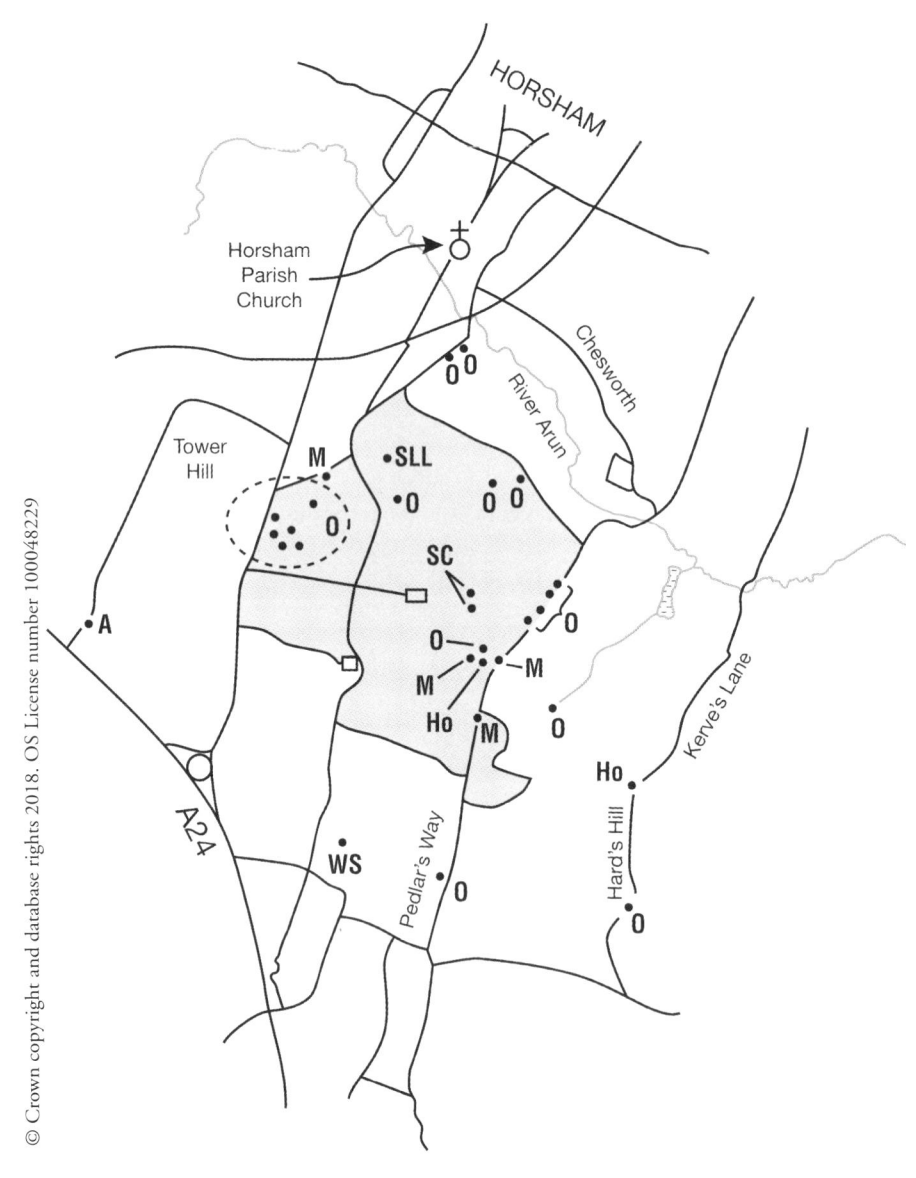

Key
M – Maple
O – English Oak
A – Ash
SLL – Small Leaved Lime
SC – Sweet Chestnut
Ho – Hornbeam
WS – Wild Service Tree

BROADBRIDGE HEATH AND WARNHAM

Broadbridge Heath, TQ 14 31, has exploded in size in the last 60 years. Bypasses have mashed it, facilitating the sprawl: the A264 bypass round the village; the A24 bypass rammed through the gap that separated it from Horsham; and now the new A264, outer southern bypass. It has good looking council housing, though.

It was originally a hamlet around the common heath, but the common was likely nibbled away at the west side by the Field Place landowners (Percy Bysshe Shelley's family), then over two thirds of the remainder was enclosed in 1858. Only the northern bit, with the cricket ground, is still registered common, and none of its heathy vegetation survives. Some of the oldest houses and cottages in Broadbridge Heath, around the north end of **Wickhurst Lane** and **Church Lane,** once marked the south eastern boundary of the common, e.g. TQ 150 313. Place names like *Broom*lands and *Goosegreen* Farm, between Broadbridge *Heath* and Warnham, commemorate that commoned past.

Underneath the pattern of this district's newest roads the alignment of the old roads is relentlessly SSW to NNE, either reflecting the alignment of Roman Stane Street, to the west, or vice versa. The ancient Sullington-Broadbridge drove continues through **Warnham**, TQ 15 33, and then becomes the A24, up to the Surrey border. The **deer park** was created in 1837 and has had a Red Deer herd since the 1850s, now run as a commercial stud with adjacent Bailing Hill Farm. It's heavily grazed and its woodland is secondary. **Lake Plantation**, TQ 157/8 325, is dark and gloomy, with conifers and 'railway station gothic' boat house ... very 'Turn of the Screw'. *Fences* are the lasting impression the deer park leaves. Warnham feels like an estate village of Warnham Court, close by. It has much solid Victorian building, some good vernacular old houses, and much use of Horsham Stone. There's a big and attractive council estate between The Street and Tilletts Lane. The parish churchyard showed some old meadow fungi even in December. It has a HUGE perched slab of Horsham Stone four paces long by 1.5 paces wide, with ripple bedding (as have many of the churchyard path slabs). Don't drop it on your foot!

Warnham's jewel is **Warnham Mill Pond** Local Nature Reserve, TQ 170 325, now squeezed between Horsham and the roaring A24 bypass. The Reserve was to be bigger, but the Council subtracted some of its area to make a golf course. It is a lovely sheet of water, with dense fringing reed beds and a backdrop of Sallow, Willow and conifers. There's Kingfisher, Great Crested and Little Grebes, and lots of wildness, fen and carr, but long lengths of friendly board walk, too, so everyone's happy. We all watched a Weasel playing and foraging round a song bird feeding station … magic. There are lots of decayed Crack Willow pollards, a dipping pond with Fringed Water Lily and good dragons and damsels. Channells Brook, the Holbrook, and Boldings Brook, all drain into it. The Mill Pond Meadow is unimproved and has Saw Wort.

It was ponded sometime around 1583, for an iron furnace worked there from that date, which produced big cannon. Parliamentary forces destroyed the furnace in 1645, during the civil war, but the pond powered a corn mill right through till the 1930s. Percy Bysshe Shelley knew it well as a youngster.

HORSHAM, DENNE PARK, CHESWORTH

Horsham, in *947 AD*, (the oldest date we have for the place name) may have been more like a New Forest glade, with herds of horses kept on heath and close-grazed lawns, by a hamlet on the edge of the Arun's meadows: *'Hors ham'*- the horse homestead. In *1800*, it was still on the edge of the huge, rough Horsham Common and the wildness of St Leonard's Forest. In *1960,* it still felt a bit rural and Wealden. The town has changed profoundly in the past 65 years, however. In *2017,* it's more like a corporate satellite, feeding capital's maw in London and the Gatwick corridor.

The old, Wealden bits are clustered around Horsham Park, The Causeway, St Mary's Church, and The Bishopric. The broach spire of **St Mary's Church** –

Denne Park's north slope, Chesworth, Horsham

156ft tall – reaches up like the arm of a drowning swimmer, above the *consumerfest*. This Norman and Early English church is grand and very 'civic', with a high painted waggon roof, covered with Horsham Slabs. The churchyard is largely wild and wooded, as is the little **Denne Road Cemetery** nearby, TQ 172 302, which has Pink Ballerina Waxcap under the trees.

As a kid I liked the displays of stuffed iridescent tropical birds in Horsham's wonderful **Museum** at the top of **The Causeway**. Those natural history collections are gone – long out of fashion, sadly – but the rambling old half timbered place is choc-a-bloc with good exhibits. The Causeway has many vernacular buildings and a nice Lime avenue. It still feels quite 'Cranford'.

The northern part of **Horsham Park,** TQ 172 311, was once within Horsham Common, and a beautiful three span girth Sessile Oak pollard, TQ 1728 3117, marks, I think, the lost boundary between the Common and the park grounds attached to Park House – until recently District Council offices and an Arts Centre. Much of the Park is playing fields, but the west and NE boundaries have some good Oak maidens.

On the (bypassed) **Worthing Road** down from **The Bishopric** is a Unitarian Chapel with *rus in urbe* grounds, and a Quaker chapel further downhill – all nice. Beyond **Tan Bridge** on the housing estate to the south is a superb 'black and white' 15th or 16th century farmhouse, with a recessed centre and Horsham Stone roof. It used to be called Needles Farm, but is now **Netherledys**, Blackbridge Lane, TQ 165 301.

There's a great feeling of release as you walk across the bridge that is *under* the railway bridge, but *over* the Arun stream and out into the greenness of **Denne Park**, TQ 167 294. It's hardly altered at all over the years. A deep gully marks the course of the Old Coach Road, up the hill from the Lodge to the plateau, and on southwards. The holloway of another drove bounds the park along its east boundary base of slope.

The mature and veteran trees are what make the Park so special (2016). I found a wasps' nest amongst the roots of one three span Oak pollard, and saw a group of Hornets fighting over a sap run on another old Oak. The ancient trees are clustered. North of the west drive Lodge, TQ 164 292, there's a group of six Oak pollards, now beginning to break up (three with scorched interiors – one dead). They are all around three spans girth, dating them back to about 1650, when the Park was new. They haven't been pollarded for over a century. There's little else left on most of the Park plain, except two Sweet Chestnut giants east of the big house (now flats). There are three good Oaks amongst sunny Bracken on the north slope. The other main cluster is on the east slope, TQ 170/1 288, near the point where the Park plain footpath meets the eastern drove (now Pedlar's Way, which also has good trees). I've counted 23 veterans, mostly Oaks, in the Park (plus another nine close by) with four good Maples, a Hornbeam and the two Sweet Chestnuts. There's a large group of mature Hawthorns in the northwest valley amongst Bracken: a fine nectar source when in blossom.

For many years the north scarp slope of Denne Park was a Larch plantation, but it was cleared recently because of infection with (so I am told) Ramorum disease, otherwise known as Larch Tree Disease or Sudden Oak Death (SOD). Now the slope is once again

THE VALE OF THE RIVER ARUN AND THE HORSHAM STONE SCARP

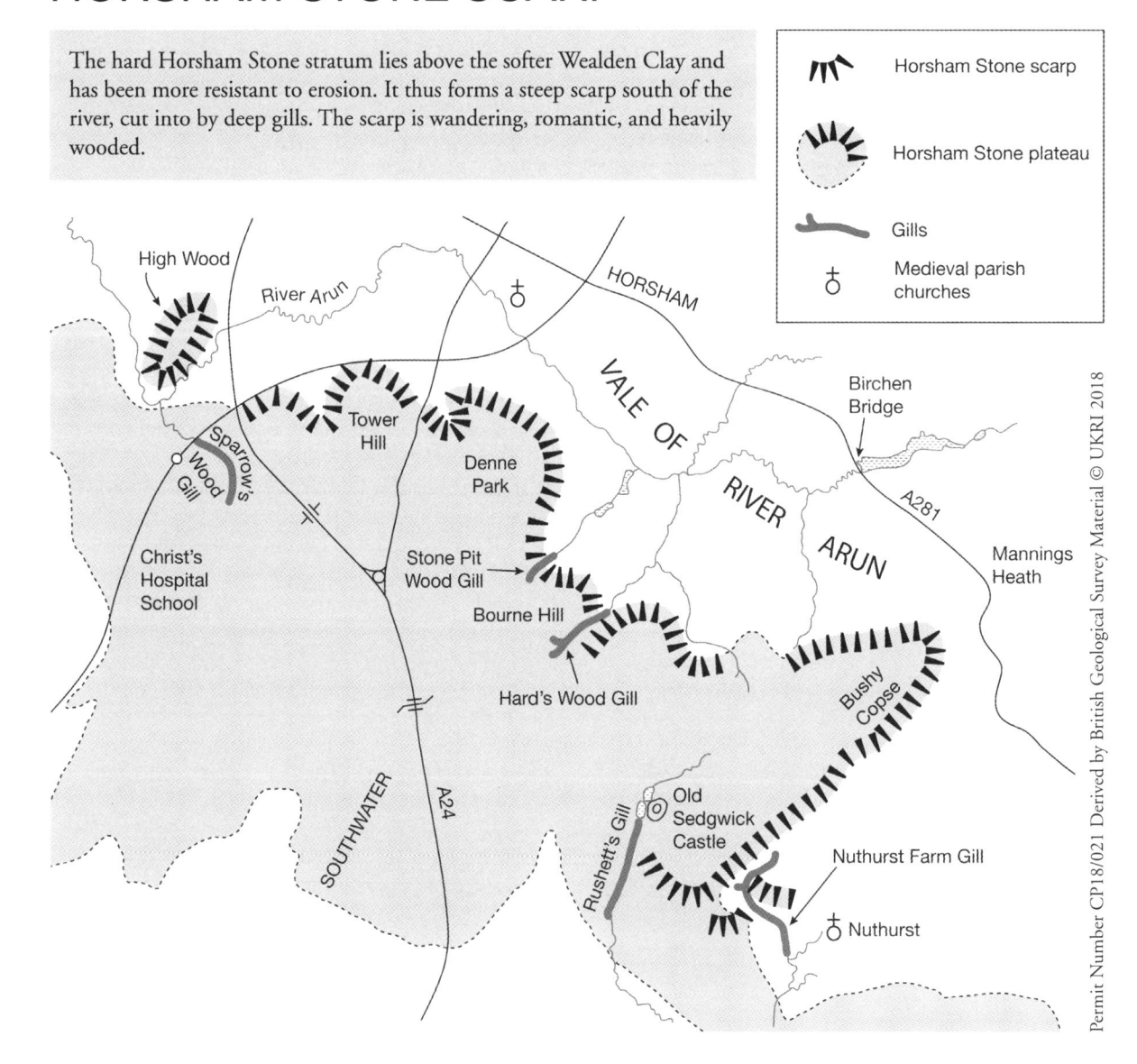

The hard Horsham Stone stratum lies above the softer Wealden Clay and has been more resistant to erosion. It thus forms a steep scarp south of the river, cut into by deep gills. The scarp is wandering, romantic, and heavily wooded.

a sunny and delightful place to walk, with Bracken, large clumps of Foxglove, and fine views.

Below Denne Hill north slope is **Chesworth**, TQ 176 295, on the banks of the Arun. It had a 900 acre deer park till c. 1550–1610, stretching east and south to include Bourne Hill, with a park lodge on the site of Bourne Hill House. Much of Chesworth mansion has gone, though most of its moat remains, with wings of 15th to 17th century date, now poshed-up and private. Queen Catherine Howard, beheaded by mad Henry the Eighth, was brought up there. The 90 acre farm around the mansion was purchased by the District Council in 1991, and is managed for public access and wildlife, with a stretch of the Arun and both wet (by the stream) and dry meadows.

West of the **Boars Head** pub, TQ 163 295, **Tower Hill** has fine views northwards across the Arun. West again, you come to **Parthings**, TQ 156 297, a fifteenth century close-studded timber framed farmhouse and pond, with old cottages and a range of old farm buildings: granary, Sussex barn and hovels. The lane continues south to the top of the hill, with views west to High Wood and north to the blue wooded Surrey Hills. All the Arun-side fields are now gone for new housing.

A CLAUDIAN[7] PROSPECT: THE HORSHAM ESCARPMENT AND THE VALE OF THE YOUNG ARUN

The clay vale of the young Arun is bounded southwards by a shadowed wooded scarp, with limpid westward skies all pink and duck egg green on March evenings. The scarp's woods are part-ancient, part-secondary. A deep ravine-like gill runs down through **Hard's Wood**, TQ 174 280. Crowds of Water Crickets, *Velia sp.*, practice their skating on its stream in spring time amongst the Bluebells. There's a much gentler gill in **Stonepit Wood**, TQ 172 285. South of **Kite's Copse**, the woodland has a line of veteran Maples along a lost trackway, TQ 182 276/7. Two gills cross the clay vale below the scarp. **Buckley Slip**, TQ 189 287, marks one of them, perhaps named after the bucks[8] of Chesworth Park, that embraced this area. Its gill soon debouches into the wooded course of the Arun, below **Birchen Bridge**, TQ 193 291, which has a roaring, foaming waterfall draining Coolhurst Mill Pond. **Kerves Brook gill** drains down from Bulls Farm. It has a fine veteran Wild Service tree on its east bank, TQ 182 282/3, and many impressive Alder stools northwards along the gill floor. Indeed, one Methusaleh forms a hollowed out 'fairy ring' of 14 paces circumference. There is a partly broken little dam, with big ripple bed Horsham Stone slabs exposed around it. The field boundaries north west of **Bull's Farm** have fine Ash, Hornbeam and Holly stools – huge, decayed and photogenic.

The scarp exists because of the resistance of Horsham Stone – bands of hard sandstone within the Wealden Clay – to down-cutting erosion by the primeval Arun. The stone fractures into large thick plates and fat slates, which have been a staple roofing, paving, and sometimes walling material of churches, manor houses, better-off farms and some barns from medieval times, and probably before. Many ponded or bushed-up pits south west of Horsham were originally quarries for this flaggy stone, and the name 'Stammerham' ('the home of the stone masons') still occurs for three farms in the area.[9]

There are old stone pits, now vegetated over, all along the top of the scarp from Broadbridge's High Wood, Denne Hill, Stonepit Wood, Hard's Wood, to Kite's Copse.

ENDNOTES

1. A 'reliquary' is a box containing a 'relic' of a saint, which could be a bit of their bone, hair, skin, or such like.
2. The Knights Templar were a kind of security police for pilgrim tourists to the Crusaders' colonies in Palestine. They were enriched by gifts of many lands, including Shipley, Saddlescombe north of Brighton, and Sompting near Worthing, from redemption-seeking feudal chiefs. The Knights Templar were finally removed from Shipley in 1326.
3. 'Vert' was woodland preserved for deer browse and shelter.
4. A 'pentice' roof is overhanging and often comes down very low.
5. St Johns Farm, on the south edge of Madgeland Wood, used to be called Heathfields Farm, and you can see why.
6. The big medieval parish of Horsham was named in two parts. That south of the Arun was 'south water' (south of the 'water', or river). That north of the Arun was 'north heath' (and was still part-heath till after the 1813 enclosure).
7. Claude Lorrain was a seventeenth century baroque French landscape painter who specialised in limpid glowing sunsets … as good, or better, than our Turner.
8. Or perhaps named after Beech trees – *boc* – growing there.
9. Two of the farms are near Christ's Hospital and one is on the Surrey border west of Rusper. See 'The Kent and Sussex Weald', page 31, by Peter Brandon, Phillimore and Co. Ltd., (2003).

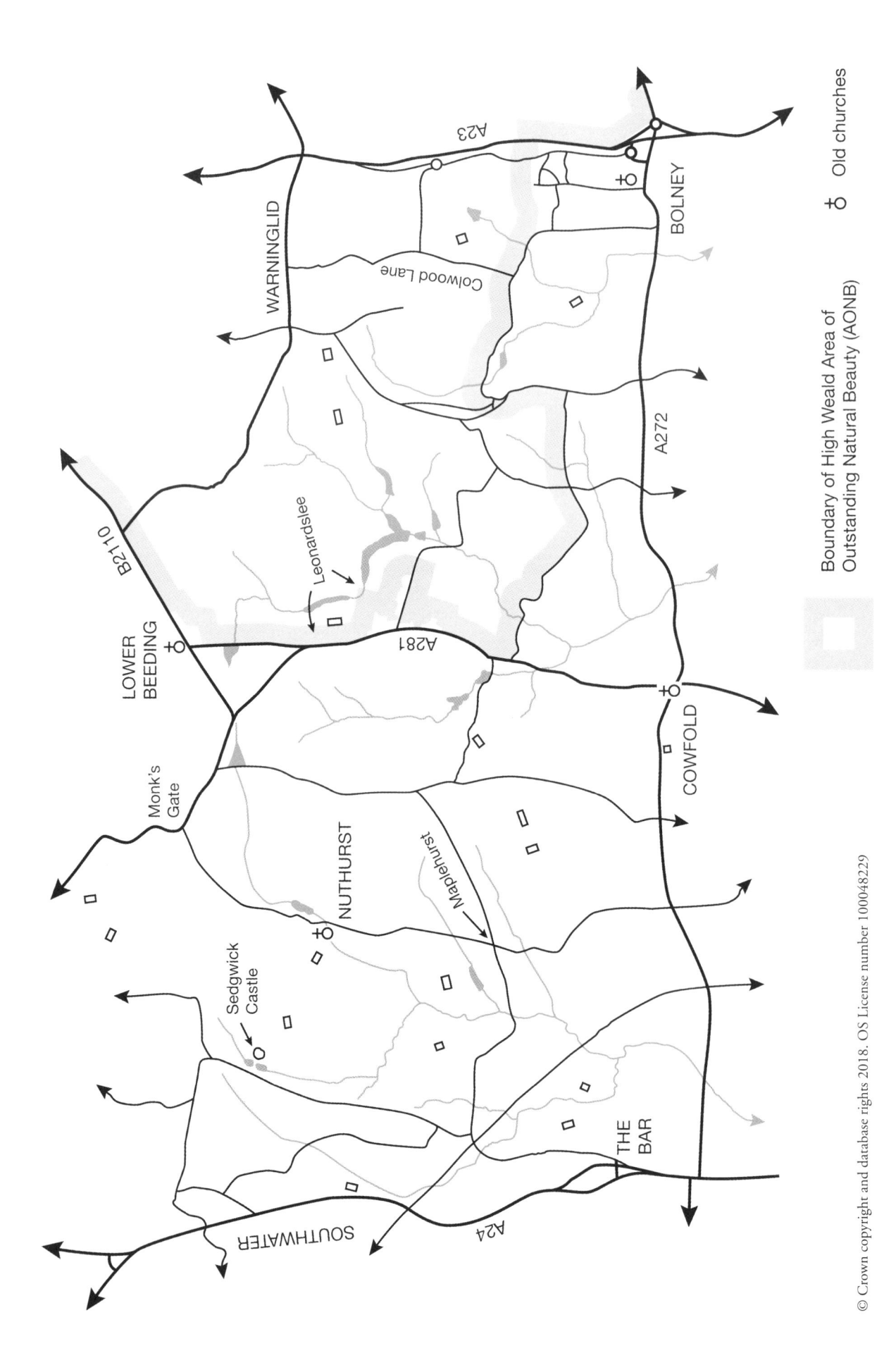

AREA GUIDE / Chapter 19: Sedgwick, Nuthurst, Leonardslee and Bolney

Boundary of High Weald Area of Outstanding Natural Beauty (AONB)

✠ Old churches

© Crown copyright and database rights 2018. OS License number 100048229

CHAPTER 19
Sedgwick, Nuthurst, Leonardslee and Bolney

At the heart of this landscape is **the old southern reach of St Leonards Forest,** surrounded by more hills, valleys and gills, and clothed in deep woods. It was heavily colonised by the very rich in Victorian times, and their mansions, mini-parks and extravagant farmhouse conversions occupy many prominences. They steal our viewpoints as well as our woods, lakes and fields.

THE SOUTHERN FOREST

Leonardslee, TQ 222 262, takes its name from the old Forest, of course, and its gardens are a true wonder. Though they lost many of their old native trees in the gales a quarter century ago they still combine elements of the older semi-natural landscape within their fantastic displays of Rhodedendrons and Azaleas.

The colours are dazzling in the Maytime gardens, but downslope from the big displays there are areas of archaic grassland with Ling Heather, Sedges, Tormentil and Lousewort. A nest of Honeybees was busy in their rot hole hive 15 feet up an old Oak maiden when we last visited, and a Cuckoo called.

Together with its old **deer park**, TQ 227 257, to the south, now re-stocked with deer, Leonardslee gives "a better idea of the old St Leonard's Forest than any other site".[1]

One midsummer dawn I walked in the deer park, as mist steamed above the lake. The heathery slopes rose to a plateau where Heath Grass, Mat Grass, *Nardus stricta*, and Sheep's Fescue survive in some grassy places. Along the eastern side Oak and Beech high forest drift down a small valley over ferny slopes. Along the north side of the lake there are several fragments of bog, which nurture ancient assemblages of species. I counted seven sedges, Marsh Pennywort and Marsh St John's Wort, Bog Pimpernel and Ivy Leaved Bellflower. I could not find the Cranberry, Sundew, Bog Myrtle[2] (this being its last recorded Sussex site) or Stag's Horn Clubmoss which Francis Rose recorded. The erstwhile best bog was overgrowing with bushes, and the Park's lower slopes have been planted with many exotic conifers which will grow to destroy the long views and compromise this best remaining fragment of the Forest's heaths.

Gosden, just south of Leonardslee, TQ 228 249, is a time haven. Its half timbered, tile hung, Horsham-slab-roofed cottage, with its veg garden and topiary cockerels, looks like a Helen Allingham painting come

OLD LEONARDSLEE: HEATH AND MEADOW

Archaic grass heath at Leonardslee, and nearby archaic meadows

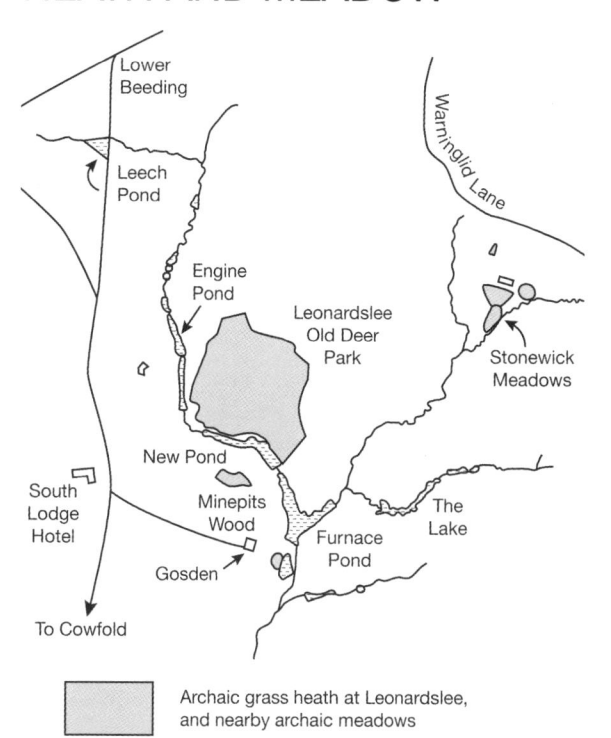

© Crown copyright and database rights 2018.
OS License number 100048229

Gosden Cottages perhaps housed the Tudor iron furnace workers

alive. The Mill Pond has a flock of white Geese, and another of Canada Geese, which honour the place's original naming: "Goose Den" – Goose wood pasture. It is tranquil (apart from the whir of a helicopter taking some VIP to the nearby Court Lodge Hotel). There's Wood Horsetail present still, Grey Wagtail on the pond bay, and Betony, Cow Wheat, Bilberry and Heather at the wood edges.

The ponds fed the Tudor iron furnace here, and the cottage perhaps housed its workers. Minepits Wood, west of Gosden, is pockmarked with old iron ore diggings. Above the Mill Pond is the Furnace Pond, now all barbed-wired-off for anglers. Below the Mill Pond is a soggy Sallow-and-Reed Mace carr, which marks the site of the primary Mill Pond, TQ 229 247. One early March day we squelched across it, clambering over mossy branches … to be rewarded by the sight of many square yards of Scarlet Elf Cup fungus amongst the Golden Saxifrage. A stag-headed little Oak pollard leans over on the south side. The footpath crosses the old pond bay and a fine waterfall roars underneath.

The woods, fields, shaws and streams south and east of Gosden around **Goodgers Farm** are delightful. You may find Wild Daffodils, as in Steep Wood. An old shepherd's caravan rusts away on a ride (2013), and in the wood on the steep north facing slope west of Long House there's a small overgrown Horsham Stone quarry, circa TQ 230 242, looking like a natural Ardingly Stone outcrop. That may be where the slabs came from for the roof of Long House, though they more likely came from the pits around the house that are now turned into ponds.

West of the A281 Horsham Road, **Westside and Newell's Rough** used to be part of the old forest, as were the Victorian mansions and their sprawling grounds along the main road. At **Westside** there's a large bosky glade, TQ 214 255, and attractive mixed woods of Birch, Beech, Spruce, Pine, Larch, and much Rhodi,

though not bad enough to make the area impassable. On at least two paths, e.g. TQ 213 257/8, a community of open ground old forest plants survives, with Green Ribbed and Common Yellow Sedges, Ivy Leaved Bellflower and Lesser Skullcap, amongst *Sphagnum* Bog Moss and Heath Plait Moss. There are Marsh Tits and Silver Washed Fritillary. **Newell's Rough** used to be leased to the Forestry Commission, but the sale of the lease to a private owner meant that it failed to benefit from the modern Commission's commitment to open access. An ornamental lake constructed after the gales, TQ 210 263, attracts Kingfishers and Brown Hawker dragons. At the Rough's north end in the old grounds of Newells are several fine groves of veteran Beech maidens, e.g. TQ 210/1/2 264/5, part within cleared glades and part embowered in Rhodi.

Lodgesale Wood, TQ 201 262, used also to be a Forestry Commission wood, and it bears a legacy of widespread Scots Pine over Birch and Bracken. Adjacent **Boyd's Wood**, TQ 199 259, has a lovely host of Wild Daffodils by its gill, with carpeting Bluebells, Butcher's Broom, and giant boundary bank Ash coppice stools.

FREE CHASE, STONEWICK, BISHOPS WOOD AND LYDHURST

To the east of Leonardslee the lovely woods are outside the ancient boundaries of St Leonard's Forest.

The Lake, TQ 234 252, above Furnace Pond, is tranquil and surrounded by dark woods. A Kingfisher has possessed it in recent years.

We picnicked on the sun drenched August slope of **Stonewick Meadows**, TQ 238/9 261, on the Woodland Trust property of William's Wood. Generation on generation of wood cutters, hay makers and herders stood where we stood in medieval forest clearings such as this. Roe Deer crashed away at our arrival. Above the Bracken the air was filled with motes … like snowflakes … myriadal flies and other tiny insects. Southern Hawker dragonflies patrolled, and the amber wings of Brown Hawkers glowed like stained glass. The meadow was a mosaic of purples of Betony and yellows of Goldenrod. There were Silver Washed Fritillary, Green Veined White and Brimstone butterflies … and a handsome Four Banded Leptura Longhorn Beetle, *Leptura quadrifasciata*, lazed on a Hogweed umbel. There were many woodland and woodland edge herbs amongst the grass. I counted 47 herbs and grasses, with Bitter Vetch and Heath Grass, Devil's Bit and Carnation Sedge. In the autumn there is Golden Waxcap fungus.

The southern lawns of Stonewick, now a nursing and rest home, are still unimproved old meadow too, (2013) and there is a further tiny meadow to the east, TQ 240 262.

Bishops Wood spans the gill below the meadows. It was part of the old episcopal manor of Stretham, near Henfield. It is now mostly planted Pine. **Dudwick Wood**, TQ 240 258, just to the south, retains its original coppice structure, though long overstood. It is dominated by Beech stools, but also English and Sessile Oak, and Scots Pine. It feels like the old swine pasture forest. There's a nice lake at **Lydhurst**, TQ 241 257. Skunk Cabbage is escaping into Dudwick Wood down its watercourse. Lydhurst is a gigantic mansion, and at the edge of its also-gigantic gardens is a metal cast statue of a World War Two Home Guard lookout. He must feel lonely there.

SPRONKETTS, EARWIG, AND CROSS COLWOOD LANES

A tangle of ancient lanes, often holloways, with tiny greens at their intersections: **Three Oaks Green**, TQ 239 244, **Bee Houses Green**, TQ 241 241, **Smith's Cross**, TQ 232 234, and **Spronketts Lane/Bull's Lane crossroads**, TQ 241 234.

Earwig Lane, TQ 242 248, is a beautiful green lane, best in autumn, very muddy in winter, between old wood banks and big trees, and with the woods of The Glen, to the east.

The Glen, TQ 243 247, is superb: a deep, humid, steep, long, tranquil, wild, varied and lovely gill. There is Shining Hookeria moss – that survivor of the Atlantic Age – and we know of 23 ancient woodland indicator plants, including Crab Apple and a few Wild Daffodils, with Anemones and Bluebells everywhere. There are fine Sessile Oaks at the north end on both slopes, e.g. a three span giant, TQ 245 251. Once we scooped up a baby Rabbit, to the grandson's delight, before letting it hip hop away. It is a place of Tawny Owls and Woodcock, fallen trees, tumbling banks, and a gurgling stream. Skunk Cabbage has escaped all the way down from stream side gardens at the north end (2012).

Spronketts Wood, TQ 244 236, shrunken by clearance for poor fields and rich mansions, is overwhelmed in parts by Rhodi thickets, with tall ornamental conifers overtopping in places. The name is a corruption of 'spring cuts', i.e. coppice wood, and coppice survives, but there seems to be no big native timber.

Opposite Colwood Park House, on the south side of Cross Colwood Lane, is delightful archaic **Colwood Meadow**, TQ 251 239. In June it has a huge display of Common Spotted Orchids, and in high summer it is dusted with the blue-mauve of Devils Bit Scabious (2012).

This is an area of ancient settlement and there are many delightful old houses, often wooden framed, like Free Chase and Barlands Farmhouses, Chargrove, TQ 247239, Chatesgrove, and Post Wood Cottages, TQ 242 250. The modern colonisation of the rich has plastered it with many painful mansions, like the plantation classical Drewitts, TQ 239 247, and modernist metal cubes at Free Chase and just south of Three Oaks Green, TQ 239 243.

Bulls and Barnfield Woods, TQ 235 239, west of Spronketts Lane, have many medium sized Oaks, much Holly, Laurel / Rhodi patches, and are bisected by a braided flat-bottomed Alder'd gill. Nice.

BOLNEY, WYKEHURST PARK AND WARNINGLID

Back in 1970, I got a summer job picking apples on the **Old Mill House Farm orchards**, west of Bolney, TQ 250 232. It was idyllic. The trees were standards you had to climb with a pointed ladder, and we spent a lot of time sitting in the crowns hailing each other like monkeys from tree to tree. It was piece work, of course, which meant we didn't *have* to work hard, and every day we lined up to collect our wages from a bloke sitting behind a little open window in the farm office.

A big chunk of those orchards are still there, some long derelict, and they've brought other parts back into production, though lots have been cleared. There's an orchard shop selling juices and ciders. The derelict trees are hoary all over with lichen, tangled with Bramble, and fallen fruit lies all around. In winter when the ground is crunchy with frost, big noisy flocks of Fieldfares feed, chirruping from the trees. In summer the air is full of Chiffchaff calls and a Fox and her cubs play. We were told that there were century old Bramley Apple trees over by the Mill House.

I was there before five a.m. at the end of one April as the stars faded. There was a February frost and April warmth, with the first apple blossom hiding amongst the grey-green lichen, over floating ground mist. First one Nightingale, then another, and a third sang forth from the dense undergrowth and collapsing trees. Tits and crows, warblers, wrens and a Stock Dove made their own tunes.

Bolney looks a pleasant village, with a fine council estate and smaller houses, and a scatter of older cottages at the south end by the church and at the north end on the site of the old Bolney Common. Yet the noise from the A23 London Road is deafening. The church is handsome, but the churchyard has been treated and has lost its old flowers and fungi. The adjacent cricket ground still has an old meadow fungal assemblage (2011).

Wykehurst Park to the north, has a pseudo-French chateau, TQ 257 243, of 1872–4, built for a mega-rich Austrian banker and now turned into flats, after a chequered history. The beautiful park has retained a feeling of unity, despite reportedly being in multiple ownership: groups of tall conifers; lots of rough, semi-improved and some unimproved pasture; a furze field, small woods, streams and ponds. South of the East Drive, TQ 281 244, there's a steep, heathy, south facing slope with Dwarf as well as Common Gorse, several Sedges, Tormentil and Small Copper butterflies.

At **Markwells Farm**, to the north of Wykehurst, there were a series of nice semi-intact meadows, TQ 265 255, where I found the huge, scarce and jewel-like "Blowfly of the Dead", *Cynomya mortuorum*. I don't know what survives of them after the recent horrendous widening operations on the A23. Part has gone, at least.

West of Bolney, **Nailard's Wood**, TQ 255 255, has been coniferised, and has a sort-of messy builders yard at its heart (2012). **Colwood Lane** has Notable Verges, circa TQ 256 264, but they seemed badly overgrown when I last visited. The conifer wood to the west, **"Piccadilly Wood"**, TQ 254 242, is an off-road four wheel drive site. The woodland is just stage scenery for the cars.

South of Nailard Wood is the **Booker's Farm Vineyard**, TQ 255 231. The vine fields are enclosed in 2m high fencing, and kissing gates let you through where the footpath crosses … a bit like being in a prison exercise yard (2012).

COWFOLD AND THE HORSHAM STONE QUARRIES

This was a country of scattered early settlement, and the names betoken that: *Wallhurst* (Briton's wood), Woldring*fold* and Cow*fold* (the suffix indicating an early forest assart), *Frith*knowle (rough, open woodland) and Home*wood* Farm (an early usage of the term '*wudu*' indicating extensive woodland).

The church and churchyard in **Cowfold** are lovely. There are fine old timber framed houses in and around Cowfold, such as Capon's Farmhouse and barn, TQ 205 227, to the west (perhaps circa 1300 in its earliest parts); Homewood Farmhouse to the east, TQ 247 226 (14th century / poshed-up); and Brook Place to the north, TQ 215 233 (Tudor / poshed-up).

Brook Place must be named after the nearby **brooks of the Cowfold Stream**, e.g. TQ 219 229, which passes southwards from its headstreams near Lower Beeding and Warninglid. The ample erstwhile farm house is evidence of the past prosperity of its lands. Brook pastures like these were once the highest value land types, with their fat cattle and lush hay crops. Now, the Cowfold Stream brooks are mostly derelict from Picts Lane, south to the A272 at Allfreys, with dense Blackthorn thickets extending out from the banks, impenetrable Brambles and big swarms of Hemlock Water Dropwort. Even the line of the public footpath has been abandoned at TQ 218 232/3. The Nightingales must love it, though, and the open parts must be fine places for marsh loving insects. Tussock Sedge is just present amongst the soggy rivulets, which are sometimes orange coloured from the iron deposits.

East and west of Cowfold, the **low ridge to the north of the A272** protects a band of Low Wealden landscape beyond, from that road's noise pollution. The low ridge is made by a hard band of Horsham Stone, and is topped by a long line of old quarries. Few of them still have stone exposures, but many are now ponds. (See 'Wealden Earth History' chapter). The tranquil narrow vale north of the ridge has large hedges and shaws, and some fine old farmhouses. Homelands Farmhouse, TQ 234 235, on Bull's Lane, is 'L' shaped, timber framed, seventeenth century or earlier, and has a little Tilgate Stone barn next to it that also looks ancient. There's an old Maple pollard and two old Oaks on the lane in front.

THE VALE OF WILD FRUIT AND SERVICE TREES

To the north west of Cowfold, the Wealden Clay vale of ancient woods, shaws and hedgerows rises northwards to Woldringfold. It is centred on the now-gone **Capon's**

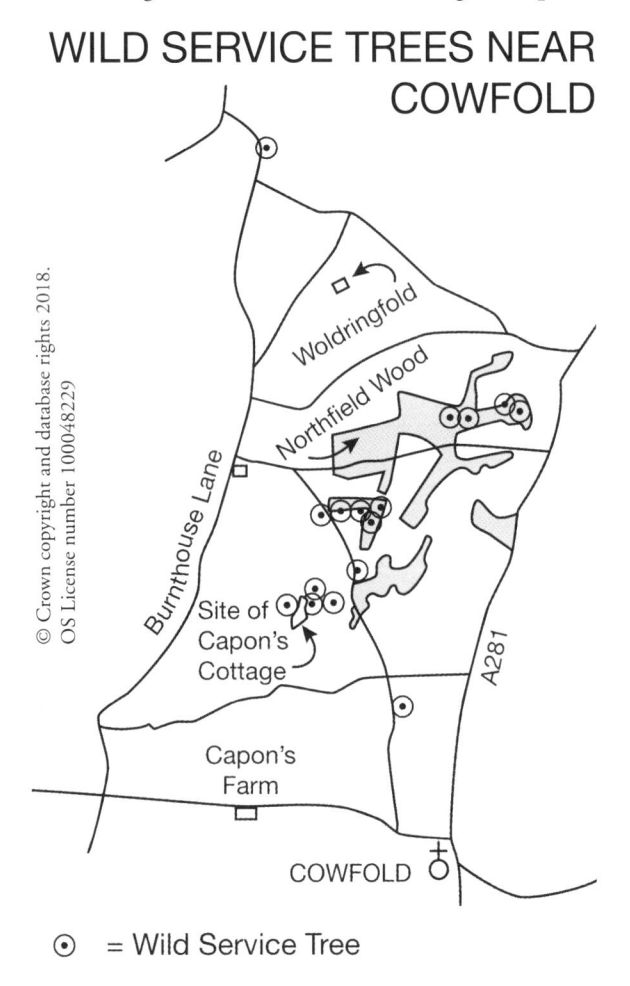

WILD SERVICE TREES NEAR COWFOLD

⊙ = Wild Service Tree

▢ = Woodland

SEDGWICK PARK MEADOWS

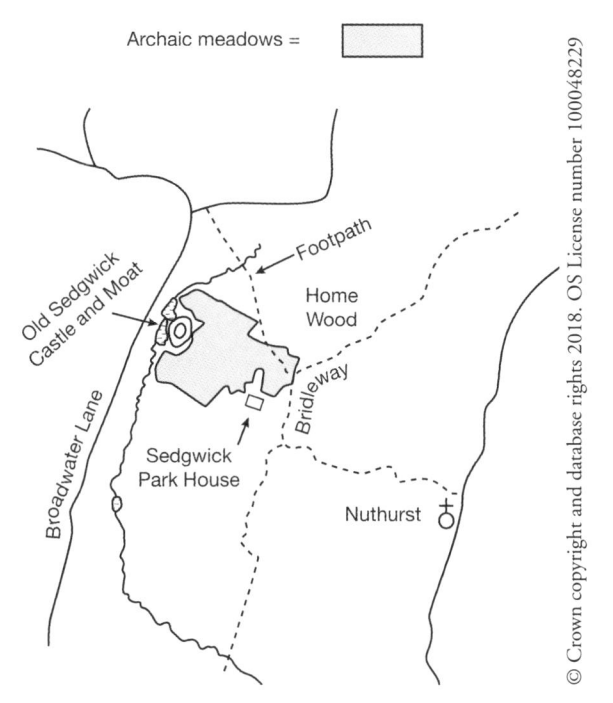

Archaic meadows = ☐

© Crown copyright and database rights 2018. OS License number 100048229

Cottage, TQ 207 234. I got to know it one August, when the hedgerows were full of fruit: lipstick red Honeysuckle and Arum berries, swelling Sloes, young Wild Service berries, Crab, Pear and Apple wildings, fattening white Hazel nuts, Spindle berries changing colour, and reddening Hips and Haws.

Around and north of the Capon's Cottage hedgerows there is an extraordinary concentration of mature Wild Service trees, and again in the Broad Shaw, east of Northfields Wood, TQ 214 241. Often these trees heavily bear fruit, and are similarly aged, tall and fine. Several are over one span in girth. Were they planted by the Hill House Farm or Woldringfold estates?

The Capon's Cottage shaw has a spiny wild pear (is this the genuinely wild *Pyrus pyraster*?) as well as three Wild Service, two primitive crabby varieties of Apple, Midland Thorn, English Elm, Cherry, Maple, Spindle, Sloe and Dogwood, and there's Butcher's Broom beneath.

Northfield Wood, TQ 209 240, is an ancient Bluebell wood, as are parts of the woods to its east, though others have been grubbed out.

Chatfield's Farmhouse, TQ 214 244, has huge chimneys. It is timber framed, with herringbone brick work and Horsham Slab roof, and its cottages are slab roofed and tile hung. Most of **Woldringfold's** park is now ploughed, and huge pylons interrupt the southwards view. There are old pear trees at **Northfield Farm** (with its tiny 'gingerbread' farmhouse) and Little Burnt House, and a good orchard at Burnt House, on the narrow and nut-laden Burnt House Lane.

SEDGWICK CASTLE AND PARK

The **medieval castle-in-the-woods**, TQ 180 269, is romantic in the old fashioned 'gothick' sense, though some romance also attaches to the Victorian mansion (Sedgwick Park) across the park … where **Alice (in Wonderland) Liddell** spent her honeymoon. That sprawling pile is a fancy of City business men, who built and have mostly since owned it.

The castle was perhaps started during the civil war of the 1140s known as 'The Anarchy', but keep, curtain walls, and two moats were built around 1258. It was demolished in the 1600s and much of the stone was probably used for the first version of Sedgwick Park house.

In the castle wood there are big groves of Male Fern and tall Redwoods (2013). On the west side yellow water lilies decorate the castle moat-pond made by the embayed Rushett's Stream. Hidden in a tangling wood on its western bank, like some lost Mayan temple, is a boarded up villa, with waterside terrace, statue, and stone galleon in full sail, a gothic frieze and a relief of Jesus' 'Ascension' in a cloud with arms outstretched, angels above and apostles below. The rest of the castle moats are deep, dry, and forested, with causeways across. The Foetid Iris flowers glow white-mauve in the gloom. The bailey in the centre has a few crumbling and ferny walls. It is a jungley place, with Swamp Cypress, fan palms, and bamboo, amongst the Bluebells, Periwinkle,

Sedgwick Castle's Elephant Tree with its small mahout

AREA GUIDE / Chapter 19: Sedgwick, Nuthurst, Leonardslee and Bolney

Ancient pollard Oak (and ladder) by the lost hilltop farmstead of Haven

Spotted Orchids and Primroses. The boat house has ripple bed Horsham slab paving and its timber roof says 1929.

There's more magic, for just north of the upper moat-pond, on the bank of Rushett Gill, stands the **Elephant Tree**, TQ 179 271, with long trunk, eyes, ears and forehead plain from two sides. An ancient, rotted and split pollard Ash of three spans girth at least, it bent to let its young mahout scramble safe into its whiskered crown.

The Rushett Gill shallows northwards from the castle towards its source at the north end of **Kite's Copse**, TQ 181 272. There are Wild Service trees in the Copse and north end of castle wood, and the wooded gill hides pits and mounds where Horsham Stone was long quarried, no doubt for castle and for mansion.

Despite all that wonder, it is the **meadows of Sedgwick Park** that most stand out. Its north meadow has much Cowslip at its west end, TQ 180 271, and in July, before the hay cut, the meadows are a pointillist pixellation of colours … with rattling Grasshoppers, droning Bumbles and jigging Meadow Browns … and Rooks a-squawking and chirping overhead. Some species are surprisingly rare (which makes one wonder about past treatment of the meadows) like Spiny Restharrow, Quaking Grass and (except in some spots) Glaucous Sedge, Burnet Saxifrage, Betony and Orchids, but rustling Yellow Rattle is gloriously dominant, with Knapweed, Meadow Vetchling, and Birds Foot Trefoil. It is a rare sight.

NUTHURST AND ITS NORTHERN WOODS

Much of the northern woods of the now-broken-up Sedgwick Park estate, along the Horsham Stone ridge, e.g. TQ 192 273 – **Home and Finche's Woods and Bushy Copse** – were coniferised. On a sunny August day some years back, things looked more hopeful, with replanting of broad leaved trees and a resurgent field layer … Violet Helleborine in flower and Silver Washed Fritillary on the wing. There are fine views south across the Nuthurst valley.

Cook's Copse, on the south side of the valley, TQ 197 267, is much more intact. It is a big and varied wood, with neatly coppiced Sweet Chestnut coups and large areas of Hazel and Ash, but few Oak. The northern gill is a dramatic vaulted space, with tall Beech – some outgrown from old coppice stools – ferny and lush.

Nuthurst Farm, TQ 189 263, a working farm (2012) west of the village, has a rambling, timber framed farmhouse with a slab roof, and next to it a sad old black Sussex barn at the point of collapse. **Nuthurst Farm Gill**, TQ 186 263, is superb: a deep, steep, narrow, primeval ravine. It has lots of Beech and Hazel coppice, much Cherry, Wild Daffodils on the east side, Bluebells, Anemones, Spurge Laurel and big Hollies.

When I last visited, **Rickfield,** TQ 196 285 and **Whytings Farms** were still working stock farms. On the lane between Nuthurst and Maplehurst there are good black-and white cottages with slab-roofs.

FROM NUTHAM TO NUTHURST

The great survivor in this landscape is the gill woodland, for there has been much shaw, hedge and small wood removal, for instance to create open surrounds for the modern mansions of Gaveston Hall and Elliotts, though much new woodland has been created, too.

Nutham Wood, TQ 165 253, epitomises these changes. Though shrunken, its heart is the wet woodland around the gill, smelling of Wild Garlic/ Ramsons, with much Alder carr. There's also a large area of old Hornbeam, and Hazel actively coppiced. It is richly varied, with Toothwort, and I counted 17 old woodland plants in one June visit. Its enchantment deserved better than the mad noise of the adjacent A24 Worthing Road.

Wooded **Stakers Gill** leads northwards to **Stakers Farm**, TQ 166 261, a fifteenth century Wealden hall house of great character. Its timber framing is uneven and wonky – like a children's drawing – and its slim chimneys are extraordinarily tall, over a slab roof. There's a perhaps-four-span Oak giant on the back lawn. It was described as 'lost in the weald' only 50 years ago.[3] That's a bad joke now, for it is as close to the Southwater Bypass as Nutham Wood.

There's more horseyculture than agriculture over much of this landscape. When **Ghyll House Farm**, TQ 177 261 was split up into field lots some years ago only two or the purchasers bought to farm, so I was told. The rest became horse grazing. One of the two hobby farm holdings, south of Limekiln Wood, TQ 185 255,

DAFFODIL COUNTRY AROUND HAVEN FARM

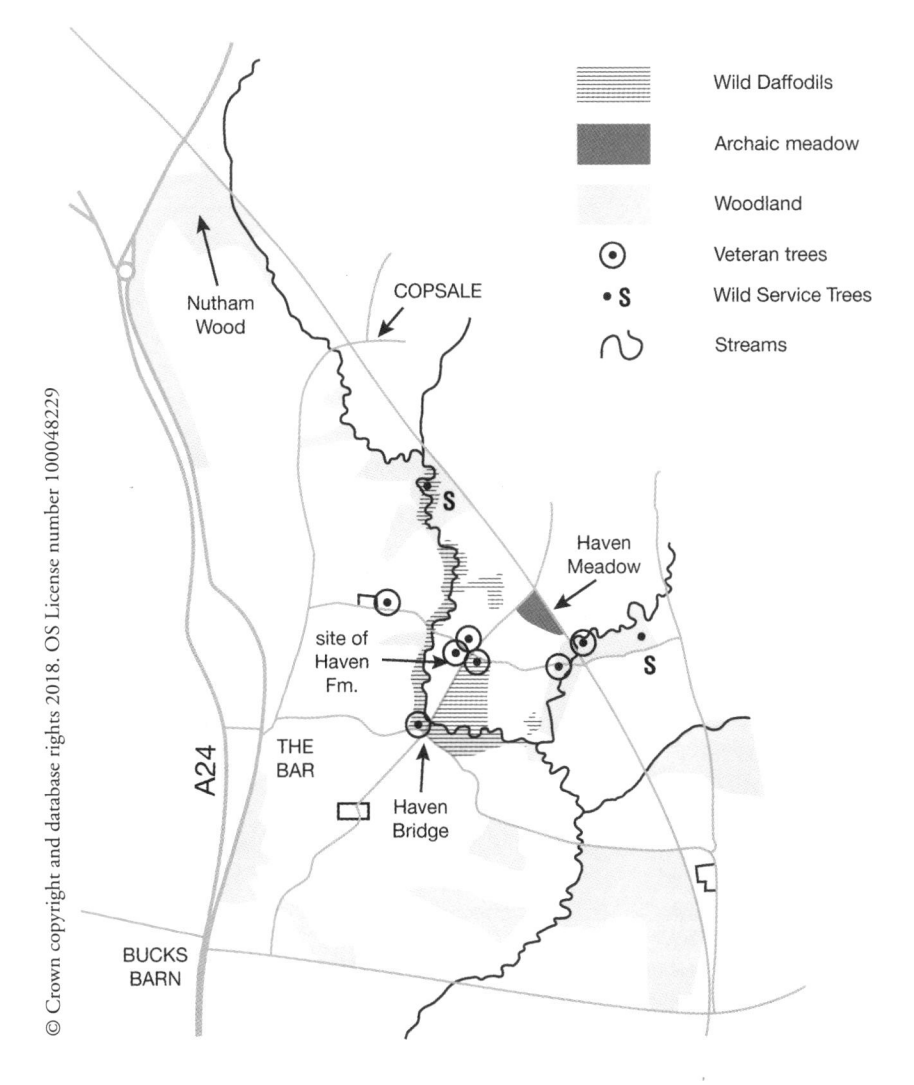

the new Elliotts plonked in the centre – a horrible antebellum mock slave plantation house. The gallops are surfaced with chipped rubber. There's no proper place for nature or food growing.

AROUND THE DOWNSLINK FROM COPSALE TO THE A272

This is a landscape I remember well from Saturday journeyings on the Horsham Flyer in the early sixties, rumbling past muddy farmyards, buttercup fields, blowsy hedges and woods, and over little farm bridges. Much of that character can still be summoned, though the farms are now mostly posh conversions, with their land as often some rich owner's playground, as farmland.

The lost **Haven Farm**, TQ 175 237, is aptly named. Its site is a small hilltop at the crossroads of a green lane and a footpath, with ancient gill woodland on three sides. All that remains of the farmstead is Horsham stone rubble, two tiny ponds, a hedged close, and three huge Oak pollards.

It is the heart of a **Wild Daffodil landscape**, and the two fields to the south, though otherwise improved, still bloom Daffodil yellow in March, as do the woods east and west of Haven Bridge, TQ 174 234, and all up the gill past Tuckman's Farm till the stream disappears under the embankment of the Downslink. In the gill woodland there is Toothwort, too, as well as Wild Service Tree.

Just before the Haven Farm green lane passes under the Downslink, the tiny triangular **Haven flower meadow** hides, TQ 177 239. Though undermanaged – rank and tussocky (2015) – it is still a paradise garden. Cowslip, Adder's Tongue Fern and Spring Sedge just cling on. In July, it is a dazzle of Yellow Rattle, Betony, Crosswort, White Clover, Buttercup, Spotted Orchis and so much more ... 53 plants seen on one visit, whilst we sat munching cake by the hedge, and the voices of the

was delightful. Run by three friends, it had chickens, Hebridean sheep and Saddleback x Old Spot pigs. Together, they bought its two fields and small woods for circa £80,000. In 2012, it was worth perhaps £240,000. Planning permission for a barn meant that the price of the land skyrocketed. They sold the produce to workmates, making no profit from it, of course. It's gone now. With land prices like that, and such competition from non-agricultural uses, what chance does sustainable and democratic farming have?

There was a Grey Wagtail pair foraging in the gill south of Ghyll House Farm. Perhaps their nest was near? **Cripps Wood**, east of Alicelands, is a Bluebell wood, TQ 177 256.

The old **Elliots Farm,** TQ 180 251, is lovely, with sixteenth century black and white timber frame, but there's no farming to be seen, for its farmland has become a sterile horse ranch, with hedgerows gone, and cyclists along the Downslink came cheerfully through the screen of trees. (It is very far gone, 2017).

South east of the meadow, on the east side of the Downslink, is the **gill wood of the lost Sunt Farm**, TQ, 180 238. The flood plain part is an Elm wood, with a fine Ash of three span girth. It is rich in the trees of ancient woodland – Wych Elm, Small Leaved Lime, Wild Service, Midland Thorn and Crab. The name 'Sunt' may indicate that this was an early swine pasture 'den' of the manor of Sompting, from which it lies exactly due north, and 11 miles distant, as the crow flies.

Narrow lanes are dangerous places nowadays, but stand with care to admire two stretches of flower-rich verge. The first is on both sides of the lane by **Joles Farm**, TQ 188 237. The splash of egg yellow Dyers Greenweed gave it away first, one afternoon in June, whilst driving past. There is Spotted Orchis and Betony, Ox Eye Daisy and Agrimony. It is now (2015) in poor condition. The second lies at **Steeds Corner**, TQ 178 248, and may be even richer in flowers, though not in colour.

BETWEEN THE BAR AND BELMOREDEAN

The four archaic meadows at **Walden Close,** TQ 188 226, on the A272 are (or perhaps *were* [4]) a jewel. The smaller, eastern two – divided by a modern drive – are the best, and are wholly unimproved. They are damp meadows, with much Pepper Saxifrage, Sneezewort, and Hemlock Water Dropwort. East of the drive there are sheets of Betony and frequent Devils Bit as well. Their recent history has been painful, and they suffered considerable neglect and damage. Yet they are/were the largest archaic meadow site for a considerable distance.

Smallham Farm, TQ 184 229, is the centre of large scale, new, broad leaved woodland creation, for instance at **Upper Soil Gill**, TQ 185 234. The fine old farm buildings seemed derelict when we last visited. Along the northern wood edge, TQ 181 234, the shreds of old meadow, with Spotted Orchis and Crosswort, Grass Vetchling and Buttercup, made a lovely midsummer picture of carmine pink and yellow. **Freeman's Wood**, TQ 180 229, is part old, part new. The brookland on its west side is lovely, with tall hedges and thick shaws.

MAPLEHURST AND HIGH HURST

Maplehurst was built around a little green, and some of the old cottages set back from the road tell where parts of the green were, before enclosure. North and south of Park Lane, TQ 194 247, there is a dairy herd (2014), cereals, tillage and haylage. **Maplehurst Farm**, just south west, TQ 185 241, has a poshed-up ancient farmhouse, but the deer and llama farm around it is regretable, with 2m fences all over and the hedge bottoms nibbled out.

Long Wood, to the south east, TQ 195 243, has blanketing Bluebells, Spurge Laurel and lots of old Hornbeam coppice stools in the upper wood. Its eastern extension at **High Hurst Copse,** TQ 202 246, is larger and even better, with Wild Service and Midland Thorn. There are many fine old Oaks around **High Hurst Manor**, and Swallows nest in the old wooden barns (now livery stables).

The Ivorys is another sprawling modern mansion, but next-door **Ivorys Farm**, TQ 198 241, though poshed-up, is old and timber framed, as are its old Sussex barns. There's much busy livery activity and small businesses in a sort-of industrial estate.

The field shaws to the east of **Micklepage Farm**, TQ 196 256, are all intact and lovely, with occasional Sessile Oak.

ENDNOTES

1. "The Habitats and Vegetation of Sussex", page 24, by Francis Rose. An essay within the 'Atlas of Sussex Mosses, Liverworts and Lichen' by Rose, Stern, Matcham and Coppins. Booth Museum of Natural History and Brighton Borough Council (1991).
2. I last saw it there in 1998.
3. 'The Buildings of England: Sussex', page 334, by Nairn and Pevsner. Penguin (1965).
4. I last saw them in 2012, when the issues had not been resolved.

AREA GUIDE / Chapter 20: Rift valley and forest: The headwaters of the Ouse

CHAPTER 20
Rift valley and forest:
The headwaters of the Ouse

The rift valley westwards of the Balcombe viaduct as far as the source of the Ouse constitutes a low Wealden 'inlier' in this corrugated High Wealden landscape of ancient woods, streams, old farms, and meandering tiny lanes.

Despite this mosaic of farmed and wooded land, there are quite large areas free of public motor roads. A walk of three miles northwards from the Slough Green ridge to the edge of Balcombe Forest can easily avoid all public roads. However, the amount of public footpaths and green lanes is also sometimes limited (for instance over the Brantridge woods, TQ 29 30, and the Borde Hill Estate, TQ 31 27) and public land with a formal freedom to roam is largely confined to the National Trust's Nymans Estate woods, the 100 acre Millenium Woodland between Cuckfield and Haywards Heath, and the Blunts Wood and Paiges Meadow Local Nature Reserve.

The A23 makes a howling gash right through this landscape, severely damaging tranquillity in a mile-wide corridor. An elderly couple whose Handcross garden backed onto the road, and who have always lived in the area, told me that they didn't notice it. Thus does long habituation erode our ability to fight back against damage to our quality of life.

NYMANS AND HIGH BEECHES TO BLACKFOLD

Two footpaths descend from Handcross eastwards into the deep woods that run continuously for 1.3 miles to Brantridge Lane: Cow Wood and Harry's Wood (both SSSI's), and Blackfold and Dencombe Woods.

Under deep February snow **Harry's Wood**, TQ 269 302, was doubly magical. A Redwing flock passed through, and a pair of Jays, and a Woodcock rose, whilst Great Spotted Woodpecker drilled. There are a scatter of fine veteran Oak and Beech, both standing and fallen. Along its higher contours it is an Oak-Hazel wood with some Beech. Ash joins in lower down over the outcropping Grinstead Clay. There's much overstood English and Sessile Oak coppice, and some part-controlled Rhodi infestation. Over the boundary on the National Trust's land a pair of Goldcrest fed on the frozen pond and bushes in Foxhole Gill, whilst we enjoyed hot tea and shortbread, grateful for the folded rubble bags between our butts and the frozen ground.

Cow Wood's 'Redwood Avenue', down in the main **Nymans valley,** is long and lovely, with alternating Wellingtonias, Coastal Redwood, and Spruce. In March, there are lots of patches of Wild Daffodils in the gullies and valley sides, TQ 267 296.

There is a low outcrop of Ardingly Sandstone rocks along the south side of the valley. Back in 1990, before my return to Sussex, my mate Paul Harmes first showed me the jewel on these rocks: mats of Tunbridge Filmy Fern, *Hymenophyllum tunbrigense*, with its translucent, one-cell-thick fronds. Not much like a fern, more like a liverwort or grandiose moss, it had clung on here in the humid microclimate of this valley for perhaps 5000 years, since the drying of the wider environment isolated it at the end of the warm and wet Atlantic Period.

It is gone, now – stolen en masse in November 2011.

The valley stream debouches into the pond of the vanished Tudor **Blackfold iron furnace**, a delightful spot, with shaded mossy banks, TQ 274 294. The furnace made pig iron for transportation to the forge at Holmsted, 1.75 miles to the south. **Blackfold's** wood and valley lie just north east, TQ 279 302. They are tranquil and remote, with a deep gill, dense plantation Larch and Norwegian Spruce over the lower slopes, but good Oaks, old Sweet Chestnut coppice and Bracken further up. (Now part-sold off as fragments, 2017). There used to be a farm on the plateau, TQ 270 301. It is long gone, but a fine three span Oak pollard survives on the farmstead site. Blackfold was a medieval swine pasture of Saddlescombe, 11.5 miles due south behind

The Brighton Line Ouse Valley Viaduct (1841): I call it the 'Rift Valley' Viaduct.

Newtimber Hill, on the Downs. Strange to think that such a tiny hamlet could once command such remote woodlands.

High Beeches Gardens, TQ 276 307, lie right across Worth Forest's old south boundary, and two veteran Oaks mark it. The Gardens nurture a series of archaic meadows and lawns. In early spring, there are superb displays of non-native Daffodils, such as the Hoop Petticoat Daffodil, *Narcissus bulbocodium*. Later, there are Green Winged Orchis, masses of Ox Eye Daisy, Yellow Rattle and Bitter Vetch. From September onwards, there's lots of Devils Bit and you may find the Pink Ballerina Waxcap, *Hygrocybe calyptriformis*, or the Indigo Pinkgill, *Entoloma chalybaeum var. lazulinum*. **Dencombe Wood,** in the gardens, has within it many fine exotics, below a canopy of maiden Oaks.

BRANTRIDGE TO BALCOMBE

At their northern end, the meadows and woods of **Brantridge,** TQ 288 302, also lie across the old Forest boundary, and the transition can still be seen. In the wood east of Brantridge Park Farm are several huge dead Beech hulks which mark the old boundary, TQ 285 306/7. The northern slope of **Knoll Wood**, TQ 292 308, ends at a large bank. Beyond this is a fine old Forest remnant that is now within the large gardens of two mansions, embracing at least four superb Beech and Oak veterans. The largest Beech – of over four spans – collapsed recently, and its fallen limbs lay around, with only one still intact (2012).

Along either side of the drive to Brantridge mansion are a series of semi-improved meadows, TQ 286 306, which retain some archaic meadow plants.

Whilst **Brantridge Wood** remains largely mixed, with much Oak, Birch, Rhodi and overstood Sweet Chestnut coppice, most of **Knoll, Alder and Casteye Woods,** TQ 302 307, are heavily coniferised. **Pond Wood** has a sporting 'duck farm' in modern ponds along its gill, with a Mallard population as dense as a chicken run (2009).

South of Casteye Wood and just north of Rowhill Lane is a nice old horse pasture on the spur of a hill, crossed by a footpath. It is an SNCI. **Rowhill Pasture**, TQ 299 304, has lots of Musk Mallow, some Devils Bit and much Tormentil, though it seems to have suffered some damage.

STAPLEFIELD TO PILSTYE AND RYELANDS

Staplefield lies on the *old* London-Brighton Road, which was shifted west of there to its present alignment some two centuries ago. It was an ancient hub at the head of the navigable Ouse, and the meeting place of many outliers of southern and Downland manors.[1] The village is strung around **Staplefield Common**, which still has its old openness, with a fine cricket pitch and pub. On summer days when the mowing tractor passes over the grass (which it does too often) the air is filled with the narcotic-sweet smell of Chamomile, which is common on the west side and near the war memorial. Bits of the old archaic heathy vegetation – old meadow fungi, Betony, Heath Bedstraw et al – hold on, but need far better recognition. **Staplefield Churchyard** is much richer, TQ 277 281, with 16 old meadow Waxcap, *Hygrocybe*, fungi recorded (making it the third best site in middle Sussex) and in spring you may see Green Winged and Spotted Orchids, Pepper Saxifrage, Bitter Vetch, Zig Zag Clover, Spring Sedge, Betony, and even Cowslips just clinging on amid many other herbs and grasses. Along Brantridge Lane to the east is the horrible Old Hall mansion and park – all heavy-duty lake construction and earth moving and screen planting to keep the likes of us out. It has a mock classical temple folly on its lake island, and looks like something out of a glossy magazine advertising summat or other …

To the north things get better. West of the Lane, **Sole's Coppice**, TQ 284 292, is a mixture of ancient and secondary woodland, with some fine old Beeches along its western gill slopes. **Ditton Place**, north again, is another of those gigantic box mansions that some City type built a century ago. It is now part of a new residential complex. It served a far more useful purpose as an Inner London Education Authority special school for many years.

East of the Lane the complex of woods around **Northlands Farm** is superb. **Northlands Wood**, TQ 290 293, has a long Ardingly Sandstone outcrop along its western side. Though much of the Wood is compromised by heavy softwood planting, the rocks still nurture (2012) their old Atlantic Period relics: including Hay Scented Buckler Fern, partly shaded by Larch and Yew, Holly and Beech, but just clinging on.

Seyron's Wood, TQ 296 293, is tranquil, large and varied, with much Bracken (2012). Woodcock like it. You've got to be warped to want to shoot them (but plenty do) so great is their beauty and scarcity. There are old gnarled upturned Chestnut stools, fine maiden Oaks and Gean, and big Hazel coups. There is Shining Hookeria moss next to the stream in **Long Wood**, TQ 292 291, and, up on a sandrock outcrop on the western gill side in **Little Sion Wood**, TQ 293 288, are three old beech pollards looking down at you like trolls on the lookout for dinner …

Whitethroat Lane that winds along the northern slope of the rift valley is lovely, passing the very posh 15th century **White House,** and **Combehole Wood**, TQ 299 289, which has a winding sandrock outcrop on both slopes at its northern end. **Spicers Farm** is 15th–16th century.

Pilstye, TQ 305 284, was an early Norman or Saxon cooperative homesteading of the 'waste' by three co-cultivators, no doubt sharing a plough. Its boundaries can be traced, thanks to the work of Heather Warne.[2] Pilstye Farm (1642) and Upper Pilstye (15th century) may stand on the sites of two of the three original farmsteads of the cooperators. They chose their ground well, on south facing well-drained sandstone, bounded by stream side meadows to the south and embracing the supplementary resources of rough sandrocks, woods, and sticky clay to the north at **Rowhill** ('*Rough Hill*').

The sandrock outcrop is dramatic at its southern end, TQ 305 290, with a quarried, vertical face. There's much Pine, Holly and Rhodi, which seems to have stifled any surviving Atlantic Period flora. **Pilstye and Rowhill Woods** are wild, mixed and lovely.

To the east of the Balcombe Road is **Lower Stumble**, TQ 310 292, the new fracking site.

The three trolls of Little Sion Wood – silhouetted against a winter sunset

On the flood plain of the Ouse stream, abutting Sand's Wood is **Balcombe Marsh**, TQ 315 284, a tiny reserve of the Sussex Wildlife Trust – an unsustainably small 'precious fragment' of archaic marshland, which stands in painful contrast to the surrounding nitrogen green cattle pastures. When I first visited in the mid-sixties the sward was low, and there was a lovely flowering of Marsh Helleborine Orchis, this being one of its only two Sussex sites. By contrast recently, the herbage was as tall as a person, which seems to have killed off the almost-as-rare Cotton Grass and Meadow Thistle, as well as the Marsh Helleborine. Still, there is much that survives: Bog Pimpernel, Marsh Pennywort, Ragged Robin, Marsh Speedwell, Narrow Buckler Fern, and lots more.

Sitting on the west side of the carriage as you whiz London-wards, looking out of the window as you cross the Balcombe viaduct, you will often have peered at the ancient farmstead that comes close into view as the land rises and the viaduct ends. It is **Ryelands Farm**, TQ 320 280, and it was named for its proximity to the infant Ouse that flows under the viaduct. '*Rye*' is a corruption of '*at the ea*' ('*ater ree*'/ '*atte ree*) and 'ea' is the Saxon word for river. Both the Adur (with *Eaton* Farm at Ashurst) and the Ouse were called 'ea' as was the Thames (with *Eton* College on its banks).

BORDE HILL TO CUCKFIELD

The wet clay woods north-west of **Borde Hill,** TQ 314 270, are full of roosting pheasants after dusk. They make a right clatter if they're disturbed. The sandy fields around **Great Bentley Farm**, TQ 313 278, are large – and have been for 150 years or more. There are big views of the marching brick arches of the 1841 **Balcombe Viaduct.** In winter, the old course of the Ouse shows up as linear meanders of shallow flood, in

Horsgate Farmstead, TQ 311 251, is surrounded by beautiful semi-improved meadows of Sweet Vernal Grass, with wet areas of Soft Rush and Ladies Smock, and Birds Foot Trefoil on humps and tumps. It is a landscape of fine old Oaks. The hollow lane southwards over the valley brook is shaded and lovely.

Blunts Wood and Paige's Meadow Local Nature Reserve, TQ 317 244, is a tribute to imaginative local authority initiative. It embraces Blunt's and Paiges's Woods and eight hedged meadows across a little valley, some improved, and the rest semi-improved. The best two are at the north end next to Blunts and Paiges Woods. They have lots of colourful herbs, and Common Spotted Orchids, Common Blue butterfly and Burnet Companion moth.

The Oak-Hazel-Hornbeam woods are ancient and rich. I counted 21 ancient woodland indicator species on one visit, including Early Purple Orchis, Crab Apple, Midland Thorn and Goldilocks Buttercup, with Wood Sorrel, Golden Saxifrage and Redcurrant down in the gill. My best memory (and I went often when I worked in Haywards Heath) is of watching a pair of Treecreepers feeding their squeaking young at a nest behind peeling bark at the top of a dead Birch bole. Lovely birds. Lovely place.

THE RIFT VALLEY'S SOUTHERN SLOPES

An ancient ridge top route tracks westwards from Whiteman's Green, marking the watershed between the Ouse, to the north, and the Adur, to the south. It takes several names as it goes west: Staplefield Road, Sloughgreen Lane, Cuckfield Lane and Warninglid Lane.

North of Staplefield Road is a beautiful roadless vale of small woods, little farms, and low wooded ridges (with Toll Shaw, Hammerhill Copse and Bigges Farm upon them). Much of it is part of the Borde Hill estate. The low ridges are capped with hard Horsham Stone strata within the sunken wedge of Wealden Clay which is the central feature of the rift valley. The Wealden Clay outcrops between Sidnye Farm and Mizbrooks Farm – well-named (it means 'moss brook') because there are a series of springs eastwards from there along Spark's Lane

The soft Wealden Clay landscape of 'The Rift Valley' from Lullings, Borde Hill

... and another view of 'The Rift Valley'

pastures which are sometimes still rushy, and with traces of the old vegetation.

South of Hanlye Lane the old fields of Hanlye and Gravelye Farms have been planted up by the Borde Hill estate with broad leaved trees to make the **Millennium Wood**, TQ 317 252. They've kept nice wide rides, with good views. There are lots of overgrown Cuckfield Stone pits – some now ponds – all along the valley sides. **Penland Wood**, TQ 321 250, and the gills that drain down into it from Gravelye Farm are lovely Bluebell woods right next to the built up area. **Penland Farm** has been sold by the Borde Hill Estate for housing development. What they give with one hand (Millennium Wood) they take away with the other …

(as in the wood at TQ 297 269) marking the transition from the sandstone to the clay below.

Much of the woodland over the low ridges is heavily pitted, and many of the pits are now ponds, but it was Horsham Stone they were digging, not iron ore. On the underside of upturned root plates and along some paths there are large pieces of Horsham slabstone.

It is an 'Oak countryside'. They are everywhere. The old hedges are well managed and the tracks hard surfaced. The young woods are neat and tidy. The farmed land has large numbers of sheep, and there is livery, too, and game cover crops. Many of the ponds are infested with reared Duck. This kind of busy management means that there is an absence of archaic grassland sites.

Sidnye Farm, TQ 295 277, is a Borde Hill tenancy. The name, like Ryelands (see above), includes the old river name 'ea'.[3] **Bigge's Farm**, TQ 290 271, is 15th century, with a timber frame, and nearby **Cleaver's Farm** and **Mizbrooks** are 17th century or earlier, and timber framed.

On the tilled fields we've found a broken Bronze Age scraper, and, nearby amongst the stubble, good clusters of Bird's Nest fungi, *Cyathus olla*, with all their tiny 'eggs' nestled inside.

Hammerhill Copse and Bridge took their names from the **Holmsted Hammer Forge**, which worked until c. 1660. It took its pig iron from Blackfold (see above) and Slaugham Furnace (see below), and from Tilgate, too. The pond bay lay just west of the Ouse bridge, TQ 281 273. It was largely removed by the County Council in 1928 to use as 'fill' for road works, though a section of it survives.

North of Sloughgreen Lane there are still areas of the greatest charm, particularly around Mallion's Lane and Staplefield Lane, but eastwards, Holmstead Farm has been painfully damaged by agribusiness. The din from the A23 is relentless.

The woods around **Beacon Hall**, TQ 274 262, have some fine old Beeches, perhaps outgrown coppice, and there's Sweet Chestnut coppice east of Mallion's Lane bordering Sloughgreen Lane's north side. It's just a cosmetic fringe though, for further downslope the ancient Holmsted Wood, which remained intact till fifty years ago, is now all gone and its site used for landfill, now grassed over. The new Holmsted Farm, to its east, is a sprawling eyesore.

Mallion's Lane itself is sheer delight, TQ 276 264. Tiny and almost car-free, it winds downhill with colourful flowery verges on both sides. I counted 73 herbs and grasses in one shortish July visit. There are Orchids, Betony, and Zigzag Clover amongst much Upright Hedge Parsley, Hogweed and Knapweed. There are many damp-loving species, like Great Willowherb, Fleabane, Marsh Bedstraw, Yellow Loosestrife and False Fox Sedge. Particularly uphill, there are many woodland species that are refugees from the lost Holmsted Wood – Bluebells, Goldenrod and Wood Melic. The verges are getting coarse because they are under-managed. Visit them before they decline further.

On lower ground the Lane turns sharply northwards and a notice tells you "Warning – Ducks on the Road". It is next to a tiny streamside 'gingerbread' cottage embowered in woods, TQ 271 268. Definitely a hobbit cottage. **North Hall**, along the Lane, is also delightful, with a tiled and weather boarded barn in front of the 17th century farmhouse.

You'll have missed "the old lost road through the woods[4]", though, as you turned sharply north, for at that sharp turn the **old course of Staplefield Lane** forked southwards. That damp and winding route, TQ 270/1 265/6, was shut up some 150–200 years ago and is now just a lovely green tunnel. The little bridge over the stream has long gone and only old bricks and a broken earthenware bottle on the stream bed mark its

OLD ANSTY WOOD

Much of this big wood was destroyed between 1800 and 1870. Several beautiful fragments survive.

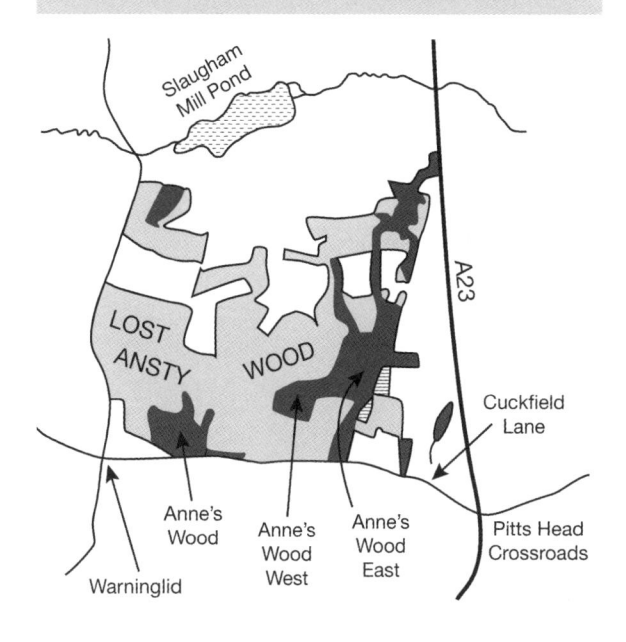

- Lost woodland
- Surviving woodland
- Archaic meadows (2011) now returning to woodland

Reproduced using c. 1870 Ordnance Survey 6 inch to 1 mile map base with the kind permission of the Ordnance Survey.

Ashfold Rough: line of funereal Beech

site. South of there the green lane has been turned into a wild garden.

Whitehouse Farm, TQ 270 262, is Tudor and timber framed, and next to it is a tiny archaic farm meadow that has good displays of Spotted Orchids (2011).

North of Cuckfield Lane a grand wood – **Ansty Wood** – stretched all the way to Warninglid from Portways Farm, just west of the A23. In 1800, it was three quarters of a mile by half a mile in size, but by 1870 it had been reduced to three scattered fragments.

Those three fragments are still superb. All three are Bluebell woods. The western fragment is now known as **Anne's Wood**, TQ 253 262. The upper part is a Sessile Oak wood of both maidens and coppice. There are two fine veteran Beech pollards and frequent Holly, with occasional Hard Fern and Wood Sorrel. Bracken is abundant. Downslope is dominated by Downy and Silver Birch. I saw a Lesser Spotted Woodpecker on the northern boundary of **Anne's Wood West,** TQ 258 263, which has a large area of big Beech veterans and old coppice on its east side, and much Birch to the west, and upslope. There's Narrow Buckler Fern and Rowan. It is very pitted. At dusk, in a 'cave' made by overhanging Beech roots, we found a 'Brambley Hedge' tableau of tiny animals having a tea party, complete with china dolls tea set. There were teddies, a red dragon, little hanging shoes, and dangling stained glass shapes. It's not the only time we've come across such things. **Anne's Wood East,** TQ 261 264, downslope on the clay, is an old coppice wood of gigantic Ash stools over young Hazel, with Alder on wet ground, and abundant Dog's Mercury. There's a three span Beech.

On the eastern boundary of East Ansty Wood is a little old **meadow**, TQ 262 264. **Portway's Farm meadow** is fast disappearing through long dereliction (2011). Only about a third is still grassland, and a quarter Bracken. The rest is invasive Ash, Sloe and Bramble. There's still a good show of Devil's Bit and Tormentil, and Meadowsweet is invasive in large parts. There are big old anthills, and Betony and Heath Bedstraw cling on. Next to the meadow, upslope, is a second archaic meadow, also at heavy risk, with abundant Tormentil and a mixed swarm of Narrow Buckler Fern and Male Fern. Both these meadows are very noisy from the nearby A23.

North of Warninglid Lane there has been much bulldozing of small woods and hedges, but much survives. **The infant Ouse**, west of Slaugham Lane, is a place of Ramsons and Reeds, Redcurrant and Alder: lush and wild. It is a mere stream, with a stoney bottom in places. Bullhead fishlings like it. On the west side of Hampshire Wood, a gill drops down from Upper Stanford in a deep, almost tranquil cleft, TQ 245 274/5. It is a delight in spring, with Bluebells, Primroses, Crab Apple blossom, and Anemones. The stream is shallow, clear and stony. Freshwater Shrimps are large and abundant, and there are a few caddis larvae. **Hampshire Wood** itself, TQ 245 277, has fine Oaks and lots of Chestnut, some recently coppiced. Part is heavily Rhodi infested (2012). On **Stanford Lane** both **Gards** (ex-Middle Stanford) and **Denman's Farmhouse**s are ancient (17th century), and **Bell's Farmhouse** down a lane to the west is 16th century, though poshed-up. **Tulley's Rough**, north of the farmhouse, is secondary Chestnut coppice and youngish Oak, but the gill stream to its south west, TQ 238 276, is lovely high Oak forest over Bluebells.

At its southern end, Stanford Lane climbs over a wooded ridge of outcropping Horsham Stone. Its woods, TQ 241 268, are a delight of Bluebells with Early Purple Orchis and Greater Stitchwort. Some of the Horsham Stone pits are flooded. **Slatehouse Farm** has a dairy herd and all the sprawling clutter of modern industrial farming. The gill wood to the north of the farmstead, TQ 243 270, though, is a lovely Bluebell wood, with much Dogs Mercury and hoary Oaks … the sound of a Woodpecker drilling, rushing water, sunlight and peace.

SLAUGHAM AND ASHFOLD

The village of **Slaugham**, TQ 257 281, has many lovely ancient cottages and bigger houses, but the atmosphere is of well-preened wealth. Not the place to buy a pint of milk. The one mile walk north to Handcross through the long-gone Slaugham deer park is still pleasant, but the tranquillity of Orange Gill woods is heavily damaged by the A23.

The best parts of the village centre are the church and churchyard and the small triangular green at the southern end of the street, abutting the churchyard. The church is a superb amalgam of periods, from the 13th to the 17th, with a lovely clutter of monuments and brasses and heraldic flummery.

The little pieces of green are still lawned by their archaic turf – beautifully maintained by mowers, now, not geese and donkeys – all furrowed and banked where centuries of cartwheels, cattle hooves and human feet have worn them down. Year on year I have seen lots of old meadow fungi upon them.

Better still are the lawns in the churchyard, with 21 species of old meadow Waxcap fungi recorded, making it the twin richest site (with Danehill churchyard) in middle Sussex. Tread carefully in late summer and autumn.

At its western end **Slaugham Mill Pond**, TQ 253 275, is true wilderness … a place of open water, spongy mint-smelling marsh, Reedmace, and tangled rotten Alders. A big fish jumps clear of the water. A pair of Great Crested Grebe sleep afloat, their heads resting on their backs and white necks plain. **Holes Wood**, TQ 255 277, bordering its north side, between the Pond and the village, is an Oak-Hazel-Bluebell Wood, with many quarry pits.

Due west of Slaugham is the little **Slaugham Common**, now all wooded. The construction of the **Furnace Pond**, TQ 249 280, actually drowned part of the common, as millers and iron masters sometimes did (as at Vale Bridge Common, Burgess Hill). In the wood below the bay, Rabbits unearth iron slag with their burrowing into the soft banks by the stream. **The Slaugham iron furnace** was working in Elizabethan times, but had disappeared by 1653.

The backbone of **Ashfold Rough**, TQ 243 283, is a north-south, half mile long bank topped with a lovely line of Beech of the most funerary and solemn appearance. All the trees are close, even bundle-planted, and lean mournfully over, often broken, some falling, many rotten. It is perhaps 150 years old. The plantation on both sides has Larch, Christmas tree and Pine coups, Birch and dense Rhodi thickets, and scattered Wellingtonias.

The Rough has gone from forest heath, to furzefield, to timber plantation in the last two centuries. Beyond its northern tip are four posh villas where a big Victorian mansion used to stand, overlooking **Ashfold Park**, which seems to have lost most of its big trees.

In the deep freeze of February 2012, local people (and us) were out tobogganing on the snowed up Park slope west of Coos Lane, TQ 250 287. The snow was like dry Ready Brek flakes, twinkling under a big yellow sun in a clear blue sky, with blue snow shadows glinting.

ENDNOTES

1   Heather Warne pers comm.
2   "Early Hamlets in the mid-Sussex Weald – a contribution for Wealden Settlement Study Circle", Heather Warne. (ct. 2010)
3   'Sidnye' is a corruption of '*southney*' – 'south of the river'.
4   From Rudyard Kipling's "The Way Through the Woods" in "Rewards and Fairies" published by Wordsworth Classics (1995)

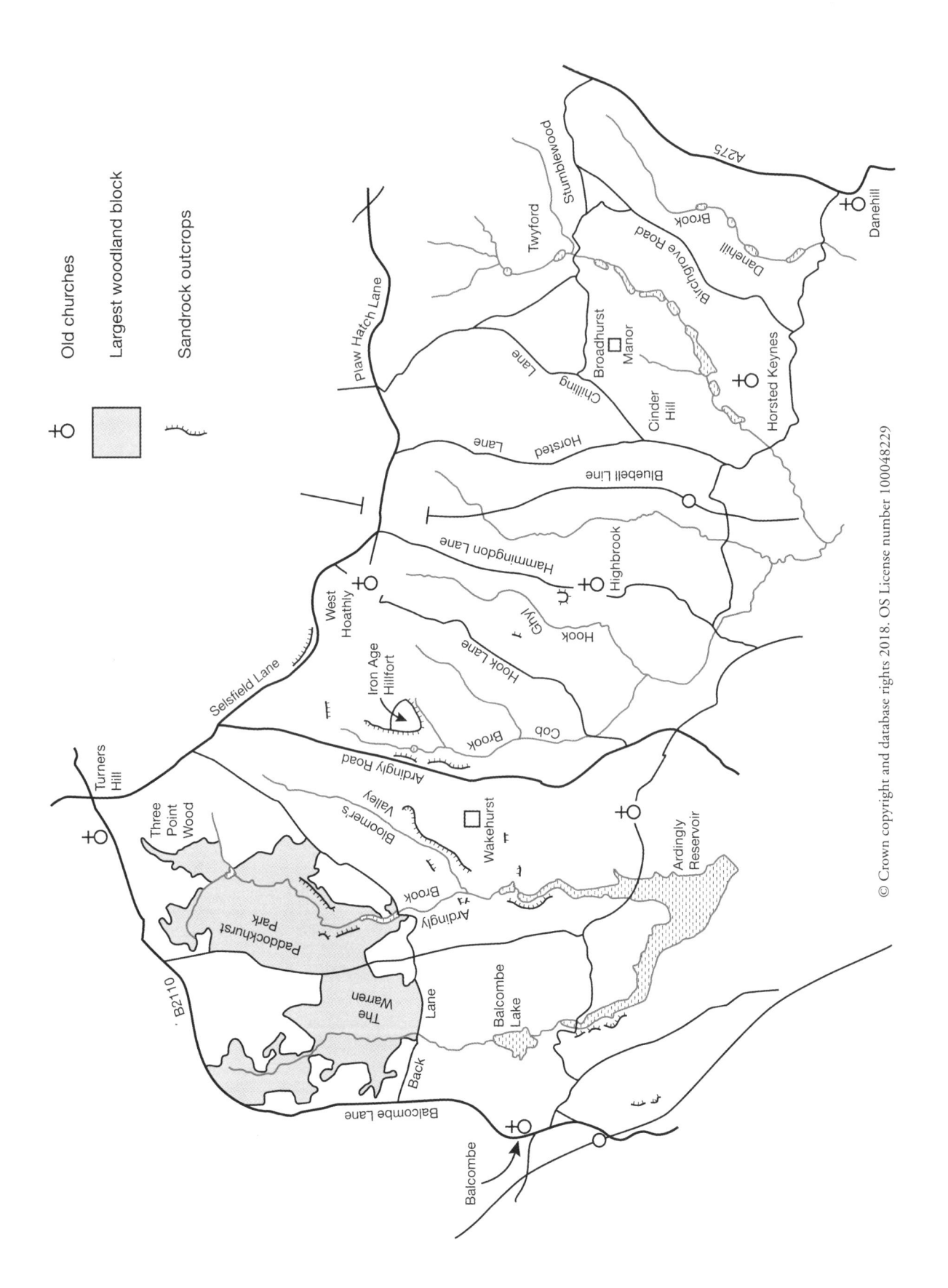

268 AREA GUIDE / Chapter 21: The Ardingly Ridgelands

CHAPTER 21
The Ardingly Ridgelands:
Balcombe, West Hoathly, Ardingly, Horsted Keynes

Looking east from Highbrook across valley and hill to Ashdown this landscape feels semi-montane … like the foothills of some larger massif.[1]

A series of high ridges march southwards for several miles across the span of this landscape. From prehistoric times travel was easiest along the spines of these ridges, and each one has its long lane or road. East-west travel, however, is inhibited by the steep clefts between the ridges, and all three western valleys have east-west valley lanes with gradients steeper than one in seven or, in the case of Cob Lane, one in five.

The Bluebell Line faithfully follows one long north-south valley and thus avoids any tunnelling except one, under the watershed/interfluve at Sharpthorne.

All of the area is within the Ouse catchment. Its highest ground forms its northern boundary and is the watershed separating it from the catchments of the Medway and Mole, to the north. This watershed is tracked by the Worth Abbey road (B2110) and the Turners Hill to Ashdown Forest road (B2028).

The geology is a layer cake of strata, from toppings of Cuckfield Stone and Grinstead Clay, down through Ardingly Sandrock and softer sand to Wadhurst Clay in the valley bottoms. These layers form giant steps down the valley sides, with the steeper strata sometimes marked out by woodland strips. To the east, the Ashdown Beds form the whole landscape.

Exposed sandrocks are a major feature of the two western valleys either side of Ardingly village, outcropping strongly at Wakehurst and Paddockhurst, and at Chiddinglye, most famously with 'Great Upon Little', the massive block balanced on its tiny 'wasp waist'.

Those two western valleys are the brightest jewels of this area, with their relict Atlantic Period (7000 to 5000 BP) plants and mini-beasts, their ancient hanging woods, and their exemplary sandrock formations. Paddockhurst Park also holds a superb assemblage of veteran Beech and Oak pollards, though they have been poorly recognised and managed. Some of the Oaks in Tilgate Wood remind one of 'old growth' maidens, so tall and sturdy are they. The SSSI gill of the Ardingly Brook – lush and humid – runs for over two miles due south through Paddockhurst Park to the Hanging Meadow at the northern tip of Ardingly Reservoir. The Chiddinglye gill, south to Burstow Bridge, is even longer – over three miles. The Langridge Wood-Ludwell Ghyl, though shorter, is even more remote. You could, in several of these gills, easily enjoy a whole day picking a slow course along them … past mini waterfalls, over rubble beds and slippery stone plates, round tiny ox-bow bends, between tall moss-and-liverwort-draped banks and gnarled tree roots, peering into deep pools, always under a dappled green canopy, with shifting shafts of sunlight. This is the nearest to being lost in the wildwood that our part of England can offer!

It is the gills which have retained their ancient woodland cover best, and in least modified form. On the higher ground there has been ancient woodland loss even in recent times, as old shaws and small woods are taken out. There has been a counter-tendency for some compensatory infilling around gill woods, as well as one large new woodland creation, between Upper and Lower Sheriff Farms, just west of Horsted Keynes Station.

One large area of plateau ancient woodland does survive at the joined woodlands of Paddockhurst Park and The Warren/Balcombe Wood, though much of it has been damaged by heavy conifer substitution. Other big plateau woods survive at Horncastle Wood and Wheeler's Wood, both on the fringe of Ashdown Forest.

Much ancient and gill woodland was destroyed by the building of Ardingly Reservoir, and the ancient drove road of Shill Lane was broken in two. Birchgrove Wood Gill and The Slade gill, Horsted Keynes, have been replaced with modern chains of fishing ponds.

Given the steeply contoured nature of much of its terrain it is surprising that there is so little archaic grassland, but 'efficient' exploitation by the large estates and modernising farms doomed most of it, and, at least till recently, one family farm was still trigger happy with herbicidal sprays along flowery verges and banks.

However, there are some fine survivals, such as along the Cob/Cockhaise Brook just east of Ardingly; at Stonelands by the White Hart pub; and at the Hanging Meadow on the Wakehurst Estate. Paddockhurst Park has good heathy remnants, particularly close to Park House, though one fine heathy sandrock site has recently been planted up with conifers. The rides and more open areas both at Paddockhurst and The Warren have interest. Much that survives hereabouts though, has suffered damage or is reduced to small fragments.

Habitation and exploitation in this landscape goes back at least to Mesolithic times, when the sandrock outcrops formed rock shelters for gatherer-hunter bands. Iron Age people built a promontory hillfort at Chiddinglye, defended on two sides by the sandrock cliffs. The Portslade-London Roman road may have been part-contemporary with the hillfort, which it passed just across the valley westwards. By Roman times much of the higher ground may have been cleared. There are several ancient names indicating open ground, such as *Feld*wyck, Sels*field*, and West *Hoath*ly, to balance the many old woodland names, such as Arding*ly*, Chidding*lye*, Wake*hurst*, Tilling*hurst*, Broad*hurst*, As*hurst*, Birch*grove*, and Hamming*den*.

In early medieval times of Wealden transhumance, the southern Downland and scarp foot manors of Ditchling, Keymer and Stanmer-Malling occupied wide strips of territory between Balcombe, Ardingly and West Hoathly, running northwards roughly around the line of the Roman road all the way to the Surrey border. To the east, Plumpton Boscage manor had the hilltop settlement at Highbrook (then Hammingden), and Birch Grove was held by Balmer, now just a Downland farm between Brighton and Lewes.

There are four big nucleated villages with churches of medieval foundation, though none of them were nucleated in early times, for this was a country of scattered farms and tiny hamlets. Ardingly, Balcombe and Horsted Keynes churches still stand apart from their current villages, which formed more democratically from scattered homes around greens. Only West Hoathly seems to have had an ongoing church hamlet of size, with its superb 15th century Priest House – my favourite old house to visit in Sussex, with its herb garden, and Flower Bees nesting in the daub above the door.

The iron industry had an Iron Age, Roman, and medieval presence, and probably influenced the building and alignment of the Roman road. There are a scatter of bloomery sites, known by the presence of slag, sometimes hearths, and sometimes place names, like *Cinder* Hill, a mile north of Horsted Keynes. With the late 15th century introduction of the water powered blast furnace the industry was transformed in scale and impact. There were smelting furnaces at Paddockhurst (Strudgate), Ardingly (Saucelands), Chiddinglye, Horsted Keynes, and Twyford (Stumbletts). There was also a forge, to make the smelted iron into goods, at Ardingly, now under the Reservoir.

Though none of their ponds have survived continuously from the Tudor hammer ponds, several are on the sites of the originals, such as the two lowest in the valley at Horsted Keynes. Slag can be found plentifully below – and on – the old pond bays, and place names survive at three of the sites: *Hammer* Wood(s), *Fire* Wood, *Cinder* Banks.

Wakehurst Place and Broadhurst Manor were the only ancient 'two fingers-to-you-lot' grand mansions, and are both now less than half their original size. Nowadays, the two giant monuments to privilege which stand out are both public schools: Worth Abbey, originally built as a private mansion for Victorian plutocrats, and Ardingly School, built by Victorian middle class educators.

It could be argued that the Agricultural Showground at Ardingly represents the same privileged interests, and that is certainly true of the threat from fracking to much of this landscape, all of which lies within the purported protection of the High Weald Area of Outstanding Natural Beauty (AONB).

CHIDDINGLY ROCKS, STONELANDS, WEST HOATHLY

The **sandrock bluffs at Chiddingly Wood**, TQ 348 320, stand up to 39 feet high, craggy and cracked, dominating both sides of its wooded valley and the side valley. They are rounded at their tops, with deep '*gulls*' (splits, often wide enough to walk through) separating huge blocks, which tip slightly, as though just about to topple down into the valley below. They have attracted people since the end of the Ice Age, at least, and their buried flint debris, and fragments of pottery, span five thousand years of the Mesolithic and early Neolithic, from about 10,000 to 5000 BP. On a picnic break, perched on top of the bluff, our walk leader[2] passed me a beautifully worked leaf arrowhead, translucently thin, about 4cm long and about 6000 years old, which they'd excavated below. I felt as reverential and nervous as if I'd being handed a new born baby! Those folk were probably living and hunting seasonally, here.

'Great upon Little' forms one separated 500 ton block, on an impossibly tiny base, which was a tourist attraction in previous centuries, as its graffiti testify, with carved dates from 1623, 1640, 1694, and 1807. Below it, in Black Dog Valley, TQ 350 320, there are lots of fallen mossy hulks, like the wilds of Oregon. I came across a Spotted Flycatcher's nest, with a neat clutch of four eggs, under a moss curtain in the side of one rotting fallen pine. The sandrocks carry the great heritage of Atlantic Period primitive plants. Most of their specialities are liverworts, including very tiny species,[3] and many are now isolated in the High Weald, hundreds of miles from their western, Welsh and Scottish redoubts. There are lots of bats using the rock fissures.

These rocks might look hard as nails, but their hard skin is only a few mm thick, and great damage can be done to them by climbing. Much more drastic damage can be done to the relict oceanic lowly plants by any sort of collection, scraping, or scrambling. This is a site where to 'tread lightly' is doubly our responsibility.

Below the rocks are little ponds, e.g. TQ 346 321, near the site of the Tudor iron furnace. The high platform between the two promontory cliffs is defended at its rear by a ditch and bank, TQ 350 323 (now hidden by a shaw) which made this a formidable six acre **hillfort**, if adequately armed. Such 'promontory forts' are rare in the Weald.

Just east of Chiddingly, is the working **Philpots Quarry**, TQ 354/5 322/3, which cuts stone from the same Ardingly Sandrock strata. There, the rock appears in a new light, warm and buff yellow, often with carbonised plant remains between the hard plates, ripple beds, fern fragments, fossil fish, and sometimes dinosaur footprints.

To the north of Chiddingly Wood, the valley becomes gentler and the sandrocks are no longer exposed, except in slight glimpses on hillside bulges. There, at **Stonelands**, TQ 348 333, is a remarkable chain of five little fields, part unimproved, part semi-improved, part grazed, part neglected. In summer, there is Devil's Bit, Betony, Harebell (just), Burnet Saxifrage, and some very colourful displays. In autumn, the unimproved slopes have another dose of colour, with King Crimson, Scarlet Hood and Parrot Waxcaps, Moor Club and Star Pinkgill fungi.

The 600 year old spire of **West Hoathly** church, TQ 363 325, is a cheering landmark for miles around. The church has Norman origins (and one wall of that time survives) though it doesn't get a mention in the Domesday Book of 1086. There are cast iron grave slabs, and the 400 year old iron workings of a clock, probably donated by one of the ironmasters. Also, a memorial to Ann Tree, burnt at the stake for her Protestantism in 1556 by Bloody Queen Mary. Down the street is the timber framed **Priest House,**[4] with House Leeks, *Sempervivum*, on the roof and a cast iron slab outside the front door to stop witches entering! It's crowded with exhibits, old fashioned and folky, and there are Plesiosaur and fossil fish vertebrae, and an Iguanodon part-femur, all under glass domes. You can buy herbs from the garden. The Swifts dart overhead.

West Hoathly Priest House: "witches' step", dinosaur fossils, bees nesting in the wattle and daub

... and if you are a witch DON'T step over the witches' step

PADDOCKHURST PARK AND THE WARREN

On 'Goblin Cliffs', looking west over the valley at the heart of **Paddockhurst Park,** are two huge coppice stools of Small Leaved Lime (2005), close together and probably once one. Down in the damp earth of the gill below, an expert[5] sieved out specimens of two tiny snails, mere pinpricks, but great rarities in this part of Britain. Amongst the grey lichen coating the bark of an Oak bole, further down the valley, close peering with an eye glass revealed the tiny pustules of Barnacle Lichen, an 'old forest' species. All those life forms signal the Park's links back to the wildwood.

The heavily wooded Park is huge, approaching the size of Petworth Park, and rivals it in beauty and interest. It was 'Wakehurst Park' for most of its more-than-600 year history,[6] but it is almost a mile[7] from Wakehurst Place. It only took its modern name when Victorian plutocrats built the mansion (now Worth Abbey School) on Paddockhurst Farm, and appended the Park to their estate. It had a warren once, but was still mapped as a Park around 1806. At some point in the 19th century it was converted to forestry. The woods are part-conifer, part Birch and Beech, and Rhodedendron continues to be a problem, though there has been much clearance.

The Park pale bank can be traced for most of its length, though Back Lane and Stoney Lane divide it. Ling Heather is common in places. The central valley is very park-like, with a new Wellingtonia avenue, low sandrocks on the west slope, high sandrocks on the east, and the gill below. There are large clusters of old Beech in the southern part, probably of 18th and 19th century origin, and many more in the north east, below and above the tall sandrock Goblin Cliffs, TQ 331 331 to TQ 334 338. It is both there and on the western pale bank that the oldest trees are to be found. Most of the veterans are Beech, but there are some old Oaks, a huge old Birch, and at least one Yew.

This Wood Ant city probably has about the same population as that of Horsham – over 50,000.

Where the drive from Park House rises eastwards to leave the park towards Newhouse Farm there is a sandrock outcrop, TQ 330 329, which has Ling and lichen heath, with several *Cladonia* lichen, Sheep's Sorrel and Fork Moss. Now Spruce has been planted right up to the rocks and all over the heath.

A long gill runs south through the Park from a pond on its northern boundary, TQ 333 340, which has white sheets of Water Crowfoot in June, Yellow Flag, Flowering Rush, many damsels and dragons, and is still, silent, and gorgeously green. The gill stream meanders freely over sandstone rubble, alongside burry old Oaks. There's Hard Fern, Polypody, Crab Apple, and Greater Water Moss at one spot. Above Strudgate hammer pond, is a disused quarry cut into the Ardingly sandstone, TQ 329 323.

The gill stream continues out of the Park southwards as the **Ardingly Brook**, e.g. TQ 330 318/9, and this lower valley is also of great beauty. There was a Tudor iron furnace, which the name **Fire Wood** commemorates, and all the way down there is much slag in the stream. There's a large derelict pump house, and an adit on the east slope, deep into the hillside, with water gushing out and white nursery egg sacs of cave spiders on the ceiling. The valley feels very Welsh, with steep open woods, Bluebells and the natural stony stream. There's Shining Hookeria moss, lots of Pignut, some Watercress, Tutsan, Primroses and Golden Saxifrage.

There are fine purlieu woods to the north and east of the Park. **Grove Wood**, TQ 329 344/5, has more than 20 ancient woodland indicator species. It is on clay in its upper parts, which explains its richness. We spotted a Hare in a field between Back Lane and the wood. **Three Point Wood** is even better, TQ 333/4 343. Its gill forms a steep gorge, with old Beech and Yew and Small Leaved Lime. There are drifts of Bluebells, some Oak high forest, dark conifer coups, extensive glades, Sweet Chestnut coppice, lots of new broad leaved planting, and some specimen Scots Pines. To the east and south of Three Point Wood is the sheep-grazed **Bramblehill valley**. There's a narrow line of unimproved Gorsey grassland along the steepest bit, TQ 339 341, on the south side. It has Quaking Grass and old herbs, but the sheep get most of it, whilst other bits are fenced out of grazing.

To the west of Paddockhurst is **The Warren**, TQ 318 323, split by Stoney Lane. The best part is on the lower ground around the gills to the west and the south, where there is open Oak wood and a mixture of conifer stands, some glades of Bracken and Ling Heather, and lovely marshy spots with *Sphagnum* Bog Mosses. Wood Ants have a big republic of circa four dozen nests – some huge – across The Warren from Balcombe Wood in the north to Great Wood in the south. This is the only Wood Ant republic that

I know of within Worth Forest east of the Brighton Line. A complete whitened skeleton of a Roe Deer lay amongst the Heather to attest to the loneliness of the place. Where **Stoney Lane** crosses the stream a sandstone platform is exposed under the bridge, with a natural swimming pool on its south side, TQ 317 320/1.

Tilgate Wood, TQ 330 309, with **Westbrook Wood** to its south, on the west side of the Ardingly Brook and the upper Reservoir, is another world … of high forest … columnar Oaks and Beeches, and rotting, busted, picturesque trees on the rumpled slopes. There

WHAT'S LOST: ARDINGLY RESERVOIR

An overlay of the modern (1978) Reservoir onto an old map base (O/S map, c. 1870). The Shell (or Shill) Brook and the Ardingly Brook lay in deep valleys with exceptionally rich patchworks of ancient woods, marshy meadows, tiny fields and old hedges, which were remote and deeply tranquil, though the Romans had crossed them with a road, and Tudor ironworks had once stood there.

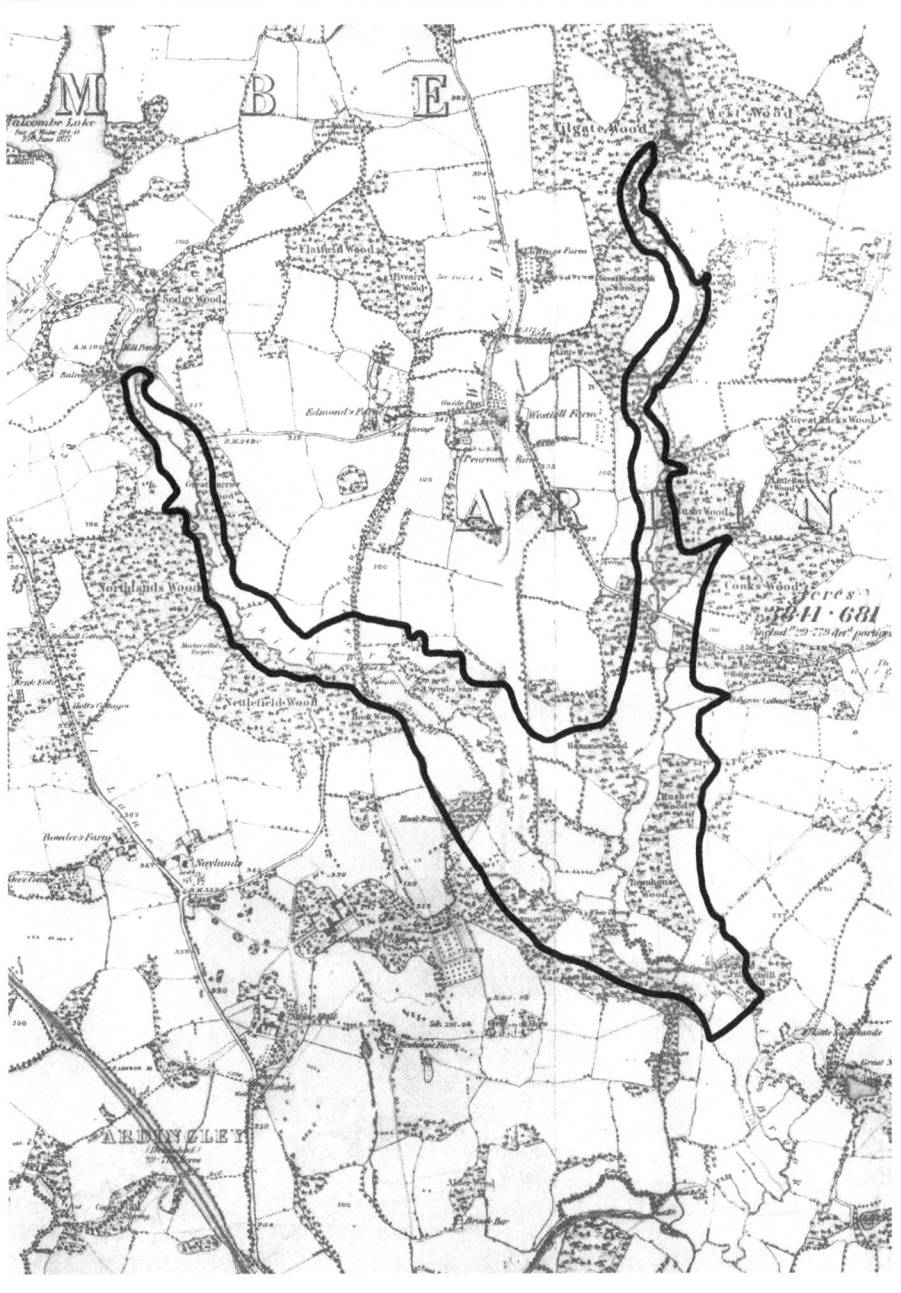

THE WAKEHURST ESTATE AND AROUND

The National Trust's **Wakehurst Estate**, e.g. TQ 33 31, (leased to Kew Gardens) runs for two miles north to south and provides a huge variety of habitats and levels of domestication. The gardens and arboreti are full of wonderful exotics, beautifully managed, which slowly increase in wildness as one descends into the valleys to the west and south, reaching an almost-naturalness in **Horsebridge Wood**, in the valley basin, TQ 332 315 – like a soggy Carboniferous mire, humid and green, with Beautiful Demoiselle flashing iridescent in the sun beams. The upper slopes of **Bloomer's Valley,** upstream, have a grassy plat gorgeous with Bluebells, and edged by a grey sandrock cliff that winds for half a mile. **West Wood Valley** has fine views from the top, and an intimate mixture of the natural and the exotic: Spotted Orchids and Purple Toothwort, fine Oaks, Handkerchief Tree, and Yellow Archangel. The paths are good, making this a superb place for folk of limited stamina and mobility, or who need to stay neat and clean.

© Crown copyright and database rights 2018. OS License number 100048229. Reproduced using c. 1870 Ordnance Survey 6 inch to 1 mile map base with the kind permission of the Ordnance Survey.

ARDINGLY RESERVOIR

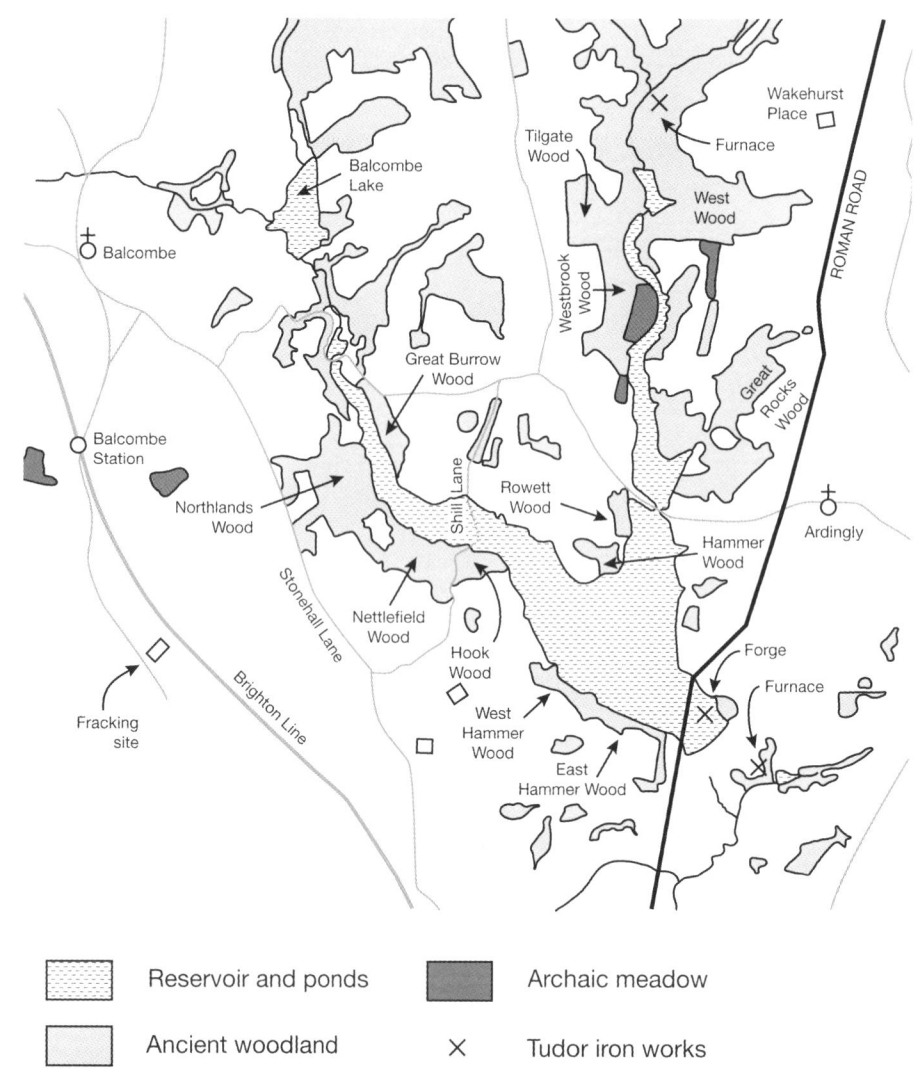

Map legend:
- Reservoir and ponds
- Ancient woodland
- Archaic meadow
- × Tudor iron works

Map labels: Balcombe Lake, Balcombe, Balcombe Station, Northlands Wood, Stonehall Lane, Brighton Line, Fracking site, Great Burrow Wood, Shill Lane, Nettlefield Wood, Hook Wood, West Hammer Wood, East Hammer Wood, Tilgate Wood, Furnace, Westbrook Wood, West Wood, Great Racks Wood, Rowett Wood, Hammer Wood, Ardingly, Forge, Furnace, Wakehurst Place, Roman Road

© Crown copyright and database rights 2018. OS License number 100048229

are ancient Atlantic Period plants, and tumbled, mossy boulders amongst the Brambles, with Wavy Silk Moss in long rats' tails … and tall sandrocks with green *Pellia* liverworts, like green flatworms, on their wet surfaces, honeycomb weathering, and *Cladonia* lichen on their tops. (Do NOT climb on the rocks or boulders. Many of their tiny plants are very special). In spring the song birds belt out their music. Below Westbrook Wood is the colourful **Hanging Meadow**, TQ 331 306. I counted 43 herbs in one steady stroll across it, including Southern Marsh Orchids and hybrid Heath x Common Spotted Orchids. Common Terns dive and chase over the Reservoir below the meadow. There are Kingfishers there, too. On sunny days in **Great Racks Wood**, TQ 335 300, on the east side of the reservoir, there are Green Tiger Beetles on the hot banks, and in spring scattered Wild Daffodil patches. Great Racks, Bushy Wood, and Tilgate Wood are within the Loder Valley Reserve (National Trust and Kew).

Tillinghurst Bank, TQ 334 307/8, can be seen right across the valley from Lullings in sultry April heat, its dusting of Bluebells like that from butterflies wings, below the contour hedge. Later, in June, its plants of old Wealden pastures are at their best: Pignut and Parsley Piert, Silver Hair Grass, Heath Grass, Tormentil, Heath Speedwell, Eggs and Bacon, Sheep's Sorrel and Sheep's Fescue (2012). At dusk, Serotine Bats patrol and Tawny Owls hoot in the woods.

BALCOMBE AND AROUND

Balcombe's little church, TQ 307 309, was a modest 13th–15th century affair, with a good stubby tower, reflecting a modest Wealden economy, but the Victorians doubled the church size after the railway came. It's almost hidden, for it lacks the lofty spires of Highbrook, Hoathly, and Horsted Keynes. The churchyard has some Waxcap fungi. The little bank to the west, down to the road, has an old meadow flora, with Betony, Bush Vetch and Grey Sedge. The village has no 'high street', but a pretty little 'square', by the old Half Moon pub, has paths radiating in all directions.

Balcombe Lake, to the north east, TQ 16 309, has Grey Wagtails on its bay, and Marsh Tits in the wet carr woods fringing the reed beds along its west side. There are fine Oaks in the shaws and small woods. The Lake drains south through Alder Wood to the mill pond of **Balcombe Mill and Mill House** (17th–19th century) hidden deep in a wooded valley.

Behind the Mill and south along the west bank of the Reservoir for a third of a mile are **sandrock outcrops**. Some are tall and dangerous, some low and rounded. Many bear a rich lower plant flora of Atlantic Period ferns, mosses and liverworts. The woodland is mostly

Looking east from Highbrook over 'The Ridgelands'

ancient, with mixed Birch, Sweet Chestnut, Oaks, Hazel and Bluebells, but much of it, down through **Northlands and Nettlefield Woods**, e.g. TQ 319 299, has been damaged by conifer substitution. One Pheasant rearing pen even surrounds a sandrock outcrop (2011). There's a big gill with tall vertical rock faces, very damp and mossy, with Rhodi, Yew, Birch and Holly. Indeed, many outcrops have Holly. The mosses and liverworts are small or tiny, dark or translucent, tufted or matting, thread like or 'leafy' … and they go by names such as Fox Tail Feather Moss and Bordered Screw Moss!

Further south again, towards the Reservoir dam, the water is fringed by the top slivers of **West and East Hammer Woods**, e.g. TQ 329 289, above the drowned site of the Tudor iron forge. You could see Common Sandpiper, and Great Crested Grebe are frequent, with Heron, Duck spp., and Coot, and there's the odd Lapwing on the exposed mud. Above those woods is **Balcombe Place**, the World War Two HQ of the Women's Land Army.

From Naylands, **Shill Lane** drops down the valley slope into Hook Wood, TQ 324 296, where its course across the old Shill Brook is submerged by the Reservoir. It re-emerges on the north bank looking like a thick shaw, but is in fact a deep, wooded **holloway**, TQ 324 300/1, climbing up the valley to **West Hill**. It is long abandoned, and the bridleway now runs up the grassy valley bottom alongside … a line medieval travellers deliberately avoided, keeping slightly up the valley side to avoid the wet and mud. You have to lift a curtain of branches to step into the holloway, made a millennium and more ago by the tenants and herders of Ditchling and Keymer manors to access their West Hill farms and *denns*, and those to the north. Inside it is airy and dark, with giant maiden Oaks. On the east bank are outgrown Beech stools, and high on the west bank are a line of veteran Ash stools, each about two spans girth. Don't go there on midsummer night. The magic must be strong. Edmond's and Lullings farmhouses are 15th century and Pearments is 17th century, all timber framed.

Two thirds of a mile north, up West Hill Lane, the verge by The Oaks is unimproved, with Bitter Vetch and Betony, TQ 326 314/5.

On the south edge of Balcombe village is an old and well-managed meadow, TQ 310/1 298/9, which has been owned jointly by the neighbouring householders for 60 years. It is very Rushy, with two Orchid species and Ox Eye Daisy. **Upper Stumble Wood gill** flows southwards from it, TQ 310 296, mossy and wet, with Golden Saxifrage, Great Scented Liverwort, Overleaf Pellia, and Ladder Flapwort. There's a small sandrock outcrop up the east slope.

Hook Farm slope: you need strong legs and lungs to farm this country

HIGHBROOK AND AROUND: HAMMINGDEN LANE, HOOK LANE AND THEIR GILLS

This is tranquil countryside.[8] The views from **Highbrook**, TQ 363 301, eastwards are like the more domestic parts of the Yorkshire Dales. You can see Plumpton Hill due south (with Blackcap and Mount Harry). Highbrook, then called Hammingden, was in the Wealden portion of Plumpton manor, known as Plumpton Boscage … and bosky it still is.

The steep valley sides have landslips, at the point where the sandstone meets the underlying Wadhurst Clay. There has been much landslipping west of **Hammenden Farm** in the steep field that the footpath descends, TQ 360 302, and it looks like there was one recently above Furtherhouse Wood, TQ 363/4 305, overlooking the **valley of the Bluebell Line**.

In that valley, east of **Newlands Cottage**, the gill bed is covered by plates of ripple bedded sandstone, TQ 367/8 311. Between there and the **Sharpthorne Tunnel**, TQ 370 320, the bed of the gill stream is plated, wide and flat, with only a thin film of *Cladophora* algae. The gradient is very shallow and there's almost no change of strata. These beds are the place to look for fossilised Iguanodon footprints! The gill woods have Wood Sorrel, Midland Thorn and its hybrids, Wych Elm (rare) and Bluebell in places. **Furtherhouse Wood**, TQ 365 305, is part-ancient, with abundant Pendulous Sedge in the secondary part. **Courtlands Wood**, TQ 368/9 316, is mostly ancient, but with much conifer substitution. There is very heavy deer pressure and, in parts, it is as poached as a cattle pasture, particularly by the stream edges. The stream passes through a tunnel under the Bluebell Line and there are lots of cave spiders on the roof.

South of **Sloe Garden Wood** (that has a steep sided gill with a mini-waterfall and little chasms) are two flower meadows with abundant Grass Vetchling in June, eg. TQ 371/2 320. On one August visit a Purple Hairstreak butterfly basked at my feet, flashing its iridescent blue-black wing patches.

West of Hammingden Lane is the lovely **Hook Valley**, with its nearly-two-mile-long serpentine, wooded gill. At the south end is **Sevenacre Wood**, TQ 355 297, with two good ponds, full of tadpoles in spring, and Herons at alert. There's a fine stand of Japanese Red Cedar nearby, and Beautiful Demoiselles in the dappled sun. Upstream is **Whitestone Wood**, TQ 360 305, with Great Woodrush, *Luzula sylvatica*, a scarce plant in Sussex. Upslope to the east, by Hammingden Lane, is the Ardingly Sandrock outcrop, TQ 362 306, after which the wood and old house is named. It is perhaps 20ft high where it faces the valley, and may be the quarry used to build Highbrook's church. It has Polypody and Narrow Buckler Fern on its lane side.

On the west side of the valley from Whitestone is **Ludwell Ghyl**, TQ 356/7 307, a lush ancient wood, with a rich ground flora and a spring at its head (Ludwell = *'hlud wielle'* = 'loud spring') flowing into an old watercress bed. It has Shining Hookeria moss, Ramsons, Golden Saxifrage and masses of Pendulous Sedge.

Upstream again, in **Hook Wood gill**, TQ 360/1 309, the bed of the stream is pebbly and exposes lots of fossils in the Wadhurst Clay. The pebbles are sometimes packed *Neomiodon* bivalves (tiny 'clams' of about a cm) forming a shelly limestone, or cemented by calcite, just leaving pock mark impressions in sandstone or mudstone. There are odd bits of tufa, too, perhaps recent … and broken slabs with sand gutters (as on every sandy beach today) … and other bits with fine markings, which could be plant or wave impressions … and all about 140 million years old! There's much Midland Thorn in the wood, with Hazel and occasional Hornbeam coppice, Holly and Oak. It's very bare on the woodland floor, except for Ramsons on wetter ground. No Bluebells. In these gill woods there is gold tinted Curled Hook Moss (very rare in Sussex) flushed by base-rich water and gradually turning into tufa.

Up slope to the west is **Hook Farm pasture**, TQ 359 312, which has partly escaped 'improvement'. Dyers Greenweed is still there, with Tormentil, Devil's Bit, and Scarlet Hood waxcap in autumn. The views south to Plumpton are lovely. On the west side of Hook Lane is the recently re-opened **Hook Quarry**, hidden behind wood and scrub, TQ 355 313. It works the upper Ardingly Sandstone, and a pebble bed above it which is rich in Ammonite fossils. A short walk up

Hook Lane takes you to a grassy plat on the east lane side, **Langridge Farm corner**, TQ 359 317/8, whose bank has Orpine and Betony, with commoner herbs, like Eggs and Bacon, Meadow Vetchling and Knapweed.

Upstream from Hook Wood Gill is **Langridge Wood**, beautifully remote and quiet, TQ 363 316/7 … just the tinkle of the brook and bird song … and two Nuthatches constantly alarming in the canopy … *huit, huit, huit!* The floor is bare though: with so many deer this is more denuded wood pasture, than coppice woodland. **Ashurst Wood**, TQ 364 321, north again, is much richer and greener, with dominant Bluebells and Anemones, and occasional Yew.

To the west of Hook Lane is **Barnlands and Coneyburrow Gill**, e.g. TQ 351 314, with much new woodland on the upper west slope, rather open woodland on the east slope, and Hornbeam hedges now lost in the new woods.

ARDINGLY, HAPSTEAD AND THE COB BROOK GILL

Ardingly church, TQ 339 298, is of the 14th century, with a sturdy 15th century tower, a timber framed porch of 1500, fine old brasses, and a veteran churchyard Yew. The church stands close to the line of the Roman road to the coast, on *Street*[9] Lane, a name which implies that medieval locals were still aware of, or used, that road. The village, nearby, was called Hapstead Green till modern times, but no part of the green survives.

To its east the land drops steeply down to the **Cob Brook meadows**. On the west side of the brook is **Withyland bank**, TQ 352 297, with lots of Burnet Saxifrage and a little Devil's Bit and Tormentil. (In poor condition, ungrazed and fenced out of management, 2016). To the south, is a **tussocky pasture**, TQ 352 294, with wet rushy gullies and stream side banks. It has Ragged Robin and Sneezewort, and Burnet Saxifrage and Pignut on the banks. Best of all is the **'little moor'**, on the eastern brook side, TQ 353/4 295/6, a damp rumpled slope with old anthills and bushes. There were (2012) big swarms of Heath Spotted Orchis and Lousewort, with Common Spotted Orchis, Heath Grass, Quaking Grass, Pepper Saxifrage, Marsh Ragwort and Zig Zag Clover – 63 herbs listed in one visit. (Ungrazed and in bad decline, July 2016).

Hapstead Wood: high forest

The **Cob Brook woods** are a delight. West of **Burstow Bridge**, TQ 359 289, there is a waterfall (loud in winter) over the weir and a tangled mixture of Bamboo and Ramsons. Going west, **Burstowhill and Motts Woods**, on the south slope, are wild and complex. There are fine Beeches on the north side, and a healthy three span girth Beech pollard on the south slope, TQ 354 290.

North of the Cob Brook meadows are **Hapstead and Moorlands Woods**, e.g. TQ 349 299, with good Oak high forest, and sunny glades. The exposed blue clay on the eroding Cob Brook banks separates like the pages of a book to reveal *Neomiodon* fossil clams like crushed rice crispies on a plate. There are thicker strata, too, and thin, crumbly iron bearing layers. On sunny days in May the Brook as far as **Hoathly Shaw**, TQ 347/8 309, has Giant Lacewing, Beautiful Demoiselle, and *Empid* and *Tachinid* flies nectaring on Ramsons and heavy scented May blossom. In the shadows of late afternoon the view south from Hoathly Shaw across to Fulling Mill Farm shows the valley slope's giant 'steps' downwards across the geological layers.

HORSTED KEYNES, CINDER HILL, BROADHURST AND BIRCH GROVE

At **Horsted Keynes,** north-going Church Lane has to swing out to go round the circular ditched and banked enclosure in which the church stands, TQ 383/4 286. If the old lane's route is dictated by the presence of the enclosure, it is likely that the enclosure is even older than the lane. Furthermore, the church's alignment is markedly NE–SW, thus aligning it with the summer solstice sunrise. It seems the church may be built on a prehistoric religious site. The church itself shows signs of great antiquity, in its cruciform plan, porticus arch,[10] Saxon doorway, and tower base. The skyscraping broach spire probably dates from about 1604. Its construction, using rope-tied wooden scaffolding, must have been extraordinarily courageous.

A footpath leads from the church down through a wood, past the **18th century watermill and 17th century mill house**, TQ 380 287, to the adjacent bay of the pond on the site of the old **iron furnace pond**. Below the bay the braided brook meanders through **Alderley Platt** wood, TQ 378 285/6. Here, it is garden-like in spring, with Anemones, Redcurrant, Primroses, Kingcups, Golden Saxifrage and lush mosses. There is much slag in the stream bed. The footpath going NW up the hill past Cinder Banks is heavily braided, and there are big pit depressions in **Pains Wood** at the top of the slope, TQ 378 290: iron ore pits, probably, from which the ore was loaded onto carts that lurched down the track to the furnace.

Next to Horsted Keynes station car park is **Leamlands Wood**, TQ 373 292, an old Hornbeam coppice at its west end, with Early Purple Orchids, but full of rotting caravans and rusting plant at its east end (2012). Is that where the old huts, carriages and caravans that housed the seasonal fruit pickers on the Cinder Hill estate[11] were left after the bushes and orchards were grubbed up? **Cinder Hill Wood**, just north, TQ 374 295, is also Hornbeam coppice, full of Bluebells and Anemones.

Cinder Hill lane goes north past the Horsted Keynes Industrial Estate (the old fruit canning and processing works) to **Cinder Hill Green**, TQ 377 297, at the fingerpost. Though only as big as a bee's knee, and with much lost under encroaching trees, the Green still has real value (2012). It has nine different grasses, including Flattened Meadow Grass, two sedges, Corn Parsley, Zig Zag Clover, Slender St John's Wort, Betony and Ox Eye Daisy. The lane divides: the west fork becomes Horsted Lane, and passes **Tanyard Farm**, where there is another old flower meadow, TQ 375/6 308 and a gnarled old Oak on the lane, whilst the east fork becomes Chilling Lane. There is a fine flowery verge at **Piplye**, TQ 383 302, with Pepper Saxifrage, orchids, Stone Parsley, and Betony. The meadow behind the hedge is nice, too.

Between these two forks is **Wickenden**. It *should* be a lovely spot, for the views are fine and it has good woods, like **Wickenden Wood**, with a Sessile Oak pollard of three spans girth by the brook edge, TQ 381 316 … but all the old grasslands are fertilised and nitrogen green … or rank and thistle infested, and all about are new fences and game cover crops. It is a sanitised place. Much the same is true of the countryside around **Broadhurst Manor**, TQ 387 300, and Cinder Hill. The larger woods are intact, but many of the shaws and hedges have been grubbed up, and archaic grasslands relentlessly removed. It must be a long time since *Greeningweed Field*, shown on an old estate map, in the crook of Oaken Wood, blazed yellow with Dyers Greenweed … or since Cowslips filled the pastures along Cinder Hill.

Broadhurst Manor (which many will remember as Carla Lane's animal sanctuary) is a huge Tudor pile, though over half of it was demolished in the late 18th century. The original south front is all giant chimneys and local stone, and the modern east front all mullioned windows and Horsham slab roofs. The west front is timber framed. Next to it is an ancient and odd looking thatched barn that may have been an outbuilding connected to the iron industry. It looks very Hobbit of the Shire. Little **Ass Wood,** east of the manor, TQ 390 300, and its twin just to the south, are full of flooded pits in the Wadhurst Clay. Were they brick pits for the house construction, or ore pits?

The big puzzle here, is when the *hurst* that Broad*hurst* was named after was grubbed up? There is an empty triangle between the lanes north of Broadhurst and Hurstwood Lane that looks as though it was the hurst site. The name Hurst*wood* Farm next to it, built in 1600, implies that the wood was still extant at that date.

South of Broadhurst, **The Slade** valley, TQ 385 295, and the **Birchgrove Wood valley**, TQ 390 294, were filled with chains of ponds (the latter 1.5 miles long) some 60 years or more ago. **Birchgrove and Warren Woods** on their south side, e.g. TQ 386 289, have much Sweet Chestnut coppice, and much new broad leaved planting. Some areas, as in The Warren, feel quite natural, others very modified.

Twyford and **Stumblewood Common**, a mile NE east of Broadhurst, make a peculiarly old fashioned area, despite the wealth of some inhabitants. Twy*ford* should really be called Tri*ford*, for there are at least three fords apparent there, e.g. TQ 396 304. After heavy rains the valley bottoms and fords are full of sand, gravel and mud that fills the gutters and begins to erode back the tarmac. They must have had a similar problem 450 years ago when **Stumbletts iron furnace** was operating, and it did not last long. The bay is broken in two place and has much slag on top, TQ 399 306. Just below it are two nice rushy semi-improved fields, grazed by old horses (2012). The only wholly unimproved bit is, paradoxically, in the garden of a 'plotlands'-

type cottage that the public footpath passes through, on the field edge. It has Spotted Orchids and nice colour. Stumblewood Common is a purlieu common of Ashdown Forest. Though bits have been enclosed, it is still a wild, rough place. Most of it is Holly, Birch, and open grown Beech over a bare forest floor, TQ 405 306/7, with mosses on the banks, and some veteran Beech on the boundary bank of Press Ridge Warren. One part, though, is still open and heathy, on the drive from Twyford Farm, TQ 398 309, with a bit of Heather and Gorse, Heath Bedstraw and Heath Speedwell. Orpine was on its lane side bank recently, though it may be gone now. There is a delightful pond just west of **Twyford Farm**, TQ 394 311. One late spring the tiny froglets covered the tracks. **Horncastle Wood** is large enough to get lost in, with a fine old Beech veteran at its heart, TQ 393 315. There is an old fashioned rough pasture dropping down from Birchgrove Lane, with Daffodils in spring, TQ 406 304/5.

Birch Grove and the valley of the Danehill Brook, e.g. TQ 399 288, have much beautiful ancient woodland, though heavily modified. The northern half, from Chelwood Gate down to Wheeler's Wood, was made into a private woodland golf course[12] for some plutocrat a few years ago, and became a real mess, with bulldozed rides and gaps. Harold Macmillan, the grouse shooting prime minister, lived in the mansion, TQ 410 304. At the southern end of the valley **Withy Wood, High Wood and Sedge Wood** have survived better, TQ 396 283. They have Shining Hookeria moss in wet flushes, with Alder Buckthorn, Pignut and Ling Heather, and Sweet Chestnut, Hazel and Hornbeam coppice. Tawny Owls hoot at dusk. **Wheeler's Wood and Newnham's Wood** have lots of Rhodi, Silver Birch and Scots Pine. They feel quite park-like in places, with mown amenity grassland in the valley bottom, and small ponds … and large herds of wild Fallow Deer (2014).

ENDNOTES

1. Which, in geological history, it was, kind of, for these ridges are some of the highest remnants of the 'Wealden Dome', an anticline which was thrust up to montane heights in early Tertiary times … and has been eroding ever since.
2. Dr Richard Carter, who with Mike Allen and Andrew Maxted, initiated a recent programme of excavation and exploration of the prehistoric usage of the Wealden sandrocks.
3. 'Southern Group meeting at Chiddinglye Rocks, West Hoathly,' by Howard Matcham, pages, 60–61, Field Bryology. (June 2009).
4. Long owned and beautifully cared for by the Sussex Archaeological Society, though they tried to sell it off a few years ago in a financial crisis. One advocate of sale argued that you didn't need publicly owned medieval houses anymore because they are all well looked after nowadays. Not for the likes of us though!
5. Dr Martin Willing, mollusc expert. *Pers comm.* The Plaited Snail and the English Chrysalis Snail are 'Atlantic' species typically found in ancient woodland. Both have their main populations in the British Isles, and the English Chrysalis Snail is almost endemic.
6. It was first recorded as a deer park after 1350.
7. In medieval times Parks were often some distance from the castle or manor house to which they belonged.
8. We walked there once during a World Cup game, and after the 3pm kick off even the country sounds – tractors, occasional cars, chain saws - were absent. Even the birds must have been watching telly.
9. The old English word 'street' was used for Roman roads.
10. A 'porticus' is a chamber, usually on the north or south arm of a cruciform plan. Most, including at Horsted, were later replaced by transepts. They are a Saxon feature, chiefly.
11. The Ashdown and General Land Company formed in 1927 to utilise most of the Broadhurst Manor Estate farmland for soft and top fruit growing. The orchards were only grubbed up in the early 1990s. *Pers comm.,* Bryan Hale, a Horsted Keynes lad and local historian. Great Nanny Pat, in my family, worked there in World War Two, with her school, in the summer.
12. The golf course cost £10 million. The owner was rumoured to have played golf there only six times. Daily Telegraph, report by Richard Eden, 6th November 2011. With that money we could build a beautiful council estate, or buy 700 acres of countryside and buildings for sustainable farming and nature conservation … even at today's lunatic land prices.

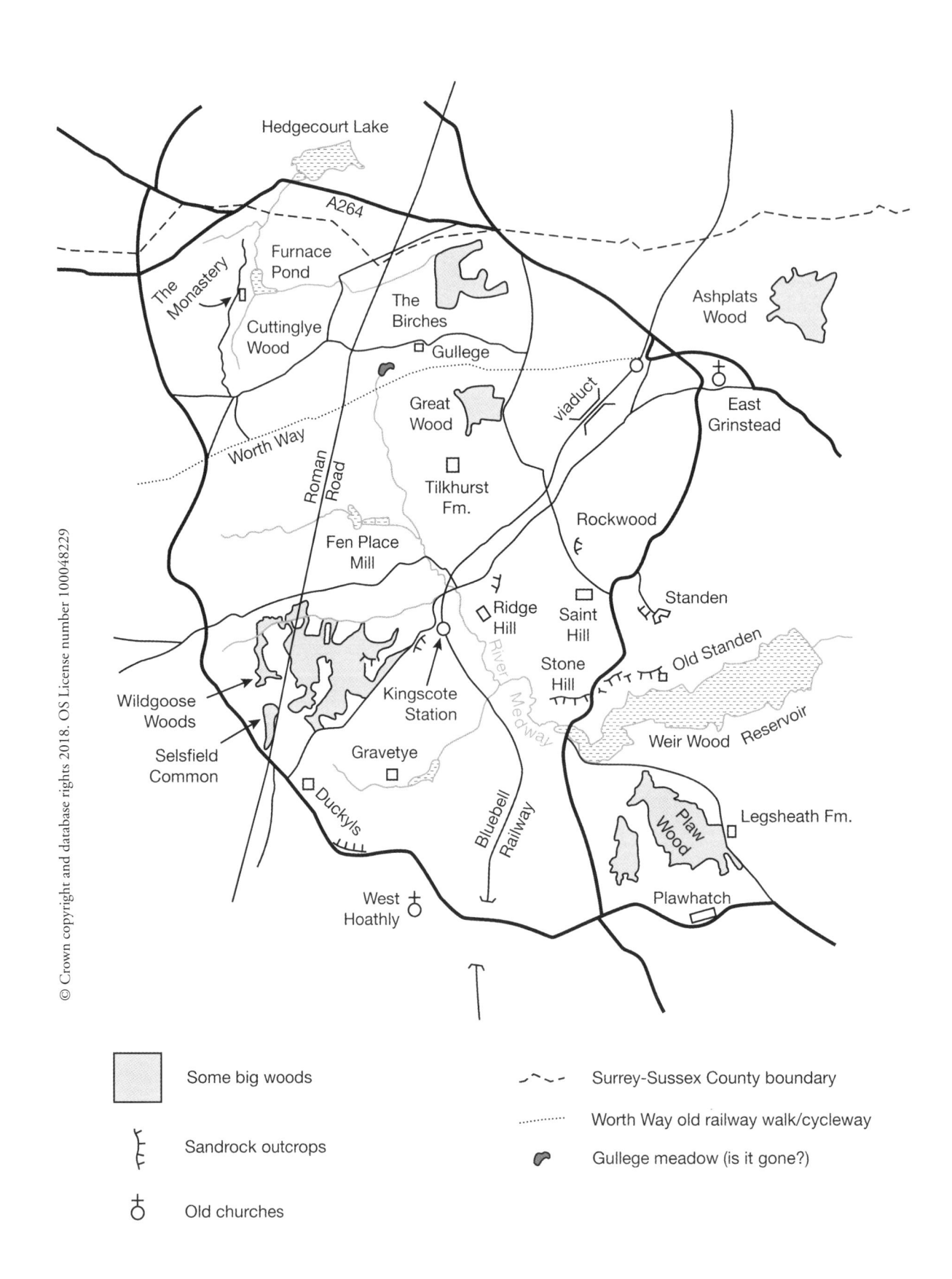

AREA GUIDE / Chapter 22: East Grinstead, Crawley Down, Gravetye and Standen

Map labels:

Hedgecourt Lake, A264, The Monastery, Furnace Pond, Cuttinglye Wood, The Birches, Gullege, Ashplats Wood, East Grinstead, Worth Way, Roman Road, Great Wood, viaduct, Tilkhurst Fm., Rockwood, Fen Place Mill, Ridge Hill, Saint Hill, Standen, Wildgoose Woods, Kingscote Station, Stone Hill, Old Standen, Weir Wood Reservoir, Selsfield Common, Gravetye, River Medway, Duckyls, Bluebell Railway, Plaw Wood, Legsheath Fm., West Hoathly, Plawhatch

© Crown copyright and database rights 2018. OS License number 100048229

Legend:
- Some big woods
- Sandrock outcrops
- Old churches
- Surrey-Sussex County boundary
- Worth Way old railway walk/cycleway
- Gullege meadow (is it gone?)

CHAPTER 22
East Grinstead, Crawley Down, Gravetye, Standen and Weir Wood Reservoir

East Grinstead church tower marks the sky line in long views from the south and west, across blue, misty wooded ridges – from Plaw Hatch Lane and Imberhorne Lane. It's oddly out of place, tall and finialed like an East Anglian wool church … not a stumpy or spired Wealden tower. The medieval church tower collapsed in 1785, and the rebuilt church emblemises the transition of this countryside from relative isolation to incorporation in the sphere of London's explosive capitalist expansion.

This landscape is divided between a relatively flat plain to the north (from East Grinstead's suburbs to Felbridge and Crawley Down) and an increasingly corrugated landscape dropping southwards (to West Hoathly and Ashdown Forest). The Worth Way disused railway line roughly divides the two parts. The northern plain is largely sandstone geologically (Upper Tunbridge Wells Sand) whereas the hills and valleys to the south are a mixture of clay land (Grinstead and Wadhurst Clays) and outcropping sandrock (Ardingly Sandstone). South of the Weir Wood Reservoir the sandstone Ashdown Beds dominate. All the area drains east to the River Medway.

A superb sandrock outcrop runs for nearly a mile past Stone Hill and Old Standen, with others at Holstein Wood, South Wood (Gravetye Estate), Rocks Wood (West Hoathly), Ridge Hill, Rockwood Park, and Standen House drive.

Till modern times the northern plain was an area of old farms (Imberhorne, Gullege, Hophurst, Gibbshaven), substantial ancient woods (Birch Wood, Cuttinglye and Furnace Woods) and a mesh of commons partly straddling the county boundary (Crawley Down, Grinstead, Hedgecourt and Copthorne). Since 1800 the naturalness of the area has suffered blow after blow. First the commons were enclosed (Grinstead and Hedgecourt soon after 1800, Crawley Down in 1848, Copthorne in 1855). Then a wave of ribbon development, commencing with the sale of the Felbridge Estate for building development in 1911, and at its height between the first and second world wars, sprawled for nearly three miles around the A264 road to Felbridge and Hedgecourt. Homesteading ripped the heart out of Cuttinglye and Furnace Woods, and (post-1945) Home Wood, south of Crawley Down. Since 1950, the suburbs of East Grinstead have spread massively along all its three main roads.

The corrugated landscape to the south, dominated by recreational country estates, was relatively undamaged, but the infrastructural needs of the adjacent urban expansion forced themselves upon it with the 1954 creation of the Weir Wood Reservoir, almost two miles long, drowning the Domesday farm of Walesbeech and the meadows and meanders of the infant Medway.

The 1983 designation of the High Weald AONB (Area of Outstanding Natural Beauty) gave some protection to the southern, hilly landscape, but the boundary (along the B2110 Turner's Hill ridge) made the excluded northern landscape even more

The sandrocks from which 'Old Standen' was named

vulnerable, and represented a political compromise with development trends far more than a genuine aesthetic judgement.

The land use patterns of the area are ancient. Both in East Grinstead parish and the western part of Worth parish (which together cover much of the area) the majority of the oldest place names denote woodland: Hacken*den*, Hazel*den*, Stan*den*, Tilk*hurst*, Cutting*lye*, Bur*leigh*, Craw*ley*, Hur*ley*, *Home Wood*. A minority imply open country: *Fel*bridge ('*fel*' = 'feld' = field, open place), *Imber*horne ('*hindberie*' = Raspberry, a heathy plant), *Laver*tye ('*Laver*' = 'lawerce' = Lark), *Grin*stead (= 'green place'), *Fen*land and Gibbsha*ven* ('*ven*' = 'fen'). Many of the farms, such as Standen and Burleigh, are recorded in the Domesday Book (1086).

The pattern of roads and tracks has an even older core. Imberhorne Lane is a continuation southwards of the long route through Tandridge from the North Downs, probably even older than the Roman road a mile to its west, which has left fewer marks on the landscape, bar a section of agger between Selsfield Common and Little Wildgoose Wood. The east-west track through Imberhorne, Gullege and Hophurst, bending south through Crawley Down, is probably Iron Age at least, and East Grinstead's High Street, Hermitage Lane, West Street and the London Road have a likely Dark Age, or earlier, provenance. All of these roads favour ridges and high ground. The old truncated green holloway to drowned Walesbeech under Weir Wood Reservoir, is one of the best places to feel the presence of the past. Some roads, such as the Turner's Hill to Grinstead road, the Selsfield Road, and Vowels Lane, are dangerous even for motorists, leave alone children and cyclists.

Though a path winds all round Weir Wood Reservoir's north bank, the reservoir edge itself is fenced off. Its western end is part-managed for nature. There are big ponds at Furnace Wood, Fen Place, Gravetye, Mill Place, and elsewhere. Most of them are not as old as they look, though earlier ones may have existed on the same sites. There are many small, flooded iron ore mine and marl pit ponds in woods and fields, and some newly created for amenity.

EAST GRINSTEAD'S EARLY FARMS

Early farms and their distant head manors to the south, before the time of the Domesday Book (1086)

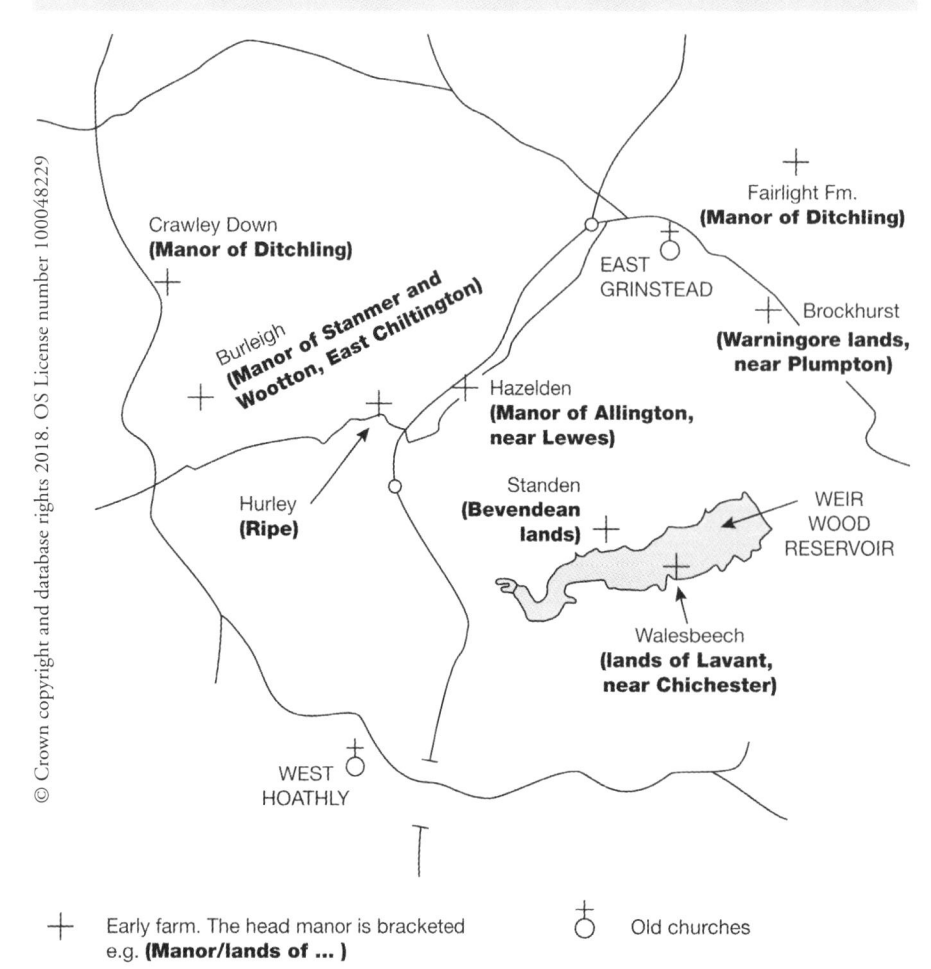

© Crown copyright and database rights 2018. OS License number 100048229

Crawley Down **(Manor of Ditchling)**

Burleigh **(Manor of Stanmer and Wootton, East Chiltington)**

Hazelden **(Manor of Allington, near Lewes)**

Hurley **(Ripe)**

Standen **(Bevendean lands)**

Fairlight Fm. **(Manor of Ditchling)**

EAST GRINSTEAD

Brockhurst **(Warningore lands, near Plumpton)**

WEIR WOOD RESERVOIR

Walesbeech **(lands of Lavant, near Chichester)**

WEST HOATHLY

✛ Early farm. The head manor is bracketed e.g. **(Manor/lands of ...)**

○ Old churches

The iron industry made a heavy impact on the area from Roman times or earlier. Four centuries ago, there were three furnaces in a chain on the infant Medway at Gravetye, Mill Place, and Stone Farm (now under the Reservoir) as well as the Warren Furnace at Furnace Wood on the infant River Eden. Warren and Gravetye furnaces were gun foundries.

There are some marvellous woods of several types – wet Alder woods, Birch, Sweet Chestnut and Hazel coppice woods, acid woods on wet sandstone, and clay woods with dense Bluebell mats. For me, the best is Cuttinglye Wood (that part not ruined by rich homesteaders), reminiscent of Britain's Atlantic fringe. Rookery and Wildgoose Woods are delightfully varied and peaceful, with occasional fine views, little lost meadows, gills and shaws. Gravetye Woods are in recovery after past damage by the Forestry Commission, but they have many of the same core qualities as Rookery and Wildgoose Woods.

Small Leaved Lime lingers to the north east and south east of Turners Hill on the infant Medway at Burleigh, in Comberdean and Great Wildgoose Woods, and in Duckell's Wood.

There is a widespread scatter of veteran trees. Many are Beech, as befits the dominant sandy soils, but there are good Ashes and Oaks too. The magnificent three span girth Oak pollard at Gullege is my favourite. The sandrock slope at Old Standen has a good cluster, including a three span girth Ash. The most famous veterans are the 300 year old Felbridge Chestnuts in a line, along the north side of Crawley Down Road.

There have been some tragic recent losses of old meadows, such as near Mill Place and Gravetye (though the Manor Hotel's archaic meadow lawn survives), whilst others are at death's door, such as those near Gullege and Rockwood Park. The Gullege meadow and that by Rookery Wood are especially rich and characterful. There are archaic flood plain meadows west of Whillet's Bridge by the Weir Wood Reservoir pondtail, and flower-rich verges and hedge banks at Hophurst Farm, Hazelden crossroads, Stonehill Road, and elsewhere.

East Grinstead has many fine old black and white timber framed houses, and others mimicking their antiquity. Most of the area's ancient owning class houses are relatively modest, like Gullege and Gravetye Manor. Those two, with Sackville College in East Grinstead, used local stone. In the eighteenth and nineteenth centuries, some big mansions like Plaw Hatch, Saint Hill and Rookwood Park were built. In the twentieth century, the Imberley/Coombe Hall estate, south west of East Grinstead, became a sort of zoo of sprawling stockbroker belt villas, as did Cuttinglye Wood. Standen House (now National Trust) is the most arty modern posh place, but at least its builders had the good grace to leave its predecessor farmstead buildings in place.

The Gravetye Estate is owned by a charity and leased to the Forestry Commission, whilst the small Standen Estate is National Trust property. Plawhatch Farm is owned by a social enterprise, collectively run on biodynamic principles. Sadly, Plawhatch Hall, once well known in the labour movement, is no longer a trade union centre.

CRAWLEY DOWN AND ITS WOODS

One spot in **Crawley Down** has strong continuity back to its past life as a breezy common, and that is the **graveyard of All Saints Church**, TQ 342 375. The church and yard were built in 1843, five years before the surrounding heath was enclosed (1848) and its ground broken up, giving the common's wild flowers just time to pile in to this refuge, like the animals entering Noah's Ark. There's Ling and Bell Heather (though the new church hall has taken out some good sward), Tufted Hair Grass, Sweet Vernal Grass, Zig Zag Clover, Eyebright, Heath Grass, Heath Woodrush, Spotted Orchids and Tormentil, all in a matrix of yellow Hawkweed colouring the whole yard. Crawley Down[1] has much good modest housing and a nice green in the middle, TQ 346 376.

The intact part of **Cuttinglye Wood**, TQ 345 388, just to the north, is like a west Welsh wood, with outgrown coppice Sessile Oak, much Bilberry, Cow Wheat, Ling Heather, Rowan, and Hard Fern. The gill is dark, steep, and inviting, with Shining Hookeria moss. There's much Beech and Pine, with Holly and Rhodi in the gill. By the footpath is a Christian monastery of the simplest kind, just single storey little wooden buildings with an indistinguishable chapel, a range of orchard trees, a woodyard, a giant Beech with a Hendrix Afro canopy, and some chickens. No fences or barbed wire, and no vile prohibitory notices. Almost no cars in the car park. I'm an atheist, but their simplicity is a model for me. You'll need a million quid for one of the big *'eff off'* villas in the rest of the wood. The **Furnace Pond**, TQ 347 390/1, is embraced by Oak and Pine woods, with yellow Water Lilies and old Swan Mussel shells on the bank. The bay must be 20ft high and the Grey Wagtails love its tumbling water. Only the east and west fringes of ancient **Furnace Wood** are intact. Its heart was homesteaded in the inter-war years, TQ 350 395. The two narrow access lanes (one a public footpath) are just the old wood's tarmaced rides. There's a mixture of bungalows and chalets, with some bigger villas. One looks like the Sopranos holiday home. **Gibbshaven Farm**, TQ 355 392, lies in the flat and lovely tree'd countryside east of the Wood. It is a wooden house of the 15th and 16th century, with a 17th century weatherboarded barn and a granary.

Ancient Burleigh Lane tracks down the steep slope south of Crawley Down across the bosky valley of the infant River Medway to **Burleigh Arches Wood**, TQ 346 363, and southwards. **Burleigh** was a swine pasture outlier of Stanmer, just outside Brighton, owned by the Archbishop of Canterbury (hence the 'Arches'). The Medway rises in Miswell Wood just west of the Turner's Hill Road, and by the stream side just east of the Road is an old damp meadow, TQ 339/340 362, with Sneezewort, Tufted Hair Grass and Devil's Bit (2011). Just south, on the edge of Turners Hill, there's a very old coppice stool of Small Leaved Lime in a back garden by the footpath, TQ 339 360. **Great Nobbs Wood** has a line of these Limes, TQ 345 365, in its west hedge.

The three ponds at **Fen Place Mill** are lovely, TQ 358 366, but the Mill and 16th century **Mill House** are poshed up, manicured and their ghosts have flown. Alexandra House was once 'Fen Place' and is now a 'Utopia Spa' …

GRINSTEAD'S WESTERN COUNTRYSIDE: KINGSCOTE TO FELBRIDGE

Between Kingscote Station and Fen Place Mill, is (was?) a lost fen meadow squeezed between the horrible road and the Medway Brook. **Ash Lea Fen Meadow**, TQ 366 361, would be dismissed at a glance by most folk – long derelict, with Bramble tangles, tall Marsh Thistle, Rushes and Tufted Hair Grass – yet it is just the kind of scruffy place where often nature is richest. When we last went (September 2011) three big gangs of Orb Weaver spiders – Marbled Orb Weaver, Four Spot Orb Weaver, Garden Cross Spider – had made their webs and were awaiting dinner. I'm sure there was plenty.

Despite some tidying up, the area around **Tilkhurst** is very attractive 'Tunnicliffe' countryside.[2] The Skylarks sing over the arable fields, and there are shaws and hedges, old woods, pits, and untidy corners. The old Tilkhurst[3] farmhouse (in origin a pre-Tudor hall house) was demolished, sadly, in 1960, just after the posh mock-Regency Tilkhurst mansion was built on the south side of **Great Wood**. That wood, TQ 371 378, is Oak over Hazel coppice, with Midland Thorn and a Sessile Oak standard. The rides are wide, grassy and flowery. Rhodi is invasive, but there's a superb specimen Wellingtonia. **Railway Shaw**, TQ 368/9 381/2, by the Worth Way, is partly a Bluebell wood, again with Midland Thorn and Anemones. **Hill Place Farmhouse**, TQ 381 373, above the wooded valley of the Bluebell Line viaduct, is the only one of the three pre-Tudor farmhouses on the south way from Grinstead to Crawley Down that survives (now Burleigh and Tilkhurst Farmhouses are gone). The wet woods below the viaduct are ancient and flowery in spring, with much Golden Saxifrage.

The prehistoric northern way from Grinstead to Crawley Down, passes via **Imberhorne**, TQ 373 383, a model nineteenth century farm, with ample barns and a grim brick farmhouse, but with good workers cottages and vegetable gardens to the south, and an unprepossessing tile hung cottage which was, in part, the medieval farmhouse. All the countryside around is threatened by East Grinstead's expansion. Half a mile westwards is old **Gullege**, a fine timber-framed house with huge chimney stacks, a south facing stone front with roof dormers, and Horsham slabs. The pollard Oak giant is on its south side, by the bridleway. North of Imberhorne, is the Alder-lined **Felbridge Water** and **The Birches**, TQ 369 390, a large, mostly ancient wet wood with abundant Ash, Chestnut coppice and Birch, over Bluebells and much Pignut in places.

Best of all, though, is the hidden **Gullege Meadow**, TQ 361 381/2, just west of Gullege. It is a *Shangri-La*, a place of utter delight, in season (2011).

Just west again, towards Hophurst Farm, along the west side base of the ancient **Worth-Grinstead parish boundary hedge**, TQ 359 380/1, is a verge of many old herbs: Saw Wort once more, Bitter Vetch, Creeping Soft Grass, Betony, Centaury, Broom, Slender St John's Wort, Heath Speedwell. The same thirty metre section of hedge holds at least six woody species, suggesting that the hedge is at least 600 years old. Its age does not surprise me. Its survival does!

EAST GRINSTEAD

East Grinstead High Street, TQ 395/6 379, is a partial refuge from the beltway sprawl westwards. It is dominated by a handsome array of ancient timber framed houses, often close-boarded to flaunt their builders' extravagance. The street was made especially wide at the middle and west end, to accommodate the medieval market. An island of old houses, Middle Row, part-replaced the market stalls in the early fifteenth century.

There was no nucleated settlement at Grinstead in the 11th century when the original church was probably built, and the High Street was likely laid out early in

Cromwell House, East Grinstead: Tudor conspicuous consumption – profligate use of timber.

East Grinstead High Street: all 'black and white' timber framing, sometimes hidden behind later stone and brick poshing up.

284 AREA GUIDE / Chapter 22: East Grinstead, Crawley Down, Gravetye and Standen

WEIR WOOD RESERVOIR

Built in 1954, the Reservoir drowned many north-south paths and lanes across the valley of the infant River Medway. It destroyed the ancient farm of Whalesbeech, a Roman ironworking site and Saxon manor mentioned in the Domesday Book (1086), with a Tudor farmhouse. It drowned many wet meadows and valleyside ancient woods.

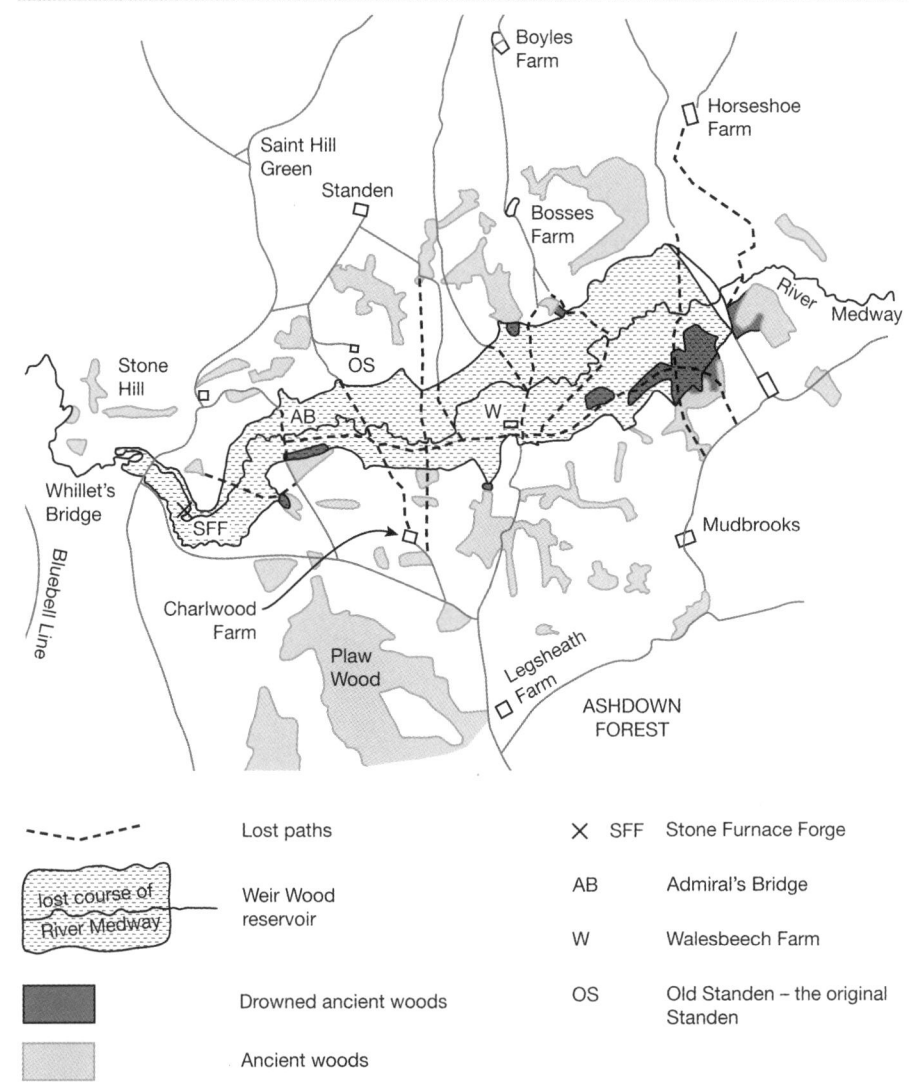

-----	Lost paths	X	SFF	Stone Furnace Forge
lost course of River Medway	Weir Wood reservoir		AB	Admiral's Bridge
			W	Walesbeech Farm
■	Drowned ancient woods		OS	Old Standen – the original Standen
	Ancient woods			

© Crown copyright and database rights 2018. OS License number 100048229

the 13th century. 19 of the houses date from the 14th, 15th and early 16th century. Another 13 are Elizabethan or Jacobean,[4] when the Tudor iron industry fuelled the town's prosperity[5] (with 22 ironworks within six miles). Cromwell House, nos. 78–80, three storied and jettied, was built with profits from the nearby Stone ironworks.[6] The bypassing of the town in the 18th and early 19th centuries by other routes to the coast, meant that its timber buildings escaped commercial pressure to replace them.

The manorial authority of Lewes Priory was replaced after the Reformation by the plutocratic Sackville family, who stamped their authority on the town with the building of Sackville College, as combined alms house and family town house c. 1608–20. It is of local stone with pretty gardens. The rebuilt church retains three iron grave slabs, and has a memorial to the three protestant martyrs burned at the stake in the street nearby (1556). The list of dead from World War One and Two on the memorial plaque is huge. There is also a memorial to a wartime airman who was a 'Guinea Pig'[7] patient of the famous East Grinstead Hospital Burns Unit – and a campaigner.

One quick escape route survives from the High Street direct to Wealden greenery, via Sackville College, on to nearby East Court Park, then lovely **Ashplats Wood**, TQ 404 388 … and away!

SOUTH TO WEIR WOOD RESERVOIR: DUNNINGS VALLEY, STANDEN, SAINT HILL

Three of the four old lanes south from East Grinstead across the Medway valley are now severed by Weir Wood Reservoir.[8] Only the **West Hoathly Road** across Whillet's Bridge, TQ 380 344, is intact. **Admiral's Bridge Lane** ends at the Reservoir and a visitors' car park, TQ 386 348. One is now partly the **Standen drive**, passing Standen House and Farm, then downhill as a wooded green lane to the Reservoir at TQ 393 350. **Harwood Lane** passes the Grinstead suburbs, then through Boyles Farm (posh, antiseptic), past Busses Farm (cattle, nice old and new buildings) to the Reservoir at TQ 398 353.

AREA GUIDE / Chapter 22: East Grinstead, Crawley Down, Gravetye and Standen

A mile south of East Grinstead rail station, and south of Turners Hill Road, the **Dunnings Valley**, TQ 38 36, is a mix of posh villas (Coombe Hall Road) and ancient woods and meadows. **Dunnings Wood**, TQ 385 364, is an open, tranquil Bluebell wood: Hazel coppice with fine tall trees, including many singled Sessile Oak, Ash, Beech, Sweet Chestnut, Birch, and frequent Holly. There's much wind-felled timber on the higher contours. On its south boundary, below Rockwood Park, is **Dunnings Meadow**, TQ 384 363. Beautiful and very derelict (2011), it has a rushy gully, with Sneezewort, big anthills, abundant Devil's Bit and Tormentil. It is disappearing under Bracken, Bramble, scrub and Hazel from the woodland edge. Only Deer hold back succession. On the south side of the Weald Landscape Trail is a **ladder of six semi-improved and unimproved meadows**, TQ 387 364, loved and well used, running for half a mile downhill towards the **Old Dunnings Mill pub**, TQ 392 368, as old as it looks. **Rockwood Park** (now flats) stands above a **sandrock outcrop**, TQ 381 363, which is now obscured by rampant Rhodedendron.

The National Trust's lovely **Standen Estate**, TQ 389 355, south of Saint Hill Green and the West Hoathly Road, used to be called Hollybush Farm, but the new Victorian owners must have thought that sounded a bit common, so they stole the name of the little Domesday farm – Standen – in the valley below. **Standen House**, designed by Philip Webb in 1891–4, looks like one of those millionaire/billionaire's places round Hampstead Heath. The gardens are on several levels, with lovely herbaceous borders and good old trees. There are beautiful views to the south and east across the Medway Valley to Plaw Hatch. The estate woods have good paths, steps and boardwalks, and there is lots of Bluebells. The nearby Weir Wood Reservoir is mostly invisible.

Old Standen – the original Standen – is down by the Reservoir edge, TQ 389 350. A magical place. Its little farm is gone and only a tin covered wooden barn survives in the hollow below the sandrocks from which it was named. (*'Standene'* = stony *'denu'* or *'denne'* = stony valley or wood pasture).[9] Its old green lane winds up the wooded scarp to the West Hoathly Road past a giant Ash and Sweet Chestnut, both of three spans girth. From here a broken sandrock scarp meanders, first Brackeny, then through the Bluebells of **The Ash Grounds**, sometimes precipitous, with fine trees, west to Stone Hill Lane.

Weir Wood Reservoir glinting through the trees from Old Standen

West of Stone Hill House is **Stone Farm Rocks**,[10] TQ 380/1 347/8, up to 6m high and 200m long, with glorious views across the valley and Reservoir. The sedimentary structures (cross-bedding, channelling, et al) of these petrified primeval dunes are very obvious, laid down over tens of thousands of years. It gets crowded with cheerful climbers, most (not all) of whom are very responsible. The arable field above the outcrop has many rock fragments too, as well as lots of slag, presumably from the site of the Tudor ironworks a few fields to the west at Mill Place. There's a further small sandrock outcrop by the bridlepath just to the west at **Stone Farm West**, TQ 377/8 349, by a little Bluebell wood. It has been partly quarried.

Great Crested Grebes sail by as you walk the **Weir Wood Reservoir** edge, and there are big rafts of duck and noisy flights of geese overhead. West of Whillet's Bridge is the lovely **pondtail of the Reservoir**, TQ 377/8 344/5, managed as a nature reserve: partly water (with a primeval swamp of giant Water Dock), partly wet unimproved meadow, partly Alder fringe and thorn scrub. We watched a Barn Owl lazily quartering the marshy fields one March, spending more time perching than hunting. There's Meadowsweet and Angelica, Knapweed, rush, sedge, and Yellow Rattle. The Moles and Grass Snakes love it. The neighbouring derelict wet fields though, are a mess of Creeping Thistle, Nettle, Dock and coarse grasses. There's a tranquil **public hide** just to the east on the Reservoir's south bank, TQ 382/3 341, where you can see Common Terns.

One small spot in the lea of the Bluebell railway embankment, **Mill Place Meadow**, TQ 374/5 344, was wonderful till recently, with Meadow Thistle, Carnation Sedge, Heath Spotted Orchis, Lousewort, Heath Grass and much else. Now it is an utter mess of thorn and Bracken, and the surviving scarce herbs (Devil's Bit, Bitter Vetch, Betony, Creeping Soft Grass) are almost

Tropical luxuriance: Water Dock in Weir Wood Reservoir's pond tail carr woodland.

gone (2014). Elsewhere around Mill Place farm are fishing ponds, horseyculture, a new vineyard, and poshed up barns and timber framed farmhouse … that modern Wealden mixture of monied leisure pursuits, replacing sustainable food growing.

Saint Hill Green, TQ 384 359, is still a sweet spot, with Helen Allingham-type cottages, but traffic prevents it being a dawdling place. It's not named after any saint, despite being indelibly associated with The Church of Scientology, for which the Manor is an HQ. 'Saint' probably comes from *'saenget'* – singed or burning hill! **Saint Hill Manor**, TQ 382 358, is late eighteenth century, of local stone, with a huge Cedar of Lebanon and a landscaped lake. There is a big yellow mock castle in the grounds. **Saint Hill Road** is very Wimbledon, with health club, rugby club and private flood lit sports fields. Wouldn't be surprised to see a cruising alien space craft full of inter-galactic millionaires land there …

The little green – **Hazleden Crossroads** – at the junction of Saint Hill and Turners Hill Roads, TQ 378 367, is rich with wildflowers: Milkwort, Purging Flax, Ling, Zig Zag Clover, Centaury, Betony, etc. A mile south, the **West Hoathly Road verge**, TQ 386 353, by a little layby, is lovely, with Dyer's Greenweed, Eyebright, Purging Flax, and Yellow Oat Grass.

Between Saint Hill and Kingscote Station is wooded country, with a core of ancient woods, much new woodland and recent planting, including some biofuel willow and some arable. To the east of **Ridge Hill Manor**, TQ 371 357, the ridge has mixed Birch, Oak and Pine, and a low sandrock outcrop, with places to scramble and holes for kids to hide in.

SELSFIELD, WILDGOOSE WOODS AND GRAVETYE

You can see why the Romans engineered their road over Selsfield. It has all-round, tip-top views to the North and South Downs. Tiny **Selsfield Common**, (National Trust), TQ 347 345, is light Oak woodland with Holly at the edges and Bilberry at the north end. Just beyond the common's north end are the wooded hollows and humps of the quarry from which the stone was hewn for Turners Hill parish church (less than a mile to the NW across the valley). Downslope, north of the Common, the **Roman road's agger** survives as a bank topped with a Holly hedge, TQ 349 348. The hedge could be four to six centuries old, judging by its varied woody species. **Rookery Wood**, below, TQ 351 351, is a patchwork of ancient and recent woodland. There's an old orchard – four Apple trees left – buried in a brackeny, sunny glade amidst imperial Ash and Oak. Downslope again, by the valley stream, is an **archaic meadow**, TQ 350 355, surrounded by encroaching shaws, with the electricity pylon cables strung overhead. It is a perfect place in late spring and early summer. The wind sighs in the trees. A Yaffle laughs. There is Heath Spotted and Common Spotted Orchis, Twayblade, Lousewort, Devil's Bit, Sneezewort, and I've never seen Bitter Vetch so common. The meadow is cut and occasionally cattle grazed (2016). Towards Rashes Farm is **Comberdean Wood**, with a line of outgrown Small Leaved Lime stools, TQ 347 350, along its southern boundary and near its spring.

The view south from East Street, (opposite Alexandra House, TQ 353 359) is of a great bowl of forest, shaws, and little fields, yellow, tawny, gold and fading green in autumn. Field-edge veteran Beech can be seen even from afar. **Great Wildgoose Wood** and **Holstein Woods** have been damaged by heavy conversion to Pine and Fir, but their gills and some slopes retain their native broadleaved trees. At the south end of Great Wildgoose Wood, three Small Leaved Lime stools survive upslope, TQ 354 346, amongst Hazel, Ash, Oak, Gean, Maple, Privet, Hornbeam, Birch and Sweet Chestnut. On the east side of Holstein Wood is a sandrock bluff partly under trees, TQ 359 352.

The **Gravetye Estate and Duckells** lie in the same 'bowl' as Wildgoose Woods, best seen from the top of the sandrock scarp just below the Selsfield Road. **West Hoathly North Rocks**, TQ 356 331, have overhangs big enough to sleep under, and there are big Beech and Oak draped over them. Below the rocks the 'bowl' is made of Wadhurst Clay, with a lower ironstone band, and Ashdown Sand exposed in the valley bottom around Gravetye and its ponds. **Rocks Wood**, TQ 356 333, on the clay, is thus quite wet, crossed by a number of streams. **Duckell's Wood**, TQ 355 341, is lovely: varied, with many colourful ornamentals, including the rare Katsura. It has an open structure, with scattered tall, often multi-stemmed Beech, areas of old Chestnut coppice, and frequent Ash. The Hornbeam on its south eastern edge make a blaze of yellow in autumn. Above the barn on the east slope is a group of old Small Leaved Lime coppice stools.

The Gravetye Estate, eg. TQ 36 34, now 643 acres, is blessed by its dedication as 'access land'. Only the large and lovely gardens surrounding the Manor, one of the classiest country house hotels in the hedge fund belt, are excluded. In early spring there are drifts of Wild Daffodils all around the **Lower Lake**, especially at the west end, and in **Warren's Wood** on either side of the drive. They colour the **Wildflower Meadow**, too, TQ 361 339, between the Manor House and the Upper Lake. Even in March the Meadow's first Wood Anemones are in bloom,[11] with the first Bulbous Buttercups and Field Woodrush. They are accompanied by planted Hoop Petticoat Daffodils, the first Snakes Head Fritillary, Spring Squill and Spring Snowflake … a delight.[12] In late summer the Meadow is purple tinted with Devil's Bit.

To the east of the Gardens, above the Lower Lake, there was until recently, a much larger archaic meadow, now gone … one of many disappointments about this estate. Its erstwhile owner, William Robinson (who got rich in late Victorian times from gardening publications, and lived there till his death in 1935) plainly had altruistic intentions in bequeathing it to a charitable foundation, that made the Forestry Commission its woodland manager. Though the Commission seem now to be restoring the natural broad leaved character of the woods they coniferised, neither the woods, nor the relentlessly improved meadows, represent how it *should* have been preserved.

At the pondtail of the Upper Lake is **The Moat**, TQ 360 338, a timber framed house of circa 1500 which was reputedly the home of the ironmasters before the **Manor House** was built by them about 100 years later (c. 1598). The Manor House is of attractive local stone, with lots of vernacular features, much wood panelling, and a lovely feeling of being in the bosom of nature, down there in the wooded valley. Sadly, it's no comfort stop for walkers who need to count their pennies.

At the north end of the Estate is another sandrock outcrop along the north side of South Wood, under the lane, TQ 364 353.

SHARPTHORNE, PLAW HATCH, LEGSHEATH

Sharpthorne is a socially mixed village, still with a pub, club, and garage. West Hoathly Station, on the Bluebell Line, is gone, and most of ancient Grinstead Wood has disappeared into the big **Sharpthorne Brickworks pit**, TQ 374 329, which excavates the Wadhurst Clay down to its lowest levels. There are fossil Horsetails, *Equisetites*, in positions of growth, with *Neomiodon* clam-like fossils.[13] Some of the fossil Ostracods (teeny little bivalve crustaceans) are so perfectly preserved that they could have been scooped from some pond yesterday. It is possible to work out what the habitats were from the species there: a mixture of temporary and permanent freshwaters. The name of one genus found there, *Theriosynoecum*, means *'companion of monsters'*, because it lived in places that the big dinosaurs sploshed through. To the north east are **Blackland Wood** (ancient, Chestnut coppice) **and Farm**, TQ 379 335, an outdoor adventure place.

East of Grinstead Lane is **Mayes Wood**, TQ 385 332, a mixed Bluebell wood of coppice Chestnut (upslope) and Hazel (downslope), Birch thickets, rides with some good flowers, and Bracken glades. The wood used to reach Plaw Hatch Lane and was continuous with Plaw Wood, till the last century. **Plaw Wood**, TQ 392 333, is much the larger of these twins, and structurally very varied. It has a good gill along its western side, with Poplar planting on the wet areas, and Shining Hookeria moss in an Alder flush. There are Beech veterans along the north eastern edge, some possible outgrown Oak coppice, much Chestnut coppice, and big coups of Norwegian Spruce, pine and other conifers. Much of the higher ground, though, is dense with Rhodedendron.

Very tired, we came out above Plaw Wood into the small fields of **Plaw Hatch Farm**, TQ 390 326, where a slow moving herd of brown and white dappled cows grazed. We spotted a man standing there with them. "*Oh no!*" I whispered to Jane, "*PLEASE not some bloke saying 'excuse me, there's no footpath here'*" …

He turned, and in the friendliest tone called "Hallo!" … and asked us where we'd journeyed. He told us all about the farm,[14] saying it was a 200 acre community owned farm that supported 12 people, had 15 acres of nursery crops, and made a profit! I struggled hard to disguise my feelings and not tear-up, so moved did I feel to be welcomed, not challenged. Upslope was a little bungalow and a grass-roofed roundhouse called Pericles, with a WELCOME sign on it, a totem pole, and a carved green man … a training project for learning disabled youngsters. We passed a sounder of happy porkers (Berks/Old Spot/Saddleback crosses) … and a small sheep flock. Near the yard (the old Plaw Hatch Hall Home Farm) are the polytunnels. There's a farm shop, with information on all its goings on, and that of its sister farm, Tablehurst, north of Forest Row and around the east of the Reservoir. They are both run on Biodynamic lines.

We walked back towards Sharpthorne in the cool of dusk across the farm fields, to avoid the murderous traffic on Plaw Hatch Lane. On the horizon across the wooded ridges was East Grinstead's church tower. The cows were being driven up the wood-edge track below to milking. There were wet cabbages. Small bats foraged in the fading glow. The western pasture was full of huge, glistening Boletes and crimson Fly Agaric. A Tawny Owl flew by in silent silhouette. A bluish mist rose on the fields, only two feet high, like dry ice on a film set. It was all so good and fine.

To the east of gloomy Plaw Hatch Hall and Legsheath Lane are the **little meadows of Legsheath Farm**, just on the north side of the Ashdown Forest pale (boundary bank). The western one, TQ 399 334/5, is damp, tussocky, heathy and rushy, with shrubs invading from its edges. It has the scarce Lemon Scented Fern, Ling heather, Marsh Violet, Sphagnum bog mosses, sedges and Tormentil. Eastwards, two other steep meadows, TQ 402 337, around the stream, are patchily unimproved and semi-improved.

The countryside around the southern banks of Weir Wood Reservoir is a rumpled patchwork of small fields, woods, hedges and big, deep pits (now wooded and often ponded). Bosky **Admirals Bridge Lane**, TQ 388 342, gives no sense of the adjacent Reservoir. The **Alder Moors**, TQ 395 341/2, are just that – a quagmiry combe bottom with much Alder, and tall Beeches on the steep banks. **Walesbeech Lane**, TQ 397 343, passes to the east. It is a lost and leaf-bestrewn holloway of old Oak, Holly, Beech and Birch, leading down to the waterside, below which was once **Walesbeech Farm,**[15] TQ 397 346. The farm may have been ancient even when listed in the Domesday Book (1086), for there was a Roman ironworking site there, and a considerable quantity of cinder could be seen in the pavements and yards about the farm.[16] It had an ornamented timber hall house of around 1500, with a jutting upper story in the Kentish fashion ('dragon-beamed'). The only local survivor of this construction, it was empty and deserted even in 1940, fourteen years before the Reservoir drowned it. Half a mile east, **Mudbrooks**, TQ 405 341, is a fine local stone farmhouse of c. 1600.

Walesbeech Farmhouse, 1940: Now drowned by the Weir Wood Reservoir

With the kind permission of the Sussex Archaeological Society

ENDNOTES

1. Crawley Down's name has the same derivation as Crawley town's: *'crau le dun'* = 'Crow glade down'. It lies on a hill marking the watershed between the Mole and Medway.
2. Charles Tunnicliffe, the painter, printmaker, and draughtsman of the countryside who died in 1979.
3. '*Tilk* hurst' = *'telga'* or *'tellow'* = young Oak, therefore 'young Oak wood'.
4. 'East Grinstead Town Trail' Published by The East Grinstead Society (1999).
5. 'East Grinstead Historic Character Assessment Report', by Roland B Harris. Sussex Extensive Urban Survey (EUS), with Mid Sussex District Council and the Character of West Sussex Partnership Programme (2005). A superb summation.
6. 'The Wealden Iron Industry', pages 100–102, by Jeremy Hodgkinson,. The History Press (2008).
7. The Hospital (and its airmen patients) were great pioneers of plastic surgery … and it still is.
   The patients called themselves 'Guinea Pigs' and formed the Guinea Pig Club for mutual support.
8. There were several other footpath routes, too.
9. In Saxon times, when Old Standen was just an assart and swine pasturage from the wildwood, it belonged to Bevendean, 18 miles south, where my family live, on the outskirts of Brighton, just over the Down from me. What did the Bevendean herders think of their long treks through the Weald to their forest huts in the autumn?
10. The rocks are an SSSI owned by the British Mountaineering Council, who have dedicated them as statutory access land, bless them.
11. Wood Anemones are a counter-intuitive feature of some Wealden archaic meadows.
12. Though the staff will be tempted to over-plant this rare natural meadow, and much new planting seems to be going on. It would be easy to damage the very 'naturalness' which William Robinson sought to foster.
13. 'English Wealden Fossils', page 33. *Op cit.*
14. And on a later visit he took us to see the cows being milked. They are 'MRI' cows – 'Meuse-Rhine-Issel' – a breed originally from the Netherlands and Germany. The herdsman was Dutch, too. The herd of 40 walked with a huge Sussex Bull (2012).
15. The 'Wale' in 'Walesbeech' really does come from '*Hwael*', the sea leviathan, used as a personal name. The 'beech' comes from '*bece*': 'stream', or, later, 'valley'. Thus, the name means 'Hwael's valley'.
16. 'East Grinstead. Notes on its Architecture. Part Two, Medieval Farms. Whalesbeech Farm', pages 6–9, by R T Mason. SAC LXXX1 (1940).

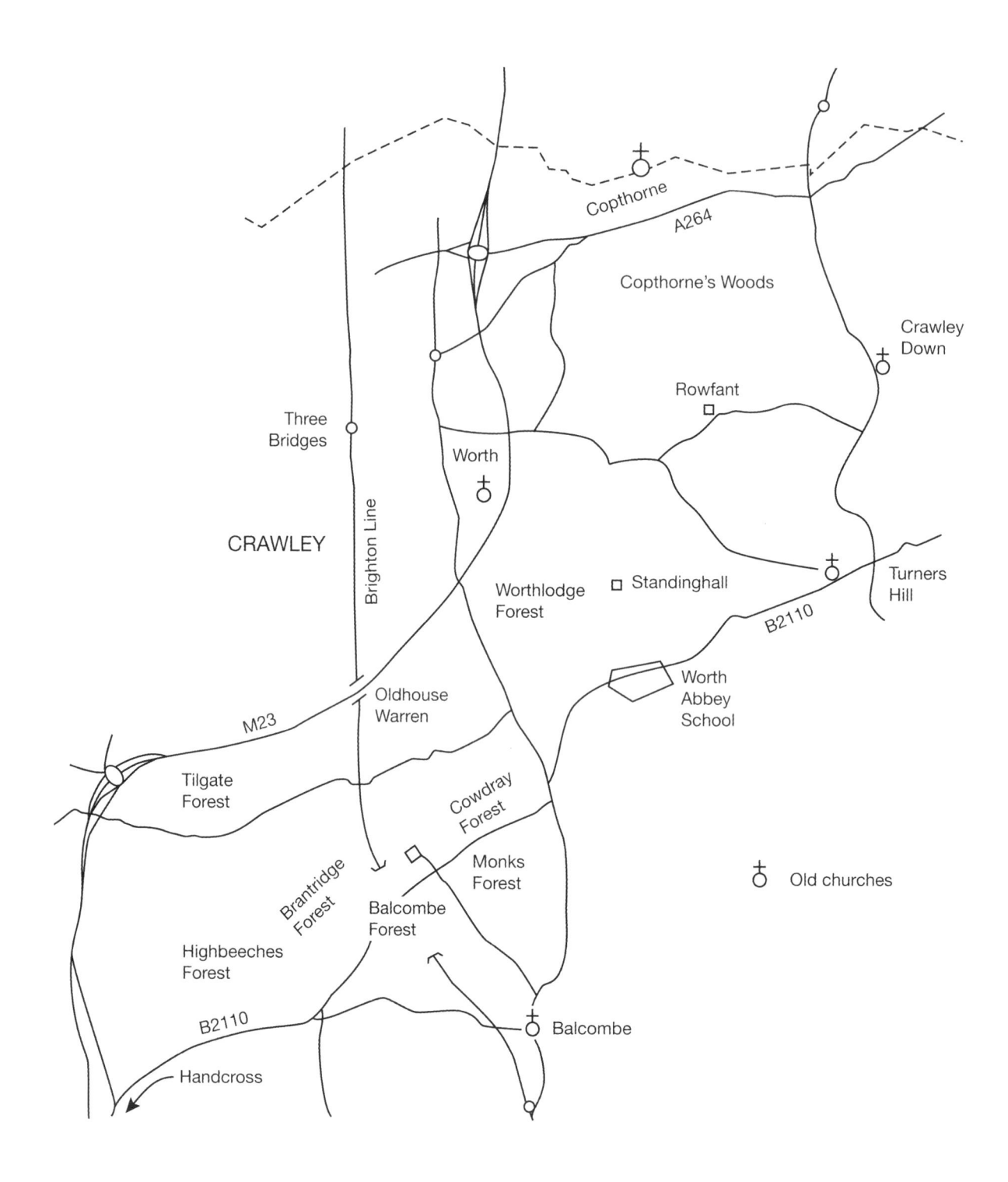

AREA GUIDE / Chapter 23: Worth Forest

CHAPTER 23
Worth Forest

(This chapter should be read in conjunction with Chapter 6: 'The forests of St Leonards and Worth').

Worth Forest is a place of many opposites. It has a more unified block of near-continuous woodland than anywhere else in middle Sussex (even St Leonards Forest), yet large parts of this woodland are oppressed by the awful din of the M23, snaking through its heart.

The Forest reaches to just a mile from the centre of Crawley, and it is bounded along most of its northern side by Crawley's spreading suburbs, yet the bulk of its woodlands have no formal public access.

The Forest is a place of peace where nature seems to rule, yet its dense coniferous plantings and dense Rhodedendron infestation over some areas, have eliminated communities of wildlife which had survived for many thousands of years.

The Forest has the same proximity to Crawley as Epping Forest does to East London. Yet Epping Forest is the pride and joy of Londoners, whilst Worth Forest is largely a secret withheld from Crawley (and London) folk.

Both nature and people get a poor deal in Worth Forest.

BALCOMBE DOWN: GREENTREES, BALCOMBE FOREST, COWDRAY AND MONKS FORESTS

These sub-forests are superb places, retaining features from the old times of medieval wood pasturage, and even – down in their damp and lush gills – from the primeval wildwood.

In the golden woods one autumn day we sat and watched a Fallow Deer stag with antlers at their most magnificent … like the forest spirit of 'Princess Mononoke'. Afterwards, in our rootling around, we found a more modest but precious wildwood denizen, the very rare and beautiful Lemon Yellow Slug, *Limax Tenellus*, with its two little black eye-stalks … We were lucky, for it normally only appears in the wettest conditions. The best time to find it is in the pouring rain. I have searched for it repeatedly in Burnham Beeches, but only found it when the rain was bucketting down. We found it in both Denches Copse, TQ 30 33, and in the woods of Greentrees Farm.

Giant Beech pollard at Greentrees, Balcombe Down

Greentrees Farm, TQ 294 326, never fails to delight. It is an ancient forest assart on the old road from Balcombe to Crawley, upon which we have recently regained our right of way. The seventeenth century Hall was burnt down in 2001, and is now replaced by a huge and domineering neo-classical status home.

Around the farmstead site, the woods and fields have superb veteran Oak and Beech pollards, some clustering in lines along ancient boundary banks. One giant Beech is over five spans in girth, TQ 297 328. To the northwest, across the fields from the farmstead and on the wood edge, there stood till recently another Beech giant of over four spans girth. Age and neglect took it, for it was perhaps two centuries out of its pollard cycle. Its limbs crashed down on all sides, to lie like the spokes of a bicycle wheel. That must have been a frightening sight. Such giants, when they go, 'explode' like that in a sort of despair of holding up their crowns any longer.

The woods immediately north of Greentrees farmstead, TQ 295 329, are secondary re-colonisations of old fields, with much Birch. They have many of the plants you would associate with such places, like Lemon Scented Fern and Narrow Buckler Fern – plants which are happy both in shady old meadows or lighter woods.

The Brighton Line's **Balcombe Tunnel** passes under the woods to the west of the farmstead, and under High Street. The fragment of old wood pasture around the Tunnel, e.g. TQ 293/4 323/4, and TQ 292 317/8, was, with Cowdray Forest, a famous resort in Victorian times, though now its fame is long forgotten. It has some fantastical Rackhamesque giant pollards.

Above the **northern Balcombe Tunnel entrance**, TQ 290 325/6, on the western side, is the most extraordinary cluster of ancient Beech pollards, with occasional Oaks. These trees look right down into the railway cutting, so you should be able to see them at a glance from your train as it rushes in or out of the tunnel. I have tried, but not yet succeeded, for my reaction time is just not quick enough … You only get a second or so. There are some ten living Beech giants and two Oaks, alongside many more dead standing hulks, many fallen, and many senescent. Many of the Beeches here (as well as further west of the tunnel, north of High Street) have trunks which are divided into a characteristic 'V' shape. Were they encouraged that way for naval ship beams, or some other lost construction purpose?

250 yards north of the northern tunnel entrance the rail cutting is crossed by an accommodation bridge, TQ 290 327, built for Greentrees Farm, but now long-disused. We've called it the **'Nature Reserve Bridge.'** It was only kept open by the passage of Badgers, and has been colonised by many old forest plants and bushes. On a springtime day Sweet Briar gave itself away by its lovely apple scent, and I counted 34 plants including Bluebells, Spotted Orchids, Primroses, Yellow Pimpernel and Wild Strawberry. There are small Blackthorn, Oak and Birch, with Brown Birch Bolete and White Coral Fungus in autumn.

Ancient Giants: the Railway Beeches above Balcombe Tunnel's north entrance.

A century ago Arthur Beckett celebrated **Cowdray Forest**, TQ 30 33, as the Magic Wood,[1] with its Beeches "so old, so huge, and so fantastic of shape". Many giants have gone since then. The bole of one vast dead four span hulk still squats by the roadside just west of the scruffy and popular car park (TQ 308 331), its poll chain-sawed right off … which probably caused its death.

The ancient trees that survive are nearly all Oak and Beech, but there are many more Oak giants than survive in St Leonards. On Balcombe Down as a whole, the ratio of Oak to Beech veterans is about 43% to 56%, whereas in St Leonards Forest it is only about 14% to 86%. Perhaps this larger presence of ancient Oaks is a sign that the relict giants on Balcombe Down have stronger links with the medieval forest than does most of St Leonard's, or the rest of Worth Forest.

Cowdray Forest has largely been replanted as mixed stands of various conifers, and many of them are now fine trees. The old forest vegetation is confined to the scattered pollards, the grassy rides and more open areas, and the east-west gill, protected by its SSSI designation. Bluebells carpet the gill, with Opposite Leaved Golden Saxifrage in the wetter areas, and you can still find Small Leaved Lime at its eastern end. Bilberry survives in at least one place and there's still a lot of Ling Heather on the plains. It is a great place for spring birdsong, and Cuckoo may still be heard there. At the western end, as the Cowdray Forest tracks begin to peter out, there are many Wild Daffodils.

Balcombe Forest, around the south end of the Balcombe Tunnel, is a wonderful place. The most intact portion lies to the west of the tunnel and is part of the small Birchanger property, whose delightful gardens themselves protect four huge old Beech pollards (2010).

Birchanger's woods, TQ 293 317, are like a fragment of the New Forest's ancient woods, with large areas of Bracken on the open forest floor, Wild Daffodils in great drifts in places, and lines of gnarled Oak and Beech pollards overhanging the gill and the gullies leading down into it. There is little dead wood, for the owners told me they take much fallen wood every year for their domestic heating system, whilst leaving the standing trees.

In the darkening evening you can hear deer shifting though the trees, and catch glimpses of parties of Fallow Deer. There is much activity, with their little paths criss-crossing even where the Bracken is dominant, and their slots (hoof prints) are everywhere. This is no surprise, for this woodland above the Tunnel is the only place across the 25 mile width of the Weald – from the North Downs to the South Downs – where deer can pass westwards and eastwards without danger from the railway, or roads or houses. This place is a bottleneck, where deer can escape the daunting obstacles to their free movement. I wonder if, in the last 60 years, it has been an important spot for the re-expansion of Roe Deer from their western refuges into East Sussex and Kent.

Between Birchanger and Handcross Lane the old forest has long been swamped by a sort of plotlands colonisation for the very rich, TQ 292 313 … with mansions hidden away in huge grounds.

The part of Balcombe Forest east of the railway line, TQ 298 320, suffers from dense Rhodedendron infestation, but there has been determined clearance in recent years, with huge moundings of bulldozed Rhodi and Sweet Chestnut stools. Crawley Lane has some fine old Oaks, TQ 299 322. Highley Manor (now a hotel) was for centuries the headquarters of Worth Forest, and later of fragmented parts of it. Nestling in the woods is Royal Oak Cottage, once a woodsmens' pub, but in its early life called the Manor House: management quarters for Balcombe Down's desmesne wood pasture.

More about Daffodils. In Worth Forest the Wild Daffodils have nothing like the widespread distribution they have in St Leonards's Forest. They are largely confined to Balcombe Down.[2] It is difficult to see any reason for this odd distribution, except that in both forests the headquarters of the species seems to be in places that were not warrened for rabbits. Could it be that Daffodils retreated under the regime of intensive rabbit farming to the redoubts in St Leonards Forest of old Shelley Deer Park and the Hyde, and in Worth Forest to Balcombe Down? After the end of warrening around 1800, they would have been able to re-expand right across St Leonard's Forest by using its pattern of long descending gills. In Worth Forest though, the pattern of drainage probably kept them bottled up in their Balcombe Down stronghold.

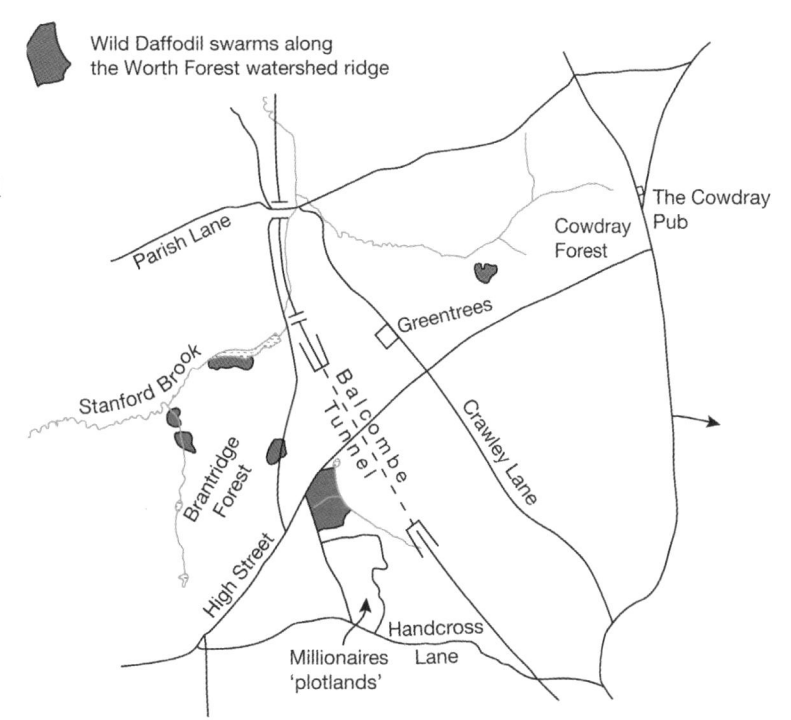

Monks Forest, TQ 305 326, has many venerable pollard trees. The best of them are in the western gill, with good numbers of ancient Oak and Beech including two giant Beech of four spans girth which were young 400 years ago. Many of the standing veterans are senescent, and need careful crown reduction and 'haloing' to free them from the overshadowing of younger trees, or they will collapse and prematurely join the fallen mouldering trunks of their erstwhile companions. The gill is a wonderful jungly place of soaring trees, a fine Sessile Oak grove, collapsed timbers spanning the mini-ravine, fern crowns, and soggy flushes with liverworts and Sphagnum Bog Moss. Nuthatch are seen and much heard, and Grey Wagtail flit in the shadows by the stony stream bed and treacherous boggy plats.

At the southern end of the Forest, **Sedgy Gill,** TQ 306 317, has a different character, for the stream there cuts down through Grinstead Clay, rather than the acidic sands of the upper gill. Bluebells dominate in springtime, under Ash and Hazel, with Midland Thorn, Redcurrant and Gooseberry.

Monks Forest may be named after a forest official – Robert Monk – in charge of the southern part of

'PILLOW MOUNDS' FOR 'CONEYS'

After the woods were cut down, commercial Rabbit (Coney) keeping became very important to the Forest economies of Worth and St Leonard's. The enclosed 'warrens' had linear 'pillow mounds' built where the bunnies could make, or were given, ready-made burrows. They were tender creatures in those days, 300 years ago. Not like now!!

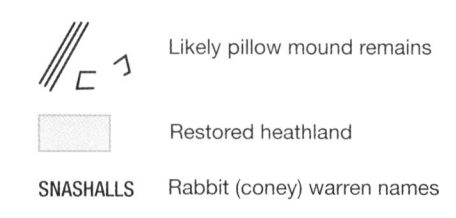

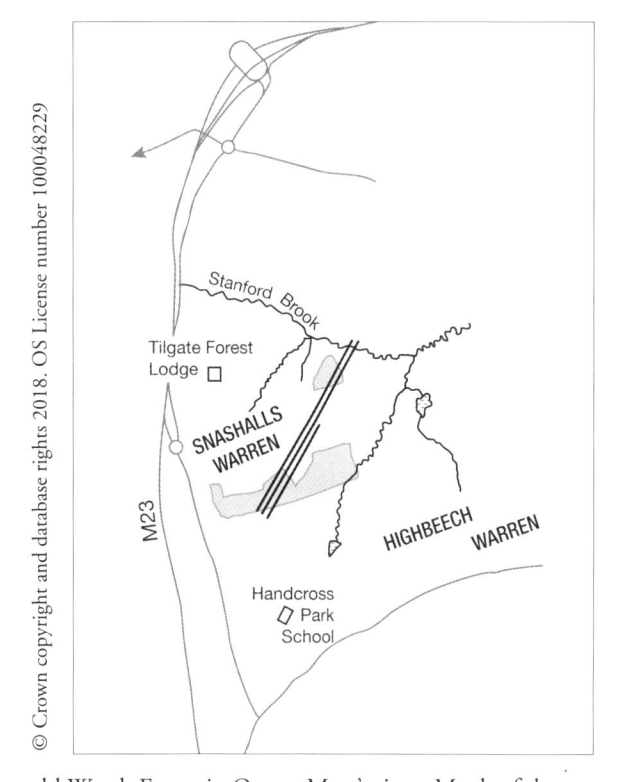

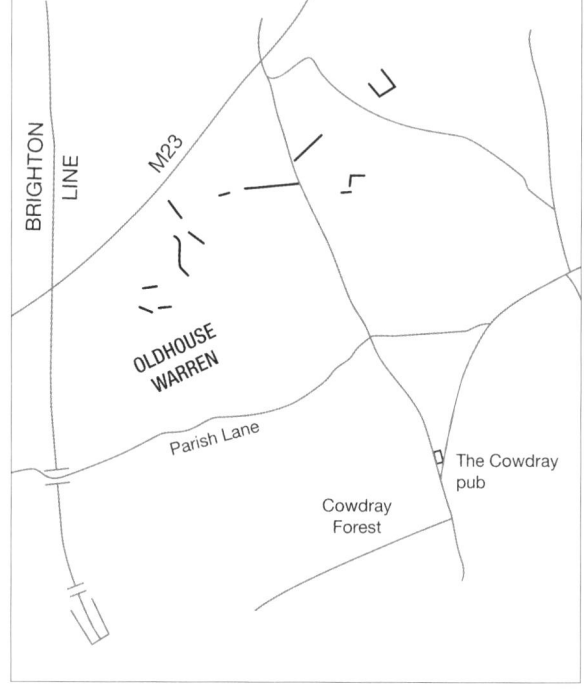

Likely pillow mound remains

Restored heathland

SNASHALLS Rabbit (coney) warren names

old Worth Forest in Queen Mary's time. Much of the flatter plateau was planted up with Sweet Chestnut coppice, presumably in the 19th century, but has been over-planted with mixed Pine, Larch and Hemlock in the 20th century. There are good heathy glades on the northern and eastern sides, with Ling Heather and young Beech, Birch and Oak. Heavy Rhododendron infestation has been brashed in some places, and there has been much replanting with broad leaved species. The main rides have been painfully resurfaced with hard core, smothering old heath and open ground ride vegetation.

TILGATE FOREST

Tilgate Country Park's lakes, gorgeous Azaleas, Rhododendrons and rare specimen trees rival Leonardslee, but it is a democratic space, with happy crowds on summer days, TQ 27 34. Anglers trundle up with their gear on wheelbarrows, and joggers do their rounds.

The Forestry Commission's woods (e.g. TQ 27 33 and 28 33) are also well managed for public access, though woefully split by the M23, which deafens large parts with its awful din. The central valley of the Tilgate Stream south of the motorway is tranquil, however, with the crowns of soaring conifers glowing golden in the rays of the afternoon autumn sun, like a scene from Oregon or Yosemite. **New Pond**, TQ 274 330, near the source of the Stream was built as a header pond for the Tilgate iron works at Furnace Green. It is a lovely quiet place, but kept very private by its anglers, with razor wire round the entrance on Parish Lane.

Though the Commission Forest has few old pollards, there are wide rides and glades, and old forest plants such as Lemon Scented Fern, Hard Fern, Ling and Bilberry have good opportunities, with all the thinning, brashing and tree harvesting. So, too, do the Wood Ants, whose thatched domed nests are to be found south of the motorway, particularly along Parish Lane, on the sunny sides of rides, and in part-shade. Much of the Forest was Sweet Chestnut coppice in early modern

CONIFERS AND FARM FIELDS HAVE REPLACED HEATH, BEECH AND OAK
Brantridge Forest looking north to Mount Pleasant

times, and the old coppice stools are resurgent in many places under the Commission's now-enlightened regime. There are some areas of dense young Pine and Birch.

There are threatening proposals for a new urbanisation within the AONB between the M23 Service Station at Junction 11 and the edge of the Forestry Commission Estate to the east. Such a development would smash the integrity of the Worth Forest landscape and the AONB south of the motorway.

The Forestry Commission used to own the **Tilgate Forest Golf Club ground**, and its heavily timbered roughs (some with much Pine, others with tall Oaks) are the heritage of their ownership. The Commission also used to own a small wood, TQ 270 329, west of New Pond. (Locked and under-managed, 2012).

Stanford Brook (as at TQ 275 321) is the strongest link with the ancient Tilgate Forest. It is unspoilt, tranquil, and lined with Oaks and Alder, though the conifers here and there crowd in from upslope. The gill is sometimes steep and narrow, sometimes gentle, often serpentine, and with little tributaries wandering off to the south. It meanders eastwards for two miles from Bensonhill Wood to the Brighton Line, where it turns north for a mile before reaching the motorway. It's got a West Country feel in places. In springtime there is lots of May blossom and occasional Rowan, with a grove of Small Leaved Lime by the pondtail to the east, TQ 283 323. Bluebells and Wood Sorrel are everywhere, with Primroses. Wild Daffodils are to the east and Anemones to the west. The ferns are gorgeous: Scaly Male, Male and Lady Ferns, Broad Buckler, Soft Shield, Hard Fern, and Bracken of course. There are Brook Lamprey and Bullhead, Caddis and Mayflies. A pollution incident at the sewage works near the spring head years ago left dead fish floating in the stream.

As part of flood control works for the suburb of Maidenbower downstream, **Clay's Lake** dam, TQ 288 326, is being massively widened and heightened to increase the lake's capacity … eliminating much of the existing lake area. In spring the yellow spikes of invasive Skunk Cabbage, rise from the lakeside mud and all the way back up Brantridge Stream to the gardens of Brantridge Forest house, TQ 285 314.

Bensonhill Wood, TQ 265 324, is a lovely Bluebell and Sweet Chestnut coppice wood, with some Sweet Chestnut and Oak standards. It has good sunny glades and rides, though it is tangled with Rhodi down in the Brook valley. One Sweet Chestnut standard is huge and leaning, TQ 267 322.

The 200 acre **Tilgate Forest Lodge estate,** TQ 26 31, though cursed by the low roar of the A23, is remarkable for its **heathland restoration project**, which since 2000, has turned poor secondary woodland back into fine heathland, TQ 265 313. It has taken place without any plant transplantation,[3] just by the reassertion of old heath plants from the seed bank, and natural dispersal. There is much Ling Heather and a bit of Bell Heather, with Dwarf and Common Gorse, Green Tiger and Minotaur Beetles. Heath Spotted Orchis recently re-appeared. The largest Ling patch has three Heather-less stripes across it, which track north eastwards for about two thirds of a mile, only stopping at Stanford Brook. These may well be the remains of pillow mounds of the old Snashall's Warren. Some years ago the **Tinker's Oak,** TQ 267 318, lost its crown in a storm, and only the broken stump remains.

High Beeches and Brantridge Forests, to the east (TQ 27 31, TQ 28 31, TQ 28 32) both have valley streams running north through beautiful Oak and mixed woodland to Stanford Brook. The forest specialities Round Leaved Water Crowfoot and Bog Pondweed are present. **High Beeches Stream** has a pond, TQ 272 317, with abundant dragons and damsels. To its east is a sunny valley, TQ 276 317 with sweet Willow Warbler and Tree Pipit music. There are crumbling Beech pollards in the gill and a Downy Birch veteran at the valley head. The forest slopes have damp flushes and marshy gullies rich with bog mosses in many colours.

Around Brantridge Stream and the pylon line are many Wood Ant nests. As autumn dusk turns to night dense conifer coups echo with the primeval grunts and whistles of rutting Fallow bucks, whilst hinds cluster in groups round the edge, like night club devotees having a fag break and a bit of fresh air. A Peregrine Falcon rises above the woods, then rows in wide circles westwards.

OLDHOUSE WARREN

Oldhouse Warren, TQ 29 34, has three main features surviving from the old, pre-modern forest. They are the *open vegetation of the ride system*; the assemblage of *veteran and ancient trees*; and the *vegetation of the two gills* – **Halfsmock Bottom** to the east with its wooded pond, and **Stanford Brook** to the west.

However, most of the Warren is dominated by conifers, planted in a great binge between 1953 and 1983. There are big stands of Norwegian Spruce, Cypress, Larch and Pine. It gets steadily noisier as one approaches the motorway. Next to the motorway, much of **Brickfield South** now sports a wooden Alamo style fort with shields, huts, fencing, and paintballs scattered around.

In the centre of the Warren and northwards towards **Flax Field**, there are very long pillow mounds, with a ditch on either side, centuries old. To the south, the Warren is crossed by the ancient west-east forest trackway, continuing the line of Parish Lane eastwards of the railway.

The *ride system* has a rich assemblage of old forest plants which are characteristic of open, disturbed and poorly drained acidic, often sandy soils. There is at least one big patch of Lily of the Valley, as well as other scarce plants like Ivy Leaved Bellflower, Bog Pimpernel, Pale, Green Ribbed, Smooth Stalked and Common Yellow Sedges, Marsh Violet, Marsh Pennywort, Lemon Scented Fern, Lesser Skullcap, and Heath Grass in matrices of Purple Moor Grass, Tormentil, and bog mosses. Even rarer species of this assemblage, such as Chaffweed and Allseed, probably also still occur in these rides, where they were known till recently, though they have drastically declined over the last century – some, such as Yellow Centaury, to local extinction. These rutted and periodically disturbed rides are also important refuges for scarce Palmate Newt, as well as for commoner species such as Smooth Newt, Common Frog, and water bugs, beetles and insect larvae. These species rely greatly upon the ephemeral pools within the deeper vehicle ruts. In autumn, but also at other damp seasons, the rides have fruitings of both woodland fungi and old grassland fungi such as Waxcaps.

In 2017 a network several km long of harsh new hard standing rides was built covering over archaic forest vegetation of heath and marsh that has survived for many millennia. It was done without any environmental assessment and without seeking the planning permission

Oldhouse Warren ride: now hardcore, smashed old sink and toilet ceramics, bits of plastic, glass and wire

that was required. Now, where once were Palmate Newts and the tiny spangles of colour from old forest herbs, there is hard core, flapping plastic, bottle tops, bits of glass and wire, smashed old sink and toilet ceramics, and a deep covering of chemically and geologically alien chalk.

As one retired estate worker said to me: *"It breaks my heart what they have done … dreadful".*

To the north of the bridlepath is an east-west boundary bank topped and surrounded by the densest cluster of *veteran trees* in the Warren, TQ 295 336. Most of them are Beech, and many of them are open grown in form. There are ancient pollard Oaks scattered singly or in small clusters around the Warren, too. The southern part has at least two ancient Yew veterans, both well over three spans girth.

Some of the veteran trees of the Warren are crowded by close-placed conifers, and are dead or dying. As in the rest of Worth Forest, there appears to be little management of the over-mature trees beyond safety hazards, and there appears to be no attempt at careful re-pollarding. Next to the timber yard I saw one felled giant Beech pollard waiting to be cut up. The Coal Tits and Siskin amongst the conifers are meagre compensation for the sadness of this.

The two gills to east and west still retain some of their old forest cover of Oak, Alder and Birch. Families of Marsh, Coal, and Blue Tit flit through, with Nuthatch

WORTH: A GIANT FOREST PARISH

Worth was a huge medieval forest parish dominated by the feudal hunting lord and his retinue, with scattered herders, peasants, woodworkers and ironworkers. This dichotomy between wealth and scarcity is emblemised by Worth parish church, a princely Romanesque late Saxon building, in a landscape which retained much forest woodland. In the last 160 years the parish has separated into fragments, as population has increased.

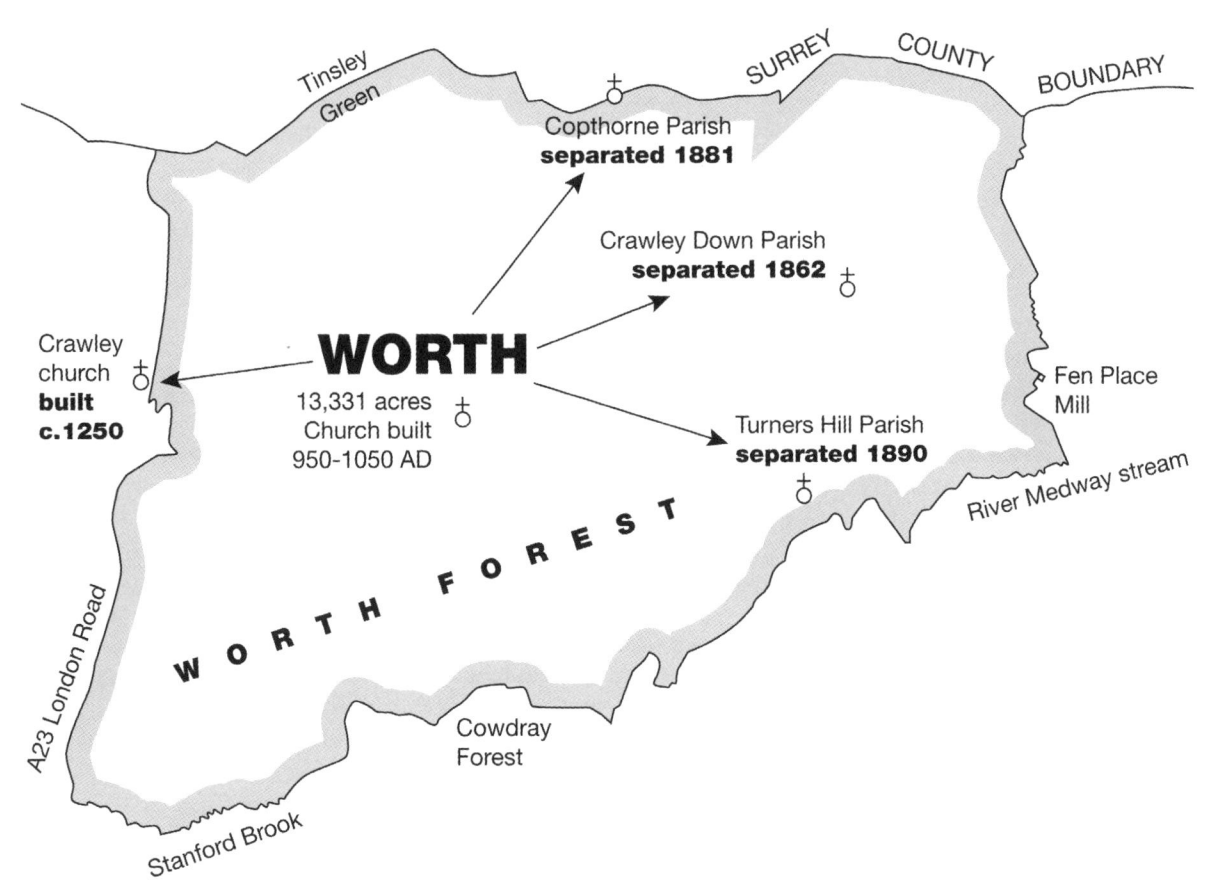

Map: Worth parish, 13,331 acres, Church built 950-1050 AD, showing Tinsley Green, Copthorne Parish separated 1881, Crawley Down Parish separated 1862, Crawley church built c.1250, Turners Hill Parish separated 1890, Fen Place Mill, River Medway stream, Worth Forest, Cowdray Forest, Stanford Brook, A23 London Road, Surrey County Boundary.

and Treecreeper. From a nearby Brackeny glade Willow Warblers sing. The pond bay of the old iron furnace at **Cruckford**,[4] TQ 290 334, has had four hundred years for the Bluebells to spread their cloak over it. It lies just north of the old forest trackway and east of its bridge over the railway. The bay (dam) is eight or nine feet tall and broken in two places, with much iron slag round.

THE MAIDENBOWER STREAMS

I remember ruefully looking out of the train window, nearly 30 years ago, as it picked up speed south of Three Bridges. The new houses of Maidenbower were spreading across the open fields towards the line. Crawley is a fine town, but it was not intended to spread this far.

Nevertheless, the planners of the new Borough Council (taking over from the Commission for the New Towns) managed to preserve and integrate fine features of the old countryside into the dense new suburb. The Maidenbower Streams are amongst the best of them. About a mile of the lowest part of wooded Stanford Brook meanders through Maidenbower, with paths along nearly all its course. It makes a completely delightful green ribbon where kids play, buggies are pushed, and dogs are walked. There is much old Hazel coppice under Oak with Gean, and all the species that delight in Wealden springtime woods: Bluebells and Primroses, Anemones, Ladies Smock, Pignut and Ramsons. I counted 14 ancient woodland plants there, and on the Worth and Brick Field Streams. The trees include Maple and a bit of Hornbeam, Crab Apple, Alder, Sallow, and some Rowan to the south ... and – most excitingly – four clusters of old coppice stools of Small Leaved Lime along Stanford Brook, and another on the banks of the Worth Stream just south of the **Frogshole Farm Pub**, TQ 297 359. There is little fly tipping, beyond a few garden clippings, which shows that these old places are loved for what they are. The biggest danger seems to be from exotic official plantings and garden escapes.

ROCK OF AGES: late Saxon pilasters and stonework at Worth Church

OLD WORTH CHURCH

This church is a very special Saxon survival, TQ 301 362. It was the cathedral of the Forest – perhaps the *minster*, a sort of head church – built in late Saxon times when Worth was part of a royal manor in a hunting forest. It wasn't built just for the local forest folk, for it is a princely space, with its huge chancel arch, high walls and high windows, like those in a castle. Its cruciform, apsidal design is a memory of the early churches of the Augustinian mission, which were built on the Roman plan by craftsmen brought from Italy or Gaul.[5]

Yet, despite the noise of the motorway close by, the old church still holds close to itself a morsel of the wildwood, for, just to its north, and partially hidden in the hedge on the north side of the Worth Way, TQ 302 363, stands what is probably the largest Small Leaved Lime in Britain, with a girth of 26 feet … a Saturn rocket of a tree.

WORTHLODGE FOREST

There is much here that is glorious, though the northern and western parts are assailed by road noise. The Oak high forest of the central gill, TQ 307 349, and the eastern and northern parts, are the best bits, though there are islands of high forest throughout, with Lemon Scented Fern. Some areas have old wood and field banks and must be old secondary woodland. The areas in the gills are the most tranquil and natural, with an alkaline influence from outcropping Grinstead Clay (with Dog's Mercury, Hazel coppice and Anemones). The conifer forest of Pine (mostly Scots), Norwegian Spruce, Fir (including Noble Fir) Larch and some Cypress, has many fine trees, and, at its best, feels like boreal woodland, whilst the open Oak high forest feels like the Forest of Dean. In autumn it is overrun with 'wood chickens' (Pheasants).

Much of the forest, particularly the south plateau, is relatively open as trees mature and are thinned, and Moor Grass, Bog Moss (in the wet spots), Ling, Bilberry, and Bracken benefit from this.

Around the northern side and its footpath entrance, TQ 301 354, there is lovely Oak and Sweet Chestnut coppice over Bluebells, with occasional Hornbeam. The road noise is deafening. One late April afternoon a Mistle Thrush, Chiffchaff and Chaffinch, were desperately trying (and failing) to sing through the din. The stream water is iron-stained, and what looks like lignite bands outcrop on the stream bank, TQ 305 360.

Oaken Wood has much old Oak over coppice, TQ 310 363. There's a lovely view of the spire of Worth church from the wood edge, across the hay fields of Worth Lodge Farm.

The long, north-south footpath from Worth Abbey to the Worth Way, e.g. TQ 313 356, has a Horse Chestnut avenue. The path and several other rides have had hard standing surfaces constructed on them which has reduced their naturalness. There is still occasional Betony, Devil's Bit, Tormentil and Tufted Hair Grass lingering from the time when conditions were more open. The ride created for the east-west pylon line, e.g. TQ 311 354, retains some openness, but Bracken and new tree growth has largely swamped its archaic grassland flowers.

STANDINGHALL FARM AND THE LIME STRONGHOLD

From the high ground on the ridge, along the downslope edge of **Rough Wood**, TQ 323 349, there are huge views northwards … nothing but sunny, forested woods in waves billowing away to the blueness of the Surrey Hills.

Though now much re-afforested, the lands around **Standinghall and Coldharbour Farms** were early – perhaps Tudor – enclosures from the hunting Forest. A 'standing' was an observation tower, built in order to keep an eye on the welfare of a forest or park, or for visitors to observe the climax of a formal deer hunt … or even to join in the gory killing of the mustered deer with crossbows.[6] The 17th century half timbered Standinghall farmhouse has gone now, but the weatherboarded black barn on its stone foundations survives.

Westwards, over the stream from the farmstead, by the public footpath (TQ 314 351/2, and TQ 315 351)

SMALL LEAVED LIME IN WORTH FOREST

Small Leaved Lime, a rare native tree, survives in sites along the east-west spinal ridge of Worth Forest, with its headquarters in Rough Wood and Brickkiln Wood. It found safe refuge on steep and soggy stream sides, often in gills. The tree has also maintained itself further downstream on the Stanford Brook in suburban Maidenbower. It was also planted widely in the post-enclosure hedgerows of Standinghall Farm. That planting was probably fortuitous. Lime hedging stakes would have been cut from coppice within nearby Rough and Brickkiln Woods. They re-grow when driven into the ground, much as Willow readily does.

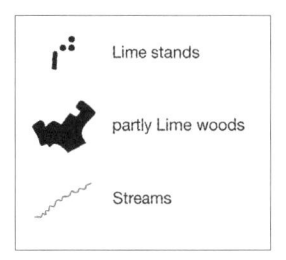

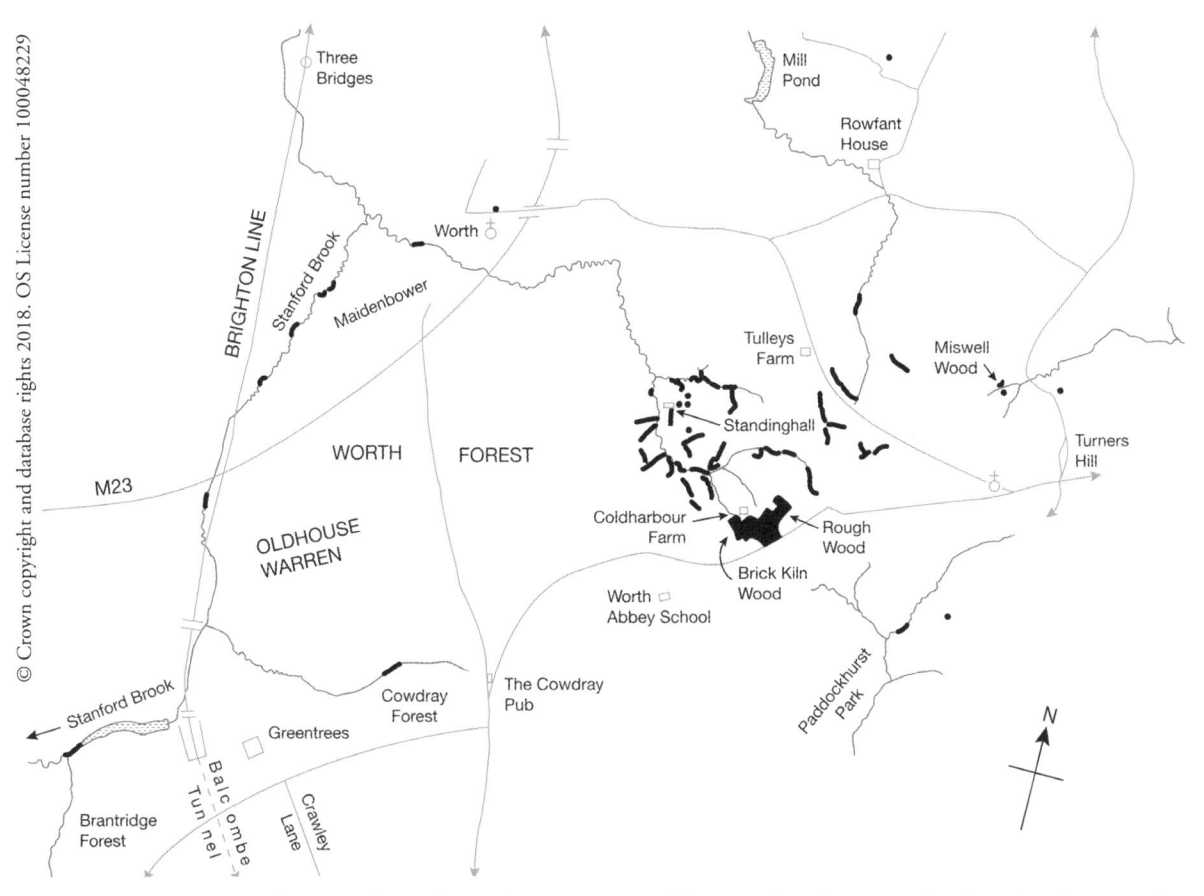

are two surviving archaic farm meadows of great beauty, with Fragrant Agrimony, Betony, Devil's Bit and myriad busy mini-beasts.

At dusk, years ago, the old timber framed Coldharbour farmhouse was deserted, empty. I couldn't resist peering through the little windows at the huge old beams and inglenook fireplace. We walked on into the darkening woods … and *then* Jane told me that as I'd peered through the windows she'd watched a movement in the roofspace … she thought I'd seen it too. I shivered. There's no such thing as ghosts, but …

This area of wooded gills, old hedges and small woods is a fine stronghold for the rare Small Leaved Lime. The bigger, more outgrown coppice stools are strung along the gills, and there are several giants, as by the **Standinghall Stream** at TQ 314 355. Many are windblown and sending up poles from their horizontal branches. There are several long lines of Limes on the long-lost field banks to the west of Standinghall Stream. The banks are difficult to detect under the brash and cut timber, but their suckering Limes stand out. Several old quarry pits have old coppice Lime stools. Often the hedgerow Limes appear to be younger, though there are at least a couple of hedgerow maidens over two spans in girth.

Upslope of the two farms, both **Rough Wood and Brick Kiln Wood** are partly Lime woods, though there are Beech and handsome old Oaks, including one veteran. Brick Kiln Wood, TQ 322 347, is a Lime coppice wood to the east of its gully stream. The poles are up to 18 inches wide, and covered with horizontal lines of pock marks made, presumably, by Woodpeckers seeking grubs. The whole character of the normally smooth grey bark is changed to look more like Gean. Rough Wood, to the east, TQ 324 349, has similar old coppice stools, particularly down in its gill … and big old maiden Oaks as well.

All the small Leaved Limes in this landscape seem to be either on the Grinstead Clay outcrop (on the upper slopes) or on Ardingly Sandstone in the valleys and gills.

TURNER'S HILL TO ROWFANT

In late autumn the beautifully kept graveyard of **Turners Hill's handsome church**, TQ 337 353, is spangled with the colours of a second summer – reds, yellows, oranges and whites – from its rich flora of old meadow fungi. Tread very carefully if you come at that time, for many of the 'fungal flowers' are tiny, and some are very rare. On an early December visit I found sixteen species, including ten Waxcaps, *Hygrocybe*, two Fairy Clubs, *Clavariaceae*, three Earthtongues, *Geoglossaceae*, and one Pink Gill, *Entolomataceae*. Yet the church is less than 120 years old … and the tower was only finished in 1924. Lord Cowdray, the local plutocrat, delayed dishing out his dosh for the tower's building "until[7] wages came down to 50% above pre-war levels" … Now *there's* Christian charity for you!

The woods west of Turner's Hill have been cut over and replanted, but, for all that, are mostly ancient. The very rare and vanishingly tiny Yellow Centaury, *Cicendia filiformis*, a kind of Gentian which likes damp sandy rides, was found in **Quarry Wood**, TQ 329 355, but it isn't suitable now, with Birch dominant, occasional Pine, Oak and Rhodi. However, there are some large old Small Leaved Lime stools, with Common Lime (which is the cross between Large and Small Leaved Lime). **Lodge Wood** is similar, with big Larch and Fir stands, and there are Small Leaved Lime stools, for instance along the ride under the power line, TQ 326 354. The woods east of Major's Hill are part of **Tulley's Farm**, and are still lovely, despite the off road motor trail gouged through, and the noise of shooting and go karting in the adjacent fields. There is much Small Leaved Lime coppice both to the west, TQ 326 356, and north, TQ 329 359, of Tulley's farmstead, and Oak, Ash, abundant Sweet Chestnut and Beech all gorgeous gold in autumn. **The Gill** (that's the name of the wood, TQ 327 363) is Sweet Chestnut coppice, but the gill which descends to the Worth Way is rich ancient woodland with some Small Leaved Lime, Bluebells, Wood Melick, Goldlilocks Buttercup etc. There's a fine three span girth Beech on the field edge, TQ 327 366, and huge old Crab Apple trees just to its north.

Trundling along in the green two coach railway train from Three Bridges[8] back in the sixties, the dark woods seemed to me to close in on both sides around **Rowfant Station**, TQ 323 367, and they do still. **Hundred Acres** wood, TQ 334 366, is big enough to get nicely lost in.

It has blocks of Larch, Scots Pine, Sweet Chestnut and Birch. There is heavy Rhodi infestation, but it doesn't badly obstruct walking. There's a central gill. Along the south edge there's Sessile Oak, Wych Elm, Gean, Rowan, English Oak, both Birches, Sallow and Hazel, which gives a idea of what the rest of the wood was like before modern plantings. Rowfant Business Centre is sited on an old brick pit there and takes in part of the wood.

Miswell and Butcher's Woods to the south east, are lovely old coppice woods, with fine old Oaks. Miswell Wood, TQ 336 359/360, has Small Leaved Lime stools on its south side. At the south end of Butcher's Wood, TQ 336 356, near the spring, there is a large open area of tall outgrown Sessile Oak coppice.

COPTHORNE COMMON AND WOODS TO ROWFANT

Copthorne Common was another of those wild places that almost made it into our time. It was still around 750 acres when it was finally broken up in 1855 – in one of the last big local enclosures. Together with Heathy and Hedgecourt Commons on its west and east sides, it sprawled along nearly two thirds of the northern boundary of Worth parish. About two thirds of it was in Surrey and a third in Sussex.

About an eighth of the old common, 86 acres, is still registered common today – retained, together with some other nearby bits, for the use of local people. Not that you'd know … for most of that rump is now incorporated in the Copthorne Golf Course. Very little of it still retains its archaic heathy vegetation. The best bit is probably a smidgeon of mown heath, TQ 322 391, in front of the Club House, on the north side of the A264. It's got abundant Ling, Tormentil and Bent Grass, with lots of Devils Bit, and scattered Dwarf Gorse and Bell Heather. To the south of the A264 much of the relict heath is very rank and there's even been recent tree planting … as if that was needed! Most of the heath is being left to disappear, though the commoner heathy species were still clinging to life when I last looked (2011).

Bashford's Wood, TQ 326 384, to the south of Copthorne Common, was once an especially lovely Bluebell wood, with much old Oak coppice. There's enough of it left to see that. There are also surviving traces of the wood's more distant past, when it was part of the wood pastures of the hunting forest, for it retains at least four giant Beech pollards of over three spans girth, and one of 2.5 spans. The wood is also now mostly incorporated into the Golf Course, and has shrunk greatly. The golf course has been mostly built upon both ancient woodland and heathland. The woodland has been whittled away for fairways, and what is left needs better treatment.

Much of the woodland south of Copthorne Common is heavily Rhodi infested. Some owners are tackling this. Some aren't. **Kings Wood**, TQ 324 378, south of Bashford's Wood, has several veteran Birch and a Small Leaved Lime coppice stool. **Copthorne Wood**, TQ 315 383, is good and bad. Much of it is old Sweet Chestnut coppice, with lots of windblown timber, and there's Cow Wheat, Rowan and abundant Birch and Holly. The din is awful to the west, from the M23 and Gatwick, but the eastern – golf course owned – part is a lot quieter. There's much Bluebell.

The old drove through **Wins Wood**, TQ 332 377, was possibly edged by an ancient Beech hedge, and several of the outgrown trees now form fine pollards. East of the drove is far less Rhodi infested than to the west (2012). Further north, on the east side of **Westlands Wood**, the bulldozer has been at work clearing woodland, TQ 335 385 … for livery pasture? It is a Bluebell Wood, but Rhodi infestation is heavy in places. **Chart's Plain** is a fine, open, airy wood, with Birch and Oak coppice co-dominant, TQ 330 388, and with a three span Beech on its northern boundary. These lovely woods are also large and wild enough to get lost in.

The last time I looked, the south pond in the woods had a notice in English AND Polish: "Poaching is illegal. You will be prosecuted".

The landscape south of Copthorne is suffering incremental development pressure and woodland loss to encroachments from the golf course, smallholders, lake fisheries, and 'horseyculture' (2012).

IRON WORKS

Old Rowfant Mill Pond, TQ 316 376, was the hammer pond for the **Rowfant Forge**, which was active till 1664. The corn mill which succeeded it worked right through to the early twentieth century. The pond is lovely, serpentine, Alder-edged and Water Lily'd, with many Dragonflies. Just to the south east, in **Horsepasture Wood**, the broken pond bay of the **Rowfant Supra Forge** can be seen, TQ 319 372. It closed earlier than the former forge, though its pond was independently useful as a header pond. The wood was heavily Rhodi infested, but much of its western end has been cleared. Good work. There is a delightful spot on the stream side where the old pondtail must have been, TQ 322 370, with a three span Beech pollard whose splintered limbs have fallen across the stream to make bridges.

Neighbouring **Layhouse Wood**, TQ 315 368, is a lovely, almost pure Oak coppice wood, much of it Sessile Oak. The prevalence of Oak coppice in this landscape (as at Chart's Plain, Layhouse, Cuttinglye, Butcher's, and Bashford's Woods) points to its usage to make charcoal for the iron works.

Rowfant House was the ironmaster's stone mansion, TQ 325 371. It is Elizabethan, though with earlier (15th century) and later parts. The late nineteenth / early twentieth century semi-industrial farm buildings at **Home Farm**, complete with factory chimney, stand out, TQ 325 376. They were derelict when I last looked in 2009. The gamekeeper said that the main building – with roof fallen in – used to have an old engine to pull sacks up, which has now gone to a museum.

ENDNOTES

1. 'The Wonderful Weald', pages 199–201, by Arthur Beckett. Methuen (1911)
2. In Birchanger's woods, in western Cowdray Forest.
3. *Pers. comm.,* Mrs Penny Mortimore and Richard Mortimore, the estate owners.
4. The name 'Cruckford' strengthens my speculation that the numbers of 'V' shaped veteran Beech and Oak nearby may be part of a local tradition of growing cruck-shaped (crooked) timber.
5. 'The English Parish Churches', page 14, by Edwin Smith. Thames and Hudson (1976).
6. 'Lodges and Standings', page 14, by Oliver Rackham. Part of 'Epping Forest through the Eye of a Naturalist', edited by M W Hanson, published by The Essex Field Club (1992).
7. 'St Leonard's, The Church on the Hill, Turner's Hill Parish Church', page 14, compiled by Eric Dawes. (2003).
8. The line closed on 1st January 1967.

© Crown copyright and database rights 2018. OS License number 100048229

CHAPTER 24
St Leonard's Forest's northern plateau

(This chapter should be read in conjunction with Chapter 6: 'The forests of St Leonards and Worth').

You have to *work* to find the beauties of St Leonard's Forest. It is a matter of rooting out the surviving high quality habitat hidden amongst the painfully damaged and modified. It is not delivered on a plate, as at Ashdown Forest. It's worth it, though.

THE DAFFODIL FOREST

Many years ago I took a springtime cycling holiday to the Wild Daffodil countryside along the Herefordshire-Gloucestershire border – Dymock, Ledbury, and Woolhope. I have cherished those memories. I had no idea, then, that I could see the same wonders much closer to home, just a mile or so from Crawley, for St Leonard's Forest has a most spectacular secret, which has been well kept.

In March and April much of the middle Forest is a glorious triumph of yellow Wild Daffodils – the primrose yellow of their outer rays and the deep yellow of the trumpets of these dainty little heralds of spring. They mass along rides, across open woodland floors, along gill sides and across relict old pastures. For some weeks in March and April they transform those places into the Plains of Heaven.

The Hyde Estate is the headquarters of the Daffodil Forest, and the estate staff clearly manage some areas with their needs in mind, like the large areas of open Daffodil woodland just north of Truckers Ghyll, for they thrive best where the shrub layer and its shade are reduced. They mass at the top of the long gills descending south westerly across the Forest: on the glorious slopes of The Steep, north of Newstead Farm; in Hydehill Wood and Old Copse at the south end of the lost medieval deer park of Shelley; around The Hyde itself; and the Wild Garden between The Hyde Mansion and the ponds of Darkalley Gill to the south.

From those heights they cascade down the gills – Newstead Gill, Hyde Gill, Darkalley and Carterslodge Gills – all the way across the middle Forest, by Hammer Pond and all across Mannings Heath Golf Course, through Cinderbank Copse, along Goldings Stream, and across the ant hilly pastures of the golf course roughs, and west of Goldings Lane to the infant Arun.

They are a true wonder.

The Daffodils display no obvious sign of anything but natural transportation across the Forest, and the forester at The Hyde told me he doesn't remember any transplantation by people taking place. For all that, it does happen. One landowner told me he'd just transplanted some bulbs from a densely flowered area of his to a bit of his nearby woodland without Daffodils. It is difficult to account for the contrast between the near-absence of the Daffodils in ancient Hoadlands Wood, TQ 256 299, and their super-abundance just to the west, at The Hyde, except by some past nudging of these sedentary beauties to adjacent sites.

I like to think that the last Black Grouse of Newstead would have hunkered down amongst Wild Daffodils, as much as Heather, and that the Tudor furnace men of the two St Leonard's iron works, in Cinderbank Wood, would have enjoyed the nodding Daffodils when they took their breaks from the heat and noise at the end of their winter firing (smelting) campaigns.

THE STEEP

This nine acre slope, TQ 242 312, part of Newstead Farm, has the very best remaining fragment of archaic cattle grazed rough pasture in this northern part of old St Leonard's Forest. It is a remarkable survival, for all around has been converted to nitrogen green intensive dairy pastures and tilled ground. It is plainly loved by its owners, though almost unknown more widely. Like The Hyde it has a most spectacular Daffodil display in springtime, but it holds much more.

Rushy gullies drain across the wet clays of its lower slope, with more close-cropped mossy lawns between them, overlooked by dryer, steeper, sandy ground

THE DAFFODIL FOREST

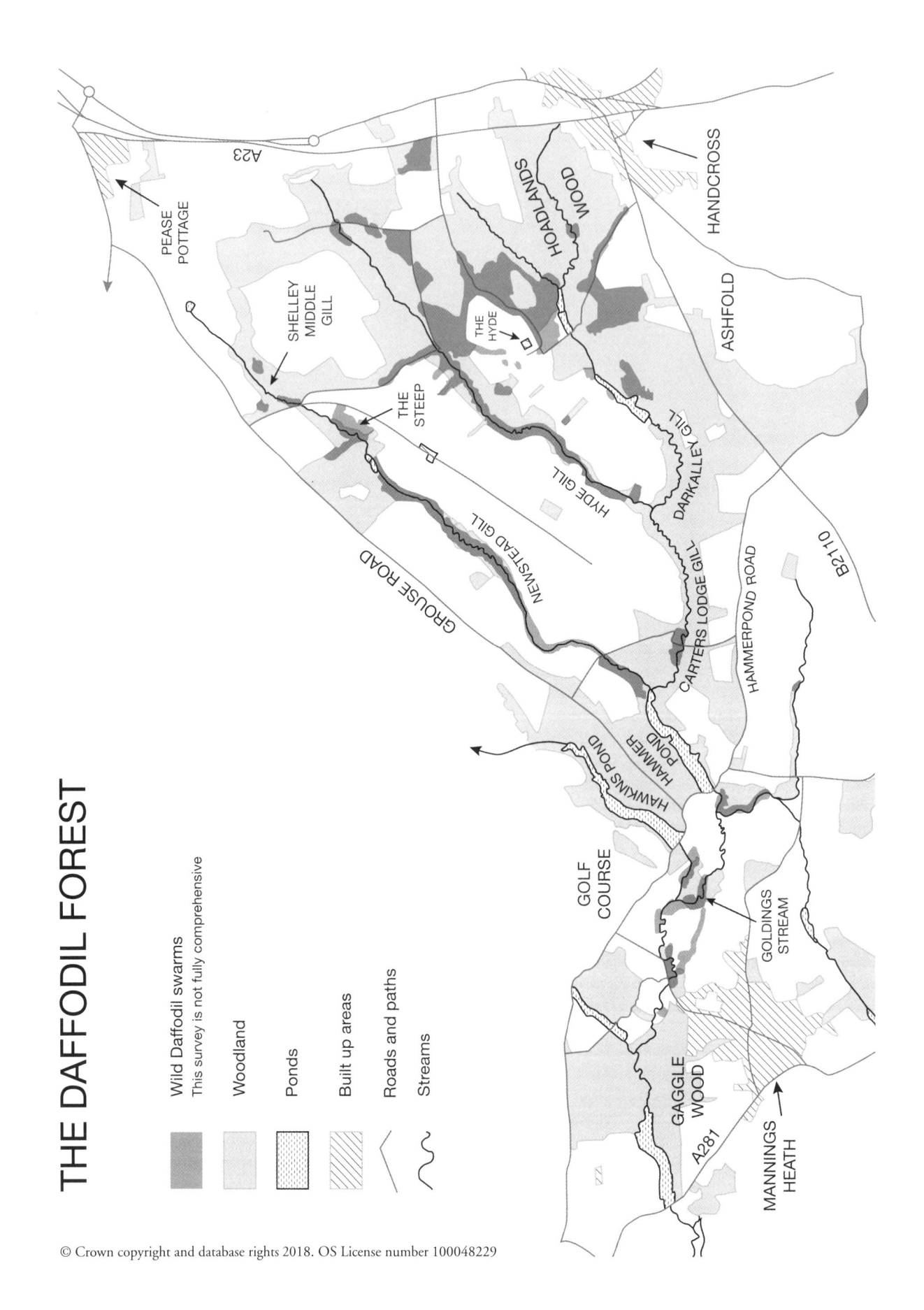

Legend:
- Wild Daffodil swarms (This survey is not fully comprehensive)
- Woodland
- Ponds
- Built up areas
- Roads and paths
- Streams

Labels on map: PEASE POTTAGE, A23, HANDCROSS, HODLANDS WOOD, ASHFOLD, SHELLEY MIDDLE GILL, THE HYDE, THE STEEP, DARKALLEY GILL, HYDE GILL, NEWSTEAD GILL, GROUSE ROAD, CARTERS LODGE GILL, HAMMERPOND ROAD, B2110, HAWKINS POND, HAMMER POND, GOLF COURSE, GOLDINGS STREAM, GAGGLE WOOD, A281, MANNINGS HEATH

© Crown copyright and database rights 2018. OS License number 100048229

Which way? ... Scented pine, hot sun, peace:
The Forestry Commission's St Leonard's Forest Estate at Greenbroom Hill.

above. In May time these lawns are purple-pink with Lousewort, and dotted yellow with Tormentil and Meadow Buttercup ... and if you look closely in the mossy sward you may find Bog Pimpernel. Adder's Tongue Fern grows in one spot. The rushy gullies harbour at least six Sedge species, Marsh Pennywort, Ivy Leaved Bellflower, Marsh St John's Wort, Creeping Forget Me Not and Lesser Spearwort. Many of these species are indicative of sites with a long historical ecological continuity.

In summer the site is busy with micromoths, bees and hoverflies, and I've seen the rare Dark Giant Horsefly, *Tabanus sudeticus*, there, many miles from its main homelands on western moors and uplands.

THE HYDE ESTATE AND THE LOST SHELLEY DEER PARK

These places are full of delights, though oppressed on their eastern side by the din of the A27. The huge boundary bank of the medieval deer park snakes across the upper ends of Newstead and Hyde Gills. It is still topped with many fine veteran Beeches. On the south side there is at least one ancient Sessile x English Oak hybrid pollard on the bank, in woodland on acidic soil, with Green Worms moss, *Plagiothecium undulatum*, Bog Moss, *Sphagnum*, and Tumble Moss, *Leucobryum glaucum*. In winter, three Woodcock started up in one place.

Shelley Middle Gill, TQ 243 318, is fine high forest of Oak, over Bluebells – a steep and romantic place with ferruginous seeps, and some Sessile Oak and Midland Thorn amongst much Downy Birch.

The Hyde wilderness garden and ponds, TQ 248 299, really 'hit the spot'. Towering, columnar Pines, young Redwood, Douglas Fir and Cypress frame the sky above. It has much of the character of Leonardslee or High Beeches, with more wildness. The lawns, which drop down to the two ponds, are a relic of the unimproved Forest grasslands, with Wild Daffodils in spring and domesticated tussocks of Ling and other Heathers in high summer. At dusk in autumn, flocks of Thrushes and Starlings circle and settle, circle and settle. A Great Spotted Woodpecker crosses the open. Song Thrushes sing as the light turns from clear, still blue to gold and red. Mistle Thrushes call from the very tops. One tiny star and the crescent moon shine, and as we walk back up the drive under the leafless woodland tracery to Handcross, the moon follows us through the trees.

Octopoid monster. St Leonard's Forest Beech giant. A 'bundle planting' or a massively outgrown hedge stool?

SAINT'S BLOOD: THE LILY BEDS

The blood of St Leonard was scattered through his forest at many spots in his fight with a dragon, and everywhere it fell Lily of the Valley sprang up (or so we tell our children, hoping thus to fire their imaginations) … but the lovely Lily Beds of the Forest, TQ 212 307, are famous enough without that legend. Few wild flower sites are so famous as to be named on Ordnance Survey maps, as they are. Lily of the Valley spangles the woods and glades between Greenbroom Hill and Scragged Oak Hill. It is a shy flowerer there, unless it gets direct sunlight, but its leaves are easily found. There's a trail bike site at the edge of the Lily Beds, with litter, shelter, and fire site mess.

St Leonard's Forest is definitely the main native stronghold of this species in Sussex. Its fame ensured the preservation of the core of the Lily Beds from the Forestry Commission's past relentless coniferisation. Now the Commission, in its modern progressive reincarnation, has re-integrated them within a restored patchwork of heath and mixed forest.

Native Lily of the Valley is a plant of dry woods and copses on both limestone and sandy soils. Till the 1930s at least it occurred in other middle Sussex woods, such as Blackbrook in Westmeston, Chiddingly in West Hoathly, Spithurst in Barcombe, at Tilgate and Worth, and in Plashett Wood, but from all those I only know it from a single site in Worth Forest now.

THE FORESTRY COMMISSION'S FOREST

One hot day in late May I picked my way through the fallen trees at **Mick's Cross**, TQ 216 302. Brightly coloured insects hovered, darted and rested amongst the mouldering hulks. The shiny Red Leafwalker hoverfly, *Xylota segnis*, and its wasp lookalike cousin the Deathskull Fly, *Myatropa florea* stared at me metallically from their sunbathing logs. Scuffing about in the mould of a broken trunk I found a large black Mealworm Beetle. We all know the larvae, famous as angler's bait and food for pet snakes and birds, but this is the beetle's ancient home, amongst the decay of forest trees.

Downhill I clambered, down into **Sheepwash Gill**, TQ 208 303, and splashed up the stream bed. I'm at eye level with a fallen log straddling the stream, that is covered in soggy mosses and Wood Sorrel leaves … and so I get to see what only close-up view makes visible, a freshly emerged Large Red Belted Clearwing moth, *Synanthedon culiciformis*, at rest. More beautiful even than the solitary wasps it has evolved to mimic, its transparent wings suffused with orange at their bases and pencilled in black along their veins, like tiny stained glass windows.

In April, there are Wood Anemone and Guelder Rose, Brimstone and Orange Tip butterflies, and we search out the golden brown drape of the rare Flagellate Feather Moss, *Hyocomium armoricum*, on a trunk just above the running stream. It is a grand place for children, with trees to climb and to swing from, nooks and streams to poke about, and good places for bonkers running.

On a soggy headstream of Sheepwash Gill, there's Marsh Violet, Bog Beacon, *Mitrula paludosa*, and Bog Pondweed, and on the hot bare ground above I watch a Green Tiger Beetle capture and eat a St Mark's Fly.

At the north end of Mick's Race in June, whilst searching for Wood Ant nests in a glade of Bracken and Heather I listen to two competing Willow Warblers singing full-tilt. A Sparrowhawk flies over … a Stock Dove croons … a Tawny Owl calls loudly … and two Cuckoos call, back and forth, back and forth in rivalry.

I could not feel more privileged for all the tea in China.

MANNINGS HEATH, THE HAMMER PONDS AND OLD IRONWORKS

I have never seen such huge Meadow Ant hills, so closely packed as here. It seemed more of a sight to expect on the African savannah. We'd crossed **Goldings Stream** east of Goldings Lane, via a fallen log amongst the Bluebells, Pignut, Redcurrant and Daffodils, and climbed up to the wood edge. There we saw this extraordinary sight … a Daffodilly field crammed tightly with huge Yellow Meadow Ant hills – up to a metre tall – all with golden crowns of moss. They stretched away right up the hill. A pair of Green Woodpeckers seemed to have taken up permanent residence, poking big beak holes in the tops and sides of the ant hills and gorging on the ants within. This field, TQ 209 291, is not the only ant hill republic on Mannings Heath Golf Course (2012). There is another large one between Goldings Stream and Hammerpond Road, TQ 212/3 292, and a small one just south of Hawkins Pond's dam, TQ 215 290.

Mannings Heath Golf Course has preserved within it a variety of relics of the old Forest landscape. **Cinderbank Copse** hides the best of them, TQ 213 290. It is a tranquil Bluebell wood with a flat Alderfield at its heart, crossed by two streams. Hawkins Stream to the north is straight and engineered, and full of iron working slag and contorted bits of iron waste. It is a leat of the Tudor St Leonards Lower Forge and Furnace. Goldings Stream to the south, is winding and deep and bordered with Daffodils, for it drains the Daffodil gills of the dissected plateau to the north. There is Hard Fern and a patch of Solomon's Seal (not native). On a tree is nailed a small poppy framed plaque in remembrance of the Halifax bomb aimer and pilot who were killed when their plane crashed in this wood in February 1945. A pond bay (dam) crosses the Alderfield, broken by Goldings Stream and festooned with Bluebells.

Both **Hawkins and Hammer Ponds** are lovely places, with woods and glades running down to them and good edging marshy vegetation. Both ponds have relict high forest of Oak and some Beech along their margins. Swallows, Martins and Swifts love to hunt aerial plankton above them.

An army of trolls: Yellow Meadow Ant hills on Mannings Heath Golf Course.

Along the west side of Hawkins Pond, e.g. TQ 216 293, are patches of heathy rough next to the golf fairways, with Dwarf Gorse, Broom and senescent Ling Heather tussocks, amongst Bracken. (At the north end of the pond this heath has been destroyed for a new vineyard, 2017).

The steep little fields west of Goldings Lane, TQ 204 292, had Highland Cattle and Daffodils when we visited, and a visiting herd of more than 60 Fallow Deer, many white, bay, fawn, and some with young pricking antlers. The woods between Mannings Heath and Coolhurst Mill Pond are tangled and wet in places, though well used by some local folk. In earlier days, this area would have had much boggy heath, for the name **Gaggle Wood,** TQ 200 290, commemorates the past presence and resinous fragrance of Bog Myrtle / Sweet Gale, *Myrica gale,* now maybe extinct in Sussex.

Coolhurst Mill Pond, TQ 195 292, is reed fringed like a Cheshire mere, with a mixture of dense, dark conifers at its eastern end and more open sunny Beech towards Birchen Bridge. Its woods look across to the handsome Victorian sandstone mansion of Coolhurst, now all flats.

Swallowfield Park, TQ 205 280, and **Holme Farm** are sandwiched between Mannings Heath and Monk's Gate, amongst thick shaws, damp and tangled woods and small fields, with some fine old Oaks. It looks like the kind of landscape likely to be targeted for housing development, and lies outside the protection of the AONB boundary despite a landscape quality which equals it in every way. **Holme Plantation**, TQ 206 279,

Island or Boundary Pond, Buchan Country Park: Dragons and Damsels a-plenty!

is beautiful, with big Bluebell displays and a fishing pond. Holme Farm is a manicured, posh conversion.

HAMMERHILL AND WARREN WOODS

Dark woods of Pine, Beech, Birch and Oak, stretch for a mile and a half between the twin hammer ponds and The Hyde. They face northwards, damp and shady, above the twists and turns of the tumbling stream in Carterslodge Gill. **Hammerhill Wood**, e.g. TQ 224 289, retains its old broadleaved high forest structure, with a carpet of Bluebells. A cleft that runs down it is a hideout for the lowliest and most ancient forest plants: the mosses Shining Hookeria, with its translucent one-cell-thick leaves perpetually moistened by running water, Green Worms, Swan's Neck Thyme Moss, Tamarisk Moss and Haircap Moss, with Wood Sorrel, and Pellia liverwort, under a canopy of young Sessile Oak, Holly and Scots Pine.

To the east, **Warren Wood**, TQ 242 292, too, retains its open high forest structure in parts. It is a magical place in spring and autumn, with deep gullies, Brackeny sunlit glades and much fallen wood and timber. The gill has Daffodils scattered at several points.

FAYGATE, HOLMBUSH, AND BUCHAN FORESTS

In 1962 and '63 we had two summer scout camps in the field above **Foxhole Pond**, in Holmbush Park, TQ 230 335. It was the era of the first great unchecked wave of agribusiness change in British farming and forestry. The surrounding Oak high forest, tangled with Rhodedendron, was being bulldozed before our eyes and planted up with commercial conifers. Still, the greatest delight of those camps was to go down to the pond in the evening with a Hazel pole fishing rod and a twig for a float, and haul out Rudd and Roach, whilst the bats played over the pond and dusk came on.

Early each morning two of us would walk down to Holmbush Farm's milking parlour and pick up two pails of fresh milk, hook them onto a wooden shoulder yolk, hitch it up, and totter back through the wood to the tents.

The pond is still nice now, though far more tamed and intensively fished, but the Forests, since then, have taken an even greater battering. Paint ball war gaming, with all its pseudo military clutter – fake missile at the entrance – has taken over most of the woods between Holmbush Farm and Foxhole Pond, TQ 231 240. Two of the best gill ponds are barbed-wired-up like post-holocaust survivalist redoubts, and the open ground of Faygate Forest and part of Black Hill was used to dump municipal waste for decades. Buchan Country Park has been broken in two by the Crawley Bypass, and the noise from the Horsham-Crawley A264 now obliterates the Forests' peace.

Parts of the old forest still live on. **Dabson and Rookfield Gills** have some of the best of them, with fine Beeches, Oaks, and Bracken glades. Downslope from Holmbush Hill there is relict old forest Oak coppice of both Sessile and English Oak, with some Sweet Chestnut and Beech stools, too. Bilberry just survives at one tiny spot. There are clusters of Beech veterans on both the east and west banks of Dabson Gill, TQ 219 334. Some pollards are grown tall, with lofty, sunny crowns, and some are senescent, with broken crowns and dead, rotting boles. There are old specimen conifers scattered around. It is a tranquil, wild place.

Rookfield Pond, TQ 213 335, is also delightful, especially at its marshy pondtail, with Emperor Dragonflies and abundant Damsels. The friendly syndicate folk who own it kindly let us walk its banks, behind the chain link fencing and padlocks. Big Carp lazed near the surface like miniature whales. The anglers only use barbless hooks, they reassured us. Jane wasn't impressed. "Fishing them out is a bit like pulling the arm on a one arm bandit when you're the owner of the machine," she said.

Buchan Country Park, TQ 240 341, is divided into a relatively domesticated eastern section, with wide strolling paths and ponds with hard revetted edges, and a wilder western section where good work is being done restoring heathland. The woods have much Birch and Pine, with some Bilberry beneath. There is Cross-leaved Heather in the cleared areas, and much hot, bare ground. Wood Ants are abundant. There are Adders still, with plenty of Lizards for their dinner.

We walked along the spongy eastern edge of **Island or Boundary Pond**, TQ 238 340, which marks the Country Park's boundary. It is the loveliest spot, with the air full of dragons and damsels, and the marsh full of old wetland plants. We walked through a grove of trees. As we passed on we heard squawks and giggles behind us, as a group of kids clambered down from the trees. We had passed unknowing right under them as they hid – completely silent – in the trees' canopy just above our heads. If only ALL children had access to such great play spaces!

To the east, the new suburb of Broadfield has preserved within it three nice ribbons of old gill woodland. The westernmost gill woodland lost a piece for the construction of the new Crawley Mosque, with its two green domes, TQ 251 346. The easternmost gill runs north into **Broadfield Pond and Park**, with its specimen conifers and beautiful little meadows, TQ 264 344 … a lovely spot.

To the south of Buchan Country Park is a tamed golf course landscape with relict thickets tangled with rhododendron, and three valley ponds. The huge Victorian mansion of Buchan Hill, now used by Cottesmore School, amazes by its sheer wasteful extravagance. It has, inevitably, a line of Wellingtonias.

LEECHPOOL AND OWLBEECH WOODS

Old purlieu woods of the Forest, they are now managed by Horsham District Council as a popular LNR (Local Nature Reserve). I heard several Yellowhammer and Willow Warbler in song on one June visit to **Owlbeech Wood**, TQ 204 317. It has an excellent heathland restoration project, with Longhorn cattle grazing three enclosures on the higher ground above the wooded Alder Gill, and the enclosures are managed for Nightjar and Woodlark, too. There are Wood Ants at one nice scruffy spot with log piles and Heather. In August, a very large flock of Swallows and Martins was hunting low flying midges over the tall pasture of St Leonards Plain, to the south, and young birds were soliciting food from their parents. The best part of **Leechpool Wood** is down in the gill, where there are many ancient woodland flowers and mosses, though it is noisy along the Horsham ring road, and Rhodedendron, Holly and Laurel darken it in places.

Owlbeech Wood is connected eastwards by mixed high forest to the Forestry Commission woodland at Highbirch Hill. **St Leonards Forest House Wood** (e.g. TQ 206 319/320) has lovely Oak standards set far apart over Bracken with a smattering of veteran Beech pollards and maidens and some Scots Pine. There is Beautiful Demoiselle in the stream along the wood's north edge.

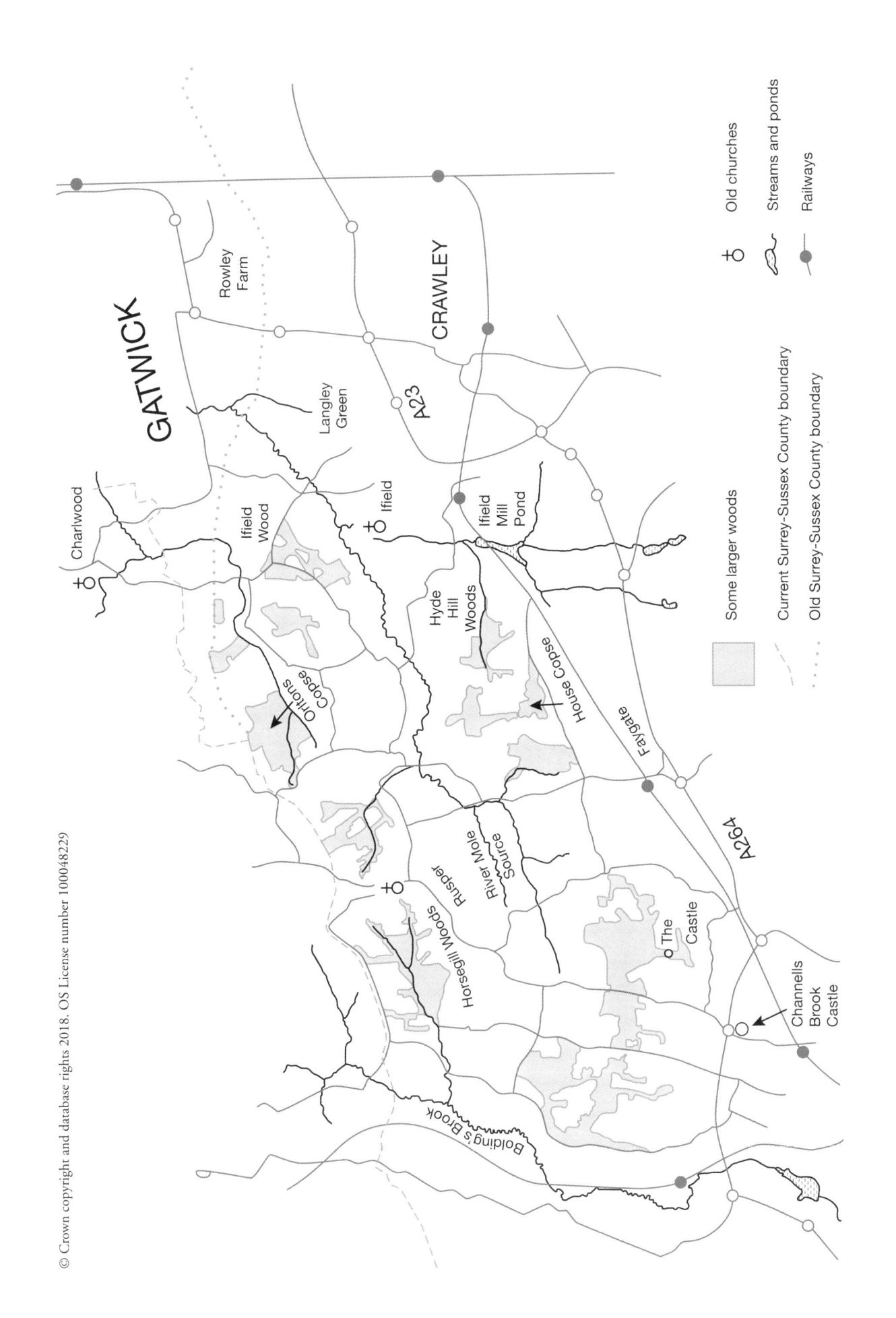

AREA GUIDE / Chapter 25: The Rusper Ridgelands – North Horsham to Ifield

CHAPTER 25
The Rusper Ridgelands – North Horsham to Ifield:
An old and threatened country

There's such a peculiar mixture of peace and roaring craziness here! Sweet music of little waters in bosky gills, whose plants cling on from wildwood times, whilst above the greenwood, huge airliners thunder like angels of death. It is a stronghold, a fortress of nature and rurality, facing the full blast of uneven and hyper-development.

Three long ridges stretching west-east protect the quietude of the little vale of the infant River Mole, so much a Surrey river, yet with its birth in the Sussex hills just south of Rusper. The *northernmost ridge* from Shiremark Farm eastwards to Prestwood, marks the Dark Age border negotiated between petty kingdoms in Surrey and Sussex, and still forms the county boundary today. Rusper village perches high on the *middle ridge*, on the old road from the Sussex coast to Dorking, through Steyning, Horsham and Newdigate. The *southern ridge* from Graylands (near Warnham Station) along Hurst Hill, past Kilnwood to Ifield Mill Pond looks south across the once-quiet vale of Faygate and Bewbush (Norman French '*Beaubusson*': 'Beautiful thicket') now bearing a roaring dual carriageway. Built development pinches great chunks out of the vale from both the Horsham and Crawley ends … and will destroy it altogether, going on present unchallenged trends.

In the early '60s, my train picking up speed going west from Ifield Station would pass over Ifield Mill Pond with meadows and fields all around, and come to a stop at Littlehaven Halt near corn fields stretching north to the Channells Brook. The Mill Pond and the Halt have been sunk in built development for several decades now.

Looking south across the Faygate Vale from Kilnwood we see the massed conifers of Holmbush and Buchan, in St Leonards Forest, and notice the contrast with the softer ridgeland woods of Oak and Ash around us, for the line of the Crawley Road (A264) marks the geological boundary between this northern Low Wealden clay country and the sandy forest lands of the High Weald.

In the times of the medieval settlers the ridges were topped with large, long woods – '*langen hursten*'. Parts of those archaic hilltop '*hursts*' still survive on the south ridge at *Hurst* Wood, and along *Hurst* Hill, and (as broken strips and pieces between giant clay pits and landfill) along *Langhurst*wood Road and Brook*hurst* Wood. They survive, too, at House Copse and Kilnwood Copse. On the middle ridge only the place name survives as *Langhurst* Hill and Farm, a mile ENE of Rusper, for the old woods have nearly all been destroyed. They are nearly gone, too, along the county boundary ridge.

Though most of the hursts have gone, and much more woodland has been cleared in recent times, archaic woodland survives plentifully along the many gills. Rusper's ridge marks the watershed between the Arun and Mole catchments, and for over a mile Highams Gill and Horse Gill descend west from Rusper towards the Arun, and Rusperhouse Gill descends east towards the Mole. Little and Great Brookhurst Gills run west into Boldings Brook. Those are all rich woods, full of special plants, particularly Coralroot Bittercress (nationally rare); Small Leaved Lime, which has its strongest Sussex fastness in the Rusper Ridgelands; and Sweet Woodruff, uncommon elsewhere in middle Sussex. Sloughbrook Gill and Reubens Gill run parallel with the infant Mole for over a mile south of Rusper, before joining it.

Shaws are still a strong heritage of this area, too. Between Rusper, Ifield, and Crawley the majority of shaws have been retained, making places like Stumbleholm Farm (Lambs Green) and Willoughby Fields (Langley Green) both by the Mole, places of trees as much as pasture. In some areas the long farming depression of a century ago has meant that fields have reverted to woods, or been planted up, on quite a large scale. Between Ifield Wood Common and Orltons Lane much of the woodland is from that era, as it is, too, north and west of Kilnwood and east of Hurst Hill.

There are several fine clusters of meadows. The loveliest I know are at Northlands and Hilltop Farms, on the ridge top north of Horsham, and at Willoughby Fields, Langley Green, next to the proposed second Gatwick runway. Fragments of wet rush meadow survive on Ifield Wood Common, and near Lambs Green. Next to Hyde Hill Woods a couple of fine flower meadows are disappearing fast to secondary woodland (2014). There are several semi-improved and unimproved meadows along the Ifield Brook. Only the Northlands / Hilltop meadows are well-managed (2012).

Historically, settlement was scattered, with small hamlets at Lambs Green, Faygate, and Friday Street. Even Ifield and Rusper were just hamlets. Ancient, timber framed farmhouses were scattered across the country on ridges, in valleys, by woods and meadows. Many survive.

Moats were obviously medieval high-fashion on the Ifield and north Horsham plains, with examples in water at Bewbush Manor House, Ifield Court and Ewhurst Place, Graylands and Holbrook (The Moated House), and Channells Brook Castle (partly wet). There are also dry and deserted moats at The Castle, near Hawkesbourne, and on the county boundary, south of Shiremark.

Little common land survived till modern times in Rusper parish, beyond small greens like Lamb's Green, which still has wide verges of 'waste'. Ifield parish, by contrast, retained its medieval commons and greens right up until 1717, when Prestwood Common was enclosed, and 1855, when much of the rest followed. It still has lovely Ifield Wood Common. Horsham's common was the largest near the area till its enclosure in 1812, and gave its name, North Heath, to the whole district of north Horsham.

The finest ancient trees are in Ifield, with the famous Oak on Ifieldwood Common, and the Ifield churchyard and Brook Cottage Yews. There is a good scatter of fine old Oaks across the area, such as the line of six on the green lane south of Nunnery Farm, and the knotty old Oak at Holbrook Park. There's a Hornbeam boundary veteran in Orlton Copse, and a crumbling pollard Hornbeam on Prestwood Lane.

The lanes are often winding and beautiful, but they are not good walking, for traffic out of Horsham and Crawley is busy and often much too fast. Only a few, like Northlands and Wimlands Roads, Orlton Lane and The Mount, remain quiet enough to walk with young children. Kilnwood still has a lovely green lane, much used by horse riders.

Us humans have been a long time here. Walking a winter ploughland we came across a broken flint blade – three to six millennia old. Close by, Hyde Hill Woods cloak the large, steep sided pits made by medieval ironstone miners … and on the slope above Bewbush the plough had freshly turned up some long-gone mason's worked fragment of local Cyrena Limestone, packed with fossil clams from the Age of Dinosaurs.

NORTH HORSHAM'S COUNTRYSIDE

The A264 north Horsham bypass has caused big severance between the north Horsham suburbs and the open country beyond the road. The bypass has cut direct and safe access along four of the five ancient north-south droves and one footpath. Now big developments are afoot which leap the bypass and will destroy the remaining half of the open north Horsham plain.

There are two medieval 'castles' on the north Horsham plain. One, **Channells Brook motte and bailey**, TQ 188 332, is now stranded just south of the bypass. It was probably made during 'The Anarchy' of King Stephen (1135–54 AD). Despite heavy noise pollution it remains a delightful *rus in urbe* morsel (2012). Its deep moat still carries the Brook around two sides – stoney bottomed, with Spleenwort, Harts Tongue, Lady and Male Ferns. Ponies graze. There are thickets of Oak and thorn, Maple, Alder and Sallow, and glades with Common Blues, Musk Mallow and Birds Foot Trefoil.

The second, **The Castle**, TQ 197 341, is to the north east, between Hawkesbourne and Owlcastle Farms. It was, perhaps, a fortified and moated farmhouse. In Maytime it is paradise. A Song Thrush serenaded me as I picked my way down the little gill from the north and the gloomy ramparts loomed up before me, but once across the breach the interior was full of light, sun and Bluebells. A Buzzard mewed above me … and there … in light and shade … a movement … a rusty red Fox cub, then another … and another … seven in all … furry, frisky and small amongst the unfurling Bracken fronds. A Bee Fly hummed near me. On the other side of the clearing was a freshly spring-cleaned Badger sett (2009).

East of **Graylands** the old northwards track crosses over **Great Brookhurst Gill**, passes over the ridge crown and over the cleft of **Little Brookhurst Gill**, TQ 182 351/2. On an April day the woods are full of dangling Green Oak Tortrix caterpillars on their almost-invisible threads up to the canopy. There's bird song everywhere. In the **gill bottom**, TQ 183 353/4, **south of Northlands Copse**, are *Viviparus* snail fossils. There's lots of Sweet Woodruff, Yellow Pimpernel, and Anemones. A Cuckoo calls. A Water Carpet moth starts and flies over the gill into the dark wood.

To the west of the track, through the trees, is the huge blue-grey wound of **Langhurstwood Quarry**, TQ 180 352, on the site of Brookhurst Farm, once a flowery place with many special plants, including Lesser Butterfly Orchis. The quarry cuts through the same Lower Wealden Clay upper beds that surface at

NORTH HORSHAM: HOW TO WRECK AN ANCIENT LANDSCAPE

The North Horsham countryside is of exceptional beauty and interest, though damaged by the Horsham Bypass. The development project shows how monstrous are the environmental consequences of our economic trajectory.

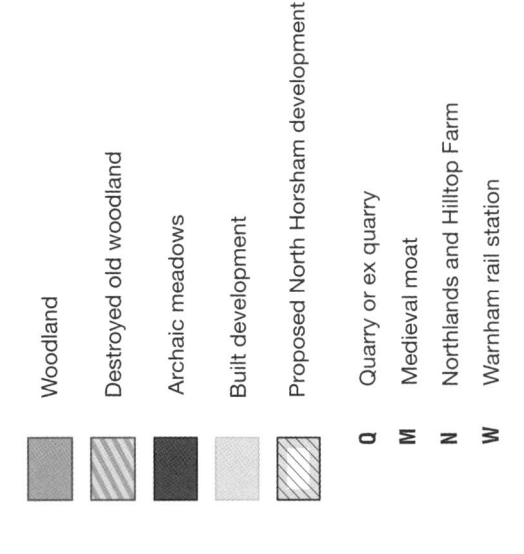

- Woodland
- Destroyed old woodland
- Archaic meadows
- Built development
- Proposed North Horsham development
- Q Quarry or ex quarry
- M Medieval moat
- N Northlands and Hilltop Farm
- W Warnham rail station

© Crown copyright and database rights 2018. OS License number 100048229

AREA GUIDE / Chapter 25: The Rusper Ridgelands – North Horsham to Ifield **313**

Kilnwood, in House Copse. It was a watery country 132 million years ago, fresh or brackish, and very 'fishy'. When we visited the quarry in 2009, there were piles of debris with Small Paludina Limestone water snail, *Viviparus*, fossils, and we found *Lepidotes* fish scales, teeth and vertebrae, sharks teeth and bone fragments. Fish ear stones (otoliths) were first discovered there, and there are reptile bone beds with Iguanodon, and horsetails, ferns and conifer shoots.

To the east of the track are the flowery meadows and pastures of **Northlands and Hilltop Farms**, e.g. TQ 187 350, divided by Northlands Road – a remarkable survival. There's Small Leaved Lime in the hedge along the lane. Swallows hunt low over the meadows, and Starlings stuff their mouths with garnered food to take back to their nestlings in the farm buildings. Some of the fields are largely unimproved, some semi-improved, but in the richer places, such as the gully east of the lane, and on damper spots, there are Ragged Robin, sedges, Sneezewort, Betony, and Zig Zag Clover, amongst Cat's Ear, vetches, Corn Mint and the grasses.

The ridgeland woods between Wimland Hill and Hurst Hill are remote, often ancient, and always lovely, with grand southerly views over the Weald. **Northland Copse**, TQ 205 347, has co-dominant Bluebell and Anemones, with Sweet Woodruff, under old coppice Hornbeam, with Ash, Crab, Gean and Midland Thorn. **Bush Copse**, TQ 202 344, is damp in parts, and once I found a beautiful iridescent blue beetle, cigar shaped, known as the Thick Legged Flower Beetle, *Ischnomera cyanea*. **Breaky Gill**, TQ 201 346, has a small Alder field lower down, with Wood Sorrel, Greasewort and Crisped Pincushion moss. Hyacinth scented **Bakehouse Copse**, TQ 199 346, feels vast, with big glades and gloomy Oaks half sunk in outgrown Hornbeam poles, and little Alder fields.

The **Hurst Hill road** forms a holloway deep in the clay up the steep slope north of old **Hawkesbourne Farm**, but it is only one braid of this important medieval road. Another four lost braids lie in **Hawkesbourne Wood**, TQ 192/3 344/5, just to the east, now all cloaked in Bluebells, old Hornbeam coppice and maiden Oaks. The farm was once a swine pasture of little Coombes, in the Adur valley near the coast. Both **Hurst Wood**, west of the Hill road, TQ 191 347, and **Rapeland Wood** to the NW, TQ 187 351/2, are made rather dark by conifer plantings in places, but still heavenly with Bluebells and Anemones in spring. Rapeland Wood has Small Leaved Lime and Wych Elm in it southern edge gill. Does **Holming Wood**, TQ 191 351, take its name from its abundant Holly?[1] It's a fine old Bluebell-Anemone wood with Pignut and Small Leaved Lime at the north tip, where there's also a good veteran Oak.

At the bottom of the hill is **Holbrook Park** – nice Victorian classical – TQ 183 338, with three good old Oaks on the lane. I asked two residents how they coped with the appalling din from the adjacent Horsham Bypass? They said they didn't notice …

RUSPER AND ITS WOODS

Rusper, TQ 20 37, is a mixed village with old council housing to the south and good vernacular buildings, including two fine old pubs, and several farmhouses on the approaches: Highams, Dial Post, and Old Park Farm Cottage. Those farms have slab roofs, as has the church, with its golden sandstone walls and sturdy late medieval tower.

The woods have survived relatively well in recent times, except to the south around Baldhorns Park, Coombers and North Grange Farms. However, the open farmland, particularly to the west around the Capel Road, and to the south, has suffered badly, with many shaws and hedges ripped out.

Horsegills Wood,[2] TQ 194 370, to the west of the village, is superb. In one late April visit I counted 27 ancient woodland indicator plants. On the edge of **Highams Gill**, e.g. TQ 196 373, I peered into a small hole in a hollow Ash stool and saw a Marsh Tit close-sitting her eggs in a nest of moss. The gill is deep, wide, long and wild, with shelly Paludina Limestone outcropping along the stream bed. In the lusher places, especially to the west, the mosses and liverworts are profuse on the crumbling banks and wet stones, with Great Scented Liverwort, Hart's Tongue Thyme Moss and Dotted Thyme Moss, alongside *Gammarus* shrimps and Water Boatmen in the pools. Rusper church bells peal, whilst Gatwick airliners rumble overhead. There were lots of Early Purple Orchids, Woodruff, Wych Elm, Midland Thorn and abundant Hornbeam. On the lower streamside to the west, the lilac blooms of Coralroot Bittercress were full-out, with their little brown bulbils in the leaf axils. This beautiful flower has its redoubts around Rusper, and in the eastern Weald, and Chilterns.

Friday Street, e.g. TQ 184/5 368, is quiet and remote. It has old cottages and the Royal Oak pub, and more ancient houses around about: at Benhams, Cripplegate, Howells and Porter's Farm. Where the stream passes under the lane there is more Coralroot, and more of it on the roadside south of Cripplegate, and on Langhurstwood Road between the clay pit and the business park.

Rusperhouse Gill, TQ 211 377, east of Rusper, shares many of the species of Horse and Highams Gills, though it is shorter. It is a Hornbeam coppice, with a veteran oak pollard on the gill bank. There's lots of Soft Shield Fern as well as Coralroot Bittercress and Sweet Woodruff. Just east, sheep had free ingress to **Dumbrells Copse**, TQ 214 382, (Hornbeam and Bluebells) the last time we looked. They had eaten it to bare ground in lots of places. Do they still?

Orlton's Copse, TQ 222 387, is a mix of gorgeous ancient woodland and old fields reverted to woodland. Ash and Pendulous Sedge have taken over the fields now, and their Hornbeam hedges grown twisted and Rackhamesque. A Jackdaw emerges from her nest hole 10ft up an Ash. The edge of the secondary woodland is marked by a sentinel Hornbeam pollard, TQ 222 387. To its west is a wide, shallow, ancient woodland valley, where beams of sunlight illuminate the fresh yellow-green leaves of Hornbeam and old Beech, like light through stained glass windows in a cathedral nave.

It would all be perfect, but for …

THE NOISE OF THE END OF THE WORLD

We found a spot to sit and eat in this true heavenly place
Of golden shafted sun and hyacinth-heavy scent
Of sheeting, drifting bluebell swarms;
Of high cathedral vaulting outgrown hornbeam stocks
And clear straight oak and ash,
Where light and sun and gold unfurling croziers of fern,
And soft slow-rotting logs be-draped with tangled moss
And freshest yellow-green wood sorrel with nodding modest blooms
Invited us.

We munched on fruit and biscuits and waited for hot tea to cool,
And watched as dumpy bumblebees worked from bell to bell,
While dancing gnats jigged up and down in light beams
Like some super-animated motes of dust.

But that was only what we **SAW**, for what we **HEARD** was hell itself

VOLCANO'S CRACK … ASTEROID IMPACT … NUCLEAR EXPLOSION
… ARTILLERY BARRAGE ON THE SOMME …

My grandparents told me what it was to witness that …
The starting of the Battle of the Somme … The noise of heaven splitting;
The roaring opening gates of hell; blasting the land from end to end …
It marked the ending of the world …

WE HEARD IT HERE

Continuous … shattering … thunder like no other … right above our heads,
As giant craft and giant craft crossed the sky above.

* * *

What thought of this would they have had, the folk who lived and worked
These woods a thousand years before?
Whose sounds in life were shouts and banter through the green,
And crash and thud of falling pole and tree;
Whose lives were marked by cattle calls, the clop of hooves,
The caw of rooks and clink of harness,
The crooning hens and twittering swallows,
And ordinary swearing, laughing, bothering human sounds.

They'd think the noise we heard could only be
The noising of the ending of the world.

How can it be that now we come to think our lives are better,
That some have to live and work **EACH DAY**
Beneath the noising of the ending of the world?

What can it be that is so good, so worthy
That it means our simple travelling is marked for all beneath us
By the noising of the ending of the world?

What deals, what sights, what loves, what curiosity
Can justify that those beneath our craft should live each day
The noising of the ending of the world?

What is it we've become that this should be
NORMALITY?

(Written on 26th April 2009, the day after we'd walked the deep Bluebell woods by Orlton Lane, just west of the runway of Gatwick Airport and below the flight path of a continuous stream of airliners rising westwards).

Rusper's fine 15th century church tower

From **The Mount**, e.g. TQ 224 381, there are fine views south across the upper Mole valley to Hyde Hill, Crawley and St Leonards Forest. The Mount Farm, TQ 227 381, and Peter's Farm, TQ 220 382, are both timber framed and 16th century in origin. **Lambs Green**, TQ 218 367, has mostly modern houses now, but Puttick's Cottages are ancient, as are Axmas Farmhouse and the cottages next to the Lamb Inn, set back from the road, presumably on the lost edge of the old green.

IFIELD: HALF TOWN, HALF COUNTRY

The Ifield countryside is mostly very flat (after all that's why the landscape of which it is a part has been cursed with Gatwick Airport) and must have been very difficult to farm, being poorly drained. It could be why so much of it, along with Charlwood to the north, remained as common until so late. It was late too, in the form of some of its commons, for both Prestwood and Ifieldwood Commons were *wooded*, long after most Wealden commons were stripped of their woods and timber. It must have been ecologically very diverse as well, with old wood pasture pollards on the north western commons, much meadow and rush pasture along the brooks and the Mole, heath at Lowfield Heath, goose lawns at Goose Green and the other Ifield greens, and tillage on the lighter ground and Mole terraces, which can be quite flinty.

Thus, in medieval times, the parish had a northern wet and wooded part with much common and deer park, and a southern part with more tillage and possibly open fields (around Goffs Park). That division corresponds roughly to the current split between the built up part of the historic parish, now in Crawley, and the still-rural part.

Ifieldwood Common, TQ 24 38, retains a continuity of woodland cover, though it was worn thin a century ago, when much of the western and southern common was grazed tussock pasture. Two ancient pollard Oaks dominate a tiny green, TQ 243 387/8, next to Oak Tree Farmhouse (now sadly lost to a big new building). The biggest is almost four spans in girth, tall and healthy, and may be 500 years old – an acorn in early Tudor times. Maple and Midland Thorn, Aspen, Hornbeam, Crab, Gean, and woodland herbs like Primrose, Wood Speedwell, Wood Sedge, Wood Melic and Bluebell survive, but their distribution is scattered by centuries of cattle grazing. The Oaks are often scrubby and open grown. The richest woodland seems to be in the south, TQ 242 382, and the largest bit of old grassland on the common survives there, sheep grazed when we last looked, with rushes, Tufted Hair Grass and old anthills, TQ 243 382. Old Purple Moor Grass 'hassocks' still survive in places under woodland trees, though the Moor Grass itself has mostly gone. It is a wet place.

Your feet can also sink in marshy parts of **Prestwood Copse**, all that's left of Prestwood Common, TQ 232 393. The Copse is old Hornbeam stools and Bluebells, rather open away from the bridlepath, with a scattered ground flora, but the old plants are all there, including Sanicle, Melic, Anemone and Midland Thorn (2009). The field hedges, Prestwood Lane and the bridleway are all on ruler-straight surveyor's alignments, made presumably at its enclosure in 1717. The wood lane is a place of riding stables, and there's builders rubble and stable manure dumped. The majority of **Great Burlands** wood, TQ 237 395, has been cleared for livery grazing, except for lollipop Oaks, and tatty Bluebells. Indeed, horseyculture rules around Prestwood, Ifieldwood, and The Mount, a legacy perhaps, of the sale of The Mount Estate in small lots, each now with its attendant clutter.

Ifield church and Rectory Farm are the chief parts of a huddle of old buildings, one meadow away from Ifield Brook. The shingled Victorian spire can be seen from the flat open country to the west. The church is lovely, with two characterful 14th century knightly effigies of the de Ifelde family. Wood from the County Oak,[3] cut down in 1847, was used for the vestry built that year. The churchyard has a grand old Yew.[4] The Farm's ancient barn is now a theatre. Upon enclosure in 1855 the core of **Ifield Green**, TQ 250 378, was kept as a sports and cricket ground (which it had been since 1721) with a little allotment site. They remain today.

Ifield Mill Pond, TQ 244 362, powered an ironworking forge in Elizabethan times. It was burnt in the British Revolution by Waller's troop of horse (1643) to prevent the royalists using it.[5] Never restored, it became a corn mill in 1683, which worked till the late 1920s. The Pond is silting up along the line of the rail causeway across it. North of the railway is nicer than the heavily trampled southern pond edge, and was part-covered with water lilies on our last visit, with Bulrush, Purple Loosestrife, Reedmace, Yellow Loosestrife, and Grey Wagtail on the pond bay. The white, weatherboarded watermill, now restored, and Mill Cottage are pretty.

Tiny, quaint **Brook Cottage**, TQ 246 367, with its veteran three span girth Yew at the back, on the Rusper Road, marks an entrance to **Ifield Meadows**, e.g. TQ 246 370. They run for almost a mile north as far as the Mole, past the church, between Ifield Brook and the urban edge, some unimproved, some semi-improved, much derelict and wooding-up, some horse grazed. Footbridges have been put across the ditches and streams, and paths mown. At the southern end is a strip of ancient woodland with huge old Hornbeam, and Oak and Alder. Local children (and adults) must love this place (2012). Every community should have somewhere like this.

Ifield Court's moat is in water, enclosing a grassy field within, TQ 246 383, where the house once stood, till burnt down. It was

Rus in urbe. Ifield Mill Pond

WOODLAND CHANGE AT IFIELD

Whilst the woodland at Orltons Copse and Ifield Wood Common has remained somewhat intact since the 18th century, much woodland was destroyed on the site of the enclosed Prestwood Common. The late 19th and early 20th century agricultural depression and the end of commons grazing encouraged the growth of much new woodland.

Ancient woodland

Recent woodland

Woodland destroyed in last 150 years

rebuilt to the east. The old

© Crown copyright and database rights 2018. OS License number 100048229

A ghost of the past. Small Leaved Lime on the bank of the 'Secret River' Mole, Gatwick. To be destroyed for a 2nd runway?

farmyard was disused on our last visit, with the slab roof of its Tudor granary half collapsed. **Ewhurst Place** and **Ewhurst Wood**, deep in Crawley now, are picturesque *rus in urbe*. The Place's moat, TQ 258 374/5, has some open water and much mud, with Bogbean, Kingcups and Reedmace, and the rambling, timber framed house's gardens form a good, respectful setting. The Wood, TQ 262 375, split by the A23, is Ash / Oak standards over Hazel, with much Bramble, thorn and Holly.

FAYGATE, KILNWOOD AND HYDE HILL

Summer of 1962. I am camping with the scouts in the fields of Holmbush Forest. We all get sent on a wide game around the local countryside. Without a thought we cross the Crawley Road and the railway line at Fullers Shaw, below Kilnwood. One of us has the idea of putting a coin on the line and waiting for the train to squash it. We sit in the line-side grass and wait. The train comes … and gently stops in front of us. The driver leans out of the window and asks us what we are doing? I can't remember what was said, except that he wasn't greatly bothered, but he settled himself back in his seat and the train rumbled on …

Summer of 2014. The railway's dangers pale beside the dangers of the Crawley Road … We'd be mad to let our kids cross it nowadays – a dual carriageway packed close with speeding, blaring traffic.

The jewel in the crown of this countryside is House Copse, but there are many other jewels, too … the Hyde Hill woods and meadows; the landscape of old shaws in North Bewbush and Stumbleholm; the gills and old secondary woodland of Furze Field and Burnt Stubbs; the scarp and its old woods below Kilnwood's green lane. All are threatened by building development and oppressed by the din from Gatwick and the Crawley Road. In a rational system this landscape would be as highly valued as Epping Forest and the New Forest. It is more beautiful than much of the South Downs National Park and deserves the same protection as them.

House Copse, TQ 228 358, (an SSSI) is the securest stronghold of Small Leaved Lime in its Rusper Ridgeland fastness. Why it dominates this wood, though scarce or gone elsewhere in the Weald, must remain a puzzle. Perhaps the Ridgeland's medieval remoteness from the busy coast – squeezed between St Leonard's Forest and the county border – preserved it from the enthusiastic browsing and brashing for winter forage (it is a very sweet 'bite') that eliminated it from more southerly wood pasture *'denns'*? Old Lime coppice stools fill the wood from east to west, sometimes mixed with Hornbeam coppice, often under Oak standards (and with occasional Oak coppice stools, as at the east end). Some of the Lime coppice stools are huge, and form 'fairy rings' of smaller stools (as at Courtlands Wood). The outgrown poles are most impressive to the northwest, where they are as big as standards. There is at least one Wild Service, and Midland Thorn, Guelder Rose, Crab and Aspen (just), big sheets of Bluebell and Anemone, and Pignut. It is a flat and often wet wood, despite being perched on the ridge, but very varied, with areas of Birch and Sallow, dense Holly and Bracken. You leave the wood feeling you have been in a grand old temple, so monumental is its presence and so full of wonder does it make you feel on a sunny spring evening.

Beyond Kilnwood's green lane the view opens across the vale. The three woods on the slope below are largely ancient. There are flooded quarry pits dug for Horsham Stone in **Fuller's Shaw**, TQ 221 347. **Kilnwood Copse**, TQ 224 352, has Small Leaved Lime, and areas that have been cleared in the recent past, and some still bearing conifers, but its Bluebells are wonderful. **Capon's Grove**, TQ 230 354 is also ancient.

One early February day, walking north across the wet open ground between House Copse and the Stumbleholm Woods, we started up a Green Sandpiper. Long way from home – that bird of gloomy forest pools far to the continental north and east! **Stumbleholm Woods**, e.g. TQ 225 365, are perhaps only a century old, full of pioneer Ash and Primroses in spring. **Stumbleholm Farm**, TQ 229 369, is some of the best of the Low Weald, by the plain of the wooded, young River

'The Secret River' linear ancient woodland: The riverbed of the Mole near Gatwick. Is this to be destroyed for a second runway?

Mole. It's a cattle farm with an old tiled farmhouse by a pond, its brindled cattle filling three big sheds in winter (2014). At dusk Redwings flock along the shaws and hedges, wild duck scud overhead, and, as darkness falls, a flock of wild geese honk from the muddy pastures, disturbed by we muttering humans in the night.

Hyde Hill Woods, TQ 233 363, mostly ancient, are now growing over to high forest. Along the Hyde Hill Brook the outgrown Hornbeam and tall Oaks give the same sense of vaulted interior space as in House Copse and Orltons Copse. There is Small Leaved Lime.

LANGLEY GREEN'S MEADOWS AND SHAWS, LOWFIELD HEATH AND ROWLEY

Still earmarked for a second Gatwick runway, the archaic landscape of the young River Mole, of Langley Green and Bonnet's Lane, is a most remarkable survival. Its present patterning of flower meadow after flower meadow, lazy, free-wandering river, all embraced by bounding curtain on curtain of tall timber, can be traced in near-all its present exactitude back 140 years, to the early 1870s, on the very first public Ordnance Survey map.

Its springtime woodland herbs (Bluebell, Anemone, Soft Shield Fern and Yellow Archangel) which decorate the pencil lines of copse and woody shaw, point back to the deeper wildwood past. So, too, does the presence of Midland Thorn, Hornbeam and rare Wild Service Tree. The ancient name **Lang*ley*** (Saxon: 'long *glade*') **Green**, and maybe **Amber*ley* Farm** too, confirms that settlement and farming were a matter of mere openings in a forest right up to early historical times.

Its flatness is its extra virtue – the source of its tranquillity. Its flatness is what gives the Mole its freedom to wander, to twist and to bend, and what brings a double sense of calm, of peace, to the dog walkers and children, cricketers and footballers, wildlifers, pony riders, strolling couples and picnicking families who have made it their own.

25.8 ha / 64.3 acres at **Willoughby Fields**, between the Mole and Langley Green is designated as a **Site of Nature Conservation Importance (SNCI),** but its footprint does not cover anything like the full area of high landscape and wildlife value. There are **sports pitches and play areas** at **Willoughby Fields** and **Cherry Lane, Langley Green,** but they largely respect and retain the ancient boundary shaws. Some of the meadows are used for livery grazing. Some are cut for hay … or just for tidiness. Many are unmanaged, and the Oaks, Hawthorn and Sallow are seeding into the old pastures.

The course of the **Mole** is largely hidden below steep banks, patched in shadier parts by Harts Tongue Thyme Moss, Dotted Thyme Moss, Greasewort, Great Scented Liverwort, Crescent Cup Liverwort and other lowly plants. Ducks and other water birds hide down there, and Wild Garlic, Pendulous Sedge, Angelica and Harts Tongue Fern grow tall. Beautiful Demoiselle and Kingfisher breed there.

The **shaws, small copses of ancient woodland, thorn brakes, and stream banks** have abundant Bluebells and are daisy-white with Greater Stitchwort in springtime. Then they are full of the music of Song Thrush and Warblers, Nightingale, too. Yellowhammers breed there.

The **shaws** are full of the handsomest maiden Oak, Ash, and Maple, with a Hazel, Sloe, Hawthorn and Holly understorey. Brown Hairstreak and Speckled Wood are their special butterflies.

The **pastures** are different field-to-field. One red-purple with Knapweed. One (heavily horse grazed) red-purple with Bartsia. One yellow with Birds Foot Trefoil, Fleabane and Creeping Cinquefoil. Others Rushy, with Ladies Smock (Milkmaids), and stately Marsh Thistle, or invaded by Creeping Thistle. Sweet Vernal Grass dominates in springtime, and Yorkshire Fog and Bent grasses in high summer. There are Green Veined Whites in spring and Common Blues, Browns and Skippers in high summer. In the damp winter meadows, you may see a ghostly white Egret on watch … **and 'on watch' is what we all must be to prevent the destruction of this lovely place …**

The old, linear course of **Langley Green** meandered for more than a mile and can still be traced, lined with trees, mostly lanky Oaks, now marking the urban

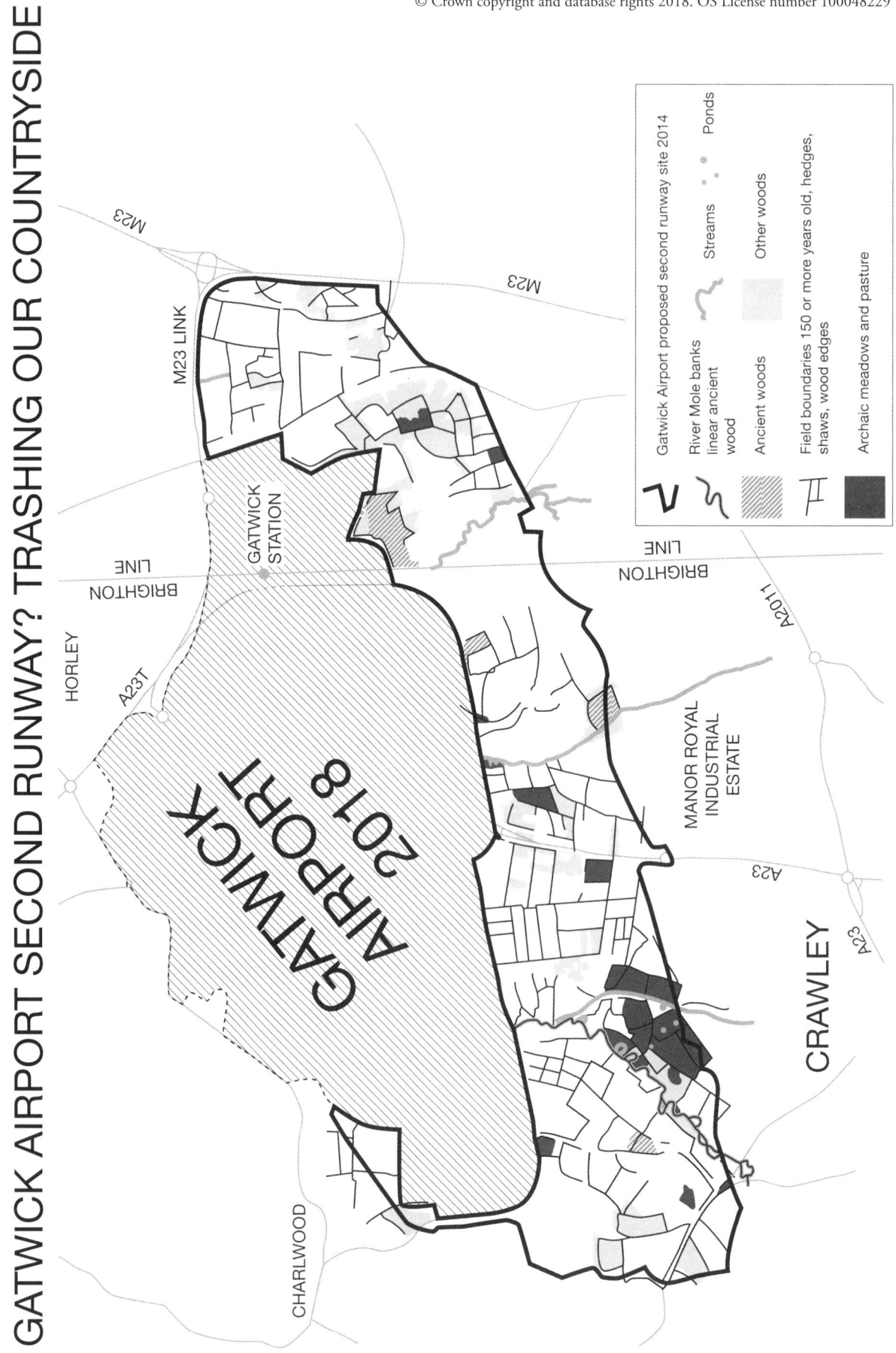

GATWICK AIRPORT SECOND RUNWAY? TRASHING OUR COUNTRYSIDE

320 AREA GUIDE / Chapter 25: The Rusper Ridgelands – North Horsham to Ifield

edge. At its eastern end, where it is bounded on both sides by industrial estates, TQ 265/6 386, it has kept its original dimensions. Its old ditches, particularly the southern, have banks with good gradation from water and mud-loving vegetation to an archaic meadow flora (2014). There's Sneezewort and Meadowsweet, Purple Loosestrife, Codlins and Cream, Eared Willow, rushes, Figwort and Fleabane. To the north is tiny **Oak Cottage**, TQ 266 390, perhaps 350 years old, now sunk amongst factories and offices, though once on the edge of Lowfield Heath, and taking its name from the long-gone County Oak, down the lane.

A scatter of other old houses which once edged Lowfield Heath still survive, now set back from the enclosure surveyor's straight Poles Lane. The chief of them is seventeenth century **Charlwood House**, TQ 263 398, hiding its elaborate timber framing, heavy chimneys and slab roof behind high hedges.

Lowfield Heath itself, TQ 267 395, enclosed in 1846, is now maize fields, livery pastures, and some strips of woodland, often pines. The Victorian church, TQ 274 400, is all that survives of the village amongst hotels and airport industrial clutter.

Rowley and its farm, pastures and wood survive much better, indeed beautifully, though the airliners roar overhead, factories and big sheds encroach from the south (the latest is a new Tescos) and the airport and ring road squeeze it to the north. Its 16th century rambling farmhouse, TQ 279 396, sits on the hill, with a big tarred medieval barn, all still a working cattle farm, with a bull in a barn, poultry round a pond, a fine old pollard Oak nearby, plus two more on the lost Green by the north lodge. **Rowley Wood**, TQ 279 392, is an ancient Bluebell wood, partly coppice with standards, with Oak, Sweet Chestnut, Ash and encroaching Sycamore.

ENDNOTES

1. 'Holm' is the old name for Holly.
2. Why '*Horse* Gill'? To add to the puzzle there is a '*Horsehead* Gill in Bakehouse Copse, to the south, TQ 198 345/6.
3. The County Oak marked the Sussex-Surrey boundary and stood on the highway crossing Lowfield Heath at TQ 270 389. It is still marked on the map.
4. Owen Johnson speculates that Ifield is named after this Yew *('Y feld'* – Yew field) though a derivation from *'eg feld'* – marsh field, seems equally likely. 'The Sussex Tree Book', page 80., By Owen Johnson. Pomegranate Press (1998). Also 'The Place-Names of Sussex', *op cit*.
5. 'Wealden Iron', by Ernest Straker, G. Bell & Sons, (1931) and 'British History Online, Ifield parish: Economic History'.

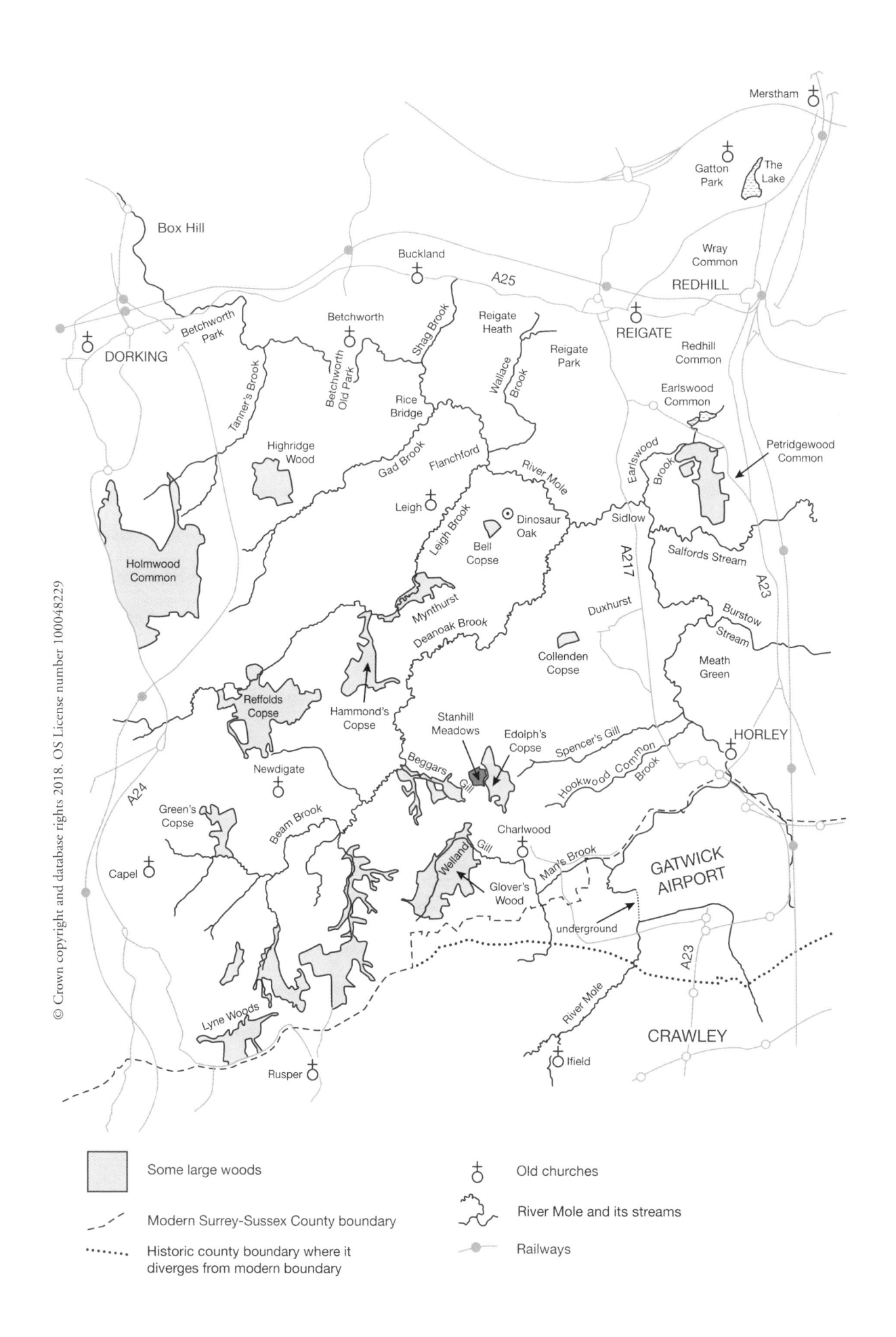

322 AREA GUIDE / Chapter 26: The Reigate and Dorking Low Weald

CHAPTER 26
The Reigate and Dorking Low Weald:

The vale of the Mole

The shadow of Gatwick

Until 60 years ago the core feature of this landscape was the vale of the River Mole, flat and peaceful, coloured by Buttercups and Loosestrife, shaded with Oaks and Alders, and speckled with quiet hamlets. It was – and still is (just) – a place of delight.

The Mole cannot be described as the area's defining feature any longer, for Gatwick Airport now dominates all. Along the ridgelands of the Surrey-Sussex border, under the airport's flight path, the noise is thunderous. It pollutes all the rest of the area as well, so that you may judge your distance and direction from the airport by the severity of the aircraft noise and the line of the planes' flight. If the airport ends up with a second runway it will strike a killing blow. If that happens, only broken fragments of this landscape will survive.

This part of the Surrey Low Weald is proof that beauty of landscape has little to do with great range of contour. Its hills are gentle, and its valleys mostly do not bother to call themselves by that term. The Wealden Clay country makes up perhaps four fifths of the area, and even over its hilliest part – between the county boundary on the Rusper ridges and Brockham, seven miles to the north – its height variation is only about 80m. Most of the area varies much less than that. The Mole wanders wherever it wills, and meets no challenge from hill or scarp between Horley and Box Hill. It twists and meanders round ox bow after ox bow, its water showing scarce signs of movement on drowsy summer days. The main hills of this place, like Stan Hill and Norwood Hill on the Paludina Limestone ridge west and north of Charlwood, grant fine views with the minimum of fuss – of green pastures, woods, hedgerows and tilled land, though marred by Gatwick's clutter to the south east.

Most of the Greensand ridge and Gault Clay under the scarp of the North Downs is similarly modest in height. Reigate Heath only rises to 90m. The Vale of Holmesdale, which is the expression of this geology to the east, through Kent, here ceases to exist, petering out in the suburbs of Reigate and Redhill, and only re-forming five miles to the west, beyond Dorking. This modesty of presence has not left the Greensand unexploited, however, and for almost a century the fine sands of the Folkestone Beds have been heavily quarried in Buckland, taking out a substantial fraction of the parish's ground, and drying out the wetlands of the Reigate Heath SSSI … and even, in the past, old Buckland village pond.

It is only to the west and to the east that the visual presence of the Greensand belt is strong. To the west, the scarp of the sandy Surrey Hills rises beyond Holmwood, the A24 and the Horsham Line. Anstiebury Iron Age hill fort perches at 247m and nearby Leith Hill is 292m. To the east, Park Hill rises to 131m (just south of old Reigate) and forms a ridge running east to Redhill Common, where it reaches 144m. Both the Leith Hill block and the Redhill ridge are outcrops of the harder Hythe Beds within the Lower Greensand.

The scarp of the North Downs forms the northern boundary of this landscape; at its highest locally at Reigate Hill, 135m, but much lower than Leith Hill and Anstiebury. The whiteness of its chalk quarries, now disused, at Brockham Hills, Betchworth Hills, and Reigate Hill forms an unmistakeable topographical marker. The entire length of the sun-drenched scarp from Box Hill to Reigate and Gatton Park is designated as an SSSI, the best long section on the whole of the North Downs, with superb ancient grasslands and rich scrub, though much has been lost to invasive poor scrub and secondary woodland.

This area was one of very late settlement, with its impeded drainage, difficult clays, and heavy woodland. Many of its settlements were not mentioned in the 1086 Domesday Book, forming mere outliers of more prosperous and peopled manorial centres on the North

GEOLOGY AND SETTLEMENT OF THE SURREY BRIGHTON LINE WEALD

Early farming settlements concentrated along the Greensands of the Vale of Holmesdale. In the Wealden Clay vale they are scattered more widely, and had their primary origin as woodland daughter settlements of the Greensand manors.

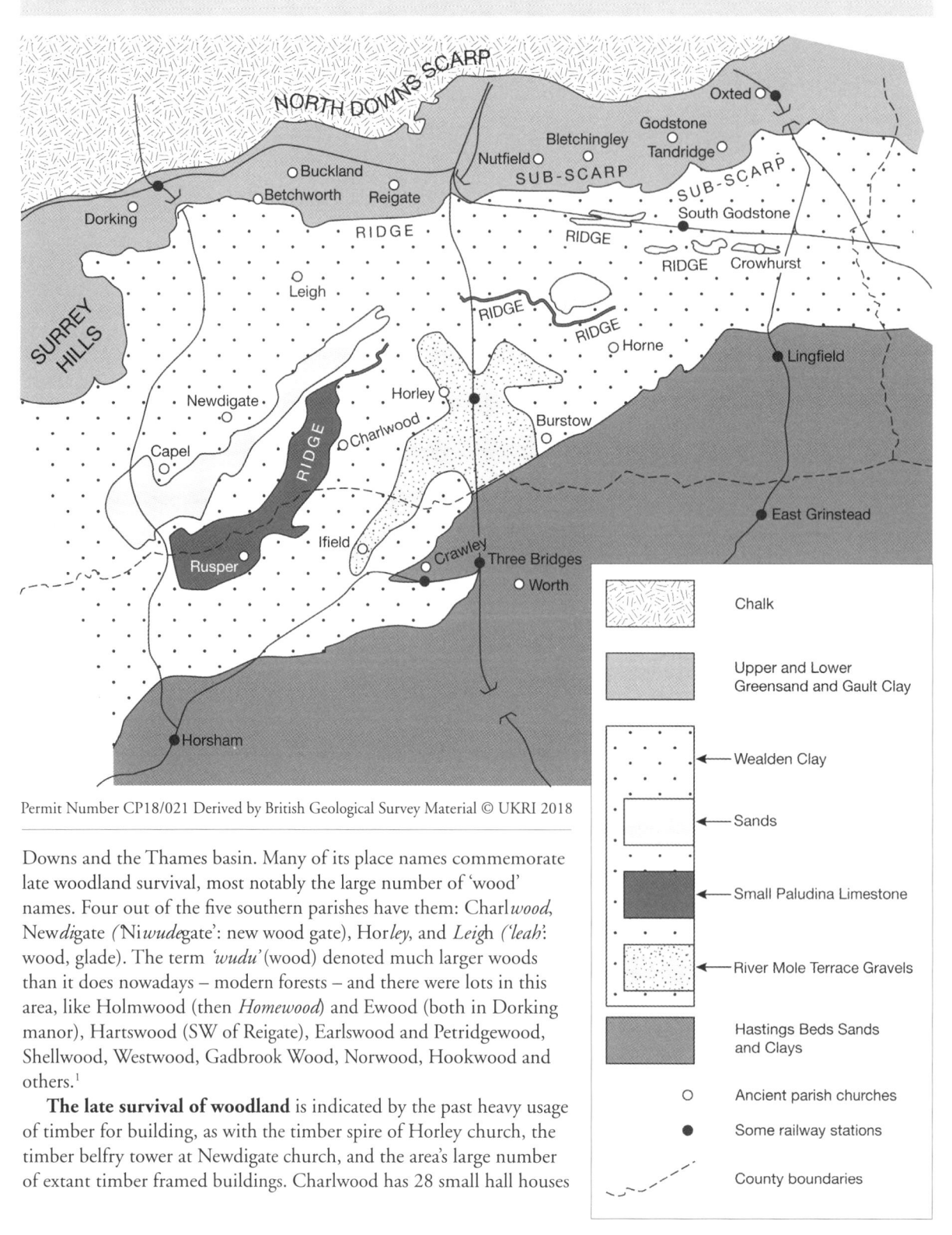

Permit Number CP18/021 Derived by British Geological Survey Material © UKRI 2018

Downs and the Thames basin. Many of its place names commemorate late woodland survival, most notably the large number of 'wood' names. Four out of the five southern parishes have them: Charl*wood*, New*d*igate ('Ni*wud*egate': new wood gate), Hor*ley*, and *Leig*h ('*leah*': wood, glade). The term '*wudu*' (wood) denoted much larger woods than it does nowadays – modern forests – and there were lots in this area, like Holmwood (then *Homewood*) and Ewood (both in Dorking manor), Hartswood (SW of Reigate), Earlswood and Petridgewood, Shellwood, Westwood, Gadbrook Wood, Norwood, Hookwood and others.[1]

The late survival of woodland is indicated by the past heavy usage of timber for building, as with the timber spire of Horley church, the timber belfry tower at Newdigate church, and the area's large number of extant timber framed buildings. Charlwood has 28 small hall houses

324 AREA GUIDE / Chapter 26: The Reigate and Dorking Low Weald

WILD AND WOODED

The early medieval vale of the River Mole was still a place of extensive forest.

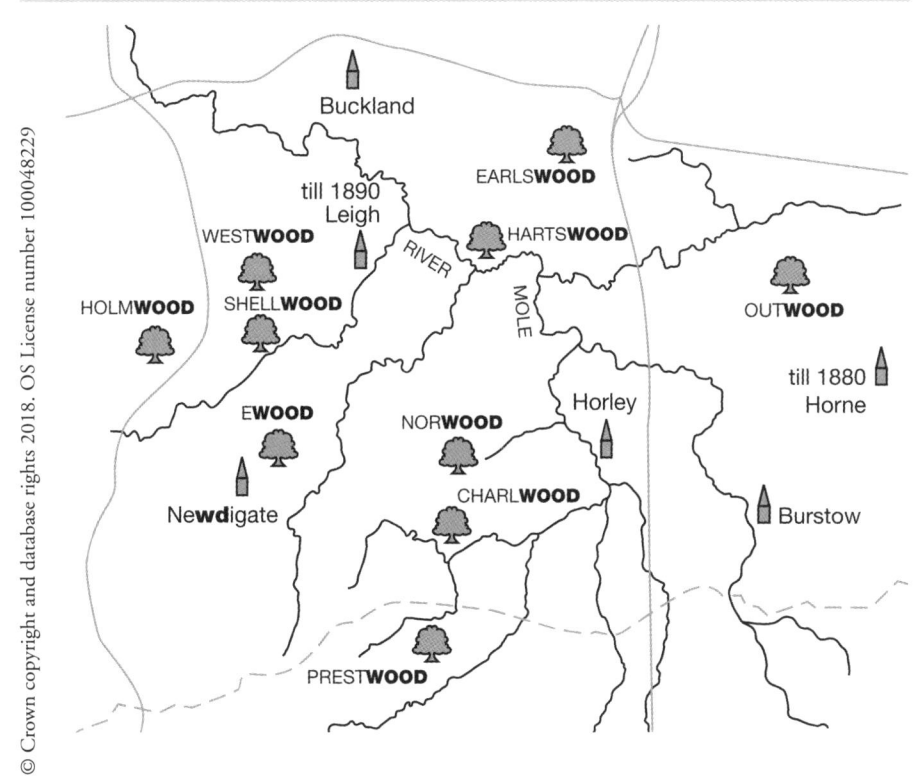

[Map showing 'Wood' place names in the Reigate and Dorking Low Weald area, including Buckland, Earlswood, Leigh (till 1890), Westwood, Hartswood, Holmwood, Shellwood, Outwood, Ewood, Norwood, Horley, Horne (till 1880), Newdigate, Charlwood, Burstow, and Prestwood. © Crown copyright and database rights 2018. OS License number 100048229]

🌳 **'Wood'** place names (Saxon 'wudu') denoting large wooded tracts (which would be called 'forests' nowadays.) Other names on the map also denote woodland: – **Buck**land ('boc'=Beech); **Leigh** and Hor**ley** ('ley'=woodland opening); Ne**wd**igate ('wd'=foreshortened 'wudu').

⛫ Surviving timber-framed medieval church belfry towers.

dating from 1401 to 1500, amongst over 80 listed buildings, more than any other Surrey village.[2]

As late as c. 1800 a lattice of commons and greens still covered much of the area, although they had lost most of their trees by then. Horley Common, with its Meath Green extension, was the largest, stretching over three miles on the River Terrace Gravels between the Burstow Stream and the Mole. Charlwood had a scatter of commons, some large, like Westfield and Lowfield Heath. Its village was formed from a collection of cottages and farms around the edge of one common. There was another commons cluster west of Leigh. Many of these commons were enclosed in the 19th century. Two remarkable clusters survived: the great commons of the towns and manors of Dorking (Holmwood and the Capel greens) and Reigate (Earlswood, Petridgewood, Redhill and Wray Commons, and Reigate Heath).

Together those preserved commons now constitute one of the two largest block of **publicly owned land in the area:** part municipal (the Reigate commons), part National Trust (Holmwood) and part parish council (the Capel greens). Surrey County Council own a mesh of statutory smallholding estates: along the Mole at Hookwood, Meath Green and Kinnersley, and around Leigh. The Forestry Commission owns Highridge Wood, south of Brockham, and the Woodland Trust owns a cluster of woods west of Gatwick – Edolph's Copse, Hammond's Copse, and part of Glover's Wood – acquired by local initiative in part to protect against the expansion of Gatwick Airport. Additionally, the Surrey Wildlife Trust has a couple of disused clay quarries – at Newdigate and Inholms, Holmwood – and manages parts of the damaged Deepdene landscape, east and west of the Dorking Bypass.

The area has no great surviving deer parks or grand feudal or aristocratic houses, and its largest landlords were mostly absentees. There were castles at Reigate, and Betchworth outside Dorking, but nothing of Reigate's is upstanding (though the castle hill is delightful) and only later ruins survive of Betchworth Castle (with wonderful fragments of the deer park). The best ornamental landscape of the rich to survive is Betchworth Oldpark (nothing directly to do with the lost castle over a mile to the west). It is a place of Claudian beauty, bosky, bisected by a meander of the Mole, with wooded slopes, old Oaks and lowing cattle. Gatton Park and its lakes, landscape gardens and woods, north of Reigate, survive in part, but the church and mansion are crowded by the sprawling post-war campus of a boarding school, and the roar of the adjacent M25 is constant. Lyne Park, on the county boundary ridges, is now bleak dairy pastures. The romantic ornamental

Charlwood's ancient churchyard Yew: burnt at its heart but still struggling on

landscape at Deepdene, Dorking, was bisected by the Dorking Bypass in 1934, and the classical mansion demolished in 1969 and replaced by an eyesore office block.

In the nineteenth and early twentieth centuries the area was heavily colonised by the new bourgeoisie and richer middle class, who added big extensions to old farmhouses, or built anew on knolls, next to woods (or replaced them) or on farmed land. These posh pads are ubiquitous in every parish … as at Broomells (Capel), Stanhill Court (Charlwood), Mynthurst (Leigh), and Buckland Lodge.

In the late nineteenth and early twentieth century, this colonisation was joined by more modest homesteading urban escapees, encouraged by farmers and landowners cashing in on this building boom in the midst of the 60 year long farming depression. Thus were the lanes and villages under the North Downs suburbanised. Parkgate woods in Newdigate became a kind of well-off plotland, and many quiet lanes in Newdigate, Capel, Beare Green, and along the ridges at Nalderswood and Norwood Hill were ribbon developed, as were the main A217 Reigate and A23 London Roads. Of course, it was ruinously worse up on the North Downs, but it was bad enough here in the Low Weald. Reigate, Redhill, and Dorking, too, expanded dramatically, sometimes rationally, with good council housing and open space provision, and sometimes with the madness of sprawling low density villa suburbs.

The decision to develop Gatwick as London's second airport in 1952 has been by far the worst single mistake. The decision was taken in breach of an undertaking made to the Chief Executive of Crawley New Town and the Ministry of Town and Country Planning that no such development would take place.[3] It imperils the very survival of the SE Surrey Low Wealden landscape, has severely ratcheted up the process of unequal regional development, made the local economy even more an appendage of the metropolis, and damaged the living conditions of many residents with noise pollution.

There was industry in this vale many centuries before, of course, mostly extractive in origin. There was a Tudor iron working furnace in Ewood, Newdigate, though the centre of the Surrey iron industry was further to the west. The Ewood site had a 90 acre pond, reputedly the biggest of its time in Surrey, which survived right up till circa 1850–60. No doubt the furnace was fired with charcoal from this huge desmesne wood, long enclosed as a deer park. A mile and a half further up the Leigh Brook towards Leigh Green (the present village) was its sister forge, commemorated by little Hammer Bridge. There was also much iron ore digging and forging in Charlwood and Horley parishes, which no doubt fed the early iron working industry in neighbouring Crawley, a medieval new town perhaps created in part to foster the iron industry.

The clay working industry – bricks and tiles, etc. – was long carried out on an artisanal scale, on farms and smallholdings. As 19th century capitalism developed, the scale of these workings became greater. Three Victorian brickfields were present on the southern, clay part of Earlswood Common, and there were brickfields at Prestwood and Mountnoddy Wood between Charlwood and the Sussex border. In the past century the workings have grown to a landscape changing scale. Capel and

Holmwood were the centre of the local industry, with the big Clock House pit east of the A24, and the Auclaye pit to its west. Both are geological SSSI's. At Beare Green is the South Holmwood pit, and there was a further pit next to Holmwood Station. A more recent working at Inholms Lane, and the big Newdigate Pit, are now nature reserves.

None of those workings yet match the landscape impacts of the greensand workings in Buckland parish, with the smaller pits west of Betchworth and at Santon (now 'restored'), south west of Reigate Heath.

As pumping ceases and workings are abandoned they fill with water, providing a new source of exploitation as commercial fishing ponds for quarry landowners, as has happened with Buckland's two main pits. If mineral working does not provide these resources then they can be purpose-made, as at the string of new fishing ponds on Greens Farm and Green Lane Farm Lakes (Newdigate), Henfold Lakes (Beare Green), and Flanchford. You put the fish in. The punters pay you to haul them out. Then they put them back – and pay to fish 'em out again.

Some ponds are much older, like The Lake and ponds at Gatton Park, the Priory Pond at Reigate, the lower of the two Earlswood Common Lakes, and Fourwents Pond on Holmwood Common. At least those that occur on the commons and public parks are free and fully accessible.

After a long period of much pollution the Mole has recovered greatly in recent years, though bad pollution incidents still occur. Its upper reaches have Eel, Brown Trout and Brook Lamprey, and both Banded and Beautiful Demoiselles flit above its waters. Kids play on the banks and in the river at Meath Green and Pixham just as they used to do and should. Tributary streams are marked by ribbons of woodland, often ancient. Tiny ox bows and high banks have grass, thorn, willow scrub, and Alder, above riffles and pools, wet rocks and seepages, and Duck Mussels can still be found. The banks, streams and gills of the Gad, Leigh, Deanoak, Beam, and Shag Brooks, the Salfords, Burstow, Gatwick Streams – and the rest – are the wildest, most natural places in this landscape.

The largest woodland block is at Holmwood Common. Though mostly less than a century and a half old, it has grown many fine Oaks, and has a good shrub layer and often dense ground cover, though without the fine springtime flower displays of ancient woods. Many other woods, like Reffolds, Glovers, South Earlswood and the Sussex border woods, are mixtures of ancient and recent woodland. Many of the Mole vale woods are small and scattered, though often ancient, and with the most intense spring displays of Bluebells. In the more acidic Greensand woods, as on Reigate Heath and Betchworth Castle Deer Park, there is Rowan and delicate sprays of Climbing Corydalis (more familiar in Welsh valley Oak woods). Beeches in Reigate Park, Deepdene, and Redhill Common mark these better drained soils.

Veteran trees are little known, but scattered broadly, without the big clusters of ancient Oaks and Beeches that old deer parks and wood pasture commons sometimes preserve. There are, however, a tribe of grotesque forest Ents at Betchworth Castle Deer Park – extraordinary Sweet Chestnuts pollards. Some other veterans are well known, like the churchyard Yews at Capel, Horley and Charlwood, the Leigh churchyard Oak, the Woodhatch Oak, and the Oakdale Giant at Holmwood Common. Many others are hidden away, like the superb Bury's Oak on the green lane south of Flanchford, the Spencer's Gill Oaks, the boundary Oak in the northwest corner of Reigate Heath, the Leigh Place Oak, and the Rome Wood Hornbeams. Reigate Park Hill has old Downy Birch, Rowan and other good trees.

Archaic heath, moor, meadow and pasture are now desperately reduced. The wet pastures of the 1830s that Luxford[4] botanised in between Reigate and Buckland, had Royal Fern, Meadow Thistle, Marsh and Great Valerian, and Marsh Ragwort. Sand quarries and modern farming have eliminated all that. Tiny Misbrooks Green in Capel and part of Wray Common in Reigate have simplified fragments of such once-commonplace Low Wealden moor. Petridgewood Common holds one of the best remaining, though neglect is causing its disappearance (2014). Mire and bog are now locally extinct, though Reigate Heath once had a superb example. There are morsels of good acid grassland in South Holmwood Churchyard, and on Holmwood Corner Common. Neglected fragments survive just north of the Earlswood Common Lakes, too. The best example is the dry heath and acid grassland of Reigate Heath, which has survived moderately well in some spots, despite a total absence of grazing and the necessity of co-existence with the golf course and sports pitches. Stan Hill meadows, Charlwood, are some of the best remaining neutral meadows, though there are other scattered relics to be seen, mostly very small, or with varying degrees of damage.

THE VALE OF THE MOLE

When the young River Mole reaches Gatwick Airport it meets a nightmare.

Leaving verdant Willoughby Fields and Amberley Farm, on the Sussex border, it is forced into a tunnel under the Gatwick runway. Escaping from that underworld into the light, it is channelled in a **new gully round the northern edge of the airport**, e.g. TQ 262 414/5, using state-of-the-art artificial meanders, to join the Gatwick Stream unnoticed, beside giant hotels and dual carriageways. The gully is doubly protected from the airport's assault on the eye and ear by

Old Horley's medieval timber-framed spire gives the finger to the Gatwick airliners flying overhead.

a giant earth bund above its south bank. On the north side all is new Buttercup meadows, minty and reedy river banks where Reed Warblers sing, riffles, steep clay banks to attract Kingfishers, and slopes down to the water, where youngsters' splash. A strip of ancient Oak-and-Bluebell woodland, TQ 265 418 (once the boundary shaw of Gatwick Park) embraces this simulacrum of a Wealden gill. All is good taste and careful faithfulness to nature. Small Leaved Lime saplings are planted in the ancient wood, and old herbs like Ragged Robin, Oval Sedge and Grass Vetchling transposed to the new meadows. Yet behind the earth bund lies a glinting half mile of solid airport car park – larger than the whole area of Charlwood village. Like the picture of Dorian Gray, this Mole 'restoration' project is the sweet face of vileness – the screen behind which nature is gobbled up by a system unable to do otherwise.

Passing twice in a few yards under the A23, the engineered Mole finally re-joins its ancient course at **Old Horley**, TQ 276 427/8. Its church spire standing above the trees and the flowers of Church Meadow, wake us from the bad dream of Gatwick. This erstwhile hamlet on the banks of the river, was one of several around the edges of the giant Horley Common. It has the Six Bells pub, its old barn, High House (all timber framed, 16th/17th century) and St Bartholomew's church and yard. The shingled wooden spire and bell chamber stand on four rough posts at the west end of the church's north aisle. **Church Meadow**, TQ 275/6 425/6, is now beautifully restored, with much Yellow Rattle, Musk Mallow and Ox Eye Daisy. There are Beautiful Demoiselles on the river. At the north end of the pub car park, behind a fence and hidden amongst Ivy, are two giant Oak maidens each with immense boles of three spans girth. There is a veteran Yew in the churchyard, too.

A mile to the north is **Meath Green**, TQ 269 445, on the edge of the brooks where the Burstow Stream meets the Mole.[5] The brook fields and gentle river were a place of delight (2013), loved by local folk and much used by children. Some fields were cattle and sheep grazed; some on the east bank of the Mole were unused and thistly. The Mole is slow, with Bulrush 'islands' in its middle, and Yellow Water Lily, and by the confluence the east bank is wooded and wild, and the fields long, narrow and with outgrown hedgerows laid out from some past plotlands venture. The whole area around the disused farms of Landens and Meath Green (both with handsome Victorian barns) is earmarked for housing, only held up by the recession (now part-developed, 2018).

The river wanders vaguely north past Saxley Hill and **Kinnersley**, TQ 263 461, which has two fine Cedars and the remains of a big timber framed Elizabethan courtyard house, much depleted and modernised. All is green and level. Two fields north of the manor the **Salfords Stream meets the Mole**, by a footbridge which it takes 15 paces to cross from bank to bank. The river is heavily vegetated, with much Flote Grass and Water Lily, huge patches of Nettle on the banks, and much English Elm there too, and in the hedges. Forget Monet's water lily pond … just stand on this footbridge and let the grace of this placid waterland enter you. **Sidlow church**, at the road crossing, TQ 259 469, is made of flint (1861) and has a yard full of Ox Eye Daisy.

Between Sidlow and **Flanchford Bridge**, TQ 234 479, the river vale has great tranquility, for it is now three to five miles from the airport runway. The brook side meadows are lush. There are big Poplars scattered, and pussy willow catkins in springtime. Ring Necked Parakeets flash green and screeching and

Mandarin Duck sunbathe. A Skylark sings above the arable beyond the brook. The older of the little riverside woods, like **Birchett Copse**, TQ 242 471, are full of Bluebells. The slip from Birchett to **Bures Manor**, TQ 242 469, is a lovely scruffy spot of old hedges, tractor ruts and old trees, including one 3.5 span girth Oak. It leads to the manor farm buildings of brick and tarred weather boarding. The old manor was supplanted in 1876 by the much bigger **Bury's Court** half a mile further NW along the river, but that mock Tudor stone pile is now a school.

By a little green (now planted with Poplars) between Bures Manor and Bury's Court, you come across a dinosaur. As you come round the corner of the lane its bulky back appears, hunched and rough skinned like a *Tyrannosaurus* crouching over its prey. Its 'shoulder' is so broad that grass grows upon it. This monstrous Oak – **the Bury Oak** (if you don't want to call it the **Dinosaur Oak**) TQ 238 468 – is the most lovable and characterful I know in Surrey (2014). It grows next to a crumbled lime kiln, now half covered in Brambles. Go and say hallo.

One field to the west is **Bell Copse**, TQ 235 466. We were there one spring evening, when the Bluebells made rivers of lapis lazuli down the rides, the Bo Peep croziers of Lady Fern uncurled, and sunbeams shone through clouds of floating Sallow down 'snow'. To the south the ancient **Stumblehole green lane**, TQ 240 465, has much Midland Thorn and Goldlilocks Buttercup, and Whitethroat sing from the bushy tangles.

To the west of Flanchford Bridge the Mole tracks just south of the Lower Greensand ridge, and 'Santon' (sandy farm) replaces 'Clayhall' (on the Wealden Clay). Around Trumpets Hill all is as monied and tidy as a Wimbledon gated close, but around **Rice Bridge**, TQ 223 487, the rough brooks and thickets along the Mole are scruffy, thorny and wild. It is a place of fine Oaks: knotty pollards along Ricebridge Lane, and grand hedgerow maidens north of Ricebridge Farm.

To the east of Rice Bridge, TQ 227 487, the river bank is park-like, grassy with scattered trees and bushes – a lovely place to play and rest. In one ancient Oak with a torn-off limb an owl had made a nest on a shelf in the hollow bole. Orange Tip butterflies enjoy the sunshine. To the north of Rice Bridge the grassy bank is rumpled at one point, TQ 223 493, so that a sliver of archaic meadow vegetation survives, with Bog Stitchwort, Pond Sedge, Ladies Smock, Great Bird's Foot Trefoil, Meadowsweet, Water Dropwort, and Dock leaves as big as Banana leaves. Below **Wonham Mill**, TQ 223/4 496 (ancient in origin, now poshed up) the waters of **Shag Brook** are clear over a stony bed, and a Grey Wagtail perches on an upturned root plate.

From Wonham the river wiggles westwards under the Downs to the Dorking / Box Hill Gap. As it does so it passes – confusingly – through two 'Betchworth Parks'. They correspond to the old manors of East and West Betchworth. The first lies just south of Betchworth village (once *East* Betchworth) and is itself divided into two by the Mole. The part of it south of the Mole is the Old Park. The second park, a mile west, is the remains of Betchworth Castle Deer Park (once of *West* Betchworth).

Betchworth Old Park is superb, TQ 210 489. The only noises are the hum of drone flies in the sun-dappled woods, of Rooks, or fish jumping, Woodies cooing, and cattle huffing. The scarp of the Downs fills the northwards view. The M25 has turned northwards out of earshot, and the Gatwick nightmare is distant. There are many mature Oaks and a couple of good veterans. New Oaks have been planted. A Hawthorn is laden and bent in all its extremities with scarlet berries, shining like beads. The cattle pastures spread down to the Mole, that's running silver under the slopes. The **northern park**, across the river, TQ 208 493, is graced with lots of fine Oaks too, many around two spans girth and some larger. Between the two is a weir of late 18th century origin, recently restored and installed with hydroelectric turbines which feed the grid. Its presence partly explains the slowness of the Mole above it. Complaints have been made that it has caused the intermittent drying up of the river below.

The old core of **Betchworth village**, TQ 210/1 497, has some nice 'Jane Austen' type houses, a popular pub, a disused forge with the old signs and clutter in place, and a little river bridge. The lovely Norman-to-Chaucerian church is of flaking Merstham Stone of luminescent greenish white tinge, with a Horsham slab roof and a Victorian tower. It has an ancient chest carved from an Oak trunk, with three huge locks. There were dead Hornets on a window sill – definitely a good sign. Parakeets screech overhead.

The remains of **Betchworth Castle Deer Park** are scattered through the modern Betchworth Park Golf Course (founded 1910), on the Lower Greensand ridge. A windblown Lime avenue (1987 gale?) runs from the park/golf course entrance on the A25 (TQ 184 501) to the remains of the 'castle', perched startlingly close to the edge of the river cliff, TQ 190 500. It's not really a castle, but the ruins of a 15th–18th century mansion which replaced the medieval castle. South from there is a scatter of grand old Oak maidens and Sweet Chestnut monsters.

The best Deer Park fragments are north and west of the golf course club house, along the slopes down to the Mole. Don't do what I did … get a Honeybee tangled in my hair whilst peering a bit too closely at a wild colony of them in a dead Pine on a rough. I rushed across the fairway bent double and flapping my fingers through my hair to dislodge it (unsuccessfully) and wacking my head with a folded map to kill it (successfully … but only after it'd stung my scalp). It was nice to give the golfers a laugh …

The deer park slope must once have tumbled right down to the Mole, but the A25 now stops it short and makes it noisy. In spring the heavy scents of May blossom and Bluebells mingle like some dull opiate.[6] The swollen, twisted, muscled-up Sweet Chestnut pollards mass in the wood just north of the club house as though about to make one last attack on us forest killers. Best of luck to 'em. What a phantasmagoria of silent power …

There's a glade a bit further west, TQ 182/3 500, with matted Bracken and Climbing Corydalis, Rowan and Birch in fresh leaf, May trees, Chestnut giants … and two giant Oak maidens of three spans girth. These Oaks are deceptive, seeming slighter and younger than the Chestnuts, though they are older, I think. Blackcaps belt out their music. A Woodpecker drills. There is sun and the smells of spring. Life is good. West again there are more Bluebells, and a grove of clean-boled Beech giants above a Brackeny combe.

The Sweet Chestnuts must be 18th century in origin. It is odd that there are no Oak pollards. Sadly, almost nothing of the park's archaic acid grassland seems to survive. It would be good to see cattle roaming these old wood pasture fragments again.

Below the deer park and the A25 is the Mole river cliff, with Horse Chestnuts in candles and May blossom in glory. The Mole is slow and wide here, before it meets the Pixham Weir and the old Pixham Mill leet. From the **Pixham Meadow** bank, TQ 180/1 501/2, the first May Flies are in the air, and Banded Demoiselles. It is a Buttercup meadow, with Peacock butterflies on the river bank Nettles. Below the weir and footbridge is a wide pool, with a sandy 'beach', shallow riffles and a little Sallow island.

Dorking, TQ 16 49, feels like Lewes, though without the castle and abundance of old buildings. The High Street is wide because it was a market once. The big church is Victorian, with a huge spire, slate roof, ashlar stone finishings, and flint walls. Lovely stained glass. I'd like to like it, but I don't. The nicest place is **Cotmandene**, TQ 169 493, a little common south of the High Street. It's mostly amenity grassland, with old sunken tracks and steep unmown banks, the best of which is at the south end of the lane which bisects

THE BETCHWORTH TREE ENTS

Sweet Chestnut 'Ents', often pollarded, from a major 18th century planting in the old Betchworth Castle Deer Park. By comparison, the number of surviving veteran Oak Ents is very small. The mapped positions are only indicative. If Tolkien saw these ancient giants he would have loved them. The map also indicates the remains of an old Lime Avenue, much reduced by winds and time.

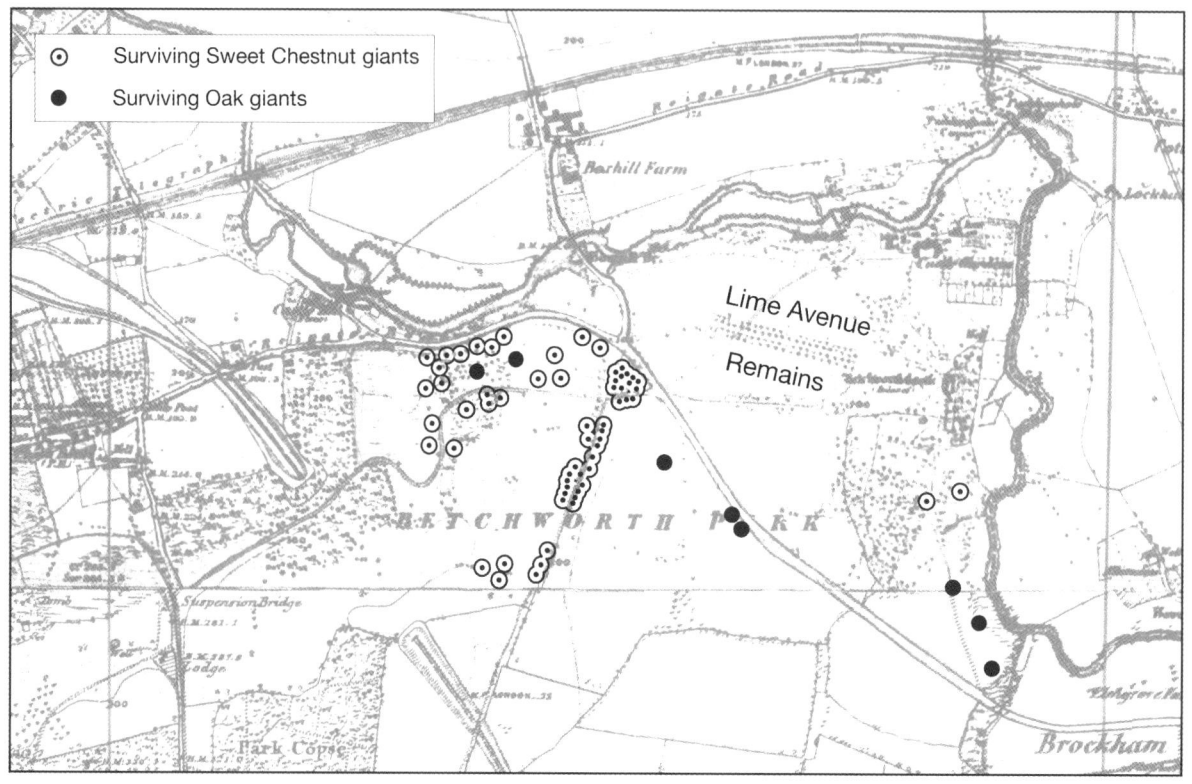

Reproduced using c. 1870 Ordnance Survey 6 inch to 1 mile map base with the kind permission of the Ordnance Survey.

'The Ents are coming!' They mass for a last attack. Betchworth Deer Park Golf Course: Sweet Chestnut Giants.

it. It has Common Blue butterflies, Bird's Foot Trefoil and the commoner old herbs. **Deepdene** was once contiguous with it, to the south, but is now separated by the wretched A24 bypass. The lawns around the vile modernist office block that replaced the fancy mansion are dotted with Harebells, but the newly planted exotic trees will shade them out in time. Brilliant work is being done to restore Deepdene's broken ornamental landscape to the west (with its ancient woods) and to the south … Great stuff.

CHARLWOOD AND ITS COUNTRY

Charlwood village, TQ 241 401, stood right in the path of the original plans for a second Gatwick runway. It was saved from that, but its fate will be little better in the long term if a re-positioned second runway is ever built.

It is exceptionally rich in ancient buildings, but, apart from the church hamlet, they are scattered and often hidden, and the on-street appearance is of Victorian and later houses. That is because this was a village of houses scattered round a common. The three main roads (Chapel Road, Pudding Lane, The Street) were all tracks across the common, enclosed only in 1846. The plain of the Mole had long had open, unenclosed ground (Low*field*, West*field* Commons) and there was much medieval iron ore working, so this would have been a place with relatively good numbers of small independent people, building the many surviving hall houses and more solid cottages.

The magnificent **church** was started only fourteen years after the Norman Conquest, and escaped big Victorian restoration. On my first visit there were Starlings nesting in the eaves, a wasps' nest and a trapped Spotted Flycatcher in the porch. There are 17th and 18th century graffiti inside the porch and scythe marks on its door stonework. The church has a Late Perpendicular carved and painted wooden screen, which survived the iconoclasm of the Reformation and is the only sizeable medieval woodwork in Surrey.[7] The church is also justly famous for its cycle of wacky frescos, mostly of about 1320. *There's a Peter Grimes-type scene of three boys being rescued from boiling by a pork butcher; a hunting scene with a greyhound chasing a hare; a hunting scene with three noble youths with hawks on their wrists being confronted by three spectral skeletons; St Margaret being swallowed by a dragon; St Margaret being spat out by the dragon; a Saxon archer …* phew!

Sadly, the 1000 year old churchyard Yew has been burnt in its core, so that a third of its canopy has died. Gatwick's noise booms from the south.

A village community trust now owns (since its closure in 2013) the old **Providence Chapel**, TQ 246 412, up Chapel Lane on the edge of the fields, wooden, weather-boarded, and with a big front verandah. Ian Nairn[8] wrote that "it would not be out of place in the remotest part of East Kentucky". The tiny graveyard of these Particular Baptists and Calvinists survives, with Great Valerian, Ox Eye Daisy, Barren Strawberry, Bugle, and other meadow herbs.

To the west of the village, below Russ Hill, is the rebuilt **Lowfield Heath Windmill**, TQ 234 407, heroically rescued in 1987 from dereliction and the threat of Gatwick's expansion and transported several miles to its new home. A post mill of around 200 years age – perhaps much more – it was once a landmark across the Mole plain, but is now somewhat incongruous in its hidden combe.

West of the village the ground rises to the Paludina Limestone ridge, straddled by **Glover's Wood**, TQ 229 409. It has much Hornbeam and Hazel coppice, with Ash, Poplar and Oak, over Bluebells. The east-west footpath through the Woodland Trust part, forms a wide ride with good scalloped glades, and masses of insects and flowers in late spring. There is an old farm pond, now with much Bog Moss, *Sphagnum*, spp., and the rare Elongated Sedge in quantity. A Small Leaved Lime has blown over at the Wood's east end and sprouted a line of fresh poles along its fallen bole, like teeth on a comb. There are Wild Daffodils in **Welland Gill** that runs through the west and inside the northern edge of the wood, perhaps uncleared since the days of the wildwood, with more Small Leaved Lime. It cuts

Charlwood's Providence Chapel "would not be out of place in the remotest part of East Kentucky"

Surviving cottage on Lady Isabella Somerset's 'Industrial Farm Colony for Female Inebriates', Duxhurst, near Horley.

down into the Paludina Limestone, and exposes fragile shaley fossils, liverworts and ferns happy in this humid green. A very scruffy Great Spotted Woodpecker leaves its nest in a rotten Hornbeam and tap, tap, taps up another tree close by.

On the same ridge less than a mile north is **Edolph's Copse**, TQ 235 424, a mixture (like Glover's) of ancient and secondary woodland, with views east across the Mole Vale. The Woodland Trust manage it beautifully, with this mixed history in mind, and it has sunny meadow areas, small ponds, wide rides, good paths, and seats. The Wild Strawberries like it. Next to it, on the west side of Stan Hill lane, are the lovely **Stan Hill Meadows**, TQ 232/3 423/4, where Cowslip and Black Sedge just cling on, with much Quaking Grass, the yellows of Fleabane and Trefoil, and patches of white Ox Eye Daisies. Just north of the meadows is old **Highworth Farm**, TQ 230 426, with black and white Tudor farmhouse, two fine tarred and weatherboarded 17th/18th century barns and 18th century hovel (cartshed). The place, though, is much poshed-up.

North of Beggarshouse Lane is **Beggars Gill**, TQ 227 422, running down to **Pock*mires* Wood**, where you may well meet Puck on a midsummer night. If he's anywhere he'll be here in these quiet greenwood gills, weaving his best magic against the Gatwick monsters that roar just to the south. **Sturtwood Farm**, TQ 214 426/7, still with all its old shaws, takes its name from the old Saxon word for tail – *steort* – the same word we still use for the little Red*start* bird.

Almost two miles northeast of Charlwood village across flat pasture lands of Oak shaws and copses is **Spencer's Gill**, and on the north bank of the Gill, marking the parish boundary, are three fine, close-grouped pollard Oaks of huge character, TQ 258 431. All are hollow. The western one has been burnt in its crown. The plough cuts across their roots far too close. All have lost much bark, and the smaller middle one has died. For all that, the older two must have balanced on this Gill bank for some four centuries. Sunning itself on the bole was a freshly emerged Small Phoenix moth, with wings patterned like the tracery of an ancient gothic window.

Just three fields away to the north is the horrible **Horse Hill oil and gas fracking / pumping site**, TQ 252 435, which has been resisted by many brave campaigners. (There's another oil well five miles north west at **Felton's Farm, Brockham**, TQ 188 486).

About 1.5 miles NNW of the Black Horse pub in Hookwood, is the low hill on which **Duxhurst** sits. The distance from the pub is significant, for it was that long distance that helped Lady Isabella Somerset[9] – big local landowner – choose Duxhurst as a suitable site for her 1895 **Industrial Farm Colony for Female Inebriates**. A string of picturesque thatched cottages serving as group homes were built around a 'village green', and there was a church and mixed farm, workrooms and recreation rooms. The biggest of the cottages, where Somerset herself lived, still stands by the 'green', TQ 257 449. The others have been lost, though the untended graveyard and many of its stones survives, hidden amongst trees, TQ 257 450/1 (2014). Odd bits of meadow survive along the Colony lane, and at its east end/south side there is a lovely archaic meadow, TQ 260 452, only about an acre, with Milkmaids and much Bugle. Opposite the end of the lane, on the east side of the A217 Reigate Road is a fine example of a Victorian small farmstead, **Lower Duxhurst Farm**, TQ 261 452. The best way to approach Duxhurst is along **Crutchfield Lane**, TQ 255 443, surely one of the nicest old lanes in the Low Weald: narrow, almost car-less, with grass on some bits, safe for children, winding, wooded, scruffy and with fine Oaks and wide verges, sometimes flowery.

AROUND NEWDIGATE AND LEIGH

Newdigate and Leigh present an appearance of bosky remoteness, with narrow roads and green lanes, although behind the screens of Oak and outgrown hedges there has been much ribbon development and an upmarket kind of plotlands creation, particularly at **Parkgate**, TQ 208 440. **Newdigate church**, TQ 197 420, epitomises the older parish, with its c. 1400 three storey, stepped Oak belfry tower, surmounted by a shingled spire. The church uses all the local stones:[10] Horsham Slab roof and walling; Paludina Limestone slabs from

Stanhill; Tilgate Stone from about a mile away; Bargate Stone from Halesbridge; Reigate Stone; Ironstone from the Henfold Plateau Gravel' and a kind of 'bubblestone'. There are several good timber framed cottages nearby, and the Six Bells pub opposite has a black tarred weatherboarded barn.

Reffolds Copse, north of the village, TQ 198 435, is nearly a mile wide, and forms the largest surviving fragment of the old Ewood. It is nearly all ancient, with areas of Oak maidens, Sweet Chestnut coppice, pure Birch stands, and invasive Sycamore. The ancient woodland dependant Ash Black Slug is there, with its mint-humbug-striped-foot, but it cannot like the big conifer coups in the south west part. A mile NE, across Broad Lane, is the Woodland Trust's **Hammond's Copse**, TQ 212 441, a lovely place, basically Oak wood with Hazel coppice, over half of which is in recovery from '70s coniferisation. There's a pond covered in Water Crowfoot in May, loads of interesting insects, and it is quite heathy in places, and wet in others.

South of Newdigate the countryside is partly intensively farmed (as around Home Farm, TQ 206 407) and partly diversified into leisure businesses (as around Green's Farm, TQ 193 411). **Green's Copse**, TQ 189 416, and the woods linked southwards are beautiful though, e.g **Lodge Copse**, TQ 190 408/9, with its noisy Rookery.

Down Hogspudding Lane, east of the village, is **Newdigate Clay Pit**, now mostly a nature reserve, TQ 203 426, and a good place to spend lazy time. There's much good rough grassland with Adder's Tongue Fern, Spotted Orchids and many other old herbs, nice scrubby bits, and ponds big and small. The largest has Catfish to 32 lb, Carp and Tench, though notoriously difficult to catch.

An old green lane went from **Ewood Furnace**, TQ 200 446, northwards past Westwood Common, through Highridge Wood and onwards, presumably much used when the iron furnace was in production. Parts of the lane now survive only as hedgeline, and the common is gone (though its boundaries are intact) as are all the other Leigh commons, except the little manicured **Leigh Church Green**, TQ 223 468 ... and a peculiar metamorphosed **Dawes Green**, TQ 215 469, which, though formally no longer a common, is managed by the parish council as a kind of recreational common more or less within its old boundaries, partly as old allotments, partly as a cricket ground, and partly as a good children's playground. A tiny enclosed meadow at the south end of the cricket ground, as well as the edges of the cricket field, retain something of the archaic herbage of the old green. So, too, does the churchyard at Leigh, with Betony and other old herbs. **Leigh Church** is much changed and its traditional timber belfry was demolished in a Victorian restoration, but there is

Newdigate church's belfry – wood, wood and more wood

original stonework on the north side, though most of the church is very flaky Reigate Stone.

A mile south of Leigh is **Mynthurst,**[11] TQ 22 45. Its woods are superb, both to the north along the **Leigh Brook**, e.g. **Rigden Rough**, TQ 221 454/5, and to the south along **Deanoak Brook**, e.g. the Ramsons wood at TQ 226 446. The Leigh Brook woods are paradisiacal at Bluebell time. Its farmed land, however, has lost many of its hedges and field boundaries, and is managed intensively for commercial dairy production, as is Norwood Place Farm to the south. There's much lush, nitrogenous green. An application for an 81 acre (that's huge) solar farm was rejected in 2015. Praise be! The old farmsteads of Herons Head, Parkhouse, Rigdens, and the rest, are all residential conversions. Depressing.

The **Gad Brook** forms Leigh's northern parish boundary and on its north side the surveyor's straight Gadbrook Road and large fields betray where the old **Gadbrook Wood Common** once was. Rough pasture still survives (2014) by the stream at **Hall Farm meadows**, TQ 210 476, and the tiny **Gadbrook Farm green** on Wellhouse Road, TQ 207/8 484/5, is very flowery, with Corn Parsley, Meadow Cranesbill and sedges (2014).

REIGATE AND ITS COMMONS AND COUNTRY

Reigate-Redhill is blessed with its commons. Every town should have kept its commons like that. Together they traverse the main geological sequence of the Low Weald.

REIGATE COMMONS

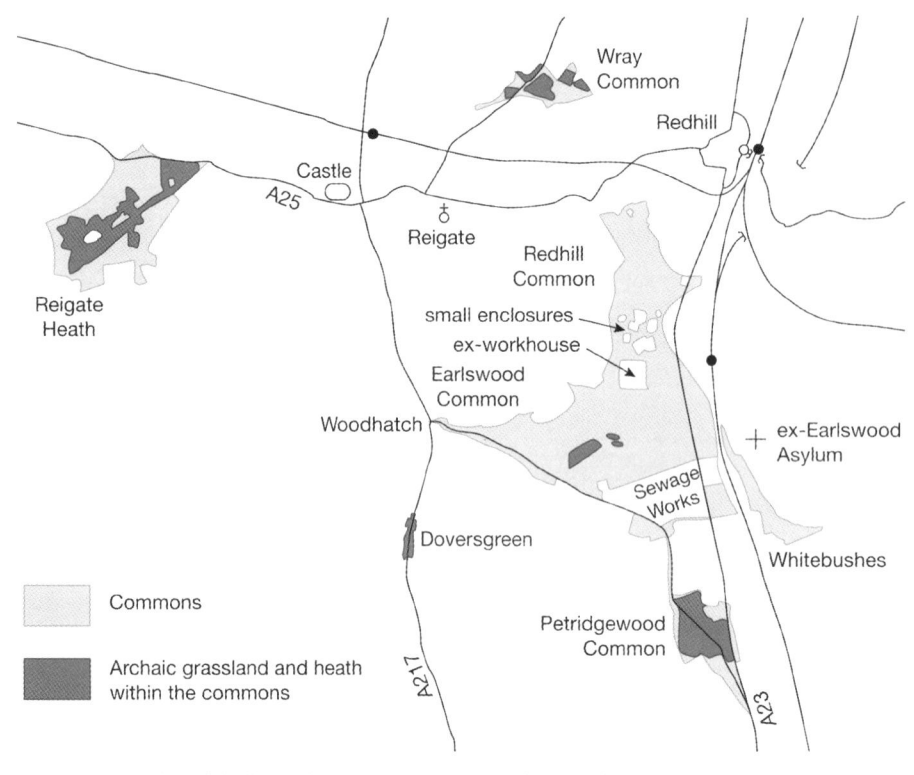

© Crown copyright and database rights 2018. OS License number 100048229

In the wooded north west corner of the common the exposed soil is black and peaty, with much Alder and Birch amongst the Oak, Rowan and Climbing Corydalis. This gives a clue to the larger tragedy of this common, which is that its primary historic character was as much that of bog and mire as of dry heath. Luxford's lists from 1838[12] make a depressing litany of its now-lost treasures: *Sundew, Cotton Grass, Marsh Lousewort, Pennyroyal, Bog Bean, Bog Pimpernel, Shoreweed, Ivy Leaved Bellflower, Heath Rush,* and *Bottle, Large Yellow, Flea, Pill, Star, Tufted* and *Carnation Sedges, et al.*

Around the Heath other wet ground was included in the SSSI. To the west, **The Alders** eponymous trees, TQ 229 500, now have roots that stand free, exposed up to one metre above the shrunken, dried out peat. To the east, **Skimmington Brooks**, TQ 240 500, with their Marsh Orchids, have dried. Willows are dying along the ditches. A dog walker told me that the brooks "used to be a swamp in winter, but now they are always as dry as a bone. They pump out the water from the (adjacent sand) quarries and then put it in the stream, rather that back in the ground". Nettles, Bramble, Himalayan Balsam and Water Dropwort have taken over from the ancient wetland vegetation.

Reigate Heath, TQ 236 503, an SSSI on the soft Folkestone Beds sands, has a very old fashioned Edwardian feel. It is dominated by its golf course (founded 1895 amongst the heather and pines) whose club house is a tile hung villa on a hilltop it shares with a black tarred smock windmill, complete with sails. The mill's ground floor is a now a chapel (you pick up the key from the clubhouse) in which the mill's centre post is suspended above you on a sagging trestle, like the sword of Damocles. There are seven round barrows in two clusters on the common, one of which, just north of the car park, is a ring barrow.

The golf club secretary told us that Adder is still present, though Grass Snake is more common. There is much Ling Heather, and Bell Heather and Dwarf Gorse hold on, with Broom and Gorse making yellow splashes. The tiny herbs of dry acid grassland seem to have fared best, and make a patchwork of buffs and subdued greens over large parts of the sports field and its surrounds at the common's east end. There is sweet scented Chamomile, Bird's Foot, Upright Chickweed, Slender Trefoil, Juniper Haircap moss, Grey Field Speedwell, Buck's Horn Plaintain and Common Stork's Bill. There are large patches of low Cladonia lichen, and Heath Grass. Elsewhere you can find Spring Sedge and the entrances to Minotaur Beetle burrows, as well as heathy micro-species of Bramble and Dandelion.

Hidden amongst the trees off the Flanchford Road is **the Heath Church**, TQ 240 502, of corrugated iron with wooden 'gothic' windows – very John Betjeman. These 'tin tabernacles' are getting as rare as hens' teeth.

West of Reigate Heath, the old centre of **Buckland**, TQ 221 508, has an over-neat green and pond, by a black tarred, weatherboarded 17th century barn with a turret, which once held the water tank supplying the village. The Reigate Road dangerously bisects the place and the local roads are lined with suburban villas. The church is of circa 1380 (restored in 1860), of Bargate Stone and ironstone rubble. The roof and the belfry and its western braced posts are of 14th century oak timber, in the tradition of the Surrey Low Weald. One remarkable north side nave window is of 14th century stained glass in rich blues and reds. North of the Green

SAND QUARRIES AND LOST WETLANDS

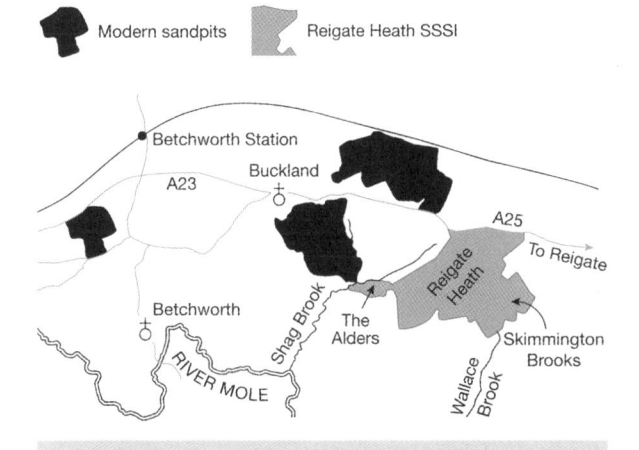

■ Modern sandpits ▲ Reigate Heath SSSI

Reigate Heath windmill and Victorian golf clubhouse

> All elements of the Reigate Heath SSSI (Site of Special Scientific Interest) – the Heath, The Alders, the Brooks – are now much drier than they were till modern quarrying. This whole landscape, with the SSSI, has lost its special wetland pasture and damp heath flora, including many rarities.

© Crown copyright and database rights 2018.
OS License number 100048229

the lane is lined with the remnants of **Rectory Green**, part of which, by Glebe House, has a Gault Clay meadow flora, now rather simplified, TQ 219 513/4.

The conjoined Redhill and Earlswood Commons cover 334 acres. **Redhill Common**, TQ 273 496, up on the Lower Greensand scarp, has superb views across the Weald from its crest, on the edge of a high grassy plat. The best spot is a long east facing scarp cut by past quarry workers and now hidden in woods. It cuts down through the Hythe Beds, exposing sands, cherts and fuller's earths.[13] It has magnificent Beeches with tangled roots along the top edges of the cliff, and much Holly and Scots Pine. Below the south facing scarp (hot, tangled and wooded) the common has many little quarry cottages nestled in dells, old pits, little twittens and small enclosures (and modern infill development) in a matrix of greens and grassy slopes. On a hummock is the lovely Victorian St John's church, of yellow brick and flint, with a spire of stone which can be seen from many spots across the Low Weald. One hot August afternoon I watched a Roe Deer buck hiding out the day amongst the grave stones – a good symbol of the town, for 'Reigate' may mean *reye gate*: 'Roe Deer gap'.

To the south, **Earlswood Common** sprawls out across the Wealden Clay in a park-like patchwork of copses and lawns. It is astonishingly litter-free. The woods are semi-natural and some must be well over a century old. The two Lakes used to be used for swimming and boating, but the wildfowl and anglers have them now. Lots of competing interests have transformed or taken bites out of the common: *the golf course (covering most of the open ground); the Brighton Line and its massive embankment; the big sewage works; the old workhouse (now a housing estate); sports grounds; allotments; brickworks (long gone); the Earlswood Asylum*[14] *(now posh apartments); and houses.* By contrast, the original vegetation that covered the entire common – ancient woods, moor and heath – is almost extinct. No ancient woods survive, and the veteran **Woodhatch Oak**, TQ 259 486, has to stand symbol for all that is gone. There is a neglected fragment of archaic grassland just north of the New Pond, TQ 268/9 485. It still has Harebells, Tormentil and Sneezewort, and in spring there is Ladies Smock, Bulbous Buttercup, and Field Woodrush amongst Red Fescue, Sweet Vernal Grass and moor grasses. It deserves to be rescued and valued.

Going south again, we come to **Petridgewood Common**, TQ 278 473. It has more of its original vegetation than the rest of the Earlswood and Redhill Commons complex, to which it is still thinly connected by a strip of roadside manorial waste. Much of its archaic wet moor and neutral grassland survives (2014). To the east of the A2044 it is managed by conservation mowing. There is much Heath Grass at the northern end, Common Spotted Orchids, Zig Zag Clover, Ox Eye Daisy and other colourful herbs. Burnet Companion moth is present. At the south end it is wetter, with much Oval Sedge and Ladies Smock. To the west of the A23, TQ 277 472, it is damp and rough, with much Tall Fescue, Tormentil, Moor Grass, *Molinia*, Grass Vetchling, Sneezewort, and Sheep's Sorrel and Sheep's Fescue on the anthills and banks. It is of high quality, but very neglected, despite the valiant efforts of good volunteers to keep the encroaching scrub under control. Ash Die Back has taken hold. It is scandalous that the money is not being found to properly conserve a public resource of this quality.

When I was a kid and we travelled up the Brighton Line I always looked out for the bit of rough open ground to the east, **Whitebushes Common**, TQ 282 480, just before the big Asylum. It sometimes

AREA GUIDE / Chapter 26: The Reigate and Dorking Low Weald had gypsies on it, and looked promising. It is still nice scruffy meadow and playing fields, crossed by paths, though most of the grassland is now improved. One ditch remains good, with False Fox Sedge, Meadowsweet, and Codlins and Cream. Sadly, the reedy ponds along the railway embankment base are now choked up.

South of Woodhatch is **Doversgreen**, TQ 257 478/9, a strip of common waste on both sides of the Reigate Road, where a mixture of old woodland flowers (Bluebells, Pignut, Goldlilocks, etc) and old wet pasture flowers survive, including Ladies Smock in a rare double petalled form.

Wray Common, TQ 266 510, on the Gault Clay, is a beautiful open place of archaic unimproved, semi-improved and improved grassland, with woodland to the south. Imprisoned, now, within a posh northern suburb, it is famous for its tower windmill of black tarred brick, with white sails and fantail. Around the windmill is a damp fragment of rush and sedge moor, with Black Sedge hanging on, Quaking Grass, and much Tufted Hair Grass. The grasshoppers keep up a great din. To the west of the A242, it is meadow-like and colourful, with much Pepper Saxifrage and lots of old herbs. An extraordinary survival.

The **church of St Mary**, TQ 259 501, stood separate from Reigate town until modern times. Its huge sandy churchyard is rough and peaceful, with Harebells round the gravestones, Burnet Saxifrage, Hawkbits, Hawkweed and Cat's Ear. Has someone been seed scattering? There are Cedars, Cypresses, Limes and Yews dotted about. The old church is externally of the fifteenth century, of soft eroding sandstone, and the tower was refaced with yellow Bath Stone almost 140 years ago.

Reigate old town, TQ 251 502, is even more like Lewes than Dorking. No surprise, since the town and castle were owned and built by the same De Warenne Earls of Surrey who owned Lewes (the first of whom was a big mate of William the Conqueror). Its castle, like Lewes, controlled the Normans escape route back to their Normandy heartland. The town has a market hall, but few obvious ancient buildings except one or two timber framed shops/houses. It is tangled all around by cars, but has so far avoided the horrors of a big bypass. **Castle Hill** dominates, with a partial moat (Reed Mace, duckweed, a big raft of Bog Bean) and an enclosed bailey with lovely flower beds. Though no old stonework survives, the whole hill with its steep and wooded outworks and labyrinthine paths, is a great place for canoodling, having a kip, a picnic, or some quiet peace.

South of the town is **Priory Park**, a delightful council-owned expanse with a museum in the old mansion that is built on the site of the Priory. To its south is the wooded ridge of **Reigate Park**, TQ 249 495, tranquil, vertiginous on the south side, and with tangled combes on its north side, with several good Oak, Beech and other veteran trees. Only a narrow strip along the top is still open ground, so the drama of Wealden views is cramped.

HOLMWOOD COMMON

The National Trust's **Holmwood Common**, TQ 175 458, is large and wild enough to get lost in (634 acres) and tranquil away from the A24 speedway through its west side. It has deep woods and thickets, rides and glades, small ponds, valleys, streams and marshy bits. At its best it has something of the qualities of the New Forest, as around **Four Wents Pond**, TQ 183 453, and the **Moor Cottage enclosure**, TQ 173/4 449.

Its original woods were lost long ago, and the first edition OS map of c 1870 shows it as rough pasture with scattered trees and shrubs, and settled edges which had the character of greens. The names *Moor*field and *Moor* Cottage attest to that past openness. It lost most of its veteran pollards, too, and the over-three-span-girth **Oakdale Giant**, TQ 170 453, seems alone in its size. The woodland is mostly Oak, often with a Holly understorey, and much Bracken. There is occasional Alder Buckthorn, Rowan, much Bramble and Honeysuckle, Sallow, and Water Pepper along the wet paths.

The relict grasslands are very simplified, probably from long dereliction or past improvement, though Tormentil is frequent. The best are on **Holmwood Corner Common**, TQ 175 442, by the bridlepath, with much Devil's Bit, and **Oakdale Green**, TQ 171 452. The **graveyard of St Mary Magdalene, South Holmwood**, TQ 171 448, better preserves the flora of the old Common, from which it is no doubt enclosed. It has Betony and Harebells (just), Ox Eye Daisy, Devil's Bit and Burnet Saxifrage.

It would be good to see docile cattle and ponies back on the Common, bringing some of the conservation services such stock supply so ably to the New Forest.

CAPEL'S COUNTRY AND ITS GREENS

I felt I knew **Capel** long before I first visited, for our mum often talked to us of the summer holidays her family spent in a friend's farmhouse between Ockley and Capel in the late 1920s. They attended Ockley and Capel churches on alternate Sundays.

In June the Swifts screech and swoop above **Capel church**, TQ 175 407, and dive to their nests under the eaves. One was found dead on the altar before the roof was repaired some years ago. There is a Yew in the yard reckoned to be 1700 years old and once part of a grove of six around a long-gone pond. In the west of the yard there is a fine three span girth Oak maiden, with catkins carrying as many Currant Galls as the currants on a Redcurrant bush on my last visit. The church masonry includes large Paludina Limestone, with fine weathered out fossil shells, ironstone galletting,[15] sandstones, chalk clunch or Reigate Stone, Horsham Stone, sandstones, and a kind of pink 'crystal[16] stone'. The countryside to its west is full of fine Oaks of two span girth and more.

Just south of **Ryersh Lane**, on the east side of a thin copse, TQ 168 408/9, the site of a lost dwelling and orchard, are a grand old hollow three span pollard Oak, ancient Ash hedge stools, another fine Oak, and an old Pear tree. These veterans often come in clusters. *Ewekene's* **Copse** (a Bluebell wood on Ryersh Lane with several fine old Oaks, TQ 171/2 413) and *Ewekene* **Farm**, bear the near-lost Saxon name for *Capel*, which is a younger Anglo-Norman name.[17] It is lovely country, though badly noise-polluted by the A24 Capel bypass.

Capel still has several greens. ***Misbrooks Green***, TQ 181 413, is the best of them, though under-managed and much in need of grazing and hay making. It keeps something of its ancient character, with Devil's Bit, Sneezewort, Betony and Pepper Saxifrage. **Misbrook** and **Brommell's Farms,** close-by on Misbrooks Green Road, also retain an old Wealden character, with their old barns, outhouses and hedgerows intact, though they are no longer working farms. ***Beare Green***, TQ 178 429, has lost its archaic character and is now manicured sports pitches and road noise. ***Clarke's Green***, TQ 172 395, is also oppressed by Capel bypass noise, but has retained a wilder character of woodland and derelict semi-improved grassland. The lanes of the parish also have much manorial waste, most of it wooded-up now, like ***Seamans Green,*** TQ 176 416, though the lanesides at the Green's south end, where it crosses the Misbrook, are colourful with tall herbs.

Temple Lane's flowery hedges lead us a beautiful way south to the high Sussex border ridge. In the brook that crosses the Lane north of **Aldurst Farm**, TQ 184/5 404/5, two fossilised Iguanodon footprints have been dug up by the farming family that live there, with a space of three generations between each finding. To the west of the Lane are the beautiful ancient woods of **Hatchlands Copse**, TQ 183 403, and **Oxpasture Copse**, TQ 182 398, and at the Lane's southern end is **Temple Wood**, a Hornbeam coppice over a sea of Bluebells. **North Barns**, TQ 190/1 389, at the wood's south corner, has a fine collection of hovels, waggon barn, granary and old cottages (2009).

South of **Lyne House**, TQ 190 384 (a brick, tile roofed pile – now flats – with picturesque pinnacles and huge new dairy stockyards) the ground drops to the densely wooded **Cowix and Gage's Gills** e.g. TQ 189 379, then rises up to **Rome Wood** and the county boundary on Capel Road. There is Sweet Woodruff, Pale Sedge, Golden Saxifrage and Wych Elm, in the gill. Where sunbeams penetrated the canopy on my last visit, a Beautiful Golden Y moth landed, and Beautiful Demoiselles flitted in numbers. It was the time of year when little Green Oak Tortrix moths are in flight, and Oak Apples flush pink amongst the leaves. The woods, however, are right under the Gatwick flight path, and airliners roar overhead. Off-road motorcyclists have gouged tracks across the gill and on both its sides.

Along the old Capel-Newdigate parish boundary, across the gill and up Rome Wood's eastern edge, e.g. TQ 192 378, is a line of veteran Hornbeam pollards and outgrown hedge stools.

ENDNOTES

1. There were fewer *'hursts'*, (large woods on hills), like Mynt*hurst* and Dux*hurst*, presumably because the country was less hilly.
2. 'Tangled Wings: Gatwick seen through green-tinted glasses', page 10, by Brendon Sewell. The Aviation Environment Federation (2012). The information is from 'Four Centuries of Charlwood Houses', by Joan Harding. The Charlwood Society (1976).
3. 'Tangled Wings', page 11, *op cit*, and 'Crawley: Old Town, New Town', edited by Fred Gray, page 35–6. Centre for Continuing Education, University of Sussex (1983).
4. 'A Flora of the Neighbourhood of Reigate', by George Luxford, ALS. (1838).
5. 'Meath' derives from *'(ge)mythe'* – 'junction of two streams'.
6. Another quote from 'Ode to a Nightingale'. John Keats.
7. 'A Guide to the Church of St Nicholas, Charlwood'.
8. 'The Buildings of England, Surrey', page 143, by Ian Nairn and Nicholas Pevsner. Penguin (1962).
9. Somerset was both passionate feminist, suffragist, social reformer, AND strictly classist and Christian. The Duxhurst Colony was divided by class, with separate establishments for the rich and famous, the middle class, and the poor. She died in 1921. From 1917 to 1923 the colony was a Children's Village, then a home for impoverished gentlefolk, which closed in the mid-thirties. After 1945 the buildings became derelict and were lost.
10. 'The Church of Saint Peter, Newdigate, Surrey: an Illustrated Guide', by Joyce Banks. On sale in the church.
11. Mynthurst means what it says: the hurst where mint grows. The name goes back to 1203 at least.
12. Luxford, *op cit*, (1838).
13. 'Early Cretaceous Environments of the Weald', page 72, by Alastair Ruffell, Andrew Ross & Kevin Taylor. Geologists Association Guide No. 55 (1996).
14. Two nieces of the Queen Mother / cousins of the Queen were holed up there for decades.
15. Small pieces of stone inserted into the mortar between the large stones.
16. Which also occurs at Rudgwick Church.
17. *Capel* simply means 'chapel', the forerunner of Capel church, built as an outlier of Dorking Manor. *Ewekene* may mean *'ea waecen'*: river-watch or guard … but what river? … the little Misbrook? The Place Names of Surrey, op cit.

AREA GUIDE / Chapter 27: The Nutfield and Godstone Low Weald

CHAPTER 27
The Nutfield and Godstone Low Weald:
Horley and Salfords to Lingfield and Oxted

I first immersed myself in this part of the Low Weald after getting entangled in heavy summer traffic on the Eastbourne Road a quarter century ago. Partly curious and partly frustrated, I drove down a side lane, then up the Enterdent Road across Tilburstow Common to the crown of the greensand ridge, where the whole Low Weald spread before me. For the rest of the afternoon I poked around the little lanes of Horne, between tall cobnut hedges, exploring farm tracks, the little church, being passed by a man and his little girl on a pony gig, and muttering delighted exclamations to myself as I passed through cool tunnels of trees, and glimpsed sunny hay meadows and cottage gardens.

It was so like my own Sussex Low Wealden landscape, beneath the South Downs. I had no idea that such quiet beauty existed on such a scale so close to the M23/M25 and the sprawling London suburbs of the North Downs. Why did everyone want to drive to Eastbourne when they had this on their doorsteps?

To be sure, the M23 is a dagger through this beauty, and I do not know how the residents of Smallfield put up with the blast of airliners overhead, coming in to land at Gatwick. It still shocks me every time I come near to the sunny slopes of the North Downs how government and business got away with constructing the M25 motorway right along the Downs' foot, smashing through the middle of a landscape that has a level of statutory protection meant to be equal to that of a National Park.[1]

The quality of this landscape *should* rationally ensure its preservation as an imperative, despite all that capitalism's hyper-development throws at it ... but it does not. The needs of capital override even the strongest statutory planning protections.

However ... when you stand in little Perry Wood (south east of Salfords station), or, eastwards, in one of the little ancient woods about the slopes of Woolborough (Saxon: *'wolf hill'*) or Outwood, there is enough there still from ancient times to imagine yourself back to the days of the wildwood, when the Wolves of the Weald still howled to the winter moon. When you stand in one of the derelict meadows of Roundabout Farm, Copthorne, amongst the sedges and rushes, the orchids and purple Betony, with black peat underfoot, you know you are standing on a relic of the once-huge moor of Copthorne Common and the other heaths of the Surrey border. When you stand in Burstow churchyard, with its tower of Wealden Oak, and walk the flowery meadows of Burstow Stream just beyond the churchyard wall, you know that the scythe men and women of Flamsteed's time[2] would recognise the scene. All is quiet both without and within Crowhurst church, perched on its hill. So quiet you can hear a bat squeaking in the roof.

This landscape is made up of three geological layers. (See map Chapter 26). The ***northernmost*** is the Vale of Holmesdale, under the North Downs, which has the youngest rocks. The M25 and the M23/M25 intersection sit upon its wooded Gault Clay band. This vale of erstwhile moor, meadow and corn, drained by the Redhill Brook and its tributaries, sits upon the Folkestone and Sandgate Beds, whose sands and Fullers Earths have been massively quarried. The Lower Greensand scarp from Redhill, past Bletchingley Castle, Tilburstow Hill, Castle Hill at Leigh Place, and on to Tandridge Park, is made up of the harder Hythe Beds sands.

The ***middle layer*** is the Wealden Clay Vale, almost five miles wide and forming the landscape's largest part. Everything about its natural landforms is gentle: softly contoured hills, plateaus and brooklands, which grade imperceptibly into two sub-scarps topped with sandy deposits. The northern sub-scarp marks a broken ridge through which the long Bletchingley Railway Tunnel passes. Crowhurst Church sits upon it. The southern sub-scarp is braced by an outcropping Small Paludina

Limestone band from Salfords to Horne. Outwood Common and windmill sit upon it, and the sands of its plateau are cut through by wooded gills draining north.

The **southern layer** is made up of the Upper Tunbridge Wells Sands and their clay bands, meeting the Wealden Clay along an oblique line between Tinsley Green and Lingfield Common, which passes Shipley Bridge, West Park, Dowlands and Chithurst Farms, and Horne Park. These sands rise gently towards the Sussex border, and their landforms scarcely differ from the clay vale to the north. Mostly they are acidic and often infertile, and can be as poorly drained as the most difficult of the Surrey Wealden Clays.

This is a landscape of infant streams and little tributaries, not rivers, for it lies across the watershed / interfluve dividing the basins of the Rivers Mole and Medway. From south to north, Copthorne Common, Outwood Windmill, Bletchingley Railway Tunnel, Tilburstow Hill and Bletchingley Church all sit on that dividing line.

To the *west of the watershed* the Redhill Brook drains Nutfield Marsh and Holmesdale Vale west of Bletchingley Church Lane. The Brook breaks southwards through the Greensand scarp at the Redhill gap to join the Nutfield Brook and Salfords Stream near Redhill Aerodrome, from where it passes under the Brighton Line to join the Mole. A second tributary of the Mole, the Burstow Stream, drains the southern part of the Mole catchment around Horley.

To the *east of the watershed*, the fingers of the River Eden – the Eden Brook (fed by Felbridge Water), the Ray[3] Brook (north of Lingfield), the Gibbs Brook, and the River Eden, drain east to a confluence between Lingfield and Edenbridge.

The floodplains to the west around Horley and to the east around Lingfield must once have been wildernesses of Alder-Sallow carr and grazing marsh. In early modern times they were converted to rich meadows, and even to deer park (at Lagham, South Godstone). They can still flood however, with dramatic effect, and climate change may make that more likely.

Nearly all this landscape's **ponds and lakes** are human-made. Hedgecourt Lake (still the largest area of water in east Surrey) and Wire Mills Lake were made for the Tudor iron industry. Some ponds powered water mills, as at Leigh Place and Bay Pond, Godstone, and Coltsford, Oxted. Others were dug as moats round farms and manor houses in high medieval times, for status and defence. Burstow parish has a cluster of these, but we come across them over the whole area, sometimes still in water (as, partly, at Lagham), sometimes buried in woodland (as on the Burstow Stream at Greatlake Farm), or just depressions in old pasture (as at Lodge Farm, Harewoods Estate). There are still many farm ponds in fields and brook pastures (with a concentration around Crowhurst) though many are now clogged with vegetation, wooded up, or managed for fishing. That is the fate of many woodland ponds too, which formed in the pits left from small scale quarrying. Others are managed for duck shooting (as at South Park).

In modern times many ponds have been created for ornament, or more recently for commercial fishing (as at Chartham Park Golf Course, or the Eden Brook south of Newchapel). Big lagoons have been created by large scale mineral quarrying in the Vale of Holmesdale, with a chain of flooded pits at Nutfield Marsh Nature Reserve, and at Godstone. There are others in the Wealden Clay Vale at Lambs Business Park, South Godstone, and Pikes Lane Brickworks, Crowhurst.

This is **a landscape of late settlement and extensive late woodland**, like the Vale of the Mole, to the west. Saxon settlements were strung along the lighter soils of Holmesdale and the greensand ridge, and are recorded in the Domesday Book of 1086: Nutfield, Bletchingley, Godstone, Tandridge, and Oxted. These had long extensions reaching south to the Sussex border, where common grazing, subsidiary farming activity, and hunting took place. These manorial extensions were organised over large distances. Tandridge parish extended like a long trunk for seven miles southwards from its church, a mere third of a mile (some 3 fields) wide for the southern 4.6 miles. A 2.5 mile long 'finger' of planned manorial settlement extended south between Earlswood Common and Horley Common. The A23 (Bonehurst Road), Gail Lane/Green Lane, and Picketts Lane are its ancient tracks, and the Brighton Line splits it. None of the modern southern parishes were then in separate existence: Horley, Burstow, Outwood, Horne, Crowhurst or Lingfield.

Saxon place names demonstrate the area's mixed character. Open areas, *'feld'*, like Nut*field*, Ling*field*, Fel*court*, Block*field*, Thunders*field* and Small*field*, existed alongside areas wild enough to support Wolves, like *Wool*borough and *Wool*pits.[4] Bletching*ley* and *Leigh*[5] in Godstone had sufficient woodland to be named by its presence in early Saxon times. Sufficient of Crow*hurst* (probably a daughter settlement of Oxted) was only cleared of its *hursts* and other large woods to make it weighty enough for parish status as late as the thirteenth century.

Prehistoric and later Roman folk had made their marks on the landscape, of course, though not enough to remove its dominant woodland cover. There are two Bronze Age round barrows just north of Godstone Green, and others probably existed nearby, or are suspected from crop marks. Prehistoric east-west trackways probably followed the Greensand ridge, the Vale of Holmesdale, the Outwood scarp, and the heathlands along the County boundary. Most tracks though, would have been aligned north-south, to cross the variety of soil types and resources people needed.

LATE SURVIVING COMMONS OF THE SUSSEX-SURREY COUNTY BORDER

The poor soils of the local Hastings Beds (largely Tunbridge Wells Sands) assisted the survival of a lattice of big commons into modern times. Most of them were only lost in the last 2.5 centuries. Some fragments still exist, but have mostly lost their open character as heaths and moors. Horley Common probably survived because it was on the poor gravelly terraces of the River Mole.

© Crown copyright and database rights 2018. OS License number 100048229

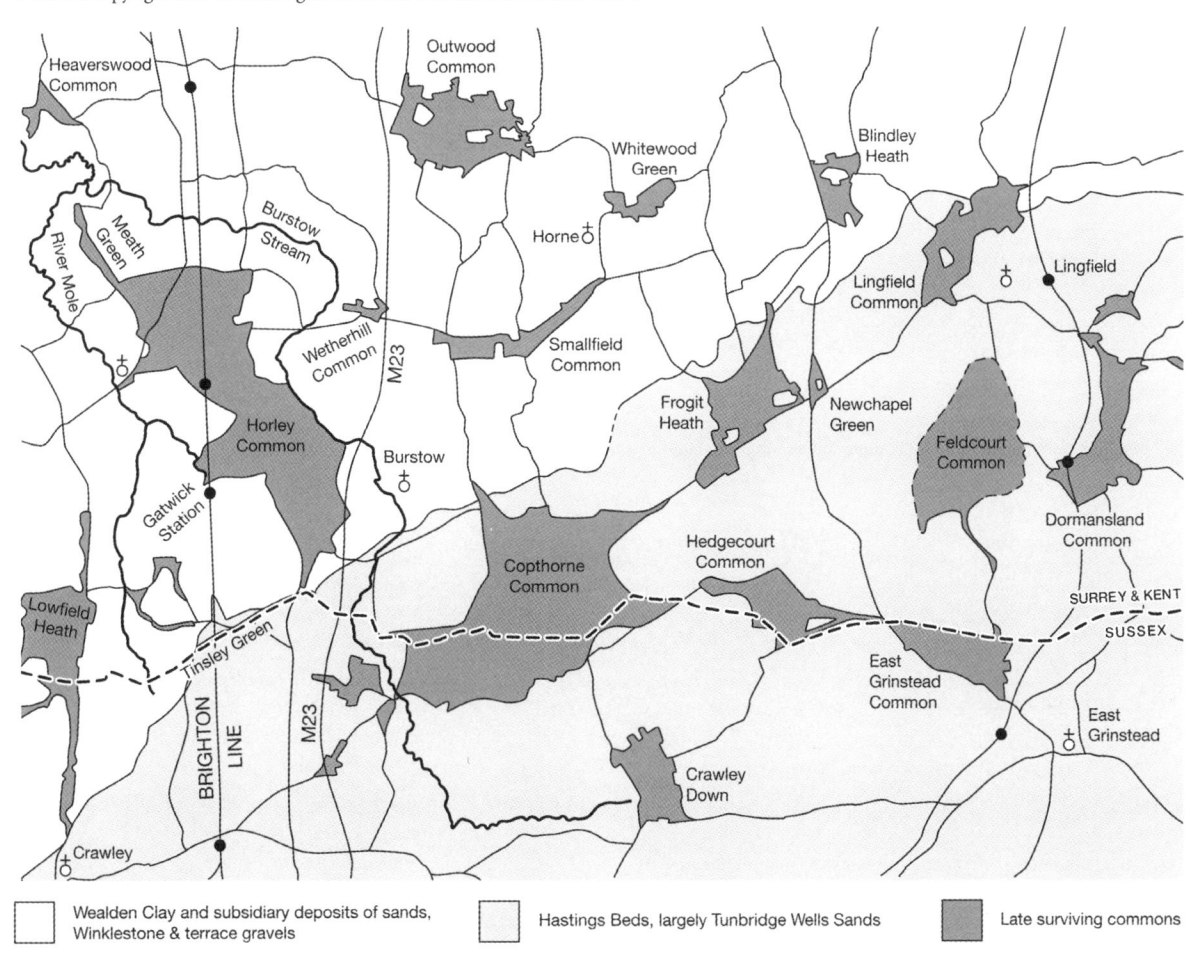

A Roman road descended the Downs through the Caterham gap, then through Godstone and Blindley Heath before crossing into Sussex at Felbridge. The place names *Stratton* Farm (now Godstone Farm) and *Stansted*[6] (near South Godstone) commemorate the road. *Flowers* Farm, Godstone, may memorialise a lost Roman villa, for 'Flower' derives from Saxon *'flor'* – floor – and perhaps there was mosaic paving there once. There was a villa too, under White Hill, and probably another east of Pendell Farm, Bletchingley. It is likely that the Roman road was an attempt to modernise a prehistoric track. The older, more rationally aligned track was probably re-asserted after the Roman occupation ended, which would explain the Saxon organisation of Tandridge parish around Tandridge Lane (just east of the Roman route) all the way south to the county boundary.

By Norman times the majority of woodland was cleared, and the **feudal ruling class organised a system of giant parks** to control enough wild land for venison production and recreational hunting. In Bletchingley two parks covered over four miles from the crest of the North Downs southwards to the Outwood scarp. Little, or North Park (1,135 acres) and Great, or South Park (1,681 acres) are commemorated by place names. Burstow's park is remembered in the place names Burstow Park Farm and Lawn Hill, and 'Outwood' was probably named after its purlieu woods. Parks once abutted Copthorne and Frogit/Frogwood Commons, and East Park and West Park place names commemorate that. There was also a large park embracing Hedgecourt Pond and Wire Mill Lake. South Godstone sits within the surviving 'pale' (boundary bank) of the 487 acre Lagham Park, where the fortifed and moated manor house of the southern of the two Godstone manors stood for centuries. The moat, some fragments of archaic grassland, and several ancient woods survive within it. All these parks were 'disparked' in the 16th and early 17th centuries.

The greensand scarp has two 'Castle Hills', though neither has an upstanding castle. 12th century Bletchingley Castle was part-demolished after the Battle of Lewes in 1264 and a mound, bank, ditch and a bit of re-fashioned masonry are left. Castle Hill, Godstone, has part of an earthwork (possibly Iron Age) in a wood right next to the noisy bypass.

Commons remained abundant in the sandy countryside of the south until a series of 18th/19th century enclosures. Lingfield had big commons on three sides – Feldcourt, Beacon Heath and Lingfield Commons – as well as lot[7] meadows down on the brooks. They were enclosed in 1809–16. Horley's giant common went slightly earlier. Some of Hedgecourt Common was enclosed in the early 18th century, and the rest, with most of Frogit Heath, was lost perhaps soon after 1810. Copthorne Common followed in 1855.

In the Wealden clay vale much of Outwood Common went after 1800, as did Smallfield Common and Whitewood Green, Horne. Blindley Heath and much brookland around it were enclosed some time earlier. However, the southern part crossed by the Ray Brook is still common and still called Blindley 'Heath', though it would be more accurate to call it Blindley 'Moor', for it is watery, not heathy. Weatherhill Common still survives in modified form, though its identity is poorly defined.

On the greensands there were Great and Little Commons north of Bletchingley, gone now, apart from a smidgeon (Little Tilgate Common) west of Little Common Lane. About 60% of Tilburstow Common survives, with Godstone Green, Nutfield Marsh, and little Broadham, Hurst and Tandridge Greens, though they have lost most of their archaic vegetation.

Public and quasi-public ownership is quite strong in this landscape, though its political profile is low. The whole six mile width of the Wealden Clay Vale just east of the M23 is in three publicly owned estates, from Castle Hill, Bletchingley, south to the site of old Copthorne Common. The National Trust owns the 430 acre Sandhills Estate under the greensand scarp, and, further south, the 2,048 acre Harewoods Estate, embracing Outwood Common. South again, in Horne, lies the West Park Estate, a Surrey County Council Smallholdings Estate of about 700 acres on either side of Chithurst Lane. The Surrey Wildlife Trust controls about 1.5 miles of flooded and worked out quarries and relict moor in the Fullers Earth vale east of Redhill, forming the Nutfield Marsh Nature Reserve. They also control Graeme Hendry Wood (another worked out part-quarry) on Tilburstow Hill, and Bay Pond Reserve east of Godstone Green. They got rid of Mary's Meadow, Crowhurst (unbelievably) despite the rarity of its ancient grassland.

Surrey Wildife Trust also manage Blindley Heath Common on behalf of the owners, Godstone Parish Council, who also own the parish's other residual commons: Tilburstowhill Common and Godstone Green (as well as Hilly Fields north of the Green with its two Bronze Age barrows). The remnants of Frogit Heath Common, with Newchapel Green, are owned by Horne Parish Council. Thus, all the relict commons of medieval Godstone Manor are in public ownership.

Lingfield Parish Council and Tandridge Distict Council together own the two Lingfield Nature Reserves (26 acres) with meadows, hedges and orchard, north of the church.

Ancient woodland clusters in two ways in this landscape. It is commonest on the poorest, wettest soils: the Tunbridge Wells Sand to the south, the Gault Clay band under the Downs, and the wettest parts of the Wealden Clay (Brook Wood and Langshott Wood, by Burstow Stream). It is most frequent too, on the steepest land: the scarps and ridges of the greensand and the Wealden Clay, and in the latter's deep gills.

On the Tunbridge Wells Sand both Baker's and Green Wood/Felcourt Wood are sizeable. The area also has fine chains of ancient woodland: Green-High-Stockriding-Chartham Woods, and Cooper's Moor-Wiremill Woods. Sweet Chestnut is a common coppice species, and there are occasional fine Beeches. The Gault Clay has ancient woodland clusters along the line of the M25 (horrendously damaged by its noise) north of Bletchingley, Godstone, Tandridge and Oxted.

On the steep greensand scarp there is a string of ancient woodland for almost five miles from Redhill to Godstone. There is another such string along the sandy ridge of the Wealden Clay at South Park, with the superb old Hornbeam coppices of Maple and Furze Woods, and another string along the Outwood ridge, on the Common and on the scarp slope at Hornecourt and the little gully woods. Steep Wealden Clay gills have preserved a fine stretch within Furze Wood, and four rich linear gill woods on the Harewood Estate. These gill woods have perhaps the greatest ecological continuity of any habitat in this landscape.

Across the Wealden Clay there is a wide scatter of small ancient woods, many of superb quality, such as Bradford Wood, with the lost medieval pale of Lagham Deer Park preserved within it. It is a place of Hornbeam and Hazel coppice.

Ancient woodland survives too, in linear form, along a number of the **oldest green lanes** – droves since the

Dark Ages or earlier. Originally corridors of cleared land, their alignments were 'fossilised' and marked by shaws, hedges and boundary timber as the clearances became generalised. Gail Lane-Green Lane, just east of Salfords, and parts of Chithurst Lane, Horne, have this woodland character. The deep **'holloways'** which cut down through the Lower Greensand ridge are wooded tunnels of trees too, in places like Little Common Lane-Pendell Road, Bletchingley, and Bullbeggars Lane and Church Lane, Godstone.

Some ancient woods have been damaged by modern conifer planting, such as a group around South Park, Bletchingley, and on the National Trust's adjoining Harewood Estate.

Secondary woods are frequent on the greensand ridge, on commons and ex-commons which have lost their grazing, and as diversification since the Victorian farming depression. The disused Fullers Earth quarries around old Nutfield on the Lower Greensand have much recent woodland, both planted and self-sown. Behind the scarp most of Tilburstowhill's woodland has either grown up on the disused common or the old quarries. The majority of Felcourt's woodland has grown up on the site of the lost common, and nearly all Frogit Heath and much of Blindley Heath commons are now woodland. The woodland around Tandridge Park is mostly modern, despite the presence of Small Leaved Lime at one spot. Ashen Plantation at Crowhurst is modern, though it may grow on the site of the *hurst* after which the parish is named. It is broad-leaved woodland, like Horley's derelict Langshott plotlands, but other modern woodlands have a more mixed character, such as Dowlands Wood in Horne. Woodland has grown up around both Hedgecourt and Wire Mill Lakes, though they were open in character historically.

This is not a countryside in which **ancient and veteran trees** are that common or recognised. The most famous are the giant Yews in Crowhurst and Tandridge churchyards. Crowhurst's Yew has a tiny goblin door, giving access into the hollow trunk big enough to hold a meeting. They are closely followed by the Plaistow Oak in Lingfield, beside the Cage and the Gun Pond. On Outwood Common, just north of the church, is a fragment of derelict wood pasture, with five or more Oak pollards, at least two of which are over three spans girth.

Most veterans are Oaks, though there are several good old Beech maidens in Chartham Wood, and a fine old Rowan at the north end of Tilburstowhill Common, by the north-south footpath. Dowlands Farmstead, south east of Smallfield, has a characterful three span Oak, recently re-pollarded, representative of a broad scattering of often hidden, isolated giants.

Heath is functionally extinct in this landscape, though abundant till post-1800. There are, however, several large and important **archaic grassland** sites. Copthorne Meadows, on that village's northern edge along the Sussex border, have a 'moor' vegetation with many scarce species, including Meadow Thistle (at its only site in SE Surrey), six sedge species, an astonishing July display of red-purple Betony, Orchids, Sneezewort, Marsh Pennywort, et al. A mile north west are two

SOME SURVIVING ARCHAIC GRASSLANDS AROUND COPTHORNE

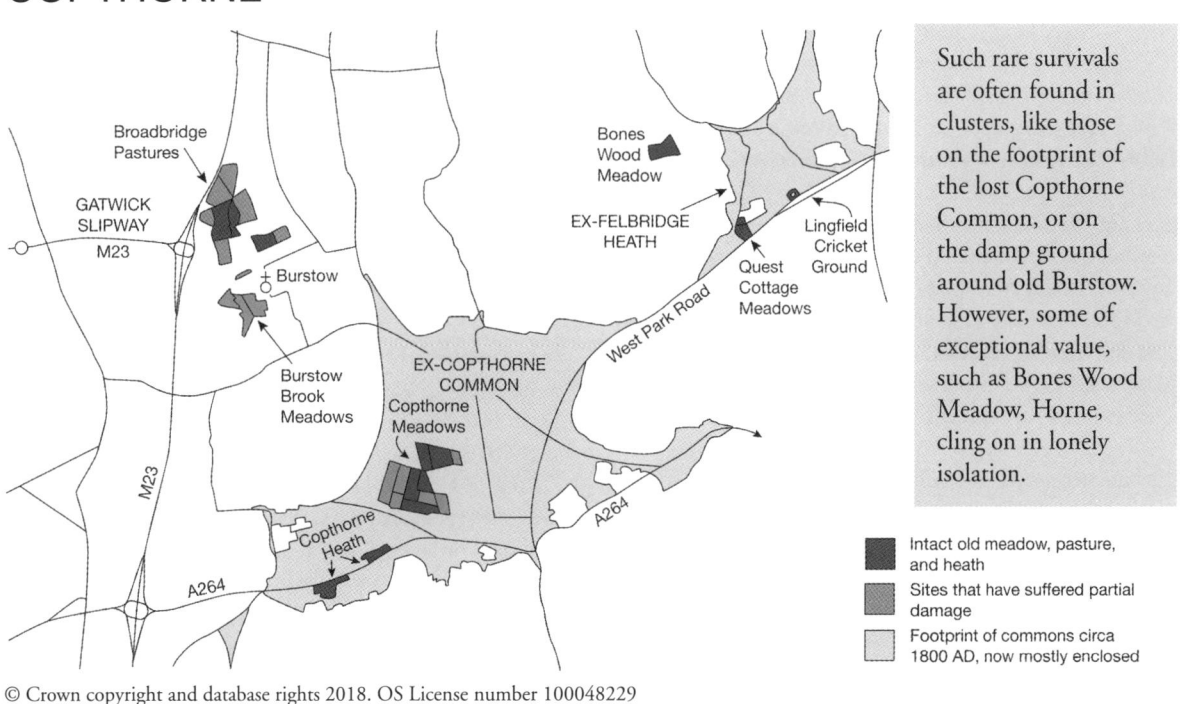

Such rare survivals are often found in clusters, like those on the footprint of the lost Copthorne Common, or on the damp ground around old Burstow. However, some of exceptional value, such as Bones Wood Meadow, Horne, cling on in lonely isolation.

■ Intact old meadow, pasture, and heath
■ Sites that have suffered partial damage
▫ Footprint of commons circa 1800 AD, now mostly enclosed

© Crown copyright and database rights 2018. OS License number 100048229

large sites: Burstow's brook meadows, and Broadbridge Pastures, right alongside the M23, wet and tussocky, with contented cattle and even wintering Snipe. Blindley Heath's 'moor' has similar tussocky vegetation, which continues in a series of farm fields to the SSE and south east. The National Trust's Harewood Estate has a group of five large archaic pastures, richly colourful in season, and there are other fine Wealden Clay sites.

Many sites are very small, like Stone House Common (a morsel of Outwood Common), and Bones Wood Meadow (on the south side of the wood, west of Bones Lane, Horne). In the Vale of Holmesdale little seems left except parts of the churchyards of Oxted, Tandridge and Bletchingley.

There are many **fine vernacular buildings**. The nearest you may get to the deep past in our built heritage is in the isolated churches of Burstow, amongst the beams of its timber belfry, and Crowhurst, so quiet on its hill. The superb cluster of timber framed houses in Old Town Lingfield, around the grand 14th/15th century church, mark its high medieval prosperity and feudal patronage. Old Oxted has a fine ancient High Street, now free of traffic. Its ancient church is half a mile to the north east. Bletchingley also has a monumental high medieval church and many ancient buildings around a triangular market space, now spoiled by the A25's traffic. Godstone's ancient Church Town has a good group of old buildings, nearly a half mile from Godstone Green.

The **pattern of modern urban settlements** seems largely a delayed product of the railway network. The Brighton Line opened in 1841, the Redhill to Tonbridge Line in 1842, and the Oxted to East Grinstead Line in 1884. Only Redhill and Horley developed greatly in the 19th century, however, and the ribbon of Brighton Line towns – Merstham, Redhill, Salfords, Horley – grew mostly in the 20th century. Indeed, Nutfield Station only opened in 1884, Gatwick Station in 1891 (to service Gatwick Racecourse) and Salfords Station in 1915 (to service new industry). South Godstone was developed in the mid 20th century on the footprint of Lagham Wood, within the lost deer park, and South Nutfield partly developed earlier on the footprint of Trindles Wood. A new centre for Oxted by the railway station was developed in the 1930s, followed by much post-war development to the north, partly in woodland. Bletchingley had no station, but both there and at Godstone and Smallfields there has been much post-1945 housing development.

The area suffers too, from a series of wasteful and irrational housing developments, on the spectrum **from plotlands to posh villas**, developed from the end of the 19th century up to the 1947 Town and Country Planning Act of the Attlee Labour government. All are wasteful in their land take and density, show gross disrespect for the wider landscapes in which they sit, and are poorly connected with services and employment. Much of Oxted has this character, as does Domewood, Dormans Park, Felbridge, Felcourt, Anglefield Corner at Blindley Heath, and many smaller ribbon developments, like Hare Lane, Blindley Heath.

Redhill Aerodrome developed (as did Gatwick) in the 1930s, in the vale formed by the confluence of the Redhill Brook and the Salfords Stream. Like Gatwick it has forced the Brook underground, though the lack of a hard runway does allow the partial retention of the grassy vale's landscape quality.

The **Fullers Earth quarries of Redhill and Nutfield** were worked at least from Roman times. The mineral's qualities as a cleanser of wool for the cloth industry may have underpinned the development of the Vale of Holmesdale villages, like Godstone. Only during and after World War Two did the quarries expand to their landscape-destroying scale, though the Fuller's Earth, in the end, was frittered away on cat litter and other trivialities alongside its strategic and medical uses. Together with the high quality builders sand pits to their east these quarryings take out much of the four mile vale between the Brighton Line and Godstone.

They are not the only culprits however, for the **M25 and M23 motorways**, built in the early 1970s, with their massive noise and air pollution, severance of communities and habitats, and intrusion, constitute a ratchet pushing forward the development of Gatwick Airport and the crazy expansion of the London megalopolis.

Surrey has always had a large gipsy community. **Travellers and show people** have been helped by locally fragmented landownership patterns to acquire homes and a bit of land for themselves, particularly to the east of Horley and Salfords, on the footprint of old Copthorne Common, and around West Park Road. It is cheering to see their ponies grazing on Nutfield Marsh Common.

THE SURREY-SUSSEX BORDER COUNTRY

The past footprint of **Copthorne Common** (the second biggest of the county border commons after Horley) can still be part-traced by its ruler-straight enclosure roads and field boundaries. The London Green Belt extends right to the Surrey county border, confining the development of urban Copthorne to the Sussex side. To the built-up area's north lie the derelict-but-intact **Copthorne Meadows**, TQ 326 398, by Roundabout Farm, with their peaty soils and time-haven flower displays. Some decades ago the last active farmer must have stashed his unwanted farm machinery in and around a Dutch barn under a hedge. Since then the barn has collapsed and the hedge has expanded into a thicket which cloaks the machinery in a tangle of branches, thorns and fallen trees. A World War Two Fordson Major tractor with spade lugs, a hand crank and glass fronted oil gauge on its bonnet, a sixties hay tedder, metal horse waggon tyres, mangles for cattle feed, and maybe even a tree-crushed threshing machine, sleep in their greenwood sepulchre (2016).

Young Oak sprigs, Bracken, Ash saplings and Bramble relentlessly invade all these fields from the hedges. Airliners thunder overhead. The seed heads of rushes are flecked with the tiny white chrysalis cases of Rush Case Bearer moths, and the place hums with busy small life forms. Wonderful … but how threatened!

To the west, beyond the woods of Heathy Ground and the M23, is ancient **Forge Wood,** TQ 295 388, around the Crawley Crematorium, and the erstwhile peaceful pastures of the Gatwick Stream. Here till the last century was **Forge Farm**, TQ 291 394, on the site of an ironworks and hammer pond (active before 1574, perhaps to the early 18th century). It is now being developed as the latest new Crawley housing district. Here the famous 'Sussex Forge' apple originated.[8]

Tinsley Green marked the old county boundary, though most of the Green lay west of the railway, where it vestigially survives as a strip of grass and Oaks amongst factories, TQ 285/6 394. **The Greyhound**, TQ 289 395 – a good and friendly pub in an ugly roadhouse – hosts the annual World Marbles Championship, a game played locally for centuries.

The ribbon development of Radford[9] Road (which continues Tinsley Green to the east) hides the mosaic of woodland, green lanes, archaic meadow fragments, ponds, shaws and outgrown hedges to its north – still threatened by the proposed Gatwick second runway. **Pickett's Wood**, TQ 295 407, is ancient, open and Brackeny, with Bluebells, Gean, and at least two good Oak pollards, probably much older than they look. Just south is **Upper Picketts Wood**, TQ 295 402, now perhaps a century old, which has acquired many ancient woodland species. It is next to an overgrown but charming meadow fragment, TQ 295/6 403/4 (2014).

The jewel in the crown of this area is ancient **Horleyland**[10] **Wood**, TQ 289 405, with fine Oak standards over Hazel coppice, and a gorgeous Bluebell display. There's a grove of Crabs whose golden apples shine like treasure trove on the flat woodland floor. There's Cow Wheat and Wood Sorrel and much Bracken (and Himalayan Balsam in places), and Deer Flies, like little (sea) crabs with wings. A new pond has been restored, and a lad fishing there told me that the fish swim away to cover every time an airliner thunders overhead … In the SW of the wood there's the stench of sewage from the huge adjacent works. To the north and NE, huge airport car parks come right up to the wood edge; a bunded balancing pond abuts the SE, and the railway bounds the west (2014). For all its beauty, this wood is a monument to the inadequacy of preserving high value sites when their landscape context

Burstow church tower's huge Oak beams take us back to medieval Worth Forest

is destroyed. Preserving such 'precious fragments' *on their own* is unsustainably tokenistic.

West of Shipley Bridge and the M23 is **Allen's Wood**, NE of Black Corner, TQ 300 401/2, with soaring trees and Brackeny glades, old coppice Oaks, and Beech on the boundaries. It sits right on the boundary between the Tunbridge Wells Sands and the Wealden Clay, thus startling you with Hard Fern and Rowan (liking the sand) and large shallow pools (as so often on clays). Open to pony grazing, it has a New Forest feel.

Burstow, TQ 312 412/3, is just a few old houses, two moated, by the ancient church, embowered in trees. It is an ancient place, possibly of pagan or early Christian worship, as the '*stow*' suffix suggests. Every time an airliner roars over you want to shake your fist at it. The timber tower and spire have huge beams that likely came from Worth Forest. The walls are of ironstone rubble, with Merstham Stone door jambs and smarter Tilgate Stone bits. Standing by the **Burstow Stream** one hot summer afternoon I heard a yowling and screeching from over the meadow. The tall grass and flowers twitched and waved, and a fighting pair of young

Muddy puddles on Tandridge's pre-Roman green lane

Foxes flashed in and out of view – oblivious to me. The fight went on across the meadow for long minutes, traceable only by the twitching grass and noise. These **Burstow Meadows,** TQ 311 417, are a quiet beauty before hay time. **Broadbridge Pastures**, TQ 308 417/8, are only three fields north of the church, and host many interesting wetland plants, like Trifid Bur Marigold, Marsh Ragwort, Bog Stitchwort, at least three sedges, and Sneezewort. The hedges are outgrown in beautiful disorder. The Burstow Stream, deep-cut and secret, winds between two of the fields, and cattle go down to drink, amongst the overhanging trees.

Just north of the A264 Copthorne Road, is **Hedgecourt Lake and Marsh**, an SSSI, TQ 352 403 … still magical in parts, though oppressed by road and airliner din. It must have been a 'Family Day' on my last July evening visit, sunny, still, hot. A Common Tern mum and dad did their Olympic moves, circling, diving, dipping to feed their two fledglings little silver fish. Reed Bunting youngsters followed their dad, and Mute Swan parents led a flotilla of five cygnets. A Garden Warbler sang from the thicket. I thought I was looking at an Eel swimming along the brown muddy bottom of the sunny western inlet, but it rose and popped its head up above the surface through a Starwort mat: a fine Grass Snake. We watched each other for nearly 10 minutes; then – slowly – it fully surfaced and wiggled away across the Starwort raft, with little fish around it. I looked at a floating young dead Pike with its huge golden eyes, black centred, and jaws like a duck's beak, full of little white teeth.

There is an area of quaking bog out towards the western pond tail water edge, covered in Bogbean, with Kingcups, Bladder Sedge, Meadowsweet, Flag and Yellow Loosestrife. It is hidden from the open water by a screen of Reed and Reed Mace. In the western carr woodland are several glades with relict moor vegetation (though Meadow Thistle is long gone). There's Pale and Smooth Stalked Sedges and Devil's Bit, with Skullcap and Marsh Pennywort (just) in the wettest glade.

Though now-scarce fen and moor plants survive (like Ling, Moor Grass, Common Valerian, with Cow Wheat) the Wildlife Trust's good managers are plainly struggling even to retain these few 'precious fragments' of rich open habitat (2013). The western end (a nature reserve) is the good part. The wildness of the open water is destroyed by the presence of many sail boats.

A mile NE down the Eden Brook, past a big commercial fishery, is the **Wire Mill Lake**, TQ 368/9 418. Much of it is lined with woods and fronted by thick Bulrush, with scattered Yellow Water Lily. There are fishing stands, a water skiing platform, and a pub/restaurant on the pond bay. There's a big excluding screen fence along the lake's south side footpath (2014). Still, a Water Shrew crossed my path, and I watched a Hobby dive on a flock of Martins and Swallows foraging over a neighbouring stables. Even damaged places have their compensations …

Just beyond East Grinstead's north western suburbs is **Chartham Wood**, TQ 377 400, a big Sweet Chestnut and Hazel coppice, with some Beech veterans and groves with fine columnar standards and dead giants. The **old road, now bridle path**, e.g. TQ 373 413, runs northwards up the middle of the **'Tandridge Trunk'** – the erstwhile narrow strip-parish of fields and woods connecting the North Downs with the Sussex border. Though many field boundaries have been taken out, the ancient woods are mostly intact, except for the clearance of High Wood west of the path. **Felcourt, Green, High,** and **Stockriding Woods** are of Oak and Hazel, over stunning Bluebells. By the bridlepath SW of Stockriding is archaic **Garfield Farm Meadow**, TQ 373 405/6, well looked after, with Zig Zag Clover, Sneezewort and Betony.

The part of **Frogit Heath** which is still common, TQ 358/9 424/5 is nearly all secondary woodland now, as is **Newchapel Green**, TQ 364 426, but still pleasant (2014), especially in autumn. **Lingfield Cricket Club field**, TQ 357/8 420, also part of the common, has a remarkable old meadow fungus flora, with seven Waxcaps and other relics of its heathy past, like Heath Grass. To their west, in the crook of East Park Lane and West Park Road are the two archaic **Quest Cottage Meadows**, TQ 352/3 417, once also part of the Heath, with some of the same fungi and much wildflower colour before haytime (2014).

LINGFIELD AND ITS SURROUNDS

Lingfield, TQ 38 43, grew enough to get mentioned in a Saxon charter of circa 880 AD, though then linked to Sanderstead on the Downs. It has two recognisable old centres. One, **Plaistow[11] Street**, has the Gun Pond, the stump of St Peter's Cross (1437), the Village Cage (an ex-holding cell: 1773) and a 4.5 span girth Oak pollard surrounded by compacted earth and tarmac – a fine and sad Methuselah. The other, **Old Town**, has the church, rebuilt in 1431 in Perpendicular style by the local feudal plutocrat. His family (the Cobhams) filled the Chancel and Lady Chapel with their gob-smacking funerary clutter of painted statuary and brasses (some 12: the "best set[12] in Surrey") in the apparel of the 14th and 15th centuries … spurs, wimples, swords from waist to feet, helms, dogs, a sea wolf and a wyvern.

One full length armoured fourteenth century knight is using a decapitated Moslem's head (in the form of a helm) as a pillow, and rests his feet on the back of a cheesed-off-looking Saracen slave. A fifteenth century armoured lord also rests his head on an old Moslem man's head (another helm). These figures of conquering Christian masters and slaughtered and enslaved Moslems in a functioning Christian church open to all seem freshly controversial in the light of similar ISIS[13] atrocities (2014).[14] Worshippers are obliged to tolerate the images of these rich lords, who forced their way in so long ago between the congregation and the altar. That is quite some cultural baggage … a bit like being forced to look at Colonel Sanders' cheery face every time you munch on a bit of fried chicken …

North of the church, the County Branch Library is housed in a wonderful 15th century hall house, complete with original fittings, ceramics, pictures and photos. On the south side, the Old Town is full of ancient brick and timber buildings, all skew-whiff and lovely. The Swifts were massed overhead on one blue skies May-time visit we made.

The straight roads north of Lingfield were made on the site of the enclosed Lingfield Common, but you can trace the old common's outlines from the surviving farmhouses that were once on its edges. There's *The Old House* (to the west: once home of Biggles' creator); *Lyne House Farm* (further west); *Pains Farm* (NW across the fields); *Coldharbour Farm* (northwards); and *Sugham Farm* (further north).

THE WEALDEN CLAY VALE – WEST OF THE M23

The **Burstow Stream** snakes through flatlands, round the north end of Horley through a landscape of well maintained thick hedges (though some have been removed), cow pastures, shaws, and old World War Two pillboxes. It bounds Brook Wood as it turns south, past Weatherhill Common and on past Thunderfield Castle. On its way it passes under Lake Lane, and between Greatlake and Littlelake Farms (with their old farmhouses). Don't go looking for a 'lake', though. That's just a lost medieval name for the Stream. *('Lacu'* = small, slow moving stream). It was also called a *'bourne'*, as survives in *Bone*hurst Road and *Bonner's* Bridge, and a *'brook'*, as in *Brook* Wood.

Langshott (the road: TQ 290 440) used to be the north edge of Horley Common. Tanyard Farmhouse and Langshott Farm/Manor Hotel, (both 17th century and timber framed) used to sit on the Common's edge. Now, a new 'Langshott' housing district is being built to the north, up to Greatlake Farm. **Brook Wood**, TQ 302 440, is wet, shady and wild. Oak (some coppiced), Ash, Hazel, Midland Thorn and Hawthorn predominate. On the ride under the power lines an Oak Eggar moth zonks about in the sun, and Silver Washed Fritillary butterflies court on the thistles and Teazel. To the SW are wooded-up derelict fields. What's left of **Weatherhill Common**,[15] TQ 304 435, is mostly Brambly Oak woodland, now, but its open western end merges with several very colourful, herb-rich pastures, grazed by a piebald mare and her foal (2104). There is much Pepper Saxifrage … and juicy blackberries of Cut Leaved Evergreen Bramble. The Impressionists would have liked the spot, for its flowers form obvious colour groups … <u>Red/purple</u>: *Knapweed, Self Heal, Red Clover and Marsh Thistle*. <u>White</u>: *Yarrow, Angelica, Upright Hedge Parsley and Burnet Saxifrage*. <u>Yellow</u>: *Birds Foot Trefoil, Cat's Ear, Square Stalked St John's Wort, Agrimony, Ragwort, Creeping Buttercup and Fleabane*.

Harrowsley and Thunderfield 'Castle' (TQ 299 425, south of Smallfield Road) together were a Saxon (or earlier) settlement of open ground and woods, on the edge of the old Horley Common. Harrowsley Farm has flat cattle pastures, with lots of Oaks, though many old hedges are gone. Thunderfield is not a 'Castle' but 2.5 concentric moats, wooded-up, which have lost their medieval manor farmstead, and are only partly in water.[16] It is now within a large plotland, with houses scattered around in big grounds. The old name (for many centuries) of Horley Common, *'Thunderfield'*, was later attached to the 'Castle'. It was originally *'Thunor's (Thor's) field (open ground)'* maybe where the god was worshipped.

North of the Burstow Stream the ground rises past the rich dairy pastures of Hathersham Farm to the **Woolborough ridge**. The lovely green corridor of **Gail Lane**, TQ 287 454, has fine Oak standards, with Wild Service and Wood Melic, Crab Apple and Field Rose, Midland Thorn, and Bush Vetch. **Perry Wood**, TQ 287 454, has a large clone of old Small Leaved Lime stools amongst the Bluebells. It is an Ash coppice wood, with Midland Thorn and Hawthorn understorey, and Bramble sub-shrub layer (2014). From there you can see north to the Downs, west to the Surrey Hills, and south to clouds sailing across the Low Weald, grey rain sheets slanting down … and the Gatwick Control Tower. Old, timber framed **Woolborough Farmhouse**, TQ 306/7 457/8, once stood alone, but modern villas now cluster with it on the hill. The views are green on green. The noise of the M23 is hellish. **Torycross Shaw**, TQ 303 460, is one of the nicest small ridge woods – a Bluebell and Hornbeam coppice, which has a spring near the top, with a mat of Thin Spiked Wood Sedge.

The ridge descends gently north to the Vale of the Salford Stream, where Redhill Aerodrome sits. West of Mason's Bridge Road the **Salfords Stream**, TQ 289 470, meanders under Crack Willow, Oak, Himalayan Balsam and Alder, past **Dean's Farm** (Tudor, timber framed, tile hung). **Green Lane**, TQ 284 469, is the lovely wooded northwards continuation of Gail Lane across the Salfords Stream.

THE WEALDEN CLAY VALE – FROM THE M23 TO THE EASTBOURNE ROAD

Chithurst Lane – an ancient farm track at its southern end, TQ 337 414 – runs north through a tunnel of trees and Bluebells from the old edge of Copthorne Common across a landscape of rich level pastures, thick hedges, Oaks and small woods. Most of this land between Dowlands Lane east to Bones Lane, and between Brick Barns Farm north to Croydonbarn Lane is in the **West Park, Surrey County Council Smallholdings Estate**. It is an old fashioned farming landscape run as three working dairy farms (2014). There's **Keepers Farm**, TQ 330 410, on Dowlands Lane, and **Holmlea Farm** and **Bysshe Court Farm**, TQ 335 429, both on Chithurst Lane. Bysshe Court Farm has based its business on Dairy Shorthorns for three generations, and they are a fine sight to see, though they hide away in the far fields between milking times. It is, maybe, the only Dairy Shorthorn farm left in Surrey. They can be milked on a low input / low output system, needing half the cattle cake that Holsteins require, and they are kept all their lives, some cows still milking at 18!

The County Council's direction of travel has been bad, though, for it has long moved from the democratic aspirations of the smallholdings legislation, which was to encourage small businesses and new entrants without family connections to landholding. The estate originally had 12 farms, but the Council has amalgamated much of the farmland and flogged off the farmsteads with bits of land attached. *Dowlands Farm, Brick Barns Farm, Palmers Farm, The Homestead, Rainscombe Farm, Chithurst Farm, Rough Beech Farm, etc. – all sold*. It is great that the estate is still publicly owned and farmed (for the smallholding estates in Sussex have all gone) but the potential of public ownership to provide an alternative to agribusiness and agricultural globalisation is still denied.

Horne Church, TQ 336 443, once had a complete timber bell tower,[17] like Burstow, but restoration got rid of that and much else. It's still worth seeing however, with a 14th century rood screen. For two miles north of the church, up and over the Outwood ridge almost to the Redhill – Tonbridge railway, you are on the **National Trust's Harewood Estate**. Very many (but not all) landscape features of the old Low Weald have been preserved or enhanced there – shaws, hedges and small woods (several modern). **The windmill at Outwood Common**, TQ 327 455, has stood since 1665 (a year[18] before the Great Fire of London) and is the oldest working post mill in the country, though damaged by a gale in 2012. The Common is mostly wooded, with frequent Hornbeam and Hazel coppice, Birch, Holly, and a cluster of old Oak pollards north of Outwood Church, c. TQ 319 461–3. **Stone House Common**, TQ 313 461/2, at its west end, is still colourful archaic grassland with five sedges. A deep gill runs through Outwood Common northwards, and there are three more on the plateau to the east, mostly cloaked in ancient woodland. There is a cluster of **five large archaic meadows east of Brown's Hill**, TQ 329 473, with all sorts of delightful old flowers, grasses, and six sedges, grazed by Sussex cattle in high summer. **Hornecourt Wood**, on the scarp, TQ 333 452, is ancient – mostly Hornbeam coppice, with fine Oaks and part-cleared conifer stands. Sadly, the tired old conflict between game bird shooting and the public is replicated on the Harewood Estate, with excluding notices just like a private estate: *"Return to footpath"; "Managed for ground nesting birds and game. Keep to footpath"; "No public right of way"* (2014).

On the north side of the Redhill – Tonbridge Line is the **Sandhills Estate**, TQ 321 495, also National Trust, but here the picture is not so happy, with many field boundaries gone and no sign of old grasslands, even on the greensand scarp slope below Castle Hill. The pond by Castlehill Farm is bolted, gated, and signed "private fishing". The best I've found of it are the two sunken holloways down the scarp either side of Castle Hill. The roar from the adjacent M23 is appalling … but when I trudged up the path towards Castlehill Farm there was a rustling … like the shaking of distant tambourines … increasing in volume as I neared a grove of Aspen – not called *Populus tremula* for nothing! There's an ancient spring-fed pond east of Outwood Lane as you touch Bletchingley. **Hevers Pond**, TQ 327 503, has all three British newts, frogs, toads and mini-beasts to enjoy.

Under the greensand scarp, both north, south and across the Bletchingley Railway Tunnel is **South Park**, e.g. TQ 341 488, a deeply tranquil place of old woods, lanes and large views. The noise of the M23 is always

Lagham Deer Park meadow from Park Hill

present, but softly, and the noise of Gatwick's planes is very distant.

Two 'time slip' encounters there one summer noon took me back to the days of the medieval deer park. Standing in dense cover, with Bracken to my chest, I realised a fine Fallow Stag was close by, browsing the Hazel and Bramble. I watched, still, until it turned its head and met my gaze. We stayed for a while in mutual inquiry, till he moved gently away. Only a few minutes before I had been munching a sarnie and drinking home-made blackberry juice, sat against an old Hornbeam, when a dark falcon glided downslope right past me to perch in a tree some 30m away. Its reddish 'trousers' gave it away … a Hobby … which had chosen her perch to watch a hidden woodland pond … seeking dragons and damsels, no doubt, and having a break from chasing Martins over the nearby farm buildings.

One other surprise has doubly endeared me to this place. Walking down the lane past **South Park Farm's** deserted barns, TQ 341 487, I copped a notice on a door in the manor house garden wall: *"Main lawn and pond can be visited. No Food or Dogs. St Mark's Foundation"*. I passed through into that immaculate garden … lawns and beds with many common flowers made special by tender care: like Red Valerian, Shasta Daisies, double flowered Sneezewort. No fence or 'ha ha' marked the end of the lawns and the beginnings of the cow pastures. Behind was the big house, a bland neo-Georgian villa replacing the old house, which had been doodlebugged with tragic fatalities in 1944. If only all our countryside offered such trusting welcome. How different, then, would be our relationships with nature!

South Park has many special places. **Maple Wood**, TQ 343/4 485, has much ancient Hornbeam coppice by the railway line. **Furze Wood**, TQ 348 488, has the deepest gill, with fern and Golden Saxifrage and Dogs Mercury leaves stained blue with birds' blackberry juice droppings. There is the cluster of lovely buildings at **Cucksey's Farm**, TQ 335 488: ancient threshing barn with wagon entrance; black weatherboarded barn and hovels; and three storey Dutch-style farmhouse looking like an old watermill. There is the **Chapel of St Mark**, by South Park Farm, converted (1909) from an old stable built in the end time of the deer park, c. 1650.

Despite this, don't be deceived by the old-fashionedness of this countryside. Several of the old woods have been heavily replanted (Poundhill, Cinderhill, Fouracre). Several of them have been part or wholly cleared (Poundhill, Sevenacre, Tye Copse, Moors Wood). Ponds in woodland and field have been packed with ducks for shooting, and the archaic grasslands and rough, scrubby corners loved by nature are gone.

The Roman road from London to Portslade Harbour ran north-south parallel with the line of Tilburstowhill Road. To the east of the modern road, opposite Yewtree Farm, TQ 357 474/5, a wide, high bank runs parallel, set back in the field and topped with Oaks, for half a mile. It was thought to be the *agger* of the Roman road, but is the outer bank of the successor medieval drove, which formed a sort of two mile long linear green[19] south of Tilburstow Hill? West of the road, on the north side of a little stream, there are several colourful old flower meadows, TQ 353 476, grazed by Sussex cattle, beyond a lovely derelict orchard with apples and pears of all sorts (2014). On the north side of ancient **Birchen Copse** is an oil drilling site, TQ 346 479.

THE WEALDEN CLAY VALE – FROM THE EASTBOURNE ROAD TO THE OXTED LINE

Lagham's medieval Deer Park (e.g. TQ 36 48) has left larger, more visible remains than the other lost parks of this area. You can trace its pale (boundary) on the Explorer map, and much of it is upstanding. It runs through lovely Bradford Wood, TQ 369 473/4, as a raised, wide bank with damp internal ditch (as deer parks often had). The most prominent built monument of the Park is the Moat, TQ 363 480, cloaked in woodland, a real wilderness, but mostly dried up in summer – wet mud, Pond Sedge and pools – except by the NW causeway, where tiny white ducks paddle. Its banks are raised 30ft above the bottom of the ditch. There was a Lodge[20] too (now gone) just north of Bradford Wood, TQ 370 476.

SOME SURVIVING ARCHAIC GRASSLAND AROUND SOUTH GODSTONE

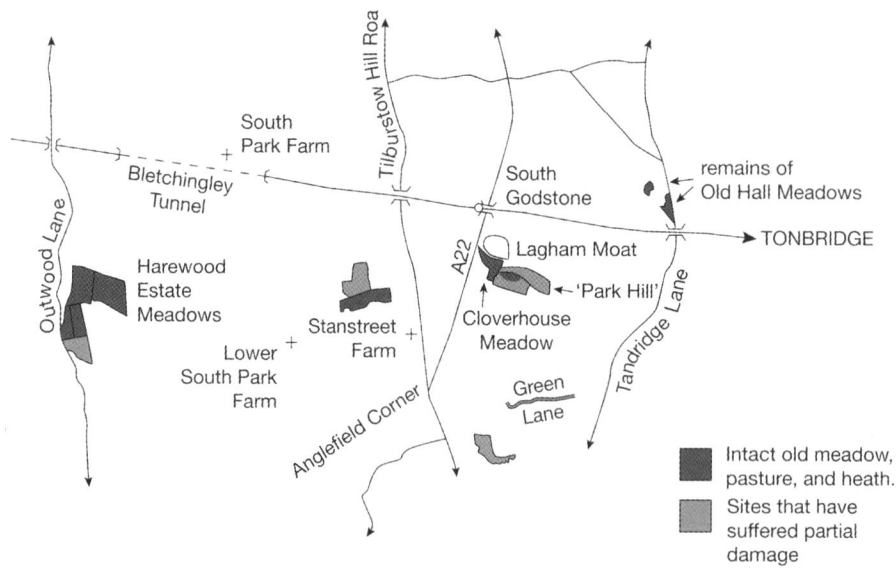

© Crown copyright and database rights 2018. OS License number 100048229

When I first properly visited **Blindley Heath Common**, TQ 366 447, some 15 years ago, it was largely covered in scrub and low Oaks, with cattle grazed glades. Now, at its centre, the feel of the old open, rushy moor is returning, with greatly expanded scrub clearance. The cattle and ponies have done a fine job trampling open new paths, bashing through Bramble, and creating a browse line under the scrub oaks. It is a wild and hopeful place. Green Frogs of huge size plop into the pools, and dragonflies patrol overhead. As is often the case, the hard-mown Cricket Pitch in the NW corner is better (2013) for old grassland fungi than the grazed Heath, hosting at least five waxcaps.

Southwards of the Common are a series of old fashioned rush pasture fields, e.g. TQ 368 440.

Crowhurst parish retains fine and tranquil Low Wealden countryside, despite agribusiness damage. One hot September afternoon I walked the field path west of Crowhurst Church, along the ridge above the Weald. There, on the roof tiles of a south facing cottage, 21 Swallows sprawled. They lay as flat as they could to catch the tiles heat … They raised their wings … They turned their brick red throats upwards to catch the sun[22] … They rolled on their sides … They could have been sunbathers on Brighton beach. **The church**, TQ 390 474, is simple and ancient, with walls of greensand rubble, Horsham slabs on the south aisle roof, a polished floor of local *Viviparus* fossil marble, a local cast iron grave slab under the altar, and a timber, shingled belfry. It stands, hilltop-high, companioned by a Yew tree said to be 4000 years old. Was it a sacred tree in *Crow Hurst?* There are two superb knightly brasses of the 15th century, in spiky armour. The bat droppings on the white altar cloth looked to me like those of Brown Long Eared Bats … which squeaked in the roof. The canopy of a side tomb has two Green Men, and a dragon nosing its own genitals and anus. What does *that* say about medieval attitudes to sex?

Within the Park are two old farmhouses of the 16th century: Posterngate and Old Hall. Just outside the Park are two earlier farmhouses of the 15th century: Yewtree and Hobbs. This hints that Lagham was disparked in the 16th century, long after substantial farmhouses had been built in the surrounding countryside. However, Lagham Manor itself (embowered within the Moat) was substantially rebuilt in 1622 at a time when a much larger park (650 acres) may have existed.[21]

If you stand on 'Park Hill', e.g. TQ 364 477, SE of the Moat, you can still see around you elements of the lost, untamed Park: *'lawn'* (where you stand), *'lag'* (the rich meadow below), and *'vert'* (the little woods to the east). There is Gorse and acid grassland around you on the hilltop, with Trailing Tormentil, several splashes of Dyers Greenweed on the break of slope, and Betony and Devil's Bit in the pasture's NW corner, amongst the trees. Between this little hill and the Moat is Cloverhouse Meadow, TQ 363 478/9, damp and rushy, with some Yellow Rattle and Sneezewort, busy Moles, and contented Four Spot Orb Weaver spiders, fat like medieval lords (2014).

Bradford Wood is the largest of the Park's surviving ancient woods (since South Godstone was built on Lagham Wood). It is a mixed coppice with Bluebells, and Bracken where the canopy is more open. A quarter mile south of the Wood is a secluded, well kept **green lane**, TQ 366 437, running east-west between Tandridge Lane and Oak Tree Farm. Between its tall hedges it is crammed with old herbs, Wintercress, Corn Parsley, et al – a fine place to learn to identify these old plants in peace.

Just over the hedge on the east of the lane north of the church is a **deserted brick kiln, Coles Barn,**[23] TQ 392 476, with a tall chimney … like a ruined Cornish tin mine (2014). There are many good

350 AREA GUIDE / Chapter 27: The Nutfield and Godstone Low Weald

You can hear the bats squeaking in the roof: Crowhurst Church

Crowhurst's giant Yew – thousands of years old perhaps

Goblin door

old timber framed houses, like **Crowhurst Place**, TQ 386 463 (much enlarged), and **Mansionhouse Farm**, opposite the church. **Mary's Meadow**, TQ 398 478/9, in the SW quarter of the crossing of the Oxted Line and the Redhill-Tonbridge Line, is a tiny triangle with an outgrown hedge ... but how rich!! Cowslips survive (just), with Pepper Saxifrage and Devil's Bit (just) amongst the colourful tall herbs.

There is a cluster of beautiful **ancient woods (Blackgrove, Moat, Stocks, et al)**, but **Ashen Plantation**, cool and tangled, TQ 383 475, west of the church, is the biggest wood, though less than 150 years old. On either side of the Redhill-Tonbridge Line are more fine old woods, like **Foyle Tolt**, TQ 389 4867, with wall-to-wall Bluebells by the Gibbs Brook. The **infant River Eden** runs close-by, and at this point, TQ 392 485, it has something of the Biblical garden. A Goldfinch charm flits along the bank, open to the wandering cattle, with good brown earth at the edge, and a wide, flat gravel riffle. In a lonely pool, shaded by Alders below a dismantled weir, little fish fry glint and swim. Isaak Walton would have loved this old fashioned place.

THE VALE OF HOLMESDALE UNDER THE NORTH DOWNS

When I was a kid, and later as an adult, I'd watch out for **'Merstham Moors'**[24] from the east side windows of the London-bound train, after we passed Redhill. At first (around 1960) I'd see inviting wet pastures and ditches and the occasional lonely walker, with the trees and fields of the ridge to the south and smallish quarry buildings to the north. As the years passed I watched as the ridge and brook pastures were gradually dug away and the quarry buildings expanded. In the end, nearly all the old view got quarried out, and was then partially re-filled and 'restored'.

When in more recent years, I got to explore the area on foot, I was amazed at the extent of the restoration project, which has created the large **Nutfield Marsh Nature Reserve**, though it by no means rubs out the insult the old landscape suffered. Indeed, more areas will be destroyed if new quarries are permitted east of Nutfield Marsh Road and east of the M23. For 1.5 miles, however, a chain of flooded sand workings, together with some relict pastures along the Redhill Stream, are now managed for nature and public recreation. At the Reserve's west end are the **Holmethorpe Lagoons**, TQ 292 515/6, next to a

The infant River Eden at Foyle Tolt

smart new housing estate. Gulls flock there in summer, with Canada Geese and a few Egyptian Geese. **The Moors**, TQ 290 513, south of the Lagoons, along the Redhill Stream are my favourite bit, with willows on the banks, sheep and cattle grazing, and shallows busy with birds at the west end. Kingfishers could turn up anywhere. East of Nutfield Road is **Mercers Country Park**, TQ 298 518. Its lake is the largest of the series, and is heavily used at the east end for windsurfing, sailing and canoeing. It has large numbers of Mallard and Teal, with Gadwall and Pochard in winter. **Spynes Mere**, TQ 306 524, with three subsidiary lakes, is the easternmost of the flooded pits. In summer there are Little Grebes with young, Great Crested Grebe, Lapwing, abundant Coot, Greylag and Canada Geese. In autumn and winter, the Reserve is good for Lapwing and you may see scarce species like Snipe, Green and Common Sandpiper … and loads of Mallard and Tufted Duck. There is lichen heath on the open shores.

It is not a place for free roaming, and views are often quite limited by fencing, tall hedges and shoreline woods. The wild floodplain that has been destroyed would itself have been rich in wildfowl, including species that will not find homes there now: Redshank and Curlew, Yellow Wagtail and Corncrake. Their preferred landscape is commemorated only by place names like 'Chil*mead*' (meadow), '*Spynes* Barn' (summer fattening pastures), 'Nutfield *Marsh*', and 'The *Moors*'.

The original **Nutfield Marsh** remains as a little common, TQ 300 515, but it is no longer marshy and has lost its archaic vegetation, except for its pond. However, one group of people, travellers, still use it as it has been used for centuries. When I was there in 2013 many of their ponies grazed whilst tethered on plug chains, whilst a travelling farrier working out of a van, shoed them for their waiting owners.

Bletchingley, TQ 326 507, was made a borough about 1210 AD. Its long, narrow 'burgage[25] plots' (now gardens) can be plainly seen on the Explorer map behind the ancient timber framed and tile hung houses of the High Street market place, interrupted only by the churchyard at the crossroads. The medieval, Tudor and Stuart prosperity of the parish can be seen in its 73 historic listed buildings and structures.

The parish church epitomises this early wealth: altered, extended, extended again, and packed with the sharp elbowed monuments of the gentry, both inside and out. The tower is 11th century; the chancel Norman too; the south aisle, Clayton Chapel and parts of the chancel are 13th century; the Ham Chapel is 14th century, and the fine south porch and other bits are 15th century. Like so many posh churches, though, it's not a homely place.

In the Vale north of the village there is a tangle of little lanes (*Sandy Lane, Stychens Lane, North Park Lane, Brewer Street, Water Lane, Church Lane, Little Common Road, Pendell Road, White Hill Lane, Place Farm Lane*) with two hamlets which still have clusters of high quality historic buildings from that prosperous past. Around *Brewer Street* there is the showy 15th century **Brewer Street Farmhouse**, TQ 323 519, with its close studded timber framing, like a blow-in from Lavenham. Round the corner is **Place Farm**, TQ 326 520/1, with a huge old barn, the remains of the Gatehouse of Bletchingley Place,[26] and a good pond across the lane. On *Pendell Road* there's the fine symmetrical, brick **Pendell House**, TQ 314 519, built by Inigo Jones in 1636; **Pendell Court**, now The Hawthorns private school; and **The**

The Tandridge churchyard Yew

Manor House, Pendell Farm – all squeezed close together in an early example of extreme gentrification.

William Cobbett[27] went to **Godstone**, TQ 34 51, in the 1820s and liked it. He'd have a shock if he saw it now. It is beset by roads and jammed with traffic (which nearly killed me once, by the Green). The Eastbourne Road and the A25 clog the place, despite a horrible bypass, and the M25 roars in the background. The ancient tumuli on the Green are long gone, but you can still see their two companions in **Hilly Field**, TQ 348 517/8, a place of welcome escape, accessed from the north side of the Green. The round barrow at its south end is partly cut into by a neighbouring garden. The north barrow is more prominent, but cut into by a quarry and its steel fence. That barrow has a ditch on its south side and a 'pillage dimple' in the top. Patches of Sheep's Sorrel, with Early Hair Grass and *Cladonia* lichens remind you that you are on the acid Folkestone Beds sands, here.

Old Godstone has two other centres. The best of them, **Church Town**, TQ 356 515, a short walk eastwards past **Bay Pond** (a rather private nature reserve and carp fishery) has all the tranquillity Godstone Green lacks, with an old school, the much-restored church, a group of old cottages and St Mary's Homes – wonderful faux-Tudor almshouses (1872) with a chapel you can visit, by G. G. Scott, who's the bloke who designed the wacky front of London's St Pancras Station. Down the lane (a holloway) is **Leigh Place and watermill**, TQ 360 508, with three ponds and much tall fencing, plus hedging to stop the likes of you and me taking a gander. It's a depressing rich folks' enclave ... which could be so much better in a different world.

It's a relief to be out in the sandy woods of **Tilburstow Hill and Common**, TQ 354 502, to climb to the top of the greensand ridge and drink in the green loveliness of the Low Weald. The woods on the scarp slope are mostly ancient.

Old **Tandridge**, TQ 374 511, is the most tranquil of the greensand ridge's ancient settlements, because the A25 curves away to its north. The ginormous **Tandridge Yew**, in the churchyard, has a powerful presence equalling (surpassing?) that of the church it has likely companioned since it was first built. Archaeologists uncovered a Saxon vault on the church's west side that was skewed in such a way as to avoid the roots of the tree, corroborating the Yew's likely prior presence.[28] It has a girth of 5.5 arm spans (over 10m/11yds). When I first saw it there was a huge outgrowth of Chicken of the Woods on its bole, some of whose limbs sweep down to make a giant 'tent'. The tree is not the only ancient life form there, for the churchyard, and the little wooded green outside, is home to Pink Ballerina waxcap, and many other archaic grassland fungi, including large troops of Golden Spindles covering much ground. **St Peter's Church** is also a monument to ancient timber, for its rafter roof and tie beam, atop the rubblestone walls, is over 700 years old. The bell turret and shingled spire, supported by massive timbers, are of the same likely date (c. 1300) and are amongst the earliest of their kind in Surrey. The nave and chancel walls date from the time of the Domesday Book (1086) though restored, and new aisles were added in Victorian times.

Just under a mile eastwards is **Broadham Green**, TQ 387 511, whose ancient sward has been reduced to boring amenity turf. Still, there are three 15th century hall houses close by: Mayflower Cottage on the east side of the Green, Old House on the west, and Stocketts Farmhouse half a mile down the lane southwards. **Hurst Green**, TQ 398 512, half a mile east on the edge of Oxted, has also had its archaic sward destroyed.

Old Oxted, TQ 384 521/2, was a little medieval town on the greensand road (now the A25), but it got stranded after the Oxted Line was constructed and New Oxted grew up around the railway station. It now appears as another unnamed suburb on the

Crowhurst Brick Kiln: the Wealden Clay was brick making country

Explorer map. It was stranded a second time in 1971 when the A25 bypass was built. It developed, probably spontaneously, in the 13th century, and it has burgage plots, especially on the south side, but it never had a market.[29] It has many fine buildings, often timber framed, of the 15th and 16th centuries, including a rare courtyard house (The George). There were four pubs on my last visit (2013): the Wheatsheaf, The Crown, The George and the Old Bell. A lane takes you north under the bypass and across the bay of the wooded Townland Pond. Just north of there is **The Mount**, TQ 380 527, which looks like a mini Silbury Hill, and was long thought to be a prehistoric burial mound. It probably wasn't. It did provide a name for *Barrow* Green, though. ('*Beorg*' = hill). Opulent **Barrow Green Court**, just over the road, is guarded by three strand barbed wire over 2m chain link fencing, warning notices ("Electronic Systems / Warning / Guard Dog Patrols"), CCTV camera on a pole, and chained gates with telephone intercom (2013). The owners must feel besieged.

Half a mile NE of Old Oxted, and perhaps half a century or more earlier, the first Oxted was built as a manorial centre on the best land. Only **St Mary's Church**, TQ 390 529, remains of it: a lovely building outside. The base of its tower is late 11th century, of Bargate Stone with much ironstone. The porch door is 14th century, with studs. The base of the south aisle and the 15th century porch are of dark and light Bargate Stone. The porch roof is of Horsham Slabs. The top of the south aisle is of clunch. The humpty tumpty churchyard has archaic grassland in parts, with a scattering of old meadow fungi. The outer part is sheep grazed.

In New Oxted, **Station Road West** is worth seeing, with its flamboyant mock Tudor buildings of the 1930s, including a little half timbered cinema …

ENDNOTES

1. The Surrey Hills AONB (Area of Outstanding Natural Beauty)
2. Flamsteed was a pioneering astronomer of the late 17th/early 18th century and was absentee rector of Burstow.
3. 'Ray' = 'at the water'. (Saxon *ea* = water, river, stream). *Atter ee* (at the water) became *atte ree*, which became *Ree*.
4. Woolpits probably means *'Wolf pit/s'* though its name is only traceable to 1738. 'The Place Names of Surrey', *op cit*.
5. Bletching*ley* and *Leigh* derive from *'legh'* – glade or forest open space.
6. Stratton was *'street farm'*, and Stansted was *'stone street'*. The Saxons called Roman roads 'streets'. 'The Place Names of Surrey', *op cit*.
7. Lot meadows were allocated into strips ('lots') for hay making, then grazed in common over the autumn and early spring.
8. Also known as the 'Cottager's Friend'; because of its dual purposes: a cider apple after picking, and a sweet apple after keeping. Page 468, 'Wealden Iron', Straker.
9. 17th century Rad*ford* Farmhouse stands near the site of the ancient *fording* of the Gatwick Stream.
10. '*Horley*land' does not take its name from its parish of Horley. It comes from '*holy* land', perhaps a memory of it being church property in the long forgotten past.
11. Plaistow = *'play stowe'* = 'play and sports place'.
12. "The Buildings of England: Surrey", page 348. Op cit.
13. ISIS: 'Islamic State of Iraq and Syria', with their medieval beheadings.
14. Though the excellent church guide recognises that "today our values are very different from those of medieval times" … but how different? Page 29.
15. Part of its east end was taken by the M23.
16. See Horley Local History Society's good website.
17. 'The Buildings of England', op cit.
18. See Outwood Windmill's good website.
19. Called 'Tilburstowhill Green' on the 1st edition 6 inch to 1 mile map (1873).
20. A new Lagham Lodge Farm was built where its old drive met Tandridge Lane.
21. See the excellent Felbridge and District History Group's publication 'Lagham Manor'. Lagham Park is not shown on John Norden's 'Map of Surrey' (1594), though Bletchingley's North and South Parks and Burstow Park are shown.
22. The nature artist C. F. Tunnicliffe has a painting of this behaviour on page 11 of "What To Look For In Autumn", a superb 'Ladybird Nature Book' with text by E. L. Grant Watson, published by Wills and Hepworth Ltd (1960).
23. There was a planning application for residential conversion (2014), so its lonely integrity may now be lost.
24. Though the moors also covered bits of Nutfield, Reigate and Gatton parishes.
25. Burgage plots were medieval borough rental properties owned by the feudal lord. They consisted of a building on a narrow street front with a long narrow strip extending behind, in the manner of open field strips. They were presumably cultivated by the tenants.
26. Bletchingley Place was the manorial centre after the feudal owners decamped from the ruined castle, on the ridge south of Bletchingley. The Place was next to North Park, commemorated in the place names North Park Lane, Farm, and Cottages, and Oldpark Wood up on the Downs. The Place was finally demolished in 1680.
27. William Cobbett, the radical farmer and journalist, wrote his 'Rural Rides' in the 1820s, and published 1830.
28. Woodland Trust website: Ancient Tree Hunt
29. 'Extensive Urban Survey of Surrey: Old Oxted'. Surrey County Archaeological Unit, Surrey History Centre, Woking, Surrey. (2003)

GLOSSARY

Agger: Embanked surface of Roman roads, as at South Godstone, Streat, Hurstpierpoint.

Alderfield: Floodplain Alder woods, often boggy.

Amplexus: The mating embrace of toads and frogs.

Ancient tree: In old age, with much decaying wood.

Ancient woodland: In continuous existence since at least 1600 AD.

Antebellum (houses): Built to mimic pre-US civil war slave plantation mansions.

AONB: Area of Outstanding Natural Beauty: of equal planning status to National Parks.

Apsidal: Typically the semi-circular (in plan) end of a church chancel. Roman origin.

Archaic: Of great age or ancient continuity of type (as in *archaic* meadow).

Assart: Piece of old woodland cleared for tillage.

Atlantic Period: Warm and wet climate from 7,000 to 5,000 BP.

Aurochsen (pl): An extinct large wild cattle species. Used to be called 'marsh cattle'.

Bailiwicks: Sub-divisions of medieval St Leonard's Forest with boundary banks and gates.

Basin (Wealden): Landscape scale depression between the North and South Downs.

Beltway: Major urban ring road with associated wasteful built sprawl. (US origin).

Biomass: The amount / weight of living organisms (or their products) in an area.

Blet: To ripen / over-ripen fruit (such as Wild Service). It enhances sugars and taste.

Bloomery: Small early iron making furnace.

Bole: Tree trunk.

Bolling: Tree trunk of a pollard.

Bosky: Covered with bushes and trees.

Boscage: Medieval term for the wooded outliers of manors, as in 'Plumpton Boscage'.

Bostals: Steep road (Saxon). Many on the Downs escarpments.

BP: Before the Present

Braided: Streams or tracks which divide and re-combine along multiple lines though moving in the same direction.

Brash: Cut younger, twiggy woody growth on a site or individual trees.

Bund: An embankment, as against floods.

Burys: Tunnelled Rabbit colonies, often in banks or mounds.

Calcareous: Containing calcium carbonate, as with chalk / limestone. Their vegetation.

Capital: An accumulation of money which is revenue generating.

Carr: Marsh or flood woodland. Alder and willow are typical.

Capitalism: Economic system based on private property, private profit, and production for the market (rather than directly for use).

Charter: These Saxon documents describe apportionments of manors, and are a major archive.

Chert: Hard silica rock. Poorer quality 'flint.' Wealden flint tends to be called 'chert.'

Clade: Here of Cuckoos. A branch / lineage of the bird which specialises in parasitising particular species (such as Dunnock).

Claudian: Here describes landscapes which evoke Claude Lorrain's paintings. He was a 17th century French baroque landscapist and his skies are better than Turner's. (Discuss).

Collateral (heirs): Descendants by an indirect line (e.g. from siblings or cousins).

Commons: Lands traditionally subject to collective rights of usage (for pasture, wood, turf, etc.). All commons now have a public right of access.

Confluence: The junction of two rivers or streams.

Conspecific: Belonging to the same species (like Brown and Sea Trout).

Coppice: A wood whose shrub layer is cut regularly for use.

Corymb: Flat topped compound inflorescences like Wild Service or Rowan or Candytuft.

Coupe: An area of woodland to be harvested for small wood or timber.

Cycle: Here of wall paintings. A set or series, or linked by a theme.

Deceit: Collective noun for Lapwings.

Dene holes: Ancient chalk extraction pits (for marl) with vertical shafts. Some at foot of Surrey Downs, as well as Kent and Essex. Good places for bats.

Denns: Outlying early medieval manorial wood pastures.

Depasture: To put out to pasture / to graze.

Depauperate: Here describes habitats / ecosystems with reduced diversity or numbers.

Desmesne: Medieval lord of the manor's in-hand land / home farm.

Detritus: Waste, debris, discards.

Diaphanous: Lace-like, gauzy, see-through, delicate.

Disparking: Removing the deer and breaking up parks – into farms, woods, mill ponds, etc.

Doggerland: The old land bridge between England's east coast and the north European plain.

Doodlebug: These 'V-1' Nazi 'flying bombs' were pilotless and jet-powered and caused horrible civilian casualties on their civilian targets in Britain and elsewhere 1944–5.

Entomology: The study of insects.

Ericaceous: Of heathers or the soils which heathers and other acid-loving plants like.

Exchange value: What a seller gets (e.g. money) for a commodity, as opposed to 'use value', which is the item's real utility. Capitalist production is driven by exchange value, not utility.

Fastnesses: Remote natural refuges / strongholds / redoubts.

Fauna: Animals of a particular place or type.

Fingerpost: Signposts with signs projecting like pointing fingers.

Flushes: Waterlogged areas (of wood or pasture) where water broadly and thinly flows downslope.

Frass: Poo or woody debris left by boring insects and other insects and animals.

Fry: Juvenile fish which have just started feeding for themselves.

Gean: Alternative name for Wild Cherry.

Gibbets: The posts from which the bodies of the executed were left to hang, sometimes on the site of their crimes.

Gill / ghyll: Deep, mostly wooded clefts carved by streams in the Weald.

Green lanes: Rough, unmetalled lanes with bounding hedges or shaws.

Greensand: Cretaceous greenish sands and sandstones, laid down in shallow marine conditions.

Grubbed: Woody vegetation which has been cleared / rooted out.

Ha ha: Boundary ditches to gardens which are invisible from distance.

Hammer ponds: Provided water power to drive old iron works' hammers and bellows. They are mostly long and narrow in Wealden valleys and gills.

Hanging wood: Wood on a steep slope.

Head deposits: Laid down in glacial times by recurrent freeze-thawing movement.

Heath: Place of heathers, with Gorse and other acid loving grasses and herbs.

Hemiparasite: Plant obtaining part of its food by parasitism, e.g. Lousewort, Yellow Rattle, Mistletoe.

Holloway: 'Sunken' lane made so by centuries of traffic. Often very deep with banks forming steep, lushly vegetated cliffs. Common in the Weald, particularly on the sandy strata.

Hovel: Here meaning an open shed or shelter, usually on a farmyard, and traditionally with a threshing barn on another side of the yard.

Improved: (Of meadows and pastures). Refers to the replacement of archaic, species-rich vegetation with simplified but highly productive vegetation.

Indicator species: Give 'shorthand' evidence of particular environmental conditions. Thus, Bluebells are an 'ancient woodland' indicator, Lungwort lichen are an 'old forest' indicator, and Dyers Greenweed is an 'archaic pasture' indicator.

Interfluve: Higher land dividing the basins / drainage areas of two rivers. (Can also be called a 'watershed').

Latifundia: Extensive / sprawling landed estates.

Leat: Artificial watercourse dug to take water to a mill's millpond.

Lepidoptera: Moths and butterflies.

Lichen: Symbiotic organisms with a 'sandwich' of algae or cyanobacteria (the 'filling') and fungi (the enclosing 'bread' layers).

Littoral: The shores of sea and lake.

Liverworts: Tiny non-vascular land plants of wet places. More primitive than mosses.

Maiden (tree): Uncoppiced, unpollarded tree (usually with a clean straight trunk).

Mahout: Asian elephant driver or keeper.

Manor: A medieval landed estate. The lord had judicial rights and kept workers in servitude.

Marl: Rock layers within the chalk with a high clay content. Used for fertiliser.

Methusaleh: A Biblical man who lived a huge age.

Microlith: Tiny worked flints typically used in clusters at the 'sharp end' of Mesolithic weapons.

Monoculture: Practice of growing single crops / species over time and over large areas. Has bad environmental effects.

Moor: Waterlogged lowland or boggy / barren upland. Can be very small, or huge (Sedgemoor).

Notable tree: Stands out locally for size. Likely to be mature, but not elderly.

Nucleated: Here, villages of clustered farmsteads and other buildings. They were rare in the Weald, where most parishes had dispersed hamlets and farms till modern times.

'Old growth' forest: Has been free of much human disturbance for a great length of time. Tends to be a US term.

Osier bed: Where Osier Willow is grown for basketry. Not common in the Weald.

Outcrop: A rock formation which breaks through to the surface (like sandrocks).

Outliers: Wealden manors were often based on or below the Downs, with distant Wealden 'outliers'.

Overstood coppice: Stools with uncut poles grown to trees.

Owning Class: Live on unearned income from profits of investments and rents.

Pale (of a park): Boundary ditch and bank, topped by fence, wall, or hedge, with the ditch inside.

Palimpsest (here of landscape): Many intersecting aspects and meanings.

Pannage: Right of common of 'mast' for pigs, comprising autumn woodland feeding on acorns, beech kernels, nuts, fruits, fungi, etc.

Park (manorial): Originally a medieval enclosure for deer. Venison was the class diet of the feudal lords.

Parker: A park keeper, safeguarding and managing the deer and their forage.

Parr: Young Salmon / Trout. Has dark 'finger marks' spaced along its flanks.

Phthalates: Type of plasticising chemicals, with negative health effects.

Pillow mounds: Human-made mounds, often with made tunnels, for rabbits to use in warrens.

Plat: Here means open grassy place, as within deer park or forest.

Plutocrat: Person of great riches, which give them power.

Poached: Often squelchy ground, heavily trampled (as by cattle) and pocked with depressions.

Pollard: Tree retaining its trunk, but with its crown of branches periodically cut.

Pondtail: End of a pond where stream enters. Often shallow with reed beds or wet woodland.

Prevernal (flowers): Late winter / early spring burst of flowers and leaves before the woodland canopy of leaves darkens the woodland floor.

Primeval: Of the earliest times.

Purlieu: Here, of woods, commons or other places surrounding forests and still partially like them.

Quartering: The systematic foraging of Owls and other animals.

Rackhamesque: Akin to the naturalistic-grotesque illustrations of Arthur Rackham (1867–1939) who excelled in gnarled, animated ancient trees.

Rank (grassland): Is ungrazed / unmown, tall, tussocky and poor in plant species.

Rapes: Sub-divisions of Sussex, probably Saxon, but best known in their Norman form. Bramber and Lewes were the capitals of their rapes.

Redoubt: Here means a last defensive stronghold for species or ecosystems.

Refugium: Here, a place of refuge for an isolated or relict population of plant, animal or ecosystem.

Relict: Thing left behind / surviving from the past (e.g. an archaic flower meadow).

Rentier: Person / class / state living on unearned rents or investment income.

Riffles: Stream / river areas of broken shallow water running over gravels / stones.

Riparian: Pertaining to the margins of a river / stream / water body.

Rus in urbe: Piece of countryside in the town, like ancient woodland in a housing estate.

Sarsens: Sandstone rocks that littered the Downs in pre-modern times. They're about 45 million years old. Also called 'grey wethers'.

Scarp: Large steep slope. (Here of the outward face of the Downs or sandstone ridges).

Shaws: Small linear woodlands, often used as field boundaries.

Small wood: Brash or coppice poles used for firewood, tools, hurdles, etc.

Sounder: Group or extended family of (older) pigs.

Span: Here, the width of an adult's arms stretch: our rough measuring unit for old trees.

Sphagnum: Type of bog moss which absorbs water and is important for peat formation.

SSSI: Site of Special Scientific Interest: a statutory designation which denotes national wildlife or geological interest.

Standard: Here, a tree grown for timber with upright, single, clear trunk with no lateral branches.

Styles (of flowers): Stalks of female sexual parts of flowers, connecting the stigma and ovary.

Stools (coppice): Low stump of a bush or tree from which a crown of coppice poles grow. They are lopped periodically from that base.

Store cattle: Young beef cattle which will be sold for finishing (fattening for slaughter).

Swine pasture: Here, Wealden medieval forest sites for seasonal pig grazing.

Transepts: Here, the 'arms' of a cross-shaped church, at right angles to the nave and chancel.

Tufa: Encrusting limestone formed by carbonate precipitation from mineral-rich streams.

Use value: The fundamental usefulness of a commodity, as opposed to its 'exchange value' (see above).

Vert: Term denoting green leafy woodland vegetation of forest or deer park protected as forage and cover for the deer.

Veteran tree: Mature tree with much decaying wood.

Warren: Enclosure for the farming of rabbits. Its managers were called 'warreners'.

Washland: Land seasonally flooded by a river or stream.

Waste: Here, old term for unimproved, untilled land. Coincides largely with modern term 'rough grazing.' Much of it was common. Includes verges, moors, marshes, etc.

Watershed: High land from which water flows down to different river basins. (Can also be called an 'interfluve'). Also the drainage basin or catchment of a river.

Weald: Here, the wide wooded vale between the North and South Downs. Historically, the term excluded part of the Low Weald. Originally meant 'forest' (as in Schwarz*wald*: Black Forest) or 'open high ground' (as in Cots*wolds*).

Winterbourne: Stream or river that flows in winter and is dry in summer.

Wood pasture: Woodland area of mixed grazing and wood and timber production. The trees would often have been pollards to raise their crowns above the reach of livestock.

Wool churches: Grand medieval churches financed by rich owners in the wool industry.

Wilding: Here, a fruit tree which has escaped from cultivation.

Ziggurat: Massive terraced, stepped pyramid or similar structure.